THE ROUGH GUIDE TO

PROVENCE
& THE CÔTE D'AZUR

ROUGH
GUIDES

Based on original text by
Neville Walker and Greg Ward

This tenth edition updated by
Brendon Griffin

Contents

INTRODUCTION   4

Where to go	5	Things not to miss	12
When to go	10	Tailor-made trips	20
Author picks	11		

BASICS   22

Getting there	23	The media	33
Getting around	26	Festivals	33
Accommodation	29	Sports and outdoor activities	34
Food and drink	31	Travel essentials	36

THE GUIDE   42

1 Marseille and around	42	5 The Haut Var and Haute Provence	198
2 Arles and the Camargue	82	6 Toulon and the southern Var	248
3 Avignon and the Vaucluse	112	7 Cannes and the western Riviera	300
4 Aix-en-Provence, the Durance and the Luberon	152	8 Nice and the eastern Riviera	342

CONTEXTS   390

History	391	Glossary of French terms	420
Books	407	Glossary of architectural terms	421
French	410		

SMALL PRINT & INDEX   422

Introduction to

Provence
& the Côte d'Azur

Seductive, sweet-scented and steeped in history, the neighbouring regions of Provence and the Côte d'Azur epitomize all that's irresistible about southern France. Each makes a fabulous destination in its own right; take a trip to both, and you can enjoy the very best France has to offer. Provence, stretching east from the River Rhône as it flows south towards the Camargue and the sea, was one of Rome's wealthiest provinces, and still abounds in extraordinary ancient relics, as well as vibrant and romantic cities like Avignon and Arles and countless alluring towns and hill villages. Named for its dazzling azure waters, the Côte d'Azur – also colloquially known as the French Riviera – consists of the fabled coast that runs from Marseille to the frontier with Italy, studded with glamorous and glitzy resorts.

France's eastern Mediterranean shoreline consists of an ever-changing series of geometric bays that give way to chaotic outcrops of glimmering rock and deep, narrow inlets, like miniature fjords – the *calanques*. Immediately behind it, the coastal hinterland is made up of range after range of steep, forested hills, while the wild, high plateaux of central Provence are cut by the deepest gorge in all Europe – the Grand Canyon du Verdon. Higher still climb the snow-peaked lower Alps and their foothills, which in the east descend right to the sea, and to the west extend almost to the Rhône. All these would count for nothing, however, were it not for the magical Mediterranean light. At its best in spring and autumn, it is both soft and brightly theatrical, as if some expert had rigged the lighting for each landscape for maximum colour and definition with minimum glare.

Food and wine are the other great pleasures of Provence. Local-grown produce – olives and garlic, asparagus and courgettes, grapes and strawberries, *cèpe* and *morille* mushrooms, almonds and sweet chestnuts – forms an integral part of the region's simple, healthy

LA CADIÈRE D'AZUR, AOL BANDOL

cuisine, while Provençal wines range from the dry, light rosés of the Côtes de Provence and Bandol to the deep and delicate reds of the Côtes du Rhône and Châteauneuf-du-Pape.

Where to go

This is a large region, and a diverse one, where contrasting landscapes encompass the rural fields and villages of inland Provence, the remote mountainous regions of the Alpes-Maritimes in the east and north, and the high-rise developments and autoroutes of the Riviera in the south. The epicentre of the Riviera, **Nice** – a vibrant and intriguing blend of Italianate influence, faded *belle époque* splendour and first-class art – makes a perfect base, with delicious food, affordable accommodation and lively nightlife. North of the city, densely wooded Alpine foothills are home to a series of exquisite **villages perchés** (medieval hilltop villages, such as **Saorge**), while to the east, the lower Corniche links the picturesque seafront towns of **Villefranche**, **St-Jean-Cap-Ferrat** and **Beaulieu**; the higher roads offer some of the most spectacular coastal driving in Europe, en route to the perched village of **Èze** and the tiny principality of **Monaco**. The Riviera's western half claims its best beaches – at jazzy **Juan-les-Pins** and at **Cannes**, a swanky centre of designer shopping and film.

The Riviera also boasts heavyweight cultural attractions, with highlights including the Picasso museum in **Antibes**, Renoir's house at **Cagnes-sur-Mer** and the superb **Fondation Maeght** and **Fernand Léger** museums in the gorgeous perched villages of **St-Paul-de-**

PROVENCE AND THE CÔTE D'AZUR

Drôme

Montélimar

Rhône Valley

Rhône

Valréas

Nyons

Bollène

Pont-St-Esprit

Vaison-la-Romaine

Bagnols-sur-Cèze

Sérignan-du-Comtat

LES DENTELLES

Mt Ventoux

MONTAGNE DE LURE

Sisteron

Orange

Châteauneuf-du-Pape

Carpentras

Villeneuve-lès-Avignon

Avignon

Fontaine-de-Vaucluse

Abbaye de Sénanque

Forcalquier

Pont du Gard

L'Isle-sur-la-Sorgue

Gordes

Roussillon

Nîmes

Apt

Manosque

St-Rémy-de-Provence

Cavaillon

Bonnieux

MONTAGNE DE LUBERON

Gréoux-les-Bains

Tarascon

LES ALPILLES

Lourmarin

Les Baux-de-Provence

Abbaye de Silvacane

Pertuis

Arles

Peti Rhône

Salon-de-Provence

Aix-en-Provence

Mt Ste-Victoire

Étang de Vaccarès

Grand Rhône

Étang de Berre

CAMARGUE

St-Maximin-la-Ste-Baume

Les Saintes-Maries-de-la-Mer

Salin-de-Giraud

Martigues

Marseille

Aubagne

La Ciotat

Toulon

Bandol

Golfe du Lion

N

0   20
kilometres

Gap

ITALY
Cuneo

Seyne-
les-Alpes
Barcelonnette

PRÉ-ALPES DE DIGNE
Mt Pelat
Allos
St-Etienne-
de-Tinée
PARC NATIONAL
DU MERCANTOUR

ALPES DE PROVENCE
Colmars

Château-
Arnoux
St-Auban
Digne-
les-Bains
Beuil
St-Martin-de-Vésubie
Tende
La Brigue

St-André-
les-Alpes
St-Sauveur-
sur-Tinée

Barrême
Annot
Puget-
Théniers

Entrevaux
Var

Moustiers-
Ste-Marie
Castellane
Sospel

Riez
Aiguines
La Palud

Verdon
Grand Canyon du Verdon
Menton
Ventimiglia

Vence
MONACO

Aups
HAUT VAR
Fayence
Grasse
Nice

Barjols
Salernes

Cotignac
Lorgues
Draguignan

Carcès
Abbaye du Thoronet

Brignoles
Fréjus
St-Raphaël
Côte d'Azur

Côte de l'Esterel

Ste-Maxime
St-Tropez

MASSIF DES MAURES

Hyères
Le Lavandou

Îles d'Hyères

MEDITERRANEAN SEA

| | TGV |

Metres
3000
2000
1500
1000
500
200
100
0

THE ART OF PROVENCE

Since the late nineteenth century, Provence and the Côte d'Azur have been home and inspiration to some of the greatest names of modern art – **Van Gogh**, **Cézanne**, **Renoir**, **Matisse** and **Picasso** among them. The brilliant **southern light** was one of the most influential factors in their work here; Matisse remarked that, had he carried on painting in the north, "there would have been cloudiness, greys, colours shading off into the distance…" Instead, during his time in Nice he produced some of his most famous, colourful works, such as Le Rideau égyptien (Interior with Egyptian Curtains) and Icare (Icarus). It was in Provence too, in Arles and St-Rémy, that Van Gogh fully developed his trademark style of bright, contrasting colours. His landscapes of olive trees, cypresses and harvest scenes, such as La Sieste (The Siesta) and Champ de Blé et Cyprès (Wheat Field with Cypresses), all pay tribute to the intensity of the **Provençal sun**. The painters in turn had a major impact on the region. Hand-in-hand with the writers and socialites who flocked to the Côte d'Azur during the interwar years, their artistic, and touristic, legacy helped to shape the Provence that exists today.

Vence and **Biot** respectively. The world's perfume capital, **Grasse**, and the ancient town of **Vence**, home to a wonderful chapel that stands as Matisse's final masterpiece, both shelter in the hills behind the busy coastal resorts, while for a real escape from the bustle of the coast, the tranquil **Îles de Lérins** lie just a few kilometres offshore from Cannes.

West of the ancient Massif of the **Esterel**, beyond the Roman towns of **Fréjus** and **St-Raphaël**, loom the dark wooded hills of the **Massif des Maures**. Here, the coast is home to the fabled hot spots of **Ste-Maxime** and **St-Tropez**, still a byword for glamour and excess more than sixty years after Brigitte Bardot put it on the jetsetters' map. In dramatic contrast, the **Corniche des Maures** stretches to the west, its low-key resorts interspersed with blissfully unspoiled strips of Mediterranean coastline. Beyond lies the original Côte d'Azur resort of **Hyères** with its elegant villas, fascinating old town, and offshore **Îles d'Hyères**, popular with nature lovers, naturists and divers.

Further west, past the great natural harbour of **Toulon** and the superb wine country of the **Bandol** AOP, lies the buzzing metropolis of **Marseille**. The region's largest city, this tough port has shucked off its once sleazy reputation to become a lively, cosmopolitan and likeable destination. On its eastern edge lie the **calanques**, a series of beautiful rocky coves protected as a national park. In their midst you will find the picture-postcard village of **Cassis**, linked to the working port of La Ciotat to the east by the spectacular **Corniche des Crêtes**. North of Marseille the elegant city of **Aix** boasts handsome stone houses, café-lined boulevards and some of the finest markets in Provence. Cézanne lived and painted here, taking his inspiration from the countryside around the nearby **Montagne Ste-Victoire**.

Beyond Aix, the Lower Rhône Valley is home to some of the most ancient cities in Provence. Both romantic **Arles** and tiny **Orange** still boast spectacular Roman structures, while **Avignon**, city of the popes and for centuries one of the great artistic centres of France, remains focused around its immaculately preserved medieval core. A short way west, officially outside Provence but an integral part of its Roman heritage, the extraordinary aqueduct known as the **Pont du Gard** stands proud after two thousand years. The stately Rhône itself runs past the vineyards of **Châteauneuf-du-Pape** and the impressive fortifications of **Villeneuve-lès- Avignon**, before meeting the sea at the lagoon-studded marshlands of the **Camargue**, with its rich wildlife including bulls, horses and flamingos.

The **Luberon** region, inland from Marseille, is a fertile rural hinterland whose delightful old villages are now dominated by second-homeowners. Nearby lie the great medieval monasteries of **Silvacane** and **Sénanque**. Beyond the plateau de Vaucluse, mighty **Mont Ventoux** dominates the horizon; a legendary challenge on the Tour de France, it attracts amateur cyclists in their thousands each summer. Immediately west, celebrated wine-producing villages nestle amid the jagged pinnacles of the **Dentelles de Montmirail**.

East of the Luberon, in the Provençal heartland, an archetypal landscape of lavender fields dotted with old stone villages stretches north towards the dramatic **Grand Canyon du Verdon**. Beyond the canyon, narrow **clues**, or gorges, open onto a secret landscape perfect for adventurous activities of all kinds, with the fortified towns of **Entrevaux** and **Colmars** defining the former frontier between France and Savoy. A third fortress town, **Sisteron**, on the Durance, marks the gateway to the mountains and the **Alps** proper, where the fine old town of **Barcelonette** provides skiing in winter and kayaking and hiking in the summer. Stretching south from here towards the **Roya Valley** and the border with Italy is the **Parc National du Mercantour**, a genuine wilderness, whose only permanent inhabitants are its wildlife: ibex, chamois, wolves and golden eagles.

When to go

Beware **the coast** at the height of summer. The heat and humidity can be overpowering and the crowds, the traffic and the costs overwhelming. For **swimming**, the best months are from June to mid-October, while sunbathing can be enjoyed any time from **February to October**. February in particular is a great month on the Côte d'Azur – museums, hotels and restaurants are mostly open, the mimosa is in blossom, and the contrast with northern Europe's climate is at its most delicious.

Inland, the lower Alps are usually under snow from late November to early April. October can erupt in storms that quickly clear, and in May, too, weather can be erratic. In **summer**, the vegetation is at its most barren save for high up in the mountains, though the lavender season tends to last from late June into early August. Wild bilberries and raspberries, purple gentians and leaves turning red to gold are the rewards of **autumn** walks. **Springtime** brings such a profusion of wild flowers you hardly dare to walk. In March, a thousand almond orchards blossom.

AVERAGE DAYTIME TEMPERATURES

	Jan	Feb	Mar	Apr	May	Jun	Jul	Aug	Sep	Oct	Nov	Dec
RHÔNE VALLEY												
Temp (°C)	7.4	6.7	10.8	15.8	17.3	25.6	27.6	27.6	23.5	16.5	10.4	7.8
Temp (°F)	45	44	51	60	63	78	82	82	74	62	51	46
CÔTE D'AZUR/RIVIERA												
Temp (°C)	12.2	11.9	14.2	18.5	20.8	26.6	28.1	28.4	25.2	22.2	16.8	14.1
Temp (°F)	54	53	58	65	69	80	83	83	77	72	62	57

Author picks

We've explored every corner of the region – here we share some top tips, favourite sights, hidden gems and quintessential Provençal experiences.

Rural markets Arriving in a charming market town such as Aups (see page 209) or Fayence (see page 218), to find its streets and squares filled with stalls overflowing with fresh local produce and seasonal delicacies, ranks among the greatest delights of exploring rural Provence.

Provence wildlife Away from the cities, Provence remains (almost) as wild as ever. The mysterious marshlands of the Camargue (see page 105) are still home to wild horses and flocks of flamingos, while eagles and mountain goats haunt the heights of the Grand Canyon du Verdon (see page 219).

Matisse's Chapelle du Rosaire, Vence Matisse famously considered this diminutive Catholic chapel (see page 338) his masterpiece, the last creative will and testament of a dying genius where the starkness of the interior only serves to heighten both the experience and the profundity of the artist's own admission "my only religion is the love of the work to be created".

MARKET NEAR MONT VENTOUX

FLAMINGOS IN CAMARGUE

Sanary-sur-Mer Fishing boats take pride of place in the perfect little harbour of Sanary-sur-Mer (see page 256), a reminder that not everywhere on the coast is geared to the whims of the super-rich. Sanary's strongest associations are with literature, not money.

The Côte d'Azur out of season May can be magical; June and September a treat. Avoid peak season and discover a kinder, gentler Côte d'Azur, where the queues are shorter and the prices generally lower – from St Tropez without tears (see page 276) to Nice when it's nice (see page 344).

Bandol rosé Rosé is the characteristic wine of the coast, perfect on a warm summer's night with seafood and a seat on the terrace. Head for Bandol (see page 254) to discover sublime rosé with a sea view.

Our author recommendations don't end here. We've flagged up our favourite places – a perfectly sited hotel, an atmospheric café, a special restaurant – throughout the Guide, highlighted with the ★ symbol.

20

things not to miss

It's not possible to see everything Provence has to offer in one trip – and we don't suggest you try. What follows is a selective and subjective taste of the region's highlights: outstanding beaches and ancient sites, natural wonders and colourful festivals. All highlights are colour-coded by chapter and have a page reference to take you straight into the Guide, where you can find out more.

1

1 CHÂTEAU D'IF
See page 66
Take a boat from Marseille to the hulking fortress which looms large in the most iconic Provence-set novel of all, Alexandre Dumas' *The Count of Monte Cristo*.

2 THE PERCHED VILLAGE OF SIMIANE-LA-ROTONDE
See page 185
One of the loveliest *villages perchés* in the region. Originally built for defence, these medieval villages are now cherished for their maze-like alleyways, mellow stone houses and spectacular settings.

3 PONT DU GARD
See page 131
Two thousand years old and still sublimely graceful, this towering Roman aqueduct spans the Gard river a few kilometres west of the Rhône.

4 FONDATION MAEGHT
See page 340
Unmissable and highly original art museum, where the building and setting are as impressive as the modern sculptures and paintings.

5 LUMA ARLES
See page 91
The most exciting piece of new architecture in France, designed by (who else but) Frank Gehry and housing an ambitious new multi-disciplinary cultural centre.

6 DINING ALFRESCO IN VIEUX NICE
See page 358
Sit outside a Vieux Nice café and watch the vibrant street life, as you tuck into *salade niçoise*, *pissaladière* or a slice of *socca* straight from the pan.

7 MARSEILLE
See page 44
Don't let its outdated reputation put you off visiting this vibrant, multi-ethnic Mediterranean metropolis with good food, great bars and culture in abundance.

8 LES BAUX
See page 94
The eleventh-century citadel and picture-perfect *village perché* of Les Baux offer incredible views south over La Grande Crau to the sea.

9 ABBAYE DE SÉNANQUE
See page 193
The beauty of the twelfth-century Cistercian abbey of Sénanque is enhanced by its position, surrounded by lavender fields.

10 THE GYPSY PILGRIMAGE, LES SAINTES-MARIES-DE-LA-MER
See page 111
An annual spectacle of music, dancing and religious ritual, dating from the sixteenth century.

11 MUSÉE CHAGALL, NICE
See page 355
Spirituality and colour combine to memorable effect in Chagall's biblical canvases.

12 GRAND CANYON DU VERDON
See page 219
Europe's largest canyon offers stunning scenery and plenty of scope for activities, from cycling to bungee-jumping.

13 PARC NATIONAL DU MERCANTOUR
See page 229
Ride, hike, canoe or ski in this Alpine wilderness that's also home to the four-thousand-year-old rock carvings of the Vallée des Merveilles.

14 FESTIVAL D'AVIGNON
See page 120
July and early August are the best months to visit Avignon, when its ancient monuments provide the backdrop to a riot of theatre, music and dance.

15 MONACO
See page 375
Experience Monaco's status as an independent principality up close by watching the changing of the guard in front of the Palais Princier.

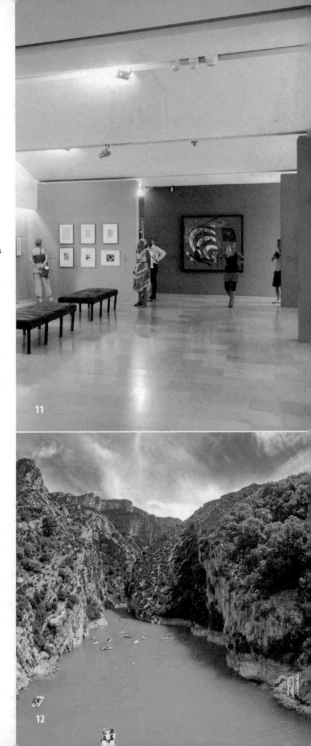

16

17

16 RIVIERA BEACHES

See page 304

From lobster and champagne on an elegant hotel beach to celebrity-spotting during the Cannes film festival, the Riviera has a beach culture all its own.

17 MONTAGNE STE-VICTOIRE

See page 165

Walk up to the top of the mountain that inspired so much of Cézanne's work.

18 WILDLIFE IN THE CAMARGUE

See page 108

Saddle up one of the white Camargue horses and explore this watery marshland on horseback.

19 AVIGNON'S PALAIS DES PAPES

See page 117

This vast medieval building was home to successive popes – and anti-popes – during Avignon's fourteenth-century heyday.

20 SCENIC THRILLS ON THE RIVIERA'S CORNICHES

See page 368

Soak up the grand coastal views along one of the world's most scintillating drives.

18

19

20

Tailor-made trips

You could never hope to see all the wonders of Provence on a single trip. We've therefore handpicked the following itineraries to help visitors with specific interests, ranging from the Roman relics of Arles to the vineyards of the Dentelles. The trips below give a flavour of what the region has to offer and what we can plan and book for you at ⓦroughguides.com/trips.

ANCIENT PROVENCE

Exploring the ancient sites of Provence, which date back even beyond the Romans and the Greeks, will take at least a week.

❶ **Vaison-la-Romaine** Walk actual Roman residential streets, complete with mosaic-floored houses, theatre and baths. See page 136

❷ **Orange** Arguably the best-preserved Roman theatre in the world is still in use for summer concerts. See page 133

❸ **Pont du Gard** Bridging a side valley a few kilometres west of the Rhône, the triple-tiered Pont du Gard is the tallest surviving Roman aqueduct. See page 131

❹ **Arles** This lovely city still holds an all-but-intact amphitheatre, plus a theatre, baths, necropolis, intriguing underground vaults, and a superb archeology museum. See page 84

❺ **St-Rémy** Just outside the modern town lie the remains of ancient Glanum, settled first by Greeks and later by Romans. See page 96

❻ **Antibes** Founded by the Greeks, Antibes has a good museum of Classical treasures. See page 320

❼ **Tende** A fascinating museum interprets the mysterious prehistoric carvings of the nearby, high-mountain Vallée des Merveilles. See page 245

SCENIC SPLENDOURS

You'll need a good two weeks to admire the full range of landscapes that Provence has to offer.

❶ **Les Calanques** Best seen on a boat tour, or from the Corniches des Crêtes coastal road between Cassis and La Ciotat, the dramatic rocky shoreline east of Marseille makes an unforgettable spectacle. See page 66

❷ **Haut Var** The dramatic rocky cliffs and pinnacles of the Haut Var are peppered with picturesque medieval villages, including gorgeous Cotignac. See page 205

❸ **Grand Canyon du Verdon** You could devote days on end to exploring the continent's deepest canyon, kayaking through its turquoise waters or hiking up to its towering peaks. See page 219

❹ **Col de la Bonette** What claims to be the highest paved road in Europe crosses this stark summit, high above the head of the verdant Tinée Valley. You'll need a head for heights! See page 237

You can book these trips with Rough Guides, or we can help you create your own. Whether you're after adventure or a family-friendly holiday, we have a trip for you, with all the activities you enjoy doing and the sights you want to see. All our trips are devised by local experts who get the most out of the destination. Visit **www.roughguides.com/trips** to chat with one of our travel agents.

❺ **The Luberon** With its wooded slopes, buttercup-filled meadows, fields of lavender and hilltop villages, the Luberon ridge rewards endless wandering. See page 186

❻ **Mont Ventoux** An infamously gruelling circuit for Tour-de-France cyclists, the loop around Mont Ventoux makes a wonderful scenic drive. See page 140

PROVENCE ON CANVAS

See Provence as the artists of the nineteenth and twentieth centuries saw it on this ten-day trail.

❶ **Arles** Van Gogh was enchanted by this ancient city, where he painted sunflowers and the *Café de Nuit*. See page 84

❷ **Martigues** Corot captured Martigues' Miroir aux Oiseaux on canvas; Picabia depicted the Étang de Berre's choppy waters. See page 76

❸ **Aix-en-Provence** Reminders of Cézanne are everywhere here, from the artist's childhood home to his studio and the mountain he painted obsessively. See page 154

❹ **Le Cannet** This unassuming Cannes suburb was home to Pierre Bonnard and now hosts the first museum dedicated to his work. See page 309

❺ **Antibes** An exuberant phase of Picasso's career is remembered at Antibes' seafront Château. See page 320

❻ **Nice** Matisse was attracted by Nice's cosmopolitan life, but Dufy's canvases in the Musée des Beaux-Arts immortalize it. See page 344

AN EPICURE'S TOUR

Allow a week for a leisurely culinary meander through the best of Provence's food and wine.

❶ **Nice** From *socca* to *salade niçoise*, Nice has a culinary heritage all its own. See page 344

❷ **Bandol** The mysterious mourvèdre grape works its magic in dark, intense reds and pale, crisp rosé. See page 254

❸ **Marseille** Provence's great port city is celebrated for bouillabaisse, the fishermen's stew that is now a gourmet treat. See page 44

❹ **Aix-en-Provence** Wonderful street markets, a restaurant on every corner and sweet *calissons* to take home as souvenirs – Provence's loveliest major city is foodie heaven. See page 154

❺ **Sisteron** The lamb from the countryside around Sisteron is renowned. See page 176

❻ **Banon** Remote, timeless Banon is home to the goats' cheese of the same name – pungent, leaf-wrapped and very, very good. See page 184

❼ **Châteauneuf-du-Pape** Rich, ruby-red wines have carried the fame of this village to the far corners of the earth. See page 131

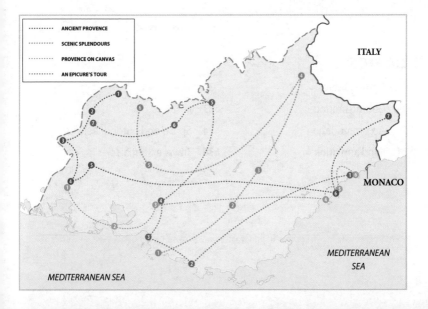

CORNICHE DE L'ESTEREL

Basics

23 Getting there

26 Getting around

29 Accommodation

31 Food and drink

33 The media

33 Festivals

34 Sports and outdoor activities

36 Travel essentials

Getting there

The quickest and cheapest way to get to Provence from the UK or Ireland is usually to fly. The region holds two of France's largest provincial airports, at Nice and Marseille, as well as lesser airports at Toulon-Hyères and Avignon. There are few direct intercontinental flights, though, so travellers from outside Europe are more likely to fly into Paris or London, then either transfer flights or complete the journey by train. For UK travellers, Eurostar rail services via the Channel Tunnel provide a fast and attractive alternative; in summer, some direct trains travel all the way to the south of France, but otherwise you'll need to change at Paris or Lille. It's also straight-forward to reach Provence by car from the UK, though it's a long drive, most comfort-ably accomplished with an overnight stop en route.

Flights from the UK and Ireland

Several **budget airlines** fly between the UK, Ireland and southern France. **Tickets** are priced for each specific flight, and vary from moment to moment. Book as early as possible for the cheapest seats. Assorted surcharges – including fees for baggage or to pay with a credit card – can easily add £30 or more each way.

Routes change frequently, and many destinations are not served all year round, so check airline websites for current options. **Ryanair** (ⓦ ryanair.com) flies to Marseille from London Stansted and Edinburgh, and to Nice from London Stansted, Dublin and Shannon. **EasyJet** (ⓦ easyjet.com) connects Nice with Belfast, Bristol, Edinburgh, Liverpool, Manchester, Newcastle and three London airports; and Marseille with Glasgow, Bristol, Luton, Gatwick and Manchester. **Flybe** (ⓦ flybe.com) links Avignon with Southampton and Birmingham, and Toulon with Southampton; and **Jet2** (ⓦ jet2.com) flies to Nice from Leeds, Manchester

and London Stansted. Ryanair also serves Nîmes from London Stansted and Luton, while easyJet flies to Montpellier from Bristol, Gatwick and Luton – both airports are just a short way west of the area covered in this book.

It's also worth checking out **national airlines** like Air France (ⓦ airfrance.com), British Airways (ⓦ ba.com) and Aer Lingus (ⓦ aerlingus.com), which these days offer reduced fares. Note, however, that as they're more orientated towards business travellers, unlike with the budget airlines it's not necessarily cheaper to fly midweek. **British Airways** flies daily from London Heathrow and London Gatwick to **Nice**, and from Heathrow to **Marseille**; low-season return fares start around £60 to Nice and £74 to Marseille. **Aer Lingus** flies from both Dublin and Cork to Nice from April to October, with return fares dropping to around €115 in low season and rising to more than €200 in summer; they also fly from Dublin to Marseille between April and September, at slightly lower prices.

Flights from the US and Canada

Very few **direct flights** connect the US and Canada with southern France. **Delta Air Lines** (ⓦ delta.com) flies nonstop from JFK in **New York** to Nice year round for around US$600–1500 return. Additionally, Canadian charter carrier **Air Transat** (ⓦ airtransat.com) links both **Montréal** and **Toronto** with Nice and Marseille in summer; fares start around Can$800 return in May, rising to around Can$1300 in July and August.

These direct flights aside, most journeys to Provence from North America will involve a **transfer**, either using an internal North American flight to hook up with the Delta or Air Transat flights or flying direct to Paris or some other major European hub and making onward connections by air or train.

Several major airlines have **scheduled flights to Paris** from the US and Canada. An off-season midweek direct return flight to Paris can be as low as US$500 including taxes from New York and Los Angeles and US$700 from Houston. From Canada, prices to Paris start at around Can$650 from Montréal or Toronto.

A BETTER KIND OF TRAVEL

At Rough Guides we are passionately committed to travel. We believe it helps us understand the world we live in and the people we share it with – and of course tourism is vital to many developing economies. But the scale of modern tourism has also damaged some places irreparably, and climate change is accelerated by most forms of transport, especially flying. We encourage our authors to consider the carbon footprint of the journeys they make in the course of researching our guides.

Air France (@airfrance.com) operates the most frequent service to Paris, with good onward connections to Provence, including frequent services to Nice, Marseille and Toulon-Hyères. Many internal Air France flights depart from Paris Orly Airport, which requires a cross-town transfer from Charles de Gaulle, but there are also internal flights to Marseille and Nice from Charles de Gaulle, which is the main portal for intercontinental flights. Another option is to fly with a European carrier – such as British Airways (@ba.com), Iberia (@iberia.com) or Lufthansa (@lufthansa.com) – to its European hub and then continue on to Paris or a regional French airport.

Flights from Australia, New Zealand and South Africa

There are **no direct flights** to Provence from Australia, New Zealand or South Africa. Most travellers from **Australia and New Zealand** choose to fly to France via London, but airlines can add a Paris leg to an Australia/New Zealand–Europe ticket. Flights via Asia or the Gulf States, with a transfer or overnight stop at the airline's home port, are generally the cheapest option; those routed through the US tend to be slightly pricier. Return **fares** start at around Aus\$900 from Sydney, Aus\$1100 from Perth, Aus\$1200 from Melbourne and NZ\$1200 from Auckland.

From **South Africa**, Johannesburg is the best place to start, with Air France flying direct to Paris from around R5000 return; from Cape Town, they fly via Johannesburg or Doha and are more expensive, starting at around R6400.

By train

The Channel Tunnel, which burrows beneath the English Channel to provide a direct train link from England, plays host to two distinct services. Eurostar carries foot passengers only, while Eurotunnel simply conveys cars and other vehicles between Folkestone and Calais, in direct competition with the ferries.

Eurostar trains depart from London St Pancras International. The fastest way to get to Provence is on the summer-only direct service to either **Avignon** (5hr 49min) or **Marseille** (6hr 26min). This runs three days weekly, increasing to five days in July and August. Return journey times back to the UK are longer, as passengers pass through security and immigration checks at Lille. Fares start at £99 return.

Most rail journeys to Provence, however, involve changing trains in either Paris (2hr 15min from London) or Lille (1hr 20min), and continuing south on a separate SNCF service. Changing in Lille usually

consists of a simple switch of platforms. Changing in Paris, however, requires you to get from the Gare du Nord, where Eurostar trains arrive, to the Gare de Lyon, the point of departure for SNCF trains to Provence and the Côte d'Azur. That's a straightforward journey, for which you catch an RER D line train from the Gare du Nord, heading in the direction "Melun/Malesherbes" or "Corbeil-Essonnes". The actual ride on the RER takes seven or eight minutes, though it takes a minimum of half an hour from the moment you get off the Eurostar train to the moment you board the SNCF service, and you should always allow at least an hour in case of delays. Don't imagine a taxi will be quicker; you may well have to wait fifteen minutes or more for a taxi, and the road journey will be slower too.

Popular destinations from London – with journey times here quoted via Paris – include Avignon (6hr 45min), Aix (7hr), Marseille (7hr), Cannes (9hr) and Nice (9hr 30min).

For the best deal on fares, buy a ticket for the entire journey through Eurostar, SNCF or an online vendor such as @loco2.com. Note that the Eurostar website tends to show many more connections via Paris than by Lille; if you'd rather change in Lille (which is simpler), it's always worth calling Eurostar by phone instead to see if anything else is available. InterRail and Eurail **passes** (see page 26) offer discounts on Eurostar trains.

Bicycles that fold are carried free of charge in Eurostar carriages. Otherwise, you can arrange for your bike to be transported either fully assembled (£35; limited spaces) or in a bike box provided by Eurostar (£30). Note that bikes over 85cm long are ineligible for Avignon and Marseille services. Finally, for visitors arriving **by air** in Paris, trains link Charles de Gaulle airport with Marseille in around four hours, with one-way fares from around €60; trains from Charles de Gaulle to Nice entail at least one change and take roughly six and a half hours, with one-way fares from around €120.

By car

Getting to Provence **by car from the UK** is relatively straightforward. The French autoroute network can be swiftly accessed by taking either a ferry from Dover or Folkestone to Calais or Dunkerque, or the Channel Tunnel to **Calais**. From there, the best route follows the E17 to the east of Paris via Troyes and Dijon, then the E15 from Beaune via Lyon to Provence. For much of the way, **traffic** is light; as a rule, congestion only ever becomes a problem south of Lyon.

The entrance to the **Channel Tunnel** is less than two hours' drive from London, off the M20 at Junction 11A, just outside Folkestone. Once there, you drive your car onto a two-tier train, which takes 35 minutes to reach Coquelles, just outside Calais. There are up to four departures per hour (one approximately every 2hr from midnight to 6am). You can turn up and buy your ticket at the check-in booths, but you'll pay a premium and at busy times booking is strongly recommended; if you have a booking, you must arrive at least forty-five minutes before departure. Note that Eurotunnel does not transport cars fitted with LPG or CNG tanks.

Standard **fares** start at £74 one-way if you book far enough ahead and/or travel off peak, rising to £105. Fully refundable and changeable FlexiPlus fares cost £219. There's room for only six **bicycles** on any departure, so book ahead in high season – fares begin from £520 each way for a bike plus rider.

The shortest **ferry** crossing connects Dover with Calais. If you're coming from the north of England or Scotland, however, you should consider P&O Ferries' overnight crossing from Hull (13hr) to Zeebrugge (Belgium), while if you live west of London, the ferries to Roscoff, St-Malo, Cherbourg, Caen, Dieppe and Le Havre can save a lot of driving time. **From Ireland**, putting the car on the ferry from Cork (14hr) to Roscoff in Brittany, or Rosslare to Cherbourg (18hr) in Normandy cuts out the drive across Britain to the Channel.

Ferry **prices** are seasonal and, for motorists, depend on the type of vehicle. In general, the further you book ahead, the cheaper the fare, while midweek and very early or late sailings are usually cheapest. At the time of writing, one-way fares with DFDS for a car and up to nine passengers are priced at £45 on the Dover–Dunkerque route and £49 on the Dover–Calais route. One-way fares from Ireland kick off at around €115 for a car and two adults.

P&O offer Dover–Calais foot passenger fares from £30 one way, while DFDS offer bicycle-plus-rider tickets from £20 one way.

AGENTS AND OPERATORS

GENERAL

French Travel Connection Ⓦ frenchtravel.com.au. Australian company offering everything to do with travel in France: accommodation, car rental, tours and even cooking classes. Eight-day tours of Provence and the French Riviera start from Aus$4498.
Viking River Cruises Ⓦ vikingrivercruises.com. French river cruises, including an eight-day trip to Avignon along the Saône and the Rhône, starting at £1495.

ACCOMMODATION

Canvas Holidays Ⓦ canvasholidays.co.uk. Tailor-made caravan and camping holidays along the Côte d'Azur.
Citadines Ⓦ citadines.com. This Europe-wide chain of apartment-hotels includes properties in Marseille and Cannes from around €75/night in high season.
Dominique's Villas Ⓦ dominiquesvillas.co.uk. Upmarket agency with a diverse range of tempting properties, mostly for larger groups.
Eurocamp Ⓦ eurocamp.co.uk. Camping holidays on the Riviera, with kids' activities and single-parent deals.
Holiday in France Ⓦ holidayinfrance.co.uk. Upmarket villas and houses to rent all over Provence, including some very large properties.
Home Away Ⓦ homeaway.co.uk. Industry leading holiday let specialist with hundreds of rental properties throughout the region, from city apartments to rural villas with pools.
HouseTrip Ⓦ housetrip.com. UK-based holiday home rental website offering a wide range of affordable family accommodation. Thousands of properties across Provence, including around five hundred in Marseille.
Gîtes de France Ⓦ gites-de-france.fr. Comprehensive array of houses, cottages and chalets throughout France.
Only Apartments Ⓦ only-apartments.com. Apartments in Provence and along the Côte d'Azur, especially in cities like Nice, Cannes and Marseille. Direct booking via the owner, from around €70/night.

ACTIVITY HOLIDAYS

Alternative Travel Group Ⓦ atg-oxford.co.uk. Five- and seven-day walking tours in Vaucluse and the Luberon, from £695.
Austin-Lehman Adventures Ⓦ austinadventures.com. US operator offering week-long hiking tours of Provence, costing from $3898.
Backroads Ⓦ backroads.com. US-based bike-tour company offering six-day Provence cycling or hiking trips – the "Classic Provence Bike Tour" starts at US$4699.
Belle France Ⓦ bellefrance.com. Walking and cycling holidays in Provence; a week in the Luberon costs from £2390.
Butterfield & Robinson Ⓦ butterfield.com. Canadian operator arranging six-day Provençal biking or walking tours; self-guided trips start at US$3495.
Cycling for Softies Ⓦ cycling-for-softies.co.uk. Easy-going cycle holiday operator to rural France, with particularly appealing itineraries in the Luberon, incorporating canoeing as well. Three-night self-guided tours from £685.
Inntravel Ⓦ inntravel.co.uk. Broad range of activity holidays, including walking and cycling, as well as property rental. A six-night cycle trip in the Camargue starts at £970.
Mountain Travel Sobek Ⓦ mtsobek.com. All-inclusive hiking trips in Provence, with travel from US; twelve days hiking from the Alps to the sea from $5995.
Walkabout Gourmet Adventures Ⓦ walkaboutgourmet. com. Australian operator offering walking tours with an emphasis

on cooking and good food. Seven-day "Pagnol's Provence" costs Aus$3950.

World Expeditions Ⓦ worldexpeditions.com. Self-guided and escorted cycling and trekking holidays, including eight-day cycling trips in Provence from £920.

RAIL & CHANNEL TUNNEL CONTACTS

Eurail Ⓦ eurail.com.
Eurostar UK ☎ 03432 186 186, Ⓦ eurostar.com.
Eurotunnel UK ☎ 08443 35 35 35, Ⓦ eurotunnel.com.
Loco2 Ⓦ loco2.com. Efficient site offering through bookings from the UK to any French station.
Man in Seat 61 Ⓦ seat61.com. Detailed advice on every aspect of travelling by train in Europe, including step-by-step accounts of how to change trains in Paris.
Rail Europe Ⓦ raileurope.com. US based booking site specialising in European rail travel.
SNCF Ⓦ en.oui.sncf. The most useful booking site for French trains.

FERRY CONTACTS

Brittany Ferries UK ☎ 0330 159 7000, Ⓦ brittany-ferries.co.uk; Republic of Ireland ☎ 021 427 7801, Ⓦ brittanyferries.ie.
Condor Ferries Ⓦ condorferries.co.uk.
Corsica Ferries Ⓦ corsica-ferries.fr.
DFDS (Dover–Calais, Dover–Dunkerque), Ⓦ dfdsseaways.co.uk.
Direct Ferries UK ☎ 03333 000 128, Ⓦ directferries.co.uk.
Ferry Savers Ⓦ ferrysavers.com.
Irish Ferries Republic of Ireland ☎ 0818 300 400, Ⓦ irishferries.com.
P&O Ferries UK ☎ 0800 130 0030, Ⓦ poferries.com.

Getting around

If you simply want to travel to and between the big-name destinations of Provence, go by train. While local bus networks operate in and around major towns, however, the only efficient way to explore the region as a whole is to use a car or bike.

By train

SNCF (Ⓦ en.oui.sncf), the national rail network, operates most rail services in Provence. High-speed **TGV** trains, capable of speeds of more than 300km/hr, link the region with Paris and the rest of France, with stations at Orange, Avignon, Aix and Marseille, before continuing via Toulon, Hyères and Les Arcs-Draguignan to serve Riviera resorts including St-Raphaël, Cannes, Nice and Monaco. Those aged between 16 and 27 might want to take advantage of the TGVmax pass (€79) which affords unlimited travel for one month on all TGV and Intercités trains requiring reservations.

Once in Provence you'll find **TER** (Transport Express Régional; Ⓦ ter.sncf.com) services more useful. These trains are often still impressively modern and comfortable, and stop at more intermediate stations. Outside peak hours (7–9am & 4.30–6.30pm) you can carry a **bicycle** free of charge on these trains, stowing it either in the baggage car or in the bicycle spaces provided. In addition to the principal lines along the Rhône Valley and the coast, a second major line heads north from Marseille through Aix and along the Durance to Manosque, Sisteron and beyond, towards Gap and Grenoble, while another line heads north from Nice towards the Italian border at Tende, linking many of the communities of the *pays-arrière niçois* with the coast.

Tickets can be bought online or at any train station (*gare SNCF*). Touch-screen vending machines with instructions in English sell tickets for express services in most stations; separate vending machines for regional (TER) services have basic English labelling. All tickets except passes or computerized tickets printed at home must be validated in the orange machines at the entrance to station platforms; it's an offence not to follow the instruction *Compostez votre billet* ("validate your ticket").

For anyone travelling in a family group, the one-day **Pass Isabelle Famille** (€35) allows a group of two adults and two under-16s unlimited travel on TER (but not TGV) trains anywhere between Fréjus and the Italian border and inland to Grasse and Tende. Provence's other rail network is the narrow-gauge **Chemins de Fer de Provence** (Ⓦ trainprovence.com), a scenic (if slow) meandering ride that connects Nice with Digne (see page 355).

By bus

Along the coast and between the major towns, Provence is well served by **buses**, with the best and most frequent routes being the fast Aix–Marseille and Marseille–Aubagne shuttles, and the services that link Nice with the other principal resorts along the Riviera. Elsewhere bus services are much less satisfactory, being geared to the needs of schoolchildren and shoppers visiting local markets, and usually both slow and infrequent – even more so during school holidays.

SNCF buses are useful for getting to places on the rail network no longer served by passenger trains, such as intermediate stops on the Manosque–Sisteron line and the entire Château Arnoux–Digne line. **Inter-urban buses** are otherwise coordinated on a departmental basis, with **timetables** and other information often available online: Ⓦ lepilote.

TOP FIVE DRIVES

Col de Turini Twisting, challenging mountain driving in the Riviera's hinterland, as driven by TV's *Top Gear* team in their search for the world's greatest road. See page 242

Corniche de l'Esterel Rust-red rocks and deep blue sea make a lasting impression on this lovely coastal drive. See page 297

Corniche des Crêtes Regular belvederes provide breathtaking coastal views from this route along Provence's highest sea cliffs. See page 70

Grand Canyon du Verdon You'll struggle to keep your eye on the wheel as you circle Europe's most spectacular gorge on the Route des Crêtes and Corniche Sublime. See page 219

Moyenne Corniche Pop on your shades and follow the tracks of a thousand car commercials on the Riviera's most glamorous drive. See page 371

com for Marseille and surroundings; ⓦwww. varlib.fr for the Var, ⓦvaucluse.fr for Avignon, the Vaucluse and around; and ⓦdepartement06.fr for Nice and the Riviera, and also for the Alpes de Haute-Provence.

Larger towns usually have a *gare routière* (bus station), often next to the *gare SNCF*. However, the private bus companies don't always work together and you'll frequently find them leaving from an array of different points (the local tourist office should be able to help locate the stop you need).

By car

Away from the big cities, Provence is a superb, scenic place to get behind the wheel. **Driving** allows you to explore the more remote villages and the most dramatic landscapes, which are otherwise inaccessible. In the **cities**, driving is much less enjoyable – the old historic parts of many towns are all but inaccessible, car crime is a problem and traffic and parking can be nightmarish, particularly in Nice and Marseille.

As for fuel, both unleaded (*sans plomb*) and diesel (*gazole* or *gasoil*) are universally available. Note that **petrol stations** in rural areas tend to be few and far between, and those that do exist usually open only during normal shop hours – don't count on being able to buy petrol at night or on Sunday. Some stations are equipped with automated 24-hour pumps, but these do not always accept foreign credit cards.

Other than in the commuter area of Marseille, **tolls** apply on the autoroutes: you pick up a ticket when you enter a toll section and pay in cash or by credit card when you leave. You can work out routes and costs of both petrol and tolls online at ⓦviamichelin. com. UK motorists can use the Liber-T automatic tolling lanes if their cars are fitted with the relevant tag; to register in advance for a tag and for more information see ⓦemovis-tag.co.uk.

Rules of the road

The French **drive on the right**. Most people used to driving on the left find it easy to adjust; the biggest problem in a right-hand-drive car tends to be visibility when you want to overtake.

Although the law of *priorité à droite* – under which you have to give way to traffic coming from your right, even when it's entering from a minor road – has largely been phased out, it still applies on some roads in built-up areas, so be vigilant at junctions. A sign showing a yellow diamond on a white background indicates that you have **right of way**, while the same sign with an oblique black slash warns you that vehicles emerging from the right have priority. **Stop signs** mean stop completely; *Cédez le passage* means "Give way".

Speed limits are 50km/hr in towns (with 30km/hr common in villages and historic towns), 80km/hr outside built-up areas and 110km/hr on dual carriageways, with a limit of 130km/hr on autoroutes in fine weather, reduced to 110km/hr in the rain. Speed limits are also lower on autoroutes that pass through urban areas, including the stretch of the A8 that runs along the Riviera. Radar and speed camera detectors are illegal.

Legal requirements

British, Irish, Australian, Canadian, New Zealand and US **driving licences** are valid in France, though an International Driver's Licence makes life easier. If the vehicle is rented, its registration document (*carte grise*) and the insurance papers must be carried. The **minimum driving age** is 18, and provisional licences are not valid.

The vehicle registration document and the **insurance papers** must be carried; only the originals are acceptable. It's no longer essential for motorists from other EU countries to buy a green card to extend their usual insurance. If you have insurance at home then you have the minimal legal coverage in France; whether you have any

ROAD INFORMATION

Up-to-the-minute information regarding traffic jams and road works throughout France can be obtained from the Bison Futé website ⓦ www.bison-fute.gouv.fr, with much of the info available in English. For information regarding autoroutes, you can also consult the bilingual website ⓦ autoroutes.fr. Once you're on the autoroute, tune in to the national 107.7FM information station for 24-hour music and updates on traffic conditions.

more than that, and (if not) whether you want to buy more, is something to discuss with your own insurance company.

If you bring a right-hand drive car from the UK, you must adjust your **headlight dip** to the right before you go. As a courtesy, change or paint your headlights to yellow, or stick on black glare deflectors. You must also affix **GB plates** if you're driving a British car, and carry a red warning triangle, a single-use breathalyzer and a spare set of headlight bulbs in your vehicle, as well as a reflective jacket that must be stored within reach of the driver's seat. Shops at ferry terminals, and on the boats themselves, sell all the required equipment.

Seat belts are compulsory for the driver and all passengers; children under 10 can only sit in the front in approved rear-facing child seats.

If you have an **accident** while driving, you must fill in and sign a *constat d'accident* (declaration form) or, if another car is also involved, a *constat aimable* (jointly agreed declaration); in the case of a rental car, these forms should be provided with the car's insurance documents.

Car rental

Car rental in France costs upwards of €230 per week (from around €70/day). Renters must be over 21 (some agencies insist on 25) and have driven for at least a year. Reserve online well in advance to get the best rates. The big-name international chains have outlets at airports, rail stations, and in most major towns and cities. Local firms can be cheaper but they won't have the agency network for one-way rentals and you should check the small print. Unless you specify otherwise, and almost certainly pay significantly extra, you'll get a car with manual (stick shift) transmission.

Note that since 2015, UK licence holders have officially been obliged to obtain **proof** that they are legally entitled to drive from the DVLA website (ⓦ gov. uk/dvla), up to 21 days before any rental. You are given a one-off code to show the rental agency; in practice few agencies seem to ask for the code, however.

CAR RENTAL AGENCIES

Avis ⓦ avis.com

Argus Car Hire ⓦ arguscarhire.com
Auto Europe ⓦ autoeurope.com
Europcar ⓦ europcar.com
Hertz ⓦ hertz.com
Holiday Autos ⓦ holidayautos.com

By scooter and motorbike

Scooters are ideal for pottering around locally, and are easy to rent. Expect to pay in the region of €35 a day for a 50cc machine. If you are over 24 years old, you don't need a licence for a 50cc moped – just passport/ ID – but otherwise you'll need a driving licence.

For anything from 50cc to 125cc you'll need to have held a driving licence for at least two years regardless of your age, while for anything over 125cc you need a full **motorbike** licence. Rental **prices** are around €60–70 per day for a 125cc bike. Crash helmets are compulsory on all bikes, and the headlight must be switched on at all times. For bikes over 125cc it is compulsory to wear reflective clothing and carry a set of spare bulbs.

By bike

As the proliferation of specialist biking tours demonstrates (see page 25), **cycling** on back roads of rural Provence can be delightful, if strenuous due to the often rugged terrain. Cycles can easily be **rented**, particularly down on the coast where several towns hold branches of the Holiday Bikes chain (ⓦ loca-bike. fr), which also rents out motorcycles and scooters. Marseille and Nice also have Paris-style credit-card-operated public bike rental stations.

Accommodation

Finding accommodation on the spot in the larger towns and cities of Provence is only likely to prove difficult during high season, July and August. On the Riviera, however, things get booked up earlier in the year: in May, the Cannes Film Festival makes it extremely difficult to find reasonably priced accommodation on the

western Riviera, while the Monaco Grand Prix creates the same problem along the coast east of Nice. In any case, booking a couple of nights in advance is reassuring at any time of year.

Hotels

Hotels in Provence, as in the rest of France, are **graded** with zero to five **stars**. The price more or less corresponds to the number of stars, though the system is a little haphazard, having more to do with ratios of bathrooms per guest than genuine quality; ungraded and single-star hotels are often very good. North American visitors accustomed to staying in rooms equipped with coffee-makers, safes and refrigerators should not automatically expect the same facilities in French hotels, even the more expensive ones – and hotels don't invariably have lifts, either. Genuine **single rooms** are rare. On the other hand, most hotels willingly equip rooms with extra beds, at a good discount. Only the very cheapest hotels these days still offer rooms without en-suite facilities, and even then they almost always have en-suite rooms as well.

Prices in the swankier **resorts** such as Cannes or St-Tropez tend to be higher than in the rest of the region – though Nice has a good supply of cheap accommodation throughout most of the year – and in high season (July–Aug), rates soar in the Côte d'Azur resorts.

Outlets of **budget motel chains** proliferate alongside autoroute exits and on the outskirts of larger towns. While characterless, these are generally inexpensive, and can make a good option for motorists, especially late at night.

Many **family-run hotels close** for two or three weeks a year in low season. In smaller towns and villages they may also shut up shop for one or two nights a week, usually Sunday or Monday. Details are given where relevant throughout this Guide, but as dates change from year to year and as some places may decide to close for a few days in low season if they have no bookings, it's always wise to call ahead to check.

Breakfast, which is seldom included in the quoted price, can add anything from €6 to €30 per person to a bill – though there is no obligation to take it. That said, in high season some hotels – particularly in popular tourist destinations – insist on half board (*demi-pension*), which includes breakfast and dinner.

France is home to a number of well-respected **hotel federations**. The biggest and most useful is *Logis de France* (☎01 45 84 70 00, ⓦlogishotels.com),

an association of more than 2800 hotels nationwide. Other, more upmarket federations include *Châteaux & Hôtels de France* (ⓦchateauxhotels.com) which offers high-class accommodation in beautiful older properties, often in rural locations.

Bed and breakfast and self-catering

In country areas especially, you're likely to come across **chambres d'hôtes** – bed-and-breakfast accommodation in someone's house, château or farm. These vary in standard, but are rarely especially cheap; with prices generally ranging from €60 to €130 for two, including breakfast, they tend to cost the equivalent of a two-star hotel. Payment is usually expected in cash. Some offer meals on request (*tables d'hôtes*), usually in the evenings only.

If you're planning to stay a week or more in one place it's worth considering renting **self-catering accommodation**. Possibilities range from urban apartments to self-contained country cottages known as **gîtes**. "Gîtes Panda" are *gîtes* located in a national park or other protected area and are run on environmentally friendly lines.

Gîtes and *chambres d'hôtes* are listed on the government-funded agency Gîtes de France (ⓦgites-de-france.com), searchable by location or theme so you can find, for example, *gîtes* near fishing or riding opportunities. Countless other agencies and websites (see page.25) also offer rental properties all over Provence, and local tourist offices maintain lists.

Hostels

At around €20–30 per night for a **dormitory bed**, usually with breakfast thrown in, youth hostels – *auberges de jeunesse* – are invaluable for single travellers of any age on a budget. Some now offer rooms, occasionally en suite, but these don't necessarily work out cheaper than rooms in inexpensive hotels. However, many enable you

---

BUDGET CHAIN MOTELS

The following motel chains are listed in approximately ascending order of price and comfort.
F1 ⓦhotelf1.com
B&B ⓦhotel-bb.com
Première Classe ⓦpremiereclasse.fr
Ibis ⓦibis.com
Campanile ⓦcampanile.com

ACCOMMODATION PRICES

Throughout this Guide we give a headline price for every accommodation reviewed. This indicates the **lowest rack rate price for a double/twin room during high season** (usually July and August). Single rooms, where available, usually cost between 60 and 80 percent of a double or twin, though many budget chain hotels do not offer discounts for single occupancy of double or triple-bed rooms. At **hostels**, we give the price for a dorm bed and, where applicable, a double room, and at **campsites**, the cost for two people, a vehicle and a tent pitch.

to cut costs by eating in cheap canteens, while in a few you can prepare your own meals in the communal kitchens.

In addition to those belonging to the two French hostelling associations listed below, there are also several independent hostels, particularly in Nice and Marseille.

Youth hostel associations

There are two rival **French hostelling associations** – the *Fédération Unie des Auberges de Jeunesse* (FUAJ: Ⓦ fuaj.org) and the much smaller *Ligue Française* (LFAJ: Ⓦ auberges-de-jeunesse.com). In either, you normally have to show a current Hostelling International (HI) **membership card** in order to stay. It's cheaper and easier to join before you leave home, provided your national youth hostel association is a full member of HI. Alternatively, you can purchase an HI card in certain French hostels (€11 over 26, €7 under 26).

Gîtes d'étape and refuges

In the countryside, another hostel-style option exists in the form of **gîtes d'étape**. Aimed at hikers and long-distance bikers, *gîtes d'étape* provide bunks and primitive kitchen and washing facilities for around €15–25 per person. They are marked on the large-scale IGN walkers' maps and listed in the Topo-guides. Mountain areas are well supplied with **refuges**, mostly run by the Fédération Française des Clubs Alpins et de Montagne (FFCAM; Ⓦ ffcam.fr). Generally only staffed in summer, these huts offer dorm accommodation and meals, and are the only available shelter once you are above the villages. Costs are around €17–26 for the night, or half that if you're a member of a climbing organization affiliated to FFCAM, plus around €20–25 for breakfast and dinner. Outside summer, some offer very limited, basic shelter at reduced cost.

More information can be found online at Ⓦ www. gites-refuges.com, where you can download four printable regional *Gîtes d'Étape et Réfuges* guides for €5 per region.

Camping

Most villages and towns in Provence have at least one **campsite** (notable exceptions being Marseille and Nice). Camping is extremely popular with the French and, especially for those from the north, Provence is a favourite destination. The cheapest sites – from around €15 – are often the **campings municipaux** run by the local authority in small communes in rural areas. Another countryside option – usually with minimal facilities – is camping **à la ferme** (on private **farmland**). Local tourist offices will usually have lists of such sites.

On the Côte d'Azur, **commercial sites** can be vast, with hundreds of pitches and elaborate facilities including swimming pools and restaurants; reckon on paying up to €40 per night for a car, tent and two people in high season on the coast. Sites are graded according to quality from one to four stars; the more stars, the better the facilities – and the higher the price. Most sites also have rental cabins, which tend to cost upwards of €100 per night.

You can search for a site by *département* via Camping France (Ⓦ campingfrance.com), Gîtes de France (Ⓦ gites-de-france.fr) or local tourist board sites. **Camping Qualité** (Ⓦ campingqualite.com) lists campsites with particularly high standards of hygiene, service and privacy, while the **Clef Verte** (Ⓦ laclefverte.org) label is awarded to sites (plus hostels and hotels) run along environmentally friendly lines.

Camping rough (*camping sauvage*) is strongly discouraged in summer due to the high risk of forest fires; in any case, you should never camp rough without first asking the landowner's permission, as farmers have been known to shoot first and ask questions later. Camping on the **beach** is not permitted.

Food and drink

Wholesome and healthy, the cooking of Provence displays all the benefits of the

Mediterranean diet, with superb fish on the coast, excellent lamb from Sisteron and, everywhere, fantastic fresh fruit and vegetables – the rewards of a sunny climate. Although the region is home to some of the world's finest and most expensive restaurants, the true glory of Provençal cuisine lies in honest home cooking based on fresh, locally sourced ingredients: in the countryside, in particular, small, family-run restaurants still serve up tasty prix-fixe feasts at traditional prices, while Nice is as good a place as any in Europe to find cheap, simple but delicious street food.

Fish and seafood are mainstays of the diet on the Mediterranean coast. At its most sublimely simple this means oursins – sea urchins – eaten raw with a sprinkling of lemon juice and a glass of crisp white wine; they're also cooked to make oursinade – a fish soup or sauce. But the region's love of fish is best reflected in the celebrated soups or stews: bourride, made with monkfish, where the cooking liquor is thickened with aïoli afterwards and served separately as a soup, and the famous bouillabaisse of Marseille, originally a humble meal cooked on the beach by fishermen but now quite a grand affair, the high cost of which reflects the quality of the ingredients used – notably rascasse or scorpion fish.

The markets of Provence are a sensual treat as well as a lively social event; the best are listed in the Guide.

Breakfast

Depending on the class of hotel or hostel, breakfast may be a simple affair of coffee and fresh baguette with jam and butter, or a much more elaborate spread involving croissants or a hot and cold buffet – though the splendour of the breakfast buffet will be reflected in the bill: a breakfast buffet in even a mid-range hotel might set you back €15, whereas a simpler bread-and-coffee affair in a cheaper hotel might be

REGIONAL DELICACIES

The "French" section of this Guide includes a **glossary** of food and drink terms (see page 414). In addition, look out for the following specialities.

Aïoli A mayonnaise-like sauce of garlic and olive oil. Un grand aïoli is an elaborate dish of salt cod, boiled beef, mutton and stewed vegetables, served with aïoli and garnished with boiled eggs and snails.
Bouillabaisse This fishermen's stew from Marseille is the most famous of all Provençal seafood dishes – at its best it's utterly delicious.
Calissons A speciality of Aix-en-Provence, these lozenge-shaped sweetmeats are made from almonds and candied lemon and are perfect with a strong espresso.
Chèvre de Banon Pungent and good, this goat's cheese from the remote village of Banon comes wrapped in chestnut leaves.
Daube de boeuf Provence's winter warmer is a beef stew enriched with red wine and seasoned with juniper, orange peel and chopped bacon.
Farcis Stuffed vegetables are a delicious speciality of the coast, but vegetarians beware – the stuffing is usually meat or sausage.
Oursins Sea urchins washed down with local white wine are the classic flavour combination if you're dining on Cassis's pretty harbour.
Pieds et paquets Sheep's trotters and stomachs may be an acquired taste, but they're a characteristic Marseille dish.
Pissaladière A sort of Provençal variation on pizza, this flat tart was developed in Nice, and consists of bread dough topped with caramelized onions, and usually with olives and anchovies too.
Pistou The Provençal equivalent of the celebrated Italian pesto sauce, made with basil, crushed garlic and olive oil.
Ravioles Ravioli is a classic Niçois dish, often stuffed with blette – Swiss chard – and daube, served with a splash of meaty daube sauce.
Rouille A thick, pinky-orange, aïoli-like sauce, made with chilli, garlic and saffron, pounded with breadcrumbs or potato, to which are added olive oil and stock. It's one of the classic accompaniments to a Provençal fish soup.
Socca Best eaten hot and fresh from the pan, this Niçois chickpea pancake is perfect street food – simple, wholesome and tasty.
Tapenade Capers, anchovies and black olives give this famous Provençal spread its pungent, salty flavour.

THE WINES OF PROVENCE

Provence has been renowned for its **wine** for well over two thousand years, since Greek settlers planted its first vineyards. While the region as a whole is especially noted for **rosé** – Provence produces almost ten percent of the world's entire supply – it's also responsible for celebrated wines ranging from the grand vintages of Châteauneuf-du-Pape to the dessert wines of Beaumes de Venise.

Eight distinct regions have their own AOC *appellations*. The **Côtes de Provence** region, scattered across eastern Provence, is by far the largest, producing almost three quarters of all Provençal wine, of which most is rosé. The **Coteaux-Varois**, inland in the centre of the region, is also dominated by rosé, while more than half the production in the **Coteaux d'Aix-en-Provence** to the west consists of reds, with **Les-Baux-de-Provence** here meriting its own *appellation*.

The most famous rosé of all comes from the **Bandol** region, centred on the eponymous coastal resort west of Toulon and relying heavily on the Mourvèdre grape variety, while west of there, towards Marseille, the **Cassis** region concentrates on dry white wines.

half that. If you're staying in a town it can be cheaper to opt out and go to a local café for a croissant, *pain au chocolat* (a chocolate-filled pastry) or sandwich, washed down with coffee or hot chocolate – though if you do so, make sure your hotel knows you're not having breakfast.

Lunch and dinner

At lunchtime, and sometimes in the evening, many restaurants and cafés offer good-value **plats du jour** (chef's specials) at prices below the **à la carte** menu prices. You'll also come across lunchtime **formules** – a menu of limited or no choice, including perhaps a main course and a drink. Most restaurants serve one or more **prix-fixe** (set-price) *menus*, which usually offer a limited selection of dishes at a reduced price, and are often available in two- and three-course versions. The usual accompaniment to a full meal is wine; stick to the house wine – often available in 25 or 50cl *pichets* (carafes) – if you want to keep the bill down.

To experience the full glory of **Provençal cooking** you really need to eat in a **restaurant**. It's still possible to eat well for €30 or less in a small, family-run place where you'll enjoy hearty, home-cooked dishes such as *daube de boeuf* or *pieds et paquets*, though the real gems are not as easy to find as they were. One appealing and affordable alternative to Provençal cuisine – particularly in Marseille – is **North African** food, while for vegetarians in particular, the numerous **pizzerias** can be a godsend; they usually advertise pizza cooked *au feu de bois* – in a wood-fired oven – and served with a drizzle of oil. Fresh **pasta**, a speciality of Nice, is affordable and often very good. **Brasseries** and **cafés** vary widely in price and style, from those that are merely large bars serving a

restricted food menu to grand (and expensive) affairs resembling the celebrated Parisian haunts of the Left Bank. Generally speaking, brasseries serve **quick meals** at any time of the day, including salads and lighter options. **Crêperies** and **salons de thé** are also good bets for light meals.

Snacks and street food

Provence – and especially Nice – is a wonderful place to eat on the hoof. Colourful **markets** are an excellent source of fresh produce, meats and cheeses, while **patisseries** often sell the delicious savoury *pain fougasse*, a finger-shaped bread that may contain olives, anchovies, sausage, cheese or bacon. Along the Riviera the **sandwich** of choice is the *pan bagnat*, a delicious mix of tuna, hard-boiled egg and bitter mesclun salad leaves drizzled with oil, usually available for around €5. **Niçois street food** includes the simple onion tart *pissaladière*, *farcis* (vegetables stuffed with a meat mixture), and hot wedges of *socca* – a pancake made with chickpea flour. In **Marseille** in particular, other options include Tunisian snacks such as *brik à l'oeuf* (a delicious filo pastry snack stuffed with soft-set egg), spicy merguez sausages and falafel.

Drinks

Coffee is the beverage of choice, served long and milky as a *café au lait* at breakfast time and drunk short and strong as an *express* (espresso) later in the day – ask for *une crème* or *une grande crème* if you want a coffee with milk, and for an Americano if you take it black. Ordinary **tea** is usually Lipton's, served in the cup with a tea bag; ask for *un peu de lait frais* if you want milk. Herb or fruit teas – known as infusions or *tisanes* – are widely available.

Draught **beer** – usually Kronenbourg – is one of the cheaper alcoholic drinks you can buy; you'll also see French and Belgian bottled beers and, in larger cities, a big international selection in Dutch- or Irish-style pubs.

Anyone in search of something stronger than wine should note that Provence is the homeland of **pastis**, the aniseed-flavoured spirit traditionally served with a bowl of olives before meals. There's also an abundance of cognac, armagnac and various flavours of *eaux de vie*, of which the most delicious is Poire Williams; *marc* is a spirit distilled from grape pulp.

The media

Anyone who can read French, or understand it when spoken, will find that the print and electronic media in France match any in the world. Otherwise, English-language newspapers are widely available, many hotels offer English-language TV, and BBC radio can easily be picked up.

Newspapers and magazines

Newsstands at airports and railway stations in Provence, and shops in the larger towns, sell **international editions** of British and North American **newspapers** and magazines.

As for the **French press**, *Le Monde* (ⓦ lemonde.fr) is the most intellectual and respected national daily, though it does now carry such frivolities as colour photos. *Libération* (*Libé* for short; ⓦ liberation.fr) is moderately left-wing, independent and more colloquial, while rigorous left-wing criticism of the government comes from *L'Humanité* (ⓦ humanite.fr), the Communist Party paper, which is struggling to survive. *Le Figaro* (ⓦ lefigaro.fr) is the most respected of the right-leaning newspapers. Visitors may well find regional newspapers such as Marseille's *La Provence* (ⓦ laprovence.com) or Nice's *Nice Matin* (ⓦ nicematin.com) more useful, for their listings rather than their indifferent news coverage.

Weekly **magazines** include the wide-ranging and left-leaning *L'Obs* (ⓦ nouvelobs.com), its right-wing counterpart *L'Express* (ⓦ lexpress.fr) and the centrist with bite, *Marianne* (ⓦ marianne.net). Look for the best investigative journalism in the weekly satirical paper *Le Canard Enchaîné* (ⓦ lecanardenchaine.fr), while *Charlie Hebdo* (ⓦ www.charliehebdo.fr) became a national bastion for free speech after the attack on its Paris offices in 2015.

Although it's aimed more at expats than visitors, the online-only **English-language magazine** *Riviera Reporter* (ⓦ riviera-reporter.com), , often contains articles of interest, as does the bi-monthly *Riviera Insider* (ⓦ riviera-press.fr).

Radio

Riviera Radio (106.5FM in France, 106.3FM in Monaco, ⓦ rivieraradio.mc) broadcasts out of Monaco and faithfully reflects its British expat audience with a homespun local-radio mix of suburban chat and middle-of-the-road hits; you can also pick up its news and events coverage on the Côte d'Azur.

Radio France (ⓦ radiofrance.fr) operates eight stations, including France Culture for arts, France Info for news and France Musique for classical music. Other major stations include Europe 1 (ⓦ europe1.fr) for news, debate and sport. Radio France International (RFI, ⓦ rfi.fr) broadcasts in French and various foreign languages, including English; listen via the website or through your phone.

Television

France 2, France 3, France 4, France 5 and Arte are the main free-to-air digital terrestrial TV channels, alongside the rolling news channel France Info, the subscription-only Canal Plus (with some unencrypted programmes) and the popular TF1 (ⓦ tf1.fr). Any number of **cable and satellite channels** are also available, including CNN, BBC World, Euronews, Eurosport and Planète+ (which specializes in documentaries).

Festivals

Provence is home to some of France's most celebrated festivals. The real heavyweights are the Avignon and Aix festivals, which use the historic settings of those two cities to stunning effect as a backdrop for high culture in early summer. Many smaller towns and villages have their own events, from traditional folk festivals to events celebrating jazz or film – in summer especially, when village noticeboards post details of the many local fetes, along with dances, night markets and so on, there's always something to catch.

Arles and Les-Saintes-Maries-de-la-Mer still stage Spanish-style *férias* or **bullfights**. The principality of Monaco makes up for its modest size with a packed programme of events of its own – including, most famously, the **Grand Prix** (🌐 acm.mc) in May (see page 381).

JANUARY TO APRIL

International Circus Festival, Monaco Mid- to late Jan. Claiming to be the world's largest circus festival, this ten-day celebration culminates with the crowning of the "Golden Clown". 🌐 montecarlofestival.mc

Fête du Citron, Menton Feb. Floats decorated entirely with lemons form part of this annual celebration. 🌐 feteducitron.com

Nice Carnival Feb–March. Massive fifteen-day carnival featuring colourful flower parades and night-time processions. 🌐 nicecarnaval.com

Fêtes des Violettes, Tourrettes-sur-Loup Weekend in late Feb or early March. Floats decorated with thousands of violets parade through the village. 🌐 tourrettessurloup.com

Printemps des Arts, Monaco March & April Classical and contemporary dance festival. 🌐 printempsdesarts.mc

MAY

Festival de Cannes Second half of May. World-famous international film festival (see page 308). 🌐 festival-cannes.com

Fête de Sainte Sarah, Les Saintes-Maries-de-la-Mer May 24–25. Romany festival celebrating Sarah, their patron saint (see page 111). 🌐 saintesmaries.com

Fête de Transhumance, St-Rémy Whit Mon, May/June. Traditional Provence festival that sees a flock of four thousand sheep parade through town. 🌐 saintremy-de-provence.com

Festival du Premier Film, La Ciotat Late May/early June. Annual film festival in the town where cinema first started (see page 72). 🌐 edencinemalaciotat.com

JUNE TO AUGUST

Fêtes de la Tarasque, Tarascon Last full weekend of June. Bull and equestrian events, fireworks and a parade of the mythical Tarasque monster through the streets (see page 103). 🌐 tarascon.fr

Festival d'Aix, Aix-en-Provence June & July. World-renowned festival of classical music and opera. 🌐 festival-aix.com

Festival des Jazz, St-Raphaël Early July. International jazz festival. 🌐 ville-saintraphael.fr

Jazz Festival, Nice Early July. Big-name jazz, soul and funk festival. 🌐 nicejazzfestival.fr

Rencontres d'Arles, Arles Early July–late Sept. Europe's most prestigious annual photography festival (see page 89). 🌐 rencontres-arles.com

Les Suds à Arles, Arles Mid-July. Festival of world music. 🌐 suds-arles.com

Festival d'Avignon July. Three-week cultural festival of theatre, contemporary dance, classical music and exhibitions (see page 120). The fringe festival is known as the Festival Off. 🌐 festival-avignon.com & 🌐 avignonleoff.com

Jazz à Juan, Juan-les-Pins Two weeks in mid-July. International jazz festival (see page 320). 🌐 jazzajuan.com

Chorégies d'Orange, Orange July. Long-established choral festival, staged in the magnificent Roman theatre (see page 134). 🌐 choregies.fr

Vaison Danse, Vaison-la-Romaine Mid- to late July. Two-week festival of contemporary dance, centring on the town's Roman theatre. 🌐 vaison-danses.com

Festival of Jewish Music, Carpentras Late July or early Aug. Celebration of Jewish musical traditions from classical to klezmer. 🌐 avignon-et-provence.com/en/agenda/festival-jewish-music-carpentras.html

International Fireworks, Monaco July & Aug. Competition of firework displays set to music. 🌐 monaco-feuxdartifice.mc

Musique à l'Emperi, Salon-de-Provence Late July–early Aug. Ten-day classical music festival in the château. 🌐 festival-salon.fr

Festival de Musique, Menton Late July–early Aug. Classical music concerts by the quayside. 🌐 festival-musique-menton.fr

Carreto Ramado, St-Rémy Aug 15. Harvest thanksgiving procession, featuring carts decorated with foliage. 🌐 saintremy-de-provence.com

SEPTEMBER AND OCTOBER

Festival International de Gastronomie, Mougins Sept. Foodie festival in a village that's famed for its gastronomy. 🌐 lesetoilesdemougins.com

Fiesta des Suds, Marseille Mid-Oct. World music and arts festival in the industrial setting of the city's docklands. 🌐 dock-des-suds.org

Sports and outdoor activities

The benign climate of Provence encourages outdoor activities of all kinds, from swimming, sailing and diving in the clear waters of the Mediterranean to adventure sports for adrenaline junkies in the Grand Canyon du Verdon.

Spectator sports

Football is the most popular spectator sport in Provence, especially in Marseille, home of Olympique de Marseille (🌐 om.net), one of the top French teams. **Motor racing** takes precedence in Monaco, while enthusiasm for **cycle racing** is as great as anywhere in France, and the annual **Tour de France** generally has a stage in Provence, most notoriously on Mont Ventoux. In and around the Camargue, the number one spectator sport is **bullfighting** (see page 87); though not to everyone's taste, it is, at least, less gruesome than the variety practised in Spain. The world-famous **Formula One Grand Prix** (see page 381) takes place in Monaco in May, while some of Provence's remote inland routes make perfect terrain for **rallying**. Monaco also hosts an international **Tennis Open** championship, April's Monte Carlo Rolex Masters (W montecarlorolexmasters.mc).

Perhaps the most characteristic Provençal sporting pastime is **pétanque**, the region's version of *boules*, which you'll see played in practically every town or village square, in parks and sometimes in purpose-built arenas. The principle is the same as in bowls, but the terrain is rough, never grass, and the area of play much smaller.

Sailing and watersports

There can scarcely be a coast anywhere in the world with as many **yachting facilities** as the Côte d'Azur, and most seaside resorts have at least one marina, often more. Of the **regattas**, Hyères hosts the Semaine Olympique des Voiles in the spring, a major sailing event that national teams often use to select their Olympic teams. In September, the attraction of St-Tropez's Les Voiles is as much glamour as sport, while Marseille's Septembre en Mer (W septembreenmer.com) offers all manner of nautical activities, from sunset sea-kayak trips along the coast to voyages on a historic barque.

The chief problem for **watersports** enthusiasts on the Côte d'Azur is simple congestion, with the thousands of yachts dodging jet skis, motorboats and windsurfers and adding up to a traffic headache. Nonetheless, the sea is warm and placid and there are plenty of places where you can rent equipment.

Elsewhere, there are opportunities for **diving** in the clear waters around Cassis, Bandol and Sanary, along the Corniche des Maures and at Saint Raphaël. **Swimming** is most enjoyable in the *calanques* of Marseille or around the quieter and more remote beaches away from the big cities; purpose-built **water parks** on the coast offer extensive facilities in exchange for their rather steep entry prices.

Outdoor and adventure activities

Provence makes a superb venue for **outdoor sports** and **adventure pursuits**. The beautiful Alpine scenery is wonderful for walking, particularly around the Grand Canyon du Verdon (see page 219) and in the Parc National du Mercantour (see page 229). The former is also popular for **hiking, rafting, canyoning, kayaking, rock climbing, hang-gliding, mountain biking** and **horseriding**; Castellane and La Palud sur verdon are the two main centres for active sports in

the gorge; nearby St-André-les-Alpes is popular for **paragliding** and hang-gliding. Gentler airborne pursuits include **hot-air ballooning** in the Pays de Forcalquier. The Camargue is Provence's most famous centre for **horseriding** (see page 107).

Cycling is popular almost everywhere, with public bike rental schemes in Marseille and Nice and ordinary rental available in most other towns; in addition, numerous organized cycling **tours** are available (see page 25). **Bike rental** information is given throughout this Guide. Cycle tourism is particularly well supported in the Luberon and Pays de Forcalquier, where you can arrange to have your luggage transported ahead of you to your next hotel. Bikes are by no means confined to paved roads: the Alpine districts of the Alpes-Maritimes and Parc du Mercantour hold signposted and mapped VTT (*vélo tout terrain*) trails for mountain-biking enthusiasts.

Skiing and snowboarding

Thanks to the unique topography of the region, it's possible to **ski** remarkably close to the coast – the closest resort to the Côte d'Azur is Gréolières-les-Neiges, a short distance from Grasse. More reliable snow and more extensive facilities are, however, found inland: at Valberg, Isola 2000, La Foux d'Allos, Auron and in the resorts around Barcelonnette.

SKI RESORTS

Auron W auron.com. Resort with 135km of pistes, mostly blue or red (easy to intermediate).

La Foux d'Allos W valdallos.com. Purpose-built, high-altitude ski resort in the Val d'Allos, which has 180km of pistes – the most extensive network in the southern Alps.

TOP TEN BEACHES

Juan-les-Pins See page 318
Plage de la Croisette, Cannes See page 305
Plage de Gigaro, La Croix Valmer See page 276
Plage Mala, Cap d'Ail See page 371
Plage Notre Dame, Porquerolles See page 269
Plage de Pampelonne, St-Tropez See page 282
Plage du Prado, Marseille See page 58
Plage de la Salis, Antibes See page 323
Les Sablettes, La-Seyne-sur-Mer See page 260
Silver beaches, Corniche des Maures See page 275

Isola 2000 Ⓦ isola2000.com. At an altitude of 2000m on the fringe of the Parc National du Mercantour, with 120km of pistes.
Valberg Ⓦ valberg.com. Resort claiming the best snow record in the region, with 90km of downhill pistes and a preponderance of red runs.
La Vallée de l'Ubaye Ⓦ ubaye.com. The region around Barcelonnette harbours several skiing resorts, including Le Sauze/Super-Sauze, Ste-Anne/La Condamine, and Pra-Loup, whose pistes link up with those of La Foux d'Allos.

Travel essentials

Costs

Provence is one of the most **expensive** French regions to visit: prices in some of the chic hot spots on the Côte d'Azur can rival those in the more prestigious arrondissements of Paris, and costs for accommodation on the coast soar during the July and August peak season when foreign visitors have to compete with the French for scarce hotel rooms.

In general the Riviera is more expensive than the rest of Provence – St-Tropez and Monaco considerably so – but even in the rest of the region you'll need to watch the pennies. For a reasonably comfortable stay, you need to allow a **budget** of around €130 (£112/$146) a day per person, assuming two people sharing a mid-priced room. By camping or staying at hostels, and being strong-willed about resisting extra cups of coffee, doses of culture and the like, you could probably manage on €85 (£73/$95) a day.

As in other European Union countries, you'll routinely find that **Value Added Tax** (*TVA*) makes up part of your hotel, restaurant or shopping bill; prices are usually quoted inclusive of the tax. At restaurants you only need to leave an additional cash **tip** if you have received exceptional service, since restaurant prices include a service charge.

EMERGENCY NUMBERS

All emergency numbers are toll-free.
Emergency calls from a mobile phone
☎ 112
Fire brigade/paramedics ☎ 18
Medical emergencies/ambulance (SAMU) ☎ 15
Police ☎ 17
Rape crisis (Viols Femmes Informations)
☎ 0800 05 95 95

Crime and personal safety

Though certain sections of **Marseille**, **Toulon** and **Nice** have a distinctly dodgy feel, violent crime against tourists is pretty rare. **Petty theft**, however, is endemic along the Côte d'Azur and also a problem in the more crowded parts of the big cities.

Make sure you have a good insurance policy (see pages 37 and 38), and take the normal **precautions**: don't flash wads of notes around; carry your bag or wallet securely and be especially careful in crowds; never leave valuables lying in view; and park your car overnight in a monitored parking garage or, at the very least, on a busy and well-lit street. Be wary of unmanned *aires* (rest areas) on the autoroute at night. It's also wise to keep a separate record of how to cancel your credit cards and report stolen phones.

Take care when **crossing roads** – inattentiveness is a problem, with many French drivers paying little heed to pedestrian crossings or lights. Do not step onto a crossing assuming that traffic will stop.

As a long-standing stronghold of the extreme right, Provence has a regrettable reputation for **racism**, directed mainly against the Arab community. If you suffer a **racial assault**, contact the police, your consulate or one of the local anti-racism organizations (though they may not have English-speakers): SOS Racism (Ⓦ sos-racisme.org) and Mouvement contre le Racisme et pour l'Amitié entre les Peuples (MRAP; Ⓦ mrap.fr). Alternatively, you could contact the **English-speaking helpline** SOS Help (daily 3–11pm; ☎ 01 46 21 46 46, Ⓦ soshelpline.org).

Electricity

Voltage is officially 230V, using **plugs** with two round pins. If you need an adapter, it's best to bring one from home, though you can find them in big department stores in France.

Entry requirements

Citizens of **EU countries** can enter France freely on a valid passport or national identity card, while those from many **non-EU countries**, including Australia, Canada, New Zealand and the United States, among others, do not need a visa for a stay of **up to ninety days**. South African citizens require a short-stay visa for up to ninety days, which costs €60.

Non-EU citizens wishing to remain **longer than ninety days** must apply for a long-stay visa, for which you'll have to show proof of income (or sufficient funds to support yourself) and medical insurance. Regulations can change, so it's advisable to check with your nearest French embassy or consulate before

> **BREXIT**
>
> The circumstances surrounding the UK's proposed withdrawal from the European Union are currently unclear. It is likewise unclear how any withdrawal will affect visas, healthcare, insurance, mobile phone roaming charges and so on. For up to date information check ⓦ www.gov.uk/visit-europe-brexit.

departure. For further information consult the Ministry of Foreign Affairs website: ⓦ diplomatie.gouv.fr.

Visa requirements for **Monaco** (an independent principality) are identical to those of France; there are no border controls between the two.

FRENCH EMBASSIES AND CONSULATES

Australia Canberra ⓦ ambafrance-au.org.
Britain London and Edinburgh ⓦ ambafrance-uk.org.
Canada Montréal ⓦ consulfrance-montreal.org; Toronto ⓦ consulfrance-toronto.org.
Ireland Dublin ⓦ ambafrance-ie.org.
New Zealand Wellington ⓦ ambafrance-nz.org.
South Africa Johannesburg ⓦ consulfrance-jhb.org.
USA Washington ⓦ ambafrance-us.org.

Health

Visitors to Provence have little to worry about as far as health is concerned. No vaccinations are required, there are no nasty diseases and tap water is safe to drink. And if you do need treatment, you should be in good hands.

Under France's excellent **health system**, all services, including doctor's consultations, prescribed medicines, hospital stays and ambulance call-outs, incur a charge that you have to pay upfront. EU citizens are entitled to a refund (usually 70 percent) of medical and dental expenses, so long as the doctor is government-registered (*un médecin conventionné*), and that you have a European Health Insurance Card (EHIC; application forms available from UK post offices or on ⓦ dh.gov.uk). Note that every member of the family, including children, must have their own card. Even with the EHIC card, it's a good idea to have additional insurance to cover the shortfall, which can be especially substantial after a stay in hospital. All non-EU visitors should ensure they have adequate medical insurance cover.

For **minor complaints**, go to a *pharmacie*, signalled by an illuminated green cross. There's at least one in every small town, and even some villages. In larger towns, at least one (known as the *pharmacie de garde*) is open 24 hours according to a rota; details are displayed in all pharmacy windows.

For anything more serious you can get the name of a **doctor** from a pharmacy, local police station, tourist office, or your hotel. Consultation fees are usually around €25. You'll be given a *Feuille de Soins* (Statement of Treatment) for later insurance claims. Any prescriptions will be fulfilled by the pharmacy and must be paid for.

In serious **emergencies** you will always be admitted to the nearest general hospital (*centre hospitalier*).

Insurance

Even though EU citizens are entitled to health-care privileges in France, they would do well to take out an **insurance policy** before travelling in order to cover against theft, loss, illness or injury. Before paying for a new policy, however, check whether you are already covered: some all-risks home insurance policies cover your possessions when overseas, and many private medical schemes include cover when abroad.

A typical travel insurance policy usually provides cover for the loss of baggage, tickets and – up to a certain limit – cash or cheques, as well as cancellation or curtailment of your journey. Most exclude so-called **dangerous sports** unless an extra premium is paid.

Internet

Even the cheapest French hotels these days, along with many cafés and bars, offer **wi-fi**; if it's important to you, make sure that it's both available and working when you check in. Occasionally it may only be accessible from the lobby or public areas. Hotels also often hold a computer or two for guest use. Internet cafés are much less common than they used to be, but on the other hand almost every **tourist office** has free wi-fi access, which you can usually use from outside even when the office is shut.

Laundry

Inexpensive self-service **laundries** or *laveries automatiques* are commonplace in Provençal towns, and are listed in this Guide for larger destinations such as Nice. They are often unattended, so bring small change. The alternative *blanchisserie* or pressing services are more expensive, as are hotel laundry services. Most hotels forbid doing laundry in your room, though you should be able to get away with a few small items.

ROUGH GUIDES TRAVEL INSURANCE

Rough Guides has teamed up with WorldNomads.com to offer great travel insurance deals. Policies are available to residents of over 150 countries, with cover for a wide range of adventure sports, 24hr emergency assistance, high levels of medical and evacuation cover and a stream of travel safety information. Roughguides.com users can take advantage of their policies online 24/7, from anywhere in the world – even if you're already travelling. And since plans often change when you're on the road, you can extend your policy and even claim online. Roughguides.com users who buy travel insurance with WorldNomads.com can also leave a positive footprint and donate to a community development project. For more information, go to ⓦ roughguides.com/shop.

LGBTQ travellers

Although conservative attitudes long meant that **LGBTQ** life in Provence was rather discreet, in the cities that have changed, both **Nice** and **Marseille** have annual gay pride celebrations. While Marseille's bar scene is low-key, Nice has a high-profile LGBTQ scene.

Attitudes are relaxed in chic resorts such as **Cannes** and **St-Tropez**, where the gay presence is long established and relatively integrated into the mainstream. Away from the coast, both **Aix** and **Avignon** have small-scale but lively bar scenes.

It's also worth checking the travel listings site ⓦ gay-provence.org and the national LGBTQ website ⓦ yagg.com.

Living in Provence

EU citizens are free to work in France on the same basis as a French citizen. This means you don't have to apply for a residence or work permit except in very rare cases. You will, however, need to apply for a Carte de Séjour from a police station within three months of your arrival. **Non-EU citizens** are not allowed to work in France unless their prospective employer has obtained an *autorisation de travail* from the Ministry of Labour before their arrival. Under the "Compétences et Talents" scheme, a four-year renewable work permit may be issued to individuals with specific skills. International students in possession of a French study visa are eligible to work around 1000 hours in any one year. Au pair visas must also be obtained before travelling to France. For queries and further information on all these issues, contact your nearest French consulate.

When **looking for a job**, start by looking at the various books on working abroad published by Crimson (ⓦ crimsonpublishing.co.uk). You can also search the online recruitment resource Monster (ⓦ monster.fr) and Job Etudiant (ⓦ jobetudiant.net), which focuses on jobs for students. In France, try the youth information agency CIDJ (Centre d'Information Jeunesse; ⓦ cidj.com), which has information about temporary jobs and about working in France; offices are located throughout France.

English-language teaching posts normally require a degree and a TEFL (Teaching English as a Foreign Language) or similar qualification. The online *EL Gazette* newsletter (ⓦ elgazette.com) is a useful source of information; so are the annual *Teaching English Abroad* published by Vacation Work, and the TEFL website (ⓦ tefl.com), with its database of English-teaching vacancies.

The Riviera has a large expat Anglophone community, and there is consequently demand for **English-language services** of various kinds, from domestic staff to *immobiliers* and experienced crew members on yachts. Riviera Radio (see page 382) often carries job ads, though these usually require fluent French. It may also be worth checking the classified sections of the *Anglo Info* websites (ⓦ riviera.angloinfo.com; ⓦ provence.angloinfo.com).

STUDY AND WORK PROGRAMMES

AFS Intercultural Programs ⓦ afs.org. Intercultural exchange organization with programmes in over fifty countries.
American Institute for Foreign Study ⓦ aifsabroad.com. Language and culture courses in Cannes over a summer, a semester or a year.

Mail

As a rule, **post offices** (*bureaux de poste* or PTTs) are open from around 8.30/9am to 6/7pm Monday to Friday, and from 8.30am to noon on Saturday; look for bright yellow *La Poste* signs. Smaller branches usually close for lunch.

For **sending mail**, standard letters (20g or less) and postcards within France cost €0.88 or €1.20 to other European Union countries. To the rest of the world it's €1.30. You can also buy stamps from *tabacs* and newsagents. To post your letter on the street, look for the bright yellow postboxes.

For **further information** on postal rates, among other things, visit ⓦ laposte.fr.

Maps

Though their town maps are often very good, tourist office hand-outs rarely contain usable regional maps. To supplement them – and the maps in this Guide – you will probably want a reasonable road map. The best are produced by Michelin (1:200,000; Ⓦviamichelin.fr) and the Institut Géographique National (IGN; 1:250,000; Ⓦ ign.fr), either as individual sheets or in one large spiral-bound *atlas routier*. **Walkers** should invest in the more detailed (1:25,000) IGN maps.

Money

France's currency, the **euro**, is divided into 100 cents (often still referred to as *centimes*). There are seven notes – in denominations of 5, 10, 20, 50, 100, 200 and 500 euros – and eight different coins – 1, 2, 5, 10, 20 and 50 cents, and 1 and 2 euros.

By far the easiest way to access your money in France is to use your credit or debit card to withdraw cash from an **ATM** (known as a *distributeur* or *point argent*); machines are ubiquitous, and most give instructions in several languages. Check with your bank before you leave home if you're in any doubt, and note that there is often a transaction fee, so it's more efficient to take out a sizeable sum each time rather than making lots of small withdrawals.

Similarly, all major **credit cards** are almost always accepted in hotels, restaurants and shops, although some smaller establishments don't accept cards, or only for sums above a certain threshold. Visa – called Carte Bleue in France – is the most widely recognized, followed by MasterCard (also known as EuroCard). American Express ranks a bit lower. Almost all credit cards charge a fee for every overseas transaction, which can really mount up if you use your card for small purchases such as parking and toll charges. It's worth obtaining a credit card that does not charge such fees, such as the Everyday card issued by Creation in the UK (Ⓦ creation.co.uk).

Opening hours and public holidays

Basic **hours of business** are Monday to Saturday 9am until noon and 2 to 6pm. In big city centres, shops and other businesses stay open throughout the day, while in July and August most tourist offices and museums are open without interruption. Otherwise almost everything – shops, museums, tourist offices, most banks – closes for a couple of hours at midday.

If you're looking to buy a picnic lunch, you'll need to get into the habit of buying it before you're ready to eat. Small **food shops** often don't reopen until halfway through the afternoon, then close again around 7.30 or 8pm.

The standard **closing day** is Sunday, even in larger towns and cities, though some food shops and newsagents are open in the morning. Some shops and businesses, particularly in rural areas, also close on Mondays.

Museums are not very generous with their hours, tending to open around 10am, close for lunch, and then run through until only 5 or 6pm. The closing days are usually Monday or Tuesday, sometimes both. We've listed the opening hours for all attractions throughout this Guide.

Phones

To call **to France** from your home country, dial your country's international access code – ☎00 from the UK, Ireland and New Zealand, and ☎011 from the USA, Canada or Australia – followed by 33 for France, and then the last nine digits of the ten-digit French number (thus omitting the initial 0).

To make a phone call **within France** – local or long-distance – simply dial all ten digits of the number. Numbers beginning with ☎08 00 up to ☎08 05 are free; those beginning ☎08 10 and ☎08 11 are charged as a local call; anything else beginning ☎08 is premium-rated, with charges varying. None of these ☎08 numbers can be accessed from abroad. Calls to mobile phones (numbers starting with ☎06) are also charged at premium rates.

To find a number try Ⓦpagesjaunes.fr; for medical emergencies, ☎15; the police, ☎17; fire and paramedics, ☎18.

NATIONAL HOLIDAYS

Jan 1 (New Year's Day) Le Jour de l'an
Easter Sunday Pâques
Easter Monday Lundi de Pâques
May 1 (May Day) La Fête du travail
May 8 (VE Day) La Fête de la Victoire 1945
Ascension Day (40 days after Easter: mid-May to early June) L'Ascension
Whitsun (7th Sun after Easter: mid-May to early June) La Pentecôte
Whit Monday (7th Mon after Easter: mid-May to early June) Lundi de Pentecôte
July 14 (Bastille Day) La Fête nationale
Aug 15 (Feast of the Assumption) L'Assomption
Nov 1 (All Saints' Day) La Toussaint
Nov 11 (Armistice Day) L'Armistice 1918
Dec 25 (Christmas Day) Noël

Mobile or cell phones

With the abolition of EU roaming charges in 2017, using a British mobile phone in France should, in theory, incur the same costs as using it back in the UK, though providers differ in their levels of geographic coverage. The cheapest option for non-EU citizens is to buy a French SIM card and pay-as-you-go at local rates.

Shopping

Provence offers a rich variety of local **crafts** and **produce** to buy as souvenirs, with everything from *santons* (nativity figures) in Aubagne or Marseille to high-quality glassware in Biot, ceramics in Moustiers-Ste-Marie, wooden items in Aiguines and fine art and handicrafts in every chic village along the Côte d'Azur.

Food can be a particular joy, from soft nougat and farmhouse honey to olive oil and fine wine, *marrons glacés* from Collobrières and *calissons* from Aix. One of the pleasures of shopping in Provence is the opportunity to taste oils and wines as you go; throughout this Guide, we've listed vineyards and wineries that offer tastings (*dégustations*).

Above all, be sure to visit at least one of Provence's legendary markets (*marchés*) for some of the best fresh produce to be found on earth. Again, we've given the relevant days for each specific destination throughout this Guide.

Most larger towns have considerable shopping facilities in the centre, including **department stores** as well as the usual range of **fashion** and **footwear** chains. The majority of Provençal towns also have sizeable edge-of-town **retail parks** that include not only mammoth supermarkets but also discount shoe and clothing retailers. Some of the Côte d'Azur resorts – in particular St-Tropez, Cannes, Nice and Monte Carlo – also hold a considerable selection of luxury stores, with all the usual international **designer** names.

Smoking

Smoking is **banned** in all enclosed public places, including public transport, museums, cafés and restaurants. It's still legal, however, on outdoor *terrasses*, so you can still finding yourself sitting next to a smoker if you dine outdoors.

Time

France is in the **Central European Time Zone** (GMT+1), one hour ahead of the UK, six hours ahead of Eastern Standard Time and nine hours ahead of Pacific Standard Time. Daylight Saving Time (GMT+2) lasts from the last Sunday in March to the last Sunday in October.

Tourist information

The **French Government Tourist Office** (Atout France) has offices throughout the world, each with its own website holding general countrywide information. For practical details on a specific location, contact the relevant regional or departmental tourist offices; details can be found at ⓦfncdt.net.

In Provence itself, practically every town (and many a village) has a tourist office – usually an **Office du Tourisme** (OT) but sometimes a **Syndicat d'Initiative** (SI). These provide local information, including maps, hotel and restaurant listings, on leisure activities, car and bike rental, bus times, laundries and countless other things. They almost always offer free wi-fi access as well, and many can book accommodation for you.

REGIONAL TOURIST WEBSITES

Alpes de Haute Provence ⓦ alpes-haute-provence.com
Bouches du Rhône ⓦ visitprovence.com
Côte d'Azur ⓦ cotedazur-tourisme.com
Var ⓦ visitvar.fr
Vaucluse ⓦ provenceguide.com

FRENCH GOVERNMENT TOURIST OFFICES ABROAD

Australia and New Zealand ⓦ au.rendezvousenfrance.com
Canada ⓦ ca.rendezvousenfrance.com
South Africa ⓦ int.rendezvousenfrance.com
UK & Ireland ⓦ uk.rendezvousenfrance.com
USA ⓦ us.rendezvousenfrance.com

Travellers with disabilities

While the French have improved facilities for travellers with disabilities, adding ramps or other forms of access to hotels, museums and other public buildings, haphazard parking habits and stepped village streets remain serious obstacles for anyone with mobility problems. All hotels are required to adapt at least one room to be wheelchair accessible, and a growing number of *chambres d'hôtes* are doing likewise. The **public transport** situation is improving as networks are modernized: Nice's Tramway, for instance, has been designed to be fully accessible.

Eurotunnel (see page 26) offers the simplest option for **travelling to France** from the UK, as you can remain in your car. Alternatively, Eurostar trains have a limited number of wheelchair spaces in first-class for the price of the regular second-class fare; reserve well in advance. While airlines are required to offer access to travellers with mobility problems, the level of service provided by discount airlines may be fairly basic. All cross-Channel ferries have lifts to and from the car deck, but moving between the different passenger decks may be more difficult.

Within France, most train stations now make provision for travellers with reduced mobility. SNCF produces a free booklet outlining its services, available at main stations and on its website for travellers with disabilities: ⓦ accessibilite.sncf.com. Note that you need to give 48 hours advance warning to receive assistance from the beginning to the end of your trip.

APF (ASSOCIATION DES PARALYSÉES DE FRANCE) CONTACTS

APF (ⓦ apf.asso.fr; in French), the French paraplegic organization, is the most reliable source of information on accommodation with disabled access and other facilities, and has representatives in each *département*.

Avignon ☎ 04 90 16 47 40
La Garde (Var) ☎ 04 98 01 30 50
Manosque ☎ 04 92 71 74 50
Marseille ☎ 04 91 79 99 99
Nice ☎ 04 92 07 98 00

Travelling with children

Children and babies are generally welcome throughout Provence, including many bars and restaurants. Hotels charge by the room, and many either have a few large **family rooms**, or charge a small supplement for an additional bed or cot. Family-run places will often babysit or offer a listening service while you eat or go out. Especially in seaside towns, most restaurants have children's menus or cook simpler food on request.

Tourist offices have details of specific **activities** for children. Children under 4 years travel free on **public transport**, while those between 4 and 11 pay half-fare. **Museums** and the like are generally free to under-12s and half-price or free up to the age of 18.

Travelling with pets from the UK

The **Pet Travel Scheme (PETS)** enables British travellers who wish to take a dog or cat to France to avoid putting it in quarantine when re-entering the UK, so long as certain conditions are met. For details, visit ⓦ gov.uk/take-pet-abroad or call the PETS Helpline (☎ 0370 241 1710).

Marseille and around

44   Marseille

66   Parc National des Calanques

69   Cassis and around

71   La Ciotat

73   Aubagne

75   L'Estaque and the Côte Bleue

76   Martigues

MUCEM

1 Marseille and around

The Marseille conurbation is the most populated and industrialized part of Provence, and indeed of southern France. After Lyon and Paris it is France's third-largest urban region, an area where tourism takes a back seat to other industries: to shipping in Marseille city, and petrochemicals around the Étang de Berre. Yet there are also wide tracts of rocky terrain and a shoreline of cliffs, jagged inlets and sandy beaches with stretches still untouched by the holiday industry. For visitors, the great attraction is Marseille itself, a vital commercial port for more than two millennia. France's second city is, for all its tough reputation, a wonderful place with a distinctive character that never ceases to surprise.

The first foreigners to settle in Provence, the ancient **Greeks** from Phocaea and their less amiable successors from **Rome**, left evidence of their presence in Marseille, where museums guard reminders of the indigenous peoples whose civilization they destroyed. The region has strong military connections. **Salon-de-Provence** holds a training school for French air-force pilots but also preserves reminders of Nostradamus; **Aubagne** is home to the French Foreign Legion but also to the characters of **Pagnol**.

There are great seaside attractions here too: the pine-covered rocks and beaches of the **Côte Bleue**; the *calanques* (rocky inlets) between Marseille and **Cassis**; the sand beaches of **La Ciotat** bay; and the dizzying, dramatic heights from which to view the coast on the **route des Crêtes**. The area also has great **wines** at Cassis, and delicious **seafood**, particularly in Marseille, home of the famous fish stew, bouillabaisse.

Marseille

In recent years **MARSEILLE** has undergone a **renaissance**, shaking off much of its old reputation for sleaze to attract a wider range of visitors. The TGV has made it accessible to northerners, the city has become one of the Mediterranean's busiest **cruise ship** ports and the shops in the streets south of La Canebière grow increasingly trendy or elegant. In 2013, the city's stint as European Capital of Culture unveiled a new face of Marseille, focused on a dramatically reworked **waterfront**. The march of progress is not, however, relentless: last year's *grand projet* still occasionally winds up as this year's broken, bottle-strewn fountain, while Marseille's easy tolerance of graffiti means it sometimes *looks* like the toughest city in France. In short, it's a rough diamond.

See past the grit, and chances are you'll warm to this vital metropolis. It has a magnetism as a true Mediterranean city, surrounded by mountains and graced with hidden corners that have the unexpected air of fishing villages. It has its triumphal architecture, too, as well as the cosmopolitan atmosphere of a major port. Perhaps the most appealing quality, however, is the down-to-earth nature of its gregarious, talkative inhabitants.

Some history
Marseille has been a **trading city** for over 2500 years, since ancient Greeks from Ionia discovered shelter in the Lacydon inlet, today the Vieux Port, and came to an agreement with the local Ligurian tribe. The story goes that the locals, noticing the exotic cargo of the strangers' boats, sent them off to the king's castle where the

Highlights

❶ Vieux Port, Marseille An intoxicating blend of food, history, water and sunlight at the very heart of France's great Mediterranean metropolis. See page 46

❷ Unité d'Habitation (Cité Radieuse), Marseille Le Corbusier's highly sculptural concrete masterpiece is a truly ground-breaking piece of modernist architecture. See page 57

❸ Bouillabaisse Marseille's very own fish stew is the true taste of the south of France – and an unmissable Marseille experience. See page 61

❹ Château d'If The most compelling of Marseille's islands was the sinister setting for Dumas' *The Count of Monte Cristo*. See page 66

❺ Calanques Whether you walk, swim or simply take a boat trip, don't miss the blinding white rocks, crystal-clear waters and fjord-like inlets of the coastal national park between Marseille and Cassis. See page 66

❻ Corniche des Crêtes Don't get blown away by the spectacular scenery (or high winds) on this scenic drive from Cassis to La Ciotat. See page 70

HIGHLIGHTS ARE MARKED ON THE MAP ON PAGE 46

1

princess's wedding preparations were in full swing. The Ligurian royal custom at the time was that the king's daughter could choose her husband from among her father's guests. As the leader of the Greek party walked through the castle gate, he was handed a drink by a woman and discovered that she was the princess and that he was the bridegroom. The king gave the couple the hill on the north side of the Lacydon, and Massalia came into being.

Since then, Marseille has both prospered and been ransacked over the centuries. It has lost its privileges to sundry French kings and foreign armies, rebuilt its fortunes, suffered plagues, religious bigotry, republican and royalist fervour and had its own Commune and Bastille-storming. It was the epic march of revolutionaries from Marseille to Paris in 1792 that gave the name to the Hymn of the Army of the Rhine that became the **national anthem** – *La Marseillaise*.

Vieux Port and around

Flanked by the twin **forts** of St-Jean and St-Nicolas – monuments in stone to the French state's traditionally wary attitude to rebellious Marseille – the **Vieux**

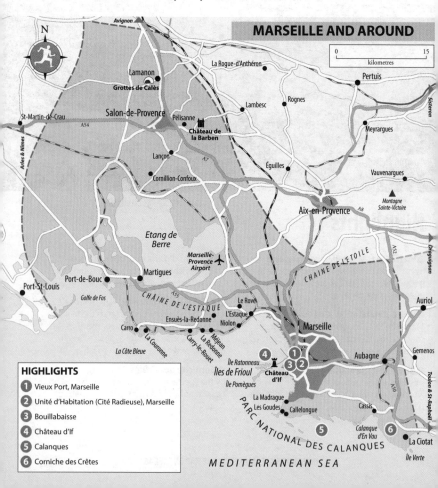

MARSEILLE AND AROUND

0 — 15
kilometres

HIGHLIGHTS

1. Vieux Port, Marseille
2. Unité d'Habitation (Cité Radieuse), Marseille
3. Bouillabaisse
4. Château d'If
5. Calanques
6. Corniche des Crêtes

MEDITERRANEAN SEA

MARSEILLE ORIENTATION

Marseille is divided into sixteen arrondissements that spiral out from the **Vieux Port**. Due north lies **Le Panier**, the old town and site of the original Greek settlement of Massalia and the impressive new cultural complex alongside the Fort St-Jean; further north still Les Docks in **Joliette** are the focus for Marseille's ambitious inner-city regeneration programmes. **La Canebière**, the wide boulevard starting at Quai des Belges at the head of the Vieux Port, is the central east–west axis of the town, with the **Centre Bourse** shopping centre and the little streets of **quartier Belsunce** to the north, and the main shopping streets to the south. The main north–south axis is **rue d'Aix**, becoming **cours Belsunce** then **cours St-Louis**, **rue de Rome**, **avenue du Prado** and **boulevard Michelet**. The trendy quarter around **place Jean-Jaurès** and **cours Julien** lies to the east of rue de Rome. On the headland west of the Vieux Port are the village-like *quartiers* of **Les Catalans** and **Malmousque** from where the **Corniche** heads south past the city's most favoured residential districts towards the beaches, bars and restaurants of the **Plage du Prado**.

Port is, more or less, the ancient harbour basin, the original inlet into which the ancient Greeks sailed, though nowadays its historic resonances are overlaid by the hubbub of sunglass-wearing idlers on the portside café terraces. The morning **fish market** on the quay, the endless queues for ferry tickets and the bustle around the **Ombrière** – a striking, mirror-ceilinged pavilion designed by Norman Foster and set back from the quayside – provide natural street theatre, while the seafood restaurants on the **pedestrianized streets** between the southern quay and cours Estienne d'Orves ensure that the Vieux Port stays busy well into the evening. The best view of the Vieux Port is from the **Jardin du Pharo**, the park of the **Palais du Pharo**, built on the headland at the harbour mouth by Emperor Napoléon III for his wife; it is now a conference centre and concert hall (ⓦpalaisdupharo. marseille.fr).

Notre Dame de la Garde

Rue Fort du Sanctuaire, 6e · **Church** Daily 7am–6.30pm · Free · **Museum** Tues–Sun 10am–5pm · €5 · ☎ 04 91 13 40 80, ⓦ notredamedelagarde.com · Bus #60 or tourist train from Vieux Port

For a sweeping view of the port, islands and Marseille's littoral, head up to the city's highest point, **Notre Dame de la Garde**, which tops the hill south of the harbour. Crowned by a monumental gold Madonna and Child and dating from the Second Empire, the church is a monstrous riot of neo-Byzantine design and the most distinctive of Marseille's landmarks. Inside, model ships hang from the rafters while the ex-votos displayed are by turn kitsch, unintentionally comic and deeply moving, as they depict the shipwrecks, house fires and car crashes from which the Virgin has supposedly rescued grateful believers. Many of the most striking are now displayed in the well-presented little **museum** beneath the basilica, which charts the history of the site.

THE MARSEILLE CITY PASS AND THE PASS MUSÉES

If you intend visiting several of Marseille's museums it's worth considering the **Marseille City Pass**, which for €26 (one day), €33 (two days) or €41 (three days) includes free admission to municipal museums, certain guided tours (see page 59), and boat travel to the Château d'If (see page 66) and free travel on métros and buses. Alternatively, you can buy a €45 **Pass Musées** from municipal museums which gives unlimited entry for a year from the date of validation. Otherwise, entry to municipal museums generally costs €5 (€8 for temporary exhibitions).

1

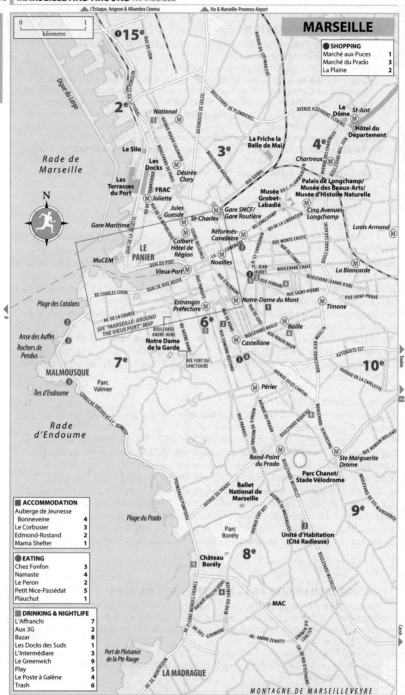

MARSEILLE

SHOPPING
Marché aux Puces	1
Marché du Prado	3
La Plaine	2

ACCOMMODATION
Auberge de Jeunesse Bonneveine	4
Le Corbusier	3
Edmond-Rostand	2
Mama Shelter	1

EATING
Chez Fonfon	3
Namaste	4
Le Peron	2
Petit Nice-Passédat	5
Plauchut	1

DRINKING & NIGHTLIFE
L'Affranchi	7
Aux 3G	2
Bazar	8
Les Docks des Suds	1
L'Intermédiaire	9
Le Greenwich	3
Play	5
Le Poste à Galène	4
Trash	6

> ## THE DESTRUCTION OF OLD LE PANIER
>
> In 1943, Marseille was under **German occupation** and Le Panier represented everything the Nazis feared and hated, an unpredictable warren providing shelter for *Untermenschen* of every sort, including Resistance leaders, Communists and Jews. They gave the twenty thousand inhabitants one day's notice to leave. While the *curé* of St-Laurent pealed the bells in protest, squads of SS moved in; they cleared the area and packed the people, including the *curé*, off to Fréjus where concentration camp victims were selected. Out of seven hundred children, only 68 returned. Dynamite was laid, carefully sparing three old buildings that appealed to the Fascist aesthetic, and everything in the lower part of the quarter, from the waterside to rue Caisserie and Grande rue, was blown up.

Abbaye St-Victor

3 rue de l'Abbaye, 7e • Daily 9am–7pm • Crypt €2 • ☎ 04 96 11 22 60, ⓦ saintvictor.net • Bus #81 from Vieux Port

Above the Bassin de Carénage and the slip road for the Vieux Port's tunnel is Marseille's oldest church, the **Abbaye St-Victor**. Originally part of a monastery founded in the fifth century on the burial site of various martyrs, the church was built, enlarged and fortified – a vital requirement given its position outside the city walls – over a period of two hundred years from the middle of the tenth century. With choir walls almost 3m thick, it looks and feels more like a fortress; it's no conventional ecclesiastical beauty. Nevertheless the **crypt**, in particular, is fascinating: a crumbling warren of rounded and propped-up arches, small side chapels and secretive passageways, its proportions are more impressive than the church above and it contains a number of sarcophagi.

Musée du Santon

47–49 rue Neuve Ste-Catherine, 7e • Tues–Sat: Jan–Nov 10am–12.30pm & 2–6.30pm; Dec Mon–Sat same hours • Free • ☎ 04 91 13 61 36, ⓦ santonsmarcelcarbonel.com • Bus #81 from Vieux Port

Close to the Abbaye St-Victor, the **Musée du Santon** is dedicated to *santons* – the Christmas figurines characteristic of the region – and has examples by some of the greatest *santon* makers from the time of the Revolution to the present. You can also see the **Carbonel atelier**, the workshop of Marcel Carbonel, one of the most renowned *santon* producers.

Maison de l'Artisanat et des Métiers d'Art

21 cours d'Estienne d'Orves, 1er • Tues–Fri 10am–noon & 1–6pm, Sat 1–6pm • Free • ☎ 04 91 54 80 54, ⓦ maisondelartisanat.org • ⓜ Vieux Port-Hôtel de Ville

Occupying beautiful, wood-beamed eighteenth-century premises on the site of Louis XIV's arsenal, the **Maison de l'Artisanat et des Métiers d'Art** hosts excellent temporary exhibitions of applied arts and crafts, providing a showcase for the region's own applied artists as well as hosting international touring exhibitions.

Le Panier

Rising above the north side of the Vieux Port, **Le Panier** is the oldest part of Marseille. This is where the Greeks built Massalia, and where, up until World War II, tiny streets, steep steps and a jumble of houses formed a *vieille ville* typical of this coast. Much of the old quarter was destroyed during World War II (see above) and replaced afterwards by solid apartment blocks in a vaguely Art Deco style. Among all this are the landmark structures that the Nazis spared: the seventeenth-century **Hôtel de Ville** on the quay; the half-Gothic, half-Renaissance **Hôtel de Cabre** on the corner of rue Bonneterie and Grande rue; and the **Maison Diamantée** of 1620, so-called for the pointed shape of its facade stonework, on rue de la Prison.

1

Musée des Docks Romains

10 place Vivaux, 2e • Tues–Sun 9.30am–6pm • €3 • ☎ 04 9191 24 62, ⓦ musee-histoire-marseille-voie-historique.fr/en • Ⓜ Vieux Port-Hôtel de Ville

After World War II, archeologists reaped some benefits from Le Panier's destruction in the discovery of the remains of a warehouse from the first-century AD Roman docks, now displayed in situ at the **Musée des Docks Romains**. You can see amphorae for oil, grain and spices in their original positions, and part of the original jetty, along with models, mock-ups and a video.

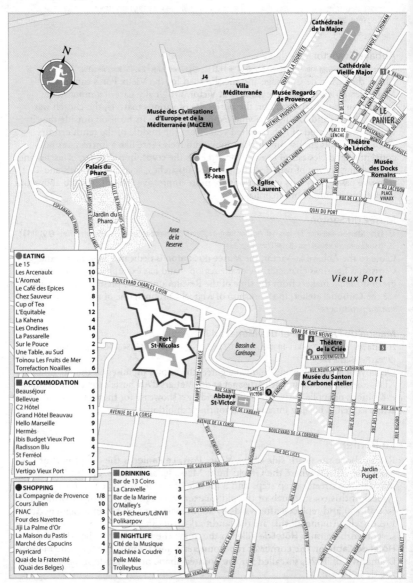

Above rue Caisserie

Above rue Caisserie, the old street patterns and architectural styles of Le Panier survive. Overlooking the small **place Daviel** is an eighteenth-century bell tower, all that remains of the Église des Accoules, destroyed in 1794 because it had served as a meeting place for counter-revolutionaries after the French Revolution. To the north of here is the vast nineteenth-century **Hôtel Dieu**, now a five-star hotel. At the junction of rue de la Prison and rue Caisserie, the steps of montée des Accoules lead up and across to **place de Lenche**, site of the Greek agora and today a good café stop.

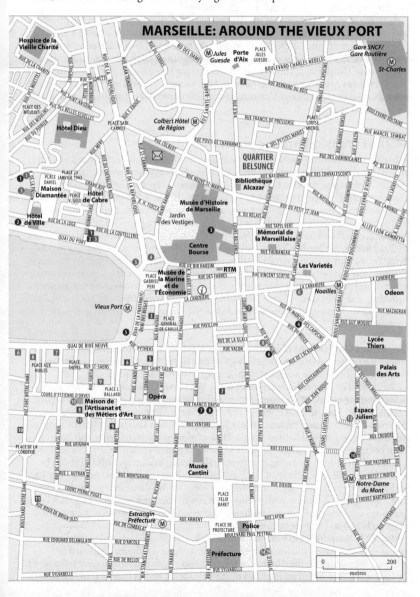

1

Hospice de la Vieille Charité

2 rue de la Charité, 2e • **Musée d'Archéologie Méditerranéenne** Tues–Sun 9.30am–6pm • €6 • ☎ 04 91 14 58 97, ⓦ musee-archeologie-mediterraneenne.marseille.fr • **Musée des Arts Africains, Océaniens et Amérindiens** Daily 9.30am–6pm • €6 • ☎ 04 91 14 58 38, ⓦ maaoa.marseille.fr • ⓜ Joliette

Climb rue du Réfuge and you'll reach a piazza with modern buildings in traditional styles, and a view of the **Hospice de la Vieille Charité** at the far end. This seventeenth-century workhouse, with a gorgeous Baroque chapel surrounded by handsome columned arcades in pink stone, is now a cultural centre, hosting excellent temporary exhibitions, two museums, a café and a bookshop.

Here, the **Musée d'Archéologie Méditerranéenne** has the second largest Egyptian collection in France after the Louvre, along with artefacts from the Middle East, Cyprus, Ancient Greece, Etruria and Rome – including a glazed brick panel from the palace of Darius in Mesopotamia, terracotta figurines from Cyprus, an extensive collection of Greek vases, and marble reliefs, antique bronzes and glass from Rome. The **Musée des Arts Africains, Océaniens et Amérindiens**, meanwhile, features beautiful *objets* from as far as Mali and Vanuatu, and rooms devoted to Mexico, Africa, Oceania and the Americas.

J4: the Euroméditerranée project

A five-square-kilometre swathe of Marseille's north side formerly dominated by port activities has since 1995 been transformed by the **Euroméditerranée** regeneration project. Gateway to the area is **Rue de la République**, a Haussmann-style boulevard that connects the Vieux Port to place de la Joliette. Its hitherto run-down buildings have been refurbished, prompting a wave of retail-based gentrification, with smart boutiques at the Vieux Port end. But the area's main visitor focus is the cluster of iconic landmarks on the J4 jetty, unveiled for Marseille's year as European Capital of Culture in 2013 and including **MuCEM**, a striking ethnographic museum. Further north, **Les Terrasses du Port** is a sleek waterside shopping mall; facing it across Quai du Lazaret is the immense former warehouse of **Les Docks**, reworked as office space with a smattering of retail and restaurants. Further north still is a cluster of new towers by star architects, including Zaha Hadid's 33-storey **Tour CMA-CGM**. Well away from the sea and radically less corporate in tone, **La Friche la Belle de Mai** is a former tobacco factory reworked as a cultural complex.

Musée des Civilisations d'Europe et de la Méditerranée (MuCEM)

Esplanade du J4/Fort St-Jean, 2e • Mon & Wed–Sun: May, June, Sept & Oct 11am–7pm; July & Aug 10am–8pm; Nov–April 11am–6pm • €9.50; free first Sun of month; English audioguide €3.50 • ⓦ mucem.org • ⓜ Vieux Port-Hôtel de Ville or Joliette

Chief symbol of Marseille's renaissance is the **Musée des Civilisations d'Europe et de la Méditerranée (MuCEM)**, a masterly conjoining of two very different structures that opened in 2013 as the centrepiece of the city's stint as European Capital of Culture. Algerian-born Provençal architect Rudy Ricciotti created a strikingly modern cube on the J4 jetty, screened behind a dark, fibre-reinforced concrete lattice that has been compared to a mantilla. This new building is joined at roof level to the restored medieval **Fort St-Jean** by means of a structurally daring footbridge. MuCEM can be entered from the waterside at J4 or from the Vieux Port through Fort St Jean: the latter is the more visually arresting route, with fine views of the Vieux Port from the ramparts and a visual *coup de théâtre* as you cross the water to enter the new building via its roof. It's worth exploring the ramped walkways that wind their way between the museum's glass walls and its concrete latticework.

MuCEM's **temporary exhibitions**, on Mediterranean-related themes, are excellent; recent examples have included a fascinating photographic exhibition dedicated to religious sites shared by the Abrahamic religions and a commendably topical show on life in Tunisia. They're staged on level two of the J4 building and in Fort St Jean (see below).

The permanent collection

Pick up a map and audioguide before visiting the **Gallery of the Mediterranean**, where English labelling is limited; there are also QR codes to scan. The collection is curated around four themes: the birth of agriculture and the emergence of gods; Jerusalem, city of three religions; citizenship and human rights; and beyond the known world. At times the definition of "Mediterranean" is stretched and some visitors may be disappointed at the lack of show-stopping exhibits – but it's engrossing enough, and the section on agriculture is genuinely informative, featuring beautiful peasant artefacts including decorative breads and water jars and an elaborately painted Sicilian farm cart. The Jerusalem section features Greek icons, a synagogue lamp from Morocco and a fourteenth-century Koran, while the citizenship and human rights section charts the emergence of democracy in Greece in the sixth and fifth centuries BC and – in stark contrast – displays a piece of the Berlin wall and a nineteenth-century guillotine. The final section focuses on the age of exploration, with beautiful globes, astrolabes and sextants and a view of Venice by Félix Ziem.

Fort St-Jean

Fort St-Jean dates from the Middle Ages, when Marseille was an independent republic; its enlargement in 1660, and the construction of Fort St-Nicolas on the south side of the port under the order of Louis XIV, represented the city's defeat as a separate entity after the king had sent in an army, suppressed the city's council, fined it, arrested all opposition and set ludicrously low limits on Marseille's expenditure and borrowing. The courtyards have been planted as a Garden of Migrations, featuring Mediterranean plants used in Christian, Jewish and Muslim medicinal tradition. You can view a seventeen-minute film on the fort's history in the Guardroom, while the Georges-Henri-Rivière building on place d'Armes close to the J4 footbridge is used for **temporary exhibitions**.

Villa Méditerranée
Esplanade du J4, 2e • Ⓜ Vieux Port-Hôtel de Ville or Joliette

Playing reluctant second fiddle to MuCEM next door, the **Villa Méditerranée** by Italian architect Stefano Boeri is almost equally striking: a glassy box daringly cantilevered over a pool that reflects the dazzling Mediterranean light. The fact that parts of the structure lie below the waterline is just one aspect of the project that has fuelled controversy and rumour since the place opened. Unveiled, like MuCEM, to coincide with Marseille's year as European Capital of Culture in 2013, it was initially dedicated "to the various forms of expression of the Mediterranean Basin", featuring both permanent and temporary exhibitions. Long regarded by many critics as lacking in any real focus, however, it's currently closed to the public with a proposed redevelopment as a replica of the Cosquer cave (see page 69).

Musée Regards de Provence
Av Vaudoyer, 2e • Tues–Sun 10am–6pm • Documentary film €4, two exhibitions €6.50; *billet couplé* to see everything €8.50 • Ⓦ museeregardsdeprovence.com • Ⓜ Vieux Port-Hôtel de Ville or Joliette

Occupying the long, low former *station sanitaire* – a fine modernist structure dating from 1948 – the **Musée Regards de Provence** opened in 2013 to display works from and about Provence, including works by Ziem, Dufy and Monticelli among others. While the artists are generally not from the front rank of international fame, standards are high and the intimate building is a delight – as understated as J4's twin icons are self-important. There's a documentary film on the history of the building, which was one of Fernand Pouillon's contributions to the reconstruction of the port after wartime devastation; he also designed the La Tourette housing complex behind the museum. The restaurant and *salon de thé* offers superb views of Fort St-Jean and the cathedral.

1

Cathédrale de la Major

Place de la Major, 2e • Mon & Wed–Sun: summer 10am–6.30pm; winter 10am–5.30pm • ☎ 04 91 90 52 87, ⓦ marseille.catholique.
fr/-La-Major-cathedrale • Ⓜ Vieux Port-Hôtel de Ville or Joliette

The **Cathédrale de la Major**, wedged between the waterfront and Le Panier, is an imposing nineteenth-century structure whose striped, neo-Byzantine bulk completely overshadows what remains of its forlorn predecessor, the Romanesque **Cathédrale Vieille Major**, which stands alongside, closed, shuttered and structurally undermined by the road tunnel beneath it.

FRAC

20 bd de Dunkerque, 2e • Tues–Sat noon–7pm, Sun 2–6pm • Tues–Sat €5; Sun free • ⓦ fracpaca.org • Ⓜ Joliette

Behind a six-storey chequered white glass facade by the Japanese architect Kengo Kuma, **FRAC (Fonds Régional d'Art Contemporain)** mounts temporary exhibitions by contemporary artists and provides a venue for experimental film, artistic workshops and conferences. It also stages exhibitions and events in other venues, including the Gare St-Charles.

La Friche la Belle de Mai

41 rue Jobin, 3e • Mon–Sat 8.30am–midnight, Sun 8am–10pm; Le Dernier Cri Mon–Thurs 10am–5pm, Fri 10am–7pm, Sat & Sun
1–7pm; Tour-Panorama Tues–Fri 2–7pm, Sat & Sun 1–7pm; skateboard park and climbing wall daily 9am–9pm • All free except for Tour-
Panorama, where price depends on exhibition • ⓦ lafriche.org • Ⓜ St-Charles or tram to "Longchamp"

Whereas much of Marseille's new infrastructure is dedicated to the consumption of culture, **La Friche la Belle de Mai** is focused equally on its production. Located well away from J4's visitor hot spots, this former tobacco factory near the Gare St-Charles has since 1992 metamorphosed into a creative quarter, with artists' studios, conservation bodies and a television studio that produces a popular soap opera, *Plus Belle la Vie*. La Friche is a venue for all kinds of performance – from circus to dance, music and theatre – and for art exhibitions; many events are free of charge. Exhibitions are staged at **Le Dernier Cri** and in the **Tour-Panorama**, which also has a vast roof terrace that hosts alfresco DJ nights and live music sets in summer (usually Fri & Sat 7–11pm; free). There's also an arthouse cinema, **Le Gyptis** (see page 65); dedicated nightclub and venue, **Cabaret Aléatoire**; puppet theatre, **Théâtre Massalia** (see page 65); plus a skateboard park and climbing wall.

La Canebière and around

La Canebière, the grandiose (if dilapidated) boulevard that runs for about 1km east from the port, is Marseille's main street. Named after the hemp (*canabé*) that once grew here and provided the raw materials for the town's rope-making trade, it was originally modelled on the Champs-Élysées, though it's no pavement-café hot spot and its shops are – with one or two exceptions – lacklustre. It is also home, at the port end, to a **maritime museum**.

Immediately north of La Canebière are the ugly **Centre Bourse** shopping centre and the **Jardin des Vestiges**, where the ancient port extended, curving northwards from the present Quai des Belges. Excavations have revealed a stretch of the Greek port and bits of the city wall with the base of three square towers and a gateway, dated to the second or third century BC.

Musée de la Marine et de l'Économie

Palais de la Bourse, 9 La Canebière, 1er • Tues–Sun 10am–6pm • €2 • ☎ 04 91 39 33 21 • Ⓜ Vieux Port-Hôtel de Ville

The evocative **Musée de la Marine et de l'Économie**, on the ground floor of the Neoclassical stock exchange, is devoted to the theme of Marseille's maritime history and contains a superb collection of model ships, including the legendary 1930s transatlantic liner *Normandie* and Marseille's very own prewar queen of the seas, the *Providence*.

Musée d'Histoire de Marseille

2 rue Henri Barbusse, Centre Bourse, 1er • Tues–Sun 9.30am–6pm • Permanent exhibition €6, permanent and temporary exhibitions €10 • ⓦ musee-histoire-marseille-voie-historique.fr • ⓜ Vieux Port-Hôtel de Ville

The **Musée d'Histoire de Marseille**, inside the Centre Bourse, shows the main finds of Marseillaise excavations. The most dramatic is the wreck of a Roman trading vessel dating from the end of the second century AD, discovered in 1967 on the site of the ancient port when the Centre Bourse was being built. There are models of the city and of its vanished nineteenth-century transporter bridge which dominated the entrance to the Vieux Port until it was blown up by the retreating Germans in 1944, plus reconstructed boats, everyday items such as amphorae and vases, and a great deal of information via text panels, film and interactive screens. The museum also hosts temporary exhibitions.

Porte d'Aix and the quartier Belsunce

The **Bibliothèque Alcazar** on cours Belsunce is one of the regeneration projects gradually supplanting the dilapidated tenements north of La Canebière, its slick modernity softened by a beaux-arts portal that recalls the old Alcazar music hall that once occupied the site and where the likes of Tino Rossi and Yves Montand performed. The continuation of cours Belsunce, rue d'Aix, stretches to **Porte d'Aix**, Marseille's Arc de Triomphe, modelled on the ancient Roman arch at Orange. This was part of the city's grandiose mid-nineteenth-century expansion which included the Cathédrale de la Major and the Joliette docks, paid for with the profits of military enterprise, most significantly the conquest of Algeria in 1830. Today it's a popular meeting place for North African men, as are the narrow streets of the **quartier Belsunce** to the east, stretching between cours Belsunce/rue d'Aix, boulevard d'Athènes and the Gare St-Charles.

Mémorial de la Marseillaise

25 rue Thubaneau, 1er • Tours Tues & Sat 10.30am & 3pm • Free; tickets from Musée d'Histoire de Marseille (see above) • ☎ 04 91 91 91 97, ⓦ musee-histoire-marseille-voie-historique.fr • ⓜ Vieux Port-Hôtel de Ville or tram to stop "Belsunce/Alcazar"

The main reason for coming to the *quartier* Belsunce is to visit the **Mémorial de la Marseillaise**, which presents the story of France's national anthem with some panache in the old real tennis court in which it was first performed in Marseille. You can listen to various versions of Rouget de Lisle's 1792 anthem – which was actually composed in Strasbourg – and discover more about the Marseille volunteers and their epic march on Paris (see page 47). Rue Thubaneau was once a notorious red light district; recent attempts to reinvent it have some way to go.

South of La Canebière

The prime **shopping quarter** of Marseille centres around three streets running south from La Canebière: rue de Rome, rue Paradis and rue St-Ferréol, which terminates

---

MARSEILLE'S COMMUNE

Within the space of four years from its completion in 1867, the Marseille **Préfecture** had flown the imperial flag, the red flag and the tricolour. The red flag was flying in 1871, during Marseille's Commune. The counter-revolutionary forces advanced from Aubagne, encountering little resistance, and took the heights of Notre Dame de la Garde from where they directed their cannon onto the Préfecture. The defeat was swifter but no less bloody than the fate of the Parisian Communards. One of the Marseillaise leaders, Gaston Crémieux, a charismatic and idealistic young bourgeois, escaped the initial carnage but was subsequently caught. Despite clemency pleas from all quarters, Thiers, president of the newly formed Third Republic and a native of Marseille, would not relent and Crémieux was shot by firing squad near the Palais du Pharo in November 1871.

1

at the pseudo-Renaissance **Préfecture**, where demonstrations in the city traditionally converge. The side streets in particular are lined with chic designer boutiques, and there's a scattering of cafés and patisseries.

Musée Cantini

19 rue Grignan, 6e • Tues–Sun 9.30am–6pm • €6; free first Sun of month • ☎ 04 91 54 77 75, ⓦ musee-cantini.marseille.fr • Ⓜ Estrangin-Préfecture

The **Musée Cantini** is the city's principal art museum devoted to paintings and sculptures of the "classic modern", from the end of the nineteenth century up to the 1960s. The Fauvists and Surrealists are well represented; there are works by Matisse, Léger, Picasso, Ernst, Le Corbusier, Miró and Giacometti.

Cours Julien and around

East of rue de Rome, the streets around **cours Julien** are full of bars and music shops, and the *cours* itself, with its pools, fountains, restaurant tables and boutiques, is populated by Marseille's bohemian crowd and its diverse immigrant community. With its small, one-off couturiers, bookshops, art galleries and engrossing markets (see page 65), by day this is one of the most pleasant places to idle in the city, though almost every surface is buried under graffiti; the atmosphere at night can be a little edgy, particularly around the métro station.

Palais de Longchamp and around

Home to two museums, the **Palais de Longchamp** was completed in 1869, the year the Suez Canal opened, bringing a new boom for Marseillaise trade. It was built as the grandiose conclusion of a now-defunct aqueduct at Roquefavour bringing water from the Durance to the city. Water is still pumped into the centre of the colonnade connecting the building's two palatial wings. Below, an enormous statue looks as if it's honouring some great feminist victory: three well-muscled women stand above four bulls wallowing in a pool from which a cascade drops the four or five storeys to ground level.

Musée des Beaux-Arts

Palais Longchamp, 4e • Tues–Sun 9.30am–6pm • €6 • ⓦ musee-des-beaux-arts.marseille.fr • Ⓜ Cinq Avenues-Longchamp or tram #2 to the same stop

The north wing of the Palais de Longchamp houses the city's restored **Musée des Beaux-Arts**, which has a fair share of old masters including paintings by Rubens, Tiepolo and Jordaens, plus works by the nineteenth-century French painters Corot and Courbet. Well represented too are Provençal landscape painters of the nineteenth century, including Félix Ziem.

Musée d'Histoire Naturelle

Palais Longchamp, 4e • Tues–Sun 9.30am–6pm • €6, €8 with temporary exhibition • ⓦ culture.marseille.fr/les-musees-de-marseille/museum-d-histoire-naturelle • Ⓜ Cinq Avenues-Longchamp or tram #2 to the same stop

The Palais de Longchamp's southeastern wing is occupied by the somewhat old-fashioned **Musée d'Histoire Naturelle** and its stuffed animals and fossils. The oldest parts of the collection date back to the cabinets of curiosity of the eighteenth century – there are some 200,000 botanical specimens alone.

Musée Grobet-Labadié

140 bd Longchamp, 1er • Tues–Sun 9.30am–6pm • €6 • ⓦ musee-grobet-labadie.marseille.fr • Ⓜ Cinq Avenues-Longchamp or tram #2 to the same stop

Opposite the Palais de Longchamp is the **Musée Grobet-Labadié**, an elegant late nineteenth-century townhouse filled with exquisite *objets d'art* representing the tastes of a typical family from Marseille's affluent merchant class at its zenith. It was closed for renovation at the time of writing.

South of the centre

Avenue du Prado, the continuation of rue de Rome, is an eight-lane highway, with impressive fountains and one of the city's biggest **daily markets** between métros Castellane and Périer. At the Rond-point du Prado, the avenue turns west to meet the corniche road.

Parc Chanot

The city's north–south axis continues as boulevard Michelet past **Parc Chanot**, the site of **Olympique de Marseille**'s ground, the **Stade Vélodrome**, recently revamped and roofed over to bring it up to UEFA Elite standards. OM's reputation for occasional brilliance means that home matches are almost always sold out, but tickets can be bought online from the team's website (@om.net). At the far side of the stadium on rue Raymond-Teisseire, the **Palais des Sports** hosts boxing matches, tennis, gymnastics and other spectacles.

Unité d'Habitation (Cité Radieuse)

280 bd Michelet, 8e • Daily 9am–6pm; solo visitors restricted to third and fourth floors and part of the roof terrace; guided tours in French Mon–Sat 2–3.30pm & 4–5.30pm; tours in English during school holidays only Fri & Sat 10am–noon • Free; guided tours €10, book via tourist office (see page 59) • @ citeradieuse-marseille.com • Bus #21 from @ Rond-Point du Prado to "Le Corbusier" stop

Set back from boulevard Michelet in the southern suburbs, Le Corbusier's **Unité d'Habitation** – also known as the **Cité Radieuse** and completed in 1952 – is a mould-breaking piece of architecture, deservedly designated a UNESCO World Heritage Site in 2016. A seventeen-storey housing complex on stilts, the Unité was the prototype for thousands of apartment buildings the world over, though close-up the difference in quality between this – the *couture* original – and the industrially produced imitations becomes apparent.

Confounding expectations, this concrete modernist structure is extremely complex, with 23 different apartment layouts, to suit single people and families of varying sizes: the larger apartments are split across two floors with balconies on both sides of the building, giving unhindered views of mountains and sea. It's a remarkably happy place; many of the original tenants are still in residence, and people chat and smile in the lobby. At ground level the building is decorated with Le Corbusier's distinctive, stylized human figure, the Modulor, while on the third floor is a **restaurant** with a terrace and superlative Mediterranean views, and a **hotel** (see page 60). The iconic, sculptural **rooftop** recreational area is probably the highlight; it's here that Le Corbusier's infatuation with ocean liners seems most obvious.

MAC

69 av de Haïfa, 8e • Tues–Sun 9.30am–6pm • €5, €8 with temporary exhibitions; free first Sun of month • @ mac.marseille.fr • Bus #23 or bus #45 from @ Rond-Point du Prado, stop "Haïfa Marie-Louise"

The southern suburbs are the setting for Marseille's contemporary art museum, **MAC**. The permanent collection, displayed in perfect, pure-white surroundings, is the continuation of the Cantini collection (see page 56) with works from the 1960s to the present. Artists include the Marseillais César and Ben, along with Buren, Christo, Klein, Niki de Saint Phalle, Tinguely and Warhol. Sculptures adorn the museum's garden.

Parc Borély

Av du Prado, 8e • **Park** Daily 6am–9pm • Free • **Botanical garden** April–Oct Tues–Sun 10am–noon & 1–6pm; Nov–March 10am–noon & 1–5pm • €3, €6 with museum • **Musée Borély** 134 av Clot Bey • Tues–Sun 9.30am–6pm • €6, including botanical garden • @ musee-borely.marseille.fr • Bus #19 or #83 from @ Rond-Point du Prado or #83 from the Vieux Port

1

The city's best green space, the **Parc Borély**, lies between avenue d'Haïfa and the sea, and has a boating lake, rose gardens, palm trees and a **botanical garden**. The eighteenth-century **Château Borély** itself is a museum of decorative arts, housing eighteenth- and nineteenth-century ceramics from the Marseille area, fashion, and Art Nouveau and Art Deco furniture, ceramics and glassware.

The corniche and south to Les Goudes

The corniche that winds south from the Vieux Port is where Marseille lets its hair down. The most popular stretch of sand close to the city centre is the Plage des Catalans, a few blocks south of the Palais du Pharo. This marks the beginning of Marseille's **corniche Président J.F. Kennedy**, initiated and partly built after the 1848 revolution. Despite its inland bypass of the Malmousque peninsula, it's a corniche as good as any on the Riviera, with *belle époque* villas on the slopes above, the Îles d'Endoume and the Château d'If in the distance, cliffs below and high bridge piers for the road to cross the inlets of La Fausse-Monnaie and the Vallon des Auffes.

Vallon des Auffes

Prior to the construction of the corniche, Malmousque and the **Vallon des Auffes** were inaccessible from the town unless you followed the "customs men's path" over the rocks or took a boat. There was nothing on Malmousque, but the Vallon des Auffes had a freshwater source and a small community of fishermen and rope-makers. Amazingly, it is not much different today, with fishing boats pulled up around the rocks, tiny jumbled houses scattered throughout, and restaurants serving the catch (see page 61). Only one road, rue du Vallon-des-Auffes, leads out; otherwise you need to take the long flights of steps up to the corniche.

Malmousque

Malmousque is a desirable residential district, home to Marseille's most distinguished hotel-restaurant, *Le Petit Nice-Passédat* (see page 62). Behind La Fausse-Monnaie inlet, a path leads to the Théâtre Silvain, an open-air theatre set in a wilderness of trees and flowers and the setting for summer concerts of jazz, chanson and pop. There's more greenery, of a formal nature, a short way further along the corniche at no. 271 in the **Parc Valmer** (daily: March, April, Sept & Oct 8am–7pm; May–Aug 8am–8pm; Nov–Feb 8am–5.30pm; free; bus #83, stop "Corniche J-Martin"), and you can explore the tiny streets that lead up into this prime district of mansions with high-walled gardens.

Plage du Prado and Montredon

The corniche J.F. Kennedy ends at the **Plage du Prado**, the city's main sand beach backed by a wide strip of lawn and overlooked by the Escale Borély bar and restaurant complex, best visited at night when it is one of the liveliest spots in town (see page 64). The promenade continues – lined intermittently with café and bar terraces – to the coastal suburb of **Montredon**, where the road curves inland just before the harbour of **Pointe Rouge**, served by ferries from the Vieux Port in summer, and an access point for the Parc National des Calanques, which stretches from here to Cassis and beyond (see page 66).

ARRIVAL AND DEPARTURE	MARSEILLE
By plane The city's airport, the Aéroport Marseille-Provence (☎0820 811 414, ⓦmarseille-airport.com), is 20km northwest of the city, linked to the *gare SNCF* by bus (every 15–20min 4.10am–12.10am; 25min; €8.30; ⓦstore.marseille.aeroport.fr/bus.html). Destinations Bristol (3 weekly; 1hr 55min); Dublin (4 weekly;	2hr 30min); Edinburgh (2 weekly; 2hr 35min); Glasgow (2 weekly; 2hr 25min); London Gatwick (1–2 daily; 1hr 50min); London Heathrow (2–4 daily; 1hr 55min); London Luton (2–4 weekly; 1hr 55min); London Stansted (2–3 daily; 2hr 5min); Manchester (2 weekly; 2hr 10min); Montreal (4–5 weekly; 8hr 10min); Paris CDG (6 daily; 1hr 25min).

By train The *gare SNCF* St-Charles (☎36 35, ⓦgares-sncf.com/fr/gare/frmsc/marseille-saint-charles) is on the eastern edge of the 1er arrondissement on square Narvik. From the station, a staircase leads down to Bd d'Athènes and on to La Canebière, Marseille's main street.

Destinations Aix-en-Provence (every 35min–1hr;46–53min); Aix-en-Provence TGV (every 30min–1hr 30min; 11–12min); Arles (every 8min–1hr 55min; 42min–1hr 3min); Aubagne (every 10min–1hr; 9–15min); Avignon (up to every 6min at peak times; 1hr 5min–1hr 55min); Avignon TGV (every 9min–1hr 5min; 39min); Cannes (every 30min–1hr; 2hr 3min–2hr 13min); Carry-le-Rouet (every 1hr–3hr; 30min); Cassis (every 30min; 22min); La Ciotat (every 10min at peak times; 29min); Les Arcs for Draguignan (hourly; 1–2hr 26min); L'Estaque (every 50min–2hr; 9–12min); Lyon Part Dieu (every 20min–1hr; 1hr 45min–3hr 35min); Martigues (every 2–3hr; 48–51min); Nice (every 30min–3hr; 2hr 36min–2hr 42min); Paris Gare de Lyon (roughly hourly; 3hr 9min–3hr 30min); St Raphaël (every 30min–3hr; 1hr 36min–1hr 42min); Salon (every 30min–2hr; 50–54min); Sisteron (4–6 daily; 2hr 7min–2hr 19min).

By bus The *gare routière* is integrated with the Gare St-Charles on rue Honnorat (☎ 04 91 08 95 95, ⓦlepilote.com), though note that buses for Cassis and La Ciotat depart from the "Castellane" halt just south of the centre.

Destinations Aix-en-Provence, via autoroute (every 5–10min; 30min–1hr); Aubagne (every 5–15min at peak times; 15min); Barcelonnette (via Digne-Les-Bains: 1–2 daily; 4hr 30min–5hr 5min); Cassis (2 daily; 50min); Grenoble (via Sisteron; 1 daily; 4hr 35min); La Ciotat (every 10min–1hr; 50min); Manosque (13 daily; 1hr 30min); Martigues (every 15–30min; 35–46min); Sisteron (3–6 daily; 2hr 15min–2hr 15min–2hr 45min).

By car Arriving by car, you'll descend into Marseille from the surrounding heights of one of three mountain ranges. Follow signs for the Vieux Port to reach the city centre.

By ferry Corsica Linea, 23 Place de la Joliette/Quai de la Joliette (☎0825 88 80 88, ⓦcorsicalinea.com), runs ferries to Corsica, Sardinia, Tunisia and Algeria.

INFORMATION

Tourist office 11 La Canebière, 1er (daily 9am–6pm; ☎0826 500 500, ⓦwww.marseille-tourisme.com). The office organizes guided tours on various themes, mostly in French but with a bilingual "Le Panier" tour (Sat 2pm).

GETTING AROUND

BY PUBLIC TRANSPORT

Bus, tram and metro Marseille has an efficient public transport network (☎rtm.fr). The métro and trams run from 5am until around 12.30/1am; buses run from 5 or 6am until 9pm, after which night bus services take over until around 12.45am.

Information You can get a plan of the transport system from *points d'accueil* at most métro stations (daily 6.50am–7.40pm) or the RTM office in the Centre Bourse, 6 rue des Fabres, 1er (Mon–Fri 8.30am–6pm). You can also download maps of a single line or the entire network on the RTM website.

Tickets and passes Flat-fee single tickets for buses, trams and métro can be used for journeys combining all three provided they take less than 1hr and involve no more than one métro ride. You can buy individual tickets (€1.70) from bus drivers, and from métro ticket offices or machines on métro stations and tram stops. Two-journey *Cartes 2 Voyages* (€3.40) and ten-journey *Cartes 10 Voyages* (€14) can be bought from métro stations, RTM kiosks and shops displaying the RTM sign. Consider also the good-value one-day *Pass XL 24h* (€5.20), three-day *Pass XL 72h* (€10.80) and seven-day *Pass XL 7 Jours* (€14.50), available from the same outlets, and for which you'll need ID and a passport pic. Tickets must be tapped on the card reader at métro gates or on board.

Ferry RTM runs a ferry between the Vieux Port and Pointe Rouge in the south of the city for easier access to the beaches and *calanques* (hourly, daily: late April to late Sept 8am–7pm; €5), and another to L'Estaque (late April to late September daily, hourly, 8.30am–7.30pm). There's also a ferry across the Vieux Port (daily, every 10min, 7.30am–8.30pm; €0.50; free for *City Pass* and *Pass XL* holders).

BY BIKE

Bike rental Blue bicycles belonging to Le Vélo scheme (ⓦlevelo-mpm.fr) can be rented from the 130 self-service rental points throughout the city, using a bank card (€1 for seven-day ticket, for the duration of which first 30min of each journey is free, €1 for each additional 30min). Electric bikes can be rented from Easymove/Velo & Oxygen, 25 Quai de Rive Neuve (daily 10am–6pm; ⓦeasymove.fr; €25/half day).

BY CAR

Car parks Cours Esplanade J4, 2e; Estienne-d'Orves, 1er; rue Breteuil, 6e; Centre Bourse, 1er; place Géneral-de-Gaulle, 1er; place Jean-Jaurès, 5e.

Car rental Avis, Gare St-Charles, 1er (☎0820 611 636, ⓦavis.com); Enterprise, 18 bd Charles Nedelec, 1er (☎04 91 05 90 86, ⓦenterprise.fr); Hertz, 31 bd Voltaire, 1er (☎04 91 05 51 20, ⓦhertz.com). All have offices at the airport.

BY TAXI

Taxis Taxi Radio Marseille (☎04 91 02 20 20); Les Taxis Marseillais (☎04 91 92 92 92).

ACCOMMODATION

Demand for accommodation in Marseille isn't as tied to the summer season as in the resorts, but even so popular hotels in good locations get booked up, so if you've a preference don't leave it too late. **Hotels** are plentiful, with lots of two- and three-star options around the Vieux Port; real budget bargains are rarer, while of late the number of luxury options has risen considerably. The simplest way to search for a **room** is through the tourist office website.

HOTELS

Beauséjour 13 rue Saint Saens ☎ 04 91 54 90 13; ⓦ Vieux Port-Hôtel de Ville. Functional, good value and fantastically located budget choice close to the Vieux Port. Rooms aren't the largest, though the optically illusional wallpaper at least enlivens the space. **€60**

Bellevue 34 quai du Port, 2e ☎ 04 96 17 05 40, ⓦ hotel bellevuemarseille.com; ⓜ Vieux Port-Hôtel de Ville. Boutique-style hotel on the port with a famous old bar, *La Caravelle* (see page 62); good views, chic decor, a/c and games consoles but no lift, so rooms on upper floors are for the fit only. **€110**

C2 Hôtel 48 rue Roux de Brignoles, 6e ☎ 04 95 05 13 13, ⓦ c2–hotel.com; ⓜ Estrangin-Préfecture. Classic modern furniture from Ron Arad, Le Corbusier and Charles Eames meets elaborate stucco work at this intimate luxury hotel, recently converted from a nineteenth-century mansion and with just twenty rooms. Facilities include a pool, spa and cocktail bar; the hotel even has its own private island. **€269**

Le Corbusier Unité d'Habitation, 280 bd Michelet, 8e ☎ 04 28 31 39 22, ⓦ hotellecorbusier.com; bus #21 from ⓜ Rond-Point du Prado to "Le Corbusier". Landmark hotel on the third floor of this renowned architect's iconic high-rise (see page 57), with fabulous views and a variety of room styles, from simple studios and a large wheelchair-accessible room to elegant suites with access to a large eighth-floor balcony. **€79**

Edmond-Rostand 31 rue Dragon, 6e ☎ 04 91 37 74 95, ⓦ hoteledmondrostand.com; ⓜ Estrangin-Préfecture. Smart, friendly three-star centrally located in the antiques district, a short walk uphill from the Vieux Port. Simple but comfortable, smallish a/c en-suite rooms, with contemporary furnishings. **€81**

Grand Hôtel Beauvau 4 rue Beauvau ☎ 04 91 54 91 00, ⓦ sofitel.accorhotels.com; ⓜ Vieux Port-Hôtel de Ville. Venerable old four-star hotel on the Vieux Port which, incredibly, first opened its doors as far back as 1816, and – uniquely – has long been a centre of production for Savon de Marseille, the city's famous soap (you can visit the workshop). The antique-contemporary rooms are well worth the money and some come with great views over the port. **€118**

Hermès 2 rue Bonneterie, 2e ☎ 04 96 11 63 63, ⓦ www. hotelmarseille.com; ⓜ Vieux Port-Hôtel de Ville. Two-star in a superb position just off the Vieux Port, with plain but comfortable rooms with flatscreen TV. Some have terraces and views and there's a roof terrace with fabulous vistas over the Vieux Port. **€74**

Ibis Budget Vieux Port 46 rue Sainte, 1er ☎ 0892 680 582, ⓦ ibis.com; ⓜ Vieux Port-Hôtel de Ville. This budget chain hotel is worth a stay for its location alone, close to the Vieux Port. Situated in a historic building, some of the rooms have timber beams – it's incredibly popular, so book ahead. **€51**

★ **Mama Shelter** 64 rue de la Loubière, 6e ☎ 04 84 35 20 00, ⓦ mamashelter.com; ⓜ Baille or Notre Dame du Mont-Cours Julien. Marseille sister of the hip Paris original, combining stylish design and boutique hotel comforts – including iMacs and free on-demand movies – at budget prices. There's a restaurant and bar, a reserved strip of beach and parking. **€79**

Radisson Blu 40 quai de Rive Neuve, 7e ☎ 04 88 44 52 00, ⓦ radissonblu.com/en/hotel-marseille; ⓜ Vieux Port-Hôtel de Ville. Stylish, primarily business-oriented modern luxury hotel with a great portside location, a health suite and an open-air pool with spectacular views. **€136**

St Ferréol 19 rue Pisançon, corner rue St-Ferréol, 1er ☎ 04 91 33 12 21, ⓦ hotel-stferreol.com; ⓜ Vieux Port-Hôtel de Ville. Three-star comforts including understated modern decor, a/c and soundproofing, plus a very central location in the main pedestrianized shopping area. **€75**

Du Sud 18 rue Beauvau ☎ 04 91 54 38 50, ⓦ hotelsud. com; ⓜ Vieux Port-Hôtel de Ville. Unassuming, decent value a/c rooms in a very central location perfect for a high-cultural soiree at the nearby Opéra. **€82**

HOSTELS

Auberge de Jeunesse Bonneveine Impasse Bonfils, Av J.-Vidal, 8e ☎ 04 91 17 63 30, ⓦ ajmarseille.org; ⓜ Rond-Point du Prado, then bus #44 (direction "Floralia Rimet", stop "Place Bonnefon") or night bus #583 from Centre Bourse. Attractive modern hostel 200m from the plage du Prado. Facilities include restaurant and bar, and rates include breakfast. Open 24hr. Closed mid-Dec to mid-Jan. **€22.90**; dorms **€24**; twins **€28.30**

Hello Marseille 12 rue Breteuil 3e ☎ 09 54 80 75 05, ⓦ hellomarseille.com; ⓜ Vieux Port-Hôtel de Ville. LFAJ-affiliated, communally minded non-profit hostel housed in a period building near the Vieux Port, with accommodation consisting of no-frills six-bed dorms. Rates include breakfast. Open 24hr. No lift. Minimum two-night stay. **€26**

★ **Vertigo Vieux Port** 38 rue Fort Notre Dame, 7e ☎ 04 91 54 42 95, ⓦ hotelvertigo.fr; ⓜ Estrangin-Préfecture. Hip backpacker hotel and hostel, with stylishly exposed beams and striking commissioned artwork. Accommodation is in simple twin rooms or four- to eight-bed mixed or female dorms, all en suite. Free breakfast. Dorms **€26**; twins **€69**

EATING

SEE MAPS PAGES 48 AND 50

Fish and seafood are the main ingredients of the Marseillais diet, and the superstar of dishes is the city's own invention, **bouillabaisse**, a saffron- and garlic-flavoured fish soup with croutons and *rouille* to throw in. There are conflicting theories about which fish should be included, though it's generally agreed that *rascasse* is essential. The other city speciality is *pieds et paquets*, mutton or lamb belly and trotters. The best, and most expensive, restaurants are close to the **corniche**, though for international choice the trendy **cours Julien** is the place to head, while **rue Sainte** is good for smart and fashionable dining close to the opera and Vieux Port. The pedestrian precinct behind the south quay of the **Vieux Port** is more tourist-oriented and fishy, while **Le Panier** has a few tiny, inexpensive bistros. You can eat good Marseille **African** food all over town, but especially in the Quartier Belsunce and the lively streets around the Marché des Capucins.

CAFÉS

Cup of Tea 1 rue Caisserie, 2e ☎ 04 91 90 84 02; Ⓜ Vieux Port-Hôtel de Ville. Gorgeous Le Panier bookshop and *salon de thé* strategically located midway up the climb from the Vieux Port to the Vieille Charité. Huge selection of speciality teas, including green tea or rooibos, as well as coffee. Mon–Fri 8.30am–7pm, Sat 9.30am–7pm.

L'Equitable 54 cours Julien, 6e ☎ 06 67 83 44 22, Ⓦ equitablecafe.org; Ⓜ Notre Dame du Mont-Cours Julien. Community-focused organic café/bar in Marseille's bohemian quarter, serving artisan beers, organic wines, teas and herbal infusions and hosting various debates and events alongside gigs, Dj sets and film screenings. Annual membership is compulsory, with fees upwards of €1. Mon 6.30–10pm, Tues 3–10pm, Wed & Thurs 3–11pm, Fri 3–11.45pm, Sat 3pm–1am.

★ **Plauchut** 168 La Canebière, 1er ☎ 04 91 48 06 67, Ⓦ plauchut.com; Ⓜ Réformés-Canebière. Beautiful old *patissier-chocolatier-glacier* and *salon de thé*, established in 1820, selling delicious home-made ice cream, croissants, *calissons* and *macarons*, plus *pogne* (a type of brioche), sandwiches and traditional *navettes* – an orange-scented biscuit sold by weight. They also host breakfast (€5.90) from 9am. Tues–Sun 8am–8pm.

Torrefaction Noailles 56 La Canebière, 1er ☎ 04 91 55 60 66; Ⓜ Noailles. Celebrated confectioner and café, with high stools, a wonderful aroma of fresh ground coffee and plenty of nougat, *calissons*, candied fruits and caramels to take away. Numerous additional branches throughout the city. Mon–Sat 7am–7pm, Sun 10am–6pm.

RESTAURANTS

Le 15 15 rue des 3 Rois, 6e ☎ 04 91 92 81 81; Ⓜ Notre Dame du Mont-Cours Julien. Exactly what you don't expect to find in the trendy streets between La Plaine and

cours Julien – resolutely straightforward bistro fare on €18.50 and €21.50 *menus*, washed down with *vin de pays*. It's not haute cuisine, and service can be on the slow side, but it's cheap, largely cheerful and often packed. Daily 7–11pm; closed 9 days in Feb and 15 in July.

★ **Les Arcenaulx** 25 cours d'Estienne-d'Orves, 1er ☎ 04 91 59 80 30, Ⓦ les-arcenaulx.com; Ⓜ Vieux Port-Hôtel de Ville. This classy place has an atmospheric and intellectual vibe, as it's also a bookshop; there's a €26 lunch *menu* and a six-course *menu découverte* for €65; otherwise, expect to pay around €21 for their version of the classic *pieds et paquets*. Mon–Sat noon–2pm & 7.30–10.30pm.

L'Aromat 49 rue Sainte, 1er ☎ 04 91 55 09 06, Ⓦ laromat.com; Ⓜ strangin-Préfecture/Vieux Port-Hôtel de Ville. Close to the Vieux Port and well regarded, with an austere modern dining room and creative dishes like fillet beef smoked with *herbes de Provence* or pork loin stuffed with Perigord truffles. Three courses with *amuse bouche* €42, *menu dégustation* €62; à la carte mains €22. Mon noon–2pm, Tues–Fri noon–2pm & 8–10pm, Sat 8–10pm.

Le Café des Epices rue du Lacydon ☎ 04 91 91 22 69, Ⓦ lecafedesepices-by-acdg.com; Ⓜ Vieux Port-Hôtel de Ville or bus #55. Candle-lit, rustic-contemporary bistro with a marked pescatarian influence and a daily vegetarian platter; lunch menu €27. Mon noon–10pm, Tues–Fri noon–2pm & 7.30–10pm, Sat noon–2.30pm & 7.30–10.30pm.

Chez Fonfon 140 Vallon des Auffes, 7e ☎ 04 91 52 14 38, Ⓦ chez-fonfon.com; bus #83. There's no debate about the quality of the bouillabaisse (€53) here; this chic restaurant overlooking a small fishing harbour is one of an elite band guarding the true recipe of the dish. Daily noon–2pm & 7–10pm.

Chez Sauveur 10 rue d'Aubagne, 1er ☎ 04 91 54 33 96, Ⓦ chezsauveur.fr; Ⓜ Noailles. Established in 1943, this modest Sicilian restaurant close to the Marché des Capucins is renowned for its excellent wood-fired pizzas, including a few made with *brousse* goat's cheese. Most priced at €12. Tues–Sat 11.30am–10.30pm.

La Kahena 2 rue de la République, 2e ☎ 04 91 90 61 93, Ⓦ lakahena.fr, Ⓜ Vieux Port-Hôtel de Ville. Great Tunisian restaurant just off the Vieux Port, with a bright, elaborately tiled interior; couscous from €10 and lamb *brochettes* for €17. There are delectable displays of sticky pastries, and a few North African bottles on the wine list. Daily noon–2pm & 7–11pm.

Namaste 43 av de Prado ☎ 04 91 80 57 94, Ⓦ namaste-13.fr, Ⓜ Castellane or Périer. if you're getting curry withdrawal symptoms, this is a more than adequate remedy, serving all the classic pan-Indian favourites (including plenty of vegetarian and vegan options) at budget prices. Mains around €12/13. Daily 6.15–10pm.

1

Les Ondines 43 av de Prado ☎09 73 133 133, ⓦlesondines.bio, ⓜEstrangin Préfecture. A relative stalwart of Marseille's growing vegan scene, *Les Ondines* proudly bills itself as the only organic certified restaurant in the city, with a changing menu of seasonal veg dishes paired with brown rice, houmous etc. Mains around €10; also does lunchboxes to take away (€8). Mon–Fri 11.45am–3pm.

La Passarelle 52 rue Plan Fourmiguier, 7e ☎04 91 33 03 27, ⓦrestaurantlapassarelle.fr; ⓜVieux Port-Hôtel de Ville or bus #82 or #83. Relaxed and informal restaurant tucked behind La Criée theatre, with a short, daily changing seasonal menu featuring the likes of seared tuna with sweet pepper hummus. Main courses around €20. The garden terrace is one of the prettiest (and most peaceful) in Marseille. Daily noon–2.30pm & 8–10.30pm; garden terrace April–Oct only.

Le Peron 56 promenade, corniche Président J.F. Kennedy ☎04 91 52 15 22, ⓦrestaurantperon.com; bus #83. The Marseille terrace experience par excellence, with a rack of tables atop a rocky, spume-lashed outcrop on the Corniche. The ravishing views are complemented by an inevitably seafood-heavy kitchen serving up the likes of Mediterranean mullet with sea urchin mayonnaise (€26) and scallops with candied pumpkin (€39). Lunch menu €55. Mon–Fri & Sun noon–2pm & 7.45–9.45pm, Sat noon–2pm & 7.45–10pm.

Petit Nice-Passédat Anse de Maldormé, corniche Président J.F. Kennedy, 7e ☎04 91 59 25 92, ⓦpassedat. fr. Gerald Passédat's gorgeous hotel-restaurant on the Corniche is the pinnacle of fine dining in Marseille, with three Michelin stars and highly inventive, seafood-based *menus* from €110 to €380. There's simpler (and cheaper) food available at the bar. Passédat also runs the cheaper *Le Môle* restaurant at MuCEM. Tues–Sat 12.30–2pm & 7.30–10pm.

★ **Sur le Pouce** 2 rue des Convalescents, 1er ☎04 91 56 13 28; ⓜSt-Charles. Lively, inexpensive Tunisian restaurant in the *quartier* Belsunce, with a huge range of couscous from €5.50 to €11, plus grills, Merguez sausages and *brochettes* from around €7. One of the city's best budget options. Daily noon–3.30pm & 6–11.30pm.

Une Table, au Sud 2 quai du Port, 2e ☎04 91 90 63 53, ⓦunetableausud.com; ⓜVieux Port-Hôtel de Ville. Michelin-starred gastronomic restaurant overlooking the Vieux Port. Chef Ludovic Turac's seafood-focused take on Provençal cooking includes dishes like seared cod with citrus zest and wood fired lobster infused with orange blossom. Mains from €28; *menus* from €58. Tues–Sat noon–1.30pm & 7.30–9.45pm, Sun noon–1.30pm.

Toinou Les Fruits de Mer 3 cours Saint-Louis, 1er ☎04 91 33 14 94, ⓦtoinou.com; ⓜNoailles. Popular with locals and visitors alike for the choice of more than forty types of shellfish, served in the restaurant and sold fresh from the counter at the front. Heaped plates of prawns, mussels and oysters start from around €10; they also do fish and chips. Daily 11.30am–10.30pm.

DRINKING

SEE MAPS PAGES 48 AND 50

Aux 3G 3 rue St-Pierre, 5e ☎04 91 48 76 36, ⓦaux3g. com; ⓜNotre Dame du Mont-Cours Julien. Marseille's only lesbian bar, close to La Plaine market and regularly packed for its weekend karaoke and DJ nights, when they spin anything from dance music to 80s hits. Gay men are welcome. Entry €10. Thurs 7.30pm–midnight, Fri 8pm–midnight, Sat 8pm–2am.

Bar de 13 Coins 45 rue Sainte Francoise ☎04 91 91 56 49; ⓜJoliette. A mural-painted icon of a corner bar in the bowels of old Marseille, frequented by writers, local characters and tourists who can actually find it. Salads, bruschettas and the like for around €12/13. Daily 9am–midnight.

La Caravelle 34 quai du Port 1e ☎04 91 90 36 64, ⓦlacaravellemarseille.com; ⓜVieux Port-Hôtel de Ville. Intimate bar and "authentic speakeasy" inside *Hotel Belle Vue* with a fantastic soundtrack of vintage jazz, soul and samba, and regular live music. Organic wines, tapas and a delightfully petite portside terrace as well. Daily 7am–2am.

Le Greenwich 142 av Pierre-Mendès-France, 8e ☎04 91 22 67 92, ⓦlegreenwich.com; bus #19. Spacious brasserie and cocktail bar by the sea in the Escale Borély complex, with a big terrace for post-beach ice creams (€9.50) and cocktails (€13 for a mojito ice). There's a full restaurant menu inside, plus Olympique de Marseille matches on TV and a house DJ. Daily 8am–midnight.

Bar de la Marine 15 quai de Rive-Neuve, 1er ☎04 91 54 95 42; ⓜVieux Port-Hôtel de Ville. A favourite bar for Vieux Port lounging, doubly famous as the apocryphal inspiration for Pagnol's Marseille trilogy (see page 74) and as a location from the film *Love, Actually*. It's open from breakfast – at lunchtime you might tuck into one of their fish or meat mains in the €15–20 range; in the evening you might tuck into tapas with wine or mojitos. Daily 7am–2am.

O'Malley's 9 quai de Rive-Neuve, 1er ☎04 91 33 65 50, ⓦomalleysmarseille.com; ⓜVieux Port-Hôtel de Ville. Classic expat-friendly Irish pub on the Vieux Port, with the familiar Celtic trappings plus live music daily at 9pm and daily happy hour (5.30–9pm), when pints are €5. Mon, Tues & Sun 3pm–1.30am, Wed & Thurs 3pm–2.30am, Fri & Sat 3pm–3.30am.

Les Pécheurs/LdNVII 43 quai de Rive Neuve ☎04 91 66 61 37, ⓦfacebook.com/LdNVII; ⓜVieux Port-Hôtel de Ville. The latest incarnation of this achingly hip bar

1

masterminded by the veteran Marseille DJs and scenesters behind *La Dame Noir* (see page 64). Very dark, very art deco and very now. Tues–Sat 6pm–2am.

Polikarpov 24 cours Honoré d'Estienne d'Orves 1er ☎04 91 52 70 30, ⊛lepolikarpov.com; ⓜVieux Port-Hôtel de Ville. Hip, LGBTQ-friendly, Russian-themed vodka bar near the Vieux Port, with regular DJ nights and a big range of vodkas, including premium brands like Grey Goose and Ketel One. Shots from €3, cocktails from €5. Daily 8am–1.30am.

NIGHTLIFE

SEE MAPS PAGES 48 AND 50

Marseille's nightlife has something for everyone, and most of what's happening is covered in the free **local arts** magazine *Ventilo* (⊛journalventilo.fr); pick it up from tourist offices, museums and cultural centres or FNAC in the Centre Bourse. FNAC, and the tourist office's ticket bureau, are the best places for **tickets and information**.

L'Affranchi 212 bd de St-Marcel, 11er ☎04 91 35 09 19, ⊛l-affranchi.com; bus #15 from ⓜSaint Marguerite Dromel, stop "St-Marcel". Concert venue in the eastern suburbs hosting club nights and live gigs, with a particular emphasis on hip-hop. There's also a DJ school. Ticket prices vary, but expect to pay around €10–15.

Bazar 90 bd Rabatau, 8e ☎06 58 52 15 15, ⊛bazar marseille.com; ⓜRond-Point du Prado. Huge, expensive mainstream superclub playing house and occasionally hosting big-name international DJs, with outdoor dancing under the palms from June to Sept. Thurs–Sat midnight–6am.

Cité de la Musique 4 rue Bernard du Bois, 1er ☎04 91 39 28 28, ⊛citemusique-marseille.com; ⓜJules Guesde. Music school and live venue close to Porte d'Aix, with an intimate cellar venue and a larger auditorium staging jazz, classical and contemporary concerts.

Les Docks des Suds 12 rue Urbain V, 2e ☎04 91 99 00 00, ⊛dock-des-suds.org; tram #2 to "Arenc le Silo". Vast warehouse that hosts Marseille's annual Fiesta des Suds and Babel Med Music world music and jazz festivals (Oct) and is a regular live venue for hip-hop, electro and global sounds.

L'Intermédiare 63 place Jean-Jaurès, 6e ☎04 91 47 01 25, ⊛facebook.com/Intermediaire.live; ⓜNotre Dame du Mont-Cours Julien. Loud, hip club and bar with regular live bands and DJs and a highly eclectic music policy, ranging from rock to electro, hip house, dance hall, reggae, cumbia, funk and world music. DJ nights 8pm–2am, live gigs from 9pm.

Machine à Coudre 6 rue Jean-Roque, 1er ☎04 91 55 62 65, ⊛bit.ly/machineacoudremarseille; tram #3 to "Rome-Davso". Music café hosting alternative rock, pop and punk acts. Generally around €5 entry. Open concert nights only; concerts start 9/9.30pm.

Pelle Mêle 8 place aux Huiles, 1er ☎04 91 54 85 26, ⊛bar-le-pelle-mele.business.site; ⓜVieux Port-Hôtel de Ville. Intimate and lively jazz club and piano bar just off the Vieux Port, with frequent live sets. Drinks prices are – by Marseille standards – a little on the high side, with a big range of whiskies from €9. Mon–Fri 5.30pm–2am, Sat 5.30pm–midnight; concerts Thurs–Sat 7/7.30–10/11pm.

Play 133 rue Breteuil ☎04 13 63 70 85, ⊛playmarseille. fr; ⓜCastellane. Friendly and unpretentious LGBTQ bar-club with a daily happy hour (7–9pm), cocktail nights, DJ sessions and the like. Wed, Thurs & Sun 7pm–2am, Fri & Sat 7pm–3am.

Le Poste à Galène 103 rue Ferrari, 5e ☎04 91 47 57 99, ⊛leposteagalene.com; ⓜNotre Dame du Mont-Cours Julien. Intimate and popular venue with regular live pop, folk, jazz, rock and electro, plus 80s and 90s DJ nights (Sat 11pm; €6), cumbia sessions (Sat 11pm; €4) and a bar. Concerts start 9pm.

Trash 28 rue du Berceau, 5e ☎04 91 25 52 16, ⊛letrashbar.com; ⓜBaille. Slick, cruisey gay men's bar with DJs and live entertainment at weekends including BDSM/fetish nights (entry €10 with *conso*). June–Sept Mon, Wed, Thurs & Sun 8.30pm–2am, Fri & Sat 9.30pm–2am; Oct–May Mon & Wed 8.30pm–2am, Fri & Sat 9.30pm–2am, Sun 3pm–2am.

Trolleybus 24 quai de Rive-Neuve, 7e ☎04 91 54 30 45, ⊛letrolley.com; ⓜVieux Port-Hôtel de Ville. Atmospheric bar, club and live venue in a series of vaulted themed seventeenth-century catacombs – currently *Marquise Rive-Neuve*, *Whisky Bar* and *La Dame Noir* – that once housed an arsenal; DJ nights have an emphasis on electro. Spirits are priced by the bottle. Thurs–Sat midnight–6am.

ENTERTAINMENT

FILM, OPERA, THEATRE AND CONCERTS

Alhambra 2 rue du Cinéma, 16e ☎04 91 03 84 66, ⊛alhambracine.com; ⓜBougainville then bus #36 to "Rabelais Frère" stop. Arthouse cinema in the north of the city with an emphasis on world cinema, occasionally showing undubbed English-language films (*v.o.*). Tickets €6.

Ballet National de Marseille 20 bd Gabès, 8e ☎04 91 32 72 72, ⊛ballet-de-marseille.com; ⓜRond-Point du Prado. The home venue of the famous dance company, founded in 1972 by Roland Petit. Now under the direction of Emio Greco and Pieter C. Scholten, the company also performs at the Opéra, Le Silo and at La Criée theatre, as well as touring worldwide.

Château de la Buzine 56 traverse de la Buzine, 11e ☎04 91 45 27 60, ⓦlabuzine.com; bus #50 from Castellane to La Valentine, then bus #51. It's a long trek from the centre, but the villa that Pagnol dreamed of turning into a *cinemathèque* is now exactly that – and a fantastic place to see his films. Matinées and evening screenings; tickets €6.90.

Le Dôme 48 av de St-Just, 4e ☎04 91 12 21 21, ⓦdome. marseille.fr; ⓜSt-Just. Marseille's large-capacity live venue, hosting big-name and middle-of-the-road acts, plus children's shows, comedy, boxing and other spectacles.

Espace Julien 39 cours Julien, 6e ☎04 91 24 34 10, ⓦespace-julien.com; ⓜNotre Dame du Mont-Cours Julien. Vibrant, municipally run arts centre staging everything from live comedy to jazz, electro and rock bands. There's a large main auditorium and a second, more intimate venue, the *Café Julien*.

La Friche la Belle de Mai 41 rue Jobin, 3e ☎04 95 04 95 95, ⓦlafriche.org; ⓜSt-Charles or tram to "Longchamp" stop. Interdisciplinary arts complex occupying a former industrial site in the north of the city (see page 54), hosting theatre, dance, live music, circus, puppetry and art exhibitions. Live DJ nights on the roof in summer.

Le Gyptis 136 rue Loubon, 3e ☎04 95 04 96 25, ⓦlafriche.org; ⓜSt-Charles. Arthouse cinema in La Friche la Belle de Mai, with a separate children's programme and occasionally showing English-language films in the original version (*v.o.*).

Odéon 162 La Canebière, 1er ☎04 96 12 52 70, ⓦodeon.marseille.fr; ⓜRéformé-Canebière or Noailles. Marseille's municipal theatre, with a wide repertoire that embraces serious drama and classic operetta as well as light classical concerts.

Opéra 2 rue Moliére, 1er ☎04 91 55 11 10, ⓦopera. marseille.fr; ⓜVieux Port-Hôtel de Ville. High opera and symphony concerts by the Orchestre Philharmonique de Marseille take place in this magnificent setting, part Neoclassical, part Art Deco. Cheapest opera tickets are for the amphitheatre at the top of the auditorium; fifty of these are held back until just before a performance.

Le Silo 35 quai Lazaret, 2e ☎04 91 90 00 00, ⓦsilo-marseille.fr; ⓜJoliette. A 1920s-built former dockside grain silo converted into a two-thousand-seat multipurpose concert venue, hosting everything from ballet to rock, swing and jazz-funk.

Théâtre de Lenche 4 place de Lenche, 2e ☎04 91 91 52 22, ⓦtheatredelenche.info; ⓜVieux Port-Hôtel de Ville. Dance, cabaret and drama is showcased at this Le Panier theatre; the resident company's repertoire ranges from Molière to Chekhov and contemporary drama.

Théâtre Massalia La Friche la Belle de Mai, 41 rue Jobin, 3e ☎04 95 04 95 70, ⓦwww.theatremassalia. com; ⓜSt-Charles or tram to "Longchamp" stop. Lively young people's theatre with inventive shows involving elements of puppetry, dance, circus and live performance, with evening and matinee shows aimed primarily at a family audience.

Théâtre National la Criée 30 quai de Rive-Neuve, 7e ☎04 91 54 70 54, ⓦtheatre-lacriee.com; ⓜVieux Port-Hôtel de Ville. Marseille's most prestigious stage for drama is home base of the Théâtre National de Marseille and an occasional venue for concerts and ballet.

SHOPPING

SEE MAPS PAGES 48 AND 50

The city's many **street markets** provide a feast of fruit and veg, olives, cheeses, sausages and roast chickens – everything you'd need for a picnic except for wine, which is most economically bought at supermarkets. The markets are also good for cheap clothes. La Plaine and Prado are the biggest; the Capucins the oldest. Marseille's Sunday flea market, **Marché aux Puces**, is a brilliant spectacle and good for serious haggling. There's a relaxed atmosphere, plenty of cafés, and everything and anything for sale. The best hunting grounds for **fashion** are in the streets off rue Saint-Ferréol, in the international boutiques of Les Terrasses du Port or in the quirkier one-off boutiques between Jean-Jaurès and La Plaine.

MARKETS

Cours Julien 6e; ⓜNotre Dame du Mont-Cours Julien. Organic produce. Wed 8am–1pm.

Marché aux Puces Av du Cap-Pinède, 15e; bus #35 from ⓜJoliette (stop "Cap-Pinède") or bus #36 from ⓜBougainville (stop "Lyon-Cap Pinède"). Though best known for the weekend flea market, this also offers food and general bric-a-brac. Food Tues–Sun 8.30am–7.30pm; flea market/bric-a-brac Sat & Sun 8.30am–2pm.

Marché des Capucins Place des Capucins, 1er; ⓜNoailles. Fruit and veg. Mon–Sat 8am–6pm.

Marché du Prado Av du Prado, 6e; ⓜCastellane or Périer. Fruit, veg, fish and general produce, plus flowers on Fri. Mon–Sat 7am–1.30pm; flowers Fri 7.30am–1.30pm.

La Plaine Place Jean-Jaurès, 5e; ⓜNotre Dame du Mont-Cours Julien. A good, large, general market. Food Mon–Sat 7.30am–1.30pm; bric-a-brac Tues, Thurs & Sat 7.30am–1.30pm; flowers Wed 7.30am–1.30pm.

Quai de la Fraternité (Quai des Belges) Vieux Port, 1er; ⓜVieux Port-Hôtel de Ville. Fish sold straight off the boats. Daily 8am–1pm.

SHOPS

La Compagnie de Provence 18 rue Francis Davso, 1er ☎04 91 33 04 17; 1 rue Caisserie, 2e ☎04 91 56 20 94; ⓦcompagniedeprovence.com; ⓜVieux Port-Hôtel de Ville. Authentic Marseille soaps and upmarket toiletries

1

that make excellent gifts. Francis Davso Mon 2–7pm, Tues–Sat 10am–1pm & 2–7pm; Caisserie Daily 10am–7pm.

FNAC Centre Bourse, 2e ☎0825 02 00 20, ⓦfnac.com; ⓜVieux Port-Hôtel de Ville. This major French chain, which also offers electronics and DVDs – and sells tickets for many arts and music events – has a good English books section. Mon–Sat 10am–7pm.

Four des Navettes 136 rue Sainte, 7e ☎04 91 33 32 12, ⓦfourdesnavettes.com; ⓜVieux Port-Hôtel de Ville. Marseille's oldest bakery is famous for its delicious, subtly orange-scented *navette* biscuits that they sell in boxes by the dozen (€17) or two dozen (€25). Mon–Sat 7am–8pm, Sun 9am–1pm & 3–7.30pm.

Jiji La Palme d'Or 16 rue d'Aubagne ☎06 19 67 39 59, ⓦfacebook.com/lechoppe.de.jiji; ⓜNoailles. Wonderland of artisanal basketwork, textiles and ceramics direct from small producers in the Maghreb. Mon–Sat 9am–7pm.

La Maison du Pastis 108 quai du Port, 2e ☎04 91 90 86 77, ⓦwww.lamaisondupastis.com; ⓜVieux Port-Hôtel de Ville. There are 95 varieties of *pastis* and absinthe on sale in this alcoholic Aladdin's cave, right on the Vieux Port. Mon–Sat 10am–7pm, Sun 10am–6pm.

Puyricard 25 rue Francis Davso 1er ☎04 91 54 26 25, ⓦpuyricard.fr; ⓜVieux Port-Hôtel de Ville. Beautifully wrapped and extremely expensive chocolates, *calissons* and sweets from Provence's most renowned *chocolatier*; the service is friendlier than you might expect. Mon–Sat 9am–7pm.

DIRECTORY

Consulates UK, 10 Place de la Joliette (☎04 91 15 72 10); USA, place Varian Fry, 6e (☎01 43 12 48 85).

Health Ambulance ☎15; doctor, SOS Médecins ☎04 91 52 91 52; 24hr casualty department at Hôpital de la Conception, 147 bd Baille, 5e (☎04 91 38 00 00); medical emergencies for travellers at SOS Voyageurs, Gare St-Charles, 3e (☎04 91 62 12 80); for out-of-hours pharmacy

(*pharmacie de garde*) see ⓦpharmaciesdegardemarseille. wordpress.com.

Laundry 19 rue St Michel (daily 7am–8.30pm).

Police Commissariat Central, 2 rue Antoine-Becker, 2e (24hr; ☎04 91 39 80 00).

Post office 25 rue Colbert, 1er.

Parc National des Calanques

One of the most delightful paradoxes of Provence is that its most pristine stretch of coast abuts its largest city. For more than 20km – from **Les Goudes** on the southern fringe of Marseille to the chic little resort of **Cassis** – the coast is a wilderness of white limestone and crystal-clear turquoise water in long, fjord-like rocky inlets known as *calanques*, largely uninhabited and accessible for the most part only on foot or by sea.

The flora of the *calanques* is exceptionally rich, while rare Bonelli's eagles are among the 67 protected bird species found here, alongside thirteen species of bats and nocturnal geckos – this entire stretch of coast, plus a further section between Cassis and La Ciotat, along the Corniche des Crêtes (see page 70), was in 2012 declared a **national park** (ⓦcalanques-parcnational.fr). The park extends offshore to protect the marine environment, which is home to coral and turtles, sea horses and sea urchins – as well as a remarkable submerged archeological site, the **Cosquer Cave** (see page 69), in the Calanque de la Triperie between Sormiou and Morgiou.

Much the most visited of the park's rocky islands are the **Île d'If** – dominated by the island fortress of the **Château d'If** – and the twin **Îles de Frioul**, a popular weekend excursion from the city. All three are within easy reach of Marseille's Vieux Port, weather permitting.

Château d'If and the Îles de Frioul

Île d'If • April–Sept daily 10am–6pm; Oct–March Tues–Sun 10am–5pm • €6• ⓦif.monuments-nationaux.fr • Various boats (ⓦfrioul-if-express.com, ⓦvisite-des-calanques.com) depart Quai de la Fraternité on Marseille's Vieux Port roughly hourly (weather permitting) for the Île d'If (20min); Frioul If Express boats continue to the Îles de Frioul (35min); returns to If or Îles de Frioul costs around €11, a round trip to all islands €16.20

"Blacker than the sea, blacker than the sky, rose like a phantom the giant of granite, whose projecting crags seemed like arms extended to seize their prey" – so the **Château**

SAFETY IN THE CALANQUES

The fragile and precious ecosystems of the *calanques* are highly vulnerable to destruction by **fire**, particularly in the summer months, with the most recent blaze in 2016 devastating thousands of acres. The risks for visitors are obvious and both smoking and lighting fires is prohibited in the massif; because of the exposed nature of the GR98 you're also advised not to attempt it in high winds. If walking, call the **Forest fire information line** (☎ 08 11 20 13 13, ⓦ www.ancien.paca.gouv.fr/files/massif/) before setting out, as from June to September access is controlled according to a colour-coded alert level: green, yellow or orange means free access; red means the massifs are closed altogether.

d'If appears to Edmond Dantès, hero of Alexandre Dumas' **The Count of Monte Cristo**, having made his watery escape after five years of incarceration as the innocent victim of treachery. In reality, most prisoners of this island fortress died before they reached the end of their sentences – unless they were nobles living in the less fetid upper-storey cells, such as a certain de Niozelles who was given six years for failing to take his hat off in the presence of Louis XIV; and Mirabeau, who had run up massive debts with shops in Aix. More often, the crimes were political. After the revocation of the Edict of Nantes in 1685, thousands of Marseillais Protestants, who refused to accept the new law, were sent to the galleys and their leaders entombed in the Château d'If. Revolutionaries of 1848 drew their last breath here, too.

The castle more or less is the Île d'If, its battlements rising almost straight from the sea. The rocky, exposed shoreline explains why when the Mistral blows it's often not possible to land here, even when ferries are still running to the Frioul islands further out.

Dumas fans will love the exhibition on the author's life; others may raise an eyebrow at the cell marked "Dantès" in the same fashion as nonfictional inmates' names. However you view it, it's a horribly well-preserved sixteenth-century edifice, the views back towards Marseille are wonderful and on a fine spring day the brilliant light and the intense colour of the sea and of the wild flowers that cover the island soften its grim countenance.

Îles de Frioul

You can combine a trip to the Château d'If with the other two Frioul islands, **Ratonneau** and the less-developed and -visited **Pomègues**; they're linked by the same ferry service as the Île d'If and joined by a causeway enclosing a yachting harbour. The islands are rich in **bird life**, including Cory's Shearwaters and Storm Petrels, and are among the driest places in France, a fact reflected in their scrubby, salt-tolerant vegetation. The human population is around one hundred. There's a cluster of cafés, restaurants and snack stops by the port on Ratonneau, but many visitors push on to the island's modest beaches, much the nicest of which is the sandy **plage de St Estève**, around a 25-minute walk from the ferry. It's overlooked by the vast Hôpital Caroline, built as a yellow fever hospital in the 1820s and gradually being restored by the city of Marseille.

Massif des Calanques

The core of the Parc National des Calanques is the mountainous limestone **Massif des Calanques**, which rises to 433m at the Sommet de Marseilleveyre south of Montredon and to 563m at Mont Puget south of the Col de la Gineste. The area's sedimentary rock was formed at the bottom of a warm sea in the Jurassic and Cretaceous periods two hundred million years ago, but the narrow, fjord-like inlets – the *calanques* or *calancas* which give the park its name – formed more recently, when sea levels dropped during a period of glaciation 1.8 million years ago.

1

The calanques

Easiest of all the **calanques** to reach are the little inlets that face west into the setting sun between La Madrague and Les Goudes, on Marseille's coastal fringe – ideal for evening swims and supper picnics. But the full majesty of the landscape begins just 2km or so to the east at the fishing settlement of Callelongue, where the road peters out and the **GR98 coastal footpath** winds its way through the rocky wilderness to Cassis (see page 69). The full hike takes around twelve hours and is arduous; there are no refreshment stops for most of the route so take plenty of water. Boat excursions offer a much less exhausting – if also potentially less rewarding – alternative.

Just two of the more distant *calanques* – **Sormiou** and **Morgiou** – are accessible by car, and even then only outside the June–August summer season; each has a small port and tiny settlement. If you're walking from Cassis, you set off along the **GR98** from Port-Miou on the western side of the town; it's about a two-hour walk to the **Calanque en Vau**, where you can climb down rocks to the shore. Intrepid pine trees find rootholds, and sunbathers find precarious ledges to laze on. Swimming in the deep-blue water between the vertical cliffs is an experience not to be missed.

ARRIVAL AND INFORMATION   THE CALANQUES

ON FOOT

You can hike through the *calanques* with a guide: itineraries range from an easy half-day walk to Calanque en Vau to a gruelling twelve-hour yomp from Marseille to Cassis (€21/28 for half day/full day, discounts for groups of more than seven; ☎ 0659 67 38 76, ⓦ randonnees-calanques.fr).

BY BUS

Bus #19 links ⓜ Rond-Point du Prado in Marseille with La Madrague de Montredon, from where bus #20 continues to Callelongue; bus #21 serves Luminy from Castellane and ⓜ Rond-Point du Prado in Marseille; and #22 serves Baumettes – which is as far as you can go on public transport if you're heading for the Calanque de Morgiou – from ⓜ Rond-Point du Prado.

BY BOAT

From Cassis Several boats offer cruises to the *calanques* from Cassis' port for €16 to €28 (ⓦ calanquesdecassis. com). You can also visit by kayak with Cassis Sports Loisirs Nautiques (☎ 04 42 01 80 01, ⓦ cassis-kayak.com) or rent a motorboat from JCF Boat Services (☎ 06 75 74 25 81, ⓦ jcfboat.com).

From Marseille Croisières Marseille Calanques runs daily two-hour (€23) and three-hour (€29) trips to the *calanques* from the Vieux Port (☎ 04 91 33 36 79, ⓦ croisieres-marseille-calanques.com). Icard Maritime (☎ 04 91 33 36 79, ⓦ visite-des-calanques.com) offers more or less identical itineraries and prices.

From La Ciotat Les Amis des Calanques Catamaran Le Citharista runs trips to the *calanques*, using, amongst

---

A HIKE TO THE CALANQUE DE SUGITON

One of the most popular routes on foot into the heart of the Parc National des Calanques leads to the **Calanque de Sugiton** from the university campus at Luminy on Marseille's southern outskirts. The round trip is 8km and takes around two and a half hours; the return leg is uphill all the way. There are no facilities, so bring whatever you need, including sunscreen and plenty of water.

Alighting at the terminus of the #21 bus, cross to the southern end of the car park where there's a barrier across the path with a national park hut to one side. From here a broad, well-marked but stony path leads to the Col de Sugiton, where a signposted side path to the right leads up to a small belvedere with breathtaking views down into the neighbouring Calanque de Morgiou – it's well worth the detour. Once you've returned to the col, a broad path curves around the left-hand hillside: take the fork sharply right after the ruined stone farmhouse to make a zigzag descent into the canyon-like Vallon de Sugiton. The path is broad and relatively easy – it's even concreted in places – until it reaches the base of the Falaise des Toits, an impressive cliff face. Here, you leave the main path, scrambling down a steep, narrow path to reach the Calanque de Sugiton, where you've earned a swim in the crystal-clear azure waters.

1

THE COSQUER CAVE

In 1991, **Henri Cosquer**, a diver from Cassis, discovered paintings and engravings of animals, painted handprints and finger tracings in a cave between Marseille and Cassis, whose sole entrance is a long, sloping tunnel that starts 37m under the sea. The cave would have been accessible from dry land no later than the end of the last ice age, and carbon dating has shown that the oldest work of art here was created around 27,000 years ago. More than a hundred animals have been identified, including seals, auks, horses, ibex, bisons, chamois, red deer and a giant deer known only from fossils. Fish are also featured, along with sea creatures that might be jellyfish. Most of the finger tracings are done in charcoal and have fingertips missing, possibly to convey bent fingers and therefore some sort of sign language. For safety reasons it's not possible to visit the cave, though diving schools in Cassis organize dives in the area.

other vessels, the catamaran *Le Citharista*, a glass-bottomed boat or (in July and Aug) a semi-rigid open boat – the latter giving the chance to take a dip (late March to end Oct except during bad weather; up to 9 daily in high season; €18–39; ☎06 09 35 25 68, ⊚ visite-calanques.fr).

INFORMATION

Tourist offices in Marseille (see page 59) and Cassis (see page 70) are useful sources of information; they sell IGN maps covering the GR98 route in detail. The national park's website has plenty of useful information in French and English (⊚ calanques-parcnational.fr).

ACCOMMODATION AND EATING

There are no settlements of any real size between Marseille and Cassis and consequently accommodation, eating and drinking options are extremely **limited**; wild camping is prohibited. Unless immediate proximity to the landscape is your top priority, you might be better off staying in Cassis.

Le Château Rte du feu de la Calanque de Sormiou around 17km from Marseille, 23km from Cassis ☎04 91 25 08 69, ⊚ lechateausormiou.fr. Meat, fish and bouillabaisse (€45; order in advance) in glorious surroundings on the *calanque* of Sormiou; expect to pay around €40 for three courses. If you book, you can drive here – the road is otherwise closed to non-residents in summer. April–Sept daily noon–3pm & 7.30–9.30pm.

Fontasse 12km west of Cassis ☎04 42 01 02 72, ⊚ hifrance.org/auberge-de-jeunesse/cassis.html. Solar-powered ecofriendly hostel in the hills above the *calanques*. It's pretty basic: there are no showers, you'll need to bring food and will be expected to help with chores. You can hike here along the GR98. Not bookable online,

bank cards not accepted and children younger than 7 not permitted. Closed early Jan to mid-March. **€15.50**

La Grotte 1 av des Pebrons, Callelongue ☎04 91 73 17 79, ⊚ lagrotte-13.com. Popular and surprisingly refined restaurant on the tiny port at Callelongue, 16km from Marseille, serving pizza from €12.50, grilled fish (€8.80), pasta and risotto. Tues–Fri noon–2pm & 7.30–9.30pm, Sat noon–3pm & 7.30–10pm, Sun noon–3pm & 7.30–9.30pm.

Le Joli Bois Rte de la Gineste ☎04 42 01 02 68, ⊚ hotel-du-joli-bois.com. Simple, pastel blue-shuttered hotel in the heart of the national park and massif, between Marseille and Cassis on the D559, with private parking for cars and bicycles. Popular with hikers. **€59**

Nautic Bar Calanque de Morgiou ☎04 91 40 06 37. On the port at Morgiou, the *Nautic* specializes in bouillabaisse (€45) and *friture* – fried fish or *girelle* crab – for around €12.50. If you book here, you can drive – the road is otherwise closed to visitors in summer. No cards. Tues–Sun 10am–10pm; closed Jan.

Cassis and around

The obvious jumping-off point for the Parc National des Calanques – which bookends it to the east and west – is the chic little fishing port of **CASSIS**, on the main coast road south from Marseille. It's hard now to imagine it as a busy industrial harbour in the mid-nineteenth century, trading with Spain, Italy and Algeria. Its fortunes had declined by the time Dérain, Dufy and other Fauvist artists started visiting at the turn of the twentieth century. In the 1920s Virginia Woolf stayed while working on *To the Lighthouse*, and later Winston Churchill came here to paint. These days it's scarcely an undiscovered secret, as one glance at property prices or the crowds in the **portside restaurants** will tell you. The place bustles with activity: stalls sell handicrafts, guitarists busk round the port and day-trippers circle the one-way system trying to find a

1

parking space. But many people still rate Cassis the best resort this side of St-Tropez, its residents above all.

The cliffs hemming it in and the value of its vineyards have prevented Cassis becoming a relentless sprawl, and the little modern development that exists is small-scale. Portside posing, eating *oursins* (sea urchins) and drinking aside, you can sunbathe on the modest **beach** and gaze up at the town's medieval **castle**, built in 1381 by the counts of Les Baux and refurbished in the twentieth century by M. Michelin, the authoritarian boss of the family tyres and guidebooks firm. It remains in private hands. If you're feeling more active you can rent **boats** in the port, go **diving** or even take an abseiling, climbing or canyoning trip in the Calanques and surrounding area with the **Bureau des Guides** (☎06 61 50 38 48, ⓦguides-calanques.com).

Musée Municipal Méditerranéen d'Art et Traditions Populaires

Rue Xavier d'Authier • Wed–Sat: June–Sept 10am–12.30pm & 2–6pm; Oct–May 10am–12.30pm & 2.30–5.30pm • Free, guided tour €3 • ☎04 42 01 88 66, ⓦcassis.fr

Cassis' small folk museum, the **Musée Municipal Méditerranéen d'Art et Traditions Populaires**, is housed in the seventeenth-century presbytery just inland from the port. It has a bit of everything: nineteenth-century paintings and photographs of Cassis and Marseille, old furniture, costumes and Roman amphorae.

Corniche des Crêtes

For those with a car or motorbike – or a bicycle and prodigious fitness – the ride along the spectacular **Corniche des Crêtes** road south from Cassis to La Ciotat (the D141) is not to be missed. From Cassis the chemin St-Joseph turns off avenue de Provence, climbs at a maximum gradient to the Pas de la Colle, then follows the inland slopes of the Mont de la Canaille. The landscape is sometimes blackened by fire, but every so often the road loops round a break in the chain to give you dramatic sea views; there are frequent stopping places from which to admire them. The **sea cliffs** of Cap Canaille visible from Cassis are among the highest in Europe, and distinctly different to the *calanques* west of Cassis in colour and geology, though they too form part of the national park.

You can **walk** from Cassis to La Ciotat in about three and a half hours: the path, beginning from Pas de la Colle, takes a precipitous straighter line, passing the road at each outer loop. The corniche is closed in high winds.

ARRIVAL AND INFORMATION   **CASSIS AND AROUND**

By bus Buses from Castellane in Marseille (2 daily; 50min) arrive at Rond-point du Gendarmerie, from where it's a short walk downhill to the port and beach.

By train The *gare SNCF* is 3.5km from town, connected by bus (7.05am–8.25pm; every 35min–1hr; 18min). Destinations Bandol (every 30min–1hr; 18min); La Ciotat (every 30min–1hr; 6min); Marseille (every 30min; 26min); St Cyr/Les Lecques (every 30min–1hr; 12min).

By car Parking in Cassis can be difficult even in low season; the multistorey car park on Av de la Viguerie is the best bet close to the port; failing that, there's a free park-and-ride

car park – Parking Relais des Gorguettes – on the outskirts, connected to the port by a shuttle bus (daily 9am–8pm, till midnight/2am July/Aug; €1.60).

Tourist office Quai des Moulins (Feb, March & Oct Mon–Sat 9.30am–12.30pm & 2–6pm; April Mon–Sat 9.30am–12.30pm & 2–6pm, Sun 9.30am–12.30pm & 3–6pm; May, June & Sept Mon–Sat 9.30am–1pm & 2–6pm, Sun 9.30am–12.30pm & 3–6pm; July & Aug Mon–Sat 9am–7pm, Sun 9.30am–12.30pm & 3–6pm; Nov–Jan Mon–Sat 9.30am–12.30pm & 2–5pm; ☎08 92 39 01 03, ⓦot-cassis. com).

ACCOMMODATION

Le Cassiden 7 av Victor-Hugo ☎04 42 01 72 13, ⓦhotel-le-cassiden.fr. Just back from the port, this two-star hotel has small, attractive modern rooms with simple decor, en-

suite showers, double glazing and a/c. Good value. **€89**

Cassis Hostel 4 av du Picouveau ☎09 54 37 99 82, ⓦcassishostel.com. Pleasant budget option in a suburban setting a short walk from the port, with double rooms and four- or six-bed dorms. There's a pool with sea views, and a kitchen. Breakfast is included. Dorms €30; doubles €85

Les Cigales 43 av de la Marne, inland just off the D559 on the edge of the village ☎ 04 42 01 07 34, ⊛ campingcassis.com. Cassis' only campsite (250 pitches) is a two-star affair amid pine trees a 15min walk from the port. Closed mid-Nov to mid-March. €25

Le Clos des Arômes 10 rue Abbé Paul-Mouton ☎ 04 42 01 71 84, ⊛ leclosdesaromes.fr. Charming, quiet hotel a short way inland from the bustle of the port, with fourteen rooms (one that sleeps four) and a lovely garden restaurant serving classic Provençal cooking. €69

Le Golfe 3 place du Grand Carnot ☎ 04 42 01 00 21, ⊛ legolfe-cassis.fr. In the middle of all the action, the rooms here have en-suite bath or shower, TV and a/c; around half of them overlook the port. There's a brasserie, bar and *glacier*. €99

Les Roches Blanches Av des Calanques ☎ 04 42 01 09 30, ⊛ roches-blanches-cassis.com. Cassis' best hotel is in an idyllic setting amid pines on the Presqu'île, west of the port. Rooms have contemporary decor, bathrooms and a/c; many have a balcony or terrace. There's a pool, plus direct access to the sea. €540

EATING AND DRINKING

Sea urchins – **oursins** – are the speciality here, accompanied by delicious white **wine** from one of the dozen vineyards that make up the Cassis *AOC*. Clairette and Marsanne are the principal grape varieties and the wines have a distinctive character: full bodied and herby but also fresh, dry and fish-friendly. Restaurant tables are abundant along the portside on Quai des Baux, Quai Calandal and Quai Barthélemy; prices vary, but the best bet is to follow your nose towards the most enticing fish smells. For picnic food, head for the **market**, held around place Baragnon east of the port on Wednesday and Friday mornings.

Les Caves du Port rue Thérèse Rastit ☎ 06 22 92 75 82. Diminutive craft beer cellar tucked away behind the port, with occasional live music. Global selection of beers from €5. Daily 9am–2am & 5pm–2am.

Le Chaudron 4 rue Adolphe Thiers ☎ 04 42 01 74 18. Esteemed old family-run bistro in the streets behind the port, with modern decor, pasta from €14 and *bavette* with shallots on the menu. *Menus* €28 and €36. March–Dec Mon & Wed–Sat 7–11pm, Sun noon–2.30pm & 7–11pm; July & Aug closed Sun lunch.

Chez Gilbert 19 quai des Baux ☎ 04 42 01 71 36, ⊛ chezgilbert.net. Renowned portside restaurant and member of the Charte de la Bouillabaisse, which guards the authentic bouillabaisse recipe (€55) – that aside, there's freshly grilled fish priced according to weight. *Menus* €35 and €40. Mon, Tues & Wed–Sun noon–2.30pm & 7–10.30pm.

La Villa Madie av de Revestel ☎ 04 96 18 00 00. With two Michelin stars and a handsome beachside terrace, this is the jewel in the crown of Cassis' fine dining scene. The likes of lobster, turbot and even caviar are treated to chef Dimitri Droisneau's signature seasonal style, with *menus* priced at €115 and €165. There's also an attached – and much more affordable – brasserie. Restaurant Mon noon–1.15pm, Thurs–Sun noon–1.15pm & 7.30–9.15pm, brasserie Mon–Fri noon–2pm; both closed Jan and early Feb.

La Ciotat

Cranes still loom over the old shipbuilding town of **LA CIOTAT**, where 300,000-tonne oil and gas tankers were built as recently as 1989. Today, the town's economy relies on property development, tourism and mooring and repairing yachts, yet it remains pleasantly unpretentious, with a golden **vieille ville** above the bustling quayside, affordable hotels and restaurants, and attractive beaches stretching northeast from the port. **Cinephiles** also have a reason to visit – the town has a strong claim to be the birthplace of the moving image.

Vieille ville

The **vieille ville**'s seventeenth-century church, **Notre Dame de l'Assomption**, has a Baroque facade – inside there's a striking early seventeenth-century painting by André Gaudion of the *Descent of the Cross* alongside modern works of art; alas, it's usually locked except during mass. The streets behind the church are uneventful and run-down in places, though the proliferation of estate agents suggests that is set to change.

1

Musée du Vieux Ciotat

1 quai Ganteaume • Mon & Wed–Sun: July & Aug 4–7pm; Sept–June 3–6pm • €3.50 • ☎ 04 42 71 40 99, ⓦ museeciotaden.org

The dignified nineteenth-century former *mairie* at the end of Quai Ganteaume houses the **Musée du Vieux Ciotat**, with fifteen rooms charting the history of the town back to its foundation by the ancient Greeks of Marseille, when local shipbuilding began. The museum also includes sections on the birth of **cinema** in the town and on *pétanque*.

Parc du Mugel

South of the Vieux Port • Daily: April–Sept 8am–8pm; Oct–March 9am–6pm • Free • Bus #30 from port, stop "Mugel"

La Ciotat's lovely botanical garden, the **Parc du Mugel**, curves around the cove of Anse du Petit Mugel, in the shadow of a strikingly odd-shaped promontory – the so-called "Bec d'Aigle" or Eagle's Beak. From the southern end of the park a path leads up through luxuriant vegetation to a narrow belvedere overlooking the sea.

Anse de Figuerolles and Gaméou

Bus #30 to Figuerolles

West of Parc du Mugel (fifteen minutes or so on foot from the port) you can reach the **Anse de Figuerolles** *calanque* down the avenue of the same name, and its neighbour, the **Gaméou**. Both have pebbly beaches and a darker rock colour from the blinding white *calanques* of Cassis and Marseille.

ARRIVAL AND INFORMATION
LA CIOTAT

By train The *gare SNCF* is 5km from the town, connected to the Vieux Port by bus #40 (every 30–40min; 20min).

Destinations Bandol (every 30min–1hr; 10min); Cassis (roughly every 30min; 6min); Marseille (every 15–30min; roughly 30min); St Cyr-Les Lecques (every 30min–1hr; 5min).

By car There's pay-and-display parking on the seafront behind the tourist office.

Tourist office Bd Anatole-France (June–Sept Mon–Sat 9am–8pm, Sun 10am–1pm; Oct–May Mon–Sat 9am–noon & 2–6pm; ☎ 04 42 08 61 32, ⓦ en.laciotat.info).

FILM IN LA CIOTAT

In 1895 **Auguste** and **Louis Lumière** filmed the first-ever moving pictures in La Ciotat and in 1904 went on to develop the first colour photographs. La Ciotat's train station has a commemorative plaque to the film **L'Arrivée d'un train en gare de La Ciotat**, which was one of a dozen or so films, including *Le déjeuner de bébé* and the comedy *L'Arroseur arrosé*, shown in the family's Château Lumière in September 1895. Apparently, the audience jumped out of their seats as the image of the steam train hurtled towards them. Three months later the reels were taken to Paris for the capital's citizens to witness cinema for the first time.

There's a solid 1950s **monument** to Auguste and Louis Lumière at plage Lumière. Nearby, at the top of allée Lumière, lies the much-altered **Château Lumière** where some of their seminal films were shot; only the grand salon is in anything like its original condition. The association that is trying to restore the building can arrange visits; enquire at the tourist office.

La Ciotat's beautiful **Eden Theatre**, on the corner of Bd A.-France and Bd Jean-Jaurès, is the world's oldest movie house, opened in 1889; it was carefully restored to coincide with Marseille's stint as European Capital of Culture in 2013 and is once again a functioning cinema, with a varied programme that includes documentaries and classics (ⓦ edencinemalaciotat.com).

THE FILM FESTIVAL

La Ciotat celebrates its relatively unknown status as the cradle of cinema with an annual **film festival**, the Festival du Premier Film Francophone, in late May, screening a selection of films before an invited jury that awards the *Lumières d'Honneur* prize. The full programme is published on the Eden Cinema's website.

BOAT TRIPS FROM LA CIOTAT

For a blissful afternoon offshore, Navette Île Verte makes the crossing to the islet of **Île Verte** (daily: April–June & Sept hourly 10am–noon & 2–5pm; July & Aug hourly 9am–6.45pm; Oct enquire at Vieux Port or call; €13 return; ☎06 63 59 16 35, ✪laciotat-ileverte.com); the lotus-eating pleasures of its rocks, woods and *calanques* aside, there's also a restaurant, *Chez Louisette* (☎06 75 50 74 98). Catamaran *Le Citharista* also makes trips to the *calanques* of **Cassis and Marseille** (see page 66).

ACCOMMODATION

Corniche du Liouquet Rte des Lecques ☎04 42 83 28 82, ✪hotel-corniche-ciotat.com. Stunningly situated by the sea to the east of town, this small three-star hotel has just twelve contemporary rooms with a/c and chic Ligne Roset furnishings. Most rooms also have a terrace. €113

La Rotonde 194 bd de la République ☎04 42 08 67 50, ✪hotel-larotonde-ciotat.fr. Good-value non-smoking two-star 200m from the port. All rooms have private bath and flatscreen TV and around half of them have balconies; cheaper rooms lack a/c. €96

Le Soleil 751 av Emile Bodin ☎04 42 71 55 32, ✪camping-dusoleil.com. The most central of La Ciotat's campsites, around 1.5km from the beach and harbour, this small two-star site has its own restaurant and takeaway. Closed Oct–March. Camping €30, mobile homes €575, bungalows €688

Vieux Port 252 quai F Mitterrand ☎04 42 04 00 00, ✪bestwestern-laciotat.com. Smart, contemporary three-star hotel right on the port, with a restaurant/bar and underground parking. Soundproofed, a/c rooms include some with sea-facing balconies. €149

EATING, DRINKING AND ENTERTAINMENT

La Ciotat's restaurants are not particularly renowned, though there is plenty of choice along the port. There's a Sunday **market** on the quay; **rue des Poilus** in the *vieille ville* is a good hunting ground for bakers, fish and fresh fruit and vegetables. La Ciotat has an animated **cultural scene**, focused on the Eden cinema (see page 72) and the Théâtre du Golfe on the seafront at Bd Anatole-France (☎04 42 08 92 87). Away from the port on place E-Gras, the Atelier Jazz Convergences (☎04 42 71 81 25), is a live **jazz** venue.

RESTAURANTS AND CAFÉS

Kitch & Cook 4 place Esquiros ☎04 42 03 91 36, ✪kitchandcook.com. Bright, funky and minimalist yet romantically tucked away on a cobbled square, this place serves up unpretentious yet creative takes on "real home cooking", with plenty of seasonal Provençal veg and a bonafide vegetarian mini-menu as well. *Menu* €31, mains around €20. Mon–Wed & Fri noon–1.30pm & 7–9.30pm, Thurs noon–1.30pm, Sat 7–10pm.

L'Office'In 18 rue des Combattants ☎04 42 36 86 25, ✪lofficein.fr. The *vieille ville's* trendiest culinary offering, a "slow food" restaurant with a pretty interior and a terrace overlooking the port, plus the likes of soba noodles with yakitori sauce (€19) or tuna with wasabi sauce (€22) on its eclectic *carte*. Menu €34. Mon & Thurs–Sun noon–2.30pm & 7–10pm.

Roche Belle Corniche du Liouquet ☎04 42 71 47 60, ✪roche-belle.fr. In an idyllic setting near the sea between La Ciotat and Les Lecques, with a shady terrace and unusual dishes like roasted pigeon with cacao jus (€30) . There's a three-course *menu* at €36.50 and they serve Bandol wines. Lunch *formule* €22; à la carte from around €28. Sept–June Tues–Sat noon–1.30pm & 7.30–9.30pm; July & Aug also open Sun same hours.

La Vieille Chouette 1 av de la Gare ☎06 09 58 42 33, ✪lavieillechouette.com. Tongue-twistingly billed as a "retro bistro/modern resto", with industrial décor and a no-nonsense menu based largely around their 100 percent made-on-the-premises burgers (from €16). Daily 11.30am–midnight.

Aubagne

Marseille's suburbs extend east along the autoroute and D8N corridor to **AUBAGNE**, set between rugged mountain ranges. With a triangle of autoroutes around it and dismal postwar developments fringing its historic core there's little reason to stay. Yet Aubagne is not without interest; it's the headquarters of the French Foreign Legion and a centre for the production of **santons**, the traditional Provençal Christmas figures. Its main claim to fame, however, is as the birthplace of writer and film-maker **Marcel Pagnol** (1895–1974).

1

Maison Natale de Marcel Pagnol

16 cours Barthelémy • April– Oct daily 9.30am–12.30pm & 2–6pm; Nov–March Mon–Sat 9am–12.30pm & 2–5.30pm • €3 • ☎ 04 42 03 49 98, ⓦ www.tourisme-paysdaubagne.fr/fr/maison-natale-marcel-pagnol

Instantly recognizable from the bust of the author and film-maker that was unveiled in 2015 on the 120th anniversary of his birth, Marcel Pagnol's birthplace is now the **Maison Natale**, which houses displays on the man and his life, as well as a fascinating fifteen-minute film (in French only). Enquire at the tourist office (see page 74) about **walks** into the surrounding countryside to visit the locations of Pagnol's films – access to the hills around Aubagne is however subject to restrictions from June to September due to the fire risk (see page 75).

Petit Monde de Marcel Pagnol

Atelier Thérèse Neveu, 4 Cour de Clastre • Tues–Sat 10am–12.30pm & 2–6pm, open Sun during the summer and winter Santon markets • Free • ☎ 04 42 03 49 98, ⓦ www.tourisme-paysdaubagne.fr/en/petit-monde-de-marcel-pagnol

The fertile soil around Aubagne makes excellent pottery, hence the town's renown for **santons** – traditional Christmas figures – and ceramics. The most impressive display of *santons* is to be found at **Le Petit Monde de Marcel Pagnol**, where two hundred finely detailed figures of Pagnol characters (including Pagnol himself) play out their parts on a model of the district, complete with farms and villages.

From mid-July to the end of August and in December, a huge daily **market of ceramics** and **santons** takes place on the central esplanade Charles de Gaulle. You can visit the potters' **workshops** that are dotted all over town at any time of the year – pick up a leaflet from the tourist office.

Musée de la Légion Étrangère

Rte de la Thuilière (D44A), *quartier* Vienot • Tues–Sun 10am–noon & 2–6pm; closed late Dec to end Jan • Free • ☎ 04 42 18 12 41, ⓦ samle.legion-etrangere.com

Aubagne's claim to fame as headquarters of the French Foreign Legion (see page 75) is commemorated by the **Musée de la Légion Étrangère**, inside the barracks in the *quartier* Vienot on the far side of the A50 autoroute from the town. Here, a sombre Salle d'Honneur pays tribute to the legion's founders and its dead, and evocative, broadly chronological displays catalogue the Legion's campaigns. Exhibits include the white *képis* familiar from cinematic depictions of Beau Geste; there's also a nod towards the impact of the Legion on popular culture, with displays of cinema posters, plus a portrait by Franz Xaver Winterhalter of the Legion's royal founder.

ARRIVAL AND INFORMATION
AUBAGNE

By train From the *gare SNCF* it's a 5min walk along Av Jeanne d'Arc to cours Foch and on to cours Barthelémy, where you'll find the tourist office.

Destinations Bandol (every 30min; 25min); Cassis (every 30min; 6min); La Ciotat (every 30min; 13min); Marseille (up to every 10min at peak times; 18–35min); Toulon (every

---

JEAN DE FLORETTE AND MANON DES SOURCES

Aubagne's **Marcel Pagnol** was an early convert to film; Alexander Korda's French-language version of his play *Marius* was an international hit as early as 1931. But it was the huge popularity in the 1980s of Claude Berri's films of Pagnol's *Jean de Florette* and *Manon des Sources*, starring Gérard Depardieu and Emmanuelle Béart, that really broadened Pagnol's international appeal. In *Jean de Florette*, an outsider inherits a property on the arid slopes of the Garlaban mountain, whose rocky crest rears north of Aubagne like a stegosaurus's back. The local peasants who have blocked its spring watch him die from the struggle of fetching water, delighted that his new scientific methods won't upset their market share.

1

THE FRENCH FOREIGN LEGION
The tradition of foreigners serving in France's armies dates back to 1346, but the **Legion** as
it exists today was created by King Louis Philippe in 1831. It received its baptism of fire in
Algeria in 1832, and was closely associated with North Africa for much of its history, founding
the garrison at Sidi Bel Abbès in 1843. The town grew to be a modern city of 100,000 and
remained the Legion's home until France withdrew from Algeria in 1962.

30min–1hr; 45min).
By bus Buses arrive at the *pôle d'échanges* alongside the
gare SNCF.
Destinations Aix (every 10–15min at peak times; 48min–
1hr 4min); Gémenos (every 25min–1hr Mon–Sat;20min);
La Ciotat (every 35min–1hr; 27–36min); Marseille (every
10min at peak times; 20min).
By car There's off-street parking in the centre of Aubagne;
on-street spaces can be scarce.

Tourist office 8 cours Barthelémy (April–June, Sept & Oct
Mon–Sat 9am–12.30pm & 2–6pm; July & Aug Mon–Sat
9am–12.30pm & 2–6.30pm, Sun 10am–12.30pm; Nov–
March Mon–Wed & Fri 9am–12.30pm & 2–5.30pm, Thurs
10am–12.30pm & 2–5.30pm, Sat 9am–12.30pm; ☎ 04 42
03 49 98, ⓦ www.tourisme-paysdaubagne.fr). The office
can provide information on Pagnol itineraries and local
potteries and *santon*-makers.

L'Estaque and the Côte Bleue

Marseille's docks finally end at the one-time fishing village of **L'Estaque**, now a suburb
of the city. Between here and Carry-le-Rouet, the hills of the **Chaîne de l'Estaque**
descend to the shore to form the first, wildest part of the coast known as the **Côte
Bleue**: a gorgeous wilderness of white rock, pines and brilliant yellow scented broom.
The shore is studded with picturesque little *calanques* where the real estate is desirable
and the water exceptionally clean; you can look across the roadstead of Marseille to
the islands and the entrance of the Vieux Port. At weekends in summer, road access to
these *calanques* is strictly limited and you may have to park some distance from the sea.

L'Estaque and around

An easy fifteen-minute train ride from the centre of Marseille – or forty minutes
by boat from the Vieux Port – the erstwhile fishing village of **L'ESTAQUE** was much
loved by painters in the nineteenth century. It was no rural paradise even in 1867,
as a gouache by Cézanne of the factory chimneys of L'Estaque shows (the painting,
originally given to Madame Zola, is now exhibited in Cézanne's studio in Aix). Yet
it still has fishing boats moored alongside yachts, lovely old villas and a short but
engrossing walk along an **art-themed trail** marked with bilingual plaques – there's a
clear map of it in the Marseille tourist office's free city guide and downloadable from
their website. In addition, its artificial **beaches** ensure that L'Estaque remains a popular
escape from the city.

From L'Estaque, the train tunnels its way westwards above the shore while the main
road, the D568, then D5, takes an inland route through **La Rove** and **Ensuès-la-
Redonne**, with smaller roads looping down to the fishing villages and summer holiday
homes of **Niolon**, **Méjean** and **La Redonne**.

Carry-le-Rouet and around

The peace and intimate scale of this coast ends at the small but bustling resort of **CARRY-
LE-ROUET**, which is popular for diving – there's a marine reserve offshore – and modestly
swanky, with a brasserie-lined marina and a casino. It was the home of the jazz singer
Nina Simone towards the end of her life, and it was here that she died in 2003.

The Côte Bleue is flatter and less rocky west of Carry towards Martigues. The town
merges into its western neighbour **Sausset-les-Pins**, where the beaches are stony and

1

artificial, without any break in the seaside houses and apartment buildings. For **beaches** it's best to head beyond Tamaris, where there are long, sandy stretches around the pleasantly downmarket family resorts of **Carro** and **La Couronne**, though you may be put off by the proximity of the petrochemical plants on the southern shore of the **Étang de Berre**.

INFORMATION   L'ESTAQUE AND THE CÔTE BLEUE

CARRY-LE-ROUET
Tourist office 11–13 Route Bleue(June–Sept Mon–Sat 9.30am–12.30pm & 2–6pm, Sun 9.30am–12.30pm; Oct–May Tues–Sat 10am–noon & 2–5pm; ☎ 04 42 13 20 36, ⓦ otcarrylerouet.fr). From the train station, turn right out onto Av Pierre Semard, which becomes Av Aristide Briand and continues to the port; the tourist office is set back from port's northeast corner.

ACCOMMODATION AND EATING

L'ESTAQUE AND AROUND
Le Cabanon Rte du Rove, L'Estaque ☎ 0488 44 32 25, ⓦ lecabanondelestaque.fr. Grilled fish and seafood in chic portside surroundings at the far end of L'Estaque's waterfront, with a shaded terrace and *plats du jour* from around €20. If you simply want a snack, try the local *chichis* (hot, doughnut-like confections) from the kiosks alongside L'Estaque's main road – they're delicious. Mon & Tues noon–3pm, Wed–Sat noon–3pm & 7–11pm.

Le Mange Tout 8 chemin du Tire-Cul, Méjean ☎ 04 42 45 91 68. Simple grilled fish and *petites fritures* (*plats* around €12–16) are served overlooking the tiny port on the *calanque* of Méjean; what's available depends on the catch of the day. Daily10am–11pm.

CARRY-LE-ROUET AND AROUND
La Brise Quai Vayssière, Carry-le-Rouet ☎ 04 42 45 30 55, ⓦ restaurant-labrise.com. A little old-fashioned but a cut above the portside brasseries, with an open terrace overlooking the harbour and plenty of lamb and fish on its €35 and €45 *menus*. July & Aug Mon & Tues 7.30–9.30pm, Wed–Sun 12.15–1.30pm & 7.30–9.30pm; Sept–June Tues 7.30–9.30pm, Wed–Sat 12.15–1.30pm & 7.30–9.30pm, Sun 12.15–1.30pm.

Lou Cigalon Chemin de Tamaris, La Couronne ☎ 04 42 49 61 71, ⓦ loucigalon.com. Three-star campsite west of Carry on a tiny, relatively peaceful sandy cove, with an extensive range of mobile homes, a restaurant, bar, pizzeria, pool and jacuzzi and wi-fi. Closed Oct–March. Camping **€36**, mobile home/week **€820**

Hôtel La Tuilière 34 av Draïo de la Mar, Carry-le-Rouet ☎ 04 42 44 79 79, ⓦ hotel-tuiliere.com. Three-star comforts 50m from the sea, west of Carry's port on the road to Sausset, with a pool, restaurant and a/c. **€103**

Martigues

MARTIGUES straddles both sides of the Caronte Canal and an island in the middle, at the southwest corner of the Étang de Berre – a 22km-long and 15km-wide lagoon ringed by oil refineries and petrochemical industries, to which the town is the maritime gateway. In the sixteenth century when the union of three separate villages – **Jonquières** to the south, **Ferrières** to the north and the island, known simply as **l'Île** – created Martigues, there were many more canals than the three that remain today.

In the centre of l'Île, in front of the sumptuous facade of the airy Église de la Madeleine, a low bridge spans the Canal St-Sébastien where fishing boats moor and houses in ochre, pink and blue look straight down onto the water. This appealing spot is known as the **Miroir aux Oiseaux** and was painted by Corot, Ziem and others at the turn of the twentieth century.

Musée Ziem

Bd du 14 Juillet, Ferrières • July & Aug Mon & Wed–Sun 10am–noon & 2–6pm; Sept–June Wed–Sun 2–6pm • Free • ☎ 04 42 41 39 60

Works by some of the artists who painted in Martigues, including Ziem's *Vieux Port de Marseille*, can be seen in the wonderful **Musée Ziem**. The collection includes works by Dérain, Dufy and Signac, while François Picabia's 1905 *Étang de Berre* shows the lagoon to be every bit as choppy as it is today. The upper floor contains local archeological and ethnological displays.

Galerie de l'Histoire de Martigues

Rond-point de l'Hôtel de Ville, Ferrières • Tues–Fri 9am–12.30pm & 2–6pm, Sat 10am–12.30pm & 2–6pm • Free • ☏ 04 42 44 34 02

Martique's well-presented local history museum, the **Galerie de l'Histoire de Martigues**, charts the town's development from prehistoric times with lavish use of old maps and visual material. The section dealing with medieval and early modern Martigues is the most engrossing.

ARRIVAL AND INFORMATION   MARTIGUES

By bus Buses from Marseille stop at the Hôtel de Police, next to the tourist office.
Destinations Aix-en-Provence (every 20min–1hr 5min; 46min–1hr 17min); Marseille (every 5–15min; 40–48min).
By train From the *gare SNCF* take bus #23 (direction "place des Aires") to the centre.
Destinations Carry-le-Rouet (every 30min at peak times; 17min); Marseille (every 30min at peak times; 53min–1hr

20min);
By car There's plentiful off-street parking close to the tourist office in Ferrières.
Tourist office Rond-point de l'Hôtel de Ville, Ferrières (June–Sept Mon–Fri 9am–6pm, Sat 9am–12.30pm & 2.30–5.45pm, Sun 9am–1pm; Oct–May Mon–Sat 9am–noon & 1.30–5pm; ☏ 04 42 42 31 10, ⓦ martigues-tourisme.com).

ACCOMMODATION

Ibis Martigues av Louis Sammut ☏ 04 42 42 05 11, ⓦ accorhotels.com. Typical Ibis value for money in a great location by the port with functional, a/c rooms with en-suite bath and flatscreen TV. **€73**
Martigues Clair 57 bd Marcel Cachin ☏ 04 42 13

52 52, ⓦ theoriginalshotels.com/hotels/martigues-clair. Rooms softened with rustic pine and natural linen represents great value for money in this boutique chain, even if it is located on a busy road. **€71**

EATING

Late June, July and August see the spectacle of the **Sardinades**, when grilled sardines are sold cheaply each evening along the quays near the *mediathèque* in the Quartier de l'Île. Aside from these, the **food** to look out for is *poutargue*, a paste made from salted mullet, and *melets*, seasoned fish-fry fermented in olive oil.
Guenat's 8 Cours de 4 Septembre ☏ 04 42 43 87 25, ⓦ restaurant-guenats.com. Popular and highly regarded

Armenian/Lebanese restaurant serving plenty of vegetarian and vegan options alongside the *brochettes*. Vegan meze €17. Wed–Sun 10am–3pm & 6pm–midnight.
Le Miroir 4 rue Marcel Galdy ☏ 04 42 80 50 45, ⓦ lemiroir.eatbu.com. Classy restaurant in a pretty waterside position in L'Île, with a two-course lunch *menu* at €20.90; three courses cost €30.90. Wed–Sat noon–2pm & 7–9.30pm, Sun noon–2pm.

Salon-de-Provence and around

Jets scream through the air above **SALON-DE-PROVENCE**, a reminder that the town's principal activities include teaching air-force pilots to fly. Salon's more enduring claims

---

SALON'S BLACK GOLD

In medieval times, Salon's economy was dependent on its tanneries, a saffron crop and flocks of sheep reputed for the quality of their mutton. True prosperity arrived in the shape of the small black olives that produced an oil, **olivo selourenco**, of great gastronomic renown. By the end of the nineteenth century the Salonais were making soap from their oil, a highly profitable commodity manufactured in appalling conditions in subterranean mills. Those to whom the dividends accrued built themselves opulent *belle époque* **villas**, the grandest of which are in the streets between the town centre and the *gare SNCF* to the west. Although most have long since been given over to other uses or divided into apartments, they give the town a quiet, surprising grace.

1

to fame are its olives and the famous predictions of **Nostradamus** which were composed here, though the museum dedicated to him is less appealing than the mementoes of Napoléon in Salon's castle, the **Château de l'Empéri**. The château rises above a **vieille ville** that was the subject of misguided modernization from the 1960s on, though recently boutiques and restaurants have recolonized it, lending it some of the animated air of the rest of the town centre – particularly on market days, when Salon bustles. A good time to visit is in July and August for the annual **classical music festival** (⟨w⟩festival-salon.fr) in the château.

The countryside **around Salon** affords glimpses of the traditional agriculture of the arid Crau region. Ten kilometres north of town, the main road and highway pass through a narrow gap in the hills by **Lamanon**, which was never much more than a stopover on the transhumance routes (used for the moving of flocks, and still followed by the Crau shepherds every June), though it does have a château, and, more interestingly, a nearby **cave-village**. South of Salon you can visit a child-friendly castle and zoo at **La Barben**.

Château de l'Empéri

Montée de Puech • Mid-April to Sept Tues–Sun 9.30am–noon & 2–6pm; Oct to mid-April Tues–Sun 1.30–6pm • €5.50, or €8 combined ticket with one other museum • ☎ 04 90 44 72 80

SALON-DE-PROVENCE

■ ACCOMMODATION	
D'Angleterre	5
Camping Nostrodamus	1
Grand Hôtel de la Poste	2
Hostellerie de l'Abbaye de Sainte Croix	4
Mas de Lure	3

● EATING	
L'Endroit	3
L'Estive	4
Kot and Sushi	2
La Salle à Manger	1

JEAN MOULIN

The northern exit from the Autoroute du Soleil to Salon-de-Provence takes you past a memorial to **Jean Moulin**, the Resistance leader who was parachuted into the nearby Alpilles range in order to coordinate the different *maquis* groupings in Vichy France. He was caught near Lyon on June 21, 1943, tortured horribly and interrogated by Klaus Barbie; he subsequently died of his injuries while on a train to Germany. In death Moulin has become the most revered of all Resistance figures, his portrait – in fedora and scarf – familiar throughout France. The bronze **sculpture**, by Marcel Courbier, is of a lithe figure landing from the sky like some latter-day Greek god, very beautiful though somewhat perplexing if you're not aware of the invisible parachute.

The centrepiece of the *vieille ville* is the **Château de l'Empéri**, a proper medieval fortress built to suit the worldliness of its former proprietors, the archbishops of Arles. It houses the **Musée de l'Empéri**, whose collections of military uniforms cover the period from Louis XIV to World War I; the sections devoted to the Revolution and Napoleon are particularly fascinating. Also included in the admission price is entry to the **Salle Théodore Jourdan**, with an exhibition of paintings and drawings by the eponymous local artist.

Maison de Nostradamus

Rue Nostradamus • Mid-April to Sept Mon & Wed–Sun 10am–12.30pm & 2–6pm; Oct to mid-April Mon & Wed–Sun 1.30–6pm • €5.10, or €7.50 combined ticket with one other museum; free first Sun of month • ☎ 04 90 56 64 31

The focus of the *vieille ville* is place des Centuries, a wide-open space fringed by café terraces. Just north of it stands the **Maison de Nostradamus**, the home, until his death, of the soothsayer. Nostradamus (see page 97) arrived in Salon in 1547 – already famous for his aromatic plague cure, administered in Aix and Lyon – and married a rich widow. After extended Italian travels, he returned to Salon, settling down to study the stars, the weather, cosmetics and the future of the world. The museum tells his multifaceted life story in a series of tableaux, and also stages temporary exhibitions. Nostradamus died in Salon in 1566; his tomb is in the Gothic **Collégiale St-Laurent**, at the top of rue du Maréchal-Joffre, north of the *vieille ville*.

Porte de l'Horloge

The principal gateway to the *vieille ville* is the **Porte de l'Horloge**, a serious bit of seventeenth-century construction, with its Grecian columns, coats of arms, gargoyles and wrought-iron campanile. Through the arch is place Crousillat, which centres on a vast mushroom of moss concealing a three-statued fountain – a wonderful spot for a café break.

Musée du Savon de Marseille

148 av Paul-Bourret • **Museum** July & Aug Mon–Sat 9.30am–noon & 2–6.30pm; Sept–June Mon–Sat 9.30am–noon & 2–5.30pm • **Factory tours** July & Aug Mon–Fri 10.30am & 2.30pm; Sept–June Tues & Thurs 10.30am, Wed 2.30pm • Free for individuals • ☎ 04 90 53 34 35, Ⓦ marius-fabre.com

To the west of the *vieille ville* and located within a working *savonnerie*, the **Musée du Savon de Marseille** tells the story of soap-making in Provence from the Middle Ages onwards. Tours of the factory give you a first-hand view of the industry.

Grottes de Calès

GR6 footpath, Lamanon • Open access daily 24hr; subject to closure during Mistral or at times of fire risk • Free

1

Above Lamanon, hidden among rocks and trees, is a remarkable troglodyte village, the **Grottes de Calès**, which was inhabited from Neolithic times until the nineteenth century. Stairs lead down into grottoes, part natural, part constructed, with hooks and gutters carved into the rock; at the centre is a sacrificial temple. Access is free, though some parts of the complex are fenced off for safety reasons: follow the Montée de Calès that ascends from opposite Lamanon's tourist office.

Château de la Barben and Zoo

Rte du Château, La Barben, 12km east of Salon, beyond Pélissanne • **Château** Feb to early March daily 2–5pm; late March to early Sept 11am–6pm; early Sept to mid-Oct Sat & Sun 2–5pm; late Oct to early Nov daily 2–5pm • €10, €17 including dungeons • ☎ 04 90 55 25 41, ⓦ chateaudelabarben.fr • **Zoo** Daily: March–June, Sept & Oct 10am–6pm; July & Aug 9.30am–7pm; Nov–Feb 10am–5.30pm • €17 • ☎ 04 90 55 19 12, ⓦ zoolabarben.com

The **Château de la Barben** was lived in for a while by Napoleon's sister, Pauline Borghese, and her apartments are still decorated in imperial style, while the rest retains a feeling of seventeenth-century luxury. Bears, elephants, big cats, hippos and a host of other non-native mammals and birds, meanwhile, are on show at the **La Barben Zoo**, which also has plenty of child-friendly entertainment such as miniature train rides.

ARRIVAL AND INFORMATION   SALON-DE-PROVENCE

By train From the *gare SNCF* on Av Émile-Zola, the long straight Bd Maréchal-Foch leads to the *vieille ville*.
Destinations Avignon (every 30min–1hr; 57min); Marseille (every 30min–1hr; 55min).
By bus The *gare routière* is at the southern end of place Jules-Morgan, on the western edge of the *vieille ville*.
Destinations Aix (every 10min–1hr; 30–36min); Arles (1 daily Mon–Fri; 1hr); Marignane Airport (every 30min;

45min–1hr 12min).
By car There's secure off-street parking close to the tourist office.
Tourist office 56 cours Gimon (June & Sept Mon–Sat 9.30am–12.30pm & 2–6pm; July & Aug Mon–Sat 9.30am–7pm, Sun 10am–1pm; Oct–May Mon–Sat 9.30am–12.30pm & 2–6pm; ☎ 04 90 56 27 60, ⓦ visitsalondeprovence.com).

ACCOMMODATION   SEE MAP PAGE 78

D'Angleterre 98 cours Carnot ☎ 04 90 56 01 10, ⓦ hotel-dangleterre.biz. Traditional and very central two star hotel, with refurbished, soundproofed a/c rooms with en-suite bath or shower and flatscreen TV. There's also a private garage. **€60**
Camping Nostradamus Rte d'Eyguières ☎ 04 90 56 08 36, ⓦ camping-nostradamus.com. Three-star campsite just off the D17 towards Eyguières, with an outdoor pool, restaurant and games facilities. Also some mobile homes (minimum two nights). Closed Nov–Feb. Camping **€21.34**, mobile homes (2 nights) **€320**
Grand Hôtel de la Poste 1 rue des Frères John et Robert Kennedy ☎ 04 90 56 01 94, ⓦ ghpsalon.com. Overlooking place Crousillat's mossy fountains and the

town's prime café terraces, with somewhat dated a/c rooms, all with TV. Some three- and four-bed rooms. No lift. **€63**
Hostellerie de l'Abbaye de Sainte Croix Rte du Val de Cuech ☎ 04 90 56 24 55, ⓦ abbaye-de-saintecroix.fr. Luxury in the atmospheric surroundings of an ancient abbey, 3km from Salon on the D16, with a/c rooms occupying the old monks' cells, each bearing the name of a saint. **€239**
Mas de Lure Rte du Val de Cuech ☎ 04 90 56 41 24, ⓦ masdelure.com. Real French country style at surprisingly affordable prices in this gorgeous period farmhouse just outside town. There's a peaceful swimming pool surrounded by woodland and the house honey is served at breakfast. Camping **€120**

EATING   SEE MAP PAGE 78

Though some of its best restaurants are out of town, central Salon is full of reasonably priced places to eat and drink, with the smarter bars and brasseries clustering at the north end of the *vieille ville*. Salon's famous olive oil can be bought at the busy Wednesday **market** on place Morgan (6.30am–1pm), the Saturday morning organic market in the town centre, or the Sunday market on place de Gaulle, along with wonderful ingredients for a picnic, from olives or

cheeses to fresh fruit and vegetables.
L'Endroit 20 montée André Viallat ☎ 04 42 86 85 32, ⓦ lendroit13300.fr. Provençal flavours meet international influences at this restaurant with a terrace in the shadow of the château; there's trout with Espelette chili paprika and lamb mousse with red wine and cranberry juice on a €29.50 *menu*. Mon & Wed 7.30–10.30pm, Tues & Thurs–Sat noon–2.30pm & 7.30–10.30pm.

L'Estive 192 av de Craponne ☏ 04 90 42 05 95. A little way out of the centre but worth it for the friendly and unpretentious service and fresh food. In keeping with the vaguely rustic theme, dishes are simple enough – sirloin steak with shallots, *andouillette* sausage in mustard sauce – but cooked to perfection. *Formule du jour* €18. Tues–Sat noon–2pm & 7.30–9.30pm.

Kot and Sushi 69 bd de la Republique ☏ 04 90 17 85 80. Highly regarded Japanese cuisine with numerous permutations of sushi, sashimi, chirashi etc. as well as specialities such as Yaki Maki, a combination of salmon, grilled eel, masago and mayonnaise. Lunchtime menus from €13.90, dinner from €18.90. Tues–Sat noon–2pm & 7–10.15pm.

La Salle à Manger 6 rue du Maréchal-Joffre ☏ 04 90 56 28 01. The most romantic and creative of central Salon's restaurants, with a beautiful, softly lit Italianate interior, excellent Provençal cooking and a sheltered courtyard garden at the back. Two courses €32; express weekday *formule* €17. Tues–Sat noon–1.30pm & 7.30–9.30pm.

Arles
and the
Camargue

84 Arles

93 La Grande Crau

94 Les Baux-de-Provence

96 St-Rémy-de-Provence

100 La Petite Crau

101 Tarascon and around

105 The Camargue

ST-RÉMY-DE-PROVENCE

2

Arles and the Camargue

The stretch of the River Rhône that flows south from Avignon to the sea has always been a vital trading route, bringing wealth and fame to the towns that line its banks. The great riverside castles at Tarascon and Beaucaire are testament to the Rhône's strategic importance, while further south, at the point where the river splits into the Petit and Grand Rhône, is Arles, once the capital of Gaul. Its great amphitheatre still seats thousands for summer entertainments, while further Roman remains survive at Glanum, on the edge of St-Rémy-de-Provence, where you can see the overlaid ruins of Greek and Roman towns.

South of Arles, spreading across the Rhône delta, the watery land of the **Camargue** has its own unique natural history and way of life. The wet expanses sustain flocks of flamingos and other birds, while black bulls and wild white horses graze along the edges of the marshes and lagoons. Every May, **gypsies** from all around the Mediterranean come to the Camarguais resort of **Les Saintes-Maries-de-la-Mer** to celebrate their patron saint.

The modest plains north and east of Arles, enclosed by the Durance and the Rhône and separated by the abrupt ridge of the **Alpilles**, are known as **La Petite Crau** and **La Grande Crau**. The villages and small towns here have retained a nineteenth-century charm, living out the traditions revived by the great Provençal poet **Frédéric Mistral**. This is the countryside that **Van Gogh** painted when he spent a year at Arles and then sought refuge in St-Rémy. Both towns celebrate his tragic brilliance.

Arles

With its sun-kissed golden stone, small-town feel and splendid setting on the east bank of the Rhône, **ARLES** is one of the loveliest cities in southern France. It's also among the oldest, with the extraordinarily well-preserved Roman amphitheatre at its heart, **Les Arènes**, as the most famous of several magnificent monuments.

Originally a Celtic settlement, Arles later became the Roman capital of Gaul, Britain and Spain, and survived the collapse of the Roman Empire as a base for the counts of Provence before unification with France. For centuries, its port prospered thanks to inland trade up the Rhône, profiting especially whenever France's enemies blockaded its eternal rival, Marseille. Decline set in with the arrival of the railways, however, and the town where **Van Gogh** spent a lonely and miserable – but highly prolific – period in the late nineteenth century was itself inward-looking and depressed.

Arles today is pleasantly laidback – at its liveliest on Saturdays, when farmers from the Camargue and La Crau come in for the weekly **market** – and a delightful place simply to stroll around. Its compact central core, tucked into a ninety-degree curve in the river, is small enough to cross on foot in a few minutes, and holds all the major sights except the **Musée Départemental Arles Antique** to the southwest, and **Les Alyscamps** necropolis and **Luma Arles** to the southeast. While ancient ruins are scattered everywhere, the heart of the Roman city, the **place du Forum**, remains the hub of popular life. Medieval Arles, on the other hand, centred on what's now the place de la République, the pedestrianized site of both the **Église St-Trophime** and the Hôtel de Ville. The one area where the city's former **walls** have survived lies to the east, in a quiet and attractive little corner. Sadly, the **riverfront**, once teeming with bars and bistros, was heavily damaged during World War II.

Highlights

❶ Les Arènes With its awe-inspiring scale, Arles' still-busy ancient Roman amphitheatre is one of Provence's most impressive Roman remains. See page 86

❷ Luma Arles You certainly can't miss this new Frank Gehry-designed aluminium tower-cultural centre, memorably described by one critic as a "stainless steel tornado". See page 91

❸ Les Baux-de-Provence Scramble over the hillsides to explore this extraordinary citadel, carved into the bleached rocks atop the Alpilles range. See page 94

❹ Carrières de Lumières A fascinating audiovisual extravaganza, projected into the cavernous interior of a former quarry in the "Valley of Hell". See page 95

❺ St-Paul-de-Mausole Home for a year to Vincent van Gogh, this psychiatric hospital in picturesque St-Rémy offers an emotive insight into the artist's suffering. See page 97

❻ Château du Roi René Tarascon's colossal riverside castle is impressive in its own right, and plays host to fascinating exhibitions on the life and lore of medieval Provence. See page 102

❼ The Camargue The expansive marshland of the Rhône delta is home to pink flamingos, white horses and unearthly, watery landscapes, as well as a colourful gypsy festival in Les Saintes-Maries-de-la-Mer. See page 105

HIGHLIGHTS ARE MARKED ON THE MAP ON PAGE 86

Roman Arles

To this day, Arles remains recognizable as the **Roman** city that was first thrust to greatness when Julius Caesar built an entire fleet here in less than a month. After using the ships to win control of Rome, he devastated Marseille for its support of his enemy Pompey, and Arles became a major port. The Mediterranean was a little closer to the city at that time, and the extensive wheatfields of the Camargue were known as the "granary of Rome".

Les Arènes

Daily: March, April & Oct 9am–6pm; May–Sept 9am–7pm; Nov–Feb 10am–5pm • €9 with Théâtre Antique (see below) • ☎ 08 91 70 03 70, Ⓦ arenes-arles.com

Constructed at the end of the first century AD, Arles' most dramatic monument, the amphitheatre known as **Les Arènes**, was the largest Roman building in all Gaul.

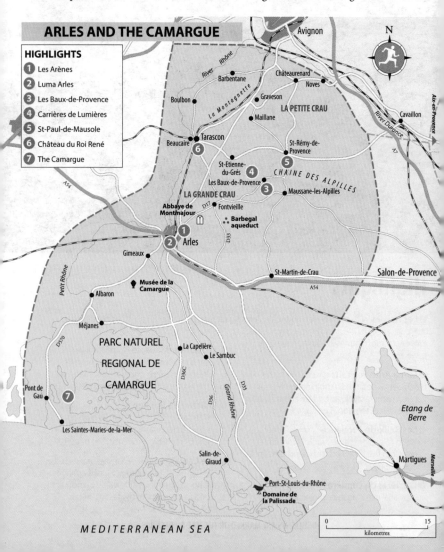

ARLES AND THE CAMARGUE

HIGHLIGHTS

1. Les Arènes
2. Luma Arles
3. Les Baux-de-Provence
4. Carrières de Lumières
5. St-Paul-de-Mausole
6. Château du Roi René
7. The Camargue

BULLFIGHTS IN THE ARLES ARENA

Bullfighting comes in two styles in Arles and the Camargue. In the local **courses camarguaises**, held at *fêtes* from late spring to early autumn (the most prestigious of which is Arles' Cocarde d'Or, on the first Monday in July), *razeteurs* run at the bulls in an effort to pluck ribbons and cockades tied to the bulls' horns, cutting them free with special barbed gloves. The drama and grace lies in the style with which the men leap over the barrier away from the bull, and in the competition for prize money. In this gentler bullfight, people are rarely injured and the bulls are not killed.

More popular, however, are the brutal Spanish-style **corridas**, consisting of a strict ritual leading up to the all-but-inevitable death of the bull. After its entry into the ring, the bull is subjected to the *bandilleros* who stick decorated barbs in its back, the *picadors*, who lance it from horseback, and finally, the *torero*, who endeavours to lead the bull through as graceful a series of movements as possible before killing it with a single sword stroke to the heart. In one *corrida* six bulls are killed by three *toreros*, for whom injuries (sometimes fatal) are not uncommon.

While outsiders may disapprove, *tauromachie* (as it's known hereabouts) has a long history in the region, and offers a rare opportunity to join in local life. It's also an opportunity to experience Arles' Roman arena in use.

Looming above the city centre, it measures 136m long by 107m wide; its two tiers of sixty arches each (the lower Doric, the upper Corinthian) were originally topped by a third, and thirty thousand spectators would cram beneath its canvas roof to watch gladiator battles and other spectacles. During the Middle Ages, it became a fortress (and effectively a miniature town), sheltering more than two hundred dwellings and three churches. Since this medieval quarter was cleared away in 1830, the Arènes has once more been used for entertainment. While it's impressive from the outside, it's only really worth paying for admission to the interior if a bullfight (see page 87), concert or other performance is taking place, when it makes an absolutely stunning venue.

Théâtre Antique

Entrance on rue du Cloître • Daily: March, April & Oct 9am–6pm; May–Sept 9am–7pm; Nov–Feb 10am–5pm • €9 with Les Arènes (see page 86) • ☎ 04 90 18 41 20

The **Théâtre Antique** is nowhere near as well preserved as the neighbouring amphitheatre. Only one pair of columns is still standing, all the statuary has been removed, and the sides of the stage are littered with broken chunks of stone. Built a hundred years before Les Arènes, it was quarried for the construction of churches not long after the Roman Empire collapsed, and later became part of the city's fortifications – one wing was turned into the **Tour Roland**, whose height gives an idea where the top seats would have been. There's little to see on an ordinary day, but it hosts performances and festivals year-round.

Thermes de Constantin

Rue du Grand-Prieuré • Daily: March, April & Oct 9am–6pm; May–Sept 9am–7pm; Nov–Feb 10am–5pm • €4 • ☎ 04 90 49 36 74

The ruins of the **Thermes de Constantin**, which may well have been the biggest Roman baths in Provence, are all that remain of the emperor's palace that extended along the Rhône waterfront. You can see the heating system below a thick Roman concrete floor and the divisions between the different areas, but there's nothing to help you imagine the original. The most striking feature, the high and rather elegant wall of an apse that sheltered one of the baths, in alternating stripes of orange brick and grey masonry, is best viewed from outside on place Constantin.

Cryptoportiques

Accessed via Hôtel de Ville, place de la République • Daily: March, April & Oct 9am–6pm; May–Sept 9am–7pm; Nov–Feb 10am–5pm • €4.50

Arles' most unusual – and spookiest – Roman remains, the **Cryptoportiques**, are reached via stairs that lead down from inside the Hôtel de Ville (see page 89). No one knows quite what these huge, dark and dank underground galleries were used for, but they may have been built simply to prop up one side of the town's level open forum, which stood above, and later became a food store or a barracks for public slaves. They're empty now, but make an atmospheric, if damp, fifteen-minute subterranean stroll.

Musée Départemental Arles Antique

Av 1ère Division France Libre • Mon & Wed–Sun 10am–6pm • €8, free first Sun of each month • ☏ 04 13 31 51 03, ⓦ www.arles-antique.cg13.fr • It's a 15min walk southwest of place du Forum, and is served by free shuttle buses from the *gare SNCF* (every 25min 7.10am–7.15pm)

The superb **Musée Départemental Arles Antique**, the best place to get an overall sense of Roman Arles, stands immediately southwest of the city centre on a spit of land between the Rhône and the Canal de l'Ecluse. Flooded with natural light and immensely

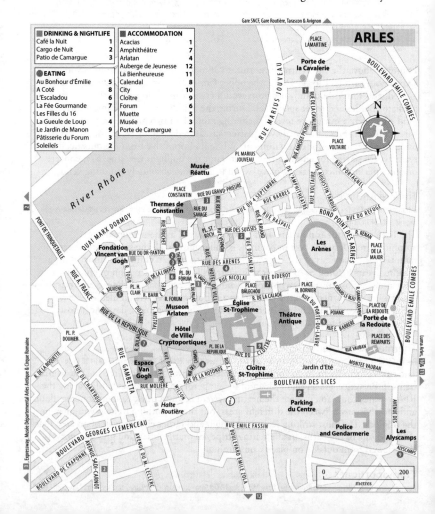

Gare SNCF, Gare Routière, Tarascon & Avignon ▲

ARLES

DRINKING & NIGHTLIFE
Café la Nuit	1
Cargo de Nuit	2
Patio de Camargue	3

EATING
Au Bonheur d'Émilie	5
A Coté	8
L'Escaladou	6
La Fée Gourmande	7
Les Filles du 16	1
La Gueule de Loup	4
Le Jardin de Manon	9
Pâtisserie du Forum	3
Soleileïs	2

ACCOMMODATION
Acacias	1
Amphithéâtre	7
Arlatan	4
Auberge de Jeunesse	12
La Bienheureuse	11
Calendal	8
City	10
Cloître	9
Forum	6
Muette	5
Musée	3
Porte de Camargue	2

THE RENCONTRES D'ARLES

Widely acknowledged to be Europe's most prestigious annual **photography festival**, the **Rencontres d'Arles** (W rencontres-arles.com) takes over more than a dozen venues throughout the city between July and late September. Visitors can either pay from €5 for admission to a single exhibition, or buy passes – €33–35 for one day, €36–42 for the whole festival – from ticket offices in the place de la République and elsewhere.

2

spacious, it starts with regional prehistory, then leads through the Roman era. The story of Arles is traced from Julius Caesar's legionnaire base and its development under Augustus, via its fourth-century status as the Christian emperor Constantine's capital of Gaul, to its importance as a trading centre during the fifth century. At that time, Emperor Honorius could say "the town's position, its communications and its crowd of visitors is such that there is no place in the world better suited to spreading, in every sense, the products of the earth."

Excellent models show the changing layout of the city and the sheer size of its monuments, while topics explored include medicine, industry and agriculture, and the use of water power. A new extension proudly displays a miraculously preserved flat-bottomed boat that was discovered in the Rhône in 2004, and is thought to have been used to transport massive blocks of stone. Overhead walkways enable visitors to admire fabulous mosaics, while sculptures on the sarcophagi salvaged from Les Alyscamps (see below) depict everything from music and lovers to gladiators and Christian miracles.

The museum is positioned on the axis of the second-century **Cirque Romaine**, an enormous chariot racetrack that stretched back 450m and seated twenty thousand spectators. Little is now discernible on the ground, however.

Les Alyscamps

Av des Alyscamps • Daily: March, April & Oct 9am–6pm; May–Sept 9am–7pm; Nov–Feb 10am–5pm • €4.50, €9 with Église St-Trophime Cloisters (see page 89) • ☏ 04 90 49 36 74

The Roman necropolis of Arles, known as **Les Alyscamps**, lies just southeast of the centre, a few minutes' walk south of boulevard des Lices. Originally much larger, it was regarded as the most hallowed Christian burial ground in all Europe long after the Roman era had ended; until the twelfth century, mourners far upstream would launch sumptuous coffins to float down the Rhône for collection at Arles. Only one of its many alleyways now survives, and even that is foreshortened by a rail line, while the finest of its sarcophagi and statues have long since disappeared. Nonetheless, ancient tombs still line the shaded walk, as painted by Van Gogh (who rendered the tree trunks azure blue), and the tranquil 400m stroll ends at the twelfth-century Romanesque church of **St-Honorat**, which is wonderfully simple, and cool on a hot day.

Place de la République

The dominant feature of the old town's central, pedestrianized **place de la République** is an obelisk of Egyptian granite. Originally it may have stood in the middle of the Cirque Romaine; it was placed here by Louis XIV, who fancied himself as a latter-day Augustus.

Also on place de la République is the palatial seventeenth-century **Hôtel de Ville**, which was inspired by the Palace of Versailles. A staircase inside leads down to the Roman **Cryptoportiques** (see page 87); in fact, the flattened vaulted roof of its entrance hall was expressly designed to minimize stress on the galleries below.

Église St-Trophime

Place de la République • **Cathedral** Mon–Sat 8am–noon & 2–6pm, Sun 9am–1pm & 2–6pm • Free • **Cloisters** Daily: March, April & Oct 9am–6pm; May–Sept 9am–7pm; Nov–Feb 10am–5pm • €5.50, €9 with Alyscamps (see page 89)

VAN GOGH IN ARLES

On February 21, 1888, **Vincent van Gogh** arrived in Arles from Paris, to be greeted by snow and a bitter Mistral wind. He started painting immediately, and within the year produced such celebrated canvases as *The Sunflowers, Van Gogh's Chair, The Red Vines* and *The Sower*. He always lived near the station, staying first at the *Hotel Carrel*, 30 rue de la Cavalerie, and then the *Café de la Gare*, until the so-called "Yellow House", at 2 place Lamartine, had been rendered fit for use as a home as well as a studio.

From the daily letters he wrote to his brother Théo, it's clear that Van Gogh found few kindred souls in Arles. He finally managed to persuade **Paul Gauguin** to join him in late October. Although the two were to influence each other substantially in the following weeks, their relationship quickly soured as the increasingly bad November weather forced them to spend more time together indoors.

Precisely what transpired on the night of December 23, 1888, will probably never be known. According to Gauguin, Van Gogh, feeling threatened by his friend's possible departure, finally succumbed to a fit of psychosis and attacked first Gauguin and then himself. He cut off the lower part of his **left ear**, wrapped it in newspaper, and handed it to a prostitute. An alternative version of the story alleges that it was in fact an infuriated Gauguin who lopped off the offending lobe with a sword, and the two artists concocted a cover story to protect Gauguin from the law.

In any event, Gauguin left Arles, and although Vincent's wound soon healed, his mental health swiftly deteriorated. In response to a petition from thirty of his alarmed neighbours, he was packed off to the **Hôtel-Dieu** hospital, where he had the good fortune to be treated by a young and sympathetic doctor, Félix Rey. Van Gogh painted Rey's portrait while in the hospital, as well as the hospital itself, whose inmates are clearly suffering from an unhappiness only Van Gogh could express. Upon leaving hospital, Van Gogh also left Arles, moving voluntarily to St-Rémy (see page.96).

IN THE FOOTSTEPS OF VAN GOGH

None of Van Gogh's paintings remains in Arles, and the Yellow House was destroyed by bombing during World War II. Vestiges of the city that he knew still survive, however. Behind the Réattu museum, lanterns line the river wall where Van Gogh used to wander, wearing candles on his hat, watching the night-time light: *Starry Night over the Rhône* shows the Rhône at Arles. The café he painted in *Café Terrace at Night* is still open for business in place du Forum, while the distinctive Pont Langlois drawbridge, which he painted in March 1888, survives on the southern edge of town. The Hôtel-Dieu hospital itself, just off rue du Président-Wilson, has become the **Espace Van Gogh**, which houses a *mediathèque* and university departments. There is a bookshop and a *salon de thé* in the arcades, and flowerbeds in the courtyard that re-create the garden that Van Gogh both painted and described.

The **Fondation Vincent van Gogh** runs a gallery and research facility at 33 rue du Dr-Fanton (Tues–Sun: early March to late April & Oct–Feb 11am–6pm; late April to Sept 11am–7pm; €9, or €12 with Musée Reattu [see page 91]; ☎04 90 93 08 08, ⓦfondation-vincentvangogh-arles.org). It owns no works by the man himself, however; changing exhibitions by contemporary artists explore themes associated with Van Gogh, but to avoid disappointment be sure you check what is on show before you pay the steep admission price.

Unusually, Arles' **Église St-Trophime** does not stand alone, but instead is simply one relatively inconspicuous facade among many on place de la République. Superb twelfth-century Provençal stone carving around its doorway depicts the Last Judgement, trumpeted by angels playing with the enthusiasm of jazz musicians; as the damned are led naked and chained down to hell, the blessed – all female and draped in long robes – process upwards.

Work on the cathedral itself started in the ninth century, on the spot where, in 597 AD, St Augustine was consecrated as the first bishop of the English. Its high nave is now decorated with d'Aubusson tapestries. The freshly restored and extraordinarily beautiful **Cloître St-Trophime**, reached by a separate entrance to the right, holds more Romanesque and Gothic stone carving, including an image of St Martha leading away the tamed Tarasque (see page 103).

Musée Réattu

10 rue du Grand-Prieuré • Tues–Sun: March–Oct 10am–6pm; Nov–Feb 10am–5pm • €8, €9 July & Aug; €12 with Fondation Vincent van Gogh (see page 90) • ☎ 04 90 49 37 58, ⓦ museereattu.arles.fr

The must-see **Musée Réattu** stands beside the river, and opposite the Roman baths, in a beautiful fifteenth-century priory. Displays range across the building's own history, including its connections with the Knights of Malta, but the museum centres on 57 ink and crayon sketches, made between December 1970 and February 1971, donated by **Pablo Picasso** in appreciation of the many bullfights he'd seen in Arles. Among the split faces, clowns and hilarious Tarasque (see page 103), there's a beautifully simple portrait of Picasso's mother, painted from life in 1923. Other twentieth-century pieces dotted about the landings, corridors and courtyard niches include Mario Prassinos' black-and-white studies of the Alpilles, and *Odalisque*, Zadkine's polychromed sculpture of a woman playing a violin. The museum also hosts very good temporary exhibitions.

Luma Arles

Parc des Ateliers 45 chemin des Minimes • Wed–Sun 11am–6pm • Price varies according to exhibition; many free • ☎ 04 88 65 83 09, ⓦ luma-arles.org

You get the feeling that however compelling the work on show at this new, multi-disciplinary "cultural centre for the 21st century", it can't help but be outshone by the glinting aluminium panels of its extraordinary, Frank Gehry-designed exterior. It looks like something between a Cape Canaveral rocket launch and a Dutch windmill as imagined by aliens, apt, perhaps, in the land of Van Gogh.

In the stepped protrusions that frame the windows there are echoes of Enric Miralles' Scottish Parliament building and the hope is that **Luma Arles** will be as transformative for the city as Kengo Kuma's V&A currently is for Dundee or Gehry's Guggenheim Museum was for Bilbao.

Work was still ongoing at the time of writing, with the grand opening scheduled for 2020. Changing exhibitions are currently held in the adjacent converted industrial buildings, and work is likewise ongoing on a public park designed by landscape architect Bas Smets.

ARRIVAL AND INFORMATION
ARLES

By train Arles' *gare SNCF* is on Av Pauline Talabot, a few blocks north of the Arènes.

Destinations Avignon (every 24min–1hr 26min; 17–20min); Avignon TGV (6 daily; 50min); Lyon (6 daily; 2hr 39min); Marseille (every 16min–1hr 25min; 45min–1hr 14min); Nîmes (6 daily; 30min); Paris (2 daily; 4hr); Tarascon (10 daily; 8–23min).

By bus Most buses arrive at the unstaffed *gare routière* alongside the *gare SNCF*, but all local services stop on Bd Georges Clemenceau, just east of rue Gambetta.

Destinations Aix (hourly via Salon de Provence; 1hr 40min); Avignon (3 daily; 1hr 5min); Avignon TGV (4 daily; 50min); Nîmes (13 daily; 30min–1hr 5min); Les Saintes-Maries-de-la-Mer (5 daily; 50min); St-Rémy (3 daily; 44min); Tarascon (roughly hourly; 20min).

By car In summer, drivers are better off parking on the periphery, such as in the Centre car park on Bd des Lices, rather than venturing into the central maze of narrow one-way streets. There's free street parking a little further out, for example on place Lamartine and near Les Alyscamps.

Tourist office Bd des Lices (Jan–March, Nov & Dec Mon–Sat 9am–4.45pm, Sun 10am–1pm; April–Sept daily 9am–6.45pm; Oct Mon–Sat 9am–5.45pm, Sun 10am–1pm; ☎ 04 90 18 41 20, ⓦ arlestourisme.com). If you plan to do a lot of sightseeing, consider buying either the €16 *Pass Avantage* or the more restricted €12 *Pass Liberté*, which offer admission to various permutations of local sites.

Bike rental 1 Véloc 12 rue de la Cavalerie (Mon–Sat 9.30am–12.30pm & 2–6pm; ☎ 04 86 32 27 05, ⓦ 1veloc. fr).

ACCOMMODATION
SEE MAP PAGE 88

Acacias 2 rue de la Cavalerie ☎ 04 90 96 37 88, ⓦ hotel-arles.brithotel.fr. Modern, simple but cheerfully decorated – and soundproofed – rooms in a friendly hotel, not far

from the train station, with free parking nearby. Closed late Oct to March. **€87**

★ **Amphithéâtre** 5–7 rue Diderot ☎ 04 90 96 10 30,

2

ⓦhotelamphitheatre.fr. Very central hotel, with inviting and charmingly decorated public spaces, and spacious a/c rooms that abound in warm colours, tiles and wrought ironwork, and have large, well-equipped bathrooms. The four-person rooms and suites are also good value. **€89**

Arlatan 26 rue du Sauvage ☎04 65 88 20 20, ⓦhotel-arlatan.fr. Set in a beautiful antique-decorated fifteenth-century mansion, this hotel has plenty of character, plus a heated swimming pool and its own garage (€12); driving the narrow streets to get here is a challenge, though. The cheapest rooms are rather small. Closed Jan. **€179**

Auberge de Jeunesse 20 av du Maréchal-Foch ☎04 90 96 18 25, ⓦfuaj.org/arles. Old-style hostel, 500m south of the centre – from the *gare SNCF*, take bus #3 to stop "Clemenceau" – with rock-hard beds in large dorms, and spartan facilities. Bike rental available. Reception 7–10am & 5–11pm (midnight in summer). Closed Nov–Feb. Rates include breakfast, served only until 9am. **€20.50**

Calendal 5 rue Porte-de-Laure ☎04 90 96 11 89, ⓦlecalendal.com. Welcoming hotel, overlooking the Théâtre Antique and glowing at sunset, with bright a/c rooms overlooking a pleasant shaded garden; rates include access to the indoor spa. **€134**

Cloître 18 rue du Cloître ☎04 88 09 10 00, ⓦlecloitre.com. Designer hotel in a peaceful but very central spot backing onto the cloisters of St-Trophime, kitted out with an intriguing mix of arty modern, shabby chic and retro. Rooms come in all shapes and sizes; one is very well adapted for wheelchair users. **€139**

Forum 10 place du Forum ☎04 90 93 48 95, ⓦhotelduforum.com. Run by the same family for almost a century, this venerable hotel, in Arles' most appealing little square, offers plain but sizeable and tasteful rooms, plus a tiny pool and a bar that's barely changed since Picasso used to hang out here. **€100**

★ **Muette** 15 rue des Suisses ☎04 90 96 15 39, ⓦhotel-muette.com. Charming old stone hotel, close to Les Arènes, where the pleasant, tranquil rooms are decked out in beiges and creams, with rough-hewn terracotta-tiled floors and lots of Van Gogh touches. Larger suites sleep up to five. Nice buffet breakfast (€10), and friendly management. Closed Jan & Feb. **€79**

Musée 11 rue du Grand-Prieuré ☎04 90 93 88 88, ⓦhoteldumusee.com. Small, good-value, family-run place, set in a seventeenth-century mansion in a quiet spot opposite Musée Réattu, with a pretty, flower-filled terrace and its own art gallery. Two-night minimum stay in summer. Closed Jan & first two weeks of March & Dec. **€96**

Porte de Camargue 15 rue Noguier ☎04 90 96 17 32, ⓦportecamargue.com. Attractive, very peaceful hotel, with light, simple rooms and a rooftop terrace, just across the Pont de Trinquetaille from the centre – parking is easier this side of the river. Closed late Oct to March. **€80**

CAMPSITES

La Bienheureuse N453, Raphèle-lès-Arles ☎04 90 98 48 06, ⓦlabienheureuse.com. Well-shaded three-star site, 7km southeast on the Aix bus route, that's the best of Arles' half-dozen campsites. Two pools, and a snack bar that serves full meals in July & Aug. Closed Oct–Feb. **€19**

City 67 rte de Crau ☎04 90 93 08 86, ⓦcamping-city.com. The closest campsite to town, 1.5km southeast on the Crau bus route, this three-star is not very attractive, but there's a certain amount of shade, plus a restaurant and a pool. Closed Oct–March. **€20**

EATING

SEE MAP PAGE 88

Arles has a good range of **restaurants** – many excellent, many cheap, and a fair number of both – while the place du Forum is the centre of **café** life. Most establishments, however, pack up for the night around 10.30pm. Saturday's **market** extends the length of Bd Georges-Clemenceau, Bd des Lices and Bd Émile-Combes, and many of the adjoining streets. A smaller food market is held every Wednesday in place Lamartine, with bric-a-brac stalls spreading down Bd Émile-Combes.

RESTAURANTS

Au Bonheur d'Émilie 5 rue Jouvène ☎04 90 98 38 71. The go-to lunch spot for Arles' vegetarians and vegans, with fresh, unfussy portions of veg, legumes and tarts, plus gluten-free options. Eat-in *formule* €9.50, takeaway €8.50. Mon, Tues & Thurs–Sat 11am–6pm.

A Coté 21 rue des Carmes ☎04 90 47 61 13, ⓦbistro-acote.com. The most affordable of two all-but-adjoining restaurants belonging to acclaimed chef Jean-Luc Rabanel, along a tiny but very central alleyway, this informal bistro has pleasant outdoor seating. Open from breakfast onwards, it serves full *menus* from €32 and *plats* such as smoked salmon with buckwheat blinis and yuzu cream from €14. At M. Rabanel's neighbouring *Atelier*, by contrast, dinner *menus* start at €95. Wed–Sun noon–3pm & 7.30–10.30pm.

L'Escaladou 23 rue Porte-de-Laure ☎04 90 96 70 43. Behind this old-fashioned facade, near the upper side of the Théâtre Antique, this local favourite holds three substantial and usually very busy dining rooms. It can be noisy and not exactly romantic, but the service is friendly, and seafood lovers are in for a real treat, in the shape of the sumptuous and magnificently garlicky €28 Arlesian bouillabaisse. The one set *menu* costs €26 for three courses. Mon, Wed & Fri–Sun noon–2pm & 7–9.30pm.

La Fée Gourmande 3 rue Dulau ☎04 90 18 26 57. This friendly, slightly kitsch little restaurant has established such a reputation for its high-class home-style cooking that reservations are essential. Changing daily specials like the house speciality, melt-in-your-mouth slow-cooked lamb, cost around €24, but there's a great-value €19 lunch *formule*. Wed–Fri 11.30am–3pm, Sat 11.30am–3pm & 7–9pm, Sun 7–9pm.

Les Filles du 16 16 rue du Dr-Fanton ✆ 04 90 93 77 36, ⓦ lrestaurantlesfillesdu16.fr. Friendly little indoor, a/c traditional bistro just off the place du Forum and run, as the name suggests, by the daughters of the original owner. The lunch *formule* costs just €16, while for dinner you can get a three-course *menu* for €29, or simply order a *plat*, such as the succulent seasonal *tellines* (tiny shellfish), or the €17 *gardiane de taureau* (bull's-meat stew). Mon–Fri noon–1.30pm & 7–9pm.

★ **La Gueule de Loup** 39 rue des Arènes ✆ 04 90 96 96 69. Cosy stone-walled restaurant, squeezed into a venerable townhouse, with the open kitchen plus four tables downstairs and the main dining room upstairs. A definite Asian influence in the cooking translates to such adventurous dishes such as bull fillet in a Thai broth (€21) Dinner *menu* €33; reservations recommended. Mon & Fri–Sun 12.15–1.45pm & 7.15–9pm, Tues noon–1.30pm & 7.15–9pm.

Le Jardin de Manon 14 av Alyscamps ✆ 04 90 93 38 68. In a relatively quiet corner spot down near Les Alyscamps (see page 89), this is worth the walk, with fairly traditional, assiduously prepared dishes such as saddle of rabbit with goat's cheese (€21), best enjoyed on the leafy terrace at the rear. *Menus* €23 or €32. Mon & Thurs–Sat noon–1.15pm & 7–9.30pm, Tues & Sun noon–1.15pm.

CAFÉS AND ICE CREAM

Pâtisserie du Forum 4 rue de la Liberté ✆ 04 90 96 03 72. *Salon de thé* with a whole patisserie full of goodies to go with the Earl Grey, plus ice cream and hot chocolate. Daily 7am–7.30pm.

Soleileïs 9 rue du Dr-Fanton ✆ 07 63 92 30 76. Delicious home-made ice cream and sorbet with all-natural ingredients including olive oil, herbs, spices and plenty of fresh fruit, plus freshly squeezed juices. April to late June Mon, Tues & Thurs–Sun 2–6.30pm; late June to late Aug Mon 2–6.30pm, Tues–Sun 2–6.30pm & 8.30–10.30pm; late Aug to Oct daily 2–6.30pm.

DRINKING AND NIGHTLIFE

SEE MAP PAGE 88

Café la Nuit 11 place du Forum ✆ 04 90 96 44 56, ⓦ restaurant-cafe-van-gogh.com. Immortalized in Van Gogh's *Café Terrace at Night* – not in his *The Night Café*, the subject of which was near the station – this long-established spot remains *the* place to enjoy Arles' charming central square. Have a drink on the terrace and you'll find yourself in quite a few holiday snaps – don't eat here, though; the food and service is very poor. Daily 9am–midnight.

Cargo de Nuit 7 av Sadi-Carnot ✆ 04 90 49 55 99, ⓦ cargodenuit.com. This lively venue puts on an excellent and eclectic line-up of live jazz, electronic and world music

concerts, and also comedy. It's only open when an event is scheduled, when the bar section also serves tapas. Schedule varies, but especially likely to be open Fri & Sat; bar opens 8pm, concerts start 9.30pm.

Patio de Camargue 49 chemin Barriol ✆ 04 90 49 51 76, ⓦ cpatiodecamargue. Arles was the original base for the world-conquering Gipsy Kings. Founder-member Chico now runs this riverfront restaurant-music venue, roughly 1km southwest of the centre, which puts on regular dinner concerts; they're typically on Sat nights, and cost upwards of €50; check website for current schedules.

La Grande Crau

The region known as **La Grande Crau** (or just La Crau) stretches east from Arles and the Rhône delta for around 30km, as far as Salon. Long ago, this was the bed of the Rhône and the Durance. Its name derives from a Greek word meaning "stony", and even though several areas are now irrigated and planted with fruit trees, protected by windbreaks of cypresses and poplars, much of it is still rock-strewn desert, unbearably hot and shadeless in summer.

Only as the Grande Crau approaches the western end of the **Alpilles**, the hills that define its northern edge – the peaks resemble the crest of a wave about to engulf the plain – does the countryside become more amenable, offering potential stop-offs at the **Abbaye de Montmajour** and the village of **Fontvieille**.

Abbaye de Montmajour

D17, 3km north of Arles • April & May daily 10am–5pm; June–Sept daily 10am–6.30pm; Oct–March Tues–Sun 10am–5pm; last admission 45min before closing • €6 • ✆ 04 90 54 64 17, ⓦ montmajour.monuments-nationaux.fr

The Romanesque ruins of the **Abbaye de Montmajour** climb the side of a small hill, next to the D17 as it sets off towards Les Baux. Visitors enter the site via the chilly crypt, and continue to the central domed chapel. A menacing stone menagerie of beasts and devils in the **cloisters** enlivens the bases of the vaulting, while long-empty tombs were carved out of the rocky hillside beyond – only one still holds its original stone lid. Be sure to climb the 124 steps of the abbey's fortified central watchtower, access to which closes much earlier than the site itself, for stunning views of La Grande Crau, the Rhône and the Alpilles. Throughout the year, the abbey hosts photographic exhibitions in association with the Rencontres d'Arles (see page 89).

Fontvieille

Little **FONTVIEILLE**, 5km northeast of Montmajour, is a site of literary pilgrimage for the French, as the setting for Alphonse Daudet's nineteenth-century *Lettres de mon moulin*, a much-loved collection of short stories that focus especially on rural Provençal life. Daudet never lived in the eponymous windmill, signposted as the **Moulin de Daudet** just south of town; it's a pretty spot, but no longer open to the public.

Barbegal aqueduct and watermill

D82, 2km south of Fontvieille • Unrestricted access at all times • Free

To see a Roman aqueduct that once served Arles, turn east from the D33 onto the D82, a couple of kilometres south of Fontvieille. After 100m the road squeezes between the ancient stone blocks of the **Barbegal aqueduct**. A footpath leads south from here, alongside successive ruined arches; with only a couple of long-standing farmhouses in sight, looking for all the world like Roman villas, the landscape feels barely changed in two thousand years. Within a few minutes, the aqueduct divides into two separate courses, one of which ends where a channel carved into the rock spills over the edge of a low bluff. Its downhill torrent originally powered the sixteen-wheel **Barbegal watermill**, which produced up to three tonnes of flour a day. Vestiges still survive, but there are no explanatory signs on the site; if you're curious to know more, head to the archeological museum in Arles (see page 88), which holds a model of the mill.

Les Baux-de-Provence

The distinctly unreal fortified village of **LES BAUX-DE-PROVENCE** perches atop the Alpilles ridge, 15km northeast of Arles. It's unreal partly because the ruins of its eleventh-century **castle** merge almost imperceptibly into the plateau, whose rock is both foundation and part of the structure, and partly because this *ville morte* (dead city), along with a vast area of the plateau around it, is accessible only via a turnstile from the living village below. Even the former bauxite quarries, cut from the jagged rocks of the **Val d'Enfer**, are now tourist attractions, home to the imaginative gallery known as the **Carrières de Lumières**. The great majority of Les Baux's visitors are day-trippers, who tend to be thinning out by 5pm. To avoid the crowds, especially in summer, come later in the day.

Brief history

When the **medieval** lords of Les Baux, who owed allegiance to none, died out at the end of the fourteenth century, the town passed to the counts of Provence and then to the kings of France who, in 1632, razed the feudal citadel to the ground and fined the population into penury. For the next two hundred years, both citadel and village were inhabited almost exclusively by bats and crows. The subsequent discovery of the mineral **bauxite** – the name derives from "Les Baux" – in the neighbouring hills brought back some life, and tourism has more recently transformed the place. Today the population stays steady at around four hundred, augmented by more than 1.5 million visitors each year.

The château

Daily: Jan, Feb, Nov & Dec 10am–5pm; March & Oct 9.30am–6.30pm; April–June & Sept 9am–7pm; July & Aug 9am–8pm; last entry 1hr before closing • €8; free audioguide in English • ☎ 04 90 49 20 02, ⓦ chateau-baux-provence.com

Although universally known as a **château**, the enormous and extraordinary **castle** at Les Baux is in truth more of a large citadel. The only gate to the complex is at the far end of the main village street. That leads first to open ground below the walls, scattered with replica siege engines and catapults that perform assorted re-enactments through the day in summer, and then to a network of footpaths over and through assorted buildings which include the ruins of the feudal castle demolished on Richelieu's orders, the partially restored **Chapelle Castrale** and the **Tour Sarrasine**. The higher you climb, the more spectacular the views become.

The village

The actual **village** of Les Baux, straggling over the hilltop just below the château, is a too-good-to-be-true collection of sixteenth- and seventeenth-century churches, chapels and mansions. Several of its most beautiful buildings are given over to museums.

In the Hôtel de Porcelet, the **Musée Yves Brayer** (March & Oct–Dec daily except Tues 11am–12.30pm & 2–5pm; April–Sept daily 10am–12.30pm & 2–6.30pm; €8;☎04 90 54 36 99, ⓦyvesbrayer.com) shows the paintings (and hats) of the twentieth-century figurative artist whose work also adorns the seventeenth-century **Chapelle des Pénitents Blancs** on place de l'Église. Changing exhibitions by contemporary Provençal artists are displayed in the **Hôtel de Manville** (hours vary; free), while the **Musée des Santons** in the old Hôtel de Ville (daily 9am–7pm; free) displays traditional Provençal nativity figures.

Carrières de Lumières

D27, 500m north of Les Baux • Daily: Jan, March, Nov & Dec 10am–6pm; April–June, Sept & Oct 9.30am–7pm; July & Aug 9.30am–7.30pm; last entry 1hr before closing • €13 • ☎ 04 90 49 20 02, ⓦ carrieres-lumieres.com

It's said that Dante took his inspiration for the nine circles of the *Inferno* from a trip he made to the valley known as the **Val d'Enfer** (Valley of Hell), immediately north of Les Baux, while staying at Arles. Jean Cocteau used its contorted rocks and bauxite quarries as a location for his 1959 film, *Le Testament d'Orphée*.

More recently, the cavernous subterranean spaces of those same quarries have been turned into an audiovisual experience called the **Carrières de Lumières**, based on the ever-dynamic projection of famous paintings across their floors and walls, ceilings and columns. The show is continuous, so you don't have to wait to go in. The effect is similar to entering an Egyptian temple that has been carved from the rock, but here you're surrounded by an endless procession of images, from entire paintings to giant blown-up details, which float and flow through the vast rectangular chambers, accompanied by music that resonates strangely in the enclosed space. The precise content changes yearly, focusing on a particular artist or school of painting. Really, though, it makes little difference; the sensation is just mind-blowing, as you wander on and through the shifting shapes and colours.

ARRIVAL AND INFORMATION   LES BAUX-DE-PROVENCE

By car Les Baux village is pedestrianized. Parking costs €5 in and below the village area, and is extremely restricted. It costs nothing at the Carrières de Lumières, though, so if you plan to walk there and back anyway it makes sense to park there in the first place.

Tourist office Maison du Roy, rue Porte Mage, at the

start of Grande-Rue (daily: April–Sept Mon–Fri 9am–6pm, Sat & Sun 10am–5.30pm; Oct–March Mon–Fri 9.30am–5pm, Sat & Sun 10am–5.30pm; ☎ 04 90 54 34 39, ⓦ lesbauxdeprovence.com).

ACCOMMODATION AND EATING

Hostellerie de la Reine Jeanne ☎ 04 90 54 32 06, ⓦ la-reinejeanne.com. The village's one moderately priced hotel, near the tourist office. Very friendly staff, simple rooms with views of the citadel, a variably priced *plat du jour*, and fish and meat dishes in the €20–25 bracket. Closed mid-Jan to mid-Feb. €59

★ **Oustau de Baumanière** ☎ 04 90 54 33 07, ⓦ oustau debaumaniere.com. Among the many luxurious options in the countryside near Les Baux, this spectacularly situated complex, immediately west of the village and stretching from below the castle rock up to the former quarries, ranks very high indeed. Accommodation of varying styles, from opulently traditional to much more contemporary, is offered in villas and buildings old and new, and there are three pools, two restaurants and a spa. Past guests have included Queen Elizabeth II. *Menus* in its most renowned restaurant, in the original hotel, start at €95 for lunch, €135 for dinner. Closed Nov–Feb, except Christmas. €338

Le Prince Noir Rue de l'Orme ☎ 04 90 54 39 57, ⓦ leprincenoir.com. An eccentric B&B in the home of an artist, in the uppermost house in the village, and which only rents three rooms: choose between a comfortable bedroom or the two luxurious suites; two-night minimum stay. Room €104; suites €153

Les Variétés 29 rue du Trencat ☎ 04 90 54 55 88, ⓦ le-varietes-aux-baux-de-provence.business.site. The village's best-value restaurant, open in the daytime only, has a lovely interior courtyard and sells elaborate salads for around €15, and tapenades and gazpacho for around €10. March–Sept Mon, Tues & Thurs–Sun 11.30am–4pm.

St-Rémy-de-Provence

The dreamy, little-changed community of **ST-RÉMY-DE-PROVENCE**, where Van Gogh sought psychiatric help and painted some of his most lyrical works, nestles against the northern base of the Alpilles, 30km from both Arles and Avignon. St-Rémy is a beautiful spot, centring on a charmingly low-key old town, the **vieille ville**, that's an enchanting tangle of narrow lanes and ancient alleyways lined with stately residences and interspersed with peaceful little squares. While it only takes a few minutes to walk from one side to the other along its main east–west axis, **rue Carnot**, it's worth exploring every nook and cranny. Despite the presence of boutiques, restaurants and a couple of cafés, the core remains surprisingly sleepy. Most commercial activity takes place instead along the busy boulevard that loops around the original walls, named Boulevard Gambetta on the north side and Boulevard Victor-Hugo on the south.

Musée des Alpilles

Place Favier • May–Sept Tues–Sun 10am–6pm; Oct–April Tues–Sat 1–5.30pm • €5 • ☎ 04 90 92 68 24

Housed in the Renaissance Hôtel Mistral de Mondragon, halfway along rue Carnot in the old town, the **Musée des Alpilles** offers an interesting overview of St-Rémy and the surrounding region. As well as a relief model of the Alpilles hills, it holds sections on folklore, festivities and traditional crafts, with an exhibit on cicadas, a symbol of Provence associated with author Frédéric Mistral. Local archeological finds are displayed in the Hôtel de Sade alongside.

Musée Estrine

8 rue Lucien Estrine • March & Nov Tues–Sun 2–5.30pm; April & Oct Tues & Thurs–Sun 10am–noon & 2–6pm, Wed 10am–6pm; May, June & Sept Tues–Sun 10am–6pm; July & Aug Tues–Sun 10am–6.30pm • €7 • ☎ 04 90 92 34 72, ⓦ musee-estrine.fr

The chief focus in the **Musée Estrine**, which occupies an eighteenth-century townhouse, is on Vincent van Gogh's one-year sojourn in St-Rémy (see page 96). A lyrical film, in French only, relates his paintings to the local landscape and flora, and a few display panels recount familiar details of the artist's life. The steep admission fee is only really worth paying if the current temporary exhibition sounds interesting, however.

NOSTRADAMUS IN ST-RÉMY

Were famed astrologer **Michel de Nostradamus** somehow to return to St-Remy, he would of course not be the slightest bit surprised to find that the house on rue Hoche where he was born on December 14, 1503, is still standing (though not open to visitors). Educated as a physician, Nostradamus first received recognition for his innovative treatment of plague victims. Only in later life did his interest in astrology and the occult lead to the publication of **The Prophecies of Michel Nostradamus**, a collection of 942 prophetic quatrains. Fearing persecution should the authorities fully understand his predictions, he deliberately wrote in an obscure and cryptic style. The end result was some extremely ambiguous French verse, which has since been the subject of numerous forgeries, urban legends and off-the-wall interpretations. Events he's been credited with predicting include the rise of Napoleon and Hitler, the Great Fire of London and the 9/11 attacks. Whether or not he foresaw the future, his success as a writer remains undisputed: the prophecies, now known as *Centuries*, have been in print since its first publication in 1551. Neither was Nostradamus himself persecuted; by the time he died in 1566, he had become Physician-in-Ordinary to King Charles IX.

2

St-Paul-de-Mausole

Av Vincent-van-Gogh, 1600m south of central St-Rémy • Daily: April–Sept 9.30am–7pm; Oct–March 10.15am–noon 1–5.15pm; last admission 30–45min before closing • €6 • ☎ 04 90 92 77 00, ⓦ saintpauldemausole.fr

The former monastery of **St-Paul-de-Mausole**, where **Vincent van Gogh** was a voluntary psychiatric patient between May 8, 1889, and May 16, 1890, is a twenty-minute walk from St-Rémy's old town. It's only 100m east of the main road south, across from Les Antiques (see below), though for a more peaceful stroll you may prefer to follow avenues Pierre-Barbier and Marie-Gasquet. Placards along this route, marked out as the "Promenade dans l'Univers de Van Gogh", show where he painted some of the 150 canvases he produced during the year, including *La Route aux Cyprès* and *Les Blés Verts*. Sadly it's characterized by suburban villas rather than sweeping vistas these days.

Visiting St-Paul-de-Mausole itself is a profoundly moving experience. Amazingly, it's still a psychiatric hospital, and although tourists are kept clear of the active area, you get a real sense of its ongoing work. Displays in the church and cloisters contrast Van Gogh's diagnosis and treatment with modern-day practices, and you can see a mock-up of his former room and walk in the glorious gardens, planted with lavender and poppies. Far from being kept under lock and key, Vincent was allowed to wander around the town and Alpilles, so long as he stayed within an hour's walk of the hospital. Art therapy forms a major component of current treatment here, and patients' work is on sale in the on-site shop.

Les Antiques

Rte des Baux-de-Provence, 1500m south of central St-Rémy • 24hr access • Free, car parking €2.80 (shared with Glanum)

Beside the main road south from St-Rémy, across from St-Paul-de-Mausole, an open patch of ground holds two Roman monuments, jointly known as **Les Antiques**, which originally marked the entrance to the town of Glanum. One is a triumphal arch celebrating the Roman conquest of Marseille, the other a well-preserved mausoleum thought to commemorate two grandsons of Augustus. Both display intricate patterning and a typically harmonious Roman sense of proportion.

Glanum

Rte des Baux-de-Provence, 1600m south of central St-Rémy • April–Sept daily 9.30am–6pm; Oct–March Tues–Sun 10am–5pm • €8, car parking €4 • ⓦ site-glanum.fr

The impressive ancient settlement of **Glanum** was dug from the alluvial deposits at the foot of the Alpilles. This site originally held a Neolithic homestead, before the Gallo-

2

THE FESTIVALS OF ST-RÉMY

The ideal time to visit St-Rémy is for one of Provence's most vibrant traditional festivals, the **Fête de Transhumance** on Whit Monday, when a flock of four thousand sheep, accompanied by goats, rams and donkeys, makes a tour of the town before being packed off to the Alps for the summer. The other major highlight in the busy local calendar is the **Carreto Ramado** on August 15, a harvest thanksgiving procession in which more than fifty mighty horses are harnessed together to haul a colossal floral float through the streets. There's also a pagan rather than workers' **Mayday** celebration, with donkey-drawn floral floats on which people play fifes and tambourines.

Greeks, probably from Massalia (Marseille), built a city here between the second and first centuries BC. Then the Gallo-Romans constructed yet another town, which lasted until the third century AD.

A footpath drops from the **visitor centre**, where models depict the site in different eras, to run through the centre of the ruins. While maps and captions line the way, getting to grips with Glanum is far from easy. Not only were the later buildings moulded on to the earlier ones, but there was also a fashion, around the time of Christ, for an archaic Hellenistic style. Greek levels can be most readily distinguished from the Roman by the stones: the earlier civilization used massive hewn rocks, as opposed to the smaller, more precisely shaped stones preferred by the Romans.

At the site's southern end, where it narrows into a ravine, a Greek edifice stands around the **spring** that made this location so desirable. Steps lead down to a pool, with a slab above for the libations of those too sick to descend. An inscription records that Agrippa restored it in 27 BC, and dedicated it to Valetudo, the Roman goddess of health. **Altars** to Hercules remain in evidence, however, while traces of a prehistoric settlement survive up the hill to the west. The Gallo-Romans directed the water through canals to heat houses and, of course, to the **baths** that lie near the site entrance. There are superb sculptures on the Roman **Temples Geminées** (twin temples), as well as fragments of mosaics, fountains of both periods and first-storey walls and columns.

ARRIVAL AND INFORMATION   ST-RÉMY-DE-PROVENCE

By bus The main bus stop is in place de la République, on the eastern edge of the old town.
Destinations Arles (3 daily; 44 min); Avignon (every 30min; 47min); Cavaillon (3 daily Mon–Sat; 35min).
Tourist office Place Jean-Jaurès, just south of the old town (mid-April to June & Sept to mid-Oct Mon–Sat 9.15am–12.30pm & 2–6.30pm, Sun 10am–12.30pm; July & Aug

Mon–Sat 9.15am–6.30pm, Sun 10am–5pm; mid-Oct to mid-April Mon–Sat 9.15am–12.30pm & 2–5.30pm; ☎04 90 92 05 22, ⓦsaintremy-de-provence.com).
Bike rental Telecycles will deliver anywhere in the area (from €20/day; ☎04 90 92 83 15, ⓦtelecycles-location. com).

ACCOMMODATION

Canto Cigalo 8a chemin de Canto Cigalo ☎04 90 92 14 28, ⓦcantocigalo.com. Very nice, peaceful country-villa hotel beside the canal, a 20min walk southeast of town, with good-sized rooms, some with a/c, and plenty of shabby-chic quilts, plus a pool and plenty of outdoor space. **€84**
Gounod 18 place de la République ☎04 90 92 06 14, ⓦhotel-gounod.com. Comfortable central hotel, where the ornately decorated rooms in the main villa combine antique furnishings with bright modern linens and musical notation murals in tribute to the eponymous composer; there's also a modern annex, plus a swimming pool. Rates include breakfast. Closed Feb & March. **€119**

★ **Hôtel du Soleil** 35 av Pasteur ☎04 90 92 00 63, ⓦhotelsoleil.com. Very welcoming hotel, set back from the main road 350m south of the centre towards Glanum, with a pool, private parking and a bar (but no restaurant). Pleasant, spacious rooms plus three self-contained apartments. Doubles **€99**; apartments **€152**
Sommeil des Fées 4 rue de 8 Mai 1945 ☎04 90 92 17 66, ⓦangesetfees-stremy.com. Five arty, minimalist, en-suite rooms in an unbeatable old-town location, above the recommended *Cuisine des Anges* restaurant, which serves a good €32 dinner *menu*. Nominally this is a B&B, but the (included) breakfast is self-service, and there's little

personal contact. €70

★ **Sous les Figuiers** 3 av Taillandier ⊙ 04 32 60 15 40, ⓦ hotelsouslesfiguiers.com. Gorgeous place just north of the old town, run by a creative photographer and painter team. Of the fourteen well-appointed rooms, the finest eleven are more expensive, with their own private garden terraces; there are no TVs, but there's a swimming pool and an on-site artist's studio (art classes available). Closed mid-Jan to mid-March. €109

CAMPSITES

Mas de Nicolas Av Plaisance du Touch ⊙ 04 90 92 27 05, ⓦ camping-masdenicolas.com. Spacious, well-shaded

four-star municipal site with its own pool, 800m from the centre on a turning off the route de Mollèges. Closed mid-Oct to mid-March. €47.20

Monplaisir Chemin Monplaisir ⊙ 04 90 92 22 70, ⓦ camping-monplaisir.fr. Family-run, five-acre, two-star campsite, 1km northwest of town along the rte de Maillane, with a pool and snack facilities. Closed late Oct to early March. €41

Pegomas 3 av Jean-Moulin ⊙ 04 90 92 01 21, ⓦ camping pegomas.com. The nearest site to the town centre, this three-star option, 1km east towards Cavaillon, has a pool, a bar and a small shop. Closed late Oct to mid-March. €36.50

EATING AND DRINKING

St-Rémy abounds in **brasseries** and **restaurants**, both within the old town (along rue Carnot in particular), and along the surrounding boulevards. It's also a great place to shop for picnic food and deli items, with **markets** on Wednesday morning in the old town, and on Saturday in place de la Mairie. The liveliest **bars** line the peripheral boulevards, especially Bd Gambetta.

L'Aile ou la Cuisse 5 rue de la Commune ⊙ 06 12 13 40 40, ⓦ restaurantlaileoulacuisse.com. Very romantic, upscale restaurant in the old town. The changing €37 dinner *menu* features succulent fish and meat specials, but doesn't include their signature whole roasted (small) chicken, which costs €24.90 à la carte. They also have a deli selling posh picnic items and delectable jams and olive oils. April to mid-Nov Mon–Wed noon–2pm & 7–9pm, Thurs & Fri noon–2pm & 7.30–9pm, Sat noon–2pm & 7.30–9.30pm, Sun noon–2.30pm & 7–9pm; mid-Nov to March Wed noon–2pm & 7–9pm, Thurs & Fri noon–2pm & 7.30–9pm, Sat noon–2pm & 7.30–9.15pm, Sun noon–2.30pm.

La Cantina 18 bd Victor Hugo ⊙ 04 90 90 90 60,

ⓦ lacantinasaintremy.com. Deliciously authentic and great value pizzeria with a colourful interior and a range of combinations both with and without tomato, most priced in the €14–15 bracket. Tues–Sun noon–2.30pm & 7–10pm.

L'Estagnol 16 bd Victor-Hugo ⊙ 04 90 92 05 95, ⓦ restaurant-lestagnol.com. Peaceful, elegant restaurant, just off the southern boulevard; pass through an inconspicuous archway to reach its light-filled dining room or the lovely garden beyond. An array of tapas (€10–15) includes Spanish standbys like *patatas bravas* and *pimientos del padron* as well as more traditional Provençal dishes and even Asian flavours, which are carried over into the seafood-heavy mains. Lunch *formule* €16. Tues–Sun noon–2pm & 7.15–9.30pm.

Gus 31 bd Victor Hugo ⊙ 04 90 90 27 61, ⓦ gussa intremy.com. Very popular and highly regarded restaurant in the old town specialising in seafood and sushi, and ranging from modest servings of Fine de Claire oysters (€10–15) to heaped mixed platters (€27–54). Tues–Sun noon–2.30pm & 7.30–10.30pm.

La Petite Crau

The plain known as **La Petite Crau**, stretching north from the Alpilles to the confluence of the Rhône and the Durance, is today richly cultivated, with cherries and peaches as its main crops. Once, however, this was a swampy wasteland, the only extensive bit of solid ground being the rocky outcrop of **La Montagnette**, which runs parallel to the Rhône for 10km. Villages are few and far between, built on the scattered bases of rock and often retaining their medieval elements of fortified walls and churches and tangled narrow streets. This is the Provence that inspired **Frédéric Mistral** and Vincent van Gogh. Although La Montagnette is lovely **walking** country, fire risk precludes access between July and mid-September.

Châteaurenard

Halfway between St-Rémy and Avignon, the main town in La Petite Crau, **CHÂTEAURENARD**, is dominated by the two remaining towers of its Romanesque and Gothic medieval **castle** (May–Sept Tues–Sat 10am–noon & 2.30–6.30pm, Sun

2.30–6.30pm; Oct–April daily except Fri 3–5pm; €4), described by Frédéric Mistral as "twin horns on the forehead of a hill". The castle's **Tour du Griffon** offers fabulous views across La Petite Crau to the Alpilles and La Montagnette.

Down below, daily life centres on a busy little loop road that circles the hill. The place is packed out every Sunday, when it hosts a massive wholesale fruit and vegetable market.

Maillane

The poet **Frédéric Mistral** was born in 1830 in **MAILLANE**, 7km northwest of St-Rémy, and buried there in 1914. Primarily responsible for the early twentieth-century revival of all things Provençal, he won the Nobel Prize for Literature in 1904. The house where he lived from 1876 onwards has been preserved intact as the **Museon Mistral**, 11 rue Lamartine (late March to mid-Oct Tues–Sun 9.30–noon & 1.30–6pm; €4; ☎04 90 95 84 19, ⓦ museemistral.fr). La Petite Crau was Mistral's "sacred triangle", and its customs and legends were a great source of inspiration to him.

Barbentane

In **BARBENTANE**, 8km northeast of Boulbon at the northern edge of La Montagnette, the fourteenth-century **Tour Anglica** keeps watch on the confluence of the Rhône and Durance. The town has two medieval gateways and a beautifully arcaded Renaissance building, the **Maison des Chevaliers**, plus a much more recent **château**, a rather gorgeous Italianate affair that's no longer open to visitors.

INFORMATION
LA PETITE CRAU

Tourist office 11 cours Carnot, Châteaurenard (June & Sept Mon–Sat 9am–noon & 2–5.45pm; July & Aug Mon–Sat 9am–noon & 2–5.45pm, Sun 10am–noon; Oct–May Mon–Sat 10am–noon & 2–5.45pm; ☎04 90 24 25 50, ⓦ chateaurenard.com).

ACCOMMODATION AND EATING

Auberge de Noves Domaine du Devès, Noves ☎04 90 24 28 28, ⓦ aubergedenoves.com. Set in extensive gardens, just west of Noves and 5km east of Châteaurenard, this beautiful farmhouse hotel boasts huge rooms, many with outdoor patios, sumptuous 1980s-style fixtures and fittings, and impeccable service. Charmingly, they classify the cheapest category as "*agréable*". Its restaurant (closed Jan to mid-Feb and Mon, Tues & Wed Oct–May) serves such delicacies as foie gras, snails, truffles and lobster, coupled with fine wines. **€225**
★ **Bastide de Boulbon** Rue de l'Hôtel de Ville, Boulbon ☎04 90 93 11 11, ⓦ labastidedeboulbon.com. Peaceful country-house hotel, set in pleasant grounds a short walk north of the village centre, and run by a friendly and obliging Belgian couple. The rooms are large and very tastefully furnished, while the evening-only dining room (closed Tues & Sat) serves romantic candlelit dinners at €37 for a three-course *menu*. Look for good-value multiday deals. Closed mid-Oct to early April. **€165**

Castel Mouisson Chemin sous les Roches, Barbentane ☎04 90 95 51 17, ⓦ hotel-castelmouisson.com. Tranquil, nicely renovated family-run hotel, a 15min walk south of the centre, with a pleasant garden and pool, but no restaurant. The cheapest rooms are very small. Closed mid-Oct to Feb. **€69**
Le Central 27 cours Carnot, Châteaurenard ☎04 90 94 10 90, ⓦ hotel-lecentral.com. Thirteen sizeable en-suite rooms above a very popular pavement brasserie. While not a place to base yourself for any length of time, it makes an inexpensive overnight stop. *Menus* €15.50 (lunch only) and €27; restaurant closed Sun. **€40**

CAMPSITE

Le Pilon d'Agel 2943 chemin du Pilon d'Agel, 3km southwest of Noves ☎04 90 95 16 23, ⓦ pilondagel.com. Good-value campsite with a pool, restaurant, kids' playground and access for people with disabilities. Open all year. **€24**

Tarascon and around

Dozing gently beside the Rhône, halfway between Arles and Avignon, the 2000-year-old city of **TARASCON** feels far removed from the tourist mainstream. Despite its imposing

2

castle, the old town centre is, apart from the arcaded rue des Halles and a couple of busy commercial alleyways, not only largely residential but also quite faded and run-down. That makes Tarascon a relaxing, atmospheric place to spend a day or two – just don't expect much drama or excitement, unless you're here for June's spectacular **carnival** in honour of the city's namesake, the amphibious monster known as the **Tarasque** (see page 103).

Château du Roi René

April daily 9.30am–5.30pm; May–Sept daily 9.30am–6.30pm; Oct–March 9.30am–12.30pm & 2–5pm • €7.50 • ☎ 04 90 91 01 93, ⓦ chateau.tarascon.fr

A vast and impregnable mass of stone, Tarascon's riverfront **Château du Roi René** has been beautifully restored to its defensive fifteenth-century stance. Those of its towers that face the enemy across the Rhône are square, while those at the back are round. Nowhere on the exterior is there any hint of softness. The interior, however, is another matter. Work on the castle began in 1400, and from 1447 onwards it was remodelled as a residence for King René of Provence, with all the luxury that the period permitted. The mullioned windows and vaulted ceilings of the royal apartments and the spiral staircase that overlook the **cour d'honneur** all have graceful Gothic lines, and assorted wooden ceilings are painted with monsters and similar medieval motifs.

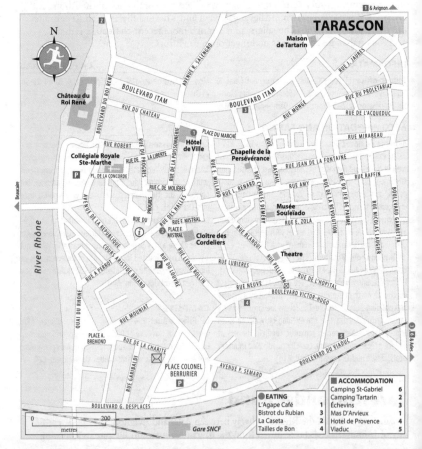

TARASCON

EATING
L'Agape Café	1
Bistrot du Rubian	3
La Caseta	2
Tailles de Bon	4

ACCOMMODATION
Camping St-Gabriel	6
Camping Tartarin	2
Échevins	3
Mas D'Arvieux	1
Hotel de Provence	4
Viaduc	5

THE TARASQUE AND TARTARIN

On the last full weekend of June, the **Tarasque**, a 6m-long dragon-like creature with glaring eyes and shark-sized teeth, storms the streets of Tarascon, its tail swishing back and forth to the screaming delight of children. The monster is said to have clambered repeatedly out of the Rhône, gobbling people and destroying the ditches and dams of the Camargue with its crocodile-like tail, until it was captured during the first century by St Martha, the sister of Mary Magdalene. It serves as a reminder of natural catastrophe, in particular floods, kept at bay here by the sometimes unreliable drainage ditches and walls. The weekend-long festivities involve public balls, bull and equestrian events, and a firework and music finale.

Another larger-than-life character – **Tartarin**, the nineteenth-century literary creation of Alphonse Daudet – is celebrated at the same time, even though his antics have left Tarascon synonymous with foolishness in French eyes. Making himself out to be a great adventurer, Tartarin scales Mont Blanc, hunts leopards in Algeria and brings back exotic trees for his garden at 55bis boulevard Itam. The address is real, though it's not open to the public or interesting to see from the outside. During the Tarasque procession, a local man, chosen for his fat-bellied figure, strolls through the town as Tartarin.

Most of the castle's huge echoing chambers are now devoid of historic furnishing. One is kitted out as an apothecary, but the rest are used for imaginative, child-friendly exhibitions that change each year, and generally play on familiar, fairy-tale images of medieval life. More authentic relics do survive here and there, as with the graffiti carvings of boats in the **Salles des Gallères**, left by captive Catalan sailors during the fifteenth century.

Visits end with a climb up to the **roof**, from which revolutionaries and counter-revolutionaries alike were thrown in the 1790s. It's now an extensive open platform, offering wonderful views in all directions.

Collégiale Royale Ste-Marthe

Place de la Concorde • Daily 8am–7pm • Free • ☏ 04 90 91 09 50

The **Collégiale Royale Ste-Marthe**, across the street from the castle, is noteworthy for its Romanesque core, the crypt of which contains the tomb of Martha, the saint credited with saving the town from the Tarasque monster (see page 103). St Martha also appears in the paintings by Nicolas Mignard and Vien that decorate its Gothic interior, along with works by Pierre Parrocel and Van Loo.

Musée Souleïado

39 rue Charles Deméry • Mon–Sat 10am–7pm • €7 • ☏ 04 90 91 08 80, ⓦ souleiado-lemusee.com

The fascinating and delightful **Musée Souleïado**, on a quiet back street, pays tribute to the family business that revived Tarascon's 200-year-old **textile** tradition of making brightly coloured, patterned, printed fabrics. Having closed down in the 1980s, the Souleïado company started operations again in 2009, and these days its dazzling creations are sold all over Provence.

Space not being at a premium, the museum spreads through a rambling old complex that also holds a courtyard tearoom. Huge rooms of artfully arranged mannequins dressed in contemporary prints are interspersed with historic exhibits, including the eighteenth-century wood blocks from which many of the *indiennage* (Indian-style) patterns are still made, and roots, shells and flowers used to create natural dyes.

A boutique sells the current Souleïado range. Men's shirts (as modelled by Picasso) typically cost around €150, and women's gear a little more, but there are discounts.

ARRIVAL AND INFORMATION
TARASCON

By train Trains from Arles (10 daily; 8–23min), Avignon (every 30min–1hr 20min; 12min) and Marseille airport (5 direct daily; 45–50min) arrive at Tarascon's *gare SNCF* on Bd Gustave-Desplaces, immediately south of the centre.
By bus Buses run from outside the *gare SNCF* to Arles (roughly hourly; 20min).

Tourist office 62 rue des Halles (June & Sept Mon–Sat 9am–12.30pm & 2–6pm; July & Aug Mon–Sat 9am–12.30pm & 2–6pm, Sun 9am–1pm; Oct–May Mon–Sat 9am–12.30pm & 2–5.30pm; ☎04 90 91 03 52, ⊛office-de-tourisme-de-tarascon.business.site).

ACCOMMODATION
SEE MAP PAGE 102

Échevins 26 bd Itam ☎04 90 91 01 70, ⊛hotel-echevins.com. Handsome old townhouse, where the large and simply designed bedrooms represent decent value for money. The attractive *Mistral* restaurant spreads across a terrace downstairs. Closed Nov–Easter. **€71**
Mas D'Arvieux Route d'Avignon, 5km northeast of Tarascon on the D970 ☎04 90 90 78 77, ⊛arvieux-provence.com. Lovely old farmhouse built on the site of a Roman villa and once frequented by Frederic Mistral, with five B&B rooms, two self-contained boutique cottages (one converted from a pigeon loft) and a studio. Doubles **€145**; cottage **€125**; studio **€120**
Hotel de Provence 7 bd Victor-Hugo ☎04 90 91 06 43, ⊛hotel-provence-tarascon.com. Lovely little hotel, with enthusiastic management. Half of the large, comfortably furnished, a/c rooms open on to a garden courtyard, the rest to a sleepy back street. No restaurant. **€71**

Viaduc 9 bd du Viaduc ☎04 90 91 16 67, ⊛hotel-duviaduc.com. Simple budget hotel near the station, with sixteen plain but clean and comfortable en-suite rooms, plus free parking but no restaurant. **€67**

CAMPSITES
Camping St-Gabriel Mas Ginoux, rte de Fontvieille ☎04 90 91 19 83, ⊛campingsaintgabriel.com. Small, verdant three-star site with a pool, focused around an old coaching inn 5km southeast of town off the Arles road. Closed mid-Nov to mid-March. **€24**
Camping Tartarin Rte de Vallabrègues ☎04 90 91 01 46, ⊛campingtartarin.fr. Well-shaded two-star site right beside the river, just north of the château, with its own bar, restaurant, pool and even mini-golf. Closed mid-Nov to mid-March. **€24.20**

EATING
SEE MAP PAGE 102

L'Agape Café 13 Place du Marché ☎04 90 93 88 87. Cheap and cheerful café serving more than serviceable steak and chips, panini, brochettes, salads and the like with a smile. The three-course lunch *formule* is fantastic value at only €10.90. Tues–Sat 7.30am–6pm.
Bistrot du Rubian 5 rue de Charretiers ☎04 90 99 87 58, ⊛bistrot-du-rubian.fr. Though a bit of a trek from the town centre, this place has a loyal local following and an extensive repertoire of traditional cuisine including lengthy salad and omelette lists. *Menus* €13.80 and €19. Mon noon–2pm, Tues–Thurs noon–2pm & 7–9.30pm, Fri & Sat noon–2pm & 7–10pm.
La Caseta 45 rue des Halles ☎04 90 91 07 81. This central, somewhat down-at-heel bistro in the old-town

lanes, always lively at lunchtime, nevertheless uses fresh market produce to create large salads and daily *plats* for €12–16, and also serves Spanish-style tapas. Mon 8am–3pm, Tues 6am–3pm & 7–10pm, Wed 8am–3pm & 7–10pm, Thurs–Sat 8am–3pm & 4–11pm.
Tailles de Bon 1 place Colonel Berrurier ☎04 90 91 47 74. Elegant lounge-style restaurant-bar, previously known as *Méo Bistro*, and located near the *gare SNCF*. The main selling point is a graded system of portion sizes: *prudent*, *raisonnable* and *généreux* (roughly €10–20), which means less of their bull fillets, parsley-cooked cuttlefish, duck and so on goes to waste. Mon 11.30am–2.30pm, Wed–Sun 11.30am–10pm.

Beaucaire

Facing Tarascon from the west bank of the Rhône, over in Languedoc, the rival town of **BEAUCAIRE** boasts a better-preserved maze of medieval streets. A more pleasant place simply to stroll around, it has even fewer facilities, and the only real sight is its ruined **castle**. Although it's just 1km away, walking across the busy river bridge can be an unappealing prospect in the heat of summer.

Château Royale de Beaucaire

Northern end of the old town • **Castle and gardens** April to mid-Oct Wed–Sat 9.30am–6pm; July & Aug 9.30am–6pm; mid-Oct to March Wed–Sat 10am–5pm • Free • **Musée Auguste-Jacquet** April to mid-Oct Wed–Sat 9.30am–12.30pm & 2–6pm; July & Aug

Wed–Sun 9.30am–12.30pm & 2–6pm; mid-Oct to March Wed–Sat 2–5pm; Nov–March Mon & Wed–Fri 10am–noon & 2–5pm, Sat & Sun 9am–noon & 2–5pm • €5 • ☎ 04 66 59 90 07

To reach the **Château Royale de Beaucaire**, thread your way north through the old town to the hill at the far end, atop which its one surviving tower far surmounts those of Tarascon across the river. Visitors are permitted to ramble freely around the ruins and **gardens**, with only the old dungeon off-limits. A modern building, by the gardens houses the **Musée Auguste-Jacquet**, which has a small but interesting collection of Roman and other archeological relics, and displays documents relating to Beaucaire's medieval fair, once among the largest in Europe.

2

INFORMATION

Tourist office 8 rue Victor Hugo (April–Sept daily 9.30am–12.30pm & 2–6pm; Oct–March Tues–Sat 9.30am–12.30pm & 2–5pm; ☎ 04 66 59 26 57, ⓦ provence-camargue-tourisme.com).

EATING

Le Vintage 30 quai du Général-de-Gaulle ☎ 09 67 10 94 27. The most stylish of several café-restaurants lined up facing the canal not far from the bridge, with variously priced, traditionally French/Provençal two-course lunch *formules* in the €15–25 range. Tues–Sun noon–10.30pm.

The Camargue

Spreading across the Rhône delta, and defined by the Petit Rhône to the west, the Grand Rhône to the east, and the Mediterranean to the south, the drained, ditched and protected land known as the **CAMARGUE** is utterly distinct from the rest of Provence. With land, lagoon and sea sharing the same horizontal plain, its shimmering horizons appear infinite.

The whole of the Camargue is a **Parc Naturel Régional**, which sets out to maintain an equilibrium between tourism, agriculture, industry and hunting on the one hand, and the indigenous ecosystems on the other. When the Romans arrived, the northern part of the Camargue was a forest; they felled the trees to build ships, then grew wheat. These days, especially since the northern marshes were drained and re-irrigated with fresh water after World War II, the main crop is **rice**. There's still some wheat, though, along with **vines** – which, because their stems were underwater, survived the nineteenth-century phylloxera infestation that devastated every other wine-producing region in France – as well as fruit orchards and the ubiquitous rapeseed.

The Camargue is effectively split into two separate sections by the large **Étang de Vaccarès** at its heart – a lagoon that, along with its islands, is out of bounds to tourists. Most visitors focus their attention on the western half, which is home to the Provençal Camargue's one sizeable town, lively **Les Saintes-Maries-de-la-Mer**, and also most of its commercial attractions, such as wildlife parks and activity operators. For drivers who don't mind scurrying, though, it is possible to take a quick look at both the western and eastern portions within a single day-trip.

There's no **ideal season** to visit. **Mosquitoes** can make the Camargue unbearable from March to November; they're less prevalent beside the sea, but elsewhere you'll need serious chemical weaponry. Biting flies are also a problem, as are the strong autumn and winter **winds**, which make cycling hard despite the flat terrain. And finally, the summer can be so hot and humid that the slightest movement is an effort.

The western Camargue: the road to Saintes-Maries

The **western** side of the Camargue is busy all summer with tourists, who flock down its main artery, the D570, towards **Les Saintes-Maries-de-la-Mer**. For a true sense of what

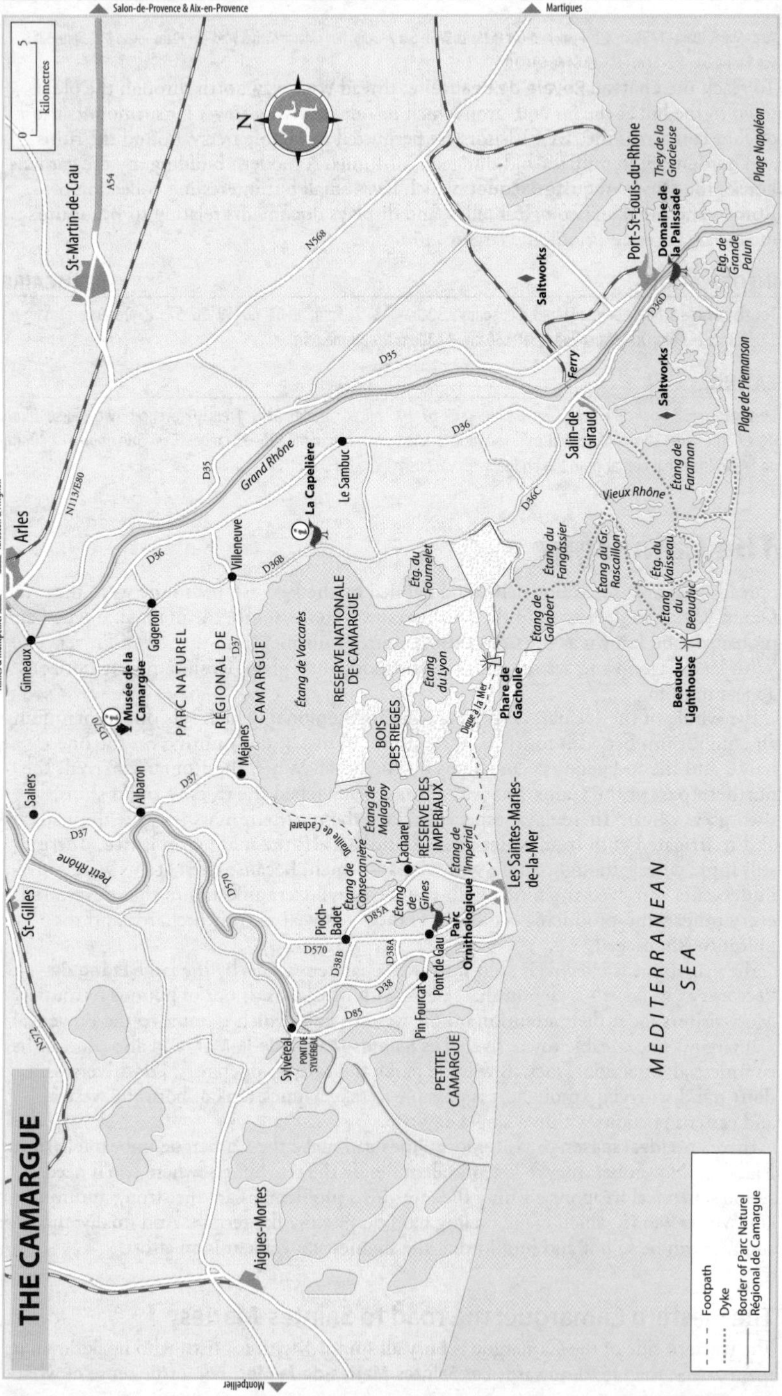
THE CAMARGUE
Salon-de-Provence & Aix-en-Provence
Martigues
Tarascon & Avignon
Nîmes & Montpellier
Montpellier
0 kilometres 5
N
St-Martin-de-Crau
A54
N568
N113/E80
Arles
Gimeaux
Saliers
St-Gilles
Petit Rhône
Grand Rhône
Musée de la Camargue
Gageron
Albaron
Méjanes
Villeneuve
La Capelière
Le Sambuc
Salin-de Giraud
Port-St-Louis-du-Rhône
Domaine de la Palissade
They de la Gracieuse
Plage Napoléon
Etg. de Grande Palun
Saltworks
Saltworks
Ferry
Plage de Piemanson
Vieux Rhône
Etang de Faraman
Etang du Gr. Rascaillon
Etg. du Vaisseau
Etang du Beauduc
Beauduc Lighthouse
Etang du Fangassier
Etang de Galabert
Etg. du Fournelet
Phare de Gacholle
Digue à la Mer
PARC NATUREL
RÉGIONAL DE
CAMARGUE
Étang de Vaccarès
RESERVE NATIONALE DE CAMARGUE
BOIS DES RIEGES
Etang du Lyon
Etang de Malagroy
RESERVE DES IMPERIAUX
Etang de l'Impérial
Draille de Cacharel
Étang de Consecanière
Cacharel
Étang de Gines
Pioch-Badet
Parc Ornithologique
Pont de Gau
Pin Fourcat
Les Saintes-Maries-de-la-Mer
Sylvéréal
PONT DE SYLVÉRÉAL
PETITE CAMARGUE
Aigues-Mortes
N572
MEDITERRANEAN SEA
D35
D36
D36B
D36C
D36D
D37
D570
D85
D85A
D38
D38A
D38B
Footpath
Dyke
Border of Parc Naturel Régional de Camargue

makes the region special, take the time to explore the marshes and dunes en route, or follow the waterfront nature trails.

Musée de la Camargue

D 570, 10km southwest of Arles • Daily: April–Sept 9am–12.30pm & 1–6pm; Oct–March 10am–12.30pm & 1–5pm • €5 • ☎ 04 90 97 10 82, ⓦ museedelacamargue.com

The main **information centre** for the Camargue lies in a working roadside farm, 10km out of Arles towards Saintes-Maries. The adjoining **Musée de la Camargue** documents the history, traditions and livelihoods of the Camarguais people, with particular emphasis on rice, wine and bulls. Overall, the displays are excellent, albeit largely in French only, and include films, photos and some rather extraordinary 3D images from the 1930s.

A 3.5km **trail** loops through the adjacent farmland, giving the opportunity to see how the traditional Provençal farmhouse (*mas*) related to the land around it. An observation tower at the end offers an overview of the mingled marsh and farmlands.

Draille de Cacharel

The best **hiking trail** in the western Camargue follows a drover's path, the 9km **Draille de Cacharel**, between Cacharel, 4km north of Saintes-Maries, and the D37 just north of Méjanes. Running initially along the narrow strip that separates two lesser lagoons, the Étang de Consecanière and the Étang de l'Impérial, it then skirts the western shoreline of the Étang de Vaccarès.

Parc Ornithologique de Pont de Gau

Pont de Gau, 4km north of Les Saintes-Maries-de-la-Mer • Daily: April–Sept 9am–7pm; Oct–March 10am–6pm • €7.50 • ☎ 04 90 97 82 62, ⓦ parcornithologique.com

For anyone interested in seeing the birdlife of the Camargue, the engrossing **Parc Ornithologique de Pont de Gau** makes a great stop before you reach Saintes-Maries. Clearly marked paths lead around and over three separate lagoons in a 30-acre marsh, making birdwatching easy. Much of it is closer to the main road than you might prefer, but that doesn't seem to bother the abundant flamingos, and for that matter you may well see horses wading knee-deep in water too. Signs and information are plentiful,

---

TOURS AND ACTIVITIES IN THE CAMARGUE

Many visitors explore the Camargue entirely by car, simply admiring the view as they drive to and from Les Saintes-Maries-de-la-Mer. You'll get a much better sense of the region, however, by signing up for the many **outdoor activities** on offer.

Canoeing and kayaking Canoe and kayak lessons are available from Kayak Vert in Sylvéréal, beside the Petit-Rhône on the D38C, 17km northwest of Saintes-Maries (☎ 04 66 73 57 17, ⓦ kayakvert-camargue.fr) and cost from €10 for 1hr.

Cycling Bikes can be rented in Saintes-Maries from Le Vélociste, place Mireille (☎ 04 90 97 83 26, ⓦ .levelociste. fr) and Le Vélo Saintois, 19 rue de la République (☎ 04 90 97 74 56, ⓦ levelosaintois.camargue.fr). In Salin-de-Giraud, try Mas St Bertrand (☎ 04 42 48 80 69, ⓦ mas-saint-bertrand.com). All charge around €15/day.

Horseriding Around thirty Camargue farms offer horseriding, costing from around €25/hr up to €100/day. Recommended options along the rte de Arles,

which leads into Saintes-Maries, include Chez Elise (☎ 06 24 28 30 82, ⓦ elise-camargue.fr); you can find full lists at ⓦ saintesmaries.com and ⓦ promenades-a-cheval.com.

Jeep safaris Camargue Safari (☎ 04 90 93 60 31, ⓦ safari-4x4-gallon.camargue.fr) offers jeep safaris from Arles or Saintes-Maries, from €36 for 3hr.

River trips The paddle-steamer *Le Tiki III* offers 90min trips from the mouth of the Petit Rhône, 2.5km west of Saintes-Maries (mid-March to Oct 1–5 daily; €12; ☎ 04 90 97 81 68, ⓦ tiki3.fr), and so too does the *Camargue* from the port in Saintes-Maries, just west of the tourist office (mid-March to mid-Oct 1–4 daily; €12; ☎ 06 17 95 81 96, ⓦ bateau-camargue.com).

2

BULLS, BIRDS AND BEAVERS: CAMARGUAIS WILDLIFE

The Camargue is a treasure-trove of bird and animal species, both wild and domestic. Neither of its most famous denizens – its **bulls** and **white horses** – are truly wild, though both roam in semi-liberty. A distinct breed of unknown origin, the Camargue horse is born dark brown or black, and turns white around its fourth year. It is never stabled, surviving the humid heat of summer and the wind-racked winter cold outdoors.

The **gardians** (herdsmen) who ride the horses are similarly hardy. Still conforming, to some extent, to the popular cowboy myth, they play a major role in preserving Camarguais traditions. Their traditional homes, or *cabanes*, are thatched, windowless one-storey structures, with bulls' horns over the door to ward off evil spirits. Throughout the summer, the *gardians* are kept busy, with spectacles involving bulls and horses in every village arena; winter is a good deal harder. Although ever fewer Camarguais property owners can afford the extravagant use of land required to rear bulls, an estimated 2500 *gardians* remain active, of whom around ten percent are women.

Camargue **wildlife** ranges from wild boars, beavers and badgers, tree frogs, water snakes and pond turtles, to marsh and seabirds, waterfowl and birds of prey. The best time for **birdwatching** is the mating season, from April to June. Of the region's fifty thousand or so **flamingos**, ten thousand remain during the winter (Oct–March) when the rest migrate to north Africa. Born grey, they turn pink aged between 4 and 7. Their tendency to trample young rice shoots in the paddy fields is an ongoing problem for park managers.

The rich **flora** of the park includes reeds, wild irises, tamarisk, wild rosemary and juniper trees. Growing up to 6m tall, the junipers form the Bois des Rièges on the islands between the Étang de Vaccarès and the sea, part of the central **National Reserve** to which access is restricted to those with professional research credentials.

while some of the less easily spotted species, such as owls and vultures, are kept in aviaries. In a rather cruel twist, wild cranes choose to nest on the roofs above their caged *confrères*.

Les Saintes-Maries-de-la-Mer

Although most visitors to the Camargue head straight to **LES SAINTES-MARIES-DE-LA-MER**, 37km southwest of Arles, this commercialized seaside village has much more in common with France's other Mediterranean beach resorts than with the wild and empty land that surrounds it. That said, Saintes-Maries is an attractive little place. A line of **beaches**, sculpted into little crescents by stone breakwaters and busy with bathers and windsurfers in summer, stretches east from its central core of white-painted, orange-tiled houses, while the pleasure **port** to the west offers boat trips to the lagoons and fishing expeditions. With its seafront *arène* staging bullfights, cavalcades and other entertainment, and musicians playing in the street, a stay of a night or two can be fun.

Église des Saintes-Maries

Place Jean XXIII • Rooftop Daily: July & Aug Mon–Sat 10am–sunset, Sun 1pm–sunset; March–June & Sept to mid-Nov Mon–Sat 10am–noon & 2–5pm, Sun 2–5pm • €3

The spider's-web tangle of streets and alleyways at the heart of old Saintes-Maries, filled with everything from supermarkets and delis to bucket-and-spade shops and art galleries, opens out into spacious squares on all sides of the grey-gold Romanesque **Église des Saintes-Maries**. Fortified in the fourteenth century in response to frequent attacks by pirates, the church has beautifully pure lines and fabulous acoustics. During the era of Saracen raids, the high, barrel-vaulted interior provided shelter for all the villagers; it even holds its own freshwater well.

At the far end, steps lead down to the low **crypt**, where the tinselled, sequined and dark-skinned statue of Sarah (see page 111) is surrounded by candles. The naïve ex voto paintings behind glass upstairs were dedicated in thanks for blessings and cures. Access to certain areas has been restricted since precious relics were stolen in 2009.

Although you can't climb to the top of the tower, you can pay to scramble onto and over the church **roof**, for great views across town.

ARRIVAL AND INFORMATION LES SAINTES-MARIES-DE-LA-MER

By bus Buses from Arles (5 daily; 50min) arrive at the north end of place Mireille, 400m short of the sea.

By car In summer, the paid parking spots along the seafront tend to fill up early; there's usually more space in the free car parks that face the lagoon inland, not far west.

Tourist office 5 av Van-Gogh, on the seafront (daily: Jan, Feb, March, Nov & Dec 9am–5pm; April–June & Sept 9am–7pm; July & Aug 9am–8pm; Oct 9am–6pm; ☏ 04 90 97 82 55, ⓦ saintesmaries.com).

ACCOMMODATION

Between April and October, and especially during the Romany festival (see page 111), book **accommodation** well in advance. Don't worry if you can't find a room in Saintes-Maries itself; appealing options are scattered throughout the nearby marshlands.

LES SAINTES-MARIES-DE-LA-MER

Bleu Marine 15 av du Dr-Cambon ☏ 04 90 97 77 00, ⓦ hotel-bleu-marine.com. Friendly, peaceful retreat at the western end of town, with simple but immaculate rooms, a nice pool and easy parking. **€94**

Camping Le Clos du Rhône Rte d'Aigues-Mortes, 800m west of Saintes-Maries ☏ 04 90 97 85 99, ⓦ camping-leclos.fr. Busy four-star site at the mouth of the Petit Rhône, not far west of central Saintes-Maries along an easy seaside path, and offering a pool, laundry and shop, but not all that much shade. Closed early Nov to March. **€31**

Le Dauphin Bleu/La Brise de Mer 31 av G-Leroy ☏ 04 90 97 80 21, ⓦ hoteldauphinbleu.fr. White-painted hotel-restaurant, on the seafront a few hundred metres from the centre at the east end of the beach road. The nicest of the rather austere rooms have balconies overlooking the

sea, and cost around €40 extra. **€99.10**

★ **Mangio Fango** Rte d'Arles ☏ 04 90 97 80 56, ⓦ hotel mangiofango.com. Tranquil farmhouse, over-looking the Étang des Launes 600m north of central Saintes-Maries. Stylish, comfortable rooms (ask for one at the back, with a balcony), pricey restaurant, spa and steam room, and a pool surrounded by lush foliage. Closed Dec–March, except Christmas & New Year. **€165**

Méditerranée 4 av F-Mistral ☏ 04 90 97 82 09, ⓦ hotel-mediterranee.org. Decked out in jolly flowers, this simple budget hotel has pretty Provençal-style rooms and is on the main restaurant street, seconds from the sea. The cheapest rooms share toilets, and there are some well-priced four-person options. **€58**

OUT OF TOWN

Cacharel Rte de Cacharel, 4km north of Saintes-Maries on the D85A ☏ 04 90 97 95 44, ⓦ hotel-cacharel.com. Sixteen luxurious rooms in an old farm, with open fires to warm you in winter, a pool to cool off in summer, and horseriding available year-round. No restaurant. **€151**

Flamant Rose D37, Albaron, 23km north of Saintes-

HIKING THE DIGUE À LA MER

Anyone wanting to drive between the western and eastern halves of the Camargue has to trace a long curve around the inland end of its central lagoon. For **hikers**, however, there's a much more direct route: the **Digue à la Mer**. Constructed late in the nineteenth century to stop the incursions of seawater that had previously precluded agriculture in the southern Camargue, this low-lying sea dyke stretches across the mouth of the Rhône. Walking the rough, narrow track along the top is a wonderful wilderness experience, with open water to either side, flamingos and other birds flying overhead, and the wind roaring in your ears.

While the dyke itself is roughly 12km long, connecting trails at either end make it possible to walk the whole way between Les Saintes-Maries-de-la-Mer and Salin-de-Giraud. The entire 31km route takes around six hours, with no facilities en route, so most visitors content themselves with an out-and-back return trip from one end or the other. The **Phare de la Gacholle** lighthouse in the middle, open as an information centre on summer weekends, makes an obvious turnaround point (July & Aug Sat & Sun 11am–5pm).

If you're coming from **Saintes-Maries**, simply head 1km east of town, staying close to the sea; the trail starts from the Plage de l'Est. Coming from **Salin-de-Giraud**, you can park beside the Étang de Fangassier at trailheads either 7km west or 13km northwest of town.

Maries and 14km southwest of Arles ☎ 04 90 97 10 18, ⓦ leflamantrose.com. Pleasant, inexpensive roadside hotel-restaurant, where the brightly decorated rooms have been attractively updated even if the common areas are rather plain. The dining room (closed Tues & Wed Sept–March) serves good *menus* from €26. **€70**

Hostellerie du Pont de Gau Rte d'Arles, Pont de Gau, 4km north of Saintes-Maries ☎ 04 9049 96 99, ⓦ pontdegau.com. Simple but pleasant motel-like rooms alongside a really excellent restaurant near the Parc Ornithologique. Closed Jan to mid-Feb. **€86**

Lou Mas Doù Juge Rte du Bac-du-Sauvage, Pin Fourcat, 10km northwest of Saintes-Maries ☎ 04 66 73 51 45, ⓦ loumasdoujuge.com. Attractive B&B on a working farm out in the countryside beside the Petit Rhône. Simple, old-fashioned rooms, with evening meal and horseriding available if requested in advance. **€95**

Mas de Pioch Pioch-Badet, 10km north of Saintes-Maries ☎ 04 90 97 50 06, ⓦ masdepioch.com. Great-value B&B in a converted nineteenth-century hunting inn just off the main road, offering large rooms, capable of sleeping up to six, plus a pool. Book well in advance. **€55**

EATING AND DRINKING

Of a summer evening, Saintes-Maries gets very lively indeed, with flamenco or gypsy-jazz guitarists and buskers everywhere. **Camarguais specialities** include *tellines*, tiny, shiny shellfish served with garlic mayonnaise; *gardianne de taureau*, bull's meat cooked in wine, vegetables and Provençal herbs; eels from the Vaccarès; rice, asparagus and wild duck; and *poutargue des Saintes-Maries*, a mullet roe dish. The town **market** is held on place des Gitans every Monday and Friday.

Brûleur de Loups 67 av Gilbert-Leroy ☎ 04 90 97 83 31, ⓦ lebruleurdeloups.com. Smart, all-round Provençal restaurant, facing the beach; its terrace is among the few places hereabouts where you get a sea view while you eat. Seafood-rich *menus* from €22, with a nice €26.50 option. Mon & Thurs–Sun noon–2.30pm & 7–10pm, Tues noon–2pm; closed mid-Nov to mid-Dec.

El Campo 13 rue Victor Hugo ☎ 04 90 97 84 11, ⓦ restaurant-elcampo.com. Locally famous gypsy restaurant with regular and authentic live flamenco (complete with dancing), and heaped plates of Spanish and Provençal cuisine. Paella and a free glass of sangria €14. Surcharge of €3.50–5 on flamenco nights. Mon & Tues 5.30–10pm, Wed–Sun noon–2pm & 7–10pm; closed Jan.

Les Embruns 11 av de la Plage ☎ 04 90 97 92 40. Welcoming brasserie on the seafront road, just 100m from the old-town bustle, with a street terrace and a bright, modern dining room. Seafood specials include fresh oysters or mussels, a daily catch for well under €20 and stuffed squid, and there's a simple but good-value €19.50 *menu*. Daily 8am–11pm.

The eastern Camargue

Cut through by the final canalized stretch of the Grand Rhône, the **eastern** side of the Camargue is much less visited than its counterpart to the west. Less agricultural and more industrial, it nonetheless holds its share of wildlife reserves and tranquil refuges, as well as the sleepy village of **Salin-de-Giraud**.

The chief business here is the production of **salt**. Evaporation was originally undertaken by the Romans in the first century AD; the Camargue now holds one of the world's largest saltworks, and the saltpans and pyramids add an extra-terrestrial feel.

Although the D35 and D36 are the principal access routes, respectively paralleling the east and west banks of the Grand Rhône all the way from Arles, the **D36B** along the eastern edge of the Étang de Vaccarès is more scenic.

La Capelière

D36B, 23km south of Arles and 19km northwest of Salin-de-Giraud • April–Sept daily 9am–1pm & 2–6pm; Oct–March daily (except Tues) 9am–1pm & 2–5pm • €3 • ☎ 04 90 97 00 97

La Capelière, the main information centre for the eastern Camargue, holds rather faded displays on local wildlife and how to see it. Outside, a short but excellent 1.5km initiation trail circles a small lagoon, with superb **birdwatching** opportunities along the way from camouflaged hides equipped with telescopes.

Salin-de-Giraud

SALIN-DE-GIRAUD, just west of the Grand Rhône in the Camargue's southeastern corner, is an industrial village, based on the saltworks company and its chemical

THE LEGEND OF SARAH AND THE GYPSY FESTIVALS

Les Saintes-Maries-de-la-Mer is famous for its annual **gypsy festival**, on May 24–25, when Romanies celebrate **Sarah**, their patron saint. According to legend, **Mary Jacobé**, the aunt of Jesus, and **Mary Salomé**, the mother of two Apostles, along with Mary Magdalene and various other New Testament characters, were driven out of Palestine and put on a boat without sails and oars.

The boat drifted effortlessly to an island in the mouth of the Rhône where the Egyptian sun god Ra was worshipped. Here Mary Jacobé, Mary Salomé and **Sarah**, their servant, set about spreading the Gospel, while the rest headed off for other parts of Provence. Sarah, who was herself Egyptian, was according to some accounts the former wife of Pontius Pilate, repudiated for becoming a Christian.

In 1448 the women's relics were "discovered" in the fortress **church** of Saintes-Maries on the former island, around the time that the Romanies were migrating into the area from the Balkans and from Spain. It's thought the two strands may have been reunited in Provence.

The gypsies adopted Sarah as their patron saint – the French word for gypsies, *gitans*, originated as a corruption of "Egyptian" – and have been making their **pilgrimage** to Saintes-Maries since the sixteenth century. It's a time for weddings and baptisms as well as music, dancing and fervent religious activities. On May 24, after Mass, the shrines of the saints are lowered from the high chapel to an altar where the faithful stretch out their arms to touch them. Then the statue of Sarah is carried by the gypsies to the sea. On the following day the statues of Mary Jacobé and Mary Salomé, sitting in a wooden boat, follow the same route, accompanied by mounted *gardians* in full Camargue dress and Arlesians in traditional costume. The bishop then blesses the sea, the Camargue, the pilgrims and the gypsies, from a fishing boat, before the procession returns to the church with much bell-ringing, guitar-playing, tambourine-bashing and singing. Another ceremony in the afternoon sees the shrines lifted back up to their chapel.

A separate pilgrimage, on the Sunday closest to October 22, is dedicated solely to Mary Jacobé and Mary Salomé; the gypsies do not participate.

factory; its tall, terraced workers' houses were built on a strict grid pattern during the Second Empire.

There's nothing really to see in Salin, nor even a town centre. For a look at the lunar landscape of the **salt piles** – the saltworks cover 110 square kilometres and produce a million tonnes a year for domestic use and export – visit the viewing point a short way south, just off the D36D. A regular **ferry**, the *Bac de Barcarin*, crosses the Grand Rhône from Salin (daily every 15min; vehicles €6); at **Port-St-Louis-du-Rhône**, just downstream, the rice and salt of the Camargue are loaded onto ships, and a small fishing fleet is still active.

Domaine de la Palissade

Just off the D36D, 7km southeast of Salin-de-Giraud • Feb & Nov Wed–Sun 9am–5pm; March to mid-June & mid-Sept to Oct daily 9am–5pm; mid-June to mid-Sept daily 9am–6pm • €3 • ☎ 04 42 86 81 28, ⊕ palissade.fr

Beside the Grand Rhône, just short of the sea, the **Domaine de la Palissade** is a natural sanctuary devoted to the fauna and flora of its neighbouring lagoons. As well as a small and rather dull visitor centre, it holds a good 9km **trail** past duck and flamingo nesting grounds, as well as a shorter 1.5km path. In summer, one- or two-hour guided **horseback** tours, by advance reservation only, cost €19 and €32 per person respectively.

ACCOMMODATION AND EATING   THE EASTERN CAMARGUE

Mas de Peint Le Sambuc, 13km north of Salin-de-Giraud on the D36 ☎ 04 90 97 20 62, ⊕ masdepeint. com. The most luxurious accommodation in the eastern Camargue. Centred on a seventeenth-century farmhouse, this rural getaway offers opulent rooms and a gourmet restaurant. Closed mid-Nov to mid-April. **€275**

Saladelles 4 rue des Arènes, Salin-de-Giraud ☎ 04 42 86 83 87, ⊕ hotel-restaurant-lessaladelles.fr. Nice little family-run hotel, with simple but bargain-priced rooms – the cheapest share bathrooms and WCs – and a popular restaurant on its shaded terrace that serves *menus* from €16 for lunch, €27 for dinner. **€37**

Avignon and the Vaucluse

114 Avignon

128 Villeneuve-lès-Avignon

131 Pont du Gard

131 Châteauneuf-du-Pape

133 Orange

136 Vaison-la-Romaine

138 The Dentelles

140 Mont Ventoux and
around

144 Carpentras

146 Pernes-les-Fontaines

147 Venasque

147 L'Isle-sur-la-Sorgue

148 Fontaine-de-Vaucluse

150 Cavaillon

Avignon and the Vaucluse

Above its confluence with the Durance, the Rhône served for centuries as the frontier between Provence and France. On the Provençal side Avignon, the magnificent city of the popes, squared off against heavily fortified Villeneuve-lès-Avignon, across the river in France. Those two towns, with their historic monuments and shared summer festival, are now the region's most popular visitor destinations. To the east and north, however, what's now the Vaucluse *département* is also home to enticing smaller towns such as Orange and Vaison-la-Romaine, each boasting remarkable Roman remains, while the Pont du Gard, an astonishing and sublimely elegant Roman aqueduct-bridge, lies a short way west of the Rhône.

3

The **villages** and **countryside** of the Vaucluse also hold great appeal. Just north of Avignon, the vineyards of **Châteauneuf-du-Pape** – whose rich red wines rank among the most famous, and delicious, in the world – adorn a rich green sweep of wine-producing country that stretches northeast past the jagged limestone hills of the **Dentelles** to the bare, imposing slopes of **Mont Ventoux**, a legendary challenge for cyclists both professional and amateur. Gorgeous little hill towns and rural communities that make wonderful overnight stops include **Séguret**, **Pernes-les-Fontaines** and **Fontaine-de-Vaucluse**, home to the mysterious source of the River Sorgue.

As an area with a distinct identity, the Vaucluse dates back only as far as the Revolution. It was created to tidy up assorted bits and pieces: the Papal Enclave of the Comtat Venaisson that became part of France in 1791, the principality of Orange won by Louis XIV in 1713, and sundry parts of Provence that didn't fit happily into the initial three *départements* drawn up in 1791. That said, its **boundaries** are basically natural – the River Rhône to the west, Mont Ventoux to the east, the northern boundary of the huge Vaucluse plateau to the north, and the River Durance to the south.

Avignon

Capital of the Catholic Church during the early Middle Ages and for centuries one of the major artistic centres of France, **AVIGNON** remains an unmissable destination. And indeed, during the **Festival d'Avignon** in July, it becomes *the* place to be in Provence.

Bounded to both north and west by a ninety-degree bend in the Rhône river, central Avignon is encircled by low medieval **walls**. With all the gates and towers restored, the ramparts give cohesion to the historic core, marking it off from the sprawling modern city beyond. Despite their menacing crenellations, however, the walls were never a formidable defence, even when girded by a now-vanished moat. The major monuments occupy a compact quarter near the river, just beyond the principal **place de l'Horloge**, which itself stands at the northern end of rue de la République, the chief axis of the old town.

Avignon can be dauntingly crowded, and stiflingly hot, in summer. But it's worth persevering, not simply for the colossal **Palais des Papes** and the fine crop of museums and ancient churches, but also for the sheer life and energy that throbs through its lanes and alleyways.

FONTAINE-DE-VAUCLUSE

Highlights

❶ Palais des Papes Avignon's most spectacular monument makes a superb backdrop for the Festival d'Avignon, held each July. See page 117

❷ Villeneuve-lès-Avignon More laidback than its bigger cousin across the river, Villeneuve has no shortage of impressive sights. See page 128

❸ Pont du Gard For almost two thousand years, this magnificent triple-tiered aqueduct-bridge has spanned the Gard river. See page 131

❹ Vaison's haute ville Across the river from the Roman ruins of Vaison's town centre, visitors can climb through quiet medieval streets to reach a ruined clifftop castle. See page 137

❺ Les Dentelles This region of jagged limestone pinnacles is home to some exceptional and varied wines, as well as plenty of good hiking trails. See page 138

❻ Mont Ventoux Western Provence's highest summit, a fabled target for amateur and professional cyclists alike, offers unrivalled panoramas. See page 140

❼ Fontaine-de-Vaucluse Enjoy a ravishing riverside stroll to reach the dramatic and intriguing source of the River Sorgue. See page 148

HIGHLIGHTS ARE MARKED ON THE MAP ON PAGE 116

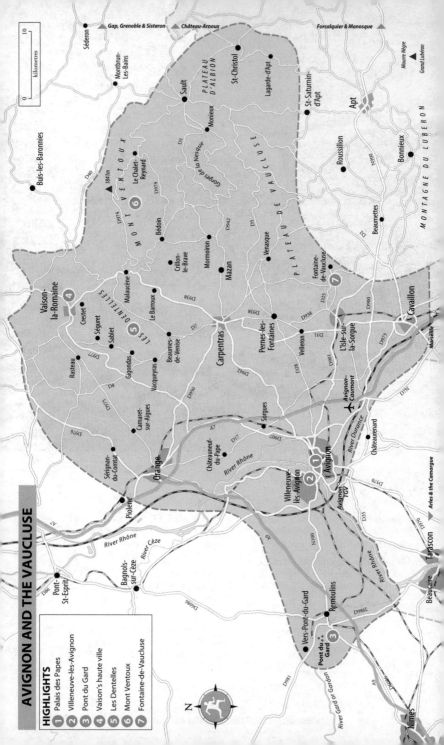

AVIGNON AND THE VAUCLUSE

HIGHLIGHTS

1. Palais des Papes
2. Villeneuve-lès-Avignon
3. Pont du Gard
4. Vaison's haute ville
5. Les Dentelles
6. Mont Ventoux
7. Fontaine-de-Vaucluse

0 — 10 kilometres

Gap, Grenoble & Sisteron   Château-Arnoux   Forcalquier & Manosque

Séderon
Montbrun-les-Bains
Buis-les-Baronnies
Mont Nègre
Grand Luberon
MONTAGNE DU LUBERON
St-Christol
Sault
Plateau d'Albion
Monieux
Lagarde-d'Apt
St-Saturnin-d'Apt
Apt
Roussillon
Bonnieux
Beaumettes
1841m
MONT VENTOUX
Le Chalet-Reynard
Gorges de la Nesque
Bédoin
6
Crillon-le-Brave
Mormoiron
Mazan
Venasque
Plateau de Vaucluse
Fontaine-de-Vaucluse
7
Vaison-la-Romaine
4
Crestet
Malaucène
Le Barroux
LES DENTELLES
5
Séguret
Sablet
Beaumes-de-Venise
Carpentras
Pernes-les-Fontaines
Velleron
L'Isle-sur-la-Sorgue
Cavaillon
Marseille
Rasteau
Gigondas
Vacqueyras
Camaret-sur-Aigues
Sorgues
Avignon-Caumont
Châteaurenard
Sérignan-du-Comtat
Orange
Châteauneuf-du-Pape
River Rhône
Avignon
1
Villeneuve-lès-Avignon
2
Avignon TGV
River Durance
Arles & the Camargue
Piolenc
Pont-St-Esprit
Bagnols-sur-Cèze
River Cèze
River Rhône
Remoulins
Châteaurenard
Tarascon
Beaucaire
Vers-Pont-du-Gard
Pont du Gard
3
River Gard or Gardon
Nîmes

N

POPES AND ANTIPOPES – THE INTRIGUING HISTORY OF AVIGNON

The first **pope** to come to Avignon, **Clement V**, was invited by the astute King Philippe le Bel ("the Good") in 1309, ostensibly to protect him from impending anarchy in Rome. In reality, Philip saw a chance to extend his power by keeping the pope in Provence, during what came to be known as the Church's "Babylonian captivity". Clement's successor, **Jean XXII**, had previously been bishop of Avignon, so he reinstalled himself quite happily in the episcopal palace. The next Supreme Pontiff, **Benedict XII**, acceded in 1334; accepting the impossibility of returning to Rome, he demolished the bishop's palace to replace it with an austere fortress, now known as the **Vieux Palais**.

Gregory XI finally moved the Holy See back to Rome in 1378, but that didn't mark the end of the papacy in Avignon. After Gregory's death in Rome, dissident local cardinals elected their own pope here, provoking the Western Schism, a ruthless struggle to control the Church's wealth. That lasted until **Benedict XIII** – now officially considered to have been an **antipope** – fled into self-exile near Valencia in 1409. It was Benedict who built Avignon's still-surviving walls in 1403, when under siege by French forces loyal to Rome. Avignon itself remained papal property until the Revolution.

As home to one of the richest courts in Europe, fourteenth-century Avignon attracted princes, dignitaries, poets and raiders, who arrived to beg from, rob, extort and entertain the popes. According to Petrarch, the overcrowded, plague-ridden papal entourage was "a sewer where all the filth of the universe has gathered".

Palais des Papes

Daily: March 9am–6.30pm; April–June, Sept & Oct 9am–7pm; July 9am–8pm; Aug 9am–8.30pm; Nov–Feb 9.30am–5.45pm; last ticket 1hr before closing • €12, €14.50 with Pont St-Bénézet (see page 120); interactive "Histopad" guide included in ticket price • ☎ 04 32 74 32 74, ⓦ www.palais-des-papes.com

Perched at the north end of the walled city, overlooking the Rhône, Avignon's vast **Palais des Papes** soars above the cobbled place du Palais. Although the palace was built primarily as a fortress, and equipped with massive stone vaults, battlements and sluices for pouring hot oil on attackers, the two pointed towers that hover above its gate are incongruously graceful. Inside, so little remains of its original decoration and furnishings that you could easily be misled into imagining that all the popes and their retinues were pious and austere. There's hardly a whiff of the corruption and decadence of fat, feuding cardinals and their mistresses; the thronging purveyors of jewels, velvet and furs; the musicians, chefs and painters competing for patronage; and the riotous banquets and corridor schemings.

Vieux Palais

Visits to the Palais des Papes follow a linear course; everything is clearly labelled, but the suggested route is far from clear unless you use your Histopad (see above). It begins in the original **Vieux Palais**, constructed from 1335 onwards, during the papacy of Benedict XII. The first building you enter, the **Pope's Tower** – also known as the Tower of Angels – is accessed via the vaulted **Treasury**, where the Church's deeds and finances were handled. Four hidden holes in the floor of the smaller downstairs room, now covered by glass, held the papal gold and jewels. Stairs lead down from here to the **Papal Gardens**, currently under archeological investigation.

The **Chambre du Camérier** or Chamberlain's Quarters, off the Jesus Hall upstairs from the Treasury, holds further cunningly concealed storage cavities. In the adjoining **Papal Vestiary**, the pope had a small library and would dress before receiving sovereigns and ambassadors in the **Consistoire** of the Vieux Palais, on the other side of the Jesus Hall.

On the floor above, the **kitchen** offers powerful testimony to the scale of papal gluttony, with its square walls becoming an octagonal chimney piece for a vast central cooking fire. Major feasts were held in the **Grand Tinel**, or dining room, where only the pope was allowed to wield a knife. Gutted by fire in 1413, it was known as the **Burned**

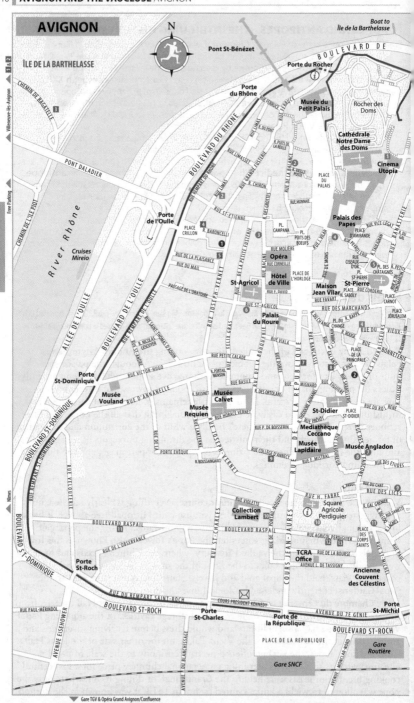

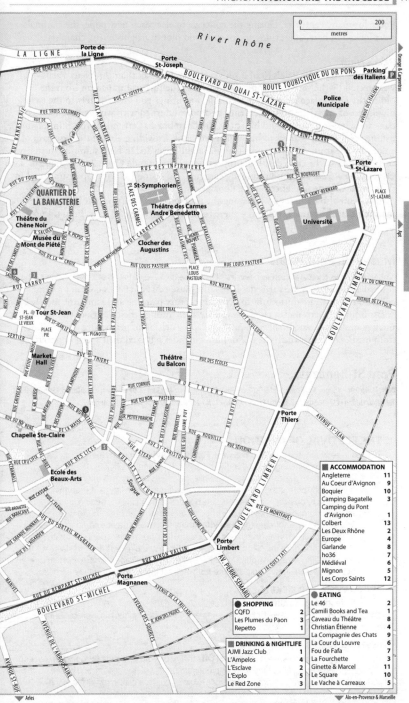

ACCOMMODATION

Angleterre	11
Au Coeur d'Avignon	9
Boquier	10
Camping Bagatelle	3
Camping du Pont d'Avignon	1
Colbert	13
Les Deux Rhône	2
Europe	4
Garlande	8
ho36	7
Médiéval	6
Mignon	5
Les Corps Saints	12

EATING

Le 46	2
Camili Books and Tea	1
Caveau du Théâtre	8
Christian Étienne	4
La Compagnie des Chats	9
La Cour du Louvre	6
Fou de Fafa	7
La Fourchette	3
Ginette & Marcel	11
Le Square	10
Le Vache à Carreaux	5

SHOPPING

CQFD	2
Les Plumes du Paon	3
Repetto	1

DRINKING & NIGHTLIFE

AJMI Jazz Club	1
L'Ampelos	4
L'Esclave	2
L'Explo	5
Le Red Zone	3

3

Room for many centuries. During the conclave to elect each new pope, the cardinals were locked in here, adjourning to conspire and plot in neighbouring chambers.

Palais Neuf

Despite its name, the **Palais Neuf** is only a few years newer than the Vieux Palais – it was erected by the very next Pope, Clement VI. The physical transition from the old to the new palace is now imperceptible, but brings you immediately to the twin highlights of any visit. Both Clement's **bedroom**, adorned with wonderful entwined oak- and vine-leaf motifs, and his study, the **Chambre du Cerf**, filled with hunting and fishing scenes, bear witness to his secular concerns. Providing almost the first dash of colour on the tour, the two rooms get unbearably crowded in high summer. Austerity then resumes in the cathedral-like proportions of the **Grande Chapelle**, or **Chapelle Clementine** – 52m long and originally carpeted and festooned with tapestries – and in the similar **Grande Audience** on the floor below.

The circuit also includes a walk along the **roof terraces**. Don't put off by signs insisting that the terrace is closed – these refer to the terrace café only. Press on upwards to enjoy the tremendous views.

Musée du Petit Palais

Palais des Archevêques, place du Palais des Papes • Daily (except Tues) 10am–1pm & 2–6pm • Free • ☎ 04 90 86 44 58, ⓦ petit-palais.org

Immediately north of the Palais des Papes, the **Musée du Petit Palais** contains a vast collection of first-rate thirteenth- to fifteenth-century painting and sculpture, mostly by artists from northern Italian cities. As you advance through the collection, you can watch them grapple with, and finally conquer, the representation of perspective – a revolution from medieval art, in which the size of human figures reflected their social importance.

Pont St-Bénézet

Daily: March 9am–6.30pm; April–June, Sept & Oct 9am–7pm; July 9am–8pm; Aug 9am–8.30pm; Nov–Feb 9.30am–5.45pm; last ticket 1hr before closing • €5, €14.50 with Palais des Papes (see page 117) • ☎ 04 32 74 32 74, ⓦ avignon-pont.com

---

THE FESTIVAL OF AVIGNON

Starting in early July, the annual, three-week **Festival d'Avignon** focuses especially on theatre, while also featuring classical music, dance, lectures and exhibitions. The city's great buildings make a stunning setting, while the streets throng with bright-eyed performers eagerly promoting their shows. Everywhere stays open late, and everything from accommodation to obscure fringe events gets booked up very quickly; getting around or doing anything normal becomes virtually impossible.

Founded in 1947 by actor-director **Jean Vilar**, the festival hosts theatre companies from across Europe. Each year, one or two "associate artists" from other countries curate contemporary works from their land of origin. While big-name directors draw the largest crowds to the main venue, the Cour d'Honneur in the Palais des Papes, lesser-known troupes and directors also stage new works, and the festival spotlights a different culture each year.

PROGRAMME AND TICKETS

The main **festival programme** is usually available from the second week in May on ⓦ festival-avignon.com, while **tickets** go on sale in mid-June, and remain available until three hours before each performance.

FESTIVAL OFF

The fringe contingent known as the **Festival Off** (ⓦ avignonleoff.com) adds an additional element of craziness and magic, with a simultaneous programme of innovative, obscure and bizarre performances. A *Carte d'Abonnement Public* for €16 gives you thirty percent off all fringe shows.

Now a somewhat bizarre sight, merely jutting halfway out to the Île de Barthelasse, the twelfth-century **Pont St-Bénézet** originally stretched for 900m, following a sinuous course right across the island and all the way to Villeneuve. It was the only bridge to cross the Rhône between Lyon and the Mediterranean. A picturesque ruin since being destroyed yet again by a flood in 1668, with just four of its 22 arches surviving, the bridge is famous less for its truncated state than for being the **Pont d'Avignon** immortalized in the famous song *Sur le pont d'Avignon* ("… *l'on y danse, l'on y danse* …"). The song has existed in various forms for five centuries, but the words and tune we know today come from nineteenth-century French operettas. It's generally agreed the lyrics should really say "*Sous le pont*" (under the bridge) rather than "*Sur le pont*" (on the bridge); the reference is either to general revelry on the island on feast days, or to the thief and trickster clientele of a tavern there dancing with glee at the arrival of more potential victims.

The narrow bridge itself is open for visits. Displays beneath its landward end explain the history of both bridge – which may have been erected on the site of a larger Roman bridge by the eponymous Bénézet, who later became the patron saint of architects – and song. After that, you're free to walk to the end and back, and dance upon it too for that matter.

Rocher des Doms

Commanding lovely views from its hilltop position north of the Palais des Papes, down to the Pont St-Bénézet and across the river, the peaceful **Rocher des Doms** park is the best place in the city for a picnic. The steep climb up is rewarded with relaxing lawns, fountains and ducks, as well as a little café.

The **Cathédrale Notre Dame des Doms** (daily: July & Aug 7am–7pm; Sept–June 8am–6pm), immediately south of the park, is topped by an enormous gilded Virgin on its belfry. It might once have been a luminous Romanesque structure; sadly, though, its interior has had a bad attack of Baroque and the result is a stifling clutter.

Place de l'Horloge

Frenetically busy year-round, the café-lined **place de l'Horloge** holds Avignon's imposing **Hôtel de Ville** and **clock tower**, as well as the **Opéra**. Around the square, on rues de Mons, Molière and Corneille, famous faces appear in windows painted on the buildings. Many depict historical visitors to the city, who described the powerful impact of hearing over a hundred bells ring at once. On Sunday mornings – traffic lulls permitting – you can still hear myriad different peals from nearby churches, convents and chapels.

Palais du Roure

3 rue Collège du Roure • Tues–Sat 10am–1pm & 2–6pm, guided tour 11am • Free • ☎ 04 13 60 50 01

The beautiful fifteenth-century **Palais du Roure** stands just south of the place de l'Horloge. Originally home to a family of Florentine bankers, it's now a centre for Provençal culture. You can take a quick peek at its gateway and courtyard for free, or pay to wander through its ground floor, filled with portraits and antique furniture. Only if you coincide with each morning's guided tour, however, can you venture upstairs to see Provençal costumes, publications and presses, century-old photographs of the Camargue and an old stagecoach.

Maison Jean Vilar

8 rue de Mons • Daily: July 11am–8pm; Sept–June 11am–6pm; note that hours can vary, especially during the festival • Free • ☎ 04 90 86 59 64, ⓦ maisonjeanvilar.org

3

The seventeenth-century Hôtel de Crochans, east of the place de l'Horloge, is home to the **Maison Jean Vilar**. Named after the theatre director who set up the "Week of Dramatic Art" in 1947 – the forerunner of the Festival d'Avignon – it houses festival memorabilia, an excellent library dedicated to the performing arts, and recordings of everything from Stanislavski to the previous year's street theatre.

Quartier de la Banasterie

The **quartier de la Banasterie**, immediately east of the Palais des Papes and north of place Pie, dates almost entirely from the seventeenth and eighteenth centuries. With tourism largely kept in check, this remains an atmospheric and beautiful district, particularly at night. Its heavy wooden doors, with their highly sculptured lintels, today bear the nameplates of lawyers, psychiatrists and doctors. The tangle of tiny and largely pedestrianized streets between Banasterie and **place des Carmes** holds plenty of tempting café and restaurant stops.

3

Place Pie and around

Avignon's main **pedestrianized area** stretches between the chain-store blandness of rue de la République – south of the place de l'Horloge – and the amazing modern **market hall** on **place Pie**, covered in a living wall of greenery and active every morning except Monday. To the northwest is the Renaissance **church of St-Pierre** (Mon–Wed & Sun 10am–1pm, Thurs–Sat 10am–1pm & 2–6pm), with handsome doors sculpted in 1551, and an altarpiece from the same period.

South of place Pie, the **Chapelle Ste-Claire** is where the poet Petrarch first saw and fell in love with Laura, during the Good Friday service in 1327, as recorded in a note in his copy of Virgil. A little way east is the atmospheric **rue des Teinturiers**, a centre for calico printing during the eighteenth and nineteenth centuries. The cloth was washed in the Sorgue canal alongside, though the four mighty watermills that survive no longer turn.

Musée Angladon

5 rue Laboureur • April–Oct Tues–Sun 1–6pm; Nov–March Tues–Sat 1–6pm • €8 • ☎ 04 90 82 29 03, ⓦ angladon.com

The **Musée Angladon** displays what remains of the private art collection of Parisian *couturier* Jacques Doucet. While the older works are largely unexceptional, the superb contemporary collection includes Modigliani's *The Pink Blouse*, various Picassos, including a self-portrait from 1904, and Van Gogh's *The Railroad Cars*, his only Provençal painting on permanent display in the region.

Musée Lapidaire

27 rue de la République • Tues–Sun 10am–1pm & 2–6pm • Free • ☎ 04 90 84 75 38, ⓦ musee-lapidaire.org

The **Musée Lapidaire**, a former Baroque chapel also known as the Musée d'Archéologie or Galerie des Antiquités, is home to larger pieces from the archeological collection of its sister museum, the Musée Calvet (see below). Besides some stunning Greek urns and vases, it abounds in Roman and Gallo-Roman sarcophagi, and early renditions of the mythical Tarasque (see page 103).

Musée Requien

67 rue Joseph-Vernet • Tues–Sat 10am–1pm & 2–6pm • Free • ☎ 04 90 82 43 51, ⓦ museum-requien.org

Founded in the nineteenth century, and centring on an old-school collection of stuffed and fossilized natural-history specimens, the **Musée Requien** can be thoroughly inspected in the space of quarter of an hour. Its oldest exhibits, such as ancient trilobites, a huge tyrannosaurus skull and assorted Neanderthal bones, fit more comfortably with modern visitors than do its more recent stuffed tiger and wolf.

Musée Calvet

65 rue Joseph-Vernet • Daily except Tues 10am–1pm & 2–6pm • Free • ☎ 04 90 86 33 84, ⓦ musee-calvet.org

The excellent, airy **Musée Calvet** is housed in a lovely eighteenth-century palace. Highlights include Antonio Forbera's extraordinary *Le Chevalet du Peintre*, a trompe-l'oeil painting from 1686 depicting the artist's easel, complete with sketches and palette; a wonderful gallery of languorous nineteenth-century marble sculptures, among them Bosio's *Young Indian*; and works by Soutine, Manet and Joseph Vernet, as well as Jacques-Louis David's subtle, moving *Death of Joseph Barra*. Look out, too, for the easily missed Flemish room behind the ticket desk. There are also some much more ancient artefacts, including enigmatic stelae from the fourth century BC, carved with half-discernible faces, and assorted ancient Egyptian treasures.

Musée Vouland

17 rue Victor-Hugo • Tues–Sun 2–6pm • €6 • ☎ 04 90 86 03 79, ⓦ vouland.com

Near Porte St-Dominique on the west side of the walled city, the **Musée Vouland** is filled to bursting with the fittings, fixtures and furnishings enjoyed by French aristocrats both before and after the Revolution. It's laid out like a still-occupied house, with most of the contents barely labelled or railed off, and there's a certain pleasure in the playful juxtaposition of items from different eras.

Collection Lambert

5 rue Violette • July & Aug daily 11am–7pm; Sept–June Tues–Sun 11am–6pm • €10 • ☎ 04 90 16 56 20, ⓦ collectionlambert.fr

Avignon's major contemporary art gallery, the thoughtfully curated **Collection Lambert**, has been hugely expanded since collector Yvon Lambert donated his lovingly amassed artworks to the city in perpetuity in 2011. Its superb spaces are used to house large-scale temporary exhibitions, one of which each year is usually devoted to a specific contemporary artist, and to show off the results of previous such shows. The permanent display includes pieces created by Jean-Michel Basquiat for Lambert's Paris gallery in 1988, as well as works by Cy Twombly, Anselm Keifer and Roni Horn.

ARRIVAL AND DEPARTURE   **AVIGNON**

By car Driving into Avignon involves negotiating a nightmare of junctions and one-way roads. The cheapest and easiest parking options for day-trippers are two free, guarded car parks, connected with the town centre by free electric shuttle buses: Île Piot (daily 24hr), which is actually part of the Île de la Barthelasse between Avignon and Villeneuve, and Parking des Italiens (Mon–Sat 7.30am–8.30pm), beside the river immediately northeast of the old town. The oversubscribed parking spaces inside the city walls are expensive, starting at around €2/hr; check whether your hotel offers free or discounted parking.

By train Avignon's *gare SNCF* is just outside the walls south of the old city. The TGV station, 2km south of the city and served by high-speed trains en route between Paris and the Riviera, is linked by regular trains with the *gare SNCF* (5min), as well as frequent buses into town (every 20min; 40min; ⓦ tcra.fr). A taxi into town (call ☎ 04 90 82 20 20) can cost

€15 or more.

Destinations (gare SNCF) Arles (every 20min–1hr 50min; 16–19min); Carpentras (every 30min at peak times; 30min); Cavaillon (every 30min–1hr 50min at peak times; 34min); Lyon (up to every 6min at peak times; 1hr 40min–2hr 45min); Marseille (up to every 6min at peak times; 1hr 5min–1hr 55min); Orange (every 6–30min at peak times; 14–20min); Tarascon (roughly every 30min–1hr; 12min); Valence (roughly every 20–40min at peak times; 1hr 20min).

Destinations (gare TGV) Aix-en-Provence TGV (22 daily; 25min); Lille-Europe (roughly every 1–2hr; 4hr 9min–5hr 5min); London St Pancras (roughly hourly up till around 4pm; 5hr 5min–7hr 14min); Lyon TGV (8 daily; 50–53min); Marseille (every 9min–1hr 5min; 39min); Paris (14 daily direct; 2hr 40min); Paris CDG Airport (4 daily; 3hr 11min–3hr30min); Valence TGV (8 daily; 30–35min).

3

By bus Avignon's *gare routière* is alongside the *gare SNCF*, just outside the walls south of the old city; for timetables, visit ⓦ sudest-mobilites.fr and ⓦ cars-lieutaud.fr.

Destinations Aix-en-Provence (7 daily; 1hr 15min); Arles (3 daily; 1hr 5min); Carpentras (roughly every 30–45min; 35–45min); Cavaillon (4–5 daily; 35min–1hr); Digne (2 daily; 3hr–3hr 30min); L'Isle-sur-la-Sorgue (12 daily; 45min); Orange (every 30min–1hr; 1hr); St-Rémy (every 30min; 47min).

By plane Avignon-Caumont Airport, 8km southeast of the centre (☎ 04 90 81 51 51, ⓦ avignon.aeroport.fr), is connected with Birmingham and Southampton on Flybe (ⓦ flybe.com). It's connected to the town centre and *gare TGV* on bus #22 (€1.40).

GETTING AROUND

By bus The main TCRA local bus stops are on cours Président-Kennedy and outside Porte de l'Oulle facing the river (tickets €1.40 each; book of ten tickets €12.50; one-day pass €3.50; ⓦ tcra.fr).

By boat A free boat service crosses the river from east of Pont St-Bénézet to the Île de la Barthelasse, site of the city's campsites (mid-Feb to March & Oct–Dec Wed 2–5.15pm, Sat & Sun 10am–11.45pm & 2–5.15pm; April–June &

Sept daily 10am–12.15pm & 2–6.15pm; July & Aug daily 11am–8.45pm).

By bike Provence Bike, immediately east of the *gare SNCF* at 7 av St-Ruf (☎ 04 90 27 92 61, ⓦ provence-bike.com), rents bicycles, scooters and motorbikes.

By taxi There is a taxi rank on place Pie (☎ 04 90 82 20 20, ⓦ avignontaxis.fr).

INFORMATION AND TOURS

Tourist office 41 cours Jean-Jaurès, at the southern end of the city (April–Oct Mon–Sat 9am–6pm, Sun 10am–5pm; July daily 9am–7pm; August daily 9am–6pm; Nov–March Mon–Fri 9am–6pm, Sat 9am–5pm, Sun 10am–1pm school holidays only; ☎ 04 32 74 32 74, ⓦ avignon-tourisme.com).

Boat trips In summer, from a base just south of place

Crillon, Cruises Mireio (☎ 04 90 85 62 25, ⓦ mireio.net) offer various themed dinner cruises upstream towards Châteauneuf-du-Pape and downstream to Arles (from around €40/person, meal included), as well as four-day trips to the Camargue (from €650/person).

ACCOMMODATION   SEE MAP PAGE 118

Even outside festival time, when rates rise even higher than the typical high-season figures quoted here, finding a **room** in Avignon can be a problem: cheap hotels fill fast, so book in advance. **Villeneuve-lès-Avignon**, across the river, often has more availability. Between the two, the Île de la Barthelasse is an idyllic spot for **camping**. The tourist office keeps track of hotel vacancies.

Angleterre 29 bd Raspail ☎ 04 90 86 34 31, ⓦ hotel dangleterre.fr. Located in a quiet neighbourhood in the southwest corner of the old city, well away from night-time noise, this is a traditional hotel with plain, low-priced rooms, many of them very small but equipped with reasonable bathrooms. **€90**

Au Coeur d'Avignon 9 rue du collège d'Annecy ☎ 06 87 72 32 77, ⓦ aucoeurdavignon.com. Newly renovated *chambres d'hôtes* in an elegant seventeenth century house with plenty of mosaic tiled floors and four en-suite rooms (plus two apartments) finished in suitably tasteful period style. Most come with a private terrace and there's also a garden, swimming pool and on-trend *bar à vin*. **€166.50**

★ **Boquier** 6 rue du Portail Boquier ☎ 04 90 82 34 43, ⓦ hotel-boquier.com. Extremely welcoming little hotel near the tourist office, with funkily decorated, widely differing, and consistently inexpensive en-suite rooms, some very small, some sleeping three or four. **€69**

Colbert 7 rue Agricol Perdiguier ☎ 04 90 86 20 20, ⓦ avignon-hotel-colbert.com. At the south end of

town and handy for local trains and buses, this hotel has warmly and imaginatively decorated rooms, mostly large and all a/c, plus a pleasant central courtyard complete with fountain. The helpful owners are always ready with suggestions. Closed Nov–March. **€74**

Europe 12 place Crillon ☎ 04 90 14 76 76, ⓦ heurope. com. Very comfortable upscale hotel, in a sixteenth-century townhouse. Unpretentiously classy, it's set back in a shaded courtyard, with bright, modern, soundproofed rooms, home-made breakfasts and an excellent restaurant. **€240**

Garlande 20 rue Galante ☎ 04 90 80 08 85, ⓦ hotel degarlande.com. Stylish little family-run hotel, in a pedestrian street near the Palais des Papes. Each of the eleven generally spacious rooms has its own colour scheme and Provençal touches, as well as a decent bathroom with bath or shower. **€84**

ho36 17 rue de la République ☎ 04 32 40 50 60, ⓦ ho36 hostels.com/avignon. Stylish, independent hostel, in a prime central location on the main street, that's swiftly become a major favourite among young international visitors. Rooms are clean and fresh, with a/c; choose between dorms sleeping 4–8 in individually curtained beds, and en-suite private doubles. Kitchen facilities are minimal, but the on-site wine bar serves tapas plus continental breakfasts. Dorms **€22**; doubles **€65**

Médiéval 15 rue Petite Saunerie ☎ 04 90 86 11 06, ⓦ hotelmedieval.com. Very central hotel in a fine seventeenth-century townhouse, with very reasonable rates (even during the festival) and a lovely garden courtyard, but somewhat plain rooms of widely varying sizes. **€78**

Mignon 12 rue Joseph-Vernet ☎09 70 35 37 67, ⓦhotel-mignon.com. The decor may be a little fussy for some tastes, but this small hotel is amazing value for money considering its spotless little rooms and fantastic location on a chic street. Closed Jan. **€69**

Les Corps Saints 17 rue Agricol Perdiguier ☎04 90 86 14 46, ⓦhotel-les-corps-saints.fr. Fresh and contemporary two-star in a great location just off the main drag; there's a steep narrow staircase to reach the upper floors. Continental breakfast not included (€5–9). Closed first two weeks in Jan. **€58**

CAMPSITES

Camping Bagatelle 25 allée Antoine-Pinay, Île de la Barthelasse ☎04 90 86 30 39, ⓦcampingbagatellecom. This wooded three-star campsite is the closest to Avignon

city centre, visible as you cross the Daladier bridge; take bus #20 from the post office, or a 15min walk from place de l'Horloge. It's nothing special, but there's a laundry, shop and café, as well as basic hostel facilities, with beds in two-, four- or six-person dorms, plus private rooms sleeping from two to four, with and without en-suite bathrooms. All hostel rates include breakfast. Open all year. Camping **€30.98**; dorms **€23.17**; doubles **€62**

Camping du Pont d'Avignon 10 chemin de la Barthelasse, Île de la Barthelasse ☎04 90 80 63 50, ⓦaquadis-loisirs.com. Well-shaded four-star site, with a lovely pool, on the island directly facing Pont St-Bénézet across the river, a fair walk from the centre but accessible on bus route #20. Closed mid-Nov to Feb. **€23.60**

Les Deux Rhône Chemin de Bellegarde, Île de la Barthelasse ☎04 90 85 49 70, ⓦcamping2rhone.com. Avignon's smallest campsite, around 3km from the city centre on the north side of the island, and equipped with pool and restaurant; bus #20 ("Gravière" stop). Open all year. **€19.51**

3

EATING

SEE MAP PAGE 118

Avignon has an enormous number of **restaurants**. The terrace café-brasseries on place de l'Horloge and rue de la République serve quick, if not necessarily memorable, meals; place des Corps-Saints holds elbow-to-elbow tables beneath the plane trees in summer; and the pedestrian lanes are packed with atmospheric possibilities.

RESTAURANTS

Le 46 46 rue de la Balance ☎04 90 85 24 83, ⓦle46 avignon.com. This smart modern bistro, with a streetfront terrace near the Palais des Papes, serves superb regional dishes using fresh market produce. At lunchtime, you can get a €12.50 *plat du jour*, usually fresh fish, or a large salad; dinner is à la carte, with starters at around €10 and mains €19. Summer Mon–Sat noon noon–2pm & 7–10pm; winter Mon–Wed & Fri noon–2pm & 7–10pm, Thurs noon–2pm, Sat 7–10pm.

Caveau du Théâtre 16 rue des Trois Faucons ☎04 90 82 60 91. Friendly bistro, with pretty painted walls, jolly red tables out on the street, and occasional live jazz, serving delicious dishes like smoked duck breast salad. Two-course lunch *menu* €13, three-course lunch *menu* €16, dinner *menu* €29. Tues–Sat noon–2pm & 7–10pm.

★ **Christian Étienne** 10 rue de Mons ☎0484 88 51 27, ⓦchristian-etienne.fr. Avignon's best-known gourmet restaurant, housed in a twelfth-century mansion, with a terrace overlooking the place du Palais. Mouthwatering delights might include a whole menu devoted to truffles, or steamed Norwegian arctic cod with a soya and galangal infusion and buckwheat noodles. Dinner *menus* range from €85 to €130 but you can also sample the restaurant's pleasures on a three- or two-course, no-choice €35/€48

lunch *menu*. Jan–June & Aug–Dec Mon, Tues & Fri–Sun noon–1.30pm & 7.30–9pm; July daily noon–1.30pm & 7.30–9pm.

La Cour du Louvre 23 rue St-Agricol ☎0 09 70 35 15 86. Hidden peacefully away from the old-town bustle in a delightful interior courtyard at the end of a *cour*, with a romantic atmosphere and good Mediterranean cooking. *Menus* start at €34.90. Mon–Sat noon–2.15pm & 7–10pm.

Fou de Fafa 17 rue des Trois Faucons ☎04 32 76 35 13, ⓦrestaurantfoudefafa.com. Wonderful mouthful of a name with food to match, eschewing interior bling to concentrate on cooking that's made this place a real foodie destination, and all at affordable prices. Dishes aren't especially showy but they are beautifully executed, with options such as fish of the day with squid ink risotto, and pumpkin ragu with beans, lentils and roasted polenta featuring on a €29 dinner *menu*. Max four people per party. Tues–Sat 7pm–11pm.

La Fourchette 17 rue Racine ☎04 90 85 20 93, ⓦla-fourchette.net. Bright, busy yet refined restaurant serving up classic and sophisticated fish and meat dishes – try the scallop mousseline with saffron – with a two course *Coup de Fourchette* lunch *menu* (€26) and a €38 dinner *menu*. Mon–Fri 12.15–1.45pm & 7.15–9.45pm; closed first 3 weeks in Aug.

Ginette & Marcel 27 place des Corps-Saints ☎04 90 85 58 70. The most attractive of several restaurants on this lively, youthful little square. If you sit outside, be sure to have a peek at the interior – it's a fun evocation of a 1940s French grocery, filled with funky bric-a-brac. Hot and cold *tartines* are the speciality (€4–8), and with soup of the day

3

priced at €4.60, you can get a substantial meal for around €10–12. Daily 10.30am–11pm.

Le Square Square Agricol Perdiguier ⓣ04 88 61 26 47. There's nothing very exceptional about the food in this outdoor café/brasserie, in a spacious park behind the tourist office, but it makes a great spot for a summer-morning coffee, or a simple lunchtime salad, plat or risotto for around €10 – and there's free wi-fi here too. March–Oct daily 8am–sunset.

CAFÉS, WINE BARS AND SALONS DE THÉ

Camili Books and Tea 155 rue de la Carreterie ⓣ04 90 27 38 50, ⓦcamili-booksandtea.com. Cosy tearoom, with a garden patio, selling organic and fairtrade tea, coffee and juices, as well as home-made cakes, pastries and snacks. It also doubles as a book exchange, with an enormous stock of English titles, and offers English and French classes,

watercolour painting and crochet workshops. Tues–Sat noon–7pm.

La Compagnie des Chats 19 rue de Lices ⓣ06 01 29 36 75. Avignon's charming contribution to Europe's increasingly popular cat café culture, with a clowder of roaming ksitties to pamper as you enjoy a *tartine* (around €10) or a two or three course lunch *formule* (€10/15). Tues–Thurs 11am–6.30pm, Fri & Sat 11am–10pm.

Le Vache à Carreaux 14 rue Peyrollerie ⓣ04 90 80 09 05, ⓦvache-carreaux.com. This intimate, homely wine bar styles itself a "*restaurant de fromage et vins*". Cheese is indeed prominent on the food menu, which features €12.50 baked half-camemberts alongside the likes of chicken with comté, mozzarella and chorizo (€15). Bottles of Côtes-du-Rhône from €19, Châteauneuf-du-Pape from €19. Daily: may–Sept noon–3pm & 7pm–1am; Oct–April 7pm–1am.

DRINKING AND NIGHTLIFE

SEE MAP PAGE 118

Though Avignon saves a lot of its energy for the festival, the city is busy with **nightlife** and **cultural events** year round, particularly café-theatre, and plenty of **classical concerts** are performed in churches, usually for free.

BARS AND CLUBS

AJMI Jazz Club La Manutention, 4 rue Escalier Ste-Anne ⓣ04 90 86 08 61, ⓦjazzalajmi.com. This popular club, in a busy arts complex behind the Palais des Papes, hosts a year-round programme of major acts and some adventurous new jazz and improvised music; check the website for the latest schedule. Hours vary.

L'Ampelos 11 rue du Vieux Sextier ⓣ09 84 27 57 97, ⓦlampelos.fr. Proudly one hundred percent biodynamic, this rustic-contemporary wine bar-cave changes its by-the-glass selection every Thursday, with cheese and charcuterie served at weekends. Tues & Wed 10am–8pm, Thurs, Fri & Sat 10am–11pm.

L'Esclave 12 rue Limas ⓣ04 90 85 14 91. Avignon's best-known gay and lesbian bar, with regular DJs, drag shows and karaoke nights at ground level, and more intimate areas upstairs. Daily 11.45pm–7am.

L'Explo 2 rue des Teinturiers ⓣ04 90 31 06 35. This corner bar is craft beer heaven, with an ever evolving range of local and national craft and organic brews, often accompanied by live music, while the riverside terrace makes for a sweet alfresco drinking spot in summer. Tues–Sat 5pm–1.30am.

Le Red Zone 25 rue Carnot ⓣ04 90 27 02 44. Sweaty,

very crimson club where DJs play anything from salsa to electro according to the night. Tues–Sat midnight–7am.

THEATRE AND CINEMA

Cinéma Utopia La Manutention, 4 rue Escalier Ste-Anne ⓣ04 90 82 65 36, ⓦwww.cinemas-utopia. org. Part of a hip converted warehouse complex that also includes a bistro and the *AJMI Jazz Club* (see above), this wildly popular venue shows a busy repertory programme of films from all over the world, many in *version originale* (undubbed).

Opéra Grand Avignon/Confluence 1 Place de L'Europe ⓣ04 90 14 26 40, ⓦoperagrandavignon.fr. Avignon's most prestigious stage for classical opera and ballet is currently housed in a temporary structure, Opéra Confluence, located opposite the Gare TGV.

Théâtre du Balcon 38 rue Guillaume-Puy ⓣ04 90 85 00 80, ⓦtheatredubalcon.org. Venue staging everything from African music and twentieth-century classics to contemporary works.

Théâtre des Carmes André Benedetto 6 place des Carmes ⓣ04 90 82 20 47, ⓦtheatredescarmes.com. Set up by, and now named after, one of the founders of Festival Off (see page 120), this theatre specializes in avant-garde performances.

Théâtre du Chêne Noir 8bis rue Ste-Catherine ⓣ04 90 86 74 87, ⓦchenenoir.fr. Programmes at this eclectic theatre range anywhere from mime or musicals to Molière.

SHOPPING

SEE MAP PAGE 118

CQFD 16 Place de la Principale ⓣ04 90 85 29 86. "Quirky Ethical French Designs" is how this shop's eponymous acronym translates, and it does pretty much what it says on the tin with original designs by local and national makers

– everything from Fair Isle-style jacquard sweaters from Normandy to beautiful hand-painted penknives crafted in Chambéry. Mon 1.30–7pm, Tues–Sat 10am–7pm.

3

Les Plumes du Paon 91 rue Bonnetterie ☏ 06 68 32 91 56, ⓦ lesplumesdupaon.com. A vintage-chic "cabinet of curiosities", selling and exhibiting the work of local artists in a myriad of creative disciplines – clothes, jewellery, sculpture, furniture, ceramics and more. Tues–Fri 11am–7pm.

Repetto 8 rue Joseph-Venet ☏ 04 90 32 29 83, ⓦ repetto.com. This showpiece outlet of the Parisian ballet brand is a good place to pick up classic ballerina pumps – they also sell classy leather accessories, as well as serious dance gear and tutus. Mon 2–7pm, Tues–Sat 10am–1pm & 2–7pm.

DIRECTORY

Laundry Lav'matic, 9 rue du Chapeau-Rouge (with wi-fi; daily 7am–8.30pm); Blanchisseuse, 24 rue Lanterne (Tues–Fri 9am–6.30pm, Sat 10am–12.30pm).
Markets Flea market: place des Carmes (Sun morning). Flowers: place des Carmes (Sat morning). Food: in the covered Les Halles market on place Pie (Tues–Fri 6am–1.30pm; Sat & Sun 6am –2pm).
Medical emergencies Doctor/ambulance ☏ 15; Hospital,

Centre Hospitalier H. Duffaut, 305 rue Raoul-Follereau (☏ 04 32 75 33 33, ⓦ ch-avignon.fr).
Police Municipale 13 bd du Quai St-Lazare ☏ 04 90 85 13 13.
Post office Cours Président-Kennedy (Mon–Fri 8.30am–12.30pm & 1.30–6pm, Sat 9.15am–noon).
Swimming pool Piscine Jean Clement, 9km east of the centre at Chemin de la Martelle, Montfavet (☏ 04 90 31 38 73).

Villeneuve-lès-Avignon

Pretty and prosperous, though little more than a village at its core, **VILLENEUVE-LÈS-AVIGNON** (also spelled Villeneuve-lez-Avignon) rises up a rocky escarpment above the west bank of the Rhône, looking down across the river upon its older and larger neighbour from behind far more convincing fortifications. Despite ongoing rivalry, Villeneuve has effectively been a suburb of Avignon for most of its history, holding palatial residences constructed by the cardinals and a great monastery founded by Pope Innocent VI.

Officially belonging to Languedoc rather than Provence, Villeneuve might be better known were it further from Avignon, whose **monuments** it can almost match for colossal scale. It is, however, a very different – and really rather sleepy – kind of place, where daily activity centres around the little place Jean-Jaurès. As such, it retains a repose and a sense of timelessness that bustling Avignon lacks. In summer it provides venues for the Avignon Festival (see page 120), but whatever time of year you visit it's certainly worth a day spent exploring.

Market days in Villeneuve's place Charles-David are Thursday, for food, and Saturday for bric-a-brac.

Fort St-André

Fort St-André Daily: June–Sept 10am–6pm; Oct–May 10am–1pm & 2–5pm • €6, €9 with La Chartreuse • ☏ 04 90 25 45 35, ⓦ fort-saint-andre.monuments-nationaux.fr • **Abbey** Tues–Sun: March & Oct 10am–1pm & 2–5pm; April 10am–1pm & 2–6pm; May–Sept Oct–March 10am–6pm • Gardens €7, gardens and guided tour of abbey €14 • ☏ 04 90 25 55 95, ⓦ abbayesaintandre.fr

Originally, Villeneuve-lès-Avignon was enclosed within the walls of its mighty castle, the enormous **Fort St-André**. Then, in 1770, the Rhône shifted its course roughly 1km south, and the fort lost its strategic importance. Now basically a hollow shell, it can be reached by climbing either the montée du Fort from place Jean-Jaurès, or the "rapid slope" of rue Pente Rapide, a cobbled street of tiny houses that leads off rue des Recollets on the north side of place Charles-David.

Once inside the bulbous, double-towered gateway that penetrates the fort's vast white walls, you find yourself on what used to be the town's narrow main street. Buying a ticket for the fort itself allows you to continue up the street, passing tumbledown ruins, and then walk along the parapets, where a cliff-face terrace offers tremendous views of both modern Villeneuve and Avignon across the river. You can also pay separately to visit its former **abbey**, now privately owned, which offers further magnificent views, as well as gardens of olive trees, ruined chapels, lily ponds and dovecotes.

If you're a fan of post-impressionist painter Émile Barnard you might want to shell out for a guided tour of the abbey interior, where some of the vaulted ceilings are adorned with his early twentieth century murals.

La Chartreuse du Val de Bénédiction

58 rue de la République • Daily: April–Sept 9.30am–6.30pm; Oct–March 10am–5pm • €8, €9 with Fort St-André (see above) • ☎ 04 90 15 24 24, ⓦ chartreuse.org

La Chartreuse du Val de Bénédiction, one of the largest Carthusian monasteries in France, spreads below the Fort St-André. Founded by the sixth of the Avignon popes, Innocent VI, it was sold off after the Revolution. Gradually restored in the twentieth century, the buildings are totally unembellished, and except for the Giovanetti frescoes in the chapel beside the refectory, all the artworks have been dispersed. Visitors are free to wander around unguided, through the three cloisters, the church, chapels, cells and communal spaces, which have little to see but plenty of atmosphere to absorb. At various points you can also enter some lovely gardens. This is one of the finest venues of the Festival of Avignon (see page 120).

Musée Pierre-de-Luxembourg

3 rue de la République • Feb–April, Nov & Dec Tues & Thurs–Sun 2–5pm, Wed 10am–noon & 2–5pm; May–Oct Tues–Sun 10am–12.30pm & 2–6pm • €3.80 • ☎ 04 90 20 49 66

The **Musée Pierre-de-Luxembourg**, just off place Jean-Jaurès, holds treasures from the fourteenth-century **Église Collégiale Notre Dame** nearby, including a rare fourteenth-

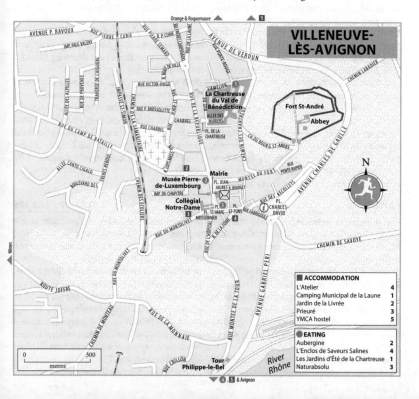

century smiling Madonna and Child carved from a single tusk of ivory. The collection also features several paintings taken from the Chartreuse, including the stunning *Coronation of the Virgin*, painted in 1453 by Enguerrand Quarton.

Tour Philippe-le-Bel

Feb, March, April & Nov Tues & Thurs–Sun 2–5pm, Wed 10am–noon & 2–7pm; May–Oct Tues–Sun 10am–12.30pm & 2–6pm • €3.50 • ☎ 04 32 70 08 57

The stout **Tour Philippe-le-Bel**, south of the centre alongside the main road from Avignon, was built to guard the western end of Avignon's Pont St-Bénézet (see page 120). The rather tricky climb to the top is rewarded with an overview of Villeneuve and Avignon.

ARRIVAL AND INFORMATION   VILLENEUVE-LÈS-AVIGNON

By bus The #5 bus (every 20min) takes 5min to ply between Villeneuve's tourist office and Avignon's Porte de l'Oulle.
Tourist office Place Charles-David (April–June & Sept Mon–Sat 9am–12.30pm & 2–6pm; July & Aug Mon–Sat

9am–6pm & Sun 9am–1pm; Oct–March Mon–Fri 9am–12.30pm & 2–5pm, Sat 9am–12.30pm; ☎ 04 9003 70 60, ⊕ ot-villeneuvelezavignon.fr).

ACCOMMODATION   SEE MAP PAGE 129

Villeneuve is more a **boutique** destination than a mere alternative to Avignon, with a handful of charming, good-value hotels and B&Bs. Rates rise during July's festival.

★ **L'Atelier** 5 rue de la Foire ☎ 04 90 25 01 84, ⊕ hoteldelatelier.com. Very tasteful rooms in a charming sixteenth-century house with a central stone staircase bathed in light, plus huge open fireplaces and a well-shaded courtyard garden with terraces. **€98**

Camping Municipal de la Laune Chemin St-Honoré ☎ 04 90 25 76 06, ⊕ camping-villeneuvezavignon. com. A spacious, well-shaded three-star site off the D980, north of both town and fort near the sports stadium and municipal swimming pool, on local bus route #5. Closed mid-Oct to March. **€31**

Jardin de la Livrée 4bis rue du Camp de Bataille ☎ 0486 81 00 21, ⊕ la-livree.fr. Five clean, comfortable, garden-facing B&B rooms in a renovated period house in the centre of the village, with a swimming pool; rates include parking and breakfast, and there's an appealing

Mediterranean restaurant downstairs. The one drawback is the noise of passing trains. **€100**

Prieuré 7 place du Chapitre ☎ 04 90 15 90 15, ⊕ leprieure.com. Much the most luxurious option in Villeneuve, this spacious former priory stands in peaceful flower-filled gardens. Its opulent rooms abound in tapestries, finely carved doors, old oak ceilings and other baronial trappings, while the top-quality dining room serves Provençal cuisine with a gourmet twist. Closed Jan to mid-Feb & Nov **€329**

YMCA hostel 7bis chemin de la Justice ☎ 04 90 25 46 20, ⊕ ymca-avignon.fr. Beautifully situated hostel, overlooking the river by Pont du Royaume (the extension of Pont Daladier). Rooms come with either double beds or bunk beds, each holding up to four people, and there's also an open-air swimming pool. Stop "Pont d'Avignon" on buses heading from Avignon to Villeneuve, "Gabriel Péri" in the other direction. **€38**

EATING   SEE MAP PAGE 129

Most of Villeneuve's **restaurants** are special-treat places for day-trippers from Avignon, though place Jean-Jaurès holds a handful of pleasant **cafés** where you can enjoy a simple snack with your drink.

Aubergine 15 rue de la République ☎ 04 90 90 05 64, ⊕ aubergine-villeneuve.restaurant. This conspicuous bistro serves good-value local food at tables out on the central square, with more of a plant based approach than most. They do a delicious veggie platter for €12, spinach fritters and butternut velouté for €9 and meatier mains in the €15 range. Daily 8am–midnight.

L'Enclos de Saveurs Salines 9 Impasse du Rhône ☎ 04 90 89 53 52, ⊕ saveurs-salines.fr. Customise your own

groaning platter of seafood at this perennially popular restaurant – from €34 for one person, up to €110 for a feast with crab and lobster. Or just opt for a simple salmon steak (€16). Daily 11am–2pm & 6–10pm.

★ **Les Jardins d'Été de la Chartreuse** Cloître St-Jean, La Chartreuse ☎ 04 90 15 24 23, ⊕ chartreuse.org. A truly memorable experience; in summer only, you can thread your way through the labyrinthine old monastery (you don't have to pay for admission) to find this open-air restaurant in a secluded courtyard. Some tables have lovely sunset views. Friendly service and *menus* of substantial Provençal cuisine from €14 (vegetarian *menu* €20), plus early-evening drinks and snacks. June–Aug daily 11.30am–10pm.

Naturabsolu 10 place St-Marc ☎09 50 76 05 97. Predominantly vegan and organic restaurant, with indoor and outdoor seating, which serves a daily €16 raw plate as well as large salads and very tempting desserts (€7), along with fresh smoothies and juices. Daily specials can include cheese, however. Mon, Tues, Thurs & Sat noon–2pm &7–9.30pm, Sun 7–9pm.

Pont du Gard

The beautiful and extraordinary **Pont du Gard**, the tallest aqueduct-bridge in the Roman world, stands 25km west of Avignon. Spanning the Gard river, a tributary of the Rhône that's also known as the Gardon, it's officially in Languedoc-Roussillon, but as the single most stunning ancient site in the Rhône Valley it's a destination no visitor to Provence should miss.

Towering almost 50m above the river, the bridge was constructed around 50 AD. It stretched for 490m between the steep cliffs on either bank, with triple tiers that originally held 47 arches – a total of twelve are now missing to either side – and was a crucial component of a 50km aqueduct that supplied fresh water to the city of Nîmes for 150 years.

Now a UNESCO World Heritage Site, the Pont du Gard is inevitably something of a tourist trap, especially since the river itself is unspoiled enough for visitors to be able to picnic beside it, and even swim in it – so irresistible in summer that many families come for a full day. With almost no other buildings around, though, there's usually enough room for everyone, and as the whole area is pedestrianized, it's surprisingly peaceful.

The Pont du Gard site

400 rte du Pont du Gard, Vers-Pont-du-Gard • Opening hours vary; check website • €9.50; July & Aug evening visits €5 • ☎ 04 66 37 50 99, Ⓦ .pontdugard.fr

All access to the Pont du Gard is via an entrance complex from which the bridge itself is out of sight. Be sure to visit the huge underground **museum** here, below the ticketing booths, souvenir shops and café. Much of it is devoted to the surprisingly fascinating topic of **Roman plumbing**, ranging through sewers and siphons, pipes and hypocausts, fountains and baths as well as of course as aqueducts, with large reconstructions of the quarry and work site showing how it was all put together.

A paved trail leads in a few hundred metres to the left bank of the river, where your first view of the bridge, with the sheer scale of its arches, and the wooded cliffs to either side, is absolutely breathtaking. While you can follow footpaths up the hillside to reach, within five minutes, the topmost tier of the structure, you are only permitted to **cross the Pont du Gard** along the lowest of its three levels. On the far side, on the broad terrace that offers the best overall views, a little snack bar sells coffee, drinks and ice creams, and there's also a full-service restaurant.

Châteauneuf-du-Pape

The large village of **CHÂTEAUNEUF-DU-PAPE**, halfway along the back road between Avignon and Orange, takes its name from the summer palace of the Avignon popes. However, its fame derives neither from the views down the Rhône Valley from its ruined fourteenth-century château, nor from its photogenic medieval streets. Instead, of course, it's the local **vineyards** that produce the magic, with the grapes warmed at night by large pebbles that cover the ground and soak up the sun's heat by day. Their rich ruby-red wine ranks among the most renowned in France, though the lesser-known white, too, is delicious.

3

3

SAMPLING THE WINES OF CHÂTEAUNEUF-DU-PAPE

During the first full weekend of August, the **Fête de la Véraison** celebrates the ripening of the grapes, with free *dégustation* (tasting) stalls throughout the village, as well as parades, dances, equestrian contests, folklore floats and so forth. As well as wine, a good deal of grape liqueur (*marc*) is imbibed.

At other times, free **tastings** are available all over the village. The tourist office maintains up-to-date listings of which local estates offer tastings, English-language tours and so on. No single outlet sells all the Châteauneuf-du-Pape wines; the best selection under one roof is at **La Maison des Vins**, 8 rue du Maréchal Foch (May–Sept daily 10am–1pm & 2–6pm; Oct–April Mon–Thurs & Sun 10am–12.30pm & 2–6pm, Fri & Sat 10am–12.30pm & 2–6.30pm; ☎04 90 83 70 69, ⊛www.vinadea.com).

As in so many Provençal villages, commercial activity is largely confined to the main road that loops around the base of Châteauneuf's small central hill. Walk up from the busy little **place du Portail**, and as soon as you step off the pedestrian route towards the castle, you're in a delightful tangle of sleepy, verdant alleyways. As for the **château** itself, which can also be reached by car, a couple of deceptively intact walls still crown the top of the hill, but they simply define a hollow shell, which is freely accessible at all times.

Musée du Vin Brotte

Bd Pierre-de-Luxembourg • Daily: mid-April to May & mid-Sept to mid-Oct 9am–1pm & 2–7pm; June to mid-Sept 9am–7pm; mid-Oct to mid-April 9am–noon & 2–6pm • Free • ☎04 90 83 59 44, ⊛www.brotte.com

Despite being run by one specific wine-producing firm to promote its own products, the best place to learn about the local wines in Châteauneuf-du-Pape is the **Musée du Vin Brotte**, southwest of the centre towards Avignon. As well as providing a good historical overview of the wine industry, covering the geology of the region and the nineteenth-century phylloxera epidemic that devastated all French wines, it illustrates traditional tools and techniques, offers free tasting, and, of course, sells Brotte wines.

INFORMATION

CHÂTEAUNEUF-DU-PAPE

Tourist office Place du Portail (May, June & Sept Mon–Sat 9.30am–6pm; July & Aug Mon–Sat 9.30am–6pm, Sun 9.30am–12.30pm; Oct–April Mon–Sat 9.30am–12.30pm & 2–6pm; ☎04 90 83 71 08, ⊛chateauneuf-du-pape-orange-tourisme.fr/tourisme).

ACCOMMODATION AND EATING

Garbure 3 rue Joseph-Ducos ☎04 90 83 75 08, ⊛www.la-garbure.com. Cosy, very central village hotel, with eight cheerful rooms, and an excellent restaurant. Dinner *menus* from €22 and terrace seating across the street. Garage parking €12. Restaurant closed Mon & Sun; hotel closed 3 weeks in Nov. **€120**

Mère Germaine 3 rue Commandant-Lemaître ☎04 90 22 78 34, ⊛lameregermaine.fr. Lively and very pleasant small hotel-restaurant, in the heart of the village, with eight welcoming rooms; rates include breakfast and parking. Well-crafted Provençal cuisine on *menus* from €30 for lunch (daily), €45 for dinner. Restaurant closed Sun evenings and Wed in winter. **€80**

Sommellerie 2268 rte de Roquemaure ☎09 70 35 60 29, ⊛la-sommellerie.fr. A charming, renovated country house, 3km north of the village, with fourteen modern pastel-painted rooms, two larger suites and a pool. The restaurant (Tues–Sat) produces superb dishes, such as roast duck with mustard and honey, on *menus* starting at €14 for lunch, €32 for dinner. Closed Jan. **€155**

Le Verger des Papes 4 montée du Château ☎04 90 83 50 40, ⊛vergerdespapes.com. This delightful restaurant, well away from the traffic near the château at the top of the hill, serves traditional food on a peaceful panoramic terrace with *menus* at €23 for lunch, €34 for dinner. March & Nov to mid-Dec Tues–Thurs & Sun noon–2pm Fri & Sat noon–2pm & 7–9pm; April & Oct Tues, Wed & Sun noon–2pm, Thurs–Sat noon–2pm & 7–9pm; May, June & Sept Tues & Sun noon–2pm, Wed–Sat noon–2pm & 7–9pm; July & Aug Tues–Sat noon–2pm & 7–9pm, Sun noon–2pm.

Orange

Thanks to its spectacular **Roman theatre**, the small town of **ORANGE**, well west of the Rhône 20km north of Avignon, is famous out of all proportion to its size. Now home to fewer than thirty thousand citizens, it was founded as Aurisio in 35 BC; only much later did its name become conflated with the fruit and the colour. In the eighth century, Charlemagne made it the seat of the counts of Orange, a title that passed to the Dutch crown in the sixteenth century. The family's best-known member was Prince William, who ascended the English throne with his consort Mary in the 1688 "Glorious Revolution", and whose supporters in Ireland established the Protestant Orange Order.

Now known as the Théâtre Antique, the Roman theatre is the one must-see attraction. Otherwise, with its medieval street plan, fountain-studded squares, houses with ancient porticoes and courtyards, and Thursday-morning **market**, Orange is an attractive enough place to stroll around, but the only reason to stay more than a day or two is to use it as a quiet base for exploring the region.

3

Théâtre Antique

Daily: March & Oct 9.30am–5.30pm; April, May & Sept 9am–6pm; June–Aug 9am–7pm, closing early on event days; Nov–Feb 9.30am–4.30pm • €9.50 including audioguide and Musée d'Art et Histoire (see page 134); €8.50 for last hour of each day (not including audioguide) • ☎ 04 90 51 17 60, ⓦ theatre-antique.com

The enormous wall of the **Théâtre Antique**, at the southern end of Orange's medieval centre, dominates the entire town. Said to be the world's best-preserved Roman theatre, it's the only one with its stage wall still standing. Around 55 AD, audiences of ten thousand could spend their days off watching farce, clownish improvisations, song and dance and, perhaps, for the sake of a visiting dignitary, a bit of Greek tragedy in Latin. Having survived periods as a fortification, slum and prison before its careful

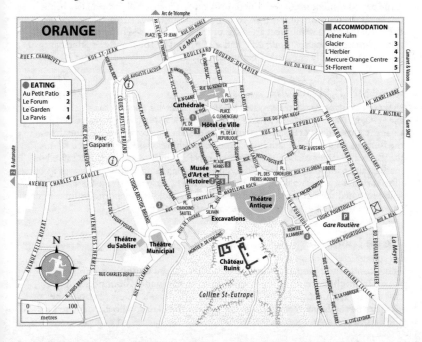

ORANGE

ACCOMMODATION
Arène Kulm	1
Glacier	3
L'Herbier	4
Mercure Orange Centre	2
St-Florent	5

EATING
Au Petit Patio	3
Le Forum	2
Le Garden	1
La Parvis	4

THE CHORÉGIES

When Orange's **choral festival**, known as the **Chorégies** (☎04 90 34 24 24, ⓦchoregies.fr), began in 1879, it marked the first performance at the Théâtre Antique in 350 years. The festival these days consists of performances scattered throughout July, with a varied programme of opera, oratorios and orchestral concerts. Tickets cost anything from €10 to €275, and go on sale in October of the preceding year. Check the Théâtre's website (ⓦtheatre-antique.com) for a calendar of other events and exhibitions.

---

reconstruction in the nineteenth century, the Théâtre still hosts **musical performances** in summer, and is also open as an archeological site.

Spreading a colossal 36m high by 103m wide, the Théâtre's outer face resembles a monstrous prison wall, despite the ground-level archways that lead into the backstage areas. Inside, an excellent free audioguide paints an evocative picture of its history and architecture. The enormous **stage**, originally sheltered by a mighty awning, could accommodate vast numbers of performers, while the acoustics allowed a full audience to hear every word. Though missing most of its original decoration, the inner side of the wall above the stage is extremely impressive. Below columned niches, now empty of their statues, a larger-than-life statue of Augustus, raising his arm in imperious fashion, looks down centre stage. Seating was allocated strictly by rank; an inscription "EQ Gradus III" (third row for knights) remains visible near the orchestra pit. Arches along the uppermost internal passageway now hold audiovisual displays, including footage of rock festivals held here during the 1970s.

Spectators who grew bored during the day-long performances could slip out of the west door to a semicircular complex cut into the rock. Some archeologists suggest this held baths, a stage for combats and a gymnasium equipped with three 180m running tracks; others say it was the forum, or even a circus.

The best **viewpoint** over the entire theatre, on St-Eutrope hill immediately behind, can be accessed – without paying – from both east and west. As you look down towards the stage, the ruins at your feet are those of the short-lived seventeenth-century castle of the princes of Orange. Louis XIV had it destroyed in 1673, and the principality of Orange was officially annexed to France forty years later.

Musée d'Art et Histoire

Rue Madeleine Roch • Daily: March & Oct 9.45am–5.30pm; April, May & Sept 9.15am–6pm; June–Aug 9.15am–7pm; Nov–Feb 9.30am–noon & 1–4.30pm • €5.50, or €9.50 with Théâtre Antique (see page 133) • ☎04 90 50 17 60, ⓦtheatre-antique.com

Orange's **Musée d'Art et Histoire**, across from the Théâtre, covers local history from the Romans onwards, and also hosts temporary exhibitions. Artefacts taken from the Théâtre complex include the largest known Roman land-survey maps, carved on marble (and badly damaged when the museum collapsed in 1962), along with a couple of sphinxes and a mosaic floor. The two upper levels, dedicated to the Gasparin family who promoted the safeguarding of Roman Orange, hold family portraits, mementoes and a reconstructed *salon*.

Arc de Triomphe

Av de l'Arc de Triomphe • 24hr access

The second major Roman monument in Orange, the impressive, triple-bayed **Arc de Triomphe**, occupies a lozenge-shaped traffic island 400m north of the city centre. Built around 20 BC, its intricate friezes and reliefs celebrate the victories of the Roman Second Legion against the Gauls, who are depicted naked and chained.

ARRIVAL AND INFORMATION

ORANGE

By train The *gare SNCF* is on Av Frédéric-Mistral, 800m east of the centre.

Destinations Avignon (every 30min at peak times; 14–23min); Paris (3 daily; 3hr 16min–3hr 39min).

By bus The *gare routière* is on Bd Edouard-Daladier, 250m east of the theatre.

Destinations Carpentras (roughly every 1hr–2hr; 45min–1hr); Châteauneuf-du-Pape (6 daily; 30min); Séguret (every 1–2hr; 47min); Sérignan (9 daily; 15min); Vaison (every 1–2hr; 1hr).

By car There's very limited parking in the city centre. For short stays (of less than 2hr 16min, to be precise), use the metered parking along cours Aristide Briand; for overnight stays use the underground car park east of the theatre near the bus station, entered from Bd Edouard-Daladier.

Tourist office The tourist office is a short walk from the centre at 5 cours Aristide Briand (July & Aug Mon–Sat 9am–6pm, Sun 9am–12.30pm; Sept–June 9am–12.30pm & 2–6pm; ☎04 90 34 70 88, ⓦ orange-tourisme.fr).

ACCOMMODATION

SEE MAP PAGE 133

Almost all Orange hotels charge for **parking**, typically around €10 – and often that's for a public car park several hundred metres away.

Arène Kulm 8 place de Langes ☎04 90 11 40 40, ⓦ hotel-arene.fr. Very presentable hotel, spreading through five buildings on a quiet, pedestrianized – though not especially attractive – square, with spacious rooms, two pools and an Italian restaurant. **€160**

Glacier 46 cours Aristide Briand ☎04 90 34 02 01, ⓦ le-glacier.com. Comfortable, cosy Provençal-style rooms with pretty quilts and floral curtains. All en suite and a/c, they vary widely in size and amenities; the smallest are tiny. Good breakfasts are available in the little pavement café downstairs. Nov–Feb closed Fri–Sun. **€79.50**

L'Herbier 8 place aux Herbes ☎04 90 34 09 23, ⓦ lherbierdorange.com. A good budget option, set in a seventeenth-century house overlooking a pretty square very near the Théâtre Antique. Rooms are simple and clean, and include some good-value family options; all have at least showers. **€69**

Mercure Orange Centre 258 route de Caderousse ☎04 90 34 24 10, ⓦ hotel-orange-saintflorent.com. Though it's not exactly central, at least this chain hotel has free parking, leafy surrounds and a swimming pool to go with its clean, comfortable rooms. Decor is contemporary-functional and breakfast is included. **€139**

St-Florent 4 rue du Mazeau ☎04 90 34 18 53, ⓦ hotel-orange-saintflorent.com. Very central, inexpensive hotel, with appealingly kitsch decor and a wide range of rooms; some have four-poster beds, all are en suite, and there are some extremely cheap singles. **€65**

EATING

SEE MAP PAGE 133

Au Petit Patio 58 cours Aristide Briand ☎04 90 29 69 27. Provençal restaurant, in a very pleasant garden courtyard tucked away not far west of the theatre. It's especially appealing at lunchtime, when €19 buys two courses plus wine and coffee; dinner *menus* cost €28 or €39, and abound in zestful local produce. Mon, Tues, Fri & Sat noon–1.15pm & 7–9.15pm, Wed & Thurs noon–1.15pm.

Le Forum 3 rue du Mazeau ☎04 90 34 01 09, ⓦ restaurant-leforum-orange.fr. Small, intimate restaurant near the Théâtre. Lunch and dinner *menus* (€15 and €29 respectively) revolve around seasonal ingredients; in January, truffles feature heavily, while in May, it's asparagus. Often booked up, so reserve ahead. Mon & Wed–Sun noon–1.30pm & 7–10pm.

Le Garden 6 place de Langes ☎04 90 11 40 40, ⓦ restaurant-le-garden.fr. Serving Orange for more than a century, with wraparound floor to ceiling windows that make for a bright, airy eating space. Relatively adventurous mains such as duck cooked with pear and chicken with cèpes and pecans are in the €20–25 range, while the lunch two/three-course lunch *formule* is €16.90/19.90. Daily noon–2pm & 7–10pm.

Le Parvis 55 cours Pourtoules ☎04 90 34 82 00, ⓦ leparvisorange.com. Michelin-Starred restaurant in a renovated townhouse by the Théâtre, with exposed beams, heavy tablecloths and a low-lit romanticism setting the tone for finely worked takes on seasonal Provençal cooking. Dinner *menus* start at €34; six course tasting *menu* €65. Sun reservations only. Tues–Sat noon–1.45pm & 7.30–9pm, Sun noon–1.45pm.

Sérignan-du-Comtat

Pretty little **SÉRIGNAN-DU-COMTAT**, 8km northeast of Orange, is noteworthy as the former home of pioneering entomologist Jean Henri Fabre. A statue of Fabre stands beside the red-shuttered *mairie*, while his former home, the **Harmas**, is open to visitors, and the **Naturoptère** alongside also honours his work.

Harmas Jean Henri Fabre

Rte d'Orange • April–June Mon, Tues, Thurs & Fri 10am–12.30pm & 2.30–6pm, Sat & Sun 2.30–6pm; July & Aug Mon–Fri 10am–12.30pm & 3.30–7pm, Sat & Sun 3.30–7pm; Sept & Oct Mon, Tues, Thurs & Fri 10am–12.30pm & 2–5pm, Sat & Sun 2.30–6pm • €6, or €10 with Naturoptère (see below) • ☎ 04 90 30 57 62, ⓦ museum-paca.org

A remarkable self-taught scientist, **Jean Henri Fabre** (1823–1915) is famous primarily for his insect studies, but he also composed poetry, wrote songs and painted his specimens with artistic brilliance. In his 40s, with seven children to support, he was forced to resign from his teaching post at Avignon because parents and priests considered his lectures on the fertilization of flowering plants licentious, if not downright pornographic. His friend John Stuart Mill bailed him out with a loan, and in due course he moved on to Sérignan, where he spent his final 36 years. His house, which he named the **Harmas** – Latin for fallow land – is on the village's western edge.

Inside, you can look round Fabre's study, with its specimens of insects and other invertebrates and his complete classification of the herbs of France and Corsica. The strong sense of a person in love with the world he researched is echoed in Fabre's extraordinary **watercolours** of the fungi of the Vaucluse, displayed in stunning colours and hallucinogenic detail on video screens on the ground floor. You're also free to wander round the **garden**, where more than a thousand species grow in wild disorder, exactly as the scientist wanted it.

Naturoptère

Chemin du Grès • July & Aug Mon 10am–9pm, Tues–Fri 10am–6.30pm, Sat & Sun 1.30–6.30pm; Sept–June Mon, Tues, Thurs & Fri 9am–12.30pm & 1.30–5pm, Wed, Sat & Sun 1.30–6pm • €7, or €12 with Harmas Jean Henri Fabre (see above) • ☎ 04 90 30 33 20, ⓦ naturoptere.fr

Constructed to eco-conscious specifications, and topped by a roof of soil and grass, the **Naturoptère** stands across a small lane from the Harmas. It hosts changing exhibitions each year, which honour the legacy of Jean Henri Fabre by examining such themes as the role of insects, or carnivorous plants, and are generally aimed at school students.

Vaison-la-Romaine

Charming **VAISON-LA-ROMAINE**, 27km northeast of Orange, offers visitors an irresistible two-for-one deal. Standing to either side of a deep gorge cut by the River Ouvèze, and connected by a single-arched Roman bridge, its two very distinct halves consist of a spectacular hilltop **medieval village**, and a lively modern town that also boasts a splendid array of **Roman ruins**.

Throughout its history, Vaison has shifted back and forth across the river, depending on whether its inhabitants needed the protection afforded by the forbidding hill to the south. The delightful *ville perché* there, now known as the **haute ville** and topped by a ruined twelfth-century castle, was the site of Vaison's original Celtic settlement. The **Romans**, however, built their homes on the flatter land north of the river, and that's where most of the shops and restaurants are now concentrated. As a result, the *haute ville* remains self-contained and largely unspoiled, despite attracting throngs of day-trippers.

Roman ruins

Av Général-de-Gaulle • Daily: Early Feb, March, Nov & Dec 10am–noon & 2–5pm; April & May 9.30am–6pm; June–Sept 9.30am–6.30pm; Oct 10am–noon & 2–5.30pm • €9)

Vaison's two excavated Roman residential districts, the **Vestiges de Puymin** and the **Vestiges de la Villasse**, lie either side of the modern town's main street. While you can peek through the railings for free, you'll get a much better sense of the style and luxury of the era if you pay for admission, which includes access to the excellent museum.

Vestiges de Puymin

Vaison's eastern cluster of Roman remains, the **Vestiges de Puymin**, stretches up a gentle hillside. The ground plans of several mansions and houses are discernible in the foreground, along with a colonnade known as the *portique de Pompée*, while the **museum** slightly higher up holds all sorts of detail and decoration unearthed from the ruins. Everyday artefacts include mirrors of silvered bronze, lead water pipes, weights and measures, taps shaped as griffins' feet and dolphin doorknobs, and there are some impressive statues and stelae. A rather thrilling tunnel through the hillside leads to an ancient **theatre**, which still seats seven thousand people during the July **dance festival** (ⓦvaison-danses.com).

Vestiges de la Villasse

Vaison's smaller, western Roman ruins, the **Vestiges de la Villasse**, reveal a clear picture of the layout of a comfortable, well-serviced town of the Roman ruling class. As well as a row of arcaded shops, they include patrician houses (some with intact mosaics), a basilica and the baths.

Cathédrale Notre Dame

Cours Talignan, west of Roman ruins • Daily 10am–noon & 2–5pm • Free

The apse of the former **Cathédrale Notre Dame** is a confusing overlay of sixth-, tenth- and thirteenth-century construction, some of it using pieces quarried from the Roman ruins. Its **cloisters** are fairly typical of early medieval workmanship, pretty enough but not wildly exciting.

Haute ville

From the south side of the **Pont Romain**, the sturdy ancient bridge across the River Ouvèze, a cobbled lane climbs upwards towards place du Poids and the fourteenth-century gateway to the medieval **haute ville**. More steep zigzags take you past the Gothic gate and overhanging portcullis of the belfry and into the heart of this sedate but very gorgeous *quartier*. There are pretty fountains and flowers in all the squares, and right at the top, from the ruined twelfth- to sixteenth-century **castle**, you'll have a great view of Mont Ventoux. In summer, Vaison's Tuesday **market** spreads up into the *haute ville*.

ARRIVAL AND INFORMATION

VAISON-LA-ROMAINE

By bus Buses from Carpentras (5 daily; 50min) and Orange (every 1–2hr; 1hr) pull in at the *gare routière* on Av des Choralies, 500m east of the centre.

By car Parking is free throughout Vaison; if there's no room to park on the central place du Chanoine-Sautel, try Quai Pasteur down by the river.

Tourist office Place du Chanoine-Sautel, between the two Roman sites (mid-March to May & Sept to mid-Oct Mon–Sat 9.30am–noon & 2–5.45pm, Sun 9.30am–noon; June Mon–Fri 9.30am–1pm & 2–5.45pm, Sat 9.30am–noon & 2–5.45pm, Sun 9.30am–noon; July & Aug Mon–Fri 9.30am–6.45pm, Sat & Sun 9.30am–12.30pm & 2–6.45pm; mid-Oct to mid-March Mon–Sat 9.30am–noon & 2–5.45pm; ☎04 90 36 02 11, ⓦvaison-la-romaine.com).

ACCOMMODATION AND EATING

Vaison has many good **restaurants**, on both sides of the river. The places in the *haute ville* cannot be beaten for their lovely views, but for a more local feel stick to the modern town.

L'Auberge de la Bartavelle 12 place Sus-Auze ☎04 90 36 02 16, ⓦrestaurant-bartavelle.fr. A lively place in an otherwise drab square in the modern town, immediately south of place Montfort, serving decent and affordable specialities from southwest France – rabbit ravioli, *confit de canard* and the like – on *menus* costing from €17 lunch, €23 at dinner. Black-and-white photos honour the author Marcel Pagnol. Tues–Thurs & Sat 12.15–1.30pm & 7.15–9.30pm, Fri 7.15–9.30pm, Sun 12.15–1.30pm; closed Jan.

★ **Le Beffroi** Rue de l'Évêché ☎04 90 36 04 71, ⓦle-beffroi.com. Beautiful, luxurious rooms in a sixteenth-century residence in a lovely setting in the *haute ville*, with a pool. There's a great restaurant, too, with a terrace that enjoys unsurpassable views over the valley. Hotel closed late Jan to early April & mid-Nov to mid-Dec; restaurant closed Tues, and Nov–Easter. **€95**

Burrhus 1 place Montfort ☎ 04 90 36 00 11, ⓦ burrhus. com. Modern, freshly styled bedrooms in the heart of town, with tiled floors and very comfortable beds. The cheapest rooms are very small, and the square gets noisy at weekends, but the sunny breakfast balcony is a real plus. **€65**

Camping du Théâtre Romain Chemin du Brusquet, off Av des Choralies, quartier des Arts ☎ 04 90 28 78 66, ⓦ camping-theatre.com. Small, four-star campsite, 500m northeast of the centre and 150m from the Roman theatre, with good facilities, including a pool, and an emphasis on peaceful family fun. Reserve well ahead in summer. Closed early Nov to mid-March. **€27.90**

★ **L'Évêché** 14 rue de l'Évêché ☎ 0406 03 03 21 42, ⓦ eveche.free.fr. Lovely B&B in the *haute ville*, with five comfortable modern rooms and a homely atmosphere. Enjoy coffee and croissants on the little terrace at the back. **€90**

La Fête en Provence Place du Vieux Marché ☎ 04 90 36 36 43, ⓦ hotellafete-provence.com. Gorgeous, comfortable, contemporary rooms, studios and duplex apartments, surrounding a pool and flower-decked patio, in the *haute ville*. There's also a romantic restaurant (closed Wed July & Aug and Tues & Wed Sept–Dec). **€80**

La Lyriste 45 cours Taulignan ☎ 04 90 36 04 67. Of several restaurants spreading across the pavements of this quiet boulevard, just north of place Montfort, the *Lyriste* stands out for its changing, high-quality *menus*, based around such tried and tested staples as smoked salmon, prawns and steaks. Two-course lunches for €14.50 and a simple but great value €21 *menu découverte* in the evening. Tues & Thurs noon–1.30pm & 7.15–9.30pm, Wed noon–1.30pm, Fri noon–1.30pm & 7.15–10pm, Sat 7.15–9.30pm, Sun noon–1.30pm.

O' Natur'Elles 36 place Montfort ☎ 04 90 65 81 67. Organic bistro on the modern town's main square, specializing in succulent savoury mixed platters of local delicacies like *pissaladière* and tapenade. At €16–25, they're not particularly cheap, but they're ideal for vegetarians. Meat and fish mains are also available, for around €20. Mon–Sat noon–2pm.

Les Tilleuls d'Élisée 1 av Jules-Mazen, chemin du Bon-Ange ☎ 04 90 35 63 04, ⓦ vaisonchambres.info. Five pretty, peaceful and great-value B&B rooms in a family home, a short walk west of the Vestiges de la Villasse; breakfast in the garden is a delight in the summer. **€80**

The Dentelles

Running northeast to southwest between Vaison and Carpentras, the jagged hills known as the **Dentelles de Montmirail** are best appreciated from the level fields, orchards and vineyards that lie to their south and west. Although the connection with "teeth" (*dents*) might seem appropriate, the range is in fact named after lace (*dentelle*), as its pinnacles slant and converge like the contorted pins on a lace-making board. To geologists, the Dentelles are Jurassic limestone folds, forced upright and then eroded by the wind and rain.

On the western and southern slopes lie the **wine-producing villages** of Gigondas, **Beaumes-de-Venise**, **Séguret**, **Vacqueyras** and, across the River Ouzère, **Rasteau**. The Dentelles are also good for long **walks**, happening upon mysterious ruins or photogenic panoramas of Mont Ventoux and the Rhône Valley, and for **rock climbing**; tourist offices can provide full information on both. The Col de Cayron pinnacle is prized by serious climbers, while all you need to tackle the Dent du Turc are decent shoes and a head for heights.

Musée du Vigneron

Rasteau, 10km west of Vaison on the rte de Roaix • Mon & Wed–Sat: April–June & Sept 2–6pm; July & Aug 11am–6pm • €2 • ☎ 04 90 83 71 79, ⓦ beaurenard.fr

The **Musée du Vigneron**, on the D975 just east of the tiny, ivy-covered village of **RASTEAU**, offers a good introduction to the art and science of winemaking. For the serious wine enthusiast, the old bottles, nineteenth-century agricultural implements, pickers' baskets and root injectors for fighting phylloxera are less interesting than the instructive displays on geology, soil, vine types, parasites and wine growing throughout the world. Visits culminate with free tastings and no obligation to buy.

Séguret

The most immediately attractive of the Dentelles villages, **SÉGURET**, 10km southwest of Vaison, is an alluring spot that blends into the side of a rocky cliff, with a ruined castle soaring high above. With its steep cobbled streets, vine-covered houses and medieval structures, including an old stone laundry and a belfry with a one-handed clock, it embodies the charms of Provence.

Gigondas

Known as "Jocunditas" (light-hearted joy) in Roman times, the village of **GIGONDAS** sits at the base of a hill 7km south of Séguret. The **Église Ste-Catherine** higher up offers superb views over limestone pinnacles emerging from the vineyards below. Vestiges of the old fortifications and château top a separate eminence in the village's upper reaches.

Gigondas' wine has the highest reputation of all the Dentelles *appellations*; almost always red, and quite strong, it has a back taste of spice or nuts and is best aged at least four or five years. The **Gigondas La Cave co-operative**, at 589 Route de Vaison, to the southwest of the village (April, May & Oct Mon–Sat 9am–12.30pm & 2–7pm, Sun 10am–12.30pm & 2–6pm; June–Sept Mon–Sat 9am–7pm, Sun 10am–12.30pm & 2–6pm; Nov–March Mon–Sat 9am–12.30pm & 2–6pm, Sun 10am–12.30pm & 2–6pm; ☎04 90 65 83 78; ⓦcave-gigondas.fr) run tours and tastings (€7–10), including wines from the Vacqueyras and Beaumes de Venise *appellations*.

Vacqueyras

Three kilometres south of Gigondas, the village of **VACQUEYRAS** is best known as the birthplace of a troubadour poet called **Raimbaud**, who wrote love poems to Beatrice in Provençal and died in the Crusades in 1207. One of the many Dentelles villages with its own *appellation*, Vacqueyras hosts an annual **wine festival** (July 13 & 14), and a wine-tasting competition on the first weekend of June.

Beaumes-de-Venise

The picturesque village of **BEAUMES-DE-VENISE**, on the southern flank of the Dentelles, is home to the region's most distinctive wine, a sweet muscat. Topped by a Romanesque bell tower, the village's twelfth-century church, **Notre Dame d'Aubune**, reflects the key local concern in the trailing vines and classical wine containers sculpted over the door.

Cave Balma Venitia

228 rte de Carpentras • Daily: mid-April to Sept 9.30am–7pm; Oct to mid-April 10am–12.30pm & 2–6pm • ☎04 90 12 41 00, ⓦbeaumes-de-venise.com

The best place to buy the Beaumes-de-Venise muscat is the **Cave Balma Venitia**, set in a huge low building beside the D7, 1km west of the centre. Pale amber in colour, with a hint of roses and lemon, the wine can usually convince the driest palates of its virtue; if you remain resistant, the *cave* also sells red, rosé and white Côtes du Rhône Villages, and the light Côtes du Ventoux.

Le Barroux

East of the Dentelles, on the Vaison–Malaucène road, the largely untouristed **LE BARROUX** is a perfect *village perché*, where the narrow, twisting streets climb up to a **château** (April & May Sat & Sun 10am–7pm; June daily 2.30–7pm; July–Sept daily 10am–7pm; Oct daily 2–6pm; €5; ⓦchateau-du-barroux.com). Dating from the twelfth to the eighteenth century, it was restored just before World War II, only to be set on fire by the Nazis in 1944. The blaze burned for ten days, but the castle was restored again between 1960 and 1990.

INFORMATION

THE DENTELLES

GIGONDAS
Tourist office Rue du Portail (Jan–March, Nov & Dec Mon–Fri 9.30am–12.30pm & 2–5pm; April–June, Sept & Oct Mon–Sat 9.30am–12.30pm & 2–6pm; July & Aug Mon–Sat 9am–12.30pm & 2.30–6.30pm, Sun 9.30am–12.30pm; ☏ 04 90 65 85 46, ⓦ ventouxprovence.fr).

BEAUMES-DE-VENISE
Tourist office Maison des Dentelles, 140 place du Marché (April–June, Sept & Oct: Mon–Sat 10am–12.30pm & 2–6pm; July & Aug Mon–Sat 9.30am–12.30pm & 2.30–6.30pm, Sun 9.30am–12.30pm; Nov Mon–Sat 10am–12.30pm & 2–5.30pm; Dec–March Mon–Fri 10am–12.30pm & 2–5.30pm; ☏ 04 90 62 94 39, ⓦ ventoux-provence.fr).

ACCOMMODATION AND EATING

SÉGURET
★ **Bastide Bleue** Rte de Sablet ☏ 04 90 46 83 43, ⓦ bastidebleue.com. This delightful rural villa, at the foot of the hill below Séguret, offers simple but attractive en-suite rooms, plus a pool. Its rustic dining room (Sept–June closed Tues & Wed), serves good *menus* from €28 in the evening. €81.50

GIGONDAS
★ **Les Florets** Rte des Dentelles ☏ 04 90 65 85 01, ⓦ hotel-lesflorets.com. Charming hotel, 2km north of Gigondas towards Séguret, with elegant and very comfortable rooms and an excellent restaurant (closed Wed all day & Thurs lunch) that serves *menus* from 26 at lunch, €43 at dinner. Closed Jan to mid-March. €135
Gîte d'Etape des Dentelles Gigondas ☏ 04 90 65 80 85, ⓦ gite-dentelles.com. This simple, inexpensive gîte, at the entrance to the village, offers two large shared dorms, ten very plain double rooms, and one triple, none of them en suite. Closed Jan & Feb. Dorms €18; doubles €40
L'Oustalet Place du Village ☏ 04 90 65 85 30, ⓦ restaurant-oustalet.fr. Thanks to a dynamic young chef, this modern restaurant, with seating indoors and out on a pleasant shaded terrace, offers the best dining in the village centre. Full dinner *menus* start at around €40. They also offer three contemporary styled rooms. Wed–Sat noon–3pm &

7–10pm; also Sun noon–2pm in summer. €160

VACQUEYRAS
Montmirail Just south of the village centre ☏ 04 90 65 84 01, ⓦ hotelmontmirail.com. Villa hotel in spacious grounds with a pool and a good Provençal restaurant, serving lunch *menus* from €27 (lunch) and €30 (dinner). Closed Nov to mid-April. €100

BEAUMES-DE-VENISE
Amerigo Vespucci 210 av Jules-Ferry ☏ 09 70 35 79 70, ⓦ lerelaisdesdentelles.fr. Formerly the *Relais des Dentelles*, just south of the village centre, across the river, this hotel reopened as a guesthouse some years back, with plain, inexpensive rooms, but its reputation rests on its restaurant, serving good Provençal food for lunch (from €16.50) and dinner (€29) daily. €69

LE BARROUX
Les Géraniums Place de la Croix ☏ 04 90 62 41 08, ⓦ hotel-lesgeraniums.com. Small, peaceful, comfortable and unpretentious hotel in the heart of the village, with spacious rooms and views of the Dentelles. Its popular *terrasse* restaurant serves decent food on lunch and dinner *menus* for €19 and €35 respectively. Closed Dec–Feb. €85

Mont Ventoux and around

Visible from the valleys of the Rhône, Luberon and Durance, the 1912m summit of **MONT VENTOUX** looms high on the horizon east of the Dentelles. White with snow, black with storm-cloud shadow or reflecting myriad shades of blue, the barren pebbles of its topmost 300m are like a coloured weather vane for all of western Provence. From a distance the mountain looks distinctly alluring; indeed, the fourteenth-century Italian poet Petrarch climbed the heights simply for the experience, although the local guides he chartered for the two-and-a-half-day hike considered him completely crazy. Small wonder – weather conditions at the top can be ferocious. The northern Mistral accelerates across Ventoux at up to 250km/hr, and wind, rain, snow and fearsome sub-zero temperatures are constant threats.

These days, for drivers at any rate, the expedition to the summit is straightforward, thanks to a zigzagging 42km road that loops up and back at typical gradients of around nine percent. It starts and ends at two little towns, just 13km apart on the mountain's western flanks: **Malaucène**, southeast of Vaison-la-Romaine; and prettier **Bédoin**, northeast of Carpentras. Both towns make good bases.

Mont Ventoux is most famous, however, for the challenge it presents to **cyclists**. Countless amateurs flock to emulate the legendary athletes of the Tour de France by completing the gruelling counterclockwise ascent from Bédoin.

Malaucène

Unless you happen to coincide with its Wednesday-morning market, there's no great reason to stop in the small town of **MALAUCÈNE**, 10km southeast of Vaison-la-Romaine, other than to use it as a base for seeing Mont Ventoux. At its southern end, the narrow main road curves west to avoid the massive bulk of a medieval church. It meets the D974, the access road to Mont Ventoux, in the town centre just beyond, where you'll find several pavement cafés and small hotels.

Crillon-le-Brave

The tiny hilltop village of **CRILLON-LE-BRAVE**, 4km west of Bédoin, dates largely from the sixteenth century, when the Duke of Crillon provided such sterling service as a general that King Henry IV designated his home as being "brave". Almost all its oldest buildings now form part of an exquisite luxury hotel (see page 142).

Bédoin

BÉDOIN, 15km northeast of Carpentras and 13km southeast of Malaucène, is a large and rather pretty village that's bustling for most of the year with cyclists, walkers and day-trippers heading to and from Mont Ventoux. Commercial activity is concentrated along a plane-tree-lined boulevard that doubles as the D974, where assorted bars, cafés, hotels and restaurants jostle in amiable competition.

The road to the summit

Whether you start the ascent from Bédoin – the route traditionally followed by cyclists – Malaucène, or indeed from Sault to the east, the defining moment for anyone **climbing Mont Ventoux** comes when you pass beyond the well-shaded woodlands lower down and reach the pitiless exposed pebblescape that lies above the tree line.

The deforestation of Mont Ventoux dates from Roman times. By the nineteenth century it had got so bad that the entire mountain appeared shaved. Oaks, pines, boxwood, fir and beech have since been replanted and the owls and eagles have returned, but the greenery is unlikely ever to reach the summit again.

As a result, the final 6km of the road up the eastern side of the mountain, from the Chalet Reynard way station, is utterly unforgiving for cyclists. A poignant shrine 1km short of the top commemorates the great British cyclist **Tom Simpson**, who died here from heart failure in 1967 on one of the hottest days ever recorded in the Tour de France. Popular legend has it that his last words were "Put me back on the bloody bike."

Surrounded by hardy scientific and meteorological observatories, the **summit** itself offers one of the most wonderful panoramas, not just in France, but in all Europe. Note that between November and May, the road is covered by snow and impassable, with only the tops of the black and yellow poles beside the road still visible.

Sault

At **SAULT**, 26km southeast of the summit of Mont Ventoux, the steep forested rocks give way to fields of lavender, cereals and grazing sheep. Wild products of the woods – *lactaire* and *grisel* mushrooms, truffles and game, as well as honey and lavender products – are bought and sold at its Wednesday **market**. Autumn is the best time for these local specialities.

Gorges de la Nesque

The spectacular **GORGES DE LA NESQUE**, south of Ventoux, stretches for 20km beside and beneath the D942, between Carpentras and Sault. This magnificent, little-known canyon was carved by the River Nesque, although the river itself is seldom visible from the road that clings to the rocks high above, and burrows repeatedly through cliff-edge tunnels.

The 200m-high **Rocher du Cire** on the canyon's southern side, 5km southwest of the village of Monieux, is coated in wax from the hives of wild bees. Men from the village are said in days gone by to have abseiled down the rock to gather honey.

INFORMATION AND ACTIVITIES

MONT VENTOUX AND AROUND

MALAUCÈNE
Tourist office 3 place de la Mairie (Mon–Sat 9.30am–12.30pm & 2–6pm; ☎04 90 65 22 59, ⓦ ventouxprovence.fr).

BÉDOIN
Tourist office 1 rte de Malaucène (Mon–Fri 9.30am–12.30pm & 2–5.30; also Sat during school holidays; ☎04 90 65 63 95, ⓦ ventouxprovence.fr).
Bike rental Bédoin Location, chemin de la Ferraille (☎04 90 65 94 53, ⓦ bedoin-location.fr) rents out bikes (€55/day) and can arrange for van transportation to the summit, from where you cycle back down.

ACCOMMODATION AND EATING

MALAUCÈNE
Le Domaine des Tilleuls Rte du Mont Ventoux ☎04 90 65 22 31, ⓦ hotel-domainedestilleuls.com. Country-house hotel, set in wooded grounds just outside the village at the foot of Mont Ventoux, with twenty rustic, slightly faded but spacious and comfortable rooms, but no restaurant. Closed mid-Nov to late March. €95

CRILLON-LE-BRAVE
Hotel Crillon-le-Brave Place de l'Église ☎04 90 65 61 61, ⓦ crillonlebrave.com. Staying in this very charming luxury hotel, you feel as though you have your own home in a peaceful medieval village. The lavish guest rooms spread through eight historic houses, with their own street doors; some occupy entire floors. Between them, two restaurants (one specialising in light seasonal cooking and the other fine dining) serve lunch and dinner *menus* starting at €36 and up to €135 for ten courses. Restaurants closed in winter. €450

BÉDOIN
Camping Le Pastory Rte de Malaucène ☎04 90 12 85 83, ⓦ camping-le-pastory.com. Pleasant, simple little two-star campsite, in a peaceful rural setting 1km northwest of the village on the D19. Closed mid-Oct to March. €14.50

L'Escapade Place Portail l'Olivier ☎04 90 65 60 21, ⓦ lescapade.eu. Plain, good-value hotel on Bédoin's main square, with free parking opposite and a decent restaurant downstairs (closed all day Thurs & Fri lunch). Closed mid Nov to mid-March. €75

Le Grillon 341 av Barral des Beaux ☎04 90 65 66 89. Centring on a wood-burning grill, this cosy central restaurant offers pavement tables beneath an enormous plane tree. The €21 lunch *menu* includes a tasty cod *cassolette*, while dinner brings the choice of a standard €26.50 *menu* or a seafood-heavy €46 variant, including two flame-grilled lobster dishes. Mon & Fri–Sun noon–3pm & 7–11pm, Tues noon–3pm, Thurs 7–11pm.

SAULT
Le Louvre Place du Marché ☎04 90 64 08 88, ⓦ louvre-provence.com. This very appealing little pastel-painted hotel offers sixteen tasteful en-suite rooms, and is cycle-friendly even by local standards. It opens onto a peaceful square behind the main drag that's almost entirely filled with tables from its restaurant, which serves traditional Provençal food on *menus* costing €23 and up. €87

Carpentras

With a population of around thirty thousand, **CARPENTRAS** is a substantial city for this part of the world. It's also an old one, first recorded in 5 BC as the capital of a Celtic tribe. The Greeks who founded Marseille came here to buy honey, wheat, goats and skins, and the Romans also had a base in Carpentras. Today, it's a faded provincial town, where restored squares and fountains alternate with decaying streets of seventeenth- and eighteenth-century houses, some forming arcades over the pavement. However, even in its grandest sections, like the eighteenth-century shopping gallery in the **Passage Boyer**, an alarming number of businesses seem to be closed down – to experience it at its liveliest, come during the last fortnight in July for the **Estivales**, a series of music, theatre and dance performances staged in front of the cathedral.

A bird's-eye view of Carpentras clearly shows its ancient perimeter line (rues Vigne, des Halles, Raspail, du Collège and Moricelly), encircled in turn, further out, by the ring of broader boulevards that follow the line of the medieval town wall. Of this, only the massive, crenellated **Porte d'Orange** and the odd rampart remain.

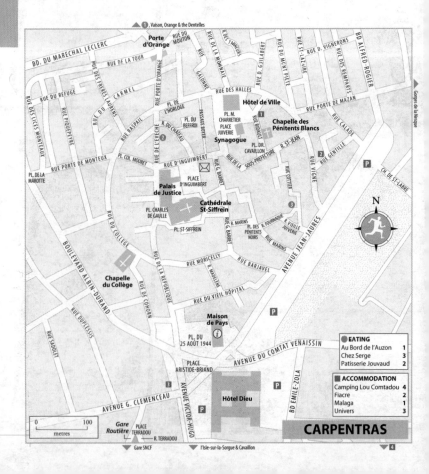

EATING
Au Bord de l'Auzon	1
Chez Serge	3
Patisserie Jouvaud	2

ACCOMMODATION
Camping Lou Comtadou	4
Fiacre	2
Malaga	1
Univers	3

CARPENTRAS

> ## CARPENTRAS MARKET
> Friday is the major **market** day in Carpentras, with the **fruit and vegetables** that appear so early in the lowlands of Vaucluse available everywhere. **Flowers and plants** are sold on avenue Jean-Jaurès, and **antiques and bric-a-brac** on rue Porte-de-Monteux and place Colonel-Mouret. **Truffles** – the fungi, not the chocolate kind – are also a local speciality, on sale on place du 25 Août 1944 between the annual St-Siffrein fair (Nov 24–27) and the start of March, and again from May until August.

Jewish Carpentras

A seventeenth-century construction on fourteenth-century foundations, the **Synagogue** on Place Juiverie (visitors received Mon–Thurs 10am, 11am, 2pm, 3pm & 4pm, Fri 10am, 11am, 2pm & 3pm; closed Jewish holidays; free; ☎ 04 90 63 39 97, ⚲ synagoguedecarpentras.com), is the oldest surviving place of Jewish worship in France.

The **Porte Juif**, on the southern side of the fifteenth-century Cathédrale St-Siffrein nearby, is so named because Jews used to pass through it to enter the cathedral in chains. Inside, whether coerced, bribed or otherwise persuaded, they would be unshackled as converted Christians. The door itself bears strange symbolism of rats encircling and devouring a globe.

Carpentras hosts an annual **Festival of Jewish Music**, ranging from classical to klezmer, in late July or early August.

L'Inguimbertine À L'Hôtel Dieu

Place Aristide-Briand • Guided tours first Sat of the month 4–5.30pm; by reservation only • Free • ☎ 04 90 63 04 92, ⚲ inguimbertine.carpentras.fr

Carpentras' huge **Hôtel Dieu**, built as a hospice in the eighteenth century, now houses a cultural centre comprising the municipal archives, a state-of-the-art library and various museum collections, incorporating some of the artefacts previously on display in the old Comtadin and Duplessis museum.

At the time of writing, renovations were still ongoing, with the museum collections closed to the public, though the library hosts lectures and temporary exhibitions, usually free – check the website for details.

ARRIVAL AND INFORMATION   CARPENTRAS

By train To relieve commuter congestion, the long-defunct train link between Avignon and Carpentras' *gare SNCF*, 400m southwest of the centre, has recently reopened.
Destinations Avignon (every 30min at peak times; 30min).

By bus Buses arrive either at the *gare routière* on place Terradou (from Avignon, Vaison and other points north and west), or on Av Victor-Hugo (from Marseille, Aix and Cavaillon).
Destinations Avignon (roughly every 30–45min; 35–45min); Cavaillon (5 daily; 50min); Gigondas (10 daily; 30min); L'Isle-sur-la-Sorgue (4 daily; 24min); Marseille airport (3–4 daily; 2hr –2hr 15min); Orange (roughly every 1–2hr; 45min–1hr); Vaison (5 daily; 50min).

Tourist office 97 place du 25 Août 1944, on the south side of the old town (Mon & Wed–Sat 9.30am–12.30pm & 2–6pm, Tues 9.30am–12.30pm & 3–6pm; ☎ 04 90 63 00 78, ⚲ ventouxprovence.fr).

ACCOMMODATION   SEE MAP PAGE 144

Camping Lou Comtadou Rte St-Didier, 881 av Pierre-de-Coubertin ☎ 04 66 60 07 00, ⚲ campingloucomtadou.com. Very pleasant, well-equipped three-star campsite, in shaded rural surroundings 1km south of the centre. Closed Nov–Feb. **€25**

Fiacre 153 rue Vigne ☎ 04 90 63 03 15, ⚲ hotel-du-fiacre.com. Grand eighteenth-century townhouse, with a central courtyard and nicely decorated rooms, two with terraces and two with balconies. The friendly owners can help plan walking and cycling tours. **€80**

Malaga 37 place Maurice-Charretier ☎ 04 90 60 57 96, ⚲ hotel-malaga-carpentras.fr. Eight clean en-suite rooms, perfectly satisfactory for budget travellers and centrally located above a decent pavement brasserie. **€49**

Univers 110 place Aristide-Briand ☎ 09 70 35 08 14, ⓦ hotel-univers84.com. The bedrooms inside this imposing old building, near the tourist office, are plain, but large and comfortable, and there's no quarrelling with the low prices, especially for the four-person rooms. **€66**

EATING

SEE MAP PAGE 144

The winding streets of Carpentras' ancient core hold plenty of small **restaurants**, while brasseries spread across the larger squares to the south. The local sweet speciality is the **berlingot**, a small, striped fruit *bonbon*.

Au Bord de l'Auzon 40 rue de l'Evêché ☎ 04 90 28 11 53, ⓦ auborddelauzon.fr. A charming and entirely unexpected little wooden chalet with an almost jungle-like, bamboo-covered terrace by the river Auzon, north of the city centre. Seasonal, organic and vegetarian/vegan-friendly, with afternoon tea served on the terrace. *Menus* from €16. Tues–Fri noon–3.30pm & 7–9.30pm, Sat 7–9.30pm.

Chez Serge 90 rue Cottier ☎ 04 90 63 21 24, ⓦ chez-serge.com. Welcoming bistro in an old mansion, serving changing daily *plats* in the courtyard beneath the shade of a huge tree. The great-value lunch *menu* is €19.50, dinner *menus* start at €32, with a major emphasis on truffles in season. Daily: June–Sept noon–2pm & 7.30–10pm; Oct–May noon–1.30pm & 7.30–9.30pm.

Patisserie Jouvaud 40 rue de l'Evêché ☎ 04 90 63 15 38, ⓦ patisserie-jouvaud.com. This cosy tearoom and patisserie, which also has three tables on the pedestrian street outside, makes a fabulous stop-off for tea and cakes. Daily 9am–7.30pm.

Pernes-les-Fontaines

The delightful small town of **PERNES-LES-FONTAINES** lies 6km south of Carpentras. Everything in Pernes – from the 36 fountains for which it's named to the ramparts, gateways, towers, covered market hall, Renaissance streets and half a dozen chapels – seems to blend into a single complex structure, and the passages between its squares feel more like corridors between rooms. What's particularly appealing, though, is that it's barely commercialized at all, and always seems to be so very quiet. Anyone hankering after a spot of shopping will be disappointed; others can simply enjoy having the place to themselves.

Of Pernes' fourteenth-century ramparts, only three gates now remain. The most impressive, the sixteenth-century **Porte Notre Dame**, was the northern entrance to the walled town. Accessed via a narrow medieval stone bridge that crosses a surviving section of the ancient moat, it leads to an elegant **cormorant fountain** and seventeenth-century market hall. Up to the right, the massive twelfth-century keep of the castle of the counts of Toulouse, now known as the **Tour Ferrande**, has been turned into a clock tower by the simple expedient of sticking two big clocks onto it halfway up. Inside, immaculately preserved fourteenth-century **frescoes** portray scenes from the legend of William of Orange and the life of Charles of Anjou.

Continue west along rue Gambetta to reach **Porte Villeneuve**, flanked by two imposing round towers, which opens off the main road through town, avenue Jean-Jaurès. Alternatively, head south from Porte Notre Dame on rue Raspail, and you'll come to the other remaining gate, **Porte St-Gilles**.

INFORMATION

PERNES-LES-FONTAINES

Tourist office 72 cours Frizet (June Mon–Fri 9am–noon & 2–5.30pm, Sat 9am–12.30pm & 2–5pm; July & Aug Mon–Fri 9am–noon & 2–5.30pm, Sat 9am–12.30pm & 2–5pm, Sun 9.30am–12.30pm; Sept–May Mon–Fri 9am–noon & 2–5.30pm, Sat 9am–12.30pm; ☎ 04 90 61 31 04, ⓦ tourisme-pernes.fr).

ACCOMMODATION AND EATING

Au Fil de Temps 51 place Louis-Giraud ☎ 04 90 30 09 48. Very charming restaurant in the old town, serving creative Provençal cuisine on *menus* starting at €26 for a two-course lunch, and ranging from €40 to €60 for dinner. There's a focus on unusual ingredients, such as rare tomato varieties. Wed–Sun noon–1.30pm & 7.30–9.30pm.

★ **La Margelle** 56 place Louis-Giraud ☎ 04 90 40 18 54, ⓦ lamargellehotel-pernes.fr. This stylish, good-value hotel, stretching back from Pernes' southern boulevard ring to a sleepy old square, holds six smart upgraded rooms plus a luxury apartment. A high-class garden restaurant (closed Mon & Sun) serves a lunch *formule* at €16 and *menu* at €38. **€120**

Venasque

The gorgeous, perfectly contained village of **VENASQUE** perches atop a spur of rock 9km east of Pernes, just before the D4 starts to wind over the Plateau de Vaucluse towards Apt. Oddly, only its upper end needed to be fortified, and remains screened off by a curtain wall punctuated by three round towers. Like so many Provençal villages, Venasque swings between its sleepy winter state and being a tourist honeypot in summer. The best time to visit is in May and June, before the main season begins, and when the daily **market** sells succulent local cherries.

Baptistère de l'Église Notre Dame

Place du Presbytère • Daily: early Jan to early April & early Oct to early Dec 9.15am–1pm & 2–5pm; early April to early Oct 9am–1pm & 2–6.30pm • €3 • ☎ 04 90 66 62 01

The remarkable **Baptistère** (baptistery) behind the **Église Notre Dame** at the lower end of Venasque ranks among the oldest religious buildings in France. Erected on the site of a Roman temple dedicated to Venus, surviving vestiges of which include a sarcophagus from 420 AD, it's thought to have been Christianized later in the fifth century.

INFORMATION   **VENASQUE**

Tourist office Grande Rue (April–Oct Tues 2–5.30pm, Wed–Sat 10am–12.30pm & 2–5.30pm; ☎ 09 67 50 11 66, ⓦ ventouxprovence.fr).

ACCOMMODATION AND EATING

La Maison Provençal 40 Grand Rue ☎ 04 90 66 02 84, ⓦ lamaisonprovencale.fr. Individually styled – if simple and unpretentious – rooms in a friendly, accommodating and very popular *chambre d'hôte*, with fabulously romantic views from the breakfast terrace. **€60**

Remparts Rue Haute ☎ 04 90 66 02 79, ⓦ hotelles remparts.com. Set into the ramparts at the top of the main street, the ivy on its walls rippling in the wind, this beautifully rustic hotel offers eight pretty rooms, and superb views from its panoramic dining room, where lunch *menus* start at €22, dinner at €27. There's even a vegetarian *menu* (€27). Closed mid-Nov to mid-March. **€90**

L'Isle-sur-la-Sorgue

Halfway between Carpentras and Cavaillon to the south, and 23km east of Avignon, **L'ISLE-SUR-LA-SORGUE** straddles five branches of the River Sorgue, with little canals and waterways running through and around the centre. Once filled with otters and beavers, eels, trout and crayfish, the river powered **medieval industries** including tanneries and dyeing works. It still holds huge waterwheels, but these days they turn for show only, and L'Isle has become an immensely popular day-trip destination. It's at its most cheerful on Sundays, when an **antiques market** spills out across town; local produce is available both then and at the smaller Thursday market.

While there are few sights to head for, the central **place de l'Église** and **place de la Liberté** do provide reminders of past prosperity, most obviously in the Baroque seventeenth-century **church** (Tues–Sat: July & Aug 10am–noon & 3–6pm, Sun 3–6pm; Sept–June 10am–noon & 3–5pm), by far the richest religious edifice for many kilometres around. Each column in the nave supports a sculpted Virtue: whips and turtledoves are Chastity's props, a unicorn accompanies Virginity, and medallions and inscriptions carry the adornment down to the floor.

ARRIVAL AND INFORMATION   **L'ISLE-SUR-LA-SORGUE**

By train The *gare SNCF* is a short walk southwest of the centre.
Destinations Avignon (every 30min–1hr; 30min); Cavaillon (every 30min–1hr 30min; 7min).

By bus Buses arrive beside pont Gambetta, on the southeast edge of the old centre.

Destinations Avignon (12 daily; 45min); Cavaillon (4 daily; 24min); Fontaine-de-Vaucluse (8 daily; 15min).

By car Although car parks are scattered all around the periphery, parking can be all but impossible on market days; if you're driving here on Thursday or Sunday, it's worth having a Plan B in mind.

Tourist office Place de la Liberté (April–June & Sept Mon–Sat 9am–12.30pm & 2.30–6pm, Sun 9am–12.30pm; July & Aug Mon–Sat 9am–12.30pm & 2.30–6pm, Sun 9am–1pm; Oct–March Mon–Sat 9am–12.30pm & 2–5.30pm, Sun 9am–12.30pm; ☎ 04 90 38 04 78, ✺ oti-delasorgue.fr).

ACCOMMODATION AND EATING

★ **La Prévôté** 4 rue Jean-Jacques Rousseau ☎ 04 90 38 57 29, ✺ la-prevote.fr. Charming hotel, arrayed around a quiet courtyard behind the church in the heart of the old town. The five rooms are decked out in beautiful terracotta tiles, wooden beams and Provençal quilts; a small, superb restaurant, downstairs in the old sacristy (closed Tues & Wed), serves top-quality *menus* from €24 for lunch, €46 for dinner. **€160**

La Sorguette 871 rte d'Apt ☎ 04 90 38 05 71, ✺ camping-sorguette.com. The three-star municipal campsite enjoys a lovely riverside location, 1km east of the

centre on the Apt road, and offers teepees and yurts as well as tent pitches. Closed mid-Oct to mid-March. **€26**

Vivier 800 cours Fernande Peyre ☎ 04 90 38 52 80, ✺ levivier-restaurant.com. For a true feast, you can't do better than this lovely gourmet restaurant, 1km northeast of the centre, where three-course *menus* start at €28 lunch, €60 at dinner. Late May to mid-Sept Wed–Fri noon–1.30pm & 7.30–9.30pm, Sat 7.30–9.30pm, Sun noon–1.30pm; mid-Sept to late May Wed–Fri & Sun noon–1.30pm & 7.30–9.30pm, Sat 7.30–9.30pm.

Fontaine-de-Vaucluse

The ancient riverside village of **FONTAINE-DE-VAUCLUSE**, 7km east of L'Isle-sur-la-Sorgue, provides the only access to the spectacular source of the Sorgue river, a short but beautiful walk beyond. As a result, it's all but overwhelmed by summer day-trippers. While the source itself is well worth seeing, Fontaine-de-Vaucluse is something of a tourist trap. Arrive in the evening, though, after the crowds have gone, and it makes a pleasant overnight stop.

At the centre of the village, a mossy waterwheel stands alongside a bridge that spans the already broad Sorgue. On the northern bank, around the circular place de Colonne, six enormous plane trees spread to form a canopy over the eponymous column in the middle. Visitors can only follow the Sorgue upstream from here on foot.

The source of the Sorgue

Thanks to a geological anomaly, all the rainwater that falls on the vast chalk plateau atop the hills east of Fontaine-de-Vaucluse is funnelled into a single channel. Measured at 630 million cubic metres per year, the most powerful natural spring in Europe emerges from a mysterious tapering fissure at the foot of towering 230m cliffs, to become the Sorgue river.

To reach the **source of the Sorgue**, follow a gentle 500m footpath, known as the chemin de la Fontaine, along the north bank from Fontaine-de-Vaucluse. Even with the usual crowds, it's a lovely walk, climbing through a narrowing gorge with the glorious green river cascading beneath thickly wooded slopes to your right.

Most visitors continue beyond the safety barriers at the path's far end, stepping gingerly down the rubble-strewn slopes to get close-up views of the limpid pool of azure-blue water that wells up from an otherworldly cavern – in technical parlance, a **sinkhole**. Don't even dream of entering the abyss; scuba divers have reached the astonishing depth of 205m below the surface, while remote-controlled cameras have descended more than 300m without reaching the bottom.

Le Musée d'Histoire Jean Garcin 39–45: L'Appel de la Liberté

Chemin de la Fontaine • April–Sept Mon & Thurs–Sun 11am–1pm & 2–6pm • €7 • ☎ 04 90 20 24 00, ✺ vaucluse.fr

An incongruous presence amid the fast-food outlets and souvenir shops on the riverside path, **Le Musée d'Histoire Jean Garcin 39–45** is an excellent history museum devoted to the story of France under Nazi occupation. Its two dominant themes are **shortages** – illustrated by such recipes as biscuits made without eggs, and fried potato peelings – and **collaboration**, with a section listing the worst offenders entitled "They sold their souls". The museum's presence here in the Vaucluse is justified by displays on the attacks carried out by local resistance fighters, though you'll need good French to make head or tail of it.

Musée du Monde Souterrain

Chemin de la Fontaine • Daily: mid-Feb to April & Oct to mid-Nov 2–6pm; May–Sept 10am–12.30pm & 2–7pm; last admission 1hr before closing; hourly tours in French only • €6 • ☎ 04 90 20 34 13

To learn more about the source of the Sorgue, stop off at the **Musée du Monde Souterrain** (also known as the Ecomusée du Gouffre) on the riverside path, best suited to French speakers. Volunteers eager to communicate their passion for crawling in the bowels of the earth lead forty-minute tours through mock-up caves and passages, while displays document the intriguing history of the exploration of the spring. The museum winds up with a collection of subterranean concretions, ranging from huge, jewellery-like crystals to pieces resembling fibre optics.

Moulin à Papier Vallis Clausa

Chemin de la Fontaine • Daily: late Jan & Dec 10am–12.30pm & 2–5.30pm; Feb, March & Nov 10am–12.30pm & 2–6pm; April & Oct 9.30am–12.30pm & 2–6.30pm; May, June & Sept 9.30am–12.30pm & 2–7pm; July & Aug 10am–7pm • Free • ☎ 04 90 20 34 14, Ⓦ moulin-vallisclausa.com

Fontaine's first water-powered paper mill was built in 1522, while the last ceased operations in 1968. The medieval method of pulping rags to paper has been re-created in the **Moulin à Papier Vallis Clausa**, where flowers are added to the pulp and the resulting paper is printed with drawings, poems and prose, ranging from Martin Luther King's "I Have A Dream" to cloying homilies and delightful etchings.

The south bank of the Sorgue

You can escape the crowds in Fontaine-de-Vaucluse by walking on the **south bank** of the river. There's no access to the source, but follow signs to Petrarch's house, and you'll swiftly find yourself in a lovely shaded park. The ruined thirteenth-century **castle** perched on the outcrop above originally belonged to the bishops of Cavaillon. No formal path leads to the top, but with good shoes you can scramble up the rough hillside to reach what's now just a hollow shell, with great views over the village. Stay well clear of the dangerous, unprotected drop-offs.

Musée Bibliothèque Francois Pétrarque

Across the bridge south of the river • April–Sept Mon & Thurs–Sun 11am–1pm & 2–6pm • €3.50 • ☎ 04 90 20 37 20

Seven centuries ago, the poet Petrarch spent sixteen unrequited years pining in Fontaine-de-Vaucluse, then as now a rustic backwater, for his beloved Laura. The pretty little **Musée Bibliothèque Francois Pétrarque** explains Petrarch's role in early Renaissance culture, with somewhat scanty displays complemented by a small gallery of modern paintings.

ARRIVAL AND INFORMATION   FONTAINE-DE-VAUCLUSE

By bus Buses from L'Isle sur la Sorgue (8 daily; 15min) arrive in the village centre.

By car Parking can be hard to find; the largest car park is a short walk south of the river (€4).

Tourist office In the village centre, on the south side of the bridge (April–Sept Mon–Sat 10am–5pm, Sun 9.30am–1pm; Oct–March Mon–Fri 9am–12.30pm & 1.30–5pm; ☎04 90 20 32 22, ⓦoti-delasorgue.fr).

Canoe rental In summer, Kayak Vert (☎04 90 20 35 44, ⓦcanoevaucluse.com) rents canoes either for short paddles, or for a fairly effortless 8km trip down to L'Isle-sur-la-Sorgue.

ACCOMMODATION AND EATING

★ **Auberge La Figuière** Chemin de la Grangette ☎04 90 20 37 41, ⓦlafiguiere-provence.fr. Simple but attractive B&B rooms in the heart of the village, with terracotta tiles, tasteful Provençal furnishings and excellent walk-in showers. With tables spread across a pleasant flower-filled courtyard, the restaurant downstairs (closed Mon) serves a great-value €26 menu. Closed Dec to mid-Feb. **€67**

Restaurant Philip Chemin de la Fontaine ☎04 90 20 31 81. This gorgeous riverside spot is sure to catch your eye as you walk up to the spring. At the very least, it's worth enjoying a quick drink on the bar section of its long, peaceful terrace, but the food is a lot better than you might expect, with full *menus* starting at €31. Easter–Sept daily noon–8pm.

Hôtel du Poète ☎04 90 20 34 05, ⓦhoteldupoete. com. Despite its uninspiring exterior, this former water mill, just outside the village below the main D25 on the river's north bank, offers luxurious accommodation, with large, comfortable rooms and a pool, but no restaurant. Closed mid-Nov to early March. **€98**

Cavaillon

Approaches to **CAVAILLON**, directly south of L'Isle-sur-la-Sorgue and 25km southeast of Avignon, pass through fields of fruit and vegetables, watered by the Durance and Coulon rivers. Market gardening is a major business, and Cavaillon, its Roman origins notwithstanding, is known simply as a **melon** town. The melon in question – the Charentais, a small pale-green ball with dark green stripes and brilliant orange flesh – is honoured by a **melon festival** in mid-July.

Cavaillon itself is pleasant enough, but somewhat run-down, and there's no great reason to linger long. All that remains of Roman Cavaillon is the **Arc de Triomphe** on place du Clos, which on Mondays is surrounded by the weekly **market**.

Cathédrale St-Véran

April–Sept Mon–Sat 8.30am–noon & 2–6pm; Oct–March Mon–Sat 9am–noon & 2–5pm • Free

On the south side of Cavaillon's archaic-looking, thirteenth-century **Cathédrale St-Véran**, God appears above a sundial looking like a winged and battered Neptune. Inside, in the St-Véran chapel above the altar, there's a painting of St Véran hauling off a slithery reptile known as Couloubre, who terrorized the locality at the dawn of the Christian era.

ARRIVAL AND INFORMATION

CAVAILLON

By train Trains from L'Isle-sur-la-Sorgue (every 30min–1hr 30min; 7min) pull in at the *gare SNCF* on Av Pierre-Semard, 250m east of the centre.

By bus The bus station, alongside the *gare SNCF* on Av Pierre-Semard, sees buses from L'Isle-sur-la-Sorgue (4 daily; 24min) and Pernes-les-Fontaines (4 daily; 33min).

Tourist office Place François-Tourel – marked by a giant melon (April–June & Sept Mon–Sat 9am–12.30pm & 1.30–6pm, Sun 9am–1pm; July & Aug Mon 9am–1pm & 2–6pm, Tues–Sat 9am–12.30pm & 1.30–6pm, Sun 9am–1pm & 2–6pm; Oct–March Mon–Fri 9am–noon & 1.30–5pm, Sat 9am–noon; ☎04 90 71 32 01, ⓦluberoncoeurdeprovence.com).

ACCOMMODATION AND EATING

Côté Jardin 49 rue Lamartine ☎04 90 71 33 58, ⓦcotejardin-cavaillon.com. A very inviting clutch of tables grouped around a stone fountain in a leafy terrace garden, specialising in fresh and seasonal ingredients to create dishes that change every month. *Menu* at €29. Tues–Sat noon–2pm & 7–9pm, Sun noon–2pm.

Le Parc 183 place François-Tourel ☎04 90 71 57 78, ⓦwww.hotelduparccavaillon.com. Elegant, good-value and very welcoming former *maison bourgeoise*, in the centre beside the tourist office; its flamboyant decor suits the building, though some of the rooms themselves are rather plain. Hearty buffet breakfasts (€11) are served in an attractive courtyard. €69

Le Prévut 353 av de Verdun ☎04 90 71 32 43, ⓦrestaurant-prevot.com. Lunch *menus* at this long-standing local favourite, 1km southeast of the tourist office, are priced at €35, while dinner *menus*, organized around seasonal themes or ingredients such as melons or mushrooms, vary from €60 to €135. Tues–Sat noon–1.30pm & 7.30–9.30pm.

Toppin 70 cours Gambetta ☎04 90 71 30 42, ⓦhotel-cavaillon.com. This appealing, central *Logis de France* offers large, warmly decorated and comfortable rooms and a stone-arched breakfast area, but no restaurant. €65

3

Aix-en-Provence, the Durance and the Luberon

154 Aix-en-Provence

165 Around Aix-en-Provence

167 Along the Durance

180 Pays de Forcalquier

186 The Luberon

SISTERON

Aix-en-Provence, the Durance and the Luberon

A wide, rushing torrent in winter that reduces to a dribble in summer, the Durance is one of the great Alpine rivers of France, slashing 320km southwest from its source near Briançon to its confluence with the Rhône near Avignon. Four *départements* converge where the Durance meets the Verdon, a few kilometres northeast of the Pont Mirabeau. Three of the four – the Alpes de Haute Provence, the Vaucluse and the Bouches du Rhône – are at their most atypical here. The portion of the Alpes de Haute Provence west of the Durance lacks the genuine Alpine majesty of the area to the east; the Luberon's history of dissent during the Wars of Religion distinguishes it from the papal tradition of the Vaucluse as a whole; and the pastoral charms of the Coteaux d'Aix and grandeur of the Montagne Ste-Victoire contrast strongly with the metropolitan feel of the Marseille conurbation. Unrepresentative of their *départements*, together these regions offer a distillation of all that, for visitors, seems most typically Provençal – of lavender and honey, crumbling hilltop villages and ancient abbeys, lively markets and excellent cuisine rooted in the *terroir*.

The charms of **Aix-en-Provence** – the region's only real city – are commonly sung. With a historic core as perfect as any in France, it glories in the medieval period of independent Provence, the riches of its seventeenth- and eighteenth-century growth and the memory of its most famous sons, Zola and Cézanne.

To the north of Aix, the transition between Mediterranean and Alpine France becomes clear along the valley of the Durance. Downstream, the fruitful countryside between sleepy **Cadenet** and bustling **Pertuis** is classically Provençal, but east of Pertuis, the landscape becomes wilder, the valley narrowing to a rocky gorge at the Défilé de Mirabeau. To the north, **Manosque** offers a rare taste of urban life, while dramatic **Sisteron** acts as a gateway to the Alps and as the northern point of departure from Provence. West of the Durance, the delights of the **Pays de Forcalquier** include the venerable town of **Forcalquier** itself and the remote and beautiful hilltop village of **Simiane-la-Rotonde**.

Sweeping further to the west, the great green surge of the **Luberon** massif is as lauded as any landscape in France, not least in the books of Peter Mayle, and its beautiful villages are nowadays distinctly chic. Its principal centre, **Apt**, is a lively market town slowly evolving in the face of the influx of wealthy Parisians and foreigners that has transformed the surrounding districts. The attractions of the countryside are diverse: the multihued ochre mines of **Bruoux**, **Rustrel** and **Roussillon**, the abandoned villages at **Buoux** and **Oppède-le-Vieux**, the immaculate village of **Gordes** and the twelfth-century Cistercian monasteries at **Sénanque** and **Silvacane**.

Aix-en-Provence

With its colourful markets, splashing fountains, pavement cafés and general air of civilized ease, **AIX-EN-PROVENCE** measures up to the popular fantasies of the Provençal

ATELIER CÉZANNE

Highlights

❶ Cézanne's Aix Visit the artist's atelier, tour his childhood home then explore a living Cézanne landscape in the country around Montagne Ste-Victoire. See pages 160, 161 and 165

❷ Forcalquier Discover this once grand, now slumbering, historic town, and its beautiful, unspoilt *pays*. See page 181

❸ Ochre in the Luberon Brilliant colour enfolds the friendly villages of Rustrel and Roussillon, and enlivens the extraordinary mine of Bruoux. See page 191

❹ Medieval hilltop villages Though Gordes is the best known, Lacoste, Saignon and Simiane-la-Rotonde are equally picturesque and far less busy. See pages 185, 186 and 196

❺ Abbaye de Sénanque The ancient Cistercian monastery is as much a symbol of Provence as the lavender fields surrounding it. See page 193

❻ Abandoned hilltop ruins Quiet and crumbling, Oppède-le-Vieux and the Fort de Buoux provide an atmospheric insight into life in the medieval *villages perchés*. See pages 187 and 194

HIGHLIGHTS ARE MARKED ON THE MAP ON PAGE 156

good life better than any city in the region. It's a stunning place, its riches based on landowning and the liberal professions. Hundreds of foreign students, particularly Americans, study in Aix, bolstering the city's youthful feel; law, humanities and arts faculties of the university Aix shares with Marseille are partly based here, where the original university was founded in 1409 and there is a prestigious politics faculty. In the nineteenth century Aix was home to two of France's greatest contributors to painting and literature, **Paul Cézanne** and his close friend **Émile Zola**. A series of brass

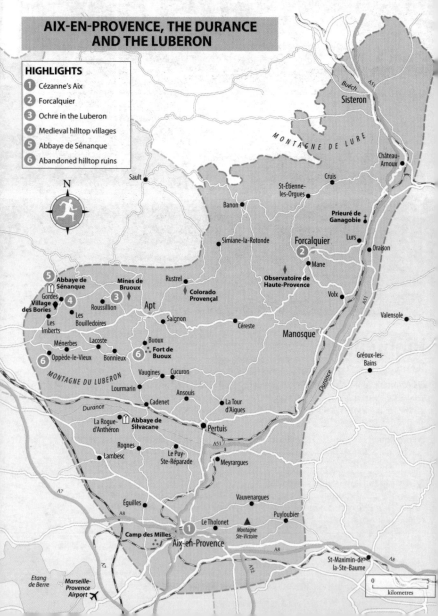

AIX-EN-PROVENCE, THE DURANCE AND THE LUBERON

HIGHLIGHTS

1. Cézanne's Aix
2. Forcalquier
3. Ochre in the Luberon
4. Medieval hilltop villages
5. Abbaye de Sénanque
6. Abandoned hilltop ruins

studs set into the pavements now allows visitors to follow a Cézanne trail through the heart of the city.

The old city, **Vieil Aix**, defined by its ring of boulevards and the majestic **cours Mirabeau**, is in its entirety the great monument here, far more compelling than any single attraction within it. With so many streets alive with people, so many tempting restaurants, cafés and shops, plus the best markets in Provence, it's easy to pass a day or two wandering around without any itinerary or destination. Beyond Vieil Aix, there are a few museums in the **quartier Mazarin** south of cours Mirabeau and, further out, the **Vaserely Foundation**, **Cézanne's studio** and the Cézanne family home, **Jas de Bouffan**. Aix also makes an ideal base for **excursions** into the beautiful surrounding countryside, a landscape made famous by Cézanne.

Some history

Aix began life as Aquae Sextiae, a Roman settlement based around its **hot springs** – there's still a thermal establishment on the site of the Roman baths in the northwest corner of the *vieille ville*. From the twelfth century until the Revolution Aix was the capital of Provence. In its days as an independent fiefdom, its most beloved ruler, **King René of Anjou** (1409–80), held a brilliant court renowned for its popular festivities and patronage of the arts. René introduced the muscat grape to the region, and today he stands in stone in picture-book medieval fashion, a bunch of grapes in his left hand, looking down the majestic seventeenth-century replacement to the old southern fortifications, the cours Mirabeau.

4

Cours Mirabeau

As a preliminary introduction to life in Aix, take a stroll beneath the gigantic plane trees of **cours Mirabeau**, stopping off along the way at one of the many cafés along its sunny north side. In contrast, the shady south side is decidedly businesslike, lined with banks, offices and shops lodged in seventeenth- to eighteenth-century mansions. These have a uniform hue of weathered stone, with ornate wrought-iron balconies and Baroque decorations, at their heaviest in the tired old musclemen holding up the porch at no. 38.

Opposite is Aix's most famous café, **Les Deux Garçons** (see page 163) with a reputation dating back to World War II of serving intellectuals, artists and their entourage; earlier still, Cézanne was a customer. The interior is all mirrors with darkening gilt panels and reading lights that might have come off the old Orient Express.

Vieil Aix

To explore the heart of Aix, wander north from cours Mirabeau and then anywhere within the ring of *cours* and boulevards. The layout of **Vieil Aix** is not designed to assist your sense of direction, but it hardly matters when there's a fountained square to rest at every 50m and a continuous architectural backdrop of treats from the sixteenth and seventeenth centuries.

Starting from the eastern end of cours Mirabeau, heading north into place de Verdun brings you to the **Palais de Justice**, a Neoclassical construction on the site of the old counts of Provence's palace. Count Mirabeau, the aristocrat turned champion of the Third Estate, who accused the États de Provence, meeting in Aix for the last time in 1789, of having no right to represent the people, is honoured here by a statue and allegorical monument.

Further west, in place de l'Hôtel de Ville at the heart of Vieil Aix, a massive foot hangs over the architrave of the old corn exchange, now a library and post office. It belongs to the goddess Cybele, dallying with the masculine Rhône and Durance. On the west side of the *place*, the **Hôtel de Ville** itself displays perfect classical proportions and filigreed wrought iron above the door. Alongside stands a **clock tower** that gives the season as well as the time.

South of place de l'Hôtel de Ville is the elegant, cobbled eighteenth-century Rococo **place d'Albertas**, which occasionally hosts concerts in summer. The square is just off rue Espariat, which runs west to place du Général-de-Gaulle and has a distinctly Parisian style. Many of Aix's classiest boutiques are clustered in this area.

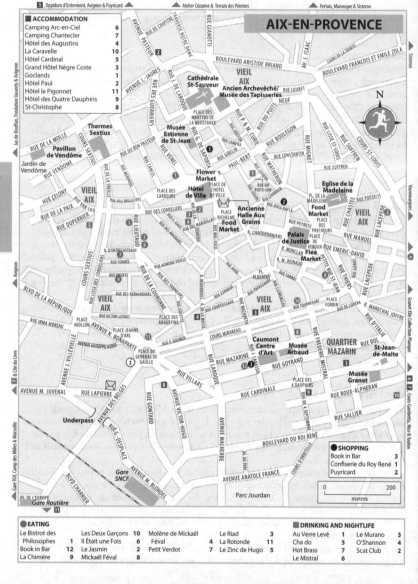

AIX-EN-PROVENCE

■ ACCOMMODATION

Camping Arc-en-Ciel	6
Camping Chantecler	7
Hôtel des Augustins	4
La Caravelle	10
Hôtel Cardinal	5
Grand Hôtel Nègre Coste	3
Goclands	1
Hôtel Paul	2
Hôtel le Pigonnet	11
Hôtel des Quatre Dauphins	9
St-Christophe	8

● EATING

Le Bistrot des Philosophes	1	Les Deux Garçons	10	Molène de Mickaël	4	Le Riad	3
Book in Bar	12	Il Était une Fois	6	Féval	4	La Rotonde	11
La Chimère	9	Le Jasmin	2	Petit Verdot	7	Le Zinc de Hugo	5
		Mickaël Féval	8			

■ DRINKING AND NIGHTLIFE

Au Verre Levé	1	Le Murano	3
Cha do	5	O'Shannon	4
Hot Brass	7	Scat Club	2
Le Mistral	6		

● SHOPPING

Book in Bar	3
Confiserie du Roy René	1
Puyricard	2

0 — 200 metres

Cathédrale St-Sauveur

34 place des Martyrs de la Résistance • Daily 8am–noon & 2–6pm; free tours of cloisters every 30min 10–11.30am & 2.30–5.30pm; west doors Mon–Sat 11.15–11.45am • ☎ 04 42 23 45 65, ⓦ cathedrale-aix.net

> **AIX FOR LESS**
>
> The **Citypass #provenceaixperience** (€25/24hr, €34/48hr, €43/72hr) gives free admission to Aix's principal museums, plus a free guided tour of the city, a free ride on the tourist train and discounts or special offers in various restaurants, shops and local businesses.

North of place de l'Hôtel de Ville lies the **Cathédrale St-Sauveur**, a conglomerate of fifth- to sixteenth-century buildings full of medieval art treasures. The cathedral's most notable artwork is *The Burning Bush*, a triptych commissioned by King René in 1475; it's generally on view from the first Sunday of Advent to Three Kings, and from Easter to Whitsun, as well as during the summer. The carved pillars of the beautiful Romanesque **cloisters** are perhaps the best sculptures in the cathedral. The four corner pillars depict the four beasts of the Revelation: man, the lion, the eagle and the bull. Also remarkable are the cathedral's **west doors** (ask at the bureau des Guides booth for someone to open them), carved by Toulon carpenter Jean Guiramand in the early sixteenth century. They depict four Old Testament prophets and twelve sibyls, the wise women of antiquity who supposedly prophesied Christ's birth, death and resurrection.

Musée des Tapisseries

28 place des Martyrs de la Résistance • Mon & Wed–Sun: mid-April to mid-Oct 10am–12.30pm & 1.30–6pm; mid-Oct to mid-April 10am–12.30pm & 1.30–5pm • €3.70 • ☎ 04 42 23 09 91

The former bishop's palace, the **Ancien Archevêché**, is the setting, each July, for part of Aix's grandiose music festival. It also houses the **Musée des Tapisseries**, a collection of wonderful tapestries. Highlights include the musicians, dancers and animals in a 1689 series of grotesques; nine scenes from the life of Don Quixote, woven in the 1730s, including one with a club-footed cat being divested of its armour by various *demoiselles*; and four superbly detailed *Jeux Russiens* (*Russian Games*) from a few decades later. A ground-floor gallery hosts temporary exhibitions, and there's also a section given over to the costumes, stage designs and history of the music festival.

Musée du Vieil Aix

17 rue Gaston de Saporta • Mon & Wed–Sun: mid-April to mid-Oct 10am–12.30pm & 1.30–6pm; mid-Oct to mid-April 10am–12.30pm & 1.30–5pm • €3.70 • ☎ 04 42 91 89 78

Close to the cathedral, Aix's local history museum, the **Musée du Vieil Aix**, occupies the magnificent late seventeenth-century Hôtel d'Estienne de St-Jean. Its collections encompass furniture, costume, *santons* and faïence and include a section on the Fête-Dieu (Corpus Christi); this late spring religious festival was highly popular in Aix until the start of the twentieth century and was celebrated with a procession, feasts and plays.

Quartier Mazarin

Taking rue Clemenceau south over cours Mirabeau brings you into the heart of the **quartier Mazarin**, built in five years in the mid-seventeenth century by the archbishop brother of the cardinal who ran France when Louis XIV was a baby. It's a very dignified district, and very quiet, centred on the beautiful **place des Quatre Dauphins** with its four-dolphin fountain.

Musée Granet

Place St-Jean-de-Malte • Tues–Sun: late June to mid-Oct 10am–7pm; mid-Oct to late June noon–6pm • €6, €8 during summer exhibition (includes Granet XXe – Collection Planque, see page 160) • ☎ 04 42 52 88 32, ⓦ www.museegranet-aixenprovence.fr

The former priory of the Knights of Malta, east of the place des Quatre Dauphins, is home to the most substantial of Aix's museums, the **Musée Granet**. Covering art and archeology, the museum exhibits finds from the Oppidum d'Entremont (see page 161), a Celto-Ligurian township 3km north of Aix, along with the remains of the Romans who routed them in 124 BC. Its paintings are a mixed bag, from Italian, Dutch and French art of the seventeenth to nineteenth century, via works by Cézanne, who studied on the ground floor of the building, to modernist pieces by Giacometti, Picasso and others. Rather overshadowing the permanent collection is the excellent annual **summer exhibition**.

Caumont Centre d'Art

3 rue Cabassole • Daily: May–Sept 10am–7pm; Oct–April 10am–6pm • €6.50, €14 including temporary exhibitions; audioguide €3 • ☎ 04 42 20 70 01, ⓦ caumont-centredart.com

Among the finest of the Quartier Mazarin's *hôtels particuliers*, the **Hôtel Caumont** was built in 1715 for the marquis de Cabannes as a town residence in the Parisian manner, its facade facing onto an enclosed court. Following extensive renovation it is now the **Caumont Centre d'Art**, hosting two big-name temporary exhibitions each year. Recent subjects have included Canaletto and the fabled Liechtenstein collection. Admission also gives access to the restored gardens and to the historic rooms, furnished to suggest the domestic life of Pauline, marquise de Caumont in the eighteenth century. You can also see a documentary on Cézanne's life in the region.

Granet XXe – Collection Planque

Chapelle des Pénitents Blancs, place Jean-Boyer • Tues–Sun: mid-June to mid-Oct 10am–7pm; mid-Oct to mid-June noon–6pm • €6, €8 during summer exhibition; includes Musée Granet (see page 159) • ☎ 04 42 52 88 32, ⓦ www.museegranet-aixenprovence.fr

A renovated seventeenth-century chapel a short walk east of the Quartier Mazarin is the setting for **Granet XXe – Collection Planque**, the Musée Granet's twentieth-century annexe. It houses some three hundred works from the collection of the late Swiss artist Jean Planque, who died in 1998; artists represented include Renoir, Monet, Van Gogh, Picasso, Dufy and Léger.

Jas de Bouffan

17 rte de Galice • ⓦ cezanne-en-provence.com/les-sites-de-cezanne/bastide-du-jas-de-bouffan

The man who came to be regarded as the father of modern painting cut a lonely figure for much of his life, spurned by the Parisian art establishment and happier away from the capital in his beloved Aix. **Paul Cézanne** was born in Vieil Aix at 28 rue de l'Opéra, the son of a hatter of Italian descent turned prosperous banker, but he grew up in a grand eighteenth-century house west of the city, where, from vantage points in the lovely garden, he painted such works as *Le Bassin du Jas de Bouffan en hiver*. Long since subsumed into the Aix suburbs, the house, known as **Jas de Bouffan**, can only be visited on a tour, which must be prebooked at the tourist office (see page 162), though no tours were operating at the time of writing due to renovation work; check the website for updates.

Fondation Vasarely

1 av Marcel-Pagnol • Daily 10am–6pm • €9 • ☎ 04 42 20 01 09, ⓦ fondationvasarely.org • Bus #2 (direction "Bouffan", stop "Vasarely")

The hill of the Jas de Bouffan area is dominated by the **Fondation Vasarely**, a bold modernist building in black and white geometric shapes created by the Hungarian-born artist Victor Vasarely in 1976. The building's seven hexagonal principal spaces are hung with 42 of Vasarely's monumental kinetic tapestries and paintings; the Fondation also hosts concerts, conferences and temporary exhibitions.

Atelier Cézanne

9 av Paul-Cézanne • Feb Tues–Sat 9.30am–12.30pm & 2–5pm; March, Oct & Nov daily 9.30am–12.30pm & 2–5pm; April & May daily 9.30am–12.30pm & 2–6pm; June–Sept daily 9.30am–6pm; visits (restricted to around 30min) at set times only: 9.30am, 10am, 10.30am, 11am, 2pm, 2.30pm, 3pm & 4pm; guided tours in English 3.30pm; all admissions via website reservation only • €6.50, guided tours €9.50 • ☏ 04 42 21 06 53, ⓦ cezanne-en-provence.com/les-sites-de-cezanne/atelier-de-cezanne • Bus #5 (direction "Parc Relais Brunet") or #12 (direction "Couteron"), stop "Cézanne", or a 10min walk uphill from the north end of the *vieille ville*

Cézanne used many studios in and around Aix, but at the beginning of the twentieth century, four years before his death, he had a house built for the purpose overlooking Aix from the north. By this stage in his life Cézanne had achieved both financial security and the recognition that had so long eluded him. It was here that he painted the *Grandes Baigneuses*, the *Jardinier Vallier* and some of his greatest still lifes. The **Atelier Cézanne** has been left exactly as it was at the time of his death in 1906: coat, hat, wine glass and easel, the objects he liked to paint, his pipe, a few letters and drawings – everything save the man himself, who would probably have been horrified at the thought of it being open to the public. The guides are true enthusiasts, and provided the atelier isn't too busy a visit is a real joy.

Terrain des Peintres

Av Paul Cézanne • Free access • Bus #12 (direction "Couteron", stop "Les Peintres")

Two kilometres north of the Atelier Cézanne up the hill of Les Lauves is the **Terrain des Peintres**, an informal Mediterranean garden on the spot where, towards the end of his life, Cézanne painted **Montagne Ste-Victoire** over and over again. Despite the suburban development that nowadays covers Les Lauves, the view is intact, and this is still the highest vantage point in Aix from which to view the mountain. At the top of the garden plaques depict several of the Montagne Ste-Victoire canvases, though they're scarcely necessary, as it would be impossible to imagine this now as anything other than Cézanne's landscape.

Oppidum d'Entremont

960 av Fernand Benoit • April & May Mon & Wed–Fri & 1st weekend of the month 9am–noon & 2–6pm; June–Sept Mon & Wed–Sun 9am–noon & 2–6pm; Oct–March Mon & Wed–Fri & 1st weekend of the month 9am–noon & 2–5pm • Free • ⓦ asso-archeo-entremont. com • Bus #11 (direction "Village du Soleil", stop "Entremont")

On the northern outskirts of Aix-en-Provence behind impressive ramparts is the Celto-Ligurian archeological site of **Oppidum d'Entremont**, for a brief period the chief settlement of one of the strongest confederations of indigenous people in Provence. Built around 175 BC, it was divided into two parts: the upper town, where the warriors are thought to have lived; and the larger lower town for artisans and traders. Though much of the site remains unexcavated the distinction is still clear, with the latter the more interesting to explore, and there are helpful signs in English. The site lay on an important trade crossroads from Marseille to the Durance Valley and from Fréjus to the Rhône. Marseille merchants finally persuaded the Romans to dispose of this irritant to their expanding business. The elevated site ensures sweeping views across Aix towards the Montagne Ste-Victoire.

Camp des Milles

40 chemin de la Badesse, Les Milles • Daily 10am–7pm • €9.50 • ☏ 04 42 39 17 11, ⓦ campdesmilles.org • Bus #14 from Aix

Southwest of the city in the district of Les Milles is the **Camp des Milles**, a former tile factory which was used on the outbreak of war in 1939 to intern enemy aliens including many distinguished German artists and intellectuals who had already fled the very enemy France was facing. From June 1940 on the story darkened; first Vichy used the site as a transit and internment camp for "undesirables" and then, following the German occupation of southern France in 1942, it became a place from which the Fascist authorities deported Jews to Drancy and from there to Auschwitz. There's now an extensive exhibition on three floors, including a permanent exhibition commemorating the 11,400 Jewish children deported from France to Auschwitz. In the former guards' canteen you can also see murals created by interned artists in the early stages of the war.

ARRIVAL AND INFORMATION   AIX-EN-PROVENCE

By train Aix's *gare TGV* lies 8km southwest of the town, and is connected to town by bus (every 15min; 23min). Local trains, including those from Marseille, arrive at the old *gare SNCF* on rue Gustave-Desplaces.

Destinations Manosque/Gréoux Bains (5 daily; 55min–1hr 5min); Marseille (roughly every 20min at peak times; 46–56min); Paris Gare de Lyon (roughly every 30–45min; 3hr 40min–3hr 50min); Pertuis (3 daily; 37–46min); Sisteron (6 daily; 1hr 18min–1hr 27min).

By bus Aix's *gare routière* is on Av de l'Europe, southwest of place du Général-de-Gaulle along Av des Belges.

Destinations Aix TGV (every 15min; 23min); Apt (4 daily; 1hr 32min–1hr 55min); Arles (hourly via Salon de Provence; 1hr 40min); Aubagne (every 10–15min at peak times; 48min–1hr 4min); Cavaillon (5 daily; 1hr 20min–1hr 30min); La Ciotat (8 daily; 1hr–1hr 20min); Éguilles (every 15–55min; 18min); Forcalquier (3 daily; 1hr 20min–1hr 30min); Manosque (roughly hourly; 55min–1hr); Marseille, via autoroute (every 5–10min; 30min–1hr); Marseille-Provence Airport (4 daily; 25min); Martigues (every 20min–1hr 5min; 46min–1hr 17min); Nice (5 daily; 2hr 20min–3hr 45min); Pertuis (every 10min–1hr; 35–45min); Puyloubier (every 30min–1hr 45min; 45min); Salon (every 10min–1hr; 30–36min); Sisteron (5 daily; 1hr 40min–2hr); Vauvenargues (hourly; 32min).

Tourist office 300 av Giuseppe Verdi, in the allées Provençales shopping mall just west of cours Mirabeau (April–Sept Mon–Sat 8.30am–7pm, Sun 10am–1pm & 2–6pm; Oct–March Mon–Sat 8.30am–6pm; ☎ 04 42 16 11 61, ⓦ aixenprovencetourism.com). Here you can find plenty of touch-screen information, details on the Cézanne trail in and around Aix, and on-site box office and accommodation booking services.

GETTING AROUND

By bus Local bus services are provided by Aix en Bus (☎ 0970 80 90 13, ⓦ aixenbus.fr), with the small electric Les Diablines vehicles able to access the narrow streets of the old city; a single ticket costs €0.80, a ten-journey "Ticket 10 Voyages" €6.50.

By taxi Taxi Radio Aixois (24hr; ☎ 04 42 27 71 11, ⓦ taxiaix. fr); Radio Taxi Mirabeau (☎ 04 42 21 61 61).

Car rental Avis, Plateau de l'Arbois near the *Gare TGV* (☎ 0820 61 16 37); Budget, *Gare TGV* (☎ 04 88 19 20 33); Europcar, 55 bd de la République (☎ 0825 35 83 58).

Bike rental Aix'Prit Vélo, 8 av St-Jérôme (☎ 04 42 21 24 05, ⓦ aixpritvelo.com). Rental from €16/day.

ACCOMMODATION   SEE MAP PAGE 158

If you're planning to visit in the summer, particularly during the June and July festivals, it's worth reserving accommodation well in advance.

Hôtel des Augustins 3 rue de la Masse ☎ 04 42 27 28 59, ⓦ hotel-augustins.com. Stunning three-star hotel in a converted medieval monastery just off the cours Mirabeau. Very central and atmospheric, with gothic stone vaulting and modern comforts. **€109**

La Caravelle 29 bd Roi-René ☎ 04 42 21 53 05, ⓦ lacaravelle-hotel.com. Well-maintained, friendly and soundproofed hotel set back slightly from the boulevards ringing Vieil Aix. The more expensive rooms overlook courtyard gardens; some have a/c. **€89**

Hôtel Cardinal 24 rue Cardinale ☎ 04 42 38 32 30, ⓦ hotel-cardinal-aix.com. A clean, peaceful and welcoming small hotel in the *quartier* Mazarin, with a/c and 29 rooms furnished in period style, including six suites with kitchenette. **€80**

Grand Hôtel Nègre Coste 33 cours Mirabeau ☎ 04 42 27 74 22, ⓦ hotelnegrecoste.com. Splendidly situated hotel in a handsome eighteenth-century house with comfortable, soundproofed, high-ceilinged a/c rooms, recently refurbished in contemporary style. There's also private parking. **€129**

Goclands 50 chemin de Brunet ☎ 04 42 27 74 22, ⓦ hotelnegrecoste.com. "Green open co-living" at this chilled villa-hostel and garden in the Aix suburbs. Sociable, living room-esque common areas with heaving bookshelves and simple dorm rooms with painted bunk beds. Take bus #7, 10 or 11 from the city centre; stop "Bellevue". Deals on longer stays. **€27.60**

Hôtel Paul 10 av Pasteur ☎ 04 42 23 23 89, ⓔ hotel. paul@wanadoo.fr. A rare one-star cheapie in the centre of Aix, though on a busy road. It's nothing fancy, but all rooms have shower and WC and the more expensive ones face the leafy garden at the back. There's storage for bikes and motorbikes on site and public car parking nearby. **€55**

Hotel le Pigonnet 5 av du Pigonnet ☎ 04 42 59 02 90, ⓦ hotelpigonnet.com. Five-star luxury in the beautiful setting of an eighteenth-century *bastide* surrounded by lush gardens, 10min on foot from the *quartier* Mazarin with a spa and a fancy restaurant, *La Table du Pigonnet*. **€325**

Hôtel des Quatre Dauphins 54 rue Roux-Alphéran ☎04 42 38 16 39, ⊛lesquatredauphins.fr. Small two-star hotel with plenty of warm, old-world charm in the peaceful *quartier* Mazarin, with a/c and small, prettily furnished en-suite rooms in traditional Provençal style. **€89**

St-Christophe 2 av Victor-Hugo ☎04 42 26 01 24, ⊛hotel-saintcristophe.com. Comfortable three-star hotel above a smart brasserie close to the tourist office and cours Mirabeau, with touches of Art Deco and a/c, soundproofed rooms, plus parking. **€76**

CAMPSITES

Camping Arc-en-Ciel Pont des Trois Sautets, 50 av Henri Malacrida ☎04 42 26 14 28, ⊛campingarcenciel. com. Close to *Chantecler* on Aix's southeastern outskirts, this four-star site is not particularly big, but it has a pool, *pétanque* and barbecue facilities. Bus #13 (direction "Le Tholonet", stop "les Trois Sautets". Closed Oct–April. **€21.40**

Camping Chantecler 41 av du Val St-André ☎04 42 26 12 98, ⊛campingchantecler.com. Four-star site 3km southeast of town. Excellent facilities include a pool, volleyball court and restaurant. Bus #4 from *gare SNCF* (stop "Val St-André"). Open year-round. **€32.20**

EATING

SEE MAP PAGE 158

Aix is stuffed full of places to eat. **Place des Cardeurs**, west of the Hôtel de Ville, is nothing but restaurant, brasserie and café terraces; **rue de la Couronne** on the western fringe of Vieil Aix has several worthwhile options, and the elegant café-brasseries lining **cours Mirabeau**, though occasionally pricey, are tempting. That said, Aix's restaurant scene repays careful exploration, as some of the best places are away from these hot spots.

CAFÉS AND BARS

Book in Bar 4 rue Cabassol ☎04 42 26 60 07, ⊛www. bookinbar.com. Charming café and *salon de thé* in Aix's English bookshop, with extra seating upstairs, selling scones, cakes , smoothies, iced tea and espresso. Mon–Sat 9am–7pm.

★ **Les Deux Garçons** 53 cours Mirabeau ☎04 42 26 00 51, ⊛les2garcons.fr. This good-looking brasserie – a favourite haunt of Albert Camus, back in the day – undoubtedly trades on its past glories, but the period interior is lovely and the brasserie food is good, if not cheap. *Plats du jour* cost around €20. The terrace is Aix's best for people-watching over a cocktail or *pression*. Daily 7am–1am.

La Rotonde 2a place Jeanne d'Arc ☎04 42 91 61 70, ⊛larotonde-aix.com. Trendy brasserie on a prime site at the western end of cours Mirabeau next to the taxi rank, with a wide terrace, cocktails and clubby ambience. Breakfast from €3.90; sharing plates of fried squid or wood-fired vegetables for around €20 as well as a full pizza menu. Daily 7.30am–1.30am.

RESTAURANTS

Le Bistrot des Philosophes 20 place des Cardeurs ☎04 42 21 64 35, ⊛lebistrotdesphilosophes.com. One of the classier offerings on tourist-oriented place des Cardeurs, with hearty *plats* and a spacious outdoor terrace. Landes duck breast in fig sauce, potato gratin, ceps and candied shallots €25; chicken supreme stuffed with crayfish in lobster sauce €25. Daily noon–2.30pm & 7–10.30pm.

La Chimère 15 rue Brueys ☎04 42 38 30 00, ⊛lachimerecafe.com. Fun, distinctive restaurant and bar with over-the-top Baroque decor, red plush all around, tapas at the bar and plenty of choice on the eclectic €29 *menu*; à la carte mains €19–29. Mon–Sat 7pm––2am.

Il Était une Fois 4 rue Lieutaud ☎04 42 58 78 56, ⊛iletaitunefois-aix.fr. Stylish but simple modern dining room, where the €19.50 lunch *formule* and dinner *menu* (main courses €22–26) include dishes such as shrimp dumplings with candied lemon and guinea fowl stuffed with goat cheese and rosemary polenta cream. Mon & Thurs–Sun noon–1.30pm & 7.30–9.30pm.

Le Jasmin 6 rue de la Fonderie ☎04 42 38 05 89, ⊛lejasmin.net. Charming little Iranian restaurant on the old town's eastern fringe, with a *brochette*-dominated *carte* and €25 and €31 *menus*. Mon–Sat noon–2pm & 7–11pm.

Mickaël Féval 11 petite rue St Jean ☎04 42 93 29 60, ⊛mickaelfeval.fr. Formerly the diffusion spin-off from renowned chef Pierre Reboul's former *restaurant gastronomique*, this place is now the home base of fellow gastronome and Michelin starred chef, Mickaël Féval. His finely wrought creations grace a lunchtime *menu du marché* (€37) and evening *menus tentation* (€68) and *seduction* (€95), as well as a fish menu (€84). Tues–Sat noon–2pm & 7.30–10pm.

Molène de Mickaël Féval 31bis rue Manuel ☎04 42 39 81 88, ⊛restaurantmolene.com. Dedicated gourmet seafood restaurant from one of Aix's most high profile chefs, with his trademark sense of curation brought to both lunch *menus* (€33 and €46) and their evening equivalents (€57 & €82), across dishes such as red tuna in a soya a mint reduction. Tues–Sat noon–2pm & 7.30–10pm.

★ **Petit Verdot** 7 rue Entrecasteaux ☎04 42 27 30 12, ⊛lepetitverdot.fr. Booking is advised at this amiable restaurant, where an interior decorated with recycled wine boxes sets the scene for seasonally changing dishes like *pata negra* ham in honey and mustard sauce (€22) or turbot with vanilla oil and sesame (€23). Mon–Sat 7pm–midnight.

Le Riad 21 rue Lieutaud ☎04 42 26 15 79, ⊛leriad. com. Upmarket Moroccan restaurant with plush ambience and a pretty garden at the back, serving tagines from

4

€14 and with a €35 *menu*. Daily noon–2.30pm & 7.30–10.30/11pm.

★ **Le Zinc de Hugo** 22 rue Lieutaud ☎04 42 27 69 69, ⓦzinc-hugo.com. Funky, rustic modern bistro and wine bar with hearty portions of beautifully presented food and a wood-fired grill taking pride of place; a side of Black Angus beef to share is priced at €65. Tues–Thurs noon–2.30pm & 7–10.30pm, Fri & Sat noon–2.30pm & 7–11pm.

DRINKING AND NIGHTLIFE   SEE MAP PAGE 158

For **drinking**, Aix's preferred style is to lounge on a café or brasserie terrace rather than cram into a noisy bar; there are plenty of the former and a (lively) handful of the latter. For **what's on information** check out the tourist office website (ⓦaixenprovencetourism.com), where you can also book tickets for events in Aix and elsewhere. Aix nightlife is at its best during the summer **festivals**, when much of the entertainment happens in the streets.

Au Verre Levé 15 rue Granet ☎04 86 31 08 15. Attractive hole-in-the-wall *cave à vin* with a scattering of pavement tables, specialising in local, organic and biodynamic wines. Perfect for a quiet drink or two. Tues–Sat 4pm–11.30am.

Cha do 46 cours Sextius ☎04 42 27 70 63. Trendy gay bar and café on the western fringe of Vieil Aix, with "Happy Mix" DJ nights on Sat, *pressions* from €5 and cocktails from €8. Tues & Thurs–Sat 7pm–2am.

Hot Brass 1857 chemin d'Eguilles, Célony ☎04 42 20 83 03, ⓦhotbrassaix.fr. Famous former jazz club, more electronic superclub than live venue these days, but still attracting some big names. An onsite restaurant, swimming pool and summer terrace ramp up the luxe factor. Free shuttle buses from the Rotonde in Aix from midnight. Entry €10 with free shot. Fri & Sat midnight–6am.

Le Mistral 3 rue Frédéric Mistral ☎06 21 75 24 97, ⓦmistralclub.fr. Another legendary nightlife spot, going since 1952, and Central Aix's liveliest club. Regular guest DJs and a music policy that spans electro, techno and house. Entry price varies, and it's sometimes free. Tues–Sat midnight–6am; summer daily, same hours.

Le Murano 24 rue de la Verrerie ☎06 49 88 00 52. Buzzy and small live venue, handily located on Vieil Aix's main late-night strip and with a variety of themed nights from jazz to burlesque; cover charge varies. Smart dress code. Mon–Sat midnight–6am.

O'Shannon 30 rue de la Verrerie ☎04 42 23 31 63. Boisterous, student-friendly Irish pub that's just about the liveliest spot for serious drinking in Aix. Mon–Fri & Sun 4pm–2am, Sat 1pm–2am.

Scat Club 11 rue de la Verrerie ☎04 42 23 00 23, ⓦscatclub.free.fr/scatnet. All kinds of rock, funk, soul, reggae and R&B – the best live music venue in Vieil Aix. Free admission. Tues–Sat 11pm–6am.

ARTS AND ENTERTAINMENT

La Fontaine d'Argent 5 rue de La Fontaine-d'Argent ☎04 42 38 43 80, ⓦlafontainedargent.com. Café-theatre with a diverse programme and an emphasis on comedy and children's theatre. Performance times vary.

Grand Théâtre de Provence 380 av Max Juvénal ☎0820 13 20 13, ⓦlestheatres.net. Aix's main stage presents the international stars of classical music and dance in suitably imposing, modern surroundings opposite the Pavillon Noir. Performances generally start at 8.30pm.

Institut de l'Image Cité du Livre 8–10 rue des Allumettes ☎04 42 26 81 82, ⓦinstitut-image.org. Aix's main arthouse cinema, in a former match factory turned arts centre next to the Pavillon Noir. Programmes include retrospectives of big-name international directors. Performance times vary.

Le Pavillon Noir 530 av Wolfgang Amadeus Mozart ☎04 42 93 48 00, ⓦpreljocaj.org. Architecturally impressive modernist performance base for the internationally renowned Ballet Preljocaj, designed by Algerian-born Provençal architect Rudy Ricciotti. The venue also hosts touring productions. Performance times vary, but generally start between 6.30pm and 8.30pm.

Le Renoir 24 cours Mirabeau ☎0892 68 72 70, ⓦlescinemasaixois.com. Mainstream multiscreen cinema occasionally showing English-language films in their original language; its sister cinemas are the Cézanne on rue Marcel Guillaume, and the Mazarin on rue Laroque.

Théâtre du Jeu de Paume 17–21 rue de l'Opéra

AIX-EN-PROVENCE MARKETS

Aix's **markets** – possibly the best in all Provence – are not to be missed. On Tuesdays, Thursdays and Saturdays the whole of Vieil Aix is taken up with stalls. Fruit, vegetables and regional specialities are sold on **place des Prêcheurs** and **place Richelme** (8am–1pm), and **Place de l'Hôtel de Ville** is filled with lilies, roses and carnations (8am–12.30pm) – there's another flower market (Mon, Wed, Fri & Sun) on place des Prêcheurs. Beyond the Palais de Justice, **place de Verdun** hosts the flea market (Tues, Thurs & Sat, 8am–1pm). Clothes are sold on **cours Mirabeau** on Tuesdays and Thursdays (8am–1pm), and on Saturdays around the Palais de Justice (8am–1pm).

AIX-EN-PROVENCE FESTIVALS

Aix hosts an ever-evolving calendar of festivals and events, encompassing everything from books to tennis tournaments, and from music in the street to an Iron Man in May (Ⓦironmanpaysdaix.com). The undoubted highlight of the festival calendar is the **Festival D'Aix-en-Provence** (Ⓦfestival-aix.com), dedicated to opera and classical concerts and with an international reputation. It's held in July; ticket prices for major events can really scale the heights – as much as €290 or as relatively little as €30 (and as little as €10 for some of the lesser names), though you won't necessarily have an unrestricted view if you opt for the cheapest. Tickets can be purchased from February through the festival website, from the box office on place de l'Archevêché (Ⓣ0820 922 923), or at FNAC stores.

Ⓣ0820 13 20 13, Ⓦlestheatres.net. Aix's "second stage" is an intimate yet grand 493-seat venue for mainstream and musical theatre, in eighteenth-century Rococo surroundings. Performances generally start at 8.30pm.

SHOPPING   SEE MAP PAGE 158

Book in Bar 4 rue Cabassol Ⓣ04 42 26 60 07, Ⓦwww. bookinbar.com. Aix's English-language bookshop is a charming place to browse, with a café (see page 163). It also organizes signings and has a regular English-language book club. Mon–Sat 9am–7pm.

Confiserie du Roy René 11 rue Gaston de Saporta Ⓣ04 42 26 67 86, Ⓦcalisson.com. The place to go for Aix's speciality almond and melon sweets, *calissons*. Lozenge-shaped gift boxes full of them come in a range of sizes and cost €12.90–37.90. Mon–Thurs & Sun 10am–1pm & 2–7pm, Fri & Sat 10am–7pm.

Puyricard 7–9 rue Rifle-Rafle Ⓣ04 42 21 13 26, Ⓦpuyricard.fr. Chocolates of the highest quality, manufactured in the village of the same name just north of Aix. They're not cheap: some of their products costs well over €100. Mon–Sat 9am–7pm.

DIRECTORY

Health Centre Hospitalier, Av des Tamaris (Ⓣ04 42 33 50 00); SAMU Ⓣ15; SOS Médecins Ⓣ04 42 26 24 00.
Laundry 36 cours Sextius; 60 rue Boulégon; 3 rue de la Fonderie.

Police Av de l'Europe (Ⓣ04 42 93 97 00); emergency Ⓣ17.
Post office 2 rue Lapierre (Mon–Fri 9am–6.30pm, , Sat 9am–noon & 2–5pm).

Around Aix-en-Provence

There is gorgeous countryside to be explored around Aix, particularly to the east, where you'll find **Cézanne**'s favourite local subject, the **Montagne Ste-Victoire**. In addition, there is the ancient site at **Oppidum d'Entremont** and Picasso's château in **Vauvenargues**. North of the city, the vineyards of the **Coteaux d'Aix** stretch towards the **Abbaye de Silvacane** and the River Durance. Southwest of the city the sombre **Camp des Milles** is a reminder that the effects of the holocaust reached even this beautiful part of the world.

The Montagne Ste-Victoire circuit

The 60km **Montagne Ste-Victoire circuit** makes a scenically rewarding day-trip from Aix-en-Provence. Leaving the city, the D10 road east to Vauvenargues passes the quarry of **Bibémus**, painted by Cézanne (guided walks in French April–Oct daily 10am; €7.70; book at Ⓦaixenprovencetourism.com), and the lake and barrage of Bimont.

Vauvenargues

At **VAUVENARGUES**, 14km from Aix-en-Provence, the weatherbeaten, red-shuttered fourteenth-century **château** bought by Picasso in 1958 overlooks the village with nothing between it and the slopes of the mountain. **Picasso** lived here till his death in 1973, and is buried in the gardens, his grave adorned with his sculpture *Woman with a Vase*. The château is no longer open to the public.

CLIMBING THE MONTAGNE STE-VICTOIRE

Though the daunting appearance of its sheer, 500m southern face suggests otherwise, it is perfectly possible to **climb** the **Montagne Ste-Victoire**. Just about the quickest way up is from the Puits d'Auzon car park at Col des Portes on the north side; the ascent to the summit – the 1011m **Pic des Mouches** – takes an hour and you'll need forty minutes for the return leg. From Puyloubier the route is longer and more difficult, the ascent taking two hours with an hour and a half to return. The GR9 footpath runs the length of the crest, following some breathtakingly vertiginous cliff faces; continuing along it you'll reach a pilgrimage chapel and the monumental **Cross of Provence**. Several routes ascend to the cross from the northwestern side of the mountain.

Whatever route you take it's a reasonably serious hike, requiring stamina, sun cream, a hat and at least a couple of litres of water per person. Access to the entire massif is controlled in summer according to the same traffic-light system used in the *calanques*, and at times of particularly high **fire risk** there may be no access at all; call ☎0811 20 13 13 before setting off to find out what the day's risk level is. For more **information** visit the **Maison Ste-Victoire** (daily 9.30am–5pm; ☎04 13 31 94 70), on the D17 in the hamlet of St-Antonin-sur-Bayon on the south side of the mountain, where they also offer free guided walks, and run a restaurant (daily 9.30am–6pm).

Puyloubier

East of Vauvenargues, the D10 splits, with the right fork eventually leading to **PUYLOUBIER**. Here you can visit the French Foreign Legion's **Pensioners' Château**, which sits in a magnificent landscape surrounded by vineyards 1.5km from the crossroads in Puyloubier at the end of the chemin de la Pallière. Its small **museum** (Tues–Sun 10am–noon & 2–5pm; free, but donation requested) is one for the military buffs, its extensive collection of uniforms including an intriguing series of handkerchiefs printed with instructions on everything from hygiene to boot care and how to assemble a revolver. A shop sells Legion sweatshirts, books and souvenirs, as well as their own wines.

Le Tholonet

From Puyloubier, the D17 skirts the spectacular southern side of Montagne Ste-Victoire to **LE THOLONET**, with its Italianate seventeenth-century château (closed to the public). On the east side of the village, an old windmill, the **Moulin de Cézanne** (hours vary according to exhibitions; call ☎04 42 66 76 28 for information), serves as an exhibition space for art and sculpture, with a bronze relief of Cézanne himself on a stele outside.

The Le Tholonet region also has its own tiny AOC, the **Vins de Palette**, comprising just 23 hectares and a handful of producers: Château Crémade, rte de Langesse (☎04 42 66 76 80, ⓦchateaucremade.com); Château Henri Bonnaud, 585 chemin de la Poudrière (☎04 42 66 86 28, ⓦchateau-henri-bonnaud.fr); and Château Simone, chemin de la Simone (☎04 42 66 92 58, ⓦchateau-simone.fr).

EATING LE THOLONET

Chez Thomé La Plantation, Av Louis Destrem ☎04 42 66 90 43, ⓦchezthome.fr. Popular restaurant set back from the main crossroads in Le Tholonet, with tables under the trees, hearty classics like slow-cooked lamb shank, *pieds et paquets* or chateaubriand with ceps, and a *menu* at €28. Tues, Wed, Fri & Sat noon–11pm, Thurs & Sun noon–3pm.

The Route des Vins

To the north and west of Aix-en-Provence, the vineyards of the **Coteaux d'Aix** fan out across a broad belt of countryside between the city and the River Durance. At

35 square kilometres, this is the second-largest AOC in Provence after the Côtes de Provence itself, and one that is still forging its reputation. The soil is particularly suited to the production of great red wines, with Grenache, Syrah, Cabernet Sauvignon and Vermentino the main grape varieties grown. The rich and fruity rosés go well with Provençal dishes like *bourride*; white wines are much less common, but are fresh and fragrant.

A signposted **Route des Vins** follows a circuit through the heart of the AOC, beginning and ending in the village of **ÉGUILLES**, 9.5km west of Aix on the D17; along the circuit the opportunities to stop and try the wines are fairly frequent. Some of the vineyards produce *vin cuit*, a Provençal curiosity that is heated during maturation.

Alongside its winery, **Château Lacoste** at Le Puy Ste-Réparade, 20km north of Éguilles, close to the Durance, has an impressive contemporary **art centre** by Japanese architect Tadao Ando (March–Oct daily 10am–7pm; Nov–Feb Mon–Fri 10am–5pm, Sat & Sun 10am–7pm; €15; ⓦchateau-la-coste.com), and an art and architecture walk featuring sculptures by Louise Bourgeois, Alexander Calder and others.

INFORMATION	THE ROUTE DES VINS
Tourist office The office at 15bis rue du Grand Logis, Éguilles (June to mid-Sept Mon–Fri 9.30am–12.30pm & 2–5.30pm, Sat 9.30am–1pm; mid-Sept to May Mon–Fri	9.30am–12.30pm & 2–5.30pm; ☎04 42 92 49 15) can supply a list of wine producers with opening times and information about the Route des Vins.

Abbaye de Silvacane

D561A, La Roque d'Anthéron • April & May Tues–Sun 10am–1pm & 2–5.30pm; June–Sept daily 10am–6pm; Oct–March Tues–Sun 10am–1pm & 2–5pm • €7.50 • ☎04 42 50 41 69, ⓦabbaye-silvacane.com

Just off the D561A a little to the east of the village of La Roque d'Anthéron stands the **Abbaye de Silvacane**, built by the same order and in the same period as the abbeys of Sénanque (see page 193) and du Thoronet (see page 206), although the "wood of rushes" from which the name Silvacane derives had already been cleared by Benedictine monks before the Cistercians arrived in 1144. As at the other two great monasteries, the architecture of Silvacane reflects the no-nonsense rule of St Benedict (Benoît) in which manual work, intellectual work and worship comprised the three equal elements of the day.

The stark, pale-stoned church and its surrounding buildings and cloisters look pretty much as they did seven hundred years ago, with the exception of the refectory, rebuilt in 1423 and given Gothic ornamentation that the earlier monks would never have tolerated. The windows in the church would not have had stained glass either. The only heated room would have been the *salle des monies* where the work of copying manuscripts was carried out, and the only areas where conversation would have been allowed were the *salle capitulaire*, where the daily reading of "the Rule" and the hearing of confessions took place, and the *parloir* (literally, a room for talking in).

Along the Durance

Some 26km from Aix-en-Provence, the D543 from Éguilles reaches the broad River Durance at the **Pont de Cadenet**, an incongruously impressive structure – particularly in summer, when the mighty Alpine river it crosses is often reduced to a dribble. The countryside on the river's north bank shelters below the massifs of the Grand and Petit Luberon and is Mediterranean in climate – hot and dry, fragrant with pines and wild thyme, ablaze with yellow and gold honeysuckle and immortelle, and alive with the quick movements of sun-basking lizards. The Durance Valley is highly fertile and yields the region's classic crops, including all the ingredients for ratatouille, while the lower slopes of the Luberon massifs are dotted with cherry trees and vines, grown both for wine and grapes. Because of the importance of agriculture, the villages here are still very Provençal in character, with fewer Parisians and other foreigners than in the northern Luberon.

As a touring base **Cadenet** has its charms, while the market town of **Pertuis** has the best transport links in the area. The beautiful villages of **Lourmarin**, **Vaugines** and **Cucuron** sit amidst vineyards and the unspoiled countryside of the Grand Luberon foothills, while **La Tour d'Aigues** and **Ansouis** boast elegant châteaux.

East of the dramatically narrow Défilé de Mirabeau and north of its confluence with the Verdon, the Durance has a somewhat different character. The Alps are close here, the river itself is exploited for electricity generation and the valley is busier and more urbanized. The major centres are **Manosque**, a bustling market town, and **Sisteron**, dominated by its splendid citadel. Between the two, the A51 Marseille–Grenoble autoroute speeds along the River Durance, bypassing the industrial town of **St-Auban** and its older neighbour **Château-Arnoux**, renowned for its superb restaurant, *La Bonne Étape*. The views from the fashionable little village of **Lurs** and the ancient **Prieuré de Ganagobie** have not been affected, nor has their isolation. **Volx** is the site of an impressive museum devoted to the olive.

Cadenet

The main road heading north to Lourmarin detours round **CADENET**, lending the place a sleepy charm with few of the chichi airs of the villages to the north. The central place du Tambour d'Arcole holds a statue of a manic drummer-boy, hair and coat-tails flying as he runs. The monument commemorates André Étienne for his inspired one-man diversion that confused the Austrians and allowed Napoleon's army to cross the River Durance in 1796.

Château de Cadenet

Off chemin des Rougettes • Free access

An energetic walk or short drive via cours Voltaire and chemin des Rougettes brings you to the crumbly remains of Cadenet's **château**, which was destroyed with pickaxes during the Revolution; most of what remains dates from the sixteenth and eighteenth centuries. It's a bit of a scramble to explore it properly but it's an intriguing ruin, with hidden stairwells and chambers built into the rock face. It's much more extensive than it first appears, and there are wonderful views over the village's huddled rooftops and the valley of the Durance beyond. On a hot day you'll most likely have it to yourself, with only the deafening noise of the *cigales* for company.

ARRIVAL AND INFORMATION
CADENET

By bus Infrequent buses on the Apt–Aix route stop in the centre of the village.
Destinations Aix-en-Provence (4 daily; 50min–1hr); Lourmarin (15 daily; 7–14min).

Tourist office 11 place du Tambour d'Arcole (April–Sept Mon, Wed, Fri & Sat 9.30am–12.30pm & 2–6pm; Oct–March Mon & Fri 9.30am–12.30pm & 2–5pm, Sat 9.30am–12.30pm; ☎ 09 72 60 79 05, ⊛ marie-cadenet.fr).

ACCOMMODATION AND EATING

Les Aromates 2 place du Tambour d'Arcole ☎ 04 90 68 35 35, ⊛ restaurant-lesaromates-cadenet.fr. Centrally located restaurant with such dishes as *chèvre mousseline*, skirt steak and duck *andouillette* on a €18 *menu du jour*. Mid-April to Oct Tues, Wed & Fri–Sun noon–2pm & 7–9pm, Thurs noon–2pm; Nov to mid-April Tues, Wed, Fri & Sat noon–2pm & 7–9pm, Thurs noon–2pm.

L'Auberge de la Fenière Rte de Lourmarin ☎ 04 90 68 11 79, ⊛ aubergelafeniere.com. Chic four-star rural hotel and *restaurant gastronomique* midway between Cadenet and Lourmarin, using absolutely fresh ingredients to create seriously gourmet concoctions on its €55–130 *menus*. There's also a bistro serving simpler food on a €39 brunch *menu*. Wed–Sun 12.30–1.30pm & 7.30–9.30pm. **€160**

Les Jardins Ajoucadou Chemin des Balerys, rte de Lourmarin ☎ 06 76 85 95 85, ⊛ lesjardinsajoucadou. com. Idyllic country house just outside of town off the road north to Lourmarin. Three themed rooms decorated in classic Provençal style and leading onto the garden terrace. A swimming pool as well. **€150**

Lourmarin

LOURMARIN stands at the bottom of a *combe*, or narrow valley, 4km north of Cadenet, its Renaissance **château** lording it over the village from a small rise to the west. The most famous literary figure associated with Lourmarin is the writer **Albert Camus**, who spent the last years of his life here and is buried in the cemetery. Nowadays the village is extremely chic, and often overrun with visitors in summer.

Château de Lourmarin

Jan Sat & Sun 10.30am–12.30pm 2.30–4.30pm; Feb, Nov & Dec daily 10.30am–12.30pm & 2.30–4.30pm; March, April & Oct daily 10.30am–12.30pm & 2.30–5pm; May & Sept daily 10am–12.30pm & 2.30–6pm; June–Aug daily 10am–6.30pm • €6.80 • ☎ 04 90 68 15 23, 🌐 chateau-de-lourmarin.com

A fortress once defended this strategic vantage point, but the current **Château de Lourmarin** dates from the sixteenth century when comfort was beginning to outplay defence – hence the generous windows. Since 1929 the château has belonged to the University of Aix, who use it to give summer sabbaticals to artists and intellectuals. Many have left behind works of art, which you can see as you stroll through vast rooms with intricate wooden ceilings, massive fireplaces and beautifully tiled floors. **Concerts** are held in the spring and summer and art **exhibitions** of all sorts are staged.

ARRIVAL AND INFORMATION
LOURMARIN

By bus Infrequent buses on the Apt–Aix route stop in the centre of Lourmarin village.
Destinations Aix-en-Provence (4 daily; 1hr 10min); Apt (4 daily; 40min); Cadenet (4 daily; 19min).
Tourist office Place H. Barthélemy (April–Sept Mon–Sat 9am–12.30pm & 1.30–6pm, Sun 10am–12.30pm & 1.30–6pm; Oct–March Tues–Sat 9am–noon & 1.30–5.30pm; ☎ 04 90 68 10 77, 🌐 lourmarin.com); they organize Camus-themed literary walks.

ACCOMMODATION AND EATING

La Cordière Impasse de la Cordière ☎ 06 81 02 18 04, 🌐 cordiere.com. Secluded and exquisitely curated *gîte*, comprising a self-contained apartment and studios, all steeped in authentic period Provençal charm. Pets welcome with advance notice. No arrivals on Sun. **€80**

Les Hautes Prairies Rte de Vaugines ☎ 04 90 68 02 89, 🌐 campasun-lourmarin.eu. Three-star campsite with a pool, restaurant and a choice of pitches, chalets or mobile homes to rent. Two-night minimum stay. Closed Nov–March. Camping **€51.10**; chalets **€719** per week; mobile homes per week **€731.60**

Hostellerie Le Paradou Rte d'Apt ☎ 04 90 68 04 05, 🌐 hotelparadou.com. Thai-style decor and a Thai restaurant (two-course lunch *formule* €18.50) are the distinguishing features of this small, secluded hotel set in spacious grounds just outside the village off the D943 to Apt. **€105**

Moulin de Lourmarin Rue du Temple ☎ 04 90 68 06 69, 🌐 moulindelourmarin.com. The luxury place to stay in the heart of the village, this eighteenth-century former oil mill has seventeen rooms and two suites, stylish Provençal decor and a restaurant (lunch *formule* from €26). **€120**

La Récréation 15 rue Philippe de Girard ☎ 04 90 68 23 73. Restaurant and *salon de thé* which serves everything from omelettes and salads to meat and fish – much of it organic – on a pretty shaded terrace, with *menus* at €23, €29.50 and €36, as well as a dedicated organic menu at €37 and a vegan option at €20. Mon & Thurs–Sun noon–2pm & 7–9.30pm.

THE WARS OF RELIGION IN THE LUBERON

During five days in April 1545 a great swathe of the Petit Luberon, between **Lourmarin** and **Mérindol**, was burnt and put to the sword; three thousand people were massacred and six hundred sent to the galleys. Their crime was having Protestant tendencies in the years leading up to the devastating **Wars of Religion**. Despite the complicity of King Henri II, the ensuing scandal forced him to order an enquiry that then absolved those responsible – the Catholic aristocrats from Aix.

Lourmarin itself suffered minor damage but the castle in Mérindol was violently dismantled, along with every single house. Mérindol's remains, on the hill above the current village on the south side of the Petit Luberon, are a visible monument to those events, and to this day the area remains sparsely populated.

Cucuron

East of Lourmarin on the D27, **CUCURON** is large but extremely fetching, with some of its ancient ramparts and gateways still standing and a bell tower with a delicate campanile on the central place de l'Horloge. Cucuron had a glimpse of fame when it was taken over by the film industry for the shooting of Rappeneau's 1995 movie *The Horseman on the Roof*, based on a Giono novel and, at the time, the most expensive French film ever made; the village has been revisited by film location crews many times since.

Cucuron's main business, however, is olive oil; there's a twelfth-century **mill** in a hollow of the rock face on rue Moulin à l'Huile that is still used to press olives. At the top of the rock a scrubby open **park** surrounds the surviving *donjon* of the citadel; the journey up to the castle above the Tour de l'Horloge takes you through the oldest and most beautiful parts of the village.

At the other end of Cucuron is the **Église Notre Dame de Beaulieu**, which contains a seventeenth-century altarpiece in coloured marble originally commissioned for the Chapelle de la Visitation in Aix-en-Provence. From the end of May to the middle of August a huge felled poplar leans against the church, a tradition dating back to 1720 when Cucuron was spared the plague. On rue de l'Église, a short way from the church, is a small **museum** (Tues & Wed 10am–12.30pm & 3.30–7pm; Thurs–Sun 3.30–7pm; €2) on local traditions and early history, with a collection of daguerreotypes.

INFORMATION	CUCURON

Tourist office 12 Cours St-Victor (April–Sept Tues–Sat 9.30am–12.30pm & 2–6pm; Oct–March Tues–Fri 9.30am– 12.30pm & 2–5pm, Sat 9.30am–12.30pm; ☎04 90 77 28 37, ⓦcucuron-luberon.com).

ACCOMMODATION AND EATING

Les Chambres de Charlotte 39 rue de la Place ☎06 19 63 50 73, ⓦles-chambres-de-charlotte.com. Three *chambres d'hôtes* and one suite in a pretty, blue-shuttered townhouse in the centre of the village, with tiled floors and beamed ceilings. **€79**

Hôtel de L'Étang Place de l'Étang ☎04 90 77 21 25, ⓦhoteldeletang.com. *Logis de France*-affiliated hotel-restaurant on the north side of the village, by the *Étang* – a pond shaded by plane trees – with a/c double rooms and a restaurant downstairs (under separate management; closed Mon and Sun evening in winter) that's open daily for lunch and dinner, with *menus* from €17/€28. **€84**

La Petite Maison Place de l'Étang ☎04 90 68 21 99, ⓦlapetitemaisondecucuron.com. In the shade of plane trees by the side of the *Étang*, this Michelin-starred restaurant serves seasonal Provençal dishes with luxurious cosmopolitan touches, with *menus* at €60 and €98. Wed–Sun 12.30–2pm & 8–10pm; winter closed Sun.

Ansouis

Halfway between Cucuron and Pertuis, the immaculate hilltop village of **ANSOUIS** is crowned by a superb **château** (guided tours Mon & Thurs–Sun: early April to mid-June & mid-Sept to Oct 3pm; mid-June to mid-Sept 3pm & 4.30pm; €10; ☎04 90 77 23 36, ⓦchateauansouis.fr), which was lived in by the same family from the twelfth century until it was sold at auction in 2008; a millennium old, it owes its present appearance to its gradual transformation from fortress to noble residence during the seventeenth century. The town's austere thirteenth-century **church**, dedicated to St Martin, abuts against the château's outer defences. At the foot of the village on rue du Vieux Moulin is the **Musée Extraordinaire de Georges Mazoyer** (daily: June–Sept 10am–7pm; Oct–May 2–6pm; €3.50; ☎04 90 09 82 64; ⓦmusee-extraordinaire.fr), an eccentric miscellany of Luberon fossils, Provençal furniture, paintings by the artist Georges Mazoyer and a blue coral grotto.

Musée des Arts et des Métiers du Vin

Rte de Pertuis, 5km from Ansouis on the D56 • April–June & Sept & Oct Mon & Sun 2.30–6pm, Tues–Sat 10am–12.30pm & 2.30–6pm; July & Aug daily 10am–12.30pm & 3–7.30pm • €5 • ☎04 90 09 83 33, ⓦchateau-turcan.com

A working *domaine* is the setting for the **Musée des Arts et des Métiers du Vin**, a spacious museum devoted to the wine industry and its associated trades, just east of Ansouis. Among the exhibits are an eighteenth-century wine press, bottles and glassware and a section on the craft of cooperage.

EATING
ANSOUIS

La Closerie Bd Platanes ☎ 04 90 09 90 54, ⓦ lacloserie ansouis.com. Strategically located midway between Ansouis' tourist car park and the château, this classy restaurant serves *quail pastilla* with spices and baba ganoush, with a €35 lunchtime *menu Clin d'Oeil*, a €52 *menu Saison* and a €75 *menu Faim Palais*. Mon, Tues, Fri & Sat lunch & dinner, Sun lunch only.

Pertuis

The one sizeable town this side of the Durance is **PERTUIS**, likeable enough but of interest primarily as a transport hub and as an inexpensive touring base. Like so many towns in the area, it only really comes to life on **market** day, which here is on Friday. In August there's a **big-band festival** (ⓦ festival-jazz-bigband-pertuis.com). The town centres around place Parmentier, rue Colbert – the main clothes shopping street leading up to place Jean-Jaurès – and the more historic place Mirabeau just to the north.

Val Joanis

West of Pertuis, just off the D973 to Cadenet • Mon–Fri 10am–12.30pm & 2–5pm, Sat 10am–1pm & 2–5.30pm; Fri & Sat garden closes 4.30pm on fair weather days for weddings • Winery free; gardens €3 • ☎ 04 90 79 20 77, ⓦ val-joanis.com

On the western fringes of Pertuis, the **gardens** and **winery** of **Val Joanis** surround the sixteenth-century *bastide* of the same name. The gardens are an attempt to re-create an eighteenth-century garden with both ornamental and productive elements, including a traditional kitchen garden and a beautiful long arbour planted with rambling roses. The vineyard produces increasingly respected Côtes du Luberon wines; there are opportunities to taste these – the reserve rosé is particularly fine – and the estate's olive oil.

ARRIVAL AND INFORMATION
PERTUIS

By train Pertuis is served by the TER (regional train network) from Marseille and Aix-en-Provence. The *gare SNCF* is 1km south of town.

Destinations Aix-en-Provence (3 daily; 37–46min); Marseille (6 daily; 1hr 5min–2hr 15min).

By bus The *halte routière* is on place Garcin, within easy walking distance of the centre.

Destinations Aix-en-Provence (every 10min–1hr; 35–

45min); Cadenet (up to 14 daily; 20min).

Tourist office Le Donjon, place Mirabeau (Mon–Thurs 10am–noon & 2.30–6pm, Fri 9am–12.30pm & 2.30–6pm, Sat 9.30am–noon & 2.30–6pm; ☎ 04 90 79 15 56, ⓦ ville-pertuis.fr).

Bike rental Bikes, including mountain bikes (VTT) and electric bikes, can be rented at Vélo Luberon, impasse François Gernelle, ZAC St-Martin (☎ 04 90 09 17 33).

ACCOMMODATION AND EATING

Le Boulevard 50 bd J. Baptiste Pécout ☎ 04 90 09 69 31, ⓦ restaurant-leboulevard.com. Pretty, a/c upstairs dining room just south of the town centre, serving the likes of, *pieds et paquets* with Pertuis potatoes, a €19 lunch *menu*, €32 *menu Durance* and a €42 *menu Gourmand*. Mon & Thurs–Sat noon–1.30pm & 7.30–9.30pm, Tues & Sun noon–1.30pm.

Hôtel du Cours 100 place Jean-Jaurès ☎ 04 90 79 00 68, ⓦ hotel-du-cours.fr. Located in the centre of town, this small, family-run hotel has twenty renovated rooms with en-suite bath or shower, plus private parking; cheapest rooms have showers but share WC. **€45**

Les Pinèdes Av Pierre Augier ☎ 04 90 79 10 98, ⓦ campinglespinedes.fr. Four-star campsite in a pine forest east of the town centre, with a pool, paddling pool and activities for children and adults. Closed mid-Oct to early April. Camping **€25**; mobile homes (per week) **€567**

Le Village Provençal Rue B. Franklin ☎ 04 90 09 70 18, ⓦ hotel-pertuis.fr. Modern hotel in ZAC St-Martin, an industrial zone to the south of town, with a/c rooms, indoor and outdoor pools, restaurant and bowling alley. **€79**

4

Château de la Tour d'Aigues

La Tour d'Aigues • Mid-April to Sept Tues–Sat 10am–12.30pm & 2.30–6pm • €3.50 • ☎ 04 90 07 50 29

Heading northeast from Pertuis towards Grambois brings you to **LA TOUR D'AIGUES**, where the vast shell of the **Château de la Tour d'Aigues** dominates the village centre. It was half destroyed during the Revolution but the most finely detailed Renaissance decoration, based on Classical designs including Grecian helmets, angels, bows and arrows and Olympic torches, has survived on the gateway arch.

You can admire most of the ruins' glories from the outside, but there's also a **Musée de Faïence** displaying products of some of the eighteenth century's most prestigious producers, plus fragments of the château's original decorative stonework. The château is also a popular venue for concerts.

ACCOMMODATION AND EATING   LA TOUR D'AIGUES

Ô P'tit Chef 51 rue Antoine de Très ☎ 04 90 07 34 64, ⓦ optitchef84.e-monsite.com. Popular, stone-vaulted restaurant serving simply, hearty portions of roast duck in pear sauce, Scottish salmon and the likes. Great value *menus* at €16.50 and €18.50. Occasional live music. Mon & Thurs–Sun noon–2pm, Tues noon–2pm.

Le Petit Mas de Marie 24 rue Marcel Pagnol ☎ 04 90 07 48 22, ⓦ lepetitmasdemarie.com. Three-star hotel a little to the west of the village on the road to Pertuis, with a restaurant, heated pool and garden. Closed late Jan to late Feb. **€105**

Manosque and around

MANOSQUE, 36km northeast of Pertuis, is an ancient town, strategically positioned just above the right bank of the River Durance. Its small old quarter is surrounded by nondescript blocks, and beyond them by ever-spreading industrial units and superstores. It is a major population centre in the *département* of Alpes-de-Haute-Provence, profiting from the new corridor of affluence that follows the autoroute north.

Manosque is home to the phenomenally successful soap and oil retailer **L'Occitane en Provence**, founded in 1976 by Olivier Baussan, and thus is as responsible as anywhere for propagating the idyllic image of Provence internationally. For the French, however, it is most famous as the hometown of the author **Jean Giono**. As well as mementoes of the writer, the town contains an extraordinary work of art on the theme of the Apocalypse by the Armenian-born painter **Jean Carzou**.

Vieux Manosque

Barely half a kilometre wide, **Vieux Manosque** is entered through either of its two remaining medieval gates: Porte Saunerie in the south, or Porte Soubeyran in the north, which sports a tiny bell suspended within the iron outline of an onion dome. Once you get through the gates it's a little dull, the streets lined with practical but unexciting country-town shops (and a few empty premises in the quieter stretches); **rue Grande** is by far the most enticing, with a fishmonger, a couple of *chocolatiers*, shops selling *chèvre de Banon* cheese and wine, and a branch of L'Occitane en Provence. Things get livelier for the weekly **market** on Saturday morning.

Midway between the two gates, on rue Grande, a more intricate bell tower graces the **Église de St-Sauveur**. Neither this nor the **Église de Notre Dame de Romigier**, further up the same street, is a particularly stunning church, though the walls of both bow outwards with the weight of the centuries, and the latter's Black Virgin (black due to the effect of gold leaf on wood) boasts a lengthy resumé of miracles.

At the heart of old Manosque, the **Place de l'Hôtel de Ville** is a pleasant place to linger awhile at a pavement café, though the seventeenth-century town hall itself has suffered from bland modernization.

Centre Jean Giono

3 bd Élémir Bourges • Tues–Sat: April–Sept 10am–noon & 2–6pm; Oct–March 2–6pm • €2 • ☎ 04 92 70 54 54, ⓦ centrejeangiono.com

JEAN GIONO

Born in Manosque, the novelist **Jean Giono** (1895–1970) set many of his books in his native Provence. He was imprisoned at the start of World War II for his pacifism, and again after liberation because the Vichy government had portrayed his belief in the superiority of nature and peasant life over culture and urban civilization as supporting the Nazi cause. In truth, far from being a Fascist, Giono was a passionate ecologist, and the countryside around Manosque plays as strong a part in his novels as do the characters. World War II embittered him, and his later novels are less idealistic.

Giono – who detested cities, above all Paris – never left Manosque and died here in 1970.

The attractive eighteenth-century house that is now the **Centre Jean Giono**, by Porte Saunerie, was the first house built outside the town walls. As well as manuscripts, photos, letters and a library of translations of Giono's work, the centre has an extensive video collection of films based on his novels, as well as interviews and documentaries. Giono himself did not live here, but at **Lou Paraïs**, off montée des Vraies Richesses, 1.5km north of the *vieille ville* (free guided tours Fri 2.30–4.30pm by arrangement only; also April–Sept Tues, Thurs & Sat at same times by advance reservation; see Centre Jean Giono website).

Fondation Carzou

7–9 bd Élémir Bourges • April–Oct Tues–Sat 10am–12.30pm & 2–6pm; Nov–March Wed–Sat 2–6pm • €5 • ☎ 04 92 87 40 49, Ⓦ fondationcarzou.fr

The French-Armenian painter **Jean Carzou**, a contemporary of Jean Giono, confronts the issues of war, technology, dehumanization and the environmental destruction of the planet head-on in his extraordinary, monumental **L'Apocalypse**. The work is composed of painted panels and stained-glass windows in the former church of the Couvent de la Présentation, now the **Fondation Carzou**, just up from the Centre Jean Giono. Everything from the French Revolution to Pol Pot's massacres is portrayed here, in nightmarish detail.

L'Occitane en Provence factory

ZI St-Maurice • **Museum and shop** April–Oct daily 10am–7pm; Nov–March Mon–Sat 10am–7pm • Free • **Factory** April–Oct daily; Nov–March Mon–Sat free guided tours (1hr; in French or English) by arrangement • ☎ 04 92 70 32 08, Ⓦ loccitane.com

On the far side of the A51 autoroute in the industrial quarter of St-Maurice is the **L'Occitane en Provence factory**, free guided tours of which include a film and a workshop on the ingredients used in the luxurious products. There's also an interactive museum and the brand's largest French store.

Maison de la Biodiversité

Chemin de la Thomassine • July–Sept Tues–Sat 10.30am–1pm & 3–6.30pm; Oct–June Wed 10am–12.30pm & 2–4.30pm; guided tours July–Sept Tues–Sat 10.30am & 4.30pm; Oct–June Wed 10.30am & 3pm • €4 • ☎ 04 92 87 74 40, Ⓦ parcduluberon.fr

To the northwest of Manosque, the Parc Naturel Régional du Luberon runs the **Maison de la Biodiversité**, which explains, with the help of a series of terraced gardens in the shade of a traditional Provençal *bastide*, the domestication of fruits and other crops by humankind. There's everything from palms to roses, figs and willows, plus a section devoted to old varieties of food crops.

Écomusée l'Olivier

Ancienne rte de Forcalquier, Volx • July & Aug daily 10am–1pm & 2–6pm; Sept–June Tues–Sat 10am–1pm & 2–6pm • €4 • ☎ 04 86 68 53 15, Ⓦ mb-1830.com/fr/ecomusee-olivier • Signposted off the D4096; bus #25 from Manosque

Just over 8km north of Manosque in the village of **VOLX**, the **Écomusée l'Olivier** tells, with the help of attractively laid-out interactive exhibits and audiovisual displays, the story of the olive – the "gift of the Mediterranean" – and the cultures that have nurtured it, from Provence to the eastern Mediterranean. You can taste and buy Provençal oils of exceptional quality here, and there's a restaurant.

ARRIVAL AND INFORMATION

By train The *gare SNCF* is 1.5km south of the centre along Av Jean Giono and Av Lattre de Tassigny, linked by bus (roughly hourly; 10min) to the *gare routière*.

Destinations Aix-en-Provence (5 daily; 55min–1hr 5min; Marseille (11 daily; 1hr 20min–1hr 56min; Sisteron (6 daily; 37–40min).

By bus The *gare routière* is a short walk south of Vieux Manosque on Bd Charles-de-Gaulle.

Destinations Aix-en-Provence (roughly hourly; 55min–1hr); Forcalquier (roughly every 2–3hr; 30min); Mane

MANOSQUE AND AROUND

(roughly every 2–3hr; 25min); Marseille (13 daily; 1hr 25min–1hr 50min); Sisteron (5 daily; 45min–1hr 5min); Volx (roughly hourly; 10min).

Tourist office 16 place du Dr-Joubert (April, May & Oct Tues–Sat 10am–12.30pm & 2–5.30pm; June & Sept Mon–Sat 10amam–12.30pm & 2–5.30pm; July & Aug Mon–Sat 10am–1pm & 3.30–7pm, Sun 10am–1pm; Nov–March Tues–Fri 10am–noon & 2–5pm; ☎ 04 92 72 16 00, ⓦ manosque-tourisme.com).

ACCOMMODATION AND EATING

L'Aromavin Place Marcel Pagnol ☎ 04 13 37 09 17, ⓦ laromavin-restaurant-manosque.com. Beautifully presented *cuisine de terroir* served in a fresh, modern interior, with mains priced around €15. Open for breakfast as well. Mon & Thurs–Sun 9.30am–3pm & 6.30–9.30pm.

La Bastide de l'Adrech Av des Serrets ☎ 06 18 18 17 18, ⓦ bastide-adrech.com. Lovely *chambres d'hôtes* in an eighteenth-century farmhouse just 5min from the centre of town with pretty, traditionally furnished rooms with beams and tiled floors, plus a couple of *gîtes*. Breakfast included. €110

Camping Provence Vallée Av de la Repasse ☎ 04 92 72 28 08, ⓦ provence-vallee.fr. Well-equipped three-star municipal campsite on a shady, four-hectare site with football pitch, two pools, a children's play area, *boules* pitch and a snack bar/takeaway. Closed Nov–March. €24

François 1er 18 rue Guilhempierre ☎ 04 92 72 07 99, ⓦ contact-hotel.com. Inexpensive two-star hotel in Vieux Manosque; rooms have shower, WC and flatscreen TV and there are family rooms for up to five, plus free parking for bikes and motorbikes. €53

Le Petit Lauragais 6 place du Terreau ☎ 04 92 72 13 00. *Gault Millau*-listed place serving cuisine from Provence and the southwest, with *confit* octopus with *piperade*, lamb stuffed with *chèvre*, pine nuts and rocket and a €26.50 *menu*. Mon–Fri noon–2pm & 7–9.30pm, Sat 7–9.30pm.

Le Pré St Michel 435 Montée de la Mort d'Imbert ☎ 04 92 72 14 27, ⓦ presaintmichel.com. Pleasant three-star hotel on the heights overlooking Manosque, with pretty, a/c rooms decorated in Provençal style, plus a restaurant and pool. €92

Lurs and around

Perched on a narrow ridge above the west bank of the Durance some 20km north of Manosque, **LURS** is a *village de caractère*, undeniably charming yet extremely conscious of its picturesque status. Immaculately restored houses stand amid immaculately maintained ruins; there's a tiny, Roman-style theatre, but little commerce. From the top of the village, you can see across the wide, multi-branching river to the abrupt step up to the Plateau de Valensole, with the snowy peaks beyond. To the south the land drops before rising again in another high ridge along the river, while to the west and north the views are just as extensive, from the rolling hills around Forcalquier to the Montagne de Lure. The best way to appreciate this geography is to follow the **Promenade des Évêques** – marked by fifteen small oratories – to the small chapel of **Notre Dame de Vie** along the narrowing escarpment.

The village has long been a centre for **graphic artists** and **printers**, and was home to the man who created the universal nomenclature for typefaces. An intriguing modern monument at the entrance to the village demonstrates the evolution of world alphabets using a spiral of posts.

Prieuré de Ganagobie

Signposted off the D4096 south of Ganagobie village • Tues–Sun 2.30–5.15pm, closed 1 week in mid-Jan • Free • ☎ 04 92 68 00 04, ⓦ abbaye-ganagobie.com

> ## THE DRUMMOND MYSTERY
>
> By the late 1940s Lurs was deserted save for the odd passing bandit, but it gained international notoriety in 1952 when the British scientist **Sir Jack Drummond** and his family were murdered while camping alongside the Durance below the village. The case was never satisfactorily solved: the man convicted of the murder was spared execution and ultimately released from custody, and in recent years it has been suggested that Sir Jack was a victim of the Cold War, assassinated because he was a British spy.

About 7km north of Lurs, at the twelfth-century **Prieuré de Ganagobie**, the floor of the priory church is covered with mosaics composed of red, black and white tiles: they depict fabulous beasts whose tails loop through their bodies, and the four elements represented by an elephant (earth), a fish (water), a griffon (air) and a lion (fire). Interlocking and repeating patterns show a strong Byzantine influence, and there's a dragon slain by a St George in Crusader armour. These decorations and the splendidly monumental west portal aside, the church has an almost fortress-like austerity.

After taking a look, you can stroll for a couple of minutes through the oaks and pines along the allée des Moines to reach the edge of the **Plateau de Ganagobie**, 350m above the Durance, and with excellent views.

ACCOMMODATION   LURS

Le Séminaire Le Village ☎04 92 73 49 95, ⓦbalneo therapie-remise-en-forme.com. *Gîte* and *chambres d'hôtes* housed in the old summer residence of the bishops of Sisteron; a/c rooms have en-suite bath or shower, and spa treatments are available. **€80**

The Pénitents des Mées and Château-Arnoux

North of Ganagobie, the impending confluence of the Durance and Bléone is announced by the **Pénitents des Mées**, a remarkable long line of pointed rocks on the east bank, said to be the remains of cowled monks, literally petrified for desiring the women slaves a local lord brought back from the Crusades. By the time you reach **CHÂTEAU-ARNOUX**, hills once more close in and the river takes on a smoother, more majestic prospect, with a barrage just east of the town creating a 7km-long artificial lake. Dominating the centre of the town – pounding traffic aside – is an imposing Renaissance **castle** (closed to the public), with five towers and multicoloured roof tiles. The main reason to stop, however, is to eat at *La Bonne Étape*, renowned as one of the best **restaurants** in Provence (see below).

ACCOMMODATION AND EATING   CHÂTEAU-ARNOUX

La Bonne Étape Chemin du Lac ☎04 92 64 00 09, ⓦbonneetape.com. One of Provence's best restaurants, celebrating the produce of the region without trendy foreign influences on its assorted *menus* (€75–115) there's also a good but much cheaper and highly recommended bistro, *Au Goût du Jour*, with a *menu* at €19.50. Dishes might include pigeon with seasonal fruits, tapenade sauce and spelt risotto, or veal with lemon balm sauce, creamy polenta and black and green olives. You can stay here in four-star comfort, too. July–Sept Tues–Sun: restaurant noon–1.30pm & 7.30–9.30pm, bistro noon–2pm & 7.30–10pm; Oct–June Wed–Sun: restaurant noon–1.30pm & 7.30–9.30pm, bistro noon–2pm & 7.30–10pm. **€221**

Sisteron and around

The last Provençal stretch of the Route Napoléon (see page 317) runs from Château-Arnoux to **SISTERON**, the first sight of which reveals its strategic significance as the major mountain gateway to Provence. The town, fortified since ancient times, was half-destroyed by the Anglo-American bombardment of 1944, but its **citadel** still stands as a fearsome sentinel over the city and the solitary bridge across the river. After heavy rains the Durance, the colour of *café au lait*, becomes a raging torrent pushing through the narrow Sisteron gap. Sisteron today is a lively place, its prosperity based as much on the extensive industrial zone that has grown up to the north along the D4085 as it is on tourism.

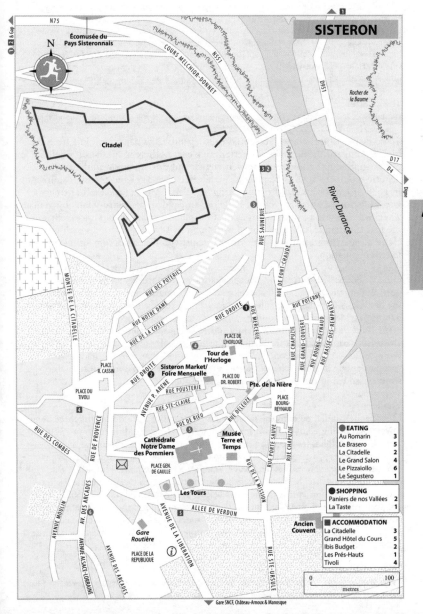

SISTERON

EATING
Au Romarin	3
Le Brasero	5
La Citadelle	2
Le Grand Salon	4
Le Pizzaiollo	6
Le Segustero	1

SHOPPING
Paniers de nos Vallées	2
La Taste	1

ACCOMMODATION
La Citadelle	3
Grand Hôtel du Cours	5
Ibis Budget	2
Les Prés-Hauts	1
Tivoli	4

NAPOLEON IN SISTERON

When **Napoleon** made his ill-fated return from exile in Elba in 1815, Sisteron gave him something of a headache. Its mayor and the majority of its population were royalist, and given the fortifications and geography of the town, it was impossible for him to pass undetected. However, luck was still with the Corsican in those days, as the military commander of the *département* was a sympathizer and removed all ammunition from Sisteron's arsenal. Contemporary accounts say Napoleon sat nonchalantly on the bridge, contemplating the citadel above and the tumultuous waters below, while his men reassembled and the town's notables, ordered to keep their pistols under wraps, looked on impotently. Eventually Napoleon entered the city, took some refreshment at a tavern and received a tricolour from a courageous peasant woman before rejoining his band and taking leave of Provence.

The citadel

Daily: Late March, April & Oct 9am–6pm; May 9am–6.30pm; June & Sept 9am–7pm; July & Aug 9am–7.30pm; first two weeks Nov 10am–5pm • €6.60 • ☎ 04 92 61 27 57, ⓦ www.citadelledesisteron.fr

To do justice to the **citadel**, you could easily spend half a day scrambling from the highest ramparts to the lowest subterranean passage. There is a leaflet in English but no guides, just audio recordings in French and English attempting to re-create historic moments, such as Napoleon's march (see page 317) and the imprisonment in 1639 of Jan Kazimierz, the future king of Poland. Most of the extant defences were constructed after the Wars of Religion, and added to a century later by Vauban when Sisteron was a frontline fort against neighbouring Savoy. No traces remain of the first Ligurian fortification nor of its Roman successor, and the eleventh-century castle was destroyed in the mid-thirteenth century during a pogrom against the local Jewish population.

As you climb up to the fortress, there seems no end to the gateways, courtyards and other defences. The outcrop on which the fortress sits abruptly stops at the lookout post, **Guérite du Diable**, 500m above the narrow passage of the Durance, and affording the best views. On the other side of the ravine, the vertical folds of the **Rocher de la Baume** provide a favourite training ground for local mountaineers.

The **Nuits de la Citadelle** festival (July and Aug; ⓦ nuitsdelacitadelle.fr) sees open-air concerts, opera, drama and dance in the grounds. There is also a **museum** with a room dedicated to Napoleon, and an exhibition on Vauban and his predecessors. The vertiginous late medieval chapel, **Notre Dame du Château**, boasts beautiful stained-glass windows added in the 1970s. It hosts art exhibitions.

Vieille ville

Outside the citadel, perhaps the most striking features of Sisteron are the three huge **towers** that belonged to the ramparts, built around the expanding town in 1370. Though one still has its spiralling staircase, only ravens use them now.

You can explore Sisteron's **lower town** along narrow passages with steep steps that interconnect through vaulted archways, known here as *andrônes*. Houses on the downslope side of rue Saunerie, overlooking the river, often descend at the back a further three or four storeys to the lanes below. In the troubled days of 1568, during the Wars of Religion, sixty lanterns were put in place to light the alleyways and deter conspiracies and plots; there's no such luxury today, and Old Sisteron can take on a spooky aspect at night. In the **upper town**, on the other side of rue Saunerie and rue Droite, the houses, like the citadel, follow the curves of the rock.

Cathédrale Notre Dame des Pommiers

Place du Général-de-Gaulle • April, May & Oct Mon & Sun 3–6pm, Tues–Sat 9am–noon & 1.30–5.30pm; June–Sept Mon 1.30–5.30pm, Tues–Sat 9.30am–noon & 1.30–5.30pm, Sun 3–6pm

The twelfth-century former **Cathédrale Notre Dame des Pommiers** has a strictly rectangular interior that contrasts with its riot of stepped roofs and an octagonal gallery adjoining a square belfry topped by a pyramidal spire. The altarpiece incorporates a Mignard painting; other seventeenth-century works adorn the chapels.

Musée Terre et Temps

Place du Général-de-Gaulle • April–Sept Tues–Sat 1.30–5.30pm• Free • ☎ 04 92 61 61 30, ⓦ sisteron.com/musee-terre-et-temps

At the rear of the cathedral, a former convent of the Visitandine order houses the **Musée Terre et Temps**, which charts the measurement of time from ancient sundials through calendars to the latest atomic clocks, in parallel with the measurement of geological time. After the thrills of the citadel it's all a bit sedate.

Écomusée du Pays Sisteronnais

Rond-point Melchior-Donnet • Mid-June to early July & late Aug to mid-Sept Tues–Sat 2–6pm; early July to late Aug Tues–Sat 10am–noon & 2–6pm, Sun 2–6pm • Free • ☎ 04 92 32 48 75, ⓦ sisteron.com/ecomusee

Occupying a striking modern structure on the north side of the citadel and with a fine view of the confluence of the Büech and Durance rivers, the small **Écomusée du Pays Sisteronnais** documents the rural life and customs of the Sisteron region, with exhibits of agricultural implements and traditional local crafts.

ARRIVAL AND INFORMATION   SISTERON

By train Sisteron's *gare SNCF* is on Av de la Libération, a short walk south of the central place de la République.
Destinations Aix-en-Provence (6 daily; 1hr 18min–1hr 27min); Château-Arnoux (2 daily; 17min); Manosque (6 daily; 37–40min); Marseille (4–6 daily; 2hr 7min–2hr 19min).

By bus Sisteron's *gare routière* is on place de la Republique near the tourist office.
Destinations Aix-en-Provence (5 daily; 1hr 40min–2hr); Château-Arnoux (roughly every 1–2hr; 15–23min); Digne (roughly every 1–2hr; 47min–1hr 10min); Manosque (up to 5 daily; 45min–1hr 5min); Marseille (3–6 daily; 2hr 15min–2hr 15min–2hr 45min).

Tourist office 1 place de la République (April– June, Sept and Oct Mon–Sat 9am–12.30pm & 2–6pm; July & Aug Mon–Sat 9am–7pm, Sun 10am–5pm; Nov–March Mon–Fri 9am–12.30pm & 2–5.30pm, Sat 9am–12.30pm; ☎ 04 92 61 36 50, ⓦ sisteron-tourisme.fr). It sells walking and cycling guides and you can pick up free maps of cycling itineraries in the region, including one that crosses the summit of the Montagne de Lure.

ACCOMMODATION   SEE MAP PAGE 177

La Citadelle 126 rue Saunerie ☎ 04 92 61 13 52, ⓦ hotel-lacitadelle.com. Inexpensive and central option overlooking the river, with a restaurant and bar. Rooms are very basic but clean, and some enjoy wonderful views; some sleep three or four. Cheaper rooms have shared facilities. €58

Grand Hôtel du Cours Allée de Verdun ☎ 04 92 61 04 51, ⓦ hotel-lecours.com. Sisteron's best – and snootiest – option is family-run, right in the centre of town, with three-star comforts, forty a/c en-suite rooms and five suites, a good restaurant and private parking. Closed Dec to mid-March. €85

Ibis Budget 1 allée des Tilleuls, Parc d'activités Sisteron-Nord ☎ 0892 68 07 55, ⓦ accorhotels.com.

Modern, well-equipped budget chain hotel, by the exit from the A51 autoroute 4km north of town, with simple en-suite a/c rooms and parking. There's a plusher *Ibis* next door. €55

Les Prés-Hauts 44 chemin des Prés Hauts ☎ 04 92 61 19 69, ⓦ camping-sisteron.com. Well-equipped four-star municipal campsite 3km north of Sisteron off the D951, with a pool, beach volleyball and a free shuttle bus to the town centre. Closed Oct–March. €22

Tivoli 21 place René Cassin ☎ 04 92 62 26 68, ⓦ hotel-tivoli.fr. Decent two-star hotel just off place de la République. Cheerful and good value, with revamped decor, restaurant, parking and a terrace with views towards the citadel. €64

EATING   SEE MAP PAGE 177

★ **Au Romarin** 103 rue Saunerie ☎ 02 40 63 15 87, ⓦ restaurant-leromarin.com. One of the more ambitious kitchens in Sisteron's old town, with *menus Gourmet*

and *Carte Blanche* in the €41–52 and €36.90–54 ranges respectively, featuring delicacies like turbot with caviar, and sweetbreads with mutton and cognac. Wed, Fri & Sat

> ## SISTERON MARKET
>
> **Place de l'Horloge**, at the other end of rue Deleuze from the cathedral, is the site for the Wednesday and Saturday **market**, where stalls congregate to sell sweet and savoury *fougasse*, lavender honey, nougat and almond-paste *calissons* that rival those from Aix-en-Provence. On the second Saturday of every month the market becomes a **fair** (*foire mensuelle*), spilling over the much larger space around the Hôtel de Ville. There are likely to be flocks of sheep and lambs, and cages of pigeons as well as stalls selling clothes and bric-a-brac.

noon–1.30pm & 7.30–9.30pm, Thurs noon–1.30pm & 7.30–9.15pm, Sun noon–3pm.

Le Brasero 27 rue Deleuze ☎ 04 92 61 56 79. Rustic pine-panelled restaurant with an old-school, Wild West feel, where you can cook your own flame grilled burgers, steak and the like at your table, as well as enjoy rarities like paella and guacamole. Good value *formules* at €14–15. Tues–Thurs & Sun noon–2pm & 7–9pm, Fri noon–2pm & 7–9.15pm, Sat noon–2pm & 7–9.30pm.

La Citadelle 126 rue Saunerie ☎ 04 92 61 13 52, ⓦ hotel-lacitadelle.com. Informal brasserie and bar with views over the Durance and a short *carte* offering salads from €10, scallop lasagne for €17 and Sisteron-style *pieds et paquets* for €15. There's also a two/three-course *formule* priced at €22/30. Daily noon–3pm & 7–10pm.

Le Grand Salon 33 place Paul-Arène ☎ 04 92 61 15 79. Centrally located café and *confiserie* overlooking the market, with good nougat and *calissons*, sandwiches and pasta for around €4–5, and a chalked-up selection of *plats du jour*. Daily: July & Aug 9am–1am; Sept–June 9am–8pm.

Le Pizzaiollo 2 av des Arcades ☎ 04 92 62 62 60, ⓦ restaurant-pizzeria-sisteron.fr. Friendly and informal, with big portions of pizza and salad plus a few local specialities, including *pieds et paquets Sisteronnais*; pizzas from €8.50, with the option of either a tomato or crème fraiche base. Daily noon–2pm & 7–10pm.

Le Segustero 7 Allée des Frênes, Val de Durance ☎ 04 92 34 75 59, ⓦ le-segustero.fr. Housed in a sympathetically renovated farm steading to the north of town, with a large garden terrace where you can enjoy the likes of Auvergne pork and rack of *Sisteronnai* lamb with herbes de Provence-infused jus. Lunch and dinner *menus* at €22 and €32. Tues–Sat noon–1.30pm & 7–9pm, Sun noon–1.30pm.

SHOPPING
SEE MAP PAGE 177

Paniers de nos Vallées 12 rue Droite ☎ 04 92 61 28 99, ⓦ paniersdenosvallees.com. Gorgeous deli selling quality local produce, including olive oil, chickpea flour, goat's cheeses, wines and chestnut purée, plus organic fruit and vegetables. Tues–Sat 9am–1pm & 3–7pm.

La Taste 224 rue Droite ☎ 04 92 61 28 99. A good bet in the old town for the flavours and scents of Provence, with everything from soaps and lavender to honey, wine, absinthe and *génépi* – a liqueur flavoured with a plant that's a member of the wormwood family. July & Aug daily 9am–7.15pm; Sept–June daily 9am–12.15pm & 3–7.15pm.

Pays de Forcalquier

Bounded in the east by the valley of the Durance, to the north by the **Montagne de Lure** and shading to the south and west into the **Parc Naturel Régional du Luberon** (see page 189), the **Pays de Forcalquier** is a beguiling mix of agrarian plenty and scenic beauty, with honey, fruit aperitifs, olive oil and cheese to savour and clear skies and pure air to enjoy. It's a region far removed from urban centres, and even the venerable capital, **Forcalquier**, has a sleepy, rural feel to it. The countryside, gentle enough around Forcalquier and the neighbouring village of **Mane**, becomes progressively wilder towards the Plateau d'Albion in the west. Here, remote villages such as **Simiane-la-Rotonde** and **Banon** have a particular charm, not yet as smart as the villages of the Luberon but easily their equal for beauty and history. It's in the more northerly villages of the Pays de Forcalquier, including Banon, that you're likely to hear Provençal being spoken and see aspects of rural life that have hardly changed over centuries. It was here too, in a tiny place called Le Contadour on the Lure foothills due north of Banon, that Jean Giono (see page 173) set up his summer commune in the 1930s to expostulate the themes of peace, ecology and the return to nature. The pristine atmospheric conditions have also attracted the attentions of astronomers, whose **Observatoire de Haute-Provence** sits in splendid isolation close to the village of **St-Michel-l'Observatoire**.

Forcalquier

Mellow **FORCALQUIER**, 11km west of the Durance on the D12, dominates the surrounding countryside, its distinctive hilly outline visible for many kilometres around. Close up, the glories of the little town's history are there for all to see, and consequently Forcalquier is as appealing as anything in the gentle, hilly countryside that surrounds it. The town is at its most animated on Mondays when the main **market** takes place.

Some history

Despite its slumbering air, Forcalquier was once a place of some significance, as its public buildings and the elaborate architectural details of its *vieille ville* betray. In the twelfth century the **counts of Forcalquier** rivalled those of Provence, with dominions spreading south and east to the Durance and north to the Drôme. Gap, Embrun, Sisteron, Manosque and Apt were all ruled from the **citadel** of Forcalquier, which even minted its own currency. When this separate power base came to an end, Forcalquier was still renowned as the **Cité des Quatre Reines**, since the four daughters of Raimond Béranger V, who united Forcalquier and Provence, all married kings. One of them, Eleanor, married Henry III of England, a fact commemorated by a modern plaque on the Gothic fountain of place du Bourguet.

Vieille ville

Looming over the central place du Bourguet, the twelfth-century former **Cathédrale Notre Dame** has an asymmetric and defensive exterior, a finely wrought Gothic porch and a Romanesque nave. Behind it are the huddled houses of the **vieille ville**, which date from the thirteenth to the eighteenth century. Bearing right along rue Plauchud from the cathedral you'll reach place St-Michel, where the fountain – a twentieth-century copy of the sixteenth-century Renaissance original – bears decorative figures engaged in bawdy activities.

East of place Vieille off rue des Lices, the house that was supposedly Forcalquier's medieval **synagogue** marks the site of the former Jewish quarter; nearby on rue des Cordeliers is the one remaining gateway to the *vieille ville*, the **Porte des Cordeliers**.

Couvent des Cordeliers

Université Européenne des Senteurs & Saveurs • Artemisia museum Feb–April & Oct–Dec Mon & Wed–Sat 10am–12.30pm & 1.30–6pm; May–Sept daily 9.30am–12.30pm & 1.30–7pm • €6 • ☎ 04 92 72 28 51, ⓦ uess.fr

---

CYCLING IN THE PAYS DE FORCALQUIER

With its beautiful landscapes and relatively quiet roads, the **Pays de Forcalquier** is wonderful territory for cycling holidays. There's a 78km signposted circuit of the region which takes in Forcalquier, Lurs, Cruis and St-Étienne-les-Orgues. For the supremely fit the most tempting route is the 18km, 1000m ascent of the Montagne de Lure, which you can tackle as a self-timed challenge using your smartphone; see ⓦ challenge-lure.com for more details.

For more **information** on cycling in the region see ⓦ leluberonavelo.com. Tourist offices have free maps with suggested routes and you can rent bikes in Forcalquier from Bachelas Cycles, 5 bd de la République (☎ 04 92 75 12 47).

The superior power of the Roman Catholic Church is represented by the **Couvent des Cordeliers**, just off boulevard des Martyrs beyond the Porte des Cordeliers. Built between the twelfth and fourteenth centuries, it bears the scars of wars and revolutions but preserves a beautifully vaulted scriptorium and a library with its original wooden ceiling. Nowadays the complex is the **Université Européenne des Senteurs & Saveurs**, and offers workshops on perfumery, aromatherapy and olfactory skills, as part of the new **Artemisia museum**. It's an interactive, scratch'n'sniff affair dedicated to the local aromatic and medicinal plants. You can wander in the beautiful restored cloister and lovely gardens, and there's a shop (same hours as museum).

The citadel

Not much actually survives of the ancient fortress of the counts of Forcalquier which once crowned the wooded hill that dominates the town, though the superb 360-degree view of the surrounding countryside is reason enough to make the steep ascent up rue St-Mary from the *vieille ville* to the **citadel**. Beside the ruins of a tower and the half-buried walls of the original cathedral of St-Mary there's a neo-Byzantine nineteenth-century chapel, **Notre Dame de Provence**, its distinctive profile visible for many kilometres around.

ARRIVAL AND INFORMATION   FORCALQUIER

By bus Buses generally drop you off at place Martial Sicard, one block back from the main place du Bourguet, except on market days when they stop at place du Bourguet.
Destinations Aix-en-Provence (3 daily; 1hr 20min–1hr 30min); Apt (4 daily; 45min); Mane (13 daily; 5min); Manosque (roughly every 2–3hr; 30min); Marseille (4 daily; 1hr 55min–2hr 20min); St-Michel-l'Observatoire (4 daily; 12min); Volx (8 daily; 15–20min).

Tourist office 13 place du Bourguet (Mon & Wed–Sat 9am–noon & 2–6pm; ☎04 92 75 10 02, ⓦhaute-provence-tourisme.com).

ACCOMMODATION AND EATING

Aïgo Blanco 5 place Vieille ☎04 92 75 27 23. Classy restaurant and *salon de thé* in the *vieille ville*, with a wonderfully shady terrace and a €19.80 lunch *menu* including tuna sashimi and wasabi asparagus, as well as salads from €16.80. Daily 9am–5pm & 6pm–midnight. Closed Jan.

La Bastide St Georges Rte de Banon, Quartier Beaudine ☎04 92 75 72 80, ⓦbastidesaintgeorges. com. Stylish four-star hotel 2km from the centre of Forcalquier, with a restaurant, heated outdoor pool and spa. A/c rooms have terraces and there are two family rooms that sleep four. €230

Camping Indigo 500m out of town on the road to Sigonce ☎04 92 75 27 94, ⓦcamping-forcalquier.com. Three-star campsite on a modest 3-hectare site, with 72 pitches and a pool; it also rents out mobile homes, for which there's a two-night minimum stay. Closed Oct–March. Camping €26; mobile homes €126

Charembeau Rte de Niozelles ☎04 92 70 91 70, ⓦcharembeau.com. Three-star hotel in a restored eighteenth-century farmhouse, 2km out of town at the end of a long drive signed off the road to Niozelles. Closed mid-Nov to Feb. €85

L'esperluette 28 bd Latourette ☎06 27 44 66 25, ⓦfacebook.com/lesperluetteforcalquier. A local favourite, this stylish and inviting little *cave à vin* cooks up bargain €17 *menus du jour* with simply prepared duck, rabbit and the likes. Mon–Thurs 9.30am–6pm, Fri 9.30am–10.30pm, Sat 9.30am–7.30pm.

Les Terrasses de la Bastide Rte de Banon, Quartier Beaudine ☎06 27 44 66 25, ⓦlesterrassesdelabastide. fr. A "semi-gastronomic" restaurant on the edge of the village by the similarly named hotel, serving Provençal cooking in a gorgeous garden. Lunch *formule* at €19 and *menus* at €30 and €35. Daily noon–1.30pm & 7–8.30pm.

SHOPPING

Distilleries et Domaines de Provence 9 av St-Promasse ☎04 92 75 15 41, ⓦdistilleries-provence. com. Just down from place Bourguet and in business since 1989, this distillery is well worth visiting to taste and buy its Henri Bardoun *pastis* and a wide range of *eaux de vie*, aperitifs and absinthe. July & Aug Mon–Sat 9am–7pm, Sun 9am–1pm; April–June & Sept–Dec Wed–Mon 10am–12.30pm & 2–6.30pm.

Mane and around

The village of **MANE**, 4km south of Forcalquier at the junction of the roads from Apt and Manosque, still has its feudal citadel – now a private residence and closed to the public – and Renaissance churches, chapels and mansions remarkably intact.

Notre Dame de Salagon

0.5km out of the village off the Apt road • Feb–April & Oct to mid-Dec Mon & Wed–Sun 10am–6pm; May & Sept daily 10am–7pm; June–Aug Mon–Wed & Fri–Sun 10am–7pm, Thurs 10am–10pm • €8 with audioguide • ☎ 04 92 75 70 50, ⓦ musee-de-salagon.com • Bus #22 from Forcalquier

Mane's most impressive building is a former Benedictine priory, **Notre Dame de Salagon**. The fortified twelfth-century Romanesque church shows traces of fourteenth-century frescoes and sculpted scenes of rural life. Archeological digs in the choir have revealed the remnants of an earlier, sixth-century church. In addition to the church, the complex comprises fifteenth-century monks' quarters, seventeenth-century stables and a smithy, which is used to display traditional farm tools; there's also an exhibition on the history of Salagon. The five **gardens** include one of aromatic plants, a medieval one with medicinal, floral and vegetable sections, a traditional Provençal garden and another which traces the geographical origins of common modern plants.

Château de Sauvan

2.5km south of Mane along the D4100 Apt road • Guided tours 3.30pm: March Sun; April & Oct to mid-Nov Thurs, Sat & Sun; May, June & Sept Mon & Thurs–Sun; July & Aug daily • €10 • ☎ 04 92 75 05 64, ⓦ chateaudesauvan.com

A few kilometres south of Mane, beyond a medieval bridge over the River Laye, you come to a palatial residence that has been called the Petit Trianon of Provence. The pure eighteenth-century ease and luxury of the **Château de Sauvan** come as a surprise in this harsh territory, leagues from any courtly city. Though there are hundreds of mansions like it around Paris and along the Loire, the residences of the rich and powerful in Haute Provence tend towards the moat and dungeon, not to French windows giving onto lawns and lake.

The furnishings are grand and the hall and stairway would take some beating for light and space, but what's best is the **setting**: the swans and geese on the square lake, the peacocks strutting by the drive and the views back to the aristocratic house itself. The gardens are slowly being restored to their historic form. Work to date has included the planting of fifty thousand lavender plants and restoration of the parterres.

Observatoire de Haute Provence

Observatoire de Haute Provence 2.5km north of St-Michel-l'Observatoire • Tours: early April to early July & early to mid Sept Wed 2.30pm, 3.30pm & 4.30pm; mid-July & Aug Tues–Thurs 2.30pm, 3.30pm & 4.30pm • €5.50 • ☎ 04 92 70 65 40, ⓦ obs-hp. fr • Bus #22 to St-Michel-l'Observatoire • **Centre d'Astronomie** Plateau du Moulin à Vent, St-Michel-l'Observatoire • Star-gazing vigils July & Aug Mon–Thurs & Sat 9.30pm; Sept Wed–Sat, plus monthly vigils on Fri & Sat in winter • €13–34 • ☎ 04 92 76 69 69, ⓦ centre-astro.fr

The tourist literature promoting the pure air of Haute Provence is not just hype. Proof of the fact is the National Centre for Scientific Research **observatory** on the wooded slopes north of the village of **ST-MICHEL-L'OBSERVATOIRE**, southwest of Mane, sited here because it has the fewest clouds, the least fog and the lowest industrial pollution in all France.

Visible from many kilometres around, it presents a peculiar picture of domes of gleaming white mega-mushrooms pushing up between the oaks. It's open for **guided tours** during which you get to see some telescopes and blank monitors, and the mechanism that opens up the domes and aims the lens. Even more exciting, however, are the night-time sky-watching vigils at the associated **Centre d'Astronomie** just east of the village itself.

4

CHÈVRE DE BANON

Banon is famous above all for its **cheese**. The *plateau des fromages* of any half-decent Provence restaurant will include a round goat's cheese marinated in brandy and wrapped in sweet chestnut leaves, but there's nothing like tasting different ages of the untravelled cheese, sliced off for you by the *fromager* at a **market** stall on place de la République (Tues mornings). As well as ensuring that you taste the very young and the well-matured varieties, they may give you an accompaniment in the form of a sprig of *savory*, an aromatic local plant of the mint family.

If you want to know more about how *chèvre de Banon* is made, visit the **Écomusée Chèvre de Banon** at the factory on route de Carniol (April–June, Sept & Oct Mon–Fri 2.30–5.30pm; July & Aug Mon–Sat 2.30–5.30pm; visit free; *dégustation* €4.50; ☎04 92 73 25 03, ⊛fromagerie-banon.fr).

Banon

The houses of the tiny *haute ville* of **BANON**, 25km northwest of Forcalquier on the D950, form a guarding wall. Within the impressive fourteenth-century fortified gate, the **Portail à Machicoulis**, the bustle of the modern village below disappears and all is peaceful and immaculate; the houses of the rue des Arcades arch across the roadway and the village peters out just beyond the former chapel of the château at the top of the slope, with only a few stretches of ruined masonry beyond. The chapel hosts **art exhibitions** (May–Oct daily 10.30am–7pm; free). As lovely as its old quarter is, however, Banon is chiefly famous for the chestnut-wrapped **chèvre cheese** that bears the village's name (see page 184).

ARRIVAL AND INFORMATION   BANON

By bus Bus #B1 from Manosque serves Banon twice daily Mon–Fri; there's one bus to Simiane and Apt on Sat.
Tourist office Place de la République (late April to June & Sept to late Oct Mon–Fri 9am–noon & 2–5pm, Sat 9am–12.30pm & 2.30–6pm; July & Aug Mon–Sat 9am–12.30pm & 2.30–6pm; ☎04 92 72 19 40, ⊛hauteprovencepaysdebanon-tourisme.fr).

ACCOMMODATION AND EATING

L'Épi Bleu Les Gravières ☎04 92 73 30 30, ⊛camping epibleu.com. Well-equipped three-star campsite just outside the village with a restaurant, barbecue, pool and laundry. Closed Nov–March. Camping €27.50; mobile homes per week €840
La Parenthèse Rte de Forcalquier ☎09 50 79 45 71, ⊛giteabanon.fr. Stone-built *chambres d'hôtes* with doubles and a few family rooms at the entrance to the old village, popular with walkers. Closed mid-Nov to Feb. €69
Les Voyageurs Place de la République ☎04 92 73 21 02. Lively café/restaurant with a shaded terrace fronting Banon's main square, with €12 lunchtime *plats du jour* and a €27.50 *menu* with grilled lamb with tapenade and thyme. Tues–Sun: July & Aug 7am–11pm; Sept–June 7am–8pm.
Les Vins au Vert rue Pasteur ☎04 92 75 23 84. Contemporary *cave à vin* combining exposed stone with groaning wine racks with the obligatory minimalist interior. Weekdays sees *L'ardoise gourmand* (€13.50), with assorted charcuterie and cheese (€15 in the evenings with amuse-bouche), while weekends bring cuisine from around the world. Tues–Sun 10am–10pm.

The Montagne de Lure

Roads north of Banon peter out at the lower slopes of the **Montagne de Lure**. To reach the summit of the Lure, by road or the GR6, you have to head east to **St-Étienne-les-Orgues**, 12km north of Forcalquier. The footpath from St-Étienne avoids the snaking D113 and D53 roads for most of the way, but you're walking through relentless pine plantation and it's a long way (about 15km) without a change of scenery – the only relief from the forest is the twelfth-century chapel of Notre Dame de Lure, which is all that remains of a vanished abbey. Just below the summit you'll see the **ski lifts**. The mountain is the oldest skiing area in the southern French Alps, and offers green runs for beginners as well as Nordic skiing. You can rent equipment during the ski season (varies according to snow conditions, but usually Dec–March; ☎04 92 75 93 47).

When the forests stop you find yourself on a stony peak, softened only by Alpine pastures and a few stunted trees. The 1826m **summit** itself is an enclosed mass of telecommunications aerials and dishes. That said, the point of the climb is that the Lure has no close neighbours, giving you near-360-degree **views** that take in the valley of the Durance and, far to the west, Mont Ventoux. The view of the distant snowy peaks to the north is the best; if you have stamina you can keep walking towards them along the GR6 to Sisteron. The ascent (and descent) of the Montagne de Lure is also popular with **cyclists** (see page 181).

ACCOMMODATION AND EATING   MONTAGNE DE LURE

Gîte d'Étape des Crêtes de Lure St-Étienne-les-Orgues ☎04 92 73 19 14, ⓦgitesdelure.fr. Simple, modern *gîte d'étape* just below the summit of the Montagne de Lure, close to the ski runs and GR6. Accommodation is in three- to seven-bed dorms. Half-board **€40**

Saint Clair Chemin de Serre, Étienne-les-Orgues ☎04 92 73 07 09, ⓦhotel-saint-clair.com. Simply decorated rooms that are pleasant and clean enough and some have garden views. There's also a restaurant, outdoor swimming pool and a sauna. **€90**

Simiane-la-Rotonde

The spiralling cone of **SIMIANE-LA-ROTONDE**, 9.5km southwest of Banon on the D51, marks the horizon with an emphasis greater than its size would warrant. However many *villages de caractère* (Simiane's official classification) you may have seen, this is one to re-seduce you, though it is gradually acquiring the same patina of metropolitan chic as the Luberon villages to the west.

The modern village and much of the commerce – what there is of it – lies in the plain by the D51, cleanly separated from the old village's winding streets of honey-coloured stone in which each house is part of the medieval defences. As you ascend through the village you pass all sorts of eye-catching details: heavy carved doors with stone lintels in exact proportion, wrought-iron street lamps, the scrolling on the dark wooden shutters of the building opposite the covered hall of the stunning **old market**. With its columns framing open sky, the hall almost overhangs the hillside on the steepest section of the village; no longer used as a marketplace, it's now occupied by café tables.

The Rotonde

March, April & Sept to mid-Nov Mon & Wed–Sun 10am–12.30pm & 2–5pm; May–Aug daily 10am–7pm • €5.50

Simiane's zigzagging streets end at the **Rotonde**, a large domed keep with a splendid ceremonial hall within. Nineteenth-century restoration work added smooth limestone to its rough-hewn fortress stones, but the peculiar feature is the asymmetry between its interior and exterior, being hexagonal on the outside and irregularly dodecagonal on the inside. The set of the stones on the domes is wonderfully wonky and no one knows what once hung from or covered the hole at the top. In August the Rotonde is a venue for the annual international **festival of ancient music** (ⓦfestival-simiane.com).

ARRIVAL AND INFORMATION   SIMIANE-LA-ROTONDE

By bus Simiane is served by bus once weekly (on Sat) from Apt (with the same bus also serving Banon).

Tourist office In the Rotonde (mid-March to April & Sept to mid-Nov Mon & Wed–Sun 10am–12.30pm & 2–5pm;

May–Aug daily 10am–7pm; ☎04 92 73 11 34, ⓦsimiane-la-rotonde.fr). It can supply information on *gîtes* and *chambres d'hôtes* in the area.

ACCOMMODATION AND EATING

Camping de Valsaintes 7km southeast of Simiane, near Carniol ☎04 92 75 91 46, ⓦvalsaintes.com. Small

two-star *camping à la ferme*, with a pool. Closed mid-Oct to March. Camping **€14.40**; bungalows per week **€485**

Le Chapeau Rouge Rte de Banon ☏04 92 74 22 86, ⓦrestaurantlechapeaurouge04.fr. Despite an unpromising location on the main road at the edge of the village, this perennially popular restaurant serves consistently great value three-course lunches for €19.50. They also put on occasional soirées with live jazz, Latin and Caribbean music and themed *menus* to match (€30–35). Wed, Thurs & Sun 9am–5pm, Fri & Sat 9am–4pm.

Gîte de Chaloux Simiane-la-Rotonde ☏04 92 75 99 13, ⓦgite-chaloux.com. *Gîte d'étape* and *chambres d'hôtes* in an eighteenth-century farmhouse off the D51 about 3km south of the village, at the junction of the GR4 and GR6 footpaths. Dorms €20; doubles €84

La Palette Salle Couverte, Haut Village ☏04 92 7520 27. *Saladerie* and snack bar in the atmospheric old covered market hall, with salads from €14 and snacks and sandwiches from €4.50; you can sample *chèvre de Banon* here. May–Aug daily noon–2pm.

The Luberon

The great fold of rock of the Luberon runs for some 50km between the Coulon and the Durance valleys, and sits at the heart of the **Parc Naturel Régional du Luberon**. The massif is divided by the **Combe de Lourmarin**, a narrow gorge through which a lone metalled road gives access south to Cadenet and Aix-en-Provence. The **Grand Luberon** is the portion of the massif to the east of the Combe de Lourmarin, while the **Petit Luberon** is the section to the west. Though many forestry tracks cross the ridge, they are barred to cars (and too rough for bikes), and where the ridge isn't forested it opens into tableland pastures where sheep graze in summer. The northern slopes have Alpine rather than Mediterranean leanings: the trees are oak, beech and maple, and cowslips and buttercups announce the summer. But it is still very hot and there are plenty of vines on the lower slopes.

North of the massifs, the lively market town of **Apt** is the chief urban centre of the Luberon: close to it the remnants of ochre extraction have created the extraordinary **Colorado Provençal**, the vibrant orange-red landscapes of **Roussillon** and the dramatic subterranean spaces of the **Mines de Bruoux**. The most beguiling of the Luberon's **villages** stand on high ground overlooking the vale of the Calavon: **Saignon**, **Bonnieux**, **Lacoste**, **Ménerbes** and, to the north, **Gordes**. Equally beguiling – and mysterious – are the ruined villages of **Buoux** and **Oppède-le-Vieux**.

The Colorado Provençal

Parking des Mille Couleurs, 12km southwest of Simiane-la-Rotonde on the D22 near Rustrel • Free access to site; car park open daily in summer 8am–7pm, rest of year hours vary according to season • Free; parking €5 (motorbikes €2); guided tour €6 • ☏04 90 04 96 07, ⓦ colorado-provencal.com

Immediately to the east of the little village of Rustrel on the D22 lies a series of dramatic former ochre quarries known as the **Colorado Provençal**, the weathered remains of six generations of ochre extraction and iron-ore mining. You'll be given a map of the hiking trails at the car park; the site is quite extensive, with trails leading through both private and public properties, extending to 5.5km. The paths through the site lead you past pumps, quarries, streams, sluice gates and settling basins – the vestiges of nineteenth- and twentieth-century industrial activity. The quarry has weathered into striking and bizarre shapes, particularly in the spectacular area known as the Sahara, which all three trails visit; here the colours range from luminous yellow to deep red. Take good walking shoes, water and a hat – it's thirsty work – and take care along certain stretches where the cliff edges are crumbling.

Saignon

Fourteen kilometres south of Rustrel, **SAIGNON** is 4km from Apt but sits high enough to have an eagle's-eye view not just of the town, but of the whole region. From below,

OUTDOOR ACTIVITIES IN THE LUBERON

The Luberon's natural beauty acts as a perfect backdrop for all manner of **activities**. Hiking, cycling and horseriding all allow you to get to know the landscape at a relatively gentle pace, but there's plenty to please more adventurous spirits too, from ballooning to rock climbing.

Cycling The 236km bike circuit of the Luberon is particularly well supported: the Vélo Loisir en Provence scheme (ⓦ leluberonavelo.com) brings together cycle rental shops, accommodation providers, restaurateurs and others to support cycle-based tourism, providing advice, secure cycle parking, transfers from rail stations or airports and transfers of luggage as well as a breakdown service.

Horseriding There are many places where you can ride in the region, from Vaugines and Cucuron on the Luberon's southern flank to Céreste, east of Apt, Joucas near Gordes and Lauris near Cadenet. Operators that speak English include: Cap Rando (from around €65/half-day; ☎ 0483 43 12 34, ⓦ cap-rando.com); Les Cavaliers du Luberon (€80/day; ☎ 06 11 23 26 08, ⓦ cavaliers-du-luberon.fr); Cheval Enjeu (€95/day; ☎ 06 87 55 42 09, ⓦ cheval-luberon.fr); La Florentine (half-day €45; ☎ 06 62 63 13 95, ⓦ laflorentine.fr);

Ferme Équestre de Joucas (€85/day; ☎ 04 90 05 80 11, ⓦ chevauxetponeysdejoucas.ffe.com), and Centre de Randonnée Équestre Janssaud (2hr €35; ☎ 06 16 50 47 11, ⓦ janssaud.com).

Hot-air ballooning Get a bird's-eye perspective of the Luberon's ochre with a 1hr balloon ride over Roussillon (€230; ☎ 06 03 54 10 92, ⓦ montgolfiere-luberon.com).

Paragliding Take a beginner's flight over the Luberon from the ochre village of Rustrel (advance booking required; €70; ☎ 06 12 20 39 26, ⓔ aero.luberon@gmail.com).

Rock climbing Buoux is the main centre for rock climbing, with qualified instruction (from around €50) available for beginners and more advanced climbers as well as mini-climbs for children. Outfits include Provence Escalade (☎ 06 66 20 80 36) and Aptitudes Escalade (☎ 04 90 04 68 41, ⓦ aptitudes-escalade.com).

the village rises like an immense fort with natural turrets of rock; on closer inspection it has an almost troglodyte charm, its houses – some exquisitely restored, others still in a crumbly state – set among the rocky outcrops on which the village's castle once stood. The very best of the views are from the pulpit-like **Rocher de Bellevue** at the far end of the village. The panorama here is almost 360 degrees; given the exposed, windy vantage point, the experience is properly breathtaking, but bear in mind that the steps to the top are a little uneven.

ARRIVAL AND DEPARTURE
SAIGNON

Saignon is linked by an infrequent **bus** service (#109) to Apt (1–2 daily; 15min).

EATING AND DRINKING

Au Comptoir de Balthazar Place de L'Eglise ☎ 04 90 04 63 55. Tiny bistro in a charming corner spot with a shrubbery-shrouded entrance and ancient beams holding up its ceiling. Cooking is all homemade and seasonal, with a three course *menu* at €30. Reservations advised. Mon, Tues & Thurs–Sun noon–1.30pm & 7–9pm.

Fort de Buoux

Signposted off the D113; from the gateway at the end of the road it's a 400m uphill walk to the entrance • Feb–Nov daily 10am–5pm; Jan and Dec telephone for opening times • €5 • ☎ 04 90 74 25 75, ⓦ buoux-village.com

From the village of **BUOUX**, 8km south of Apt, a minor road leads the short distance to the fortified, abandoned hilltop village known as the **Fort de Buoux**; the "x" in the name is pronounced. It stands on the northern flank of the Grand Luberon massif, overlooking a canyon forged by the once powerful River Aiguebrun at the start of its passage through the Luberon.

Numerous relics of prehistoric life have been found in the Buoux Valley, and in the earliest Christian days anchorite monks survived against all odds in tiny caves and niches in the vertical cliff face. In the 1660s, Fort de Buoux was demolished by command of Louis XIV for being a centre of Protestantism, but the ruins – including cisterns, storage cellars with thick stone lids, arrow-slitted ramparts, the lower half of a Romanesque chapel and a near-intact keep – give a good impression of life here over the centuries. Today, the spot is popular with **climbers**, many of whom can be seen clinging to the cliff face as you approach the fort.

ACCOMMODATION AND EATING   BUOUX

Auberge des Seguins Buoux ☎04 90 74 16 37, ⓦaubergedesseguins.com. Nestling at the foot of a gorge close to the Fort de Buoux, this busy hotel has a restaurant (*menus* €25), pool and informal café, with accommodation in dorm beds or rooms; the cheapest rooms share WC, while for the more expensive rooms *demi-* or full *pension* is required. Closed mid-Nov to Feb. Dorms €14; doubles with shared WC €60; doubles *demi-pension* €118

Apt

The main settlement in the Luberon, **APT**, lies northeast of the Combe de Lourmarin, nestling beneath the northern slopes of the Grand Luberon on the banks of the River Coulon. Best known for its crystallized fruit and preserves, Apt, like so many of the surrounding villages, is gentrifying rapidly as foreigners and wealthy Parisians move in. For now, though, the balance between timeless market town and fashionable urban oasis is about right, and Apt is a likeable and bustling little place with one of the oldest cathedrals in Provence, excellent shops and a lively Saturday **market** (see page 190).

June brings the **Luberon Jazz Festival**, while in July **Tréteaux de Nuit** (ⓦtreteauxdenuit. com) fills four days with concerts, plays, café-theatre and exhibitions.

Cathédrale de Ste-Anne

Off rue des Marchands • Guided tours June–Oct Mon–Fri 10am, 11am, 3pm & 4pm • €5 • ☎06 88 47 23 42, ⓦapt.fr/Cathedrale-Sainte-Anne.html

The **Cathédrale de Ste-Anne** is one of the oldest cathedrals in Provence – not the most coherent architecturally, but an agreeable enough mishmash of styles. The oldest parts of the cathedral include a beautiful fourth-century carved stone ceiling in the *crypte*

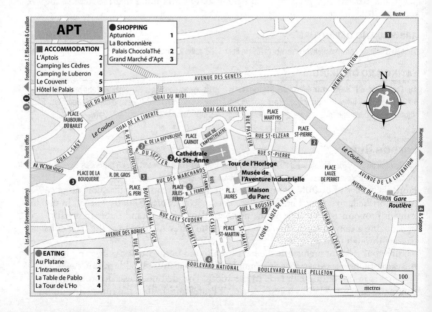

PARC NATUREL RÉGIONAL DU LUBERON

The **Parc Naturel Régional du Luberon** is administered by the Maison du Parc in Apt at 60 place Jean-Jaurès (Mon–Fri 8.30am–noon & 1.30–6pm; free; ☎ 04 90 04 42 00, Ⓦ parcduluberon.fr). It's a centre of activity with laudable aims – nature conservation and the provision of environmentally friendly tourist facilities – and also the place to go for information about the fauna and flora of the Luberon, footpaths, cycle routes, pony trekking, *gîtes* and campsites. The *maison* has a geology display and also mounts temporary exhibitions.

---

inférieure; elsewhere slabs dating from the eighth and ninth centuries were reused in the twelfth. The cathedral's chief relic is a veil said to have belonged to St Anne herself. Outside, the **Tour de L'Horloge** (bell tower) spans the rue des Marchands.

Musée de l'Aventure Industrielle

14 place du Postel • Feb–June & Sept–Dec Tues–Sat 10am–noon & 2–5.30pm; July & Aug Mon–Sat 10am–noon & 2–6.30pm • €5 • ☎ 04 90 74 95 30

Apt's industrial heritage is the subject of the **Musée de l'Aventure Industrielle**, laid out over three floors and covering the major industries of the town and surrounding area: ochre, candied fruits and the production of fine faïence. Exhibits include the re-creation of a potter's studio, plus works by the sculptor Alexis Poitevin, who was inspired by industrial themes.

Fondation J.P. Blachère

384 av des Argiles • Mon–Sat 2–6pm • Free • ☎ 04 32 52 06 15, Ⓦ fondationblachere.org

The industrial district of les Bourguignons to the west of the town is the unlikely setting for the **Fondation J.P. Blachère**, which stages a few exhibitions each year devoted to contemporary African sculpture and painting and hosts artists in residence.

Les Agnels lavender distillery

Rte de Buoux • Shop daily: April–Sept 10am–7pm; Oct–March 10am–5.30pm; 1hr guided tours May–Aug daily 11am & 4pm; Sept Mon–Fri 11am & 4pm • €6 • ☎ 04 90 04 77 00, Ⓦ lesagnels.com

A little way to the south of the town on the road to Buoux is the **Les Agnels lavender distillery**, which can be visited twice daily on a guided tour where you'll witness the distillation of lavender, aromatic plants and citrus and learn about the history and techniques behind the production of essential oils, floral waters and the like, as well as their benefits. There's a shop too, of course.

ARRIVAL AND INFORMATION   APT

By bus Buses drop you off either at the place de la Bouquerie or at the *gare routière* on Av de la Libération at the eastern end of town.

Destinations Aix-en-Provence (3 daily; 1hr 50min–2hr); Avignon (7 daily; 1hr 15min); Avignon TGV (4 daily; 1hr 23min–1hr 40min); Bonnieux (4 daily;13min); Cadenet (3 daily; 1hr); Lourmarin (3 daily; 40min); Simiane-la-Rotonde (1 weekly on Sat; 1hr 10min).

By car Arriving by car, park either along the river or to the east of the town centre.

Tourist office 788 av Victor Hugo, to the northwest of the centre (July & Aug Mon–Sat 9.30am–12.30pm & 2–6.30pm, Sun 9.30am–12.30pm; Sept–June Mon–Sat 9.30am–12.30pm & 2–6pm; ☎ 04 90 74 03 18, Ⓦ luberon-apt.fr).

Bike rental Luberon Cycles, 86 quai Général-Leclerc (☎ 04 86 69 19 00).

ACCOMMODATION   SEE MAP PAGE 188

L'Aptois 289 cours Lauze de Perret ☎ 04 90 74 02 02, Ⓦ aptois-hotel.fr. Overlooking place Lauze de Perret, this clean, simple two-star hotel is reasonably priced and cyclist-friendly, and has some rooms with disabled access and some that sleep three. **€65**

★ **Le Couvent** 36 rue Louis-Rousset ☎ 04 90 04 55 36, Ⓦ www.loucouvent.com. Lovely *maison d'hôtes* in a seventeenth-century convent in the centre of the town, with five spacious rooms, tasteful decor and a pretty private garden with pool. Breakfast is served in the former convent refectory. **€99**

Hôtel le Palais 24bis place Gabriel-Péri ☏ 04 90 04 89 32, ⌨ hotel-le-palais.com. Inexpensive two-star option bang in the centre of town, above a pizza and pasta place. There are double-glazed, pastel painted doubles and singles, and some rooms have a/c. **€67**

CAMPSITES

Camping les Cèdres 63 impasse de la Fantaisie ☏ 04 90 74 14 61, ⌨ camping-les-cedres.eu. A leafy two-star site with just 75 pitches, within easy walking distance of the town, across the bridge from place St-Pierre. Closed mid-Nov to Feb. **€12.80**

Camping le Luberon Av de Saignon ☏ 04 90 04 85 40, ⌨ campingleluberon.com. Three-star campsite, less than 2km from the centre of town, with swimming pool, restaurant, snack bar, bakery, bar and children's activities. Closed Oct–March. **€52**

EATING

SEE MAP PAGE 188

VIEILLE VILLE

Au Platane 25 place Jules Ferry ☏ 04 90 04 74 36, ⌨ restaurant-apt.fr. Full of wrought iron filigree and lush greenery, with a wonderfully leafy and secluded garden terrace. Unpretentious Provençal standbys fill the *formule/menu du midi* (€15.50/17.50) and dinner *menu* (€30.50) but the real surprise here is the set vegetarian *menu* (evenings only; €22) featuring the likes of aubergine caviar. Tues–Sat noon–2pm & 7–9pm.

★ **L'Intramuros** 120–124 rue de la République ☏ 04 90 06 18 87. Inventive bistro-style food served in eccentric, cluttered surroundings in Apt's *vieille ville*, with the likes of slow-cooked rabbit leg, baked potato stuffed with tapenade and gratin of vegetables: *plats* €18.50; pizzas €12 and up.

Tues–Sat noon–1.30pm & 7.45–9pm.

La Table de Pablo Petits Cléments, Villars ☏ 04 90 75 45 18, ⌨ latabledepablo.com. Book at least 24hr in advance to make the trek 8km north of Apt to this restaurant, close to the village of Villars, for dishes such as Gubernat duck with hazelnut crumb, smoked pork and chorizo. *Menus* €33–50. Mon, Tues, Fri & Sun noon–1.30pm & 7.30–8.45pm, Thurs & Sat 7.30–8.45pm; closed first 2 weeks Jan.

La Tour de L'Ho 125 bd National ☏ 04 90 75 24 82, ⌨ restaurant.latourdelho.fr. Seasonal French cooking in a convivial edge-of-*vieille ville* setting, with *menus* at €21.90 and €28.90. Handy when everywhere else is closed. Daily 9.30am–10.30pm.

SHOPPING

SEE MAP PAGE 188

Saturday is the best day to visit Apt, when cars are barred from the town centre to allow artisans and cultivators from the surrounding countryside to set up stalls at the town's weekly **Grand Marché**. The great local speciality of **fruits** – crystallized, pickled, preserved in alcohol or turned into jam – features at the market and in shops around town.

Aptunion Quartier Salignan, 2km from Apt on the Avignon road ☏ 04 90 76 46 66, ⌨ lesfleurons-apt.com. Fill up with goodies at the shop of this confectionery factory or, during the school holidays, come for a free tour, video and tasting. Mon–Sat 10am–12.30pm & 2–6.30pm.

La Bonbonnière Palais ChocolaThé 25 rue Eugène Brunel ☏ 04 90 74 12 92, ⌨ labonbonniere84.

com. Every sort of sweet and chocolate, as well as the Provençal speciality *tourron*, an almond paste flavoured with coffee, pistachio, pine kernels or cherries. Quality teas as well, including organic. Tues–Sat 9.30am–1pm & 2.30–7pm.

Grand Marché d'Apt Place de la Bouquerie and rue des Marchands. Though this splendid market takes place year round, summer Saturdays are the liveliest, with up to three hundred stalls selling every imaginable Provençal edible. Everyone, from successful Parisian artists with summer studios here, to military types from the St-Christol base, serious ecologists, rich foreigners and local Aptois, can be found milling around for this lively social event. Sat 8am–1pm.

The Mines de Bruoux

Rte de Croagne, Gargas • Guided tours (50min) last two weeks in March and first two weeks in Nov Tues–Sat 11am, 2pm & 3pm; April to early July and late Aug to Oct daily 10.30am, 11.30am, 2pm, 3pm, 4pm & 5pm; early July to late Aug 10.30am, 11am, 11.30am, noon, then every 20mins from 2pm–5pm, 5.30pm & 6pm; one tour daily in English early to late Aug 12.45pm; tablet guides in English on demand • Low season €7.90, high season €8.90 • ☏ 04 90 06 22 59, ⌨ minesdebruoux.fr

The extraordinary former **ochre mine** of **Bruoux** at Gargas, north of Apt on the route de Croagne, is entered via a bright orange cliff face into which a number of tall, arched entrances have been cut. These lead to a 40km network of subterranean passageways, 15m high in places. The **guided tour** takes you 650m underground, which is enough to give you a good impression of the strong colour, eerie atmosphere and strikingly beautiful, monumental form of the tunnels – altogether more reminiscent of the temple of some lost civilization than of a workaday place of mineral extraction.

Roussillon

Perched precariously atop soft rock cliffs 10km northwest of Apt, the buildings of **ROUSSILLON** radiate all the different shades of the seventeen ochre tints once quarried here. A spiralling main street leads past potteries, antique shops and restaurants up to the top of the village; it's worth the effort of walking up for the views over the Luberon and Ventoux.

Conservatoire des Ocres

Usine Mathieu, Apt road • Daily: Feb & March 10am–1pm & 2–5pm, April–June, Sept & Oct 10am–6pm; July & Aug 10am–7pm; Nov & Dec 2–5pm; guided tours (50min) available, times vary according to season • €7; joint ticket with Sentier des Ocres €7.50 • ☎ 04 90 05 66 69, ⓦ okhra.com

Just outside Roussillon, on the Apt road, an old **ochre factory** has been renovated as the **Conservatoire des Ocres**. You can look round the various washing, draining, settling and drying areas, though you probably won't get much out of a visit without joining a guided tour. It also hosts excellent exhibitions on themes related to the use and production of ochre, with accompanying workshops for both adults and children, and there's a shop selling pigments and books.

Sentier des Ocres

Daily: Last three weeks in Feb & mid-Nov to early Jan 11am–3.30pm; March 10am–5pm; April 9.30am–5.30pm; May & Sept 9.30am–6.30pm; June 9am–6.30pm; July & Aug 9am–7.30pm; Oct 10am–5.30pm; first two weeks in Nov 10am–4.30pm • €3; joint ticket with Conservatoire des Ocres €7.50 • ☎ 04 90 05 60 16

Roussillon's **ochre quarries** are close to the centre of the village and can be visited on the **Sentier des Ocres**, which is well worth the modest admission fee to see the strange landforms and vibrant colours of the former quarry, which range from soft pinks to deep orange.

There are two circuits – a shorter one and a longer one – both of which are hot work on a summer's day, but you'll get a reasonable impression of the quarries even on the shorter route. The ochre is ferrous and influences the type of vegetation found in the area, with species like heather, chestnut, laurel, furze and broom that are otherwise quite unusual in Provence.

INFORMATION   **ROUSSILLON**

Tourist office Place de la Poste (July & Aug Mon–Sat   9.30am–12.30pm & 2–6.30pm, Sun 9.30am–12.30pm; 9.30am–12.30pm   &   2–6pm;   Sept–June   Mon–Sat   ☎ 04 90 05 60 25, ⓦ otroussillon.pagesperso-orange.fr).

OCHRE QUARRYING

Ochre quarrying has been carried out in the Vaucluse since prehistoric times, producing the natural dye that gives a range of colours (which don't fade in sunlight) from pale yellow to a blood red. By the nineteenth century the business had really taken off, with first donkeys and (by the 1880s) trains carrying truckloads of the dust to Marseille to be shipped round the world. At its peak in 1929, 40,000 tonnes of ochre were exported from the region. Twenty years later it was down to 11,500 tonnes, and in 1958 production at Roussillon was finally stopped, in part because the foundations of the village were being undermined. Production continues at Gargas, east of Roussillon, and at Rustrel.

ACCOMMODATION AND EATING

Camping L'Arc en Ciel Rte de Goult ☎ 04 90 05 73 96, ⓦ camping-arc-en-ciel.fr. Three-star campsite in pine woods 2km along the D104 to Goult, with a pool, children's play area, wi-fi, shop and pizzeria. Closed Nov to mid-March. **€24**

La Maison des Ocres Rte de Gordes ☎ 04 90 05 60 50, ⓦ lamaisondesocres-hotel.com. Three-star hotel on the quieter side of the village a little removed from the tourist hubbub, with eighteen a/c rooms, some with views towards Gordes and the mountains, some with private terrace. Closed mid-Nov to Feb. **€123**

La Treille Rue du Four ☎ 04 90 05 64 47. Seasonal *cuisine du marché* under a white awning in the *vieux village*, with a €21 lunch *formule*, Luberon and Ventoux wines and the likes of fillet beef with truffle sauce or veal with asparagus from around €20. Daily 9am–5pm.

Gordes and around

GORDES, west of Roussillon and 6km north of the main Apt–Avignon road (but only as the crow flies), tumbles to spectacular effect down a steep hillside to create one of the most photographed views in all Provence. The approach at sunset is particularly memorable as the ancient stone turns gold. The village is popular with film directors, media personalities, musicians and painters, many of whom have added a Gordes address to their main Paris residence. As a result, the place is full of expensive restaurants, cafés and art and craft shops.

In the vicinity, you can see a superb array of dry-stone architecture in **Village des Bories**, as well as the **Abbaye de Sénanque**, and a couple of museums dedicated to glass and olive oil. Gordes' festival, **Les Soirées d'Été de Gordes**, held in the first two weeks of August, sees the village awash with theatrical performances, jazz and world music.

The château

Early April to mid-Oct daily 10am–12.30pm & 1.30–6pm • €5

In the past, near-vertical staircases hewn into the rock gave the only access to the summit of the village, where the church and houses surround a twelfth- to sixteenth-century **château** with few aesthetic concessions to the business of fortification. By the early twentieth century most of Gordes' villagers had abandoned the old defensive site and it lay in ruins until the village was rediscovered by artists, including Chagall and the Hungarian scientist of art and design, Victor Vasarely; it's still occasionally used for exhibitions, but is otherwise worth visiting primarily to see its monumental Renaissance staircase and chimney.

Caves du Palais St-Firmin

Rue du Belvédère • April–June & Sept to early Nov 10.30am–1pm & 2.30–6pm; July & Aug 10.30am–1pm & 2.30–6.30pm • €6 standard entry; €7.50 for cave tour and gardens (bookable by email only: caves.saint.firmin@gmail.com) • ☎ 06 61 20 36 44, ⓦ caves-saint-firmin.com

Gordes is just as warren-like below ground as it is above, as a visit to the **Caves du Palais St-Firmin** will demonstrate. It's a series of atmospherically lit interlocking stone vaults variously containing oil mills, tanks, silos, wine vats and a chapel. Burrowing into Gordes' bedrock for agricultural, craft and other purposes began in the eleventh century; in times of strife these cellars were both escape routes and places of refuge. You can also visit the impressive terraced gardens surrounding the caves, landscaped from an almost sheer rubble-strewn slope back in the 1960s.

ARRIVAL AND INFORMATION
GORDES

By bus Gordes does not lie on any major public transport routes and it's likely you'll arrive under your own steam. Infrequent buses connect it with Cavaillon, 16km to the west, and arrive at place du Château, before continuing to Roussillon. Destinations Cavaillon (4 daily; 30min); Roussillon (4 daily; 20min).

Tourist office In the château (April–Sept Mon–Sat 9am–12.30pm & 1.30–6pm, Sun 10am–12.30pm & 1.30–6pm; Oct–March 9am–noon & 1.30–5.30pm; ☎ 04 90 72 02 75, ⓦ gordes-village.com).

ACCOMMODATION AND EATING

La Bastide de Gordes In the village ☎ 04 90 72 12 12, ⓦ bastide-de-gordes.com. The most luxurious hotel in the village, furnished with eighteenth-century antiques and with stunning views over the Luberon from its pool and terrace, plus a Sisley spa. **€615**

La Bastide de Pierres Place du Château ☎ 04 90 72 18 91, ⓦ bastide-de-pierres.com. Pizza from €12 at this Italian place on the main square, as well as a variety of fresh pasta dishes in the €17 range and salads for €15. Daily 12.15–2.30pm & 7.15–9.30pm.

Camping des Sources Rte de Murs ☎ 04 90 72 12 48, ⓦ campingdessources.com. Two-star campsite 5min from the village on the D15 road to Murs, with a restaurant, bar, children's play area, minigolf, sports area and pool. Closed Oct to early April. **€38.30**

L'Estellan Les Imberts, southwest of Gordes on the D2 ☎ 04 90 72 04 90, ⓦ mas-de-la-senancole.com. This excellent restaurant occupies an old *mas* with an exceptionally pretty garden terrace. The two/three course lunchtime *formule* is priced at €21/26, while the evening *menu* (€39) may feature the likes of smoked trout with a celery and Granny Smith apple remoulade. Mid-May to Sept daily 12.15–1.45pm & 7.15–9.30pm; Oct to late Dec & mid-Feb to mid-May Wed–Sun 12.15–1.45pm & 7.15–9.30pm.

Les Romarins Rte de Sénanque ☎ 04 90 72 12 13, ⓦ masromarins.com. Overlooking the village, this three-star country-house hotel has comfortable, traditionally styled and mostly a/c rooms, plus a garden with terrace and swimming pool. **€147**

La Trinquette rue des Tracapelles ☎ 04 90 72 11 62. Perched on the westerly flanks of the village, with fantastic views from the terrace, this bistro transforms simple seasonal produce into sensational meals, from prawn ravioli to pork marinated in sage and rosemary. A two-course lunch for €26 and a three-course evening *menu* at €36. Mon & Thurs–Sun noon–10pm, Tues 7–10pm.

Village des Bories

4km southwest of Gordes on the D15, signed off the D2 to Cavaillon • Daily 9am–sunset • €6 • ☎ 04 90 72 03 48, ⓦ levillagedesbories.com

An unusual rural agglomeration, the **Village des Bories** is a walled enclosure containing dry-stone houses, barns, bread ovens, wine stores and workshops constructed in a mix of unusual shapes: curving pyramids and cones, some rounded at the top, some truncated and the base almost rectangular or square. They are cleverly designed so that rain runs off their exteriors and the temperature inside remains constant whatever the season. To look at them, you might think they were prehistoric (and Neolithic rings and a hatchet have been found on the site), but most date from the eighteenth century and were inhabited until the early nineteenth century.

Abbaye de Sénanque

4.7km northwest of Gordes, off the D177 • Guided 1hr tours in French Jan, Feb & early Nov to Dec daily 10.30am, 2.15pm & 3.30pm; March, June & Sept to early Nov 10.30am, 2.30pm, 3.30pm & 4.30pm; April Mon–Sat 10.30am, 12.45pm, 2.30pm, 3.30pm, 4.30pm & 5pm, Sun 2.30pm, 3.30pm, 4.30pm & 5pm; May Mon–Sat 10.10am, 10.30am, 12.45pm, 2.30pm, 3.30pm, 4.30pm & 5pm, Sun 2.30pm, 3.30pm, 4.30pm & 5pm; July & Aug Mon–Sat 10 daily 10.10am–4.30pm, Sun 7 tours 2–5pm; closed Sun mornings and certain religious festivals; for non-guided visits see website for hours • €7.50 • ☎ 04 90 72 18 24, ⓦ senanque.fr

The **Abbaye de Sénanque** is one of a trio of twelfth-century monasteries established by the Cistercian order in Provence, and predates both the *bories* and Gordes' castle. It stands alone, amid fields of lavender in a hollow of the hills, its weathered stone sighing with age and immutability. Though it has become one of the most familiar Provençal views, tourist numbers are tightly regulated and visitors are asked to dress modestly (no cycling gear) and to respect the silence to which the abbey is consecrated. The shop at the end of the visit sells the monks' produce, including liqueur, jams and toiletries as well as books, CDs, honey and lavender essence.

From the abbey, the loop back to Gordes via the D177 and D15 reveals the northern Luberon in all its glory.

Les Bouilladoires

The area around Gordes was famous for its olive oil before severe frosts killed off many of the trees. A still-functioning Gallo-Roman press, made from a single slice of oak 2m in diameter, as well as ancient oil lamps, jars and soap-making equipment, can be seen at the **Moulin des Bouillons** (April–Oct Mon & Wed–Sun 10am–noon & 2–6pm;

€7.50 including Musée de l'Histoire du Verre et du Vitrail) in **LES BOUILLADOIRES**, on the D148 just west of St-Pantaléon, 3.5km south of Gordes, and well signed from every junction. The ticket also gives admittance to the **Musée de l'Histoire du Verre et du Vitrail** (same hours; €7.50 including Moulin des Bouillons; ☎04 90 72 22 11, ⓦmusee-verre-vitrail.com), housed in a semi-submerged bunker next to the Moulin; the museum contains strongly coloured contemporary stained-glass creations by Frédérique Duran, the artist whose work forms the core of the collection, and plenty of historical exhibits. Outside, Duran is also the subject of the **Parc de Sculptures**, where his conspicuously totemic creations tower somewhat incongruously over pretty landscaped gardens.

Musée de la Lavande

276 rte de Gordes Coustellet • Daily: Feb–April & Oct–Dec 9am–12.15pm & 2–6pm; May–Sept 9am–7pm • €8 • ☎ 04 90 76 91 23, ⓦ museedelalavande.com

If you've travelled through Provence in high summer you will have seen, smelled and probably tasted lavender. The **Musée de la Lavande**, on the route de Gordes near the hamlet of Coustellet, offers a chance to learn more about lavender and its uses. Exhibits include copper stills dating back to the sixteenth century, plus there's a film show and free English-language audioguide, as well as the inevitable shop.

The Petit Luberon

The **Petit Luberon** has long been popular as a country escape for Parisians, Germans, the Dutch and the British – it was the setting for Peter Mayle's *A Year in Provence* (see p.xxx) – and *résidences secondaires* are everywhere. It remains a beguiling pastoral idyll, though these day's it's a rich person's retreat, its hilltop villages increasingly chic and its ruins, like **de Sade**'s **château** in **Lacoste** and the **Abbaye de St-Hilaire** near Bonnieux, being restored by their owners.

Oppède-le-Vieux

Ravishingly beautiful **OPPÈDE-LE-VIEUX**, above the vines on the steeper slopes of the Petit Luberon, maintains an aloof distance from the tourist invasion – literally so, for car-borne visitors are forced to park at quite a distance downhill and huff and puff their way up to the village along a meandering footpath. It's worth the climb. With its Renaissance gateway, the square in front of the ramparts suggests a monumental town within, and indeed at the settlement's zenith in the fourteenth century, nine hundred people lived here. But behind the line of restored sixteenth-century houses there are only the romantic, overgrown ruins that stretch up to the remains of the medieval **castle**; here and there isolated new homes have been crafted from restored fragments of the complex. "No entry" symbols warn you away from some of the more hazardous and crumbly portions of the ruin, while signs in English and French recount the history of the village. From the Vieux Château at the very top, the views are every bit as lovely as Oppède itself.

ACCOMMODATION AND EATING   OPPÈDE-LE-VIEUX

Petit Café 12 rue de Ste-Cécile ☎04 90 76 74 01, ⓦ lepetitcafe.fr. Pretty little *chambres d'hôtes* on the main square, with three simply furnished rooms in suitably rustic style, plus a bistro serving Luberon wines and simple dishes such as grilled octopus or saltimbocca alla Romana. *Menus* €21 and €32. Mon & Thurs–Sun noon–2.30pm & 7–9pm, Tues noon–2.30pm. **€140**

Ménerbes

If you head east from Oppède-le-Vieux, **MÉNERBES** is the next hilltop village you come to. It's shaped like a ship, with panoramic views from the top of the village: you can look down onto an odd jigsaw of fortified buildings and mansions, old and new. In the other direction houses with exquisitely tended terraces and gardens, all shuttered up outside holiday time, ascend to the mammoth wall of the citadel, including the beautiful house that belonged to Dora Maar (1907–97) – artist, photographer, and mistress and muse of Pablo Picasso.

Maison de la Truffe et du Vin

Place de l'Horloge • Jan–March & Dec Thurs–Sat 10am–5pm; April–Oct daily 10am–6pm • Free • ☎ 04 90 72 38 37, ⓦ vin-truffe-luberon.com

The exquisite seventeenth-century Hôtel d'Astier de Montfaucon – a former boys' school and hospital – is now home to the **Maison de la Truffe et du Vin**, which has an *oenothèque* where you can taste and buy local wines at vineyard prices, a shop selling soaps, olive oil, flavoured vinegars and (in season) fresh truffles, and a restaurant and *bar à vins*. There's a lovely garden at the back of the house.

Musée du Tire-Bouchon

Rte de Cavaillon, left off the D103 towards Beaumettes • Jan, Feb & Nov Mon–Fri 9am–12.30pm & 2–5pm; March, April & Oct Mon–Fri 9am–12.30pm & 2–6pm, Sat & Sun 10am–12.30pm & 2–6pm; May & June Mon–Fri 9am–12.30pm & 2–7pm, Sat & Sun 10am–12.30pm & 2–7pm; July–Sept daily 9am–7pm • €5 • ☎ 04 90 72 41 58, ⓦ museedutirebouchon.com

Outside Ménerbes is the wine-producing Domaine de la Citadelle's **Musée du Tire-Bouchon**, or Museum of Corkscrews, housed in a château dating back to the seventeenth century. The intriguing collection includes a Cézar compression, a corkscrew combined with pistol and dagger, others with erotic themes and many with beautifully sculpted and engraved handles. You can also visit the wine cellars for a free tasting.

Abbaye de St-Hilaire

2950 rte de Lacoste • Daily: Easter to mid-Nov & Christmas holidays 10am–6pm • €2.50 • ⓦ abbaye-saint-hilaire-vaucluse.com

The Carmelite **Abbaye de St-Hilaire**, with its fine seventeenth-century cloisters, exquisite Renaissance stairway and ancient dovecotes, is a handsome work of ecclesiastical architecture, though it's undergoing gradual restoration and at any one time parts of it may be off-limits. The abbey is tucked down a rutted track; it isn't large and you won't see much sign of life – you pay your admission fee into an honesty box – but the peace and tranquillity are impressive and the setting a delight.

ACCOMMODATION AND EATING   MÉNERBES

★ **Café du Progrès** Rue Raoul et Raymond Sylvestre ☎ 04 90 72 22 09. As featured in *A Year in Provence*, this friendly bar/*tabac* is good for simple meals and drinks, with an €18 lunch *formule*, quiches and *plats du jour*, plus a terrace with superb views over the surrounding countryside. In case you're thinking it's all delightfully rustic, check out the titles on the newsstand, which include *Die Zeit* and *The Financial Times*. Daily 6.30am–11.30pm.

Maison de la Truffe et du Vin Place de l'Horloge ☎ 04 90 72 38 37, ⓦ vin-truffe-luberon.com. Classy restaurant in the seventeenth-century Hôtel d'Astier de Montfaucon, with a luxurious, truffle-dominated menu; *menu du jour* €20. April–Oct Mon–Fri & Sun 12.30–2pm; also open evenings in summer.

Le Roy Soleil Le Fort, rte des Baumettes ☎ 04 90 72 25 61, ⓦ roy-soleil.com. Quiet and pretty hotel amid olive trees just outside the village, with a pool, 21 rooms and suites – some with terrace – and a *restaurant gastronomique*. __€155__

Lacoste

LACOSTE and its château can be seen from all the neighbouring villages, and are particularly enticing in moonlight, while a wind rocks the hanging lanterns on the narrow cobbled approaches to the château, and the castle itself is a floodlit beacon, visible from many kilometres around. These days you're as likely to hear American as French voices in Lacoste, since much of the village forms an outpost of the Savannah College of Art and Design.

The château

July & Aug daily 10am–6pm • €12 • ☎ 04 90 75 93 12, ⓦ lacoste-84.com

Lacoste **château**'s most famous owner was the Marquis de Sade, who retreated here when the reaction to his writings got too hot, but in 1778, after seven years here, he was locked up in the Bastille and the castle destroyed soon after. Semi-derelict, it was bought by *couturier* Pierre Cardin in 2001 and greatly restored, and it now hosts a **festival** of music and theatre each year in July.

In summer you can visit the château to admire Pierre Cardin's eclectic furnishings and his selection of contemporary art, though the entry price is steep for what's on offer.

ACCOMMODATION AND EATING LACOSTE

Café de France Lacoste ☎ 04 90 75 82 25. Simple rooms – cheaper ones with shared facilities – are available at this café, where the terrace offers views of Bonnieux. Three course *menu midi* €16. Daily noon–2.30pm & 7.30–9.30pm for food, later for drinks. **€40**

Bonnieux

From the *terrasse* by the old church on the heights of the village of **BONNIEUX** you can see Gordes, Roussillon and neighbouring Lacoste, 5km away. But the open aspect and lovely views aren't the only reason to pause here. Larger and livelier than its near-neighbour without being anything like as overrun as Roussillon or Gordes, Bonnieux makes an ideal touring base – if you're fit. Rising in a series of terrace-like switchbacks up a long, steep slope, it's the kind of place where you're forever huffing up the hill or tripping down it.

Bonnieux has its own **Bories**, an abandoned dry-stone-walled village, located deep in the forest south of the village off the D36 (April–Nov daily 10am–7pm; €5; ⓦ enclos-des-bories.fr). The village is also home to one of the Luberon's oldest wine-producing *domaines*, the family-owned **Château La Canorgue** on route du Pont Julien (Mon–Sat: May–Aug 9am–7pm; Sept–April 9am–noon & 2–6pm; ☎ 04 90 75 81 01, ⓦ chateaulacanorgue.com), where the production is organic and follows biodynamic principles in part. Further along the Pont Julien road you'll reach the triple-arched **Pont Julien**, which spans the River Coulon 5km north of Bonnieux, and dates back to the time when Apt was the Roman base of Apta Julia.

Musée de la Boulangerie

12 rue de la République • April–Sept Mon & Thurs–Sun 10.30am–1pm & 2.30–6pm • €4 • ☎ 04 90 75 88 34

Bonnieux has long had a reputation for the quality of its bread, and in the upper part of the old village the **Musée de la Boulangerie** is devoted to traditional baking. It's housed in a seventeenth-century former bakery with a handsomely proportioned oven of volcanic rock and a period baker's shop on the ground floor. The cellar contains baking implements, the first floor an archive and collection of cake moulds, and the second floor is devoted to the depiction and symbolism of baking, its customs and its accoutrements across the centuries.

Église Louise Bourgeois

Le Couvent d'Ô, rte de Lacoste • July & 1st ten days of Sept daily 10am–1pm & 3–6pm • €6 • ☎ 04 90 75 80 54, ⓦ egliselouisebourgeois.com

The seventeenth-century Couvent d'Ô, also known as the **Église Louise Bourgeois**, provides a graceful backdrop for several major works by French-American sculptor Louise Bourgeois. The pieces – one spider symbolizing motherhood, plus a Carrara marble font, Christ in rags and a sculpture of hands joined in prayer – were especially commissioned for the church.

ARRIVAL AND DEPARTURE BONNIEUX

By bus The Apt–Avignon bus comes no closer than the Pont Julien but the infrequent Apt–Aix service passes through the centre of the village. Destinations Aix-en-Provence (3 daily; 1hr30min–1hr 40min); Apt (4 daily; 25min).

ACCOMMODATION AND EATING

Le César Place de la Liberté ☎ 04 90 75 96 35, ⓦ hotel-restaurant-cesar-bonnieux.fr. *Logis de France* place at the top of the village, with classy furnishings in the lobby, a restaurant serving a €32 two-course *menu*, and breathtaking views from some rooms. The cheapest are in an annexe without a/c; more expensive options start at €95. **€60**

★ **Le Clos du Buis** Rue Victor Hugo ☎ 04 90 75 88 48, ⓦ leclosdubuis.com. Very pleasant three-star hotel in a former boulangerie close to the centre of the village, with eight a/c rooms, a pool, beautiful garden, private parking and views of Mont Ventoux. **€156**

Le Fournil 5 place Carnot ☎ 04 90 75 83 62, ⓦ lefournil-bonnieux.com. Lovely outer Mediterranean dishes laced with olive oil and garlic, Luberon and Ventoux wines and a pretty terrace fringing a fountain-dominated *place*. Mains such as duck with fresh salsify, and lamb with winter vegetable tajine and dates priced at €21.50 and €26.80 respectively. Wed–Fri & Sun 12.30–2pm & 7.30–9.30pm, Sat 12.30–2pm.

4

The Haut Var and Haute Provence

202 Chaîne de la Ste-Baume

205 Brignoles

205 The Haut Var

209 Aups

210 Northwest of Aups

211 Digne-les-Bains

214 Draguignan

216 North and east of Draguignan

219 Grand Canyon du Verdon

225 Lac de Castillon and around

226 Clues de Haute Provence

228 Massif les Monges

229 Parc National du Mercantour

ABBAYE DU THORONET

5 The Haut Var and Haute Provence

Stretching up into the high Alps, the unspoiled heartland of Provence is characterized by deep valleys and snowcapped mountains in the north, from which rivers flow down to the gentle undulating fields of vines, lavender, sunflowers and poppies in the south. Small towns and villages still thrive on their traditional industries of making honey, tending sheep, digging for truffles and pressing olive oil; and in isolated areas it's hard to believe this is the same country, never mind province, as the Côte d'Azur. Landscapes are exceptional, from the tranquil countryside of the Haut Var to the wild emptiness of the Plateau de Canjuers, the untrammelled forests east of Draguignan, and, most spectacularly of all, Europe's largest ravine, the Grand Canyon du Verdon.

The towns, like workaday **Draguignan**, are not the prime appeal. First and foremost, this is an area for **walking** and **climbing**, or **canoeing** and **windsurfing** on the countless lakes that provide power and irrigation. The **Grand Canyon du Verdon** is a must, even if only seen from a car. The best way to discover the area, however, is simply to stay in a village that takes your fancy – **Aups** or **Cotignac**, perhaps – eating, dawdling, and drifting into the rhythms of local life. **Food** here is quintessentially Provençal: lamb from the high summer pastures, goat's cheese, honey, almonds, olives and wild herbs. The soil is poor and water scarce, but the **wine** is still of sufficiently high quality for the Côtes de Provence *appellation* to extend to the Upper Var.

For centuries the border between Provence and Savoy ran through this part of France, a political divide embodied by the impressive fortifications of **Entrevaux** and **Colmars**, the principal town of the Haut Verdon. To this day, most of the region is not generally thought of as part of Provence. The French refer to it as the **Alpes-Maritimes**, which is also the name of the *département* that stretches from between the Haut Var and Verdon valleys to the Italian border, and includes the Riviera. Where Provence ends and the Alps begin is debatable, but the **Tinée Valley** is usually cited as definitely belonging to the latter – the mountains here are pretty serious and the Italian influence becomes noticeable – and it's hard to imagine a more Alpine settlement than **Barcelonnette**, beyond the peaks to the north.

The region's mountainous northeastern segment, **Haute Provence**, is not an easy place to live. Abandoned farms and overgrown terraces bear witness to the declining viability of mountain agriculture. But the **ski resorts** bring in money, while summer sees an influx of trekkers, naturalists and climbers. The area protected as the **Parc National du Mercantour**, covering 75km from east to west, holds no permanent inhabitants at all.

Running along the southern limit of the Alps, the **Nice–Digne rail line**, known as both the Chemins de Fer de Provence and the **Train des Pignes**, is the only remaining segment of the region's nineteenth- and twentieth-century narrow-gauge network. One of the great train rides of France, it takes in the isolated Var towns of **Puget-Théniers** and Entrevaux, and ends at low-key **Digne**, the centre of the lavender industry. Elsewhere, **public transport** is a problem except in the **Roya Valley**, over in the east, where the Nice–Turin rail line links the Italianate towns of **Tende** and **Sospel**, and also gives access to the tiny, intriguing perched village of **Saorge**. Buses are infrequent and many of the best starting points for walks or the far-flung pilgrimage chapels are off the main roads. With your own transport, you'll face tough climbs and long stretches with no fuel supplies, but you'll be free to explore the most exhilaratingly beautiful corner of Provence.

ALPINE VILLAGE OF SAORGE

Highlights

❶ Abbaye du Thoronet An exquisite rose-coloured monastic complex, and the oldest of Provence's three great Cistercian monasteries. See page 206

❷ Aups With its fabulous crop of well-priced hotel-restaurants, this lovely rural town makes a perfect overnight stop. See page 209

❸ Grand Canyon du Verdon Walk, drive, cycle, raft or bungee, but whatever you do, don't miss Europe's largest and most spectacular gorge. See page 219

❹ Parc National du Mercantour An unspoiled alpine wilderness that's home to the Vallée des

Merveilles and its mysterious 4000-year-old rock carvings. See page 229

❺ Entrevaux and Colmars-les-Alpes Both these picturesque towns retain beautifully preserved fortifications designed by Vauban. See pages 236 and 234

❻ Skiing in the Alpes-Maritimes Glide down the mountain in the resorts of Auron and Allos. See pages 238 and 233

❼ Saorge Enchanting village, perched on a sheer hillside, with a remarkable Baroque monastery and wonderful local walks. See page 244

HIGHLIGHTS ARE MARKED ON THE MAP ON PAGE 202

5

Chaîne de la Ste-Baume

East of **Aubagne** (see page 73), the urban sprawl that surrounds Marseille finally gives way to the **Chaîne de la Ste-Baume**, a sparsely populated region of rich forests. The plateau north of this stark ridge makes wonderful territory for walking and cycling, with the north-facing slopes holding a rare profusion of woods, flowers and wildlife. The entire area north to **St-Maximin**, south to **Signes**, west to **Gémenos** and east to **La Roquebrussanne** is protected. You are not allowed to camp in the woods or light fires, and an ancient royal edict still forbids the picking of orchids.

Gémenos

Thanks to the beautiful seventeenth-century **château** that serves as its Hôtel de Ville, **GÉMENOS**, 3km east of Aubagne, makes a tempting stop. Cafés, bars and patisseries surround the château, while welcoming hotels are scattered further out.

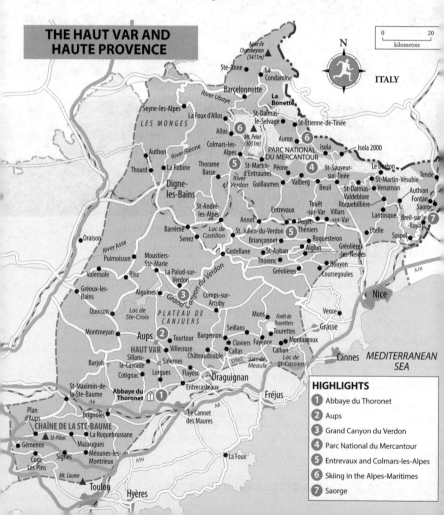

THE HAUT VAR AND HAUTE PROVENCE

HIGHLIGHTS

1 Abbaye du Thoronet
2 Aups
3 Grand Canyon du Verdon
4 Parc National du Mercantour
5 Entrevaux and Colmars-les-Alpes
6 Skiing in the Alpes-Maritimes
7 Saorge

5

THE SEASONS OF HAUTE PROVENCE

Haute Provence is a different world from season to season. In **spring** the fruit trees in the narrow valleys blossom, and melting waters swell the rivers, sometimes flooding villages and carrying whole streets away. Groves of chestnut and olive trees in the foothills bear fruit in **summer** and **autumn**, while the pine forests higher up are edged with wild raspberries and bilberries, and the moors and grassy slopes with white and gold alpine flowers. Above the line where vegetation ceases lie rocks with eagles' nests and snowcaps that never melt. In **winter** the sheep and shepherds retreat to warmer pastures, leaving the snowy heights to antlered mouflons and chamois, and camouflaged ermine. The villages, where the shepherds came to summer markets, batten down for the long cold haul, while modern conglomerations of Swiss-style chalet houses, sports shops and late-night bars come to life around the ski lifts. From November to April many of the mountain passes are closed, cutting off the northern town of Barcelonnette from its lower neighbours.

Plan-d'Aups and the Ste-Baume summit

Northeast of Gémenos, the D2 follows the narrow valley of St-Pons, past an open-air municipal theatre cut into the rock and the **Parc Naturel de St-Pons**, where beech, hornbeam, ash and maple trees surround the ruins of a thirteenth-century Cistercian abbey, before zigzagging up towards the Espigoulier pass. A footpath beyond the park soon links to the GR98, which climbs directly up the Ste-Baume massif, then follows the ridge, with breathtaking views.

At **PLAN-D'AUPS** – almost too small to count as a village, but home to a hilltop Romanesque church, tucked in among modern neighbours – the dramatic climb levels out to a forested plateau running parallel to the jagged Ste-Baume peaks, which line the southern horizon like a massively fortified wall. The **Hôtellerie de la Ste-Baume**, a pilgrimage centre 3km east of Plan d'Aups that's run by Dominican friars, is the starting point for a pilgrimage based on Provençal mythology, or simply for a walk up to the high ridge. The myth picks up the story of **Mary Magdalene**, after her arrival in Les Saintes-Maries-de-la-Mer (see page 108). For some unexplained reason, she gets transported by angels to a cave (*grotte*) just below the summit of **Ste-Baume**. There she spends 33 years, before being flown to St-Maximin-de-la-Ste-Baume (see page 204) to die.

The difficult **paths** up from the Hôtellerie are dotted with oratories, calvaries and crosses. It takes roughly an hour to reach the sombre *grotte* at the top, where Mass is held daily at 11am. The path beyond, leading to the **St-Pilon summit**, makes you wish for some of Mary's winged pilots.

East to La Roquebrussanne

East of Plan-d'Aups, the D95 crosses many kilometres of unspoiled forest. Superb cycling country, these groves of spindly, stunted oaks and beeches have exerted a mystical pull since ancient times, and were sacred to the Druids. Around the sleepy but likeable little village of **MAZAUGUES**, you pass huge, nineteenth-century covered stone wells, built to hold ice that could then be transported on summer nights down to Marseille or Toulon.

Southwest of Mazaugues, the GR99 footpath leads, after an initial steep climb, on a gentle three- to four-hour walk down to Signes. Continuing east on the D64, on the other hand, brings you to the larger but still attractive village of **LA ROQUEBRUSSANNE**, where lots of little footbridges, each leading to a private home, straddle a peaceful stream, and there's a sizeable Saturday food **market**.

Signes

Beside the lovely Gapeau stream 14km southwest of La Roquebrussanne, **SIGNES** is an appealing little village where palm trees and white roses grow around the war

5

memorial, the clock tower is more than four hundred years old, and the locals make their living from wine, olives, cereals and market gardening. Its Thursday **market** centres on place Marcel-Pagnol.

St-Maximin-de-la-Ste-Baume

In the handsome town of **ST-MAXIMIN-DE-LA-STE-BAUME**, in 1279, the count of Provence supposedly discovered a crypt containing the relics of Mary Magdalene and St Maximin, hidden during a Saracen raid. He set about building a basilica and **monastery**, which was consecrated in 1316, though construction continued until 1532. The medieval streets that surround the basilica have considerable charm, with their uniform tiled roofs at anything but uniform heights; a covered passageway south of the church leads into the arcaded rue Colbert, a former Jewish ghetto. There's also a reasonable assortment of **cafés** and **brasseries**, congregating on place Malherbe, as well as shops selling the work of local artisans.

Basilica and monastery of St-Maximin

Basilica Daily 7.30am–7.30pm · **Cloisters and chapterhouse** Daily 7.30am–7.30pm · Free

St-Maximin's substantial Gothic **basilica** is extravagantly decorated in stone, wood, gold, silk and oil paint, with highlights including beautiful wood panelling in the choir and paintings on the nave walls, as well as Ronzen's lovely *Retable de la Passion* (1520). Look out, too, for the wonderfully sculpted fourth-century sarcophagi, and the grotesque skull once venerated as that of Mary Magdalene, encased in a glass helmet framed by a gold neck and hair, in the **crypt**.

The thirteenth-century **cloisters** and **chapterhouse** of the monastery, now part of the *Couvent Royal* hotel, are much more delicate. Look down the well to see the escape route used by the Dominican friars during sixteenth-century sieges.

INFORMATION

CHAÎNE DE LA STE-BAUME

SIGNES

Tourist office In the *médiathèque* on rue Frédéric-Mistral (Sun–Fri 9am–noon & 1.30–6pm, Sat 9am–noon & 1.30–5pm; ☎ 04 94 98 87 80, ✆ signes.com).

ST-MAXIMIN-DE-LA-STE-BAUME

Tourist office Place Jean Salusse (Mon–Sat 9am–12.30pm & 2–6pm, Sun 10am–12.30pm & 2–5pm; ☎ 04 94 59 84 59, ✆ ot-stmaximin.provenceverte.fr).

ACCOMMODATION AND EATING

GÉMENOS

Relais de la Magdeleine Rond 40, av du 2ème Cuirassier ☎ 04 42 32 20 16. Luxury hotel, in a lovely, vine-covered eighteenth-century manor house in a park designed by Le Nôtre, just off the N396 route d'Aix. The restaurant (closed mid-Nov to mid-March) serves a €45 lunch *menu*, while dinner is à la carte, at around €75 for three courses. **€145**

PLAN-D'AUPS

Lou Pèbre d'Aï Quartier Ste-Madeleine ☎ 04 42 04 50 42, ✆ loupebredai.com. Comfortable, good-value roadside hotel, where five of the six sizeable, slightly old-fashioned rooms have mountain-view balconies, there's a heated pool in the garden, and the restaurant serves good seasonal *menus*, from €15 for lunch, €28–38 for dinner. **€61**

SIGNES

Château de Cancerilles Rte de Belgentier ☎ 04 94 90 81 45, ✆ chateaudecancerilles.com. Studios and apartments in the Garcia family's wonderful *chambres d'hôtes*, in an old stone farm surrounded by vines and with a glorious pool. Only rentable by the week in high season, but available by the night for the rest of the year. **€94**

ST-MAXIMIN-DE-LA-STE-BAUME

★ **Couvent Royal** Place Jean-Salusse ☎ 04 94 86 55 66, ✆ couvent-royal.fr. This imposing thirteenth-century monastery has been converted into a comfortable, highly atmospheric hotel. Some of its clean, excellent-value rooms used to be monks' cells. *Menus* in the elegant cloister restaurant start at €27. **€91**

Plaisance 20 place Malherbe ☎ 04 94 37 01 30. A short walk west of the monastery, this well-run, friendly hotel offers simple but spacious rooms in a grand townhouse, but no restaurant. **€56**

Provençal Chemin de Mazaugues ☎ 04 94 78 16 97, ⓦ camping-le-provencal.com. Three-star campsite, 2km southeast towards Marseille, with pool, bar, restaurant and shop. Closed Oct–March. **€38**

La Table en Provence 50 rue Général-de-Gaulle ☎ 04 94 59 84 61. Relaxed café-restaurant, with outdoor tables facing the basilica at the end of the main old-town shopping street, that's ideal for a satisfying lunch, with cooked dishes and salad specials, such as house foie gras with squash chutney and watercress (from €16). Tues–Thurs & Sun noon–1.30pm, Fri–Sat noon–1.30pm & 7–8.30pm.

Brignoles

BRIGNOLES, 18km east of St-Maximin, is an ordinary, reasonably well-preserved provincial centre that can make for a convenient night's stay. At its heart, beyond the sprawling commercial zones and busy ring roads, lies a gentrified, warren-like medieval hill town that's full of quiet, shaded squares and old facades with faded adverts and flowering window boxes. Rue des Lanciers, with its fine old houses where the rich Brignolais used to live, leads up from place des Comtes-de-Provence to the twelfth-century **St-Sauveur** church. Behind that, the stepped street of rue St-Esprit runs down to place Caramy, the café-lined central square of the modern town. The streets are filled by large **markets** on Wednesdays and Saturdays.

Musée du Pays Brignolais

Place des Comtes-de-Provence • April–Sept Wed–Sun 9am–noon & 2.30–6pm; Oct–March Wed–Sat 10am–noon & 2.30–5pm, Sun 10am–noon & 3–5pm • €4 • ☎ 04 94 69 45 18

Displays in the fascinating, old-style **Musée du Pays Brignolais**, housed in a thirteenth-century summer residence of the counts of Provence, dip into every aspect of local life, ranging from a paleo-Christian sarcophagus to a reinforced concrete boat made by the inventor of concrete in 1840. There's a statue of a saint whose navel has been visibly deepened by the hopeful hands of infertile women, a reconstruction of a bauxite mine, a crèche of *santos*, and some Impressionist Provençal landscapes by Frédéric Montenard.

ARRIVAL AND INFORMATION   BRIGNOLES

By bus Brignoles' *gare routière* is on place St-Louis, immediately northeast of the old town.
Destinations Aix (2 daily; 1hr 10min); Marseille (2 daily; 1hr 40min); St-Maximin (8 daily; 25min).

Tourist office Carrefour de l'Europe roundabout, north of the River Caramy (Sept–June Mon–Sat 9am–noon & 2–6pm; July & Aug Mon–Sat 9am–12.30pm & 2–7pm, Sun 9am–1pm; ☎ 04 94 72 04 21, ⓦ la-provence-verte.net).

ACCOMMODATION AND EATING

La Bastide de Messine Chemin de Cante Perdrix ☎ 04 94 72 09 06. Very nice five-room *chambres d'hôtes*, 2km northwest of the centre, in a renovated old farmhouse with a pool. **€80**

Camping de Brignoles 786 rte de Nice ☎ 04 94 69 20 10, ⓦ camping-brignoles.com. Two-star municipal campsite, in a pleasant leafy setting 1km east of the centre down the rte de Nice. Closed Nov–March. **€18.50**

L'Oustau Place Caramy ☎ 04 94 69 11 10. The pick of several similar café-restaurants on the main square, with shaded outdoor tables and a €14 daily *menu* offering the likes of grilled beef with cep sauce. Tues–Sat 6.30am–8pm, Sun 6.30am–1pm.

The Haut Var

Northeast of Brignoles, the rocky **Haut Var** holds some delightfully picturesque medieval villages, including **Cotignac** and **Villecroze**. Further north, the **Argens Valley** to the Verdon Gorge is the true heart of Provence, with its soft enveloping countryside of

5

woods, vines, lakes and waterfalls, streaked with rocky ridges before the high plateaux and mountains. To the outsider, the villages rather merge together; to know them properly you'd have to live here for winter after winter. The region is also home to the **Abbaye du Thoronet**, Provence's oldest surviving Cistercian monastery.

Barjols

Fountains are the chief attraction of **BARJOLS**, a somewhat rundown but oddly appealing old town 21km north of Brignoles. The whole place is split in two by a massive ravine that runs down the middle, and used to provide the water power for its long-defunct tanning industry, No fewer than 28 mossy springs and splendid stone water features are dotted around, mostly in Barjols' older, eastern **quartier du Réal**. The glum, rickety former tanneries have been taken over by artists and craft workers; you can visit their studios down the old road to Brignoles, further east. Looking back upwards from here at the industrial ruins is a spooky night-time experience.

Cotignac

COTIGNAC, the Haut Var's loveliest village, stands 23km northeast of Brignoles. From its photogenic place de la Mairie, rue de l'Horloge heads under the clock tower and up to the church, from which a path leads to the foot of the spectacular 80m cliff that forms the back wall of the village. A splendidly colourful and flower-bedecked, if at times nerve-racking, **cliffside trail** (April–June & Sept Mon & Wed–Sat 10am–noon & 2.30–5.30pm, Tues & Sun 2.30–5.30pm; July & Aug daily 10am–1pm & 3–7pm; Sept Tues–Sat 10am–noon & 2–6.30pm, Sun 2–6.30pm; €2) leads past a troglodyte's dream of passageways, precarious stairways and strange little structures to the two ruined towers at the summit, relics of a long-abandoned castle. The rock between them is riddled with further caves and tunnels.

Long venerated as a saviour from the plague, the miraculous Virgin in the **Chapelle de Notre Dame des Grâces**, on the summit across the valley to the south, hit the big time in 1638 when Louis XIII and Anne of Austria – married for 22 childless years – made their supplications to her. Nine months after the royal visit, the future Sun King let out his first demanding squall.

Entrecasteaux

ENTRECASTEAUX, 9km east of Cotignac along the minor D50, is scarcely more than a stone frame for its **château**, which rises from formal gardens to dominate the village.

Château d'Entrecasteaux and Le Nôtre gardens

Château Guided tours only: Easter to mid-June Sun 4pm; July to Sept daily except Sat 4pm; Aug daily except Sat 11.30am & 4pm • €10 • ☎ 04 94 04 43 95, ⓦ chateau-entrecasteaux.com • **Gardens** Dawn–dusk • Free

Both Entrecasteaux's seventeenth-century **château**, and the publicly owned **Le Nôtre gardens** that separate it from the village, are open to visitors. The château owes its current condition to Scottish painter Ian McGarvie-Munn (1919–81), who retired in 1974 after a career that included a stint as head of the Guatemalan navy, and devoted himself to this massive restoration job. Its interior is spacious, light and charmingly rustic, typified by the terracotta tiles, a style that was all the rage when the Count and Countess of Grignan used the château as their summer residence.

Abbaye du Thoronet

Off the D79, 16km southeast of Cotignac • Daily: April–Sept 10am–6.30pm; Oct–March 10am–1pm & 2–5pm • €8 • ☎ 04 94 60 43 96, ⓦ thoronet.monuments-nationaux.fr

The austere, rose-coloured **Abbaye du Thoronet**, one of Provence's three great Cistercian monasteries, stands in superb seclusion, deep in the forest of La Daboussière. Like Silvacane and Sénanque (see pages 167 and 193), it was founded in the first half of the twelfth century, but Thoronet is the oldest, and was completed in the shortest time, so its aesthetic coherence transcends its relatively modest size.

Although the monastery was abandoned in 1791, it was kept intact during the Revolutionary era. Restoration started in the 1850s, and a more recent campaign has brought it to graceful, melancholy perfection. It centres on lovely cloisters, holding a covered fountain; climb the stairs from the adjoining dormitory to admire them from the open walkway above.

Salernes

Compared with Cotignac, **SALERNES**, 13km northeast, is quite a metropolis, with a thriving tile-making industry and enough near-level irrigated land for productive agriculture. Twenty or so studios and shops, large and small, sell a huge range of **pottery** and **tiles**, while on Sunday and Wednesday a **market** takes place beneath the ubiquitous plane trees on the *cours*.

Sillans-la-Cascade

Tiny **SILLANS-LA-CASCADE**, 6km west of Salernes, is a nice, sleepy little village that has clung on to a brief stretch of ancient ramparts. Down below, on the Bresque river, a stunning **waterfall**, reached by a twenty-minute walk along a delightful and clearly signed path from the main road, gushes into a turquoise pool that's perfect for swimming.

Villecroze

Some 5km northeast of Salernes, **VILLECROZE** is a charming village – though you could drive straight through without realizing that its lovely, peaceful old quarter was even there. The inconspicuous walled medieval town, immediately south of the main D557, is entered beneath an unadorned terracotta clock tower. With its vaulted stone arcades, it's a joy to stroll around.

Like Cotignac (see opposite), Villecroze sits beneath a water-burrowed cliff. The gardens around the base are delightfully un-Gallic and informal, while intriguing **grottoes** in its flanks are open to visitors (April–June Wed–Sun 1–5pm; July & Aug daily 10am–5pm; Sept Tues–Sun 10am–noon & 2–5pm; Oct Wed–Sun 1–4pm; €4; ☎04 94 70 63 06).

The centre of community life in Villecroze, the place du Général-de-Gaulle across the road from the old town, hosts a **market** on Thursday mornings.

Tourtour

TOURTOUR, 6km north of Villecroze via the tortuous D51, sits 300m higher, atop a ridge with views extending to the massifs of Maures, Ste-Baume and Ste-Victoire. It's a tiny, tight-knit village with a seemingly organic unity, its soft-coloured stone growing into stairways and curving streets, and branching to form arches, fountains and towers. An old mill looks like it has always been in ruins, while the elephant-leg towers of the sixteenth-century bastion straddle the *mairie* as if of their own volition. The two elms on the main square, planted when Anne of Austria and Louis XIII visited Cotignac, are almost as enormous, albeit showing signs of decrepitude.

Drivers approaching Tourtour are directed to **parking spaces** a few hundred metres southeast, then walk in via open parklands surrounding a hilltop church. While that helps to preserve the central core, it inevitably also means it's rather unreal, a enclave of little galleries, tea rooms and pottery shops.

INFORMATION

THE HAUT VAR

BARJOLS
Tourist office Bd Grisolle (April–June & Sept Tues–Fri 9am–noon & 2–5pm, Sat 9am–noon; July & Aug Mon–Sat 9am–12.30pm & 2–6pm, Sun 9am–1pm; Oct–March Tues, Wed & Fri 9am–noon & 2–4pm, Thurs 2–4pm, Sat 9am–noon; ☎ 04 94 77 20 01, ⓦ barjols.fr).

COTIGNAC
Tourist office Pont de la Cassole (April–June & Sept Tues, Wed & Fri 9.30am–1pm & 2–6pm, Thurs 2–6pm, Sat 9am–

12.30pm; July & Aug Mon–Sat 9am–12.30pm & 2–7pm, Sun 9am–1pm; Oct–March Tues, Wed & Fri 9am–12.30pm & 2–4pm, Thurs 2–4pm, Sat 9am–12.30pm; ☎ 04 94 04 61 87, ⓦ ot-cotignac.provenceverte.fr).

SALERNES
Tourist office Place Gabriel-Péri (July & Aug Mon–Sat 9.15am–12.15pm & 1.45–7pm, Sun 9.30am–12.30pm; Sept–June Tues–Thurs & Sat 9.15am–12.15pm & 1.45–6pm, Fri 2–6pm; ☎ 04 94 70 69 02, ⓦ ville-salernes.fr).

ACCOMMODATION AND EATING

BARJOLS
★ **Aux Petits Oignons** 21 rue Louis Pasteur ☎ 09 80 39 13 53. Phenomenally efficient and great-value bistro, with tables out on the main square in summer. The small kitchen serves up hearty salads and substantial set *menus* from €19.50; the deconstructed steak tartare is especially recommended. Daily 11.30am–3pm & Mon, Wed, Fri & Sat 7–9pm.

Le Pont d'Or 2 rue Eugène Payan ☎ 04 94 77 05 23, ⓦ hotel-du-pont-d-or-barjols.cote.azur.fr.   Pleasant *Logis de France* hotel-restaurant where the simple old-fashioned rooms overlook the central ravine, and the dining room (closed Sun eve & Mon) serves unremarkable *menus* from €14.50. Closed Dec to mid-Jan. **€61**

COTIGNAC
Camping des Pouverels Chemin des Pouverels ☎ 04 94 04 71 91, ⓦ mairiecotignac.fr/camping. This municipal campsite, with peaceful shaded sites 2km northeast of the village towards Aups, also offers dorm accommodation. Closed Nov–March. Camping **€10**; dorms **€12**

Restaurant du Cours 18 cours Gambetta ☎ 04 94 04 78 50, ⓦ restaurant-hotelducours.fr. Sun-kissed pavement restaurant – not to be confused with the *Brasserie du Cours* – at the heart of the village's social life, decked out with bright yellow tablecloths and serving top-quality *menus* (from €13.50 for lunch, around €30 in the evening). Despite the sign, it's not a hotel. July & Aug daily noon–2pm & 7–10pm; Sept–March closed Tues eve & Wed.

Maison Gonzagues 9 rue Léon Gérard ☎ 04 94 72 85 40, ⓦ maison-gonzagues-cotignac.com. Cotignac being short of hotels, this gorgeous and very welcoming *chambres d'hôtes*, offering five antique-furnished rooms complete with four-poster beds, in a former tannery, is the best accommodation option in the village. **€115**

★ **Le Temps de Pose** 11 Place de la Mairie ☎ 04 94 77 04 69 17. This quaint, flower-bedecked café on a quiet

square makes an ideal spot for breakfast, a light lunch or a reviving cup of tea. Tasty, fresh sandwiches and quiches cost around €9.50, a large salad or daily *plat* more like €12. July & Aug daily 8.30am–10pm; Sept–Nov & Easter–June Tues–Sun 9–6.30pm.

ENTRECASTEAUX
Bastide Notre-Dame L'Adrech de Ste-Anne ☎ 04 94 04 45 63, ⓦ bastidenotredame.free.fr. Terracotta *chambres d'hôtes* just west of the village, with five pretty, colour-coordinated rooms and a pool in the shaded garden. **€102**

Lou Cigaloun 93 chemin Caravane, St-Antonin-du-Var ☎ 04 94 04 42 67, ⓦ hotel-restaurant-loucigaloun.com. The friendly, family hotel-restaurant, in Entre-casteaux's even smaller neighbour 4km east, has just six nicely modernized rooms, along with a pool and a park alongside. Its restaurant offers simple but fine cooking, with lunch from €16.90. Closed Nov–Feb. **€70**

SALERNES
L'Odyssée 5 rue des 4 Coins ☎ 04 94 68 02 32. Friendly restaurant with seating on the main square, serving changing daily *menus* that focus on local, and especially organic, produce; *plats* like steak frites or risotto typically cost €15–20. Look out for concerts and theatre performances in winter in the square. Daily (except Thurs) noon–1.30pm & 7.30–9.30pm.

SILLANS-LA-CASCADE
Les Pins 1 Grande Rue ☎ 04 94 04 63 26, ⓦ restaurant-lespins.com. The five simple en-suite rooms in this attractive hotel-restaurant, beside the main road, are well priced but very ordinary. The food, served on a colourful patio, is considerably better, with lunch at €20 and dinner *menus* from €32 (Tues–Sun 11.30am–2pm & Wed–Sat 7–9pm). The owners also run their own bakery, alongside. **€62**

5

VILLECROZE

Au Bien Être Quartier Les Cadenières ☎ 04 94 70 67 57, ⓦ aubienetre.com. Secluded and very comfortable hotel, 3km south along the D557, where French windows lead direct from the rooms to the pool. Dinner *menus* in the dining room (closed lunch Mon–Wed) start at €29. Hotel closed Oct to March. **€89**

★ **La Bohème** Villecroze ☎ 04 94 70 80 04. Delightful, very floral café and tearooms, just inside the medieval walls, with tables out on the alley, an enticing sun-trap. Breakfast (€6.50) is served, along with cooked brunches (€10), afternoon tea, smoothies and cakes. Daily 9am–1pm & 4–7pm.

Le Colombier Rte de Draguignan ☎ 04 94 70 63 23, ⓦ lecolombier-var.com. Very charming hotel-restaurant, south along the D557, with six sizeable and tastefully decorated rooms with terraces, and a lovely peaceful garden. *Menus* in the restaurant (closed Sun eve & Mon) start at €29.50. Closed mid-Nov to mid-Dec. **€95**

TOURTOUR

Bastide de Tourtour Rte de Flayosc ☎ 04 98 10 54 20, ⓦ www.bastidedetourtour.com. Upscale hotel-restaurant, housed in a modern version of a fortified farmhouse, equipped with jacuzzis, tennis courts and a gym, and serving classic local cuisine on *menus* from €29 (Sept–June closed lunch Mon–Fri). **€175**

Aups

The neat and rather charming village of **AUPS**, 10km north of Salernes, makes an ideal base for drivers touring the Haut Var or the Grand Canyon du Verdon. While it has all the facilities visitors might need, it remains a vibrant, lived-in community, still earning its living from agriculture, and at its best on Wednesdays and Saturdays, when **market** stalls fill its central squares and the surrounding streets. There's also a **truffle** market on Thursdays between November and the end of February.

Though only 500m or so above sea level, this was considered by the ancients to be the beginning of the Alps; its Roman name, Alpibus, became first Alps and then Aups. It now centres on three ill-defined and interconnected squares, where the D557 reaches the southern end of the village: **place Frédéric-Mistral**, the smaller **place Duchâtel** slightly uphill to the left and the tree-lined gardens of **place Martin-Bidouré** to the right. Beyond these, the tangle of old streets, and the sixteenth-century clock tower with its campanile, make it an enjoyable place to explore.

Musée Simon Segal

Av Albert 1er • Daily (except Tues): June–Aug Wed–Mon 11am–1pm & 4–7pm; Sept Wed–Mon 11am–1pm & 4–6pm; Oct–May by appointment only • Free • ☎ 04 94 70 00 07, ⓦ aups.fr

The finest works, not surprisingly, in Aups' **Musée Simon Segal**, in the former chapel of a convent, are by the Russian-born painter Simon Segal, and include some expressive portraits. Some of the other paintings, though, hold interesting local scenes. One depicts the Roman bridge at Aiguines, now drowned beneath the artificial lake of Ste-Croix.

ARRIVAL AND INFORMATION   **AUPS**

By bus Buses stop on place Frédéric-Mistral.   Destinations Aiguines (1 daily; 35min); Cotignac (1 daily;

REPUBLICAN RESISTANCE IN AUPS

An obelisk on Aups's **place Martin-Bidouré**, inscribed "To the memory of citizens who died in 1851 defending the Republic and its laws", commemorates a period of republican resistance all too rarely honoured in France. Peasant and artisan defiance of **Louis Napoleon's coup d'état** that year was at its strongest in Provence, and the defeat of the insurgents at the battle of Aups, on December 10, 1851, was followed by a massacre of men and women alike. The badly wounded Martin Bidouré escaped, but was swiftly found being succoured by a peasant, and was executed on this very spot. The monument also honours an unnamed man with a wooden leg, while the names of local Resistance fighters were added after World War II.

5

25min).

ACCOMMODATION AND EATING

★ **Auberge de la Tour** Rue Aloisi ☎ 04 94 70 00 30. Appealing and great-value hotel, where the beds have duvets, and the tasteful, airy, well-equipped rooms sleep up to four. They surround a sunny, peaceful, plant-filled courtyard restaurant that serves good *menus* from €25.50, so in a ground-floor room you could end up with diners right outside your window. Closed Oct–March, restaurant also closed Tues Sept–June. €53

Bastide du Calalou Moissac-Bellevue ☎ 04 94 70 17 91, ⓦ bastide-du-calalou.com. Imposing country-house hotel in a small village 5km northwest of Aups on the D9. The building itself is nothing special, but it's set in grand gardens and has 32 plush rooms, a pool and a fine restaurant serving dinner *menus* from €33. €189

Bastide de l'Estré Chemin de la Croix de Pins ☎ 04 94 84 00 45, ⓦ estre.net. B&B accommodation in an attractive rural location, off the road to Moustiers-Ste-Marie 3km north of town. There's also a *gîte* to rent, a camping barn for walkers and cyclists with dorm beds, and they serve evening

meals by reservation for €30. Dorms €30; *Gîte/* week €700

Camping Les Prés Rte de Tourtour ☎ 04 94 70 00 93, ⓦ campinglespres.com. This well-shaded two-star site, to the right off allée Charles-Boyer just 300m southeast of the town centre, has a bar, snack bar and pool. Closed Dec–Feb. €47

Grand Hôtel Place Duchâtel ☎ 04 94 70 10 82, ⓦ grand-hotel-aups.com. Traditional village hotel, just off the main square, with six plain but adequate en-suite rooms, including some that sleep up to four. The popular and hugely efficient garden restaurant in front serves excellent *menus* at €18–30.50, and there's also a nice bar. €62

St-Marc Rue Aloisi ☎ 04 94 70 06 08, ⓦ hotel-restaurant-lesaintmarc83.com. Rickety, earthy and characterful old rooms (sleeping up to five; not all en suite) in a former olive oil mill overlooking a tiny square and above a good restaurant, where a delicious roasted duck breast comes as part of the €11.50 lunch *menus*. Closed Tues & Wed Sept–June, plus second half Nov. €65

Northwest of Aups

For anyone heading northwest of Aups towards the Grand Canyon du Verdon, two little towns make potential stops. **Quinson**, which marks the start of the lower gorges, is home to a showpiece modern museum of regional prehistory, while beneath its workaday façade, **Riez** holds a smattering of Roman ruins.

Quinson

QUINSON, an old but not especially remarkable village overlooking fields of spectacular sunflowers on the attractive D13 22km northwest of Aups, sits at the head of the **Basses Gorges du Verdon**. If you haven't yet seen the Grand Canyon du Verdon, these 500m depths will strike you as quite dramatic, but they're rather difficult to reach. The GR99 trail makes a short detour to the south side of the gorge a couple of kilometres downstream from Quinson, and paths off the road between Quinson and Esparron also lead to the edge of the gorge.

Musée de Préhistoire des Gorges du Verdon

Rte de Montmeyan • **Musée** April–June & Sept daily (except Tues) 10am–7pm; July & Aug daily 10am–8pm; Oct to mid-Dec & Feb–March daily (except Tues) 10am–6pm • €8 • **Guided cave tours** July & Aug Wed & Sat 9.15am; 3hr 30min; otherwise see website • €5 (reservation essential) • ☎ 04 92 74 09 59, ⓦ museeprehistoire.com

A huge and incongruous modern edifice at the edge of Quinson, the **Musée de Préhistoire des Gorges du Verdon** was a millennium project, designed by Norman Foster and opened in 2001. While it is Europe's largest museum of human prehistory, its primary focus remains very local, charting a million years of human habitation in Provence. Highlights include a multimedia presentation of the cave of Baume Bonne and a 15m-long reconstruction of the caves of the canyon of Baudinard, with their

5

6000-year-old red sun paintings. Despite some intriguing Neolithic stelae and Bronze Age finds, though, many visitors find the museum unsatisfying, with dry-as-dust displays veering erratically between targeting kids and adults, and very poor provision for non-French speakers.

The most important local archeological site is the cave of **Baume Bonne** itself, where human occupation has been traced back 400,000 years. It's only accessible on foot, and on guided tours – which take a total of three and a half hours including the hike to and from the museum.

Riez

The main business of **RIEZ**, 21km north of Quinson, is derived from the lavender fields that cover this corner of Provence – hence the hideous **lavender distillery**, 1km south, which produces essence for the perfume industry. Riez is more village than town today, but its antiquity is readily apparent. Four stately **Roman columns** stand in a field just off avenue Frédéric-Mistral at the bottom of the main allées Louis-Gardiol, while over the river stand the disappointingly scanty remains of a sixth-century **cathedral** (open access).

For a **walk** with good views over the town, head first for the clock tower above Grande Rue, then go up the steps past the cemetery, where a stony curving path brings you to a cedar-shaded platform on the hilltop where the pre-Roman Riezians lived. The only building there today is the eighteenth-century **Chapelle St-Maxime**, with its gaudily patterned interior.

ARRIVAL AND INFORMATION   **NORTHWEST OF AUPS**

QUINSON
Tourist office Rue de St-Esprit (Mon–Fri 9am–12.30pm & 1.30–5pm, Sat 9.30am–12.30pm; ☎04 92 74 01 12, ⓦquinson.fr).

RIEZ
By bus Riez has connections with Barjols (1 daily; 45min);

Marseille (2–3 daily; 2hr); Moustiers-Ste-Marie (2 daily; 20min).
Tourist office Place de la Marie (July & Aug Mon–Sat 10am–1pm & 3.30–7pm; June & Sept Tues–Sat 10am–12.30pm & 2.30–6pm; April & May Tues–Sat 10am–12.30pm & 2–5.30pm; Oct–March Wed 10am–noon & 1–5pm; ☎04 92 77 99 09, ⓦville-riez.fr).

ACCOMMODATION AND EATING

QUINSON
Relais Notre-Dame ☎04 92 74 40 01, ⓦrelaisnotre dame04.com. Just south of the prehistory museum, this appealing, old-fashioned hotel has simple, attractive en-suite rooms, while its restaurant (closed Mon eve & Tues) serves a €20.90 vegetarian *menu*, and others from €20 to €41, with outdoor seating across the main road above a sunflower field. Closed mid-Nov to March. **€88**

RIEZ
Rose de Provence Rue Edouard-Dauphin ☎04 92 77 75 45, ⓦrose-de-provence.com. This three-star campsite, across the river 400m southeast of the centre of Riez, is a good option. Facilities on offer include a trampoline, table tennis, *boules* and a very small heated pool. Closed Oct to March. **€24.90**

Digne-les-Bains

DIGNE-LES-BAINS, 42km north of Riez and the capital of the Alpes-de-Haute-Provence *département*, is a retirement spa that's by far the largest town in northeastern Provence. While it enjoys a superb location between the Durance Valley and the start of the real mountains, and holds some interesting **museums**, it's really not a holiday destination. Consisting of a couple of busy boulevards connecting yawningly empty squares, and a small network of faded lanes in the old town, it's best seen as a convenient overnight base.

5

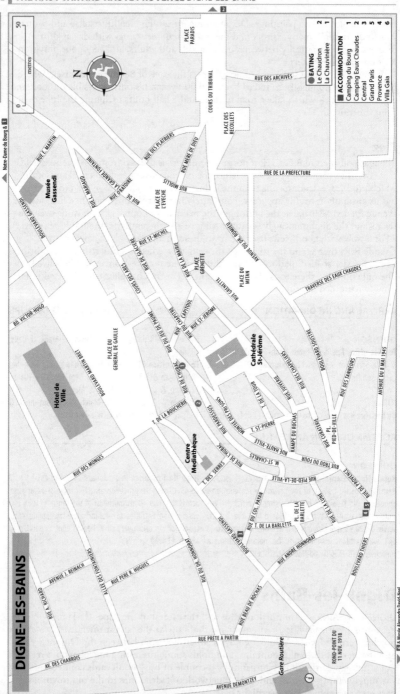

DIGNE-LES-BAINS

EATING
Le Chaudron 2
La Chauvinière 1

ACCOMMODATION
Camping du Bourg 1
Camping Eaux Chaudes 2
Central 3
Grand Paris 4
Provence 5
Villa Gaia 6

CHEMINS DE FER DE PROVENCE

Also known as the **Train des Pignes**, in honour of the pine cones originally used as fuel, the narrow-gauge **Chemins de Fer de Provence** connects Digne-les-Bains with Nice (see page 211), with stops including Annot and St-André-les-Alpes. It's a stupendous ride, with four trains daily covering the full route in 3hr 30min, for a one-way fare of €24. The scenery includes glittering rivers, lush dark-green forests, dramatic cliff faces and plunging gorges. For full details, see ⊚ trainprovence.com.

Wednesday and Saturday **markets** bring animation to the windswept **place Général-de-Gaulle**, north of the cathedral, with lavender products, including honey, in abundance.

Cathédrale St-Jérôme

Montée des Prisons • June–Oct Tues–Thurs & Sat 3–6pm

In the heart of medieval Digne, the **haute ville**, the fifteenth-century **Cathédrale St-Jérôme** has become weed-encrusted and dilapidated. Its Gothic facade is still impressive and the features inside, in particular the stained-glass windows, clearly indicate that this was once an awesome place of worship.

Musée Gassendi

64 bd Gassendi • Daily (except Tues): mid May–Sept 11am–7pm; Oct–mid May Mon & Wed–Fri 9–noon & 1.30–5.30pm, Sat–Sun 1.30–5.30pm • €6 • ☎ 04 92 31 45 29, ⊚ musee-gassendi.org

The **Musée Gassendi** commemorates seventeenth-century mathematician and astronomer **Pierre Gassendi**, who grew up in Digne. As well as displays on his life, it holds assorted, largely anonymous sixteenth- to nineteenth-century paintings, and skulls from a variety of animals from dromedaries to gorillas. The top floor is devoted to British sculptor **Andy Goldsworthy**, who from 1999 onwards created open-air sculptures in ruined structures along the ancient mountain footpaths hereabouts. Composed of cracked mud and hair, his *River of Earth* fills one enormous wall.

Musée Alexandra David-Néel

27 av du Maréchal Juin, 1.2km southwest of the centre • ☎ 04 92 31 32 38, ⊚ alexandra-david-neel.org

Exclusively dedicated to the memory of an extraordinary, tenacious explorer who spent more than fourteen years travelling the length and breadth of Tibet, the **Musée Alexandra David-Néel** (renovated in 2019) is where the redoubtable Ms David-Néel lived out the remainder of her life, eventually dying in 1969, aged 101. The house, only accessible on guided tours, is stuffed full of fascinating photographs tracing her journeys – she ran away from home for the first of countless times during her "cheerless" childhood at the age of 5, and blackened her face with lacquer to reach Lhasa in 1924 – as well as old Tibetan ornaments, masks and paintings.

ARRIVAL AND INFORMATION   DIGNE-LES-BAINS

By train The *gare Chemins de Fer de Provence* is on Av Pierre Sémard, on the west bank of the river, 750m southwest of the centre. A regular SNCF bus links it with the *gare SNCF* at St-Auban–Château-Arnoux (30min), on the Marseille–Sisteron line.

Destinations All services 4–5 daily: Annot (1hr 30min); Barrême (40min); Entrevaux (1hr 50min); Nice (3hr 15min); Puget-Théniers (2hr); St-André-des-Alpes (1hr).

By bus The *gare routière* is on Rond-point du 11 Novembre 1918.

Destinations Avignon (4 daily; 3hr 30min); Barcelonnette (2 daily; 1hr 30min); Castellane (2 daily; 1hr 10min); Marseille (4 daily; 2hr–2hr 30min); Nice (2 daily; 3hr 15min); Riez (2 daily; 1hr 15min); St-André-les-Alpes (2 daily; 1hr); Seyne-les-Alpes (2 daily; 40min); Sisteron (9 daily; 1hr 15min).

5

Tourist office Place du Tampinet (April–June & Sept–Oct Mon–Sat 9am–noon & 2–6pm, Sun 9.30am–noon & 2.30–4.30pm; July & Aug Mon–Sat 8.30am–12.30pm & 1.30–6.30pm, Sun 9.30am–noon & 2.30–4.30pm; Nov–March Mon–Fri 9am–noon & 2–5pm, Sat 9am–1pm; ☎04 92 36 62 62, ⓦot-dignelesbains.fr).

ACCOMMODATION   SEE MAP PAGE 212

Central 26 bd Gassendi ☎04 92 31 31 91, ⓦlhotel-central.com. Spacious, comfortable budget hotel, on a bustling street in the heart of town near the tourist office. The cheapest of its simple antique-furnished rooms lack en-suite facilities. €58

Grand Paris 19 bd Thiers ☎04 92 31 11 15, ⓦhotel-grand-paris.com. Seventeenth-century convent with large, tastefully decorated rooms, and a high-class gourmet restaurant (closed lunchtime Mon–Wed in low season), where excellent Provençal dinner *menus* start at €38. Breakfast is a hefty €17. Closed Dec–Feb. €110

Provence 17 bd Thiers ☎04 92 31 32 19, ⓦhotel-alpes-provence.com. Set back behind a garden courtyard, this renovated hotel, close to the centre, is bright and friendly, with cheerful if small en-suite rooms. Almost all are equipped with queen-sized double beds, but there's also one (very small) cheaper single. €64

Villa Gaia 24 rte de Nice ☎04 92 31 21 60, ⓦhotel-villagaia-digne.com. Stately, peaceful eighteenth-century country house, 3km southwest of the centre and offering ten very comfortable guest rooms of varying sizes, along with spa facilities. There's no public restaurant, but guests can have dinner for €26. Closed Nov to mid-April. €92

CAMPSITES

Camping du Bourg Rte de Barcelonnette ☎04 92 31 04 87, ⓦcampingdigne.com. Two-star municipal campsite, with a tennis court but no pool, 1.5km northeast of the centre along the D900 to Seynes-les-Alpes; follow Av Ste-Douceline left from the top of Bd Gassendi. Closed mid-Oct to March. €18.50

Camping Eaux Chaudes Av des Thermes ☎04 92 32 31 04, ⓦcampingleseauxchaudes.com. Pleasantly situated three-star campsite, 1km east of town towards the Établissement Thermal, with a couple of pools and entertainment in July and Aug. Closed Nov–March. €25.50

EATING   SEE MAP PAGE 212

★ **Le Chaudron** 40 rue de l'Hubac ☎04 92 31 24 87. This excellent old-town restaurant, run by a very friendly husband-and-wife team, offers pavement seating in summer and a cosy upstairs dining room in winter. The €31 dinner *menu* focuses on substantial baked dishes from their wood-fired oven. Mon, Tues & Fri–Sun noon–3pm & 7.30–10pm.

La Chauvinière 54 rue de l'Hubac ☎04 92 31 40 03. Intimate spot in the *haute ville*, serving traditional Provençal dishes on *menus* from €13.50 for lunch and from €28 for dinner. There's some outdoor seating on the terrace below the cathedral that's crammed with multicoloured parasols. Mon–Sat noon–2pm & 7–9pm.

Draguignan

DRAGUIGNAN, the main settlement of the inland Var, less than 30km northwest of the coast at Fréjus, is a bustling, if not particularly exciting, place that has a couple of worthwhile **museums**, a lively **market** on Wednesdays and Saturdays around place du Marché, and a striking **theatre**. Its boulevards and compact medieval centre hold enough moderately priced hotels and restaurants to make it a potential touring base.

Draguignan's compact old town is dominated by the distinctive seventeenth-century **Tour d'Horloge** (July & Aug guided tours only; free), which stands next to the twelfth-century Chapelle St-Sauveur atop a small hill just north of place du Marché.

Musée des Arts et Traditions Populaires de Moyenne Provence

75 place Georges Brassens • Tues–Sat 9am–noon & 2–6pm • €3.50 • ☎04 94 47 05 72, ⓦculture-dracenie.com

The **Musée des Arts et Traditions Populaires de Moyenne Provence**, in the old town, beautifully showcases the old industries of the Var. Nineteenth-century farming techniques and the manufacturing processes for silk, honey, cork, wine, olive oil and tiles are presented within the context of daily working lives, though some scenes are spoiled by rather dire wax models.

5

Musée Municipal

Rue de la République • Tues–Sat 10am–6pm • Free • ☎ 04 98 10 26 85

Highlights at the **Musée Municipal**, housed in a former bishop's palace, include a delicate marble sculpture by Camille Claudel; Greuze's *Portrait of a Young Girl*; two paintings of Venice by Ziem; a Renoir; and, upstairs in the library, a copy of the *Romance of the Rose* and early Bibles and maps.

Rembrandt's *Child with a Soap Bubble*, stolen from the museum in 1999, was finally recovered in 2014, when an alarm-systems technician finally confessed to having kept it on his desk at home for the previous fifteen years.

ARRIVAL   DRAGUIGNAN

By bus The *gare routière* at the bottom of Bd Gabriel-Péri, main Marseilles to Nice line at Les Arcs, 12km south. south of the centre is connected by shuttle bus with the Destinations Les Arcs (every 30min; 20min).

INFORMATION

Tourist office 2 av Lazare Carnot (July & Aug Mon–Sat 9am–12.30pm; Oct–May Mon–Fri 9am–12.30pm & 1.30–9am–12.30pm & 2.30–6pm, Sun 9.30am–12.30pm; 5pm, Sat 9am–12.30pm; ☎ 04 98 10 51 05, ⓦ tourisme-June & Sept Mon–Fri 9am–12.30pm & 2.30–6pm, Sat dracenie.com).

ACCOMMODATION AND EATING

Camping La Foux Quartier de la Foux ☎ 04 94 68 18 27, ⓦ camping-lafoux.com. This two-star campsite, 2km south towards Les Arcs, stays open year-round, and has a bar, restaurant and even mini-golf as well as a good pool complex. €24

Le Domino 28 av Carnot ☎ 04 94 67 15 33, ⓦ ledomino. fr. Fine old antique-furnished townhouse in which two pretty B&B rooms upstairs overlook the courtyard garden. Downstairs, a good restaurant (closed Sun & Mon) serves an eclectic mix of Provençal staples and world cuisines, on *menus* that start at €14 for lunch. €75

★ **La Musar'Dine** 93 chemin du Coutelet ☎ 06 88 18 50 82, ⓦ lamusardine.wordpress.com. A rare vegetarian restaurant ten minutes' walk north from the town centre but well worth the trek. Expect a vibrant array of tarts, salads

and seasonal veg all lovingly prepared from scratch, served in the delightful shady terrace. (€18 lunch, €28 dinner). Reservation essential: Daily noon–2pm & 7–9pm.

Table de Martine 18 place du Marché ☎ 04 94 68 00 09. Friendly, relaxed restaurant, with tables out on the pedestrianized street, and offering vegetarian dishes such as courgette-flower *beignets* as well as fish and meat specialities like the €24 *assiette cannibal* of carpaccio and steak tartare. Lunchtime *plats* €11, dinner *menus* from €24.50. Mon, Tues & Thurs–Sat 11.30am–3pm & 7–11pm, Sun 11.30am–3pm.

Victoria 52 av Carnot ☎ 04 94 47 24 12, ⓦ hotel-victoria-draguignan.com. Central, somewhat dated belle époque hotel, with a garden. It's on a main road, so for a quieter night, ask for a room at the back. €66

North and east of Draguignan

Of the two principal routes onwards and upwards from Draguignan, the **D955** heads north towards the mighty Grand Canyon du Verdon (see page 219), with the dramatic **Gorges de Châteaudouble** as a foretaste of the scenic splendours ahead, while the **D562** sets off northeast towards Grasse, with several medieval villages as potential detours along the way.

Between January and June, in the wonderful, almost uninhabited expanse of forest south of the D562, you may see untended cattle with bells round their necks and sheep chewing away at the undergrowth. That these animals are once more roaming the former pasturing grounds of the transhumance routes has great ecological benefits in maintaining the diversity of the forest.

Châteaudouble

Beyond the exquisitely peaceful village of **Rebouillon**, beside the River Nartuby 5km northwest of Draguignan along the D955, the scenery changes dramatically with the start of the **Gorges de Châteaudouble**. A mere scratch it may be, compared to the great Verdon gorge, but it holds some impressive sites, not least the village of **CHÂTEAUDOUBLE** hanging high above the cliffs. Nostradamus predicted that the river would grind away at the base until the village fell, but has yet to be proved right. All but deserted out of season, Châteaudouble consists of little more than a couple of churches, a handful of houses, a potter's workshop, a beekeeper and his hives, and a ruined tower and ramparts.

Callas

The village of **CALLAS**, 15km northeast of Draguignan, can be reached by turning left onto the D525 12km along the road to Grasse. It's an agreeable place to stop for lunch or spend the night, with a lovely square by the church at its highest point.

Bargemon

The steep, narrow D25 climbs through luscious valleys for 6km north of Callas before reaching the charming village of **BARGEMON**. Two immovable obstacles, an old stone fountain and a large plane tree, stand a few metres apart on the main road through; with no apparent rule as to whether either or both constitutes any kind of traffic roundabout, this little stretch does, however, form a de facto village centre, with considerable fun to be had watching from the pavement cafés as the vehicles attempt to duck and dive their way through. The ancient core of the village is immediately south, a small tangle of pedestrianized streets tucked away behind fortified gateways, while the bars and restaurants along the commercial street are kept busy in summer by throngs of well-heeled expats. Bargemon is an exclusive residential district, chosen by no less than David and Victoria Beckham as the site of their Provençal retreat. It's especially picturesque in spring, when the streets are filled with orange petals and mimosa blossom.

Musée-galerie Honoré Camos

Chapelle St-Étienne • June–Sept Wed–Sun 3.30–7pm • Free • ☎ 04 94 76 72 88

The eleventh-century Chapelle St-Étienne, outside the walled core alongside the village's small market square, houses the **Musée-galerie Honoré Camos**. As well as displays on local history, it hosts exhibitions of local painters, with a permanent collection of works by Honoré Camos himself (1906–91). The two angel heads on its high altar are attributed to the great Marseillais sculptor Pierre Puget.

Seillans

The village of **SEILLANS**, 13km east of Bargemon along the minor D19, consists of the diminutive, very picturesque *vieux village*, shielded behind medieval walls from a sprawl of modern villas. The Romanesque **Chapelle de Notre Dame de l'Ormeau**, 1km along the road to Fayence beyond, holds a wonderful Renaissance altarpiece, attributed to an inspired Italian monk; for details of guided tours, contact Seillans' tourist office (see page 218).

Collection Tanning-Ernst

Rue de l'Église • Mon–Sat 2.30–6.30pm, Sun 2.30–5.45pm • €3.50 • ☎ 04 94 76 85 91

Seillans was home to the painter **Max Ernst** (1891–1976) in his final years. He moved here in 1953, five years after marrying fellow artist **Dorothea Tanning**, whom he met after seeing her Surrealist and mildly erotic self-portrait, *Birthday*.

The three-storey **Collection Tanning-Ernst** displays that painting, along with some lesser-known lithographs by Ernst himself, and even a mirrored bed (complete with a mink bedspread) that he designed.

5

Mons

The hilltop village of **MONS**, 14km northeast of Seillans via the D53 and D563, is perched close to the highest spot in the Var. It's a very pretty little place, where the views from the open square at the southern end are said to stretch all the way to Corsica, and while there's nothing very specific to see, it's well worth a stop.

Fayence

Larger and livelier than its neighbours, **FAYENCE**, 6km east of Seillans, was known to the Romans as Favienta Loca (favourable place), and its modern charm lies in the contrast between its small-town bustle and the peaceful traffic-free side streets spilling over with flowers. The *vieille ville* curls tightly around the steep slopes of a hill. The imposing porchway of the *mairie* guards its entrance, while a fourteenth-century gateway, the **Porte Sarrazine**, plus the inevitable ateliers and souvenir shops, lie beyond. A **market** fills place de l'Église on Tuesdays, Thursdays and Saturdays.

ARRIVAL AND INFORMATION   NORTH AND EAST OF DRAGUIGNAN

SEILLANS
Tourist office Place du Thouron, beneath the Ernst exhibition (Mid Sept–mid June Mon–Fri 10am–12.30pm & 2.30–5.30pm, Sat 2.30–5.30pm; mid June–mid Sept Mon–Sat 10am–12.30pm & 2.30–6.30pm, Sun 2.30–5.45pm; ☎ 04 94 76 85 91, ⓦ seillans.fr).

FAYENCE
By bus Buses stop on the central place Léon-Roux.

Destinations St Raphaël (Mon–Sat 3 daily; 1hr 20min).
Tourist office Place Léon-Roux (mid-April to mid-June Mon–Sat 9am–noon & 2–6pm; mid-June to mid-Sept Mon–Sat 9am–12.30pm & 2–6.30pm, Sun 10am–noon; mid-Sept to mid-April Mon–Sat 9am–noon & 2–5.30pm; ☎ 04 94 76 20 08, ⓦ ville-fayence.fr).
Bookshop Librairie du Château, 1 rue St-Pierre, sells local guides and maps in English (Tues–Sat 9.30am–12.15pm & 2.15–7pm, Sun 9.30am–12.15pm; ☎ 04 94 84 72 00).

ACCOMMODATION AND EATING

CHÂTEAUDOUBLE
La Tour Place Beausoleil ☎ 04 94 70 93 08, ⓦ latour-chateaudouble.eresto.net. There's food to match the stunning location at this restaurant on the verdant central square, with a terrace overlooking the gorge, and satisfying Provençal *menus* from €27. Mon, Tues & Thurs–Sat noon–1.30pm & 7–9pm, Sun noon–1.30pm; closed evenings in winter.

CALLAS
Résidence Mart'ins 23 rue St-Eloi ☎ 06 07 45 92 56. Tiny, inexpensive B&B, adjoining the shaded place Georges-Clemenceau. **€60**
Hostellerie des Gorges de Pennafort On the D25, below the D525 ☎ 04 94 76 66 51, ⓦ hostellerie-pennafort.com. Grand hotel-restaurant, overlooking the Pennafort waterfalls 7km south of Callas, with its own heliport, pool, lake and olive grove. The restaurant (closed Mon, plus Tues lunch, Wed lunch & Sun eve) spreads across a huge outdoor terrace; *menus* range from €63 to a tear inducing €170. Closed mid-Jan to mid-March. **€210**

BARGEMON
★ **La Campana** 25 rue de la Résistance ☎ 04 94 76 63 15. Lively Provençal restaurant, with pavement

seating alongside the main street, which centres on an old-fashioned wood-burning oven and serves an aromatic and irresistible à la carte array of €8–10 starters like baked mussels or avocado and salmon salad, and €15–18 grilled or roasted meat and fish dishes. Daily (except Thurs) noon–2pm & 7.30–9.30pm.
Maison Fontaines 6 rue Morceau ☎ 04 94 47 84 11, ⓦ maisonfontaines.com. Bargemon holds no hotels, but this friendly and arty Dutch-owned B&B, in a blue-shuttered townhouse a few steps north of the old town, offers two spacious, stylish and homely rooms. Rates include a delicious and substantial breakfast. **€100**

SEILLANS
★ **Les Deux Rocs** 1 place Font-d'Amont ☎ 04 94 76 87 32, ⓦ hoteldeuxrocs.com. Exquisitely restored hotel in a townhouse by the old washhouse, opposite the two eponymous rocks on a little fountained square. It's a great place both to stay and to eat, with beautiful antiques, warm decor, and *menus* that range from €23 (lunch) to €52 (restaurant closed Sun eve, all Mon, & Tues lunch). Closed mid-Nov to mid-March. **€80**
★ **Gloire de Mon Père** Place du Thouron ☎ 04 94 60 18 65, ⓦ lagloiredemonpere.fr. Delightful restaurant,

almost filling the tiny square that squeezes between the tourist office and the village walls, and serving delicious Provençal food on dinner *menus* from €32 plus vegetarian options from €11. Daily (except Wed) noon–2pm & 7–9.30pm.

MONS

★ **Le Petit Bonheur** 1 place Frederic Mistral ☎ 04 94 76 38 09. Offering a good €23 *menu* of local specialities within the tastefully restored stone and timber restaurant or outside on a charming little square, where an ancient fountain serves to chill the wines. Tues–Sat 9am–3pm & 6–9pm.

FAYENCE

Camping Lou Cantaire D562 ☎ 04 94 76 23 77, ⓦ camping-lou-cantaire.fr. Three-star campsite in wooded surroundings 5km southwest of Fayence towards Draguignan, with a couple of pools plus, in July and Aug, kids' activities and evening entertainment. Closed mid-Oct to mid-March. **€34.80**

Farigoulette 1 place du Château ☎ 04 94 84 10 49. Peaceful restaurant, in a former stable at the top of the village, serving tasty traditional *menus* from €19 for lunch, €29 for dinner. Mon & Thurs–Sat noon–1.45pm & 7–9.30pm, plus Tues 7–9.30pm mid July–mid Aug.

Moulin de la Camandoule Chemin de Notre-Dame-des-Cyprès ☎ 04 94 76 00 84, ⓦ camandoule.com. English-owned converted mill, 1km northwest of town, which offers a dozen tasteful and comfortable rooms in really special surroundings. Their top-notch restaurant, *L'Escourtin*, serves *menus* from €26.50 at lunch, €39 at dinner (Sept–June closed Mon eve, all day Tues & Wed lunch). **€138**

Les Oliviers 18 av St-Christophe ☎ 04 94 76 13 12, ⓦ lesoliviersfayence.fr. Straightforward, friendly little modern hotel, just below Fayence on the D19, with clean a/c rooms plus a nice garden and pool, and a bar but no restaurant. **€96**

Provençal 6 rue Camille Laroute ☎ 04 94 76 24 91. Friendly restaurant with attached deli, perched just above the market square below the main road. Lunch *menus* featuring vibrant salads and roast beef for €18 are served beneath the shade of a plane tree. Daily 12.30–2.30pm & 7am–9pm; closed Nov–March.

Grand Canyon du Verdon

Europe's widest and deepest gorge, the breathtaking **Grand Canyon du Verdon** – a V-shaped chasm also known as the **Gorges du Verdon** – cuts a 21km-long east–west swathe through the limestone foothills of the Alps. Peppered with spectacular viewpoints, plunging crevices up to 700m deep, and glorious azure-blue lakes, the area is absolutely irresistible; try not to leave Provence without spending at least a day here. The river falls from **Rougon** at the eastern end of the gorge, disappears into tunnels, decelerates for shallow languid moments, and finally exits in full flow at the **Pont de Galetas** to fill the huge artificial **Lac de Ste-Croix**.

The main overnight bases near the canyon are the villages of **Moustiers-Ste-Marie** and **Aiguines** at its western end; the even smaller community of **La Palud-sur-Verdon** halfway along the north rim; and the larger town of **Castellane** beyond its eastern end.

With so many hairpin bends and twisting, narrow roads, it takes a full, rather exhausting day to **drive** right around the canyon, particularly in the fearsome midsummer traffic. The entire circuit being 130km long, many visitors choose instead to explore just one rim, along either the **Route des Crêtes** on the north side or the **Corniche Sublime** to the south. This is **cycling** country only for the preternaturally fit, but **walking** is the ideal way to explore; the best trails start on the northern side (see page 221).

Before you hike in the gorge itself, get details of the route and advice on **weather conditions**. You'll also need water, a torch for the tunnels, and warm clothing for the cold shadows in the narrow corridors of rock. Always stick to the path and don't cross the river except at the *passerelles (*footbridges); water levels change very abruptly when the dams open upstream (☎04 92 83 62 68 for recorded information), and drownings can and do occur.

Moustiers-Ste-Marie

The loveliest village on the fringes of the gorge, **MOUSTIERS-STE-MARIE** occupies a magnificent site near its western end. Set high on a hillside, 7km north of Lac de Ste-

GRAND CANYON DU VERDON

Croix but just out of sight of both canyon and lake, it straddles a plummeting stream that cascades between two golden cliffs. A star slung between the cliffs on a chain – the original incarnation of which was hung here by a returning Crusader – completes the perfect picture.

Not surprisingly, Moustiers gets very crowded in summer, when visitors throng its winding lanes and pretty bridges, and fill the many shops and galleries that sell the traditional local speciality, **glazed pottery**.

Coming here out of season is more of an unalloyed pleasure, but you can escape the commercialism year-round by puffing your way up to the aptly named chapel of **Notre Dame de Beauvoir**, high above the village proper. It's reached by a footpath along which the stone steps have been polished slippery-smooth by centuries of pilgrims' feet. The most direct route, from the east side of the village, takes around fifteen minutes each way; a longer path loops up from the west. Both are best tackled in the shade of the morning.

Musée de la Faïence

Hôtel de Ville, rue du Seigneur de la Clue • Mid-March to June, Sept & Oct daily except Tues 10am–12.30pm & 2–6pm; July & Aug daily except Tues 10am–12.30pm & 2–7pm; Nov & Dec Sat & Sun 2–5pm • €3 • ☎ 04 92 74 61 64, ⓦ moustiers.eu

Moustiers has been renowned for ceramics since the seventeenth century. Faïence (colourful tin-glazed earthenware) was first manufactured in Provence four hundred years earlier, but the art reached its apogee in Moustiers during the reign of Louis XIV. The story is told in the small but fascinating **Musée de la Faïence**, filled with spectacular examples, on the east side of the stream.

Lac de Ste-Croix

At the canyon's western end, the river emerges abruptly into the enormous turquoise reservoir of the **Lac de Ste-Croix**. From the Pont de Galetas, where the D957 crosses the river, you can often see river rafts rounding the final bend of the gorge. At **beaches** immediately north and south, rowing boats and pedalos are available to rent; when no floodgates are open, the waters are placid enough to set off upstream between the cliffs. **Swimming** is also good here, though when the lake levels are low, things can get a bit muddy around the edges.

The north rim

The spectacular and tortuous D952 runs more or less parallel to the north bank of the Verdon river for 45km east from Moustiers to Castellane. For the best close-up views of the gorge, however, head south along the **Route des Crêtes** from the village of **La Palud-sur-Verdon** halfway along.

La Palud-sur-Verdon

Peace, tranquillity and breathtaking scenery reign supreme in the principal pit stop along the northern rim, **LA PALUD-SUR-VERDON**, 20km southeast of Moustiers. Even if you're just passing through, take the time to wander around its narrow, rambling streets and pause for a meal or drink. Out of season, the village all but closes down.

Route des Crêtes

To admire the very best of the Gorges du Verdon, detour off the D952 onto the dramatic **Route des Crêtes**, which loops away both from the centre of La Palud, and from another intersection a short distance east. Along its 23km circuit, it offers a succession of stunning canyon viewpoints. There's nothing to stop you driving straight off into the abyss on its highest stretches, and at some points you look down a sheer 800m drop to the sliver of water below. As the middle section of the Route des Crêtes

5

GRAND CANYON DU VERDON ACTIVITIES

Outfitters and guides based around the gorge offer activities of all kinds. Most operate in summer only, between April and September. For general **information**, contact the Parc Naturel Régional du Verdon (ⓦparcduverdon.fr).

Only attempt to **canoe** or **raft** the full length of the gorge if you are very experienced and strong; you'll have to carry your craft for long stretches. However, you can pay (in the region of €35 for 2hr, €75 for a full day) to join a group and tackle certain stretches of the river. No trips take place during hydroelectric operations, so be prepared for disappointment.

MULTI-ACTIVITY OPERATORS

UCPA La Palud ⓣ04 92 77 30 13, ⓦucpa-vacances. com. Climbing, walking, cycling, canoeing and canyoning with trained guides.

Verdon Passion Moustiers ⓣ06 08 63 97 16, ⓦverdon-passion.com. Canyoning, climbing and paragliding.

WALKING AND CLIMBING

Des Guides pour l'Aventure La Palud ⓣ06 85 94 46 61, ⓦguidesaventure.com. Professional walking guides, rock climbers and canyoneers.

Maison des Guides du Verdon La Palud ⓣ04 92 77 30 50, ⓦescalade-verdon.fr. Association of professional guides for walks, canyoning and rock climbing.

Le Perroquet Vert La Palud ⓣ04 92 77 33 39, ⓦleperroquetvert.com. Climbing shop and *chambres d'hôtes* (see page 224).

WATERSPORTS

Aboard Rafting Castellane ⓣ04 92 83 76 11, ⓦaboard-rafting.com. Water-based activities including rafting, canoeing, canyoning, hydrospeeding and water rambling.

Raft Session Castellane ⓣ07 63 63 69 50, ⓦraft session.com. Rafting, canoeing, canyoning and aquatic hiking (where you walk, wade and swim along the gorge).

CYCLING

Location E-Bike 04 Impasse de notre Dame, St-André les Alpes ⓣ06 72 92 63 40, ⓦebike04.fr. Cycle rental with itineraries around Saint André les Alpes and also Castellane.

BUNGEE JUMPING

Latitude Challenge Marseille ⓣ04 91 09 04 10, ⓦlatitude-challenge.fr. Bungee jumps from the 182m Pont de l'Artuby.

is one-way (westbound only), you have to start from the more scenic eastern end to see it all. The road closes each winter from November 15 to March 15.

For **walkers**, the best descent to the river itself starts at La Maline, halfway along. Hiking down, then following the Verdon on the **Sentier Martel** footpath and climbing back up at **Point Sublime**, near Rougon on the D952, takes seven hours, and is best done as part of a guided group.

Unaccompanied shorter excursions into the canyon include the relatively easy **Sentier du Lézard**, marked from Point Sublime. Alternative routes, ranging from thirty minutes to four hours, offer the chance to pass through the **Couloir Samson**, a 670m tunnel with occasional "windows", and a stairway down to the chaotic sculpture of the riverbanks.

Rougon

Immediately opposite Point Sublime, at a sharp, blind curve in the D952, a narrow side road doubles back up from the main road, away from the river. It takes three sinuous kilometres to snake its way up to the hilltop village of **ROUGON**, a lovely little place that feels very far removed from the summer crowds. Assorted café and restaurant terraces offer extraordinary views out over the canyon, surrounded by majestic cliffs and stark karst crags straight from some Chinese scroll painting.

The south rim

The aptly named **Corniche Sublime**, delineating the southern rim of the Grand Canyon du Verdon, is every bit as dramatic as its northern counterpart. The precarious but exhilarating D71 follows its entire course, starting at **Aiguines** at its western end, and eventually meeting the D955 up from Draguignan at **Comps-sur-Artuby**.

Aiguines

AIGUINES, perched at the western end of the Corniche Sublime 30km north of Aups, is a charming village that effectively consists of a single long promenade high above the Lac de Ste-Croix. Sadly, its château, a confection of pepperpot towers that dazzle with their coloured tiles, is not open to the public.

Musée des Tourneurs sur Bois

Place de la Résistance • May, June, Sept & Oct Mon–Thurs 10am–6pm, Fri 10am–4pm, Sun by reservation only; July & Aug daily 10.30am–6.30pm; Nov–April by request only • €3.50 • ☎ 04 94 70 99 17, ⓦ museedestourneurssurbois.com

The interesting little **Musée des Tourneurs sur Bois**, tucked into the mall-like building that also holds the tourist office, is devoted to the craft of **wood-turning**. The local speciality here lay in transforming ancient boxwood roots into *boules* for *pétanque*; the museum holds the entire workshop of the village's last traditional craftsman, who retired in 1978. Several shops nearby sell rather beautiful wooden souvenirs and utensils.

Along the Corniche Sublime

The **Corniche Sublime** itself was built expressly to provide jaw-dropping and hair-raising views. Drivers with any fear of heights – and of course their passengers – are best advised not to come this way.

The most spectacular viewpoint of all comes towards its eastern end, 24km along from Aiguines. Overlooking the **Balcons de la Mescla**, it's a memorable *coup de théâtre*. As the view is withheld until you are almost upon it, the 250m drop at your feet comes as a visceral body blow. Beyond the Balcons, the D71 plummets southeast for its final 16km down to Comps, descending through end-of-the-earth heath and hills.

Comps-sur-Artuby

The isolated settlement of **COMPS-SUR-ARTUBY** stands 20km north along the D955 from Châteaudouble (see page 216), beyond the increasingly bleak military camp of Canjuers. Though the surrounding scenery is magnificent, the village itself holds few specific sights, other than the fortified chapel of **St André**.

Castellane

Huddled at the foot of a sheer 180m cliff, the grey and rather severe-looking town of **CASTELLANE** now serves as a gateway for visitors to the **Gorges du Verdon**, 17km southwest. In summer, thanks to its wide range of restaurants, hotels and cafés, it enjoys an animation rare in these parts.

Houses in Castellane's *vieille ville* are packed close together; some lanes are barely shoulder wide. A footpath from behind the parish church on place de l'Église winds its way up to the chapel of **Notre Dame du Roc** atop the cliff. Less demanding than it might appear, the path soon passes the machicolated **Tour Pentagonal**, standing uselessly on the lower slopes. Twenty to thirty minutes should see you at the top; you won't actually see the gorge, but there's a pretty good view of the river disappearing into it and the mountains circling the town.

GETTING AROUND GRAND CANYON DU VERDON

By bus Public transport connections are poor. You can find timetables on ⓦ lapaludsurverdon.com, but broadly speaking there's one bus between Marseille, Aix, Riez, Moustiers, La Palud, Rougon and Castellane (July & Aug Mon–Sat; Sept–June Mon & Sat only). Two daily buses also stop at Castellane en route between Gap and Digne to the northwest, and Grasse and Nice to the southeast.

INFORMATION

MOUSTIERS-STE-MARIE

Parc Naturel Régional du Verdon For information on the gorge, visit the park office, Domaine de Valx (☎ 04 92 74 68 00, ⓦ parcduverdon.fr).

Tourist office Place de l'Église (March, Oct & Nov daily 10am–12.30pm & 2–5.30pm; April–May 10am–12.30pm & 2–6pm; June & Sept 9.30am–12.30pm & 2–6pm; July & Aug Mon–Fri 9.30am–7pm, Sat & Sun 9.30am–12.30pm & 2–7pm; Dec–Feb daily 10am–12.30pm & 2–5pm; ☎ 04 92 74 67 84, ⓦ moustiers.fr).

LA PALUD-SUR-VERDON

Bureau des Guides Grande Rue (hours erratic; daily in summer, weekends only otherwise; ☎ 04 92 77 30 50, ⓦ escalade-verdon.fr); the best place to find out about guided walks, climbing, canyoning, rafting and other activities.

Tourist office The Maison des Gorges du Verdon, in the central château, incorporates the tourist office and holds displays on the gorge (daily except Tues: mid-March to mid-June & mid-Sept to mid-Nov 10am–noon & 4–6pm; mid-June to mid-July & mid-Aug to mid-Sept 10am–1pm & 4–7pm; mid-July to mid-Aug 9am–1pm & 3–7pm; ☎ 04 92 77 32 02, ⓦ lapaludsurverdon.com & ⓦ lapalud-verdontourisme.com).

AIGUINES

Tourist office Allées de Tilleul (July & Aug Mon–Fri 9.30am–6pm, Sat & Sun 10am–noon & 2–5pm; Sept–June Mon–Fri 9am–12.30pm; ☎ 04 94 70 21 64, ⓦ aiguines.fr).

CASTELLANE

Tourist office Rue Nationale (May, June & Sept Mon–Sat 9am–noon & 2–6pm, Sun 9.30am–12.30pm; July & Aug daily 9am–6.30pm; Oct–April Mon–Sat 10am–noon & 2–5pm; ☎ 04 92 83 61 14, ⓦ castellane-verdontourisme.com).

ACCOMMODATION AND EATING

MOUSTIERS-STE-MARIE

Bastide de Moustiers Chemin de Quinson ☎ 04 92 70 47 47, ⓦ bastide-moustiers.com. Moustiers' most luxurious accommodation, beside the main D952 just below the village, and run by celebrity chef Alain Ducasse. Each of the dozen exquisite rooms has its own theme, there's a herb garden, a helipad in the grounds, and the restaurant offers weekday *menus* at a (relatively) modest €65. Closed Nov–Feb, plus Tues & Wed in low season. **€360**

Clerissy Place du Chevalier du Blacas ☎ 04 92 74 62 67. Thriving pavement pizzeria and crêperie offering non-stop service during hot summer days. The wood fired pizzas start at a very palatable €8. Daily noon–2.30pm & 7–9.30pm, all day in summer.

Le Colombier Quartier St-Michel ☎ 04 92 74 66 02, ⓦ le-colombier.com. Very comfortable, good-value hotel on the main road, 600m below the village. The cheapest rooms are in the older original building, with larger and fancier options in a motel-style annexe, and there's a pleasant garden and pool, but no restaurant. Closed Nov–March. **€85**

Domaine du Petit-Lac Rte des Salles sur Verdon ☎ 04 92 74 67 11, ⓦ lepetitlac.com. Two-star campsite, beside the eponymous "little lake" halfway along the D957 between Moustiers and the Lac de St-Croix. Nice shaded sites, a bar/restaurant in July and Aug, and lots of family-oriented activities, including canoeing and mini-golf. Closed early Oct to late April. **€27**

Le Grignotière Rte de Ste-Anne ☎ 04 92 74 69 12. Escape the summer crowds by climbing just above the east side of the village to this delightful courtyard restaurant; as dusk falls, it's a haven of calm. Hearty salads for around €15, a daily *plat* for €17.50, grilled meats and fish for €19. 12.15–1.45pm & 7.15–9pm, closed all Mon & Tues lunch.

★ **Hotel-Café du Relais** ☎ 04 92 74 66 10, ⓦ lerelais-moustiers.com. Central hotel in a great location beside the main bridge, where the lovely upgraded rooms have modern bathrooms. The views are fantastic, and the brasserie serves good Provençal dishes, with a €15 lunch *formule* and dinner *menus* from €35, on a *belle époque*-style terrace overlooking the stream. Closed Nov–March, plus Tues except in July & Aug. **€90**

LA PALUD-SUR-VERDON

Auberge de Jeunesse Rte de la Maline ☎ 04 92 77 38 72, ⓦ fuaj.org. Beautifully sited, nicely modernized hostel, poised on the hillside 500m south of the village, offering beds in rooms that sleep from two to six. Rates include breakfast. Closed Sept to early April. **€21.50**

Camping Municipal Rte de Castellane ☎ 04 92 77 38 13, ⓦ camping.lapaludsurverdon.com. Two-star municipal campsite, 800m east of the village along the D952. Minimal facilities, but it's a nice setting. No reservations necessary. Closed Oct–March. **€15**

Hôtel & Spa des Gorges du Verdon Rte de la Maline ☎ 04 92 77 38 26, ⓦ hotel-des-gorges-du-verdon.fr. Smart, very comfortable and beautifully isolated, this luxurious hotel is an unlikely but welcome presence, 500m along the Rte des Crêtes from the village, just a few minutes' walk from the trails down into the gorge. Closed late Oct to early April. **€225**

Perroquet Vert Grande Rue ☎ 04 92 77 33 39, ⓦ leperroquetvert.com. This central townhouse B&B offers

three plain but comfortable bedrooms and serves as a shop-rendezvous for climbers and walkers. Closed Nov–March. **€60**
Le Provence Rte de la Maline ☎ 04 92 77 38 88. Good-value ivy-covered hotel, in a panoramic location 100m below the village, beside the Rte des Crêtes. Its large courtyard garden offers pleasant dappled shade; the perfect place to wind down over a cool drink from the bar. Rates include breakfast. Closed Dec–March. **€95**

ROUGON

Le Mur des Abeilles Eastern end of village ☎ 04 92 83 76 33. Walk right through Rougon to reach this delightful crêperie-café, where the tables on the garden terrace enjoy sublime long-range views of the canyon. Substantial crêpes cost €5.50–10, and they offer other snacks and drinks. Easter–Oct daily 10am–6pm.

AIGUINES

Altitude 823 Grande Rue ☎ 04 98 10 22 17. The best of the nine rooms in this small hotel-restaurant, at the hairpin bend where the main road reaches the centre, enjoy far-reaching views down to the lake. Breakfast is €7. Closed Nov to mid-March. **€66**
Camping Le Galetas Quartier Vernis ☎ 04 94 70 20 48. Aiguines' large and rather plain municipal campsite is a long way down from the village, almost within diving distance of the lake. Closed mid-Oct to March. **€15.50**
Hôtel du Grand Canyon du Verdon Falaise des Cavaliers ☎ 04 94 76 91 31, ⊛ hotel-canyon-verdon.com. Perched atop a dramatic precipice on the Corniche Sublime, 20km east of Aiguines, with superb views, this rather faded, old-fashioned hotel makes a great overnight stop – so long as you don't suffer from vertigo. The restaurant (closed Tues eve & Wed except July & Aug) serves good meals on *menus* from €25. Rates are for compulsory *demi-pension*. Closed Nov–March. **€85**
Le Vieux Château Place de la Fontaine ☎ 04 94 70 22 95, ⊛ hotelvieuxchateau.fr. Appealing *Logis de France* hotel, housed in an eighteenth-century coaching inn in the heart of the village, with bright, albeit simple rooms and a

nice terrace bar and restaurant that serves a €17 *menu* and a decent €13 *plat du jour*, such as beef casserole or trout. Closed Nov–March. **€85**

COMPS-SUR-ARTUBY

Grand Hotel Bain Av de Fayet ☎ 04 94 76 90 06, ⊛ grand-hotel-bain.fr. Nice old ochre-painted hotel-restaurant in the heart of town, with old-fashioned but cosy rooms, a reasonable restaurant serving *menus* from €18.50 for lunch, €20 for dinner, at pavement tables, and a sunny garden. **€68**

CASTELLANE

Camping Frédéric Mistral 12 av Frédéric-Mistral ☎ 04 92 83 62 27, ⊛ camping-frederic-mistral.fr. Small, well-shaded campsite, close to the river just 100m west of the central place Marcel Sauvaire. While hardly a rural idyll, it's very convenient for the town itself. Closed mid-Nov to Feb. **€32**
★ **Commerce** Place Marcel Sauvaire ☎ 04 92 83 61 00, ⊛ hotel-du-commerce-verdon.com. Comfortable and very central, Castellane's finest hotel holds modernized rooms that sleep up to four, plus a delightful patio, garden and pool out back. Closed Nov–Feb. **€100**
Domaine du Verdon ☎ 04 92 83 61 29, ⊛ camp-du-verdon.com. Leafy four-star campsite, 1.5km west of town, which has several pools, including one with big water slides; a restaurant and bar; and a small fishing lake. Closed mid-Sept to mid-May. **€50**
★ **Gîte Chasteuil** Chasteuil ☎ 04 92 83 72 45, ⊛ chasteuil.com. Beautiful five-room B&B, enjoying spectacular mountain views from its hillside perch in the hamlet of Chasteuil, north of the D952 7km west of Castellane, and reached by a very steep minor road with eleven switchbacks. One room has a kitchenette for guests' use and the owners will prepare picnics for €11. **€82**
Hôtel du Roc 3 place de l'Église ☎ 04 92 83 62 65, ⊛ hotel-du-roc.fr. Friendly and very inexpensive hotel on the main square, with simple but pleasant rooms and a restaurant that serves conventional *menus* from €15, with a smattering of Portuguese dishes. Closed Oct to mid-April. **€65**

SHOPPING

MOUSTIERS-STE-MARIE

La Chaîne Rte du Seigneur de la Clue ☎ 04 92 74 63 45, ⊛ moustiers-faiences.com. Irresistible ceramics shop,

selling beautiful and affordable faïence (glazed pottery) manufactured using original seventeenth- and eighteenth-century techniques. Daily 10am–7pm.

Lac de Castillon and around

Following the D955 north of Castellane brings you after 5km to the southern shore of the 100m-deep **Lac de Castillon**, created by one of the many hydroelectric projects that harvest the awesome power of the River Verdon. Slightly milky and an unearthly shade of aquamarine, the Lac de Castillon is a popular bathing spot in high summer,

5

with closely supervised **beaches**, **boats** for rent, and opportunities for **waterskiing**. At its southern tip, the D955 crosses the awe-inspiring **Barrage de Castillon**, where there's a small parking area, though bathing is forbidden. The gleam of gold in the hills above the opposite bank is the Buddhist centre of Mandarom.

With good train and road access, plenty of accommodation in the Alpine village of **St-André-des-Alpes** as well as Castellane (see page 223), and well-organized facilities for outdoor activities, this is an easy corner of Haute Provence to explore. Traditional Provence is never far away, as the sight of sheep taking over the roads en route to or from their summer pastures may remind you.

St-Julien-du-Verdon

The village of **ST-JULIEN-DU-VERDON**, 5km north of the Barrage de Castillon, was a casualty of the creation of the lake. Today it's a tiny place, with nothing to suggest that this was once Sanctus Julienetus, on the Roman road from Nice to Digne. Still, it's an appealing, quiet spot if you just want to laze about by calm water with a gorgeous mountain backdrop.

St-André-les-Alpes

Unlike so many tightly huddled Provençal villages, **ST-ANDRÉ-LES-ALPES**, 8km north of St-Julien, sprawls amid open meadows. Low-key but ever-increasing tourist development, in the form of wooden chalets and villas to all sides, gives it a straggly feel, though its central streets and squares lie open to magnificent views of the mountains. Beautiful **hiking** and **biking** trails radiate out from St-André; whether the lake itself is visible depends on current water levels, but as a rule it ends 1km or more south.

ARRIVAL AND INFORMATION   ST-ANDRÉ-LES-ALPES

By train The *gare Chemins de Fer de Provence*, across the N202 northeast of the centre, is served by trains between Digne and Nice (see page 211).
By bus Bus timetables are detailed on ⓦ haut-verdon-voyages.fr.

Destinations Castellane (1 daily in summer; 30min).
Tourist office Place Marcel-Pastorelli (April–June & Sept Mon–Sat 9am–noon & 2–6pm; July & Aug daily 9am–1pm & 2–6.30pm; Oct–March Mon–Fri 10am–noon & 2–5pm; ☎ 04 92 89 02 39, ⓦ saintandrelesalpes-verdontourisme.com).

ACTIVITIES

Paragliding and hang-gliding Aerogliss, based south of the village (☎ 04 92 89 11 30, ⓦ aerogliss.com), offers well-organized paragliding and hang-gliding around Mont Chalvet to the west. Short flights for less experienced gliders take place in the morning, and there are three-day

beginners' courses starting at €350.
Watersports Aqua Bond Rafting (☎ 06 61 99 13 79, ⓦ aquabondrafting.com) on route de Nice – the main road just south of St-André –, organizes local rafting, paddleboarding, aqua-trekking and kayaking.

ACCOMMODATION AND EATING

Camping Les Iscles ☎ 04 92 89 02 29, ⓦ camping-les-iscles.com. This large two-star municipal campsite, set in the pinewoods by the confluence of the Verdon and the Issole, offers good facilities at a very good price. Closed mid-Oct to March. **€15**

Lac et Forêt Rte de Nice ☎ 04 92 89 07 38, ⓦ lacforet.com. An imposing 1930s hotel, beside the main road, 1km south towards St-Julien. Rooms vary considerably, from what might charitably be called kitsch to stylish and smart. Lake views cost around €20 extra. Closed mid-Nov to mid-April. **€75**

Clues de Haute Provence

The arid and sparsely populated region known as the **Clues de Haute Provence** lies east of Castellane, in the Pre-Alpes de Grasse. Despite lying just a short way north of the busiest parts of the Côte d'Azur, barely 20–30km from either Vence or Grasse, it's an anomalous, little-visited pocket, where the seclusion is disturbed only by the winter influx of skiers heading to the 1777m summit of the **Montagne du Cheiron**.

The word **clues** refers to gorges cut by torrential rivers through the limestone mountain ranges. Each claustrophobic and seemingly collapsible *clue* here opens onto a wide and empty landscape of white and grey rocks with a tattered carpet of thick oak and pine forest. All the horizons are closed off by mountains, some erupting in a space of their own, others looking like coastal cliffs trailing the **Cheiron**, the **Charamel** or the 1664m-high **Montagne de Thorenc**.

Not all the passes stay open in winter. Routes that go through the *clues* rather than over passes are manageable for cyclists: this is gorgeous, clean-air, long-freewheeling and panoramic terrain. Hiking trails abound, with the **GR4** as the main through-route for walkers from Gréolières to Aiglun across the Cheiron. **Accommodation**, however, is scarce, with hotels small and scattered, and campsites, too, are thin on the ground. Even winter accommodation at **Gréolières** and **Gréolières-les-Neiges** is minimal, as visitors tend to come for a day's skiing or have their own places.

Coursegoules

Although the sleepy old hill village of **COURSEGOULES** has an undeniable charm, the bare white rocks that surround it are hardly hospitable for agriculture. The local population has declined to around three hundred or so, and many of its houses are now second homes.

Gréolières

Originally a stopping point on the Roman road from Vence to Castellane, **GRÉOLIÈRES**, 11km west of Coursegoules and significantly larger, is now surrounded by ruins, of Haut-Gréolières to the north and a fortress to the south. While the village is liveliest during the winter, it passes as a summer resort as well, and is a popular site for paragliding.

Gréolières-les-Neiges

An 18km drive around the mountains from Gréolières – first west, then doubling back east – brings you through the Clue de Gréolières to **GRÉOLIÈRES-LES-NEIGES**, barely 5km north as the crow flies. The closest ski resort to the Mediterranean, this is a centre for **cross-country skiing** (Ⓦ station-de-ski-greolieres-les-neiges.com). Nine lifts ascend Mont Cheiron in winter, while a single chairlift operates in July and August for summer panoramas. While there are no hotels, just furnished apartments, a handful of cafés and restaurants stay open year-round.

St-Auban

With its back to the mountainside, pocket-sized **ST-AUBAN** rises above the grassy valley, its wide southern views making up for the plainness of the village itself. The gash made by the River Esteron has left a jumble of rocks through which the water tumbles beneath overhanging cliffs riddled with caves and fissures. In summer, rock climbing and canyoning are possible in the narrow *clue*.

Briançonnet

Downstream (northeast) from St-Auban, 7km along the D2211, **BRIANÇONNET** enjoys a stunning location. Views from its cemetery stretch southwards past the edge of the Montagne de Charamel across kilometres of uninhabited space. The Romans had a

5

settlement here and the houses you see today are built with stones from the ancient ruins; odd fragments of Latin are still decipherable in the walls. There's just one street with a boulangerie, a *tabac*, a small museum of local history and a church.

From here you can head north across the **Col de Buis** (usually closed Nov to mid-April) to Entrevaux or Annot, or east towards the Clue d'Aiglun and the Clue de Riolan.

Route des Crêtes

Clinging to the steep southern slope of the Montagne de Charamel, the switchbacking **Route des Crêtes** (D10) requires concentration and nerve. For long stretches there are no distracting views, only thick forest matted with mistletoe. After the hamlet of Le Mas, which hangs on the edge of a precipitous spur below the road, trees can no longer get a root-hold in the near-vertical golden and silver cliffs; the narrowing road crosses high-arched bridges over cascading streams that fall to smoothly moulded pools of aquamarine.

Roughly 14km east of its junction with the D5, just before **Aiglun**, the D10 crosses the Esteron as it shoots out from the high-pressure passage (too narrow for a road) that splits the Charamel and the Montagne St-Martin. The most formidable *clue* of all, it's impossible to explore. You can, however, walk for roughly 3km south along the GR4 from the D10, 1.5km west of the *clue*, to the **Vegay waterfall**, halfway between Aiglun and Gréolières-les-Neiges, where water destined for the Esteron plummets down a vertical cliff face.

From **ROQUESTERON**, 10km east of Aiglun – and divided for a century by the France–Savoy border – you can either follow the D17 above the Esteron to the river's confluence with the Var, or take the tangled D1. That leads, via passages of rock seamed in thin vertical bands, to **BOUYON**, from where the D8 loops back to Coursegoules. Both routes lead through a succession of eagle's-nest villages.

ARRIVAL AND DEPARTURE   CLUES DE HAUTE PROVENCE

GRÉOLIÈRES   Grasse (1 on Sat and daily during winter holidays; 50min).
By bus Gréolières has very infrequent connection with

EATING

COURSEGOULES
Bistrot de Sophie 37 place Neuve ☎ 04 93 59 11 19. This simple, friendly, modern bistro caters to day-trippers with a no-nonsense lunchtime *menu du jour* that lists dishes such as "beef" or "rabbit" (€27 on Sun; €18 otherwise). Daily (except Wed) 11am–4pm.

GRÉOLIÈRES
La Vieille Auberge 7 place Pierre-Merle ☎ 04 93 59 03 02. Café-restaurant where diners can eat well and cheaply on Gréolières' central square; there are tables out on the street and a hearty €25 *menu*, rich in meaty Provençal classics. Daily 8am–7pm.

Massif les Monges

North of Digne, the mountains that reach their highest peak at **Les Monges** (2115m) form an impassable barrier, as far as roads are concerned, between the valleys that run down to Sisteron and the Durance, and those that belong to the Bléone's tributaries. There are footpaths for serious **walkers**, and just one road loops south of Les Monges linking Digne and Sisteron across the **Col de Font-Belle**. Fantastic forested paths lead off past vertical rocks from the pass.

The D900a, which follows first the course of the Bléone, and then the Bès torrent, before joining the main D900 and continuing north to **Seyne-les-Alpes**, passes many of the protected sites of the **Réserve Naturelle Géologique de Haute Provence**, where shrubs, flowers and butterflies are now the sole visible wildlife. After heavy rain the waters tear through the **Clues de Barles and Verdaches** like a boiling soup of mud.

Making a livelihood from the land here is difficult. Assorted "*marginaux*" (those into alternative lifestyles) manage to survive, making goat's cheese and doing seasonal work; the indigenous *paysans* are more likely to be opening *gîtes* and servicing the city dwellers who come for **trekking** or **skiing** trips. But it's still very wild and deserted, with little accommodation other than *gîtes* and *chambres d'hôtes*.

Seyne-les-Alpes

The hill village of **SEYNE-LES-ALPES** stands in a distinctly Alpine landscape 40km north of Digne, its highest point topped by a Vauban fort. Quiet for most of the year, Seyne experiences its main influx in winter, when three skiing stations, **St-Jean**, **Chabanon** and **Le Grand Puy**, are in operation. It also hosts the only surviving **horse fair** in southeast France, held on the second Saturday of October, and a mule breeder's competition on the second Saturday of August.

INFORMATION SEYNE-LES-ALPES

Tourist office Place d'Armes, off Grande Rue (July & Aug Mon–Sat 9am–12.30pm & 2.30–6.30pm, Sun 9.30am– 12.30pm; Sept–June Mon–Fri 9am–noon & 2–6pm; ☎04 92 35 11 00, ⊛blanche-serre-poncon.com).

ACCOMMODATION AND EATING

Au Vieux Tilleul Les Auches, 1km from town centre ☎04 92 35 00 04, ⊛vieux-tilleul.fr. Looking like a mountain chalet, and remaining open in winter, this hotel offers twenty spacious, comfortable rooms, a happy combination of pool and sauna, and a restaurant (closed Sun eve) with dinner *menus* from €23. Lunch served Aug only; closed first three weeks in Dec. **€83**

Camping Les Prairies ☎04 92 35 10 21, ⊛campinglesprairies.com. Three-star, summer-only campsite, beside the river 800m below town, with a nice pool, bar and snack bar. Closed mid-Sept to April. **€22**

Parc National du Mercantour

Strictly speaking, the **Parc National du Mercantour**, which stretches across the Alps for 75km from east to west, holds no permanent inhabitants. That's just the central core of a much wider area, however, in which the park sprawls across the peaks while a succession of delightful high-mountain valleys cradle towns that attract hikers and wildlife enthusiasts in summer and skiers in winter. The park itself, meanwhile, is crossed by numerous paths, equipped with refuge huts that provide basic food and bedding for trekkers.

The region readily divides into broadly parallel valleys, carved by rivers flowing south towards the Mediterranean. Approaching from the small town of **Barcelonnette**, north of the mountains, four potential routes cross the watershed of Mont Pelat, La Bonette, Chambeyron and their high gneiss and granite extensions. Exhilarating for (ultra-fit) cyclists, they can scare the wits out of drivers unused to vertiginous high-altitude roads. The Col d'Allos leads into the **Haut-Verdon** Valley; the Col de la Cayolle into the **Haut-Var** Valley; the road across the summit of La Bonette to the **Tinée** Valley; and the Col de Larche heads into Italy. All but the last are snowed up between November and April, and sometimes stay closed as late as June. Further east, the **Vésubie** rises just below the Italian border; like the Tinée and the Verdon it runs into the Var.

Barcelonnette

From the northern border of Provence at the broad Lac de Serre-Ponçon, the D900 follows the River Ubaye to little **Barcelonnette**, passing through a dramatic landscape

5

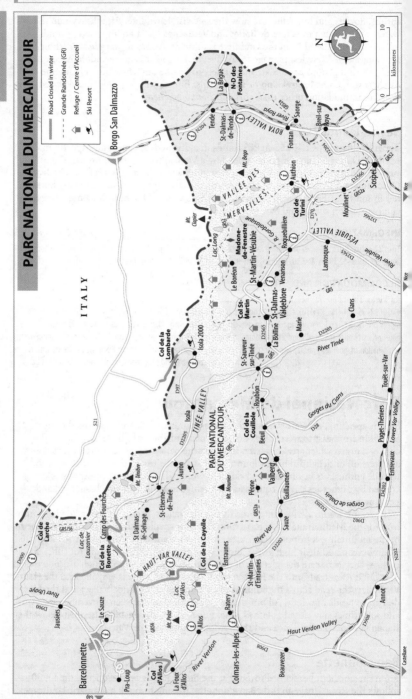

PARC NATIONAL DU MERCANTOUR

Road closed in winter
Grande Randonnée (GR)
Refuge / Centre d'Accueil
Ski Resort

N

0   10
kilometres

ITALY

Borgo San Dalmazzo

La Brigue
N-D des Fontaines
Tende
St-Dalmas-de-Tende
Saorge
Fontan
Breil-sur-Roya
River Roya
ROYA VALLEY

Mt. Bego
VALLÉE DES MERVEILLES
Authion
Col de Turini
Sospel
Moulinet
Mt. Clapier
Lac Long
Madone-de-Fenestre
Roquebillière
Rte. Gordolasque
Le Boréon
St-Martin-Vésubie
Venanson
Lantosque
VÉSUBIE VALLEY
River Vésubie

Col St-Martin
St-Dalmas-Valdeblore
Marie
Clans

Col de la Lombarde
Isola 2000
St-Sauveur-sur-Tinée
La Bolline
River Tinée

D97
Isola
TINÉE VALLEY
PARC NATIONAL DU MERCANTOUR
Roubion
Col de la Couillole
Beuil
Gorges du Cians
Touët-sur-Var
Puget-Théniers
Lower Var Valley
Entrevaux

Mt. Ténibre
Auron
St-Étienne-de-Tinée
Mt. Mounier
Péone
Valberg
Guillaumes
Sauze
River Var
Gorges de Daluis

Col de Larche
Lac de Lauzanier
Camp des Fourches
Col de la Bonette
St-Dalmas-le-Selvage
Col de la Cayolle
HAUT-VAR VALLEY
Entraunes
St-Martin-d'Entraunes
Annot
Haut Verdon Valley

River Ubaye
Jausiers
Le Sauze
Barcelonnette
Pra-Loup
Col d'Allos
La Foux d'Allos
Mt. Pelat
Lac d'Allos
Allos
Ratery
Colmars-les-Alpes
River Verdon
Beauvezer
Castellane

Nice

of tiny, irregular fields backed by the jagged silhouettes of mountains that look like something out of a vampire movie. The town owes its Spanish-sounding name, "Little Barcelona", to its foundation in the thirteenth century by Raimond Béranger IV, count of Provence, whose family came from the Catalan city. Although snow falls here at the end of the year and stays until Easter, and there are several **ski resorts** nearby, summer is the main tourist season.

Backed by views of snowcapped mountains, Barcelonnette is an immaculate little place. Its distinctive houses boast tall gables and deep eaves, while in the central square, **place Manuel**, a white clock tower commemorates the centenary of the 1848 revolution. These days the sunny squares see little more activity than gentle *pétanque* games played by old men wearing berets – a more ideal spot for doing nothing would be hard to find.

Musée de la Vallée

10 av de la Libération • Sept–mid Nov & mid Dec–early July Wed–Sat 2.30–6pm; early July–Aug daily 10am–noon & 2.30–6.30pm • €4 • ☎ 04 92 81 27 15, ⓦ barcelonnette.com

Barcelonnette has a surprising connection with **Mexico**: many local sheep farmers and wool merchants emigrated to Latin America in the nineteenth century to make their fortunes, before returning home to build their dream houses. In one of these grand villas, La Sapinière, the **Musée de la Vallée** details the life and times of the people of the Ubaye Valley, and the emigration to Mexico and the travels of a nineteenth-century explorer from the town.

ARRIVAL AND INFORMATION   BARCELONNETTE

By bus Buses from Marseille, Digne or Gap arrive on place Aimé-Gassier.

Destinations Digne (2 daily; 1hr 30min); Gap (4 daily; 1hr 30min).

Parc National du Mercantour information centre In the Musée de la Vallée, 10 av de la Libération (June to early July & Sept daily except Tues 2.30–6pm; early July to Aug daily 10am–noon & 2.30–6.30pm; ☎ 04 92 81 21 31,

ⓦ mercantour-parcnational.fr). Staff provide maps, advise on walks and mountain refuges, and explain the fauna and flora.

Tourist office Off place Frédéric Mistral (July & Aug daily 9am–12.30pm & 1.30–7.30pm; Sept & mid-Dec to June Mon–Sat 9am–noon & 2–6pm; Oct to mid-Dec Mon–Sat 10am–noon & 2–4pm; ☎ 04 92 81 04 71, ⓦ barcelonnette. com).

ACTIVITIES

Walking and biking Rando Passion/Maison de la Montagne, 31 rue Jules-Béraud (☎ 04 92 81 43 34, ⓦ rando-passion.com), provides guidance for walks and VTT mountain biking (plus rental) in summer, and offers snow-shoeing and igloo building in winter.

Water-based activities More than a dozen companies offer whitewater activities from canyoning and canoeing to rafting, including Alligator (☎ 04 92 81 06 06;

ⓦ alligator-rafting.com) and Aqua'Rider (☎ 06 32 42 50 15, ⓦ aquarider.net).

Skiing Local ski resorts include Pra-Loup (ⓦ praloup. com), where the pistes link up with La Foux d'Allos (see page 233); Ste-Anne/La Condamine (ⓦ sainte-anne. com); and Le Sauze/Super-Sauze (ⓦ sauze.com). During the skiing season, a free bus loops between the resorts and Barcelonnette.

ACCOMMODATION

Azteca 3 rue François-Arnaud ☎ 04 92 81 46 36, ⓦ azteca-hotel.fr. Pleasant hotel, in a nineteenth-century villa built by an emigrant returned from Mexico, steps away from the centre and enjoying superb views of the mountains. Avoid the overpriced "Mexican" rooms, below the breakfast terrace. **€83.50**

Camping du Plan 52 av Émile-Aubert ☎ 04 92 81 08 11, ⓦ campingduplan.fr. This three-star site is the closest to town, 500m southwest along the D902 towards the Col de la Cayolle. It centres on a chalet-style building that doubles

as shop, bar and deli. Closed Oct to mid-May. **€9**

★ **Chalet les Blancs** Hameau les Blancs, Pra Loup ☎ 04 92 84 04 21, ⓦ hotel.lesblancs.free.fr. Lovely mountain-chalet hotel, ideal for families, in a ski resort 9km drive southwest. As well as wonderful valley views and thirty large well-equipped rooms, they have a heated indoor pool and a restaurant in which full meals, with a dessert buffet, cost €25. Rates include breakfast. Summer **€78**, winter **€106**

Cheval Blanc 12 rue Grenette ☎ 04 92 81 00 19,

5

WILDLIFE OF THE MERCANTOUR

The mountains of the Mercantour are renowned as a **wildlife** habitat. Camping, lighting fires, picking flowers, playing loud music or otherwise disturbing the delicate environment is strictly forbidden.

MAMMALS

The least shy mammal hereabouts is the **marmot**, a cream-coloured, badger-sized creature often seen sitting on its haunches in the sun. Chamois, mouflon and ibex are similarly unwary of humans. The male **ibex** is a wonderful, big, solid beast with curving, ribbed horns that grow to 1m long; almost hunted to extinction, the population is now stable. Another species of goat, the **chamois**, is also on the increase; the male is recognizable by the shorter, grappling-hook horns and white beard. The **mouflon**, introduced to the Mercantour in the 1950s, is the ancestor of domestic sheep. You might also see **stoats**, rare species of **hare**, and **foxes**, the latter the most abundant predator since bears and lynxes became extinct. The most problematic predator, however, is the **wolf**, formerly extinct, but now stalking the region again, having crossed the border from Italy. With almost two thousand sheep killed by wolves each year, sheep farmers are not happy.

BIRDS

The Mercantour is a perfect home for **eagles**, which nest on the high crags. Pairs of **golden eagles** are breeding, while a rare vulture, the **lammergeier**, has been successfully reintroduced. Other birds of prey – **kestrels**, **falcons** and **buzzards** – wing their way down from the scree to the Alpine lawn and its torrents to swoop on lizards, mice and snakes. The **great spotted woodpecker** and the black-and-orange **hoopoe** are the park's most colourful inhabitants. **Ptarmigan**, which turn snowy-white in winter, can sometimes be seen in June parading to potential mates on the higher northern slopes. **Blackcocks**, known in French as *tétras-lyre* for their lyre-shaped white tails, burrow into the snow at night and fly out in a flurry of snowflakes when the sun rises.

FLORA

The **flowers** of the Mercantour are an unmissable glory. Around forty of the over two thousand species represented are unique to the region. The moment the snow melts, the lawn between the rocky crags and the tree line begins to dot with golds, pinks and blues. Rare species of **lily** and **orchid** grow, as do the elusive **edelweiss** and the wild ancestors of various cultivated flowers – pansies, geraniums, tulips and gentian violets. Rarest of all is the **multi-flowering saxifrage** (*saxifraga florulenta*), a big spiky flower that looks as though it must be cultivated, though it would hardly be popular in suburban gardens since it flowers just once every ten years. Wild strawberries, raspberries and bilberries tempt visitors into the woods.

Ⓦ chevalblancbarcelonnette.com. Good value, central *Logis de France*, consisting of a rambling labyrinth of widely varying rooms above an attractive bar and restaurant (closed Sun) where *menus* start at €22. Closed Nov. €69

Grand Hôtel 6 place Manuel ❶ 04 92 81 03 14, Ⓦ grandhotel-barcelonnette.fr. Old-fashioned but cosy and very central hotel, with 21 wood-panelled bedrooms, some capable of sleeping five. €78

Grande Épervière 18 av des Trois Frères Arnaud ❶ 04 92 81 00 70. This imposing Mexican-era mansion, sitting within its own peaceful grounds an easy 500m walk west of Barcelonnette centre, is nowadays home to an upmarket hotel. All the comfortable, sizeable guest rooms come with balconies, and there's a bar but no restaurant. €87

EATING AND DRINKING

Barcelonnette holds enough **restaurants** to feed the whole valley. At the **markets** on place Aimé Gassier and place St-Pierre (Wed & Sat), you'll find all manner of sweets, jams and alcohol made from bilberries, pâtés made from thrush, partridge and pheasant, and the local juniper liqueur, *génépi*.

Le Gaudissart Place Aimé Gassier ❶ 04 92 81 00 45, Ⓦ legaudissart.fr. Relaxed courtyard restaurant on the southern edge of the centre, serving good old-fashioned home cooking, with a daily lunchtime *plat* for €13.80 and dinner *menus* at €18.50 and €29. Mon & Sun 7.30am–2pm, Tues–Sat 7.30am–2pm & 7–9.30pm.

Poivre d'Âne 49 rue Manuel ❶ 04 92 81 48 67, Ⓦ restaurantpoivredane.eatbu.com. This welcoming restaurant, known for its hearty portions of mountain favourites, is larger than it looks; beyond its main-street terrace there's a cosy covered courtyard at the back. As well as a €15 lunch *menu* and €28 dinner *menu*, they offer churrasco grilled meats for €20.50 and cheese-and-potato *tartiflette* for €19.50. Mon–Sat noon–2pm & 7–9.30pm.

Villa Morelia Le Château, Jausiers ☎04 92 84 67 78, ⓦvilla-morelia.com. Gastronomic restaurant in a neo-Mexican folly 9km east that also houses a plush spa hotel. They serve a delicious nouvelle cuisine *menus* from €45. Jan, Feb & May–Oct daily noon–1.30pm & 7.30–9pm.

The Haut-Verdon Valley

The beautiful **Haut-Verdon Valley** forms the most direct route between Barcelonnette in the north and Castellane in the south. In its upper reaches, before it's forced to squeeze into the dramatic Gorges du Verdon, the Verdon river runs through a bucolic landscape that's at its most seductive around the pretty village of **Colmars-les-Alpes**. This is also prime ski country, especially in the vicinity of **Allos**.

To reach the valley from Barcelonnette, however, you have first to cross the 2250m **summit of the Col d'Allos**, 20km southwest of town on the D908, which is usually closed from November to May. There's no disputing the magnificence of the long-range views, or the wild flowers that bloom in springtime, but many drivers find the road itself truly terrifying. Long stretches consist of bare one-lane switchbacks, with no protective guardrails and no warning of oncoming traffic.

A **mountain refuge** on the pass, *Col d'Allos* (☎04 92 83 85 14, ⓦrefuge-col-dallos.fr; June–Sept only), marks the junction with the GR56 hiking trail, which leads west to the Ubaye Valley and Seyne-les-Alpes, and east to the Col de Larche and the Tinée Valley.

La Foux d'Allos

Scruffy **LA FOUX D'ALLOS**, peppered with vast, ugly hotels, is probably the cheapest Provençal resort in which to **ski** or snowboard, and its sixty-plus lifts and 180km of pistes are open from mid-December to mid-April. The area joins up with Pra-Loup to the north, and the resort is quite high (1800–2600m) with more than 250 snow cannons, so melting is seldom a problem.

La Foux d'Allos and its neighbours are also keen to promote themselves as **summer resorts**. A handful of lifts operate in July and August to transport mountain bikers to well-marked trails around the mountain.

Allos

The medieval village of **ALLOS**, 9km south of La Foux d'Allos, was all but destroyed by fire in the eighteenth century; one tower of the ramparts half-survived and became the current clock tower. The old livelihoods of tending sheep and weaving woollen sheets were dying out when tourism began early in the twentieth century, with the discovery of the nearby **Lac d'Allos**. Once skiing became established, Allos's agricultural days were numbered. Even so, despite all its *résidences secondaires*, it's not a bad place to spend a day or two.

Lac d'Allos

At 2228m, the round and impossibly blue surface of the **Lac d'Allos**, 13km east and 800m above Allos, reflects the amphitheatre of towering peaks that curves around its flanks. The lake nourishes trout and char in its pure cold waters, while mouflon and chamois bound around its banks. Looking towards the one-time glacier flow, you can just see the peak of **Mont Pelat**, the highest mountain in the Parc National du Mercantour.

To walk to the lake from Allos, follow the path that starts by the church. Alternatively, an uneven, single-track road weaves up 46 bends in 6km through a dense forest of larch trees to a busy car park, from which a 45-minute hike brings you to what was once the head of a glacier.

5

Colmars-les-Alpes

COLMARS-LES-ALPES, on the valley floor 7km downstream from Allos, is an extraordinarily well-preserved stronghold, whose name comes from a temple to Mars built by the Romans high on the adjacent hill. Colmars' all-but-intact sixteenth-century **ramparts**, complete with arrow slits and small square towers, were constructed on the orders of François I of France to reinforce the defences that had existed since 1381, when Colmars became a border town between Provence and Savoy. When Savoy declared war on France, in 1690, Vauban was called in to make the town even more secure, and designed the Fort de Savoie and the Fort de France at either end. Their **gateways** now form the town's two principal entrances, adorned with climbing roses.

Inside the walls, you find yourself in a quiet, atmospheric, somewhat rough-hewn old Provençal town, with cobbled streets and fountained squares. The **Fort de Savoie** is only open in summer (mid-June to mid-Sept Mon, Wed, Thurs, Sat & Sun 10am–2.30pm & 3–6.30pm, Tues & Fri 3–6.30pm; €3), when exhibitions of local customs and costumes are set up beneath the magnificent larch-timbered ceilings. All in all, there's not a lot to do in Colmars except wander around and soak up the atmosphere, or take a twenty-minute walk east to the **Lance waterfall**.

Colmars lies at the junction of the Verdon Valley road with the D78, which climbs northeast between the Frema and Encombrette mountains and descends to the Var Valley at St-Martin-d'Entraunes.

INFORMATION AND ACTIVITIES

THE HAUT-VERDON VALLEY

LA FOUX D'ALLOS

Tourist office Maison de la Foux (May–Nov Mon–Sat 10am–noon & 2–5.30pm; Dec–April daily 9.30am–noon & 2–6.30pm; ☎ 04 92 83 80 70, ⍈ valdallos.com).

Ski and bike rental SkiSet (☎ 01 41 12 97 97, ⍈ la-foux-d-allos.skiset.com).

ALLOS

Tourist office Northern end of the old village (July & Aug daily 9.30am–noon & 2–6.30pm; Sept–Oct & March–June daily 9am–noon & 2–6pm; Nov–Feb 9am–noon & 2–6pm, closed Sun; ☎ 04 92 83 02 81, ⍈ valdallos.com).

Parc de Loisirs Allos's summer-only park offers a large man-made lake, plus activities from canoeing to mini-golf (July & Aug daily 10am–6.45pm; adults €10, children €5;

☎ 04 92 83 09 45, ⍈ valdallos.com).

Parc National du Mercantour information office In the same building as the tourist office, northern end of the old village (☎ 04 93 16 78 88, ⍈ mercantour.eu).

Ski and bike rental Au Petit Allossard, rue du Pré de Foire (☎ 04 92 83 14 62, ⍈ aupetitallossard.sport2000.fr).

COLMARS-LES-ALPES

Tourist office On the main road outside the walls, facing the Porte des Glacis (July & Aug Mon–Sat 9am–12.30pm & 2–6.30pm, Sun 9.30am–noon & 2–5.30pm; Sept & May–June Mon–Sat 9am–noon & 2–6pm, Sun 9.30am–12.30pm; Oct–April Mon–Sat 9am–noon & 2–6pm; ☎ 04 92 83 41 92, ⍈ colmars-les-alpes.fr).

ACCOMMODATION AND EATING

ALLOS

Auberge Les Gentianes Grande Rue ☎ 04 92 83 03 50, ⍈ lesgentianesallos.com. Simple, inexpensive hotel-restaurant in the old village, with plain but acceptable rooms and a restaurant that serves full meals from €16. **€70**

La Ferme Girerd-Potin 5km northwest on rte de la Foux ☎ 04 92 83 04 76, ⍈ chambredhotes-valdallos. com. Sixteenth-century farmhouse, open year-round, that offers five very comfortable en-suite B&B rooms plus a three-bedroom gîte. Two-night minimum stay, half-board compulsory, so rates here include breakfast and dinner. **€116**

L'Ours Blanc Le Seignus ☎ 04 92 83 01 07, ⍈ hotel-loursblanc.com. Small hotel near the foot of the ski lifts,

with simple but bright and comfortable rooms, a warm welcome, and a restaurant specializing in hearty mountain food. Closed April, May & mid-Sept to mid-Dec. **€70**

COLMARS-LES-ALPES

Bois Joly Le Bois Joly ☎ 04 92 83 40 40. Small and very scenic campsite, amid the riverside trees a 10min walk from the village. Closed Oct–April. **€14.50**

Le France Place de France ☎ 06 29 22 42 80. Colmars' one hotel, an old-fashioned but very appealing place just across the D908 from the walled town, has a garden restaurant that serves pizza in summer, and a splendid old bar. **€65**

Gassendi Rue St-Joseph ☎ 04 92 83 43 21, ✉ gassendi@

gmail.com. This year-round *gîte d'étape* – housed in a hideously pebble-dashed monstrosity that's actually a twelfth-century Templar hospice – holds six dorms with ten beds each, and a couple of private double rooms. Rates include breakfast; an evening meal costs €15 extra. Dorms €22; doubles €60

The Haut-Var Valley

Confusingly, the dramatic **Haut-Var Valley**, carved by the upper reaches of the Var river, is entirely distinct from the region known as the Haut Var. To reach it from Barcelonnette, follow the D902 due south, climbing through a deep gorge cut by the **River Bachelard**. It then turns abruptly east, continuing beside the river as it squeezes between Mont Pelat to the south and the ridge of peaks to the north. At the *Bayasse* refuge (☎04 92 32 20 79, ✆refuge-bayasse.fr), the D902 turns south once more, towards the **Col de la Cayolle**, while a track and the GR56 continue east towards La Bonette and the Tinée Valley.

Having switchbacked down south from the Col de la Cayolle, the road becomes the D2202. The **Var** now makes its appearance, pouring southwards towards Guillaumes, and beyond that down through the **Gorges de Daluis** to Entrevaux. Many of the chapels that punctuate its banks are superbly decorated, like the Renaissance Chapelle de St-Sébastien, just north of **Entraunes**, and the church at **St-Martin-d'Entraunes**, with its Bréa retable.

Guillaumes

Tucked beneath the ruined Château de la Reine Jeanne, **GUILLAUMES**, a minor metropolis that's a favourite with cyclists in summer, served for centuries as a resting place for sheep heading between the Haut-Var summer pastures and Nice. Most flocks now travel by lorry, but the old **sheep fairs** still take place on September 16 and the second Saturday of October. Winter sees a migration in the opposite direction, as the residents of the Côte d'Azur flock to the ski resorts of Valberg and Beuil, east of Guillaumes, on the fabulous road that climbs over to the Tinée Valley.

Gorges de Daluis

The Var enters the dramatic red-rocked **Gorges de Daluis** around 5km south of Guillaumes. Drivers heading upstream here (northwards) enjoy better views; much of the downstream carriageway is in tunnels. Walkers can take a closer look at the gorge by following the 2km **Sentier du Point Sublime** from Pont de Berthéou on the D2202 to the Point Sublime itself. The Pont de la Mariée is a popular spot for **bungee jumping** (late June–early Oct Sat–Sun 11am & 1pm; €79, reservation only; ✆saut-elastique.com).

The Lower Var Valley

East of St-Julien-du-Verdon (see page 226), the N202 climbs to meet the Var river after 24km. From there, as first the D4202 and then the D6202, it follows the **Lower Var Valley** for another 40km to its semi-subterranean confluence with the Tinée, and thus provides direct access to Nice along the spectacular gorge known as the **Défilé de Chaudan**. This riverside route is also followed by the *Chemins de Fer de Provence* (see page 213), with its major highlight being the medieval fortified town of **Entrevaux**.

Annot

Surrounded by hills a couple of kilometres north of the N202, 17km east of St-Julien-de-Verdon, the town of **ANNOT** centres on a large open *cours*, lined by plane trees. This is bounded to one side by the River Vaire and to the other by a compact **vieille ville**, a flavourful tangle of pretty arcades, mysterious passageways, thick arches and gateways that lacks any businesses or tourist attractions. While not as lovely or picturesque as Entrevaux, Annot is a popular holiday centre, and makes an excellent base for walks,

5

up past strange sandstone formations to rocky outcrops with names like Chambre du Roi (the King's Chamber) and Dent du Diable (the Devil's Tooth).

Entrevaux

The absurdly photogenic village of **ENTREVAUX** stands on the north bank of the River Var 15km east of Annot, 6km beyond the southern end of the Gorges de Daluis. Entrevaux was once a key border town between France and Savoy, and the only access to its old walled centre is via a single-arched drawbridge across the rushing river. The bridge was fortified by Vauban, whose linking of the town with a ruined **château** (access at any time; €3), perched atop a steep spur 135m above the river, gives the site a menacing character. Originally the château could only be reached by scrambling up the rock, but by the seventeenth century that had become unacceptable, and Vauban built the double-walled ramp, plus attendant bastions, which zigzags up the rock with ferocious determination.

The former **cathedral** (summer 9am–7pm; winter 9am–5pm; free), in the lower part of the old town, is well integrated into the military defences, with one wall forming part of the ramparts and its belfry a fortified tower. The interior, however, is all twirling Louis Quinze, with misericords, side altars and organ as over-decorated as they could possibly be.

Musée Moto

Rue Serpente • April Sat & Sun 10am–noon & 2–6pm; May–Oct daily 10am–noon & 2–6pm • Free, donations accepted • ☎ 04 93 79 12 70

A bizarre labour of love, the **Musée Moto**, in the heart of the village, consists of a rather amazing collection of old motorcycles squeezed into a tiny house. Prize specimens include a gleaming Harley-Davidson from 1917, and a Narcisse tandem from 1951.

Puget-Théniers

East of Entrevaux, the broad Var Valley abounds in pear, apple and cherry orchards. **PUGET-THÉNIERS**, 13km along, is a presentable but not especially good-looking country town, though its **vieille ville**, on the right bank of the River Roudoule, is full of thirteenth-century houses, some still bearing symbols of their original owners' trades on the lintels. The left bank is dominated by the great semicircular apse of the Romanesque **church**, resembling a fort or prison.

On the *cours* below the old town, a statue of a naked woman with bound hands commemorates **Auguste Blanqui**, born here in 1805. A leader of the Paris Commune of 1871, Blanqui spent forty years in prison for – as the inscription states – "fidelity to the sacred cause of workers' emancipation". There are few French revolutionaries for whom the description "heroic defender of the proletariat" is so true, and none who came from a more isolated, unindustrialized region.

Touët-sur-Var

The River Cians joins the Var 8km east of Puget-Théniers. The road along this tributary, the D28 (see page 240), climbs beside the spectacular **Gorges du Cians** to reach the ski resort of Beuil. Crammed against a cliff not far beyond the confluence, **TOUËT-SUR-VAR** holds a remarkable church, built over a small torrent that's visible through a grille in the floor of the nave. The village's highest houses look as if they're falling apart, but in fact the gaps between the beams are open galleries where the midday sun can reach the rows of drying figs.

ARRIVAL AND INFORMATION   **THE LOWER VAR VALLEY**

ANNOT
By train The *gare Chemins de Fer de Provence*, on the Nice–Digne line, is not far southeast of place du Germe.

Tourist office Place du Germe, just outside the old quarter (May, June, Sept & Oct Mon–Sat 9am–noon & 2–6pm, Sun 9.30am–12.30pm; July & Aug daily 9am–1pm &

2–6.30pm; Nov–March Mon–Fri 10am–noon & 2–5pm; April Mon–Fri 9am–noon & 2–6pm; ☎04 92 83 23 03, ⓦannot-tourisme.com).

ENTREVAUX
By train The *gare Chemins de Fer de Provence* is just downstream from the centre, on the south bank.
Tourist office In the left-hand tower of the drawbridge (May–Sept daily 10am–1pm & 2–6pm; Feb–April & Oct–Dec daily 10am–12.30pm & 1.30–5pm, closed Sun mid Nov–Dec; ☎04 93 05 46 73, ⓦentrevaux.info).

PUGET-THÉNIERS
By train The *gare Chemins de Fer de Provence* is on the N202.
By bus Buses stop in front of the train station.
Destinations Annot (1 daily; 20min); Barrême (1 daily; 1hr 10min); Digne (1 daily; 2hr); Entrevaux (1 daily; 10min); St-André-les-Alpes (1 daily; 1hr).
Tourist office Alongside the *gare Chemins de Fer de Provence* (mid May–Aug Mon–Fri 9am–12.30pm & 2–6pm, Sat & Sun 9am–7pm; Sept–May Mon–Sat 9am–noon and 2–5.30pm; ☎04 93 05 05 05, ⓦpuget-theniers.fr).

ACCOMMODATION AND EATING

ANNOT
L'Avenue Av de la Gare ☎04 92 83 22 07, ⓦhotel-avenue.com. Smart little hotel, a few metres south of the old town, with small, tasteful rooms and a good restaurant that's open for dinner only, serving *menus* from €16–32. Closed Nov–March. **€90**
Beau Séjour Place du Révelly ☎04 92 83 21 08. This well-priced *Logis de France*, beside the entrance to the *vieille ville*, has sixteen clean and comfortable rooms, plus a restaurant that serves good local food both indoors and out. **€55**
La Ribière On the D908 ☎04 92 83 21 44, ⓦla-ribiere.com. Very pleasant two-star campsite, just north of town towards Fugeret; you can swim in the river alongside. Pizzas and simple meals available in summer. Closed Nov to mid-March. **€19**

ENTREVAUX
L'Ambassade Place du Marché ☎04 93 05 49 98. Appealing bar/restaurant in the walled village, with outdoor tables on an attractive lane. All of its set *menus*, starting at €17, include a plate of the delicious house

speciality, *secca* (dried beef). Mon–Sat 10am–2.30pm & 6–10.30pm.
Maison de Julie Le Plan d'Entrevaux ☎04 92 02 46 42, ⓦmaisonjulie.com. Very welcoming B&B, in a charming old house off the main road 3.5km west of town, and offering two large en-suite rooms, one sleeping two and the other four. Rates include breakfast. **€60**
Vauban 4 place Moreau ☎04 93 05 42 40, ⓦhotel-le-vauban.com. With no hotels in the old town proper, the *Vauban*, immediately across the river, is the most convenient option, with reasonable rooms – the cheapest are not en suite – and a restaurant (Nov to April closed eve) specializing in roast lamb, pasta and seafood, with *menus* from €18.50 at lunchtime, €27.50 at dinner. **€75**

PUGET-THÉNIERS
Les Acacias 1km east on the D6202 ☎04 93 05 05 25. Much the best food near Puget-Théniers. *Cuisine de terroir* drawing on local produce can be enjoyed on a €16 lunch *menu*, or for €32 in the evenings. Mon, Tues, Thurs & Sun noon–2pm, Fri & Sat noon–2pm & 7.30–9pm.

The Tinée Valley

The longest tributary of the Var, the **Tinée**, rises just below the 2800m summit of **La Bonette**, 30km southeast of Barcelonnette (see page 229) by road. The mountains on its left bank – under whose shadow **St-Étienne** and **Auron** nestle – rise up to the Italian border, while the river heads south to cut a steep, narrow valley before joining the Var 30km from the sea.

Across La Bonette

Claiming to be the highest "inter-valley" stretch of tarmac in Europe, the D64 across **La Bonette** gives a feast of high-altitude views. The actual summit of the mountain, a ten-minute scrabble up scree from a lesser loop road that branches off the main road, is not particularly exciting, and all the more ugly for its military training camp. The green and silent spaces of the long approach, however, circled by barren peaks, are magical.

From **Camp des Fourches**, before the alarming hairpins begin for the southern descent, you can hike along the **GR5/56** north, parallel with the Italian border, to the Col de Larche. While it's not exactly a stroll, once you've climbed to the Col de la Cavale (after 5km or so) it's more or less downhill all the way, with the Ubayette

5

torrent as your guide; the **Lac de Lauzanier**, 5km further along, is a spot you may never want to leave.

St-Étienne-de-Tinée

On the south side of La Bonette, the D2205 descends, with the Tinée alongside, to the little town of **ST-ÉTIENNE-DE-TINÉE**, an inward-looking but attractive community that comes to life during its sheep fairs, held twice every summer, and the Fête de la Transhumance at the end of June.

On its western side, off boulevard d'Auron, a cable car then chairlift climb to the summit of **La Pinatelle**, thereby linking the village to the ski resort of Auron; the cable car runs in summer as well (€5), with a restaurant, *Le Grizzly*, at its upper end.

Auron

Seven kilometres south of St-Étienne and accessible on a dead-end road, the resort of **AURON** (w auron.com) has 21 lifts and 135km of pistes used by skiers in winter (Dec–April; €35/day). A few remain open for hikers and mountain bikers in summer (July & Aug; €10/day).

Isola 2000

Downstream from St-Étienne, the D2205 runs between nothing but white quartz and heather. Only the silvery sound of crickets competes with the water's roar until you reach **Isola**, an uneventful village at the foot of the climb to the purpose-built ski resort of **ISOLA 2000** (w isola2000.com), a jumble of concrete apartment blocks high in the mountain, just below the tree line, built to accommodate the skiers who use its 22 lifts and 120km of pistes (Dec–April; €35/day).

From Isola, both the D2205 and the Tinée river head south through the Gorges de Valabre towards St-Sauveur-sur-Tinée. The drop in altitude is marked by sweet chestnut trees taking over from the pines.

St-Sauveur-sur-Tinée

The pleasingly sleepy village of **ST-SAUVEUR-SUR-TINÉE**, 13km south of Isola, is dominated by its medieval needle belfry. The adornments of the Romanesque gargoyled church include a fine fifteenth-century retable, behind the bloodied crucifix. There's not a lot to do here, other than sit in the sun above the river or head off along the GR52A, but it's an attractive place to pause.

From St-Sauveur, you can either head west along the D30 towards Valberg and the Haut-Var Valley, a precipitous climb, or follow the Tinée south, passing far below the charming perched villages of Marie, Clans and La Tour, all of which have medieval decorations in their churches.

Roubion

To enjoy spectacular bird's-eye views over the Tinée Valley, turn west at St-Sauveur-sur-Tinée onto the D30. After 12km of slowly snaking its way up the sheer valley walls, it passes just below the dramatic hilltop village of **ROUBION**. Park at the edge and walk up into its tangled alleyways, and the centuries simply seem to drop away. On the first Sunday of October, in a celebration of the annual **Transhumance**, the squares and streets of Roubion fill once more with sheep.

ARRIVAL AND INFORMATION   **THE TINÉE VALLEY**

ST-ÉTIENNE-DE-TINÉE
By bus Auron (1–6 daily; 15min); Isola (1–2 daily; 15min); Nice (1–2 daily; 1hr 50min); St-Sauveur-de-Tinée (1–2 daily; 30min).

Tourist office 2 rue des Communes-de-France, at the northern end of the village; doubles as information centre for the Parc du Mercantour (daily 10.30am–12.30pm & 2–6pm; ☎ 04 93 02 41 96, w auron.com, w mercantour.eu).

5

Ski rental Ski Shop Les Gentians, in Auron (ⓦauron. skimium.fr), rents ski clothing and equipment.

ACCOMMODATION AND EATING

LA BONETTE
Café A Marius Bousieyas, St-Dalmas-le-Sauvage ☎04 93 03 53 30, ⓦs405235569.siteweb-initial.fr. Tiny, isolated hostel-cum-B&B with six-bed dorms and private doubles, in a magnificent setting high on the southern flanks of La Bonette 13km north of St-Étienne. Evening meals €20. Dorms **€24**; doubles *demi-pension* **€98**

ST-ÉTIENNE-DE-TINÉE
Camping du Plan d'Eau At the edge of the village ☎04 93 02 41 57, ⓦcampingduplandeau.com. Small, summer-only municipal site, in a nice verdant location beside a little lake. Closed Oct to mid-May. **€15**

Chamois d'Or 1 av de Gaulle ☎04 93 02 44 80. Very friendly little crêperie spreading through a pretty garden facing the village's fifteenth-century church, serving simple

menus of tasty crêpes and salads for €14 and €18. June–Oct Tues–Sun noon–2pm & 7.30–9pm.

Regalivou 8 bd d'Auron ☎04 93 02 49 00, ⓦleregalivou. free.fr. Lively hotel-restaurant, perched above the village centre which has a large terrace, and stays open year-round. Fourteen en-suite rooms, and a hearty restaurant serving pizzas and grilled meats. **€65**

ROUBION
Auberge du Moulin Place Recipon ☎04 93 02 09 06. Tiny restaurant with terrace that celebrates the local hunting culture with mounted boar and stag heads on the wall. Unsurprisingly the €22 *menu* is a meat-fest of roasted ruminants and local game with rich foraged mushroom sauces. Daily 9.30am–6.30pm

Crêperie de Païsot Place Adolphe-Ramin ☎06 81 68 40 22. Right at the entrance to the village, this friendly place offers pizzas, salads and drinks as well as a full menu of inexpensive crêpes, served on an enormous sunny south-facing terrace. March, April & Sept–Dec Fri–Sun 11am–9pm; May–Aug daily 10am–9.30pm.

The Cians Valley

For anyone driving westward across Haute Provence, towards the Grand Canyon du Verdon and beyond, the compelling **Cians Valley** short-cut leaves the Tinée Valley by taking the D30 west from St-Sauveur-sur-Tinée, via Roubion on the D30. Once out of the valley, the road drops once more to reach the small ski resort of **Beuil**, where you can join the D28 to follow the wild River Cians on its compelling course south through the **Gorges du Cians**.

Beuil

Perched beneath a stern grey pyramidal peak, at the northern end of the Gorges du Cians, **BEUIL** is a sturdy old mountain village. Twisting lanes lace through its ancient core, while a verdant hilltop park stands just above. Beuil has a double identity as a low-key **ski resort**, with the nearby slopes holding 26 lifts and 58 distinct runs.

Gorges du Cians

The sinuous **Gorges du Cians** stretches south for 22km from just below Beuil to the point where the River Cians joins forces with the Var. An ominous chaos of water, tumbling between looming red schist cliffs, it's paralleled by the D28, which repeatedly burrows through tunnels in the rock on its west bank. It finally emerges into the lower Var Valley a total of 46km southwest of St-Sauveur, 2km west of Touët-sur-Var (see page 236).

INFORMATION	THE CIANS VALLEY

BEUIL
Tourist office Bd du Col Marcel Pourchier, beside the roundabout at the village entrance (Mon–Sat 9am–noon

& 2–5pm, Sun 10am–noon & 2–5pm; ☎04 93 02 32 58, ⓦbeuil.com).

ACCOMMODATION AND EATING

BEUIL
★**L'Escapade** 15 Bd du Col Marcel Pourchier ☎04 93

02 31 27, ⓦhrlescapade.fr. Cosy, Alpine-style hotel, its public spaces festooned with ancient farming implements.

The cheapest of the simple but comfortable wood-panelled rooms share toilets; en-suite rooms cost more, and some have balconies carpeted with artificial grass. The food, savoured on an outdoor terrace, is magnificent; diners start by helping themselves from a huge jar of preserved mushrooms as well as platters of pâté and *fromage de tête*, then move onto substantial meat and fish dishes, such as fillet of beef or roasted trout. *Menus* from €26 (lunch and dinner). Closed Oct–Christmas. **€65**

The Vésubie Valley

A rewarding scenic detour as you follow the Tinée Valley south from the summit of La Bonette is to head east on the D2565, 4km south of St-Sauveur-sur-Tinée, to the dramatic **Vésubie Valley**. The road first has to climb through the scattered **Commune of Valdeblore**, home to the ancient village of **St-Dalmas**, before descending to **St-Martin-Vésubie** in the Vésubie Valley itself.

South of St-Martin, road and river head for the Var, passing **Roquebillière**, the perched village of **Lantosque** and the approach to the pilgrimage chapel of **Madonne d'Utelle**. An alternative southern route from the valley crosses east to the **Col de Turini** and down the **River Bévéra** towards Sospel.

Commune de Valdeblore

Straddling the Col St-Martin between the Tinée and Vésubie valleys, the **COMMUNE DE VALDEBLORE** consists of a series of villages strung along the D2565. The most interesting, **ST-DALMAS**, was built on the remains of a Roman outpost, and lies at the strategic crossroads between the most accessible southern route across the lower Alps, linking Piedmont with Provence, and a north–south route that connects Savoy with the sea. That historical importance is clear from the dimensions of the **Église Prieurale Bénédictine** (mid-June to mid-Sept daily 3–5pm), parts of which date from the tenth century. A gruesome glazed tomb reveals a 900-year-old skeleton; more appealing are the fragments of fourteenth-century frescoes in the north chapel. The present structure is Romanesque, plain and fierce with its typically Alpine bell tower.

Across the Col St-Martin, 3km east of St-Dalmas, chairlifts at the ski resort of **La Colmiane** provide stunning views from the **Pic de Colmiane** (daily: Christmas–March 10am–4.50pm; July & Aug 10am–6pm; ski pass €22 daily, chairlift alone €6; ☎04 93 23 25 90, ⓦcolmiane.com).

St-Martin-Vésubie

The lovely little town of **ST-MARTIN-VÉSUBIE** stands at the head of the Vésubie Valley 11km east of St-Dalmas. In late spring and early autumn it makes a perfect base for exploring the surrounding mountains, while in winter you can go for wonderful walks in snowshoes, or tackle assorted cross-country skiing routes.

The main artery of the old quarter, the **rue du Docteur-Cagnoli**, is a cobbled pedestrian street of Gothic houses with overhanging roofs and balconies. A channelled stream flows down its full length along a shallow central trough, and it's punctuated by pretty little chapels like the pastel-hued **Chapelle des Pénitents Blancs**. Commanding a small terrace just off the foot of the street, St-Martin's **church** boasts a classic Baroque facade; the interior holds works attributed to Louis Bréa. Southeast of the church you can look down at the Madone de Fenestre torrent from place de la Frairie.

Alpha wolf reserve

Le Boréon, 8km north of St-Martin on the D89 • April–June, Sept, Oct & school hols daily 10am–5pm, last admission 3.30pm; July & Aug daily 10am–6pm, last admission 4.30pm • €12; €10 in winter • ☎04 93 02 33 69, ⓦ alpha-loup.com

At **LE BORÉON**, a small, scenic mountain retreat, just inside the Parc du Mercantour, the **Alpha wolf reserve** is home to three distinct wolf packs. Wolves were reintroduced to this region in 1992, and their presence remains controversial. The reserve represents an attempt to explain the often-misunderstood creatures to locals, and explore their

5

current and historic interaction with humans. Despite its shortage of English-language information and signage, it's a fascinating place to visit – and if you come in spring, you can watch the new-born cubs from three observation points.

Roquebillière

The old village of **ROQUEBILLIÈRE**, on the left bank of the Vésubie 13km southeast of St-Martin, has had to be rebuilt six times since the Dark Ages following catastrophic landslides and floods. After the last major disaster, in 1926, when half the buildings disappeared under mud, a new village was created high above the river's right bank. The wide, tree-lined avenues of the *nouveau village* lie in stark contrast to the crumpling, leaning, medieval houses bearing down over narrow passageways in the dark and sad *vieux village*.

The Gordolasque Valley

The D171 along the **Gordolasque Valley** above old Roquebillière heads northeast for 16km, with paths leading off eastwards towards the Vallée des Merveilles. From the end, hikers can continue upstream past waterfalls and high crags to Lac de la Fous, to meet the GR52 running west to Madone de Fenestre and east to the northern end of the Vallée des Merveilles (see page 245). This triangle between Mont Clapier on the Italian border (3045m), Mont Bego (2873m) to the east and Mont Neiglier (2785m) to the west is a fabulous area for walking, but not to be taken lightly. All the **mountain refuges** here belong to the Club Alpin Français (W ffcam.fr), and may well be unsympathetic if you turn up unannounced.

Col de Turini

Around 3km south of Roquebillière, the D70 leaves the Vésubie Valley to head east to the **Col de Turini**, where four roads and two tracks meet. All give access to the **Forêt de Turini**, between the Vésubie and Bévéra valleys, in which larches in the highest reaches give way lower down to firs, spruce, beech, maples and sweet chestnuts.

The road north from the col through the small ski resort of **Camp d'Argent** to L'Authion gives a strong impression of limitless space, following the curved ridge between the two valleys and overlooking a hollow of pastures. There are plenty of walks hereabouts, but the sun, the flowers and the wild strawberries and raspberries are so pleasant you might prefer simply to stop in a field and listen to the cowbells.

Utelle

Just north of the point where the Vésubie river starts to pick up speed through the gorge that leads to its confluence with the Var, 16km south of Roquebillière, the switchbacking D32 climbs east to reach yet another far-flung **chapel**, dedicated to **La Madone d'Utelle**. Set on a plateau above the village of **UTELLE**, it's high enough to be visible from the sea at Nice. According to legend, two Portuguese sailors lost in a storm in 850 AD navigated safely into port by a light they saw gleaming from Utelle. They erected a chapel here to give thanks, though the current one dates from 1806. **Pilgrimages** still take place on Easter Monday, the Monday of Pentecost, August 15 and September 8, and conclude with a communal feast on the grassy summit.

ARRIVAL, INFORMATION AND ACTIVITIES   **THE VÉSUBIE VALLEY**

ST-MARTIN-DE-VÉSUBIE
By bus There are services from Lantosque (2 daily; 30min); Nice (2 daily; 1hr 45min) and Roquebillière (2 daily; 15min).
Tourist office Place Félix-Faure (Mon–Sat 9.30am–12.30 & 2–6pm, Sun 9.30am–12.30pm; T 04 93 03 21 28,

W saintmartinvesubie.fr).
Outdoor activities Guides du Mercantour, place du Marché (T 04 93 03 31 32, W guidescapade.com), organizes canyoning, climbing, walking and skiing expeditions.

ACCOMMODATION AND EATING

COMMUNE DE VALDEBLORE

Hotel de Valdeblore Rue Central, La Bolline ☎ 04 93 03 28 53, ⊕ hotel-valdeblore.com. Simple but very charming hotel, in the heart of the westernmost Valdeblore village, 10km up from the D2205. Nine attractively modernized wood-panelled rooms, including a spacious two-room family suite. **€73**

ST-MARTIN-DE-VÉSUBIE

Camping Ferme St-Joseph Quartier St-Joseph, rte de Nice ☎ 06 70 51 90 14, ⊕ camping-alafermestjoseph. com. Small, leafy campsite, beside the lower bridge over La Madone, which offers basic but attractive rental cabins – cheaper if you use your own bedding – as well as tent pitches. Closed late Sept to late April. Camping **€17**; cabins **€57**

Châtaigneraie 145 Allée de Verdun ☎ 04 93 03 21 22, ⊕ edwards-park-hotel-chataigneraie.com   Imposing, summer-only hotel, set in lovely gardens near the village centre. Comfortable en-suite rooms that sleep up to five – many have balconies – plus a pool and a good restaurant. Closed Oct–May. **€75**

La Dame de Coeur 20 rue Cagnoli ☎ 06 84 60 82 02. Friendly little old-town café/restaurant, serving omelettes and tarts, mixed savoury platters small and large (€10/€16), pasta and simple daily *plats* (€10/€16), with tables on the pretty street alongside an old stone fountain – diners are encouraged to refill their water jugs with the icy cold spring water. Mid-July to mid-Sept Mon & Sat noon–3pm & 7–9.30pm, Tues, Thurs & Fri 7–9.30pm, Sun noon–2.30pm; mid-Sept to mid-July Fri 7–9.30pm, Sat noon–2pm & 7–9.30pm, Sun noon–2pm.

★ **La Pierre Bleue** 163 bd Raoul Audibert ☎ 04 93 03 37 86, ⊕ silvana.giordanengo.free.fr/LaPierreBleue. Delightful, secluded B&B set in lush gardens and offering five lovely en-suite rooms; the friendly hosts also cook superb dinners for €32, using fresh local ingredients. Closed Oct–May. **€112**

Treille 68 rue Cagnoli ☎ 04 93 03 30 85. Unpretentious and inexpensive restaurant on the main pedestrian street, where the shaded terrace enjoys fabulous mountain views. *Menus* from €27 for lunch, €33 for dinner, plus €10–16 pizzas in the evening only. Mid-April to June, Sept & Oct Mon & Thurs–Sun noon–2pm & 7.30–9pm, Tues noon–2pm; July & Aug Tues–Sun noon–2pm & 7.30–9pm.

The Roya Valley

The most easterly valley of Provence, the **Roya Valley** is also the most accessible, served by train lines that climb from the coast from both Nice, via the appealing town of **Sospel**, and Ventimiglia in Italy, which converge just south of **Breil-sur-Roya**. When Nice became part of France in 1860, the upper Roya Valley was kept by the new King Victor Emmanuel II of Italy to indulge his passion for hunting, despite a plebiscite in which only one person in Tende and La Brigue voted for the Italian option. Only in 1947 was the valley finally incorporated into France.

Sospel

The ruggedness of the surrounding terrain only serves to emphasize the placid idyll of **SOSPEL**, which straddles the main road and rail links from the French coast to the Roya Valley. This dreamy Italianate town, spanning the gentle River Bévéra, is worth half a day of anyone's time. Its main street, avenue Jean-Médecin, follows the river on its southern bank before crossing the most easterly of the three bridges to become boulevard de Verdun, heading for the Roya Valley.

The central bridge, the picturesque eleventh-century **Vieux Pont**, has a tower poised between its two spans for collecting tolls. The scene is made yet more alluring by the balconied houses along the lush north bank, some of which have trompe-l'oeil facades. Viewed from the east, with the hills to the west and the bridge tower reflected in the water, this scene would be hard to improve.

While some of the back streets are becoming somewhat rundown, the **Place St-Michel**, a block back from the river at the west end of town, holds a haunting series of peaches-and-cream Baroque facades. Stand facing the **Église St-Michel** with its detached, austere Romanesque clock tower, and the **Chapelle des Pénitents Gris** and **Chapelle des Pénitents Rouges** are to your left, while to the right are the medieval arcades and trompe-l'oeil decoration of the **Palais Ricci**.

The road behind the church, rue de l'Abbaye, reached via steps between the two chapels, climbs to an ivy-covered **castle ruin** that offers good views of town.

5

Breil-sur-Roya

The town of **BREIL-SUR-ROYA** sits in a deep, narrow valley 23km northeast of Sospel, over the Col de Brouis. Here, a mere 8km north of the Italian border, the River Roya has picked up enough volume to justify a barrage, behind which a placid and aquamarine lake is ideal for canoeing. A place of modest industries – leather, olives and dairy products – Breil spreads back from both banks, with the old town on the eastern edge. A Renaissance chapel, with a golden angel blowing a trumpet from its rooftop cross, faces place Biancheri, while the vast eighteenth-century **Église Santa-Maria-in-Albis** (daily 8am–6pm) by the pont Charabot is topped by a belfry with shiny multicoloured tiles. Concealed behind the faded, crumbling plasterwork of its facade, its interior is quite splendid.

Several good **walks** are signed from the village. For a short stroll, follow the river downstream past the barrage and the washhouses, then fork upwards through an olive grove to a tiny chapel and an old Italian gatehouse. The path eventually leads up to the summit of the Arpette, which stands between Breil and the Italian border.

Saorge

The fascinating and very atmospheric village of **SAORGE**, reached by a side road that climbs steeply east from the main road at **Fontan**, 7km north of Breil, consists of a tight cluster of venerable houses in grey and mismatched shades of red tumbling across a cliff-like hillside. Set against a dramatic backdrop of deep green woodlands, the scene is brightened by the church and chapel towers, shimmering with gold Niçois tiles.

While separate roads climb up to Saorge from both north and south, the village itself is entirely pedestrianized. Not only is its main alleyway too narrow for traffic, but it meanders up and down flights of steps and through crumbling arches formed by the houses. It's paralleled by lesser lanes and alleys both above and below, linked by a tracery of tiny stairways and footpaths. Tiers of slender, too-tall houses jostle to peer over each other's shoulders; the tallest tower among them belongs to the **Église St-Sauveur** (daily 9am–5pm), which holds some sumptuous ecclesiastical art. At the far southern end of the street a path leads across the cultivated terraces to **La Madone del Poggio**, an eleventh-century chapel guarded by an impossibly high bell tower topped by an octagonal spire. The chapel itself is private property.

There's magnificent **hiking** in the hills above Saorge, and through the isolated valleys that lead east towards the Italian border.

Monastère de Saorge

Daily: Feb–May & Oct 10am–12.30pm & 2.30–5.30pm; June–Sept 10am–12.30pm & 2.30–6.30pm • €6 • ☏ 04 93 04 55 55, ⊛ saorge. monuments-nationaux.fr

Remarkably for such a tiny village, Saorge is home to a French national monument, in the delightful shape of the country's only **Baroque monastery**. Reached by a footpath that climbs from near the southern end of the main street, the **Monastère de Saorge** was founded by Franciscan monks who arrived to help during a seventeenth-century plague epidemic, and were given this site by grateful villagers. Because it was in Piedmont in Italy rather than France, it avoided damage during the French Revolution, and it remains a beautiful little place, with frescoes depicting the life of St Francis in its cloisters and refectory. It now serves as a writers' retreat, with residents benefiting from the superb organic garden laid out on the terraces behind.

La Brigue

The handsome village of **LA BRIGUE**, 8km northeast of Fontan, lies on an eastern tributary of the Roya, just south of Tende, surrounded by pastures and with the perennial snowcap of Mont Bego visible to the west. Its Romanesque church, the **Église St-Martin**, is full of medieval paintings, including several by Louis Bréa, mostly

5

depicting hideous scenes of torture and death. The octagonal seventeenth-century **Chapelle St-Michel** stands alongside.

Notre Dame des Fontaines

4km east of La Brigue • May–Sept Mon–Wed & Fri–Sun 10am–12.30pm & 2–5.30pm • €4 • ☎ 04 93 79 09 34, ⓦ labrigue.fr

From the exterior, the sanctuary of **Notre Dame des Fontaines** might appear to be a plain, graceful place of retreat. Inside, however, it's more akin to a slasher movie. Painted in the fifteenth century by Jean Baleison and Jean Canavesio, the restored **frescoes** depict 38 episodes. Each one, from Christ's flagellation through the torment on the Cross to devils claiming their victims and, ultimate gore, Judas's disembowelment, is full of violent movement and colour.

Vallée des Merveilles

2hr 30min guided walks start from the Lac des Mesches, 8km west of St-Dalmas-de-Tende on the D91 • June & Sept daily 8am & 1pm; July & Aug daily 8am, 11am, 1pm & 3pm • €11 • ☎ 04 93 04 73 71, ⓦ tendemerveilles.com & ⓦ mercantour-monts-et-merveilles.com

The **Vallée des Merveilles** lies between two lakes, more than 2000m up on the western flank of Mont Bego. The first person to record his experience of this high valley of lakes and bare rock, a fifteenth-century traveller who had lost his way, described it as "an infernal place with figures of the devil and thousands of demons scratched on the rocks". These were no delusions: the rocks are carved with images of animals, tools, people working and mysterious symbols, dating from 3200 BC onwards. More are to be found in the **Vallée de Fontanable** on the northern flank of Mont Bego, and west across the southern slopes of Mont des Merveilles.

Over the centuries other travellers, shepherds and eventually tourists have carved additional engravings hereabouts. As a result, solo visitors can only explore the Vallée de Fontanable, and the Mont des Merveilles area, on a single specific path. Joining a **guided walk** instead, led by an official Mercantour guide, is highly recommended: venturing into the area alone, you could easily miss the engravings altogether, while blue skies and sun can quickly turn into violent hailstorms and lightning.

The easiest route to the Vallée des Merveilles is the 10km trek (6–8hr) that starts at *Les Mesches* refuge, 8km west of St-Dalmas-de-Tende. The first part of the climb is through woods full of wild raspberries, mushrooms and bilberries, not all of it steeply uphill. Eventually you rise above the tree line and **Lac Long** comes into view. A few pines still manage to grow around the lake, and in spring the grass is full of flowers, but a mountain wilderness encircles you. From the *Refuge des Merveilles* by the lake, you continue up through a fearsome valley where the rocks turn from black to green according to the light. From here to just beyond the **Lac des Merveilles** you can start searching for the engravings.

The path to the Vallée de Fontanable starts 4.5km further up the D91 beyond *Les Mesches* refuge, just before the Casterino information point.

Tende

TENDE, the highest town on the Roya, guards the access to the Col de Tende, which connects Provence with Piedmont but is now bypassed by a road tunnel. Part of Italy until 1947, Tende is not especially attractive, but it's a bustling place, with plenty of cheap accommodation, restaurants, bars and shops.

The town's old and gloomy houses are built with green and purple schist, but blackened by fumes from trucks crossing to and from Italy. Above them rise the cherry-coloured belfry of the **collegiate church**, the peachy-orange towers and belfries of various **chapels**, and a 20m needle of wall that's the sole relic of a long-vanished château.

The **vieille ville** is fun to wander through, looking at the symbols of old trades on the door lintels and the overhanging roofs. On place de l'Église, the **Collégiale Notre Dame de l'Assomption** is more a repository of the town's wealth than a place of contemplation, with Baroque excess throughout.

5

Musée des Merveilles

Av 16 Septembre 1947 • Mid June & mid Sept daily (except Tues) 10am–6.pm; mid Sept–mid June daily (except Tues) 10am–5pm; closed 2 weeks in Nov • Free • ☎ 04 93 04 32 50, 🌐 www.museedesmerveilles.com

Tende's beautifully designed **Musée des Merveilles** details the geology, archeology and traditions of the Vallée des Merveilles. Alongside dioramas depicting the daily lives of Copper and Bronze Age peoples, reproductions of the rock designs are displayed, with attempts to decipher the beliefs and myths that inspired them. They're placed in the context of the contemporaneous civilizations of the ancient Near East, emphasizing the motif of the primordial couple, the bull-god and the earth goddess. There's also a model of Otzï, the so-called "Iceman" whose frozen body was discovered on the Italy-Austria border in 1991. For anyone with reasonable French-language skills, it's an invaluable insight into an intriguing subject.

ARRIVAL, INFORMATION AND ACTIVITIES   THE ROYA VALLEY

SOSPEL

By train The *gare SNCF* is southeast of town on Av A-Borriglione.

Destinations Nice (hourly; 55min); Tende (8 daily; 1hr); Breil-Sur-Roya (8 daily; 1hr).

Tourist office 1 place St-Pierre (Mon 10am–12.30pm & 1.30–6pm, Tues & Thurs 9.30am–6pm, Sat 9.30am–4.45pm; ☎ 04 83 93 95 70, 🌐 sospel-tourisme.com).

BREIL-SUR-ROYA

By train The large *gare SNCF* is 600m north of the centre.

Destinations Nice (8 daily; 1hr).

Tourist office 17 place Biancheri (June–Sept Mon–Sat 9am–12.30pm & 2–6pm, Sun 9am–12.30pm; Oct–May Mon–Fri 9am–noon & 1.30–5.30pm, Sat 9am–noon; ☎ 04 93 04 99 76, 🌐 breil-sur-roya.fr).

Outdoor activities Roya Evasion, 11 bd Rouvier ☎ 04 93 04 91 46, 🌐 royaevasion.com), rents bikes and other equipment, and organizes guided canoeing and whitewater rafting trips.

SAORGE

By train Saorge shares a *gare SNCF* with Fontan. The station is a short way up the eastern valley slope from Fontan, 1.4km below Saorge itself; taxis meet all trains.

Destinations Nice (4 daily; 1hr 15min–1hr 40min).

LA BRIGUE

Tourist office Place St-Martin (Mon–Fri 9am–12.30pm & 1.30–5pm; ☎ 04 83 93 95 50, 🌐 labrigue.fr).

TENDE

By train The *gare SNCF* is set back from the top of the main street, Av 16 Septembre 1947. In addition to regular services on the same line, the Train des Merveilles (🌐 tendemerveilles.com), designed for sightseers and offering English commentary in summer, leaves Nice daily at 9.17am, and reaches Tende at 11.24am (€32 return).

Destinations Nice (2 daily; 1hr 55min).

Tourist office 103 av 16 Septembre 1947 (daily 9am–noon & 2–6pm; ☎ 04 83 93 98 82, 🌐 tendemerveilles.com).

ACCOMMODATION AND EATING

SOSPEL

Camping Mas Fleuri Quartier La Vasta ☎ 04 93 04 14 94, 🌐 camping-mas-fleuri.com. The closest of the four local campsites, 2km upstream along the D2566, this two-star site has a pool. Closed Oct–March. **€16.70**

Étrangers 7 bd de Verdun ☎ 04 93 04 00 09, 🌐 sospel. net. Smart hotel, just across the town's eastern bridge, with a covered pool; its riverfront restaurant, *Bel Aqua* (closed Tues & Wed lunch), serves lunch *menus* for €25 and dinner from €32. Closed Dec–Feb. **€70**

Relais du Sel 3 bd de Verdun ☎ 04 93 04 00 43, 🌐 relaisdusel.fr. Attractive restaurant at the east end of town, where you dine on a terrace that's well below street level and just above the river. Excellent *menus* at €19 (lunch), €25 and €35 (dinner). Tues–Sat noon–2pm &

7–9pm, Sun noon–2pm.

Souta Loggia 5 place St-Nicolas ☎ 04 93 87 93 75. Cool café/bar, stretching beneath and beyond the arcades of a fine old square just north of the river, with a hip soundtrack, plus a *menu* of €12 salads and changing *plats* including steaks and fish specials. Daily 11am–11pm.

BREIL-SUR-ROYA

Camping Azur et Merveilles 650 promenade Georges Clemenceau ☎ 04 93 62 47 04, 🌐 camping-azur-merveilles.com. The municipal two-star campsite, part of a complex that also includes a large indoor swimming pool, is in a pleasant spot by the river, just upstream from the village. Bikes available for rent. Closed Oct–March. **€19**

Roya 3 place Biancheri ☎ 04 93 04 48 10. This central

hotel has very plain, somewhat ageing rooms above a Spar supermarket. All overlook the river, some have balconies; the cheapest lack en-suite facilities. €70

SAORGE

Ca' da Barrera 1 rue Doumergue, esplanade Charles de Gaulle ☎ 06 16 44 08 26, ⓦ chambresdhotes-saorge.fr. Saorge's one accommodation option, just below the village centre and accessible on foot only, holds five smart modern B&B rooms, with superb long-range views, opening off a sleek, contemporary dining room. Rates include breakfast; dinner (€25) by reservation. €90

Lou Pountin 56 rue Revelli ☎ 04 93 04 54 90. Perched just above the main alleyway through the village, with a few tables crammed onto the pavement, this good-value pizzeria and Italian restaurant, run by a former food writer, serves a €17.50 *menu*. Daily noon–2pm & 7–9pm.

★ **Petite Épicerie** 68 rue Revelli ☎ 09 67 38 10 83, ⓦ lapetiteepiceriesaorge.blogspot.co.uk. This little grocery-deli on the main drag doubles as a great-value bistro, a social hub for locals. Tasty mixed cheese or charcuterie platters (€7.40 to €9.50), and an excellent €12.50 *plat du jour*, are served at a couple of outdoor tables.

April–June & Sept–Dec daily (except Tues) 8am–2pm & 5–8pm; July & Aug daily 8am–9pm.

LA BRIGUE

Le Mirval 3 rue Vincent-Ferrier ☎ 04 93 04 63 71, ⓦ lemirval.com. Large, renovated century-old *Logis de France* by the bridge, offering eighteen rooms overlooking the Levenza stream, and decent food in its light conservatory dining room. Rooms on *demi-pension* basis only, including breakfast and dinner; they also offer inclusive rates with guided hiking. Closed Nov–March. *Demi-pension* €106

TENDE

La Marguerita 19 av du 16 Septembre ☎ 04 93 04 60 53. Popular pizzeria, with beams strung with dried herbs and garlic, stuffed foxes on the walls and a good range of Italian specialities on the menu like cep ravioli for €12. Daily noon–2pm & 6.30–11pm; closed Tues Oct–June.

Miramonti 5 rue Antoine Vassalo ☎ 04 93 04 61 82, ⓦ lemiramonti.fr. Inexpensive and very central hotel-restaurant that's handy for the station. The cheapest of its six clean, plain rooms lack en-suite facilities. Closed mid-Nov to mid-Dec. €56

Toulon and the southern Var

250 Les Lecques and
St-Cyr-sur-Mer

254 Bandol and around

255 Cap Sicié peninsula

257 Toulon and around

263 Hyères

267 Îles d'Hyères

271 Corniche des Maures

276 St-Tropez and around

283 Massif des Maures

287 Ste-Maxime and around

288 Inland: the Argens Valley

290 Fréjus and around

294 St-Raphaël

297 The Esterel

MASSIF DES MAURES

Toulon and the southern Var

The shoreline of the Var *département* represents a sizeable chunk of the Côte d'Azur and, thus, of the fabled allure of the south of France. Though much of the coast has been developed, the resorts are mostly small, and between the oversized marinas and dull apartment complexes, the characteristic landscape of pines, glimmering rocks and translucent sea still sometimes takes precedence – cheered in February by mimosa blossom and in autumn by the brilliance of the turning vines. Development notwithstanding, this is still a coastline that conjures up the visual magic that attracted Impressionists, Post-Impressionists and their 1950s cinematic successors. The nexus of the Côte's artistic fame and cinematic glamour – but also of vulgar display and hype – is the erstwhile fishing village of St-Tropez, possessed of charisma (and peak-season crowds, and prices) that none of its neighbours can match.

Elsewhere, the pleasures are those of the seaside, which for the most part is neither conspicuously fashionable nor unduly dowdy. In the west, highlights include the wines of the **Bandol** *appellation contrôlée* and the literary and historic associations of **Sanary-sur-Mer**. **Hyères** has attracted foreign visitors since the eighteenth century, while the crystal-clear waters and pristine ecosystems of the **Îles d'Hyères** lie just offshore. To the east is the **Corniche des Maures**, a long procession of small coastal villages turned resorts, and though it's hard to gauge quite where **Cavalière**, **Pramousquier** or **Le Rayol** start or stop, each is a little paradise of dense pinewoods and clean, sandy beaches, with the sublime garden at **Le Rayol** providing a standout diversion.

Behind this coast, the mournful **Massif des Maures** is more pristine still, its endless forests sheltering ancient monasteries and the timeless agricultural industries of cork oak and chestnut. The principal villages of **Collobrières** and **La Garde-Freinet** still preserve (for now at least) some of their rural character in the face of the encroaching wealth of **St-Tropez**, its chic neighbours and beautiful peninsula. Facing St-Tropez across its bay is the middle-class resort of **Ste-Maxime**, beyond which the coast road follows the shoreline's twists and turns – without ever quite shaking off suburbia – all the way to **Fréjus**. This, the most ancient of the Var's coastal towns, is replete with monuments from its Roman and medieval heyday. The sun, sea and sand theme reasserts itself in Fréjus's twin town of **St-Raphaël**, before the coast turns wilder along the dramatically red, rocky corniche of the **Esterel**.

The Var's one great urban agglomeration – an important transport hub that you're quite likely to pass through – is the naval port (and departmental capital) of **Toulon**, blessed with a magnificent natural harbour, cursed by its past reputation for racism and sleaze, and now slowly making good the political and aesthetic mistakes of its recent past.

Les Lecques and St-Cyr-sur-Mer

Wedged between the D559 coast road and the sea at the Var's western extremity, sedate **LES LECQUES** is a beach resort, pure and simple – the coastal extension of the inland town of **ST-CYR-SUR-MER**, with which it shares a municipality.

Les Lecques is strung along a sand-and-shingle beach that curves east from the town's marina to the pleasant little fishing port of **La Madrague**, from where a wonderful 12km coastal path meanders around Pointe Grenier to the *calanque* of **Port d'Alon** – where there's a simple snack bar/restaurant, *Chez Tonton Ju* (April–Oct daily lunch

PORQUEROLLES ISLAND

Highlights

❶ Bandol appellation contrôlée Sample the fine wines and explore the peaceful wine-growing country a little way inland from the bustle of the coast. See page 254

❷ The island of Porquerolles Rent a bike to discover the pristine beaches and landscapes of the most easily accessible of the Îles d'Hyères. See page 268

❸ St-Tropez Suspend your cynicism for a day and enjoy the art, the absurdity, the glamour and sheer excess of the Côte d'Azur's best-known resort. See page 276

❹ Massif des Maures Escape the glitz and development of the coast to explore the sombre wooded hills, and the unspoiled country towns of Collobrières and La Garde-Freinet. See page 283

❺ Fréjus Founded by Julius Caesar as a naval base, Fréjus has some of the best-preserved Roman remains along this coast, including a theatre, an amphitheatre and a ruined aqueduct. See page 290

❻ The Esterel Drive or walk in the most distinctive, rugged and ancient of the coast's landscapes, the craggy, red Esterel. See page 297

HIGHLIGHTS ARE MARKED ON THE MAP ON PAGE 252

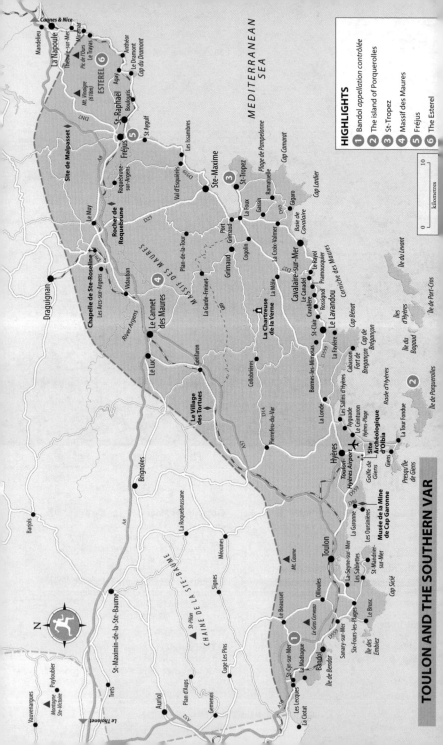

TOULON AND THE SOUTHERN VAR

HIGHLIGHTS

1. Bandol appellation contrôlée
2. The island of Porquerolles
3. St-Tropez
4. Massif des Maures
5. Fréjus
6. The Esterel

0 kilometres 10

MEDITERRANEAN SEA

only; ☎04 94 26 20 08) – before continuing to Bandol. In St-Cyr-sur-Mer proper, there is a miniature, golden **Statue of Liberty**, sculpted by Bartholdi, the artist who created its better-known New York sister.

The twin towns' other great draw is wine from the local **vineyards**, which belong to the Bandol *appellation* (see page 254).

Musée de Tauroentum

131 rte de la Madrague, between Les Lecques and La Madrague • May Sat & Sun 3–7pm; June–Sept & school holidays daily (except Tues) 3–7pm; Oct–April Sat & Sun 2–5pm • €5 • ☎04 94 26 30 46, ⊕ museedetauroentumsaintcyrsurmer.fr

Les Lecques claims to have been the Greek trading post of Tauroentum, site of a decisive naval battle between Caesar (the eventual victor) and Pompey for the control of Marseille. The remains of a **Roman villa**, now the **Musée de Tauroentum**, on the coast between Les Lecques and La Madrague, date from the first century AD and boast three extant mosaics, patches of frescoes, a couple of interesting sarcophagi, numerous beautiful Greek and Roman vases and other household items.

Centre d'Art Sébastien

12 bd Jean-Jaurès, St-Cyr-sur-Mer • Wed–Sun 10am–noon & 2–6pm • €1 • ☎04 94 26 19 20

In St-Cyr, the small **Centre d'Art Sébastien** displays the paintings and tender terracotta statues of Sébastien, the Parisian-born artist (and friend of Picasso) in a beautifully restored former caper storehouse. It also hosts regular temporary exhibitions of painting, sculpture and photography.

ARRIVAL AND INFORMATION

LES LECQUES AND ST-CYR-SUR-MER

By train The *gare SNCF* serving Les Lecques and St-Cyr-sur-Mer lies between the two at the north end of Av des Lecques, a 20min walk from Les Lecques.

Destinations Bandol (every 30min–1hr; 5min); La Ciotat (every 20min–1hr 30min; 5min).

Tourist office Place de l'Appel du 18 Juin, off Av du Port, Les Lecques (April–June & Sept–Oct Mon–Sat 9am–12.30pm & 2–6pm, Sun 10am–1pm; July & Aug Mon–Sat 9am–1.30pm & 2.30–7pm, Sun 10am–1.30pm & 2.30–5pm; Nov–March 9am–12.30pm & 2–5pm; ☎04 94 26 73 73, ⊕ saintcyrsurmer.com).

ACCOMMODATION

Les Baumelles 1 rte de la Madrague ☎04 94 26 21 27, ⊕ campinglesbaumelles.fr. A spacious three-star campsite, close to the beach between Les Lecques and La Madrague and with plenty of shade. It also rents out mobile homes by the week. Closed Oct–March. Camping **€32**; mobile home per week **€660**

Beau Séjour Les Palmiers 34 av de la Mer, Les Lecques ☎04 94 26 54 06, ⊕ beausejour-lespalmiers.fr. Pleasant former winery with fourteen individually themed rooms – from lavender to Moroccan – close to the sea, plus a restaurant serving seasonal, regional cuisine. **€150**

Grand Hôtel des Lecques 24 av du Port, Les Lecques ☎04 94 26 23 01, ⊕ grandhotel-leslecques.com. A handsome three-star hotel set in a large garden with a pool, *pétanque* pitch and tennis courts, 100m from the sea. **€159**

EATING

The widest choice of restaurants in **Les Lecques** is along the traffic-free seafront promenade near the marina, while there's a smaller cluster of unpretentious eating places around the fishing harbour at **La Madrague**. St-Cyr has a **market** on Sunday at place G. Péri in the *vieille ville* from 8am to 1pm.

Beau Séjour Les Palmiers 34 av de la Mer, Les Lecques ☎04 94 26 54 06, ⊕ beausejour-lespalmiers.fr. Hotel/restaurant with a pretty courtyard setting and Italian-influenced Mediterranean food based on local produce.

Lunch *formule* €15; *menu* €35. Live music on Fri nights over the summer. April–Oct Thurs–Sat noon–2pm & 8–10.30pm.

★ **Les 2 Soeurs** Nouveau Port des Lecques, Les Lecques ☎04 94 26 24 15, ⊕ les2soeurs.fr. Smart, friendly place right on the marina, with pizzas from €10, salads from €15.50 and regional fishy treats like bouillabaisse for €25. Daily noon–2.30pm & 7–10.30pm; closed mid-Nov to end Dec.

Bandol and around

BANDOL is a lively resort screened from the open sea by its vast marina. The town bustles with yachties and with day-trippers browsing in its many clothes shops, which range from cheap to chic. Bandol is rightly proud of its wines, which have their own, distinct *appellation contrôlée*, and sampling and buying wine is much the best reason to stop over; the attractive countryside around town also holds some gentle attractions. Other than this, the sea is the main draw, whether for beach lazing, watersports or excursions to the **Île de Bendor**, which hosts France's largest exposition of wines, spirits and alcohols.

Oenothèque des Vins de Bandol

Place Lucien Artaud • Summer Mon–Sat 10am–1pm & 3–7pm, Sun 10am–1pm; winter Mon–Sat 10am–1pm & 3–6.30pm, Sun 10am–1pm • ☎ 04 94 29 45 03, ⊕ maisondesvins-bandol.com

Given that **wine** is Bandol's main claim to fame, the obvious first port of call is the modern **Oenothèque des Vins de Bandol** at the eastern end of the Quai Charles-de-Gaulle opposite the casino. You can obtain information and maps of the various *domaines* here, but if you don't have the time for a self-guided tour of the local vineyards, this is also a good place to taste and buy, with its helpful, friendly staff.

The beaches

Bandol's most scenic sandy **beach** curves around **Anse de Rènecros**, an almost circular cove west of the port along boulevard Louis-Lumière. More secluded are the little coves and beaches along the coastal path to Les Lecques, which you reach from avenue du Maréchal-Foch on the western side of the Anse de Rènecros.

Île de Bendor

⊕ lesilespaulricard.com • Boat trips from Bandol's port: daily: April–June, Sept & Oct 7am–8pm; July & Aug 7am–1am; Nov–March 7.30am–5pm • €15

THE WINES OF BANDOL

Winemaking in these relatively infertile coastal hills dates back to the Phoenician colony that later became Roman Tauroentum. The quality of the wines – which is boosted by the unusually low yields – was acknowledged as early as the eighteenth century, when despite decrees promoting cereal production over wine, Bandol's vines were spared by official *dérogation*. The Bandol **appellation d'origine contrôlée** (or AOC) was established in 1941, making it one of France's oldest. *Domaines* were replanted with the region's traditional cinsault, grenache and **mourvèdre** grapes, the last-named of Spanish origin and the dominant grape in the superb reds and sublime pale, dry rosés; the whites, though rare, are also worth trying. Bandol **reds** must contain a minimum of fifty percent mourvèdre, though some winemakers push this percentage far higher. The result is a rich, dark red wine that develops notes of leather, truffle and black fruits as it matures.

The Bandol AOC spreads in an arc along the A50 autoroute from **St-Cyr** in the west to **Ollioules** in the east, with the densest concentration of vineyards still focused on La Cadière. Most can be visited for tasting and buying; those with international reputations include the **Domaine Tempier** at Le Plan du Castellet, 1082 chemin des Fanges (Mon–Fri 9am–noon & 2–6pm; ☎ 04 94 98 70 21, ⊕ domainetempier.com), **Château de Pibarnon** at La Cadière (Mon–Sat 9am–noon & 2–6pm; ☎ 04 94 90 12 73, ⊕ pibarnon.com) and the organic **Domaine de Terrebrune** at 724 chemin de la Tourelle, Ollioules (July & Aug 9.30am–12.30pm & 3–6.30pm; Sept–June Mon–Sat 9.30am–12.30pm & 2.30–6pm; ☎ 04 94 74 01 30, ⊕ terrebrune. fr), where there's an excellent *restaurant gastronomique*, *La Promesse* (☎ 04 94 98 79 39, ⊕ restaurant-lapromesse.fr).

If you're at all susceptible to the allure of islands, you may want to take the short boat trip from Bandol's quay to the rocky **Île de Bendor**. Uninhabited when it was bought by *pastis* tycoon **Paul Ricard** in the 1950s, it's nowadays more tourist honeypot than desert island: picnics aren't allowed and it is cluttered from end to end with attractions of various kinds, including a **museum** dedicated to Ricard advertising (summer only: daily 10.30am–12.30pm & 3–6pm; free), and the **Musée des Vins et des Spiritueux EUVS** (July & Aug only: daily except Wed 1–6pm; free), which in addition to its vast display of wines, spirits and bottles, restaurant menus and drinks lists, also hosts wine and spirits symposiums. The man who created all this, Paul Ricard, died in 1997 and is buried at the highest point of the island.

For most of the year, outdoor activities on the island revolve around the **Centre International de Plongée** (☎04 94 29 55 12, ⓦplongee-cip-bandol.fr), which offers diving training from beginner to instructor level, including classes for children from the age of 8 upwards.

6

ARRIVAL AND INFORMATION

BANDOL

By train From Bandol's *gare SNCF*, head down Av de la Gare and Av du 11 Novembre 1918 to reach the town centre and port.

Destinations Hyères (every 30min; 42min); Sanary (every 30min–1hr; 7min); Toulon (every 30 min–1hr; 19 min)

Tourist office On Bandol's quayside at allée Vivien (daily: June–Sept 9am–7pm; Oct–May 10am–6pm; ☎04 94 29 41 35, ⓦbandol.fr).

ACCOMMODATION

Golf Hotel Plage de Rènecros ☎04 94 29 45 83 ⓦgolfhotel.fr. You couldn't be closer to the beach than at this pleasant two-star hotel on the pretty sandy cove of Rènecros, a short walk from the centre of Bandol; it also has secure private parking. **€112**

Île Rousse 25 bd Louis Lumière ☎04 94 29 33 00, ⓦile-rousse.com. Bandol's top hotel is a five-star affair, with a pool, thalassotherapy spa, a private stretch of Rènecros beach, vast, light rooms and a fancy restaurant (see below). **€297**

Le Key Largo 19 corniche Bonaparte ☎04 94 29 46 93, ⓦhotel-key-largo.com. A pleasant two-star hotel right by the sea near the port. Rooms are simple but bright; some have balconies and the more expensive have views of the Île de Bendor. **€92**

EATING AND DRINKING

You'll find plenty of restaurants, brasseries and bars – some of them quite sophisticated – in the centre of Bandol, along **rue de la République** and **allée Jean-Moulin**, parallel to the port. For picnic food try the Tuesday morning **market** on the quayside.

Auberge du Port 9 allée Jean-Moulin ☎04 94 29 42 63, ⓦauberge-du-port.com. Classy restaurant and informal brasserie with a terrace facing the port: oysters for €8.50, seafood tapas from €5 and a €22 lunch *menu*. Daily 6.30–1am; last lunch orders 2.30pm, last dinner orders 11pm (10pm outside high season).

Au Fille du Temps 1 rue de la Paroisse ☎04 83 99 46 17, ⓦaufildutemps.eatbu.com. Located a little way back from the port this modern diner focuses on seafood with favourites like their generous mixed grill platter of prawns and scallops as well as less common combinations like mullet with pesto sauce, both €23. Mon & Wed–Sun 10am–3pm & 7–10.30pm, Tues 10am–3pm & 6–11pm.

Les Oliviers 25 bd Louis Lumière ☎04 94 29 33 12, ⓦthalazur.fr/bandol/hotel. Elegant Michelin starred *restaurant gastronomique* at the *Île Rousse* hotel, with delights such as scallop and truffle feuilleté with Jerusalem artichoke purée and a vermouth reduction; *menus* €58–128. Daily: July & Aug 7.15–10pm; Sept–June 12.15–2pm & 7.15–10pm.

Cap Sicié peninsula

The coastal approach to Toulon from the west takes you via the congested neck of the **Cap Sicié peninsula**. On the western side, **Six-Fours-les-Plages** sprawls between pretty **Sanary-sur-Mer** and **Le Brusc**, from where you can get boats to another of Ricard's islands, **Île des Embiez**.

The eastern side of the peninsula merges with Toulon's former shipbuilding suburb of La Seyne-sur-Mer (see page 260), while at the southern end a semi-wilderness of high cliffs and forest reigns.

6

A LITERARY HAVEN

In the interwar years, Sanary-sur-Mer was not the most fashionable place in the south of France, but its lack of cachet made it affordable to writers and intellectuals. **Aldous Huxley** wrote *Eyeless in Gaza* and *Brave New World* at his Villa Huley on allée Thérèse in between dips at the Gorguette beach; later, after the Nazis came to power, many of Germany's cultural elite found temporary refuge here. **Thomas Mann** held court at his villa on chemin de la Colline, later torn down by the Nazis to make way for coastal defences; his near-neighbour was Alma Mahler, widow of the composer, while **Brecht** sang anti-Hitler songs in the cafés on the *quai*. A plaque on the tourist office wall commemorates Sanary's German connection; the office itself will supply you with information on landmarks associated with the exiles, many of which are now marked with plaques. Huxley's villa, now known as Les Flots, and Sybille Bedford's house in chemin du Diable are among the survivors.

Sanary-sur-Mer

"Next morning the sun came through the French window, the window gave onto a balcony, the balcony to a sea front; small boats bobbing at harbour. Pretty, my mother said." Sybille Bedford, Quicksands, a Memoir

So the little harbour of **SANARY-SUR-MER**, 5km east of Bandol, seemed to the novelist and travel writer Sybille Bedford in the mid-1920s, when she saw it for the first time. And so it remains, with its pastel pink and yellow facades and comically dignified little *mairie*. The harbour preserves its fishing-port character, the headland to the west its discreetly desirable villas. It may not be the most fashionable spot in the south of France, but Sanary's intact charm draws day-trippers from a wide area, and on warm summer evenings the portside hums with life.

Literary fame aside, the pleasures of Sanary are those of the coast: café-lounging on the port and swimming or diving in the clear waters west of the town, at La Gorguette or the coves of Portissol and Cousse; the town claims to be the birthplace of scuba diving. It livens up on Wednesday, which is market day.

Tour Romane

Place de la Tour • July & Aug Mon & Thurs–Sun 10am–12.30pm & 3.30–7pm, Tues & Wed 3.30–7pm; Sept–June Wed–Fri 2.30–6pm, Sat & Sun 10am–12.30pm & 2.30–6pm • Free

The thirteenth-century **Tour Romane** by the port holds a small **museum** devoted to undersea archeology, with finds including fragments of Carthaginian amphorae dating from the fifth to the third century BC and discovered off the Île des Embiez.

ARRIVAL AND INFORMATION SANARY-SUR-MER

By train The *gare SNCF*, which Sanary shares with neighbouring Ollioules, is 2.5km northeast of the centre; buses into town (4 daily; 11min) don't necessarily link up with train arrivals.
Destinations Bandol (every 30min–1hr; 7min); Toulon (every 30min–1hr; 11min).
By bus Buses from Toulon, Bandol or Six-Fours stop at the post office, two blocks back from the port.

Destinations Bandol (hourly; 10min); Six-Fours (every 30min–1hr; 10min); Toulon (hourly; 40min).
Tourist office By the port at 1 quai du Levant (April–June, Sept & Oct Mon–Fri 9am–6pm, Sat 9am–1pm & 2–5pm; July & Aug daily 9am–7pm; Nov–March Mon–Fri 9am–12.30pm & 2–5.30pm, Sat 9am–12.30pm & 2–5pm; ☎04 94 74 01 04, ⓦsanarysurmer.com).

ACCOMMODATION AND EATING

Campasun Parc Mogador 167 chemin de Beaucours ☎04 94 84 23 75, ⓦcampasun.eu. Four-star campsite west of the town centre, with a heated pool, sports facilities and with mobile homes as well as pitches for tents or caravans. Closed Jan & Feb. **€77**
Centre Azur des UCJG 149 av du Nid ☎04 94 74 18 87, ⓦcentre-azur.com. Sanary's YMCA, in the quiet district

of Portissol, offers accommodation in canvas bungalows, or rooms with shared or private facilities. High season half or full board only. Per person, half/full board: camping **€38.90/€49.90**; doubles **€48.50/€60**
L'enK New 13 rue Louis Blanc ☎04 94 74 66 57. Creative Asian fusion cuisine with a strong fish and seafood emphasis in dishes such as prawn ravioli with a mango jus.

Menu €22.90. Daily noon–2pm & 7–10.15pm, later in high season.

Le Nautique 6 quai Général de Gaulle ☎04 94 74 00 64. Once the haunt of Sanary's interwar literary exiles, the *Nautique* is rather classy as bar *tabacs* go, with an impressive selection of cigars, cocktails, ice creams and fancy coffees. They also do a charcuterie sharing platter and a bottle of Corsican wine for €30. Daily 6.30am–2am.

★ **Quai 16** 16 quai Esmenard ☎06 31 34 62 10. Tiny place on Sanary's port – the interior is all kitchen and you

sit on the narrow terrace outside – serving traditional Provençal fare with an emphasis on fish and seafood. Service is friendly and prices good value; there's a lunchtime *formule* for €17.90 and evening *menus* at €18.90 and €29.90. Tues–Sat noon–2pm & 7–10pm, Sun noon–2pm.

La Tour 24 quai Général de Gaulle ☎04 94 74 10 10, ⓦsanary-hoteldelatour.com. Attractive and historic hotel from which Sybille Bedford first glimpsed Sanary, with a/c en-suite rooms, and a good quayside restaurant. There's also private parking. **€174**

6

Six-Fours-les-Plages

Sanary merges seamlessly along the D559 into **SIX-FOURS-LES-PLAGES**, which at first seems nothing but sprawling suburbs littered with hoardings, though it has its charms – not least its well-kept sand and shingle beaches (of which the **Plage du Cros**, just before Le Brusc, is the nicest). A small lane off the D11 Sanary–Ollioules road on the northern fringes of Six-Fours takes you to the **Chapelle de Pépiole** (daily 3–6pm), a stunning sixth-century pre-Romanesque chapel with three naves, restored during the 1950s and set in the midst of pines, cypresses and olive trees.

Le Brusc and Cap Sicié

From the pleasant harbour of **LE BRUSC**, a **coastal footpath** winds its way along the wild headlands of **Cap Sicié** itself. The path offers heady views in every direction, but as it can get pretty windy up here, exploring the cliffs should be done with a certain amount of caution even on a calm day. The sturdy sentinel of **Notre Dame du Mai** (Oct–April every first Sat morning of the month & every first and third Sun 2–6pm; May daily 9am–noon & 2.30–6pm for pilgrimages; free), once a primitive lighthouse, provides a good target. A little way back from the coast the scenic, twisting D2816 gives car access to the *cap*, its hiking trails, picnic sites and the naturist beaches on its eastern flank, but is closed to traffic from mid-June to mid-September.

Île des Embiez

ⓦlesilespaulricard.com • Ferry crossings from Le Brusc daily: Jan–March & Nov–Dec 7am–5.30pm; April–mid-June & Sept–Oct 7am–10.45pm; mid-June–Aug 7am–11.45pm; outside July & Aug later sailings are available if booked in advance; 15min; €17

Larger than its sister island to the west, Paul Ricard's second island, the **Île des Embiez**, offers more natural beauty, with a couple of pocket-handkerchief beaches and low cliffs that are a riot of flowers in spring; there's even a nature trail to follow. With its vast marina, miniature road train, tennis courts and vineyards, it's not exactly Robinson Crusoe country, however. The big draw is the **Institut Océanographique Paul Ricard** (July–Aug Mon–Fri 10am–12.30pm & 1.30–5.30pm, Sat 10am–12.30pm & 2–5.30pm; April–June & Sept–Oct Mon–Fri 10am–12.30pm & 1.30–5.30pm, Sat 2–5.30pm, Sun 10am–12.30pm; Feb–March & Nov–mid-Nov Mon–Fri 10am–12.30pm & 1.30–5.30pm, Sun 2am–5.30pm; mid-Nov–Jan Mon–Fri 10am–12.30pm & 1.30–5.30pm; €5; ⓦinstitut-paul-ricard.org), which has an aquarium and exhibitions on underwater matters.

Toulon and around

Viewed from the heights of Mont Faron or Notre Dame du Mai, it's clear why **TOULON** had to be a major port. The city stands on a magnificent natural harbour:

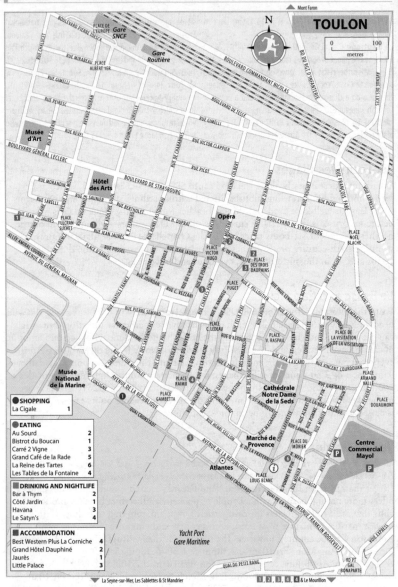

TOULON

SHOPPING
| La Cigale | 1 |

EATING
Au Sourd	2
Bistrot du Boucan	1
Carré 2 Vigne	3
Grand Café de la Rade	5
La Reine des Tartes	6
Les Tables de la Fontaine	4

DRINKING AND NIGHTLIFE
Bar à Thym	2
Côté Jardin	1
Havana	3
Le Satyn's	4

ACCOMMODATION
Best Western Plus La Corniche	4
Grand Hôtel Dauphiné	2
Jaurès	1
Little Palace	3

with the 15km shoreline of the heart-shaped bay of the Petite Rade (the inner harbour) shared between Toulon and its neighbour **La Seyne-sur-Mer** to the west. Facing the city, about 3km out to sea, is **St-Mandrier**, a virtual island connected to the Cap Sicié peninsula by the isthmus of Les Sablettes and protecting the Grande Rade (the outer harbour) both northwards and eastwards. The town is home to the French Navy's Mediterranean Fleet, continuing a **naval tradition** that dates back to the fifteenth century. The city's strategic importance made wartime destruction almost inevitable; the entire fleet was scuttled here in November 1942 to avoid it falling into the hands of the Germans, while the waterfront was severely battered during the Allied landings of 1944.

Though the high apartment buildings and wide highways slicing through the centre don't make the approach to Toulon – now also a major stopover for cruise liners – very alluring, a regeneration programme is slowly beautifying the *vieille ville*. A smart **gallery** of modern art attracts touring shows from Paris, while the town also boasts good **markets** and superb views from **Mont Faron**; in addition, there are fine sand or shingle **beaches** to the east in Le Mourillon and across the Petit Rade at La-Seyne-sur-Mer. Meanwhile, the city's **Stade Mayol** is the home of one of France's most successful rugby teams, RC Toulonnais.

Vieille ville

Toulon's **vieille ville**, crammed in between boulevard de Strasbourg and avenue de la République on the old port, has a fine scattering of **fountains**, a decent selection of shops (particularly clothing stores), and an excellent **market** (Tues–Sun) on cours Lafayette; on Fridays and Saturdays there's also a farmer's market on neighbouring rue Pierre Lendrin. The nicest (and liveliest) parts of the old town are around the **Cathédrale Notre Dame de la Seds** and the imposing nineteenth-century **Opéra**, with plenty of café terraces that offer people-watching opportunities. Big chunks of the eastern side of Vieux Toulon disappeared with the construction of the ugly but useful **Mayol** shopping centre; traffic-free Quai Cronstadt fronting the **port** is more alluring, with plenty more sunny café terraces.

Musée National de la Marine

Place Monsenergue, Quai Norfolk • Mon & Wed–Sun 10am–6pm • €6; English audioguide €2 • ☎ 04 22 42 02 01, ⓦ musee-marine.fr

The vast expanse of the **Arsenal**, on place Monsenergue, marks the western end of the *vieille ville*, with its grandiose eighteenth-century gateway leading to the **Musée National de la Marine**, where visitors are greeted by Pierre-Louis Ganne's depiction of the Battle of Trafalgar. The museum displays figureheads, an extensive collection of model ships and the control panel of the famous French aircraft carrier *Clemenceau*, as well as stark black-and-white photos that illustrate the after-effects of the scuttling of the French fleet in 1942.

Hôtel des Arts

236 bd Général Leclerc • Tues–Sun 10am–6pm • Free • ☎ 04 83 95 18 40, ⓦ hda.var.fr

Housed in the Beaux Arts former Conseil General building on boulevard Général Leclerc – Toulon's Haussmann-inspired main east–west artery – the handsome **Hôtel des Arts** attracts big touring exhibitions from the major Parisian galleries; a vigorous acquisitions policy is also helping the museum to assemble a permanent collection, embracing installation and video art alongside painting and sculpture.

Musée d'Art

113 bd Général Leclerc • Tues–Sun noon–6pm • Free • ☎ 04 94 36 81 01

The grandiose **Musée d'Art** has an eclectic collection spanning eighteenth- and nineteenth-century works by Toulon artists, paintings by Fragonard and Felix Ziem and more modern pieces by the likes of Niki de St Phalle and Yves Klein. The museum stages themed exhibitions that draw on its own collection, as well as hosting temporary exhibitions.

Around the Petite Rade

Regular municipal ferries connect Toulon's *gare maritime* with La Seyne-sur-Mer (#8M; 20min); Les Sablettes via Tamaris (#18M; 30min); and St-Mandrier (#28M; 20min) • ⓦ reseaumistral.com

It's worth taking the time to discover the attractions of Toulon's magnificent **natural harbour**, from the forts and shoreline of **La Seyne-sur-Mer** to the sandy beaches of **Les Sablettes** and the charm of the small port of **St-Mandrier-sur-Mer**.

La Seyne-sur-Mer

The loss of **LA SEYNE-SUR-MER**'s naval shipyards at the end of the 1980s took a heavy toll on this old industrial community, though a smart new waterfront complete with a public park has now taken their place. Away from the centre, La Seyne has an attractive shoreline along the Petite Rade and the Baie du Lazaret, dotted with pines and eccentric villas and popular with joggers.

Musée Naval du Fort Balaguier

924 Corniche Bonaparte • Tues–Sun: July & Aug 10am–noon & 3–7pm; Sept–June 9am–noon & 2–6pm • €3 • ☎ 04 94 94 84 72

Occupying a fort built in 1634 and later reinforced by Vauban, the **Musée Naval du Fort Balaguier** explores La Seyne's long association with naval history. In 1793, after Royalists had handed Toulon over to the British and Spanish fleet, it was the scene of fierce fighting between the British and Napoleon's forces, during which the British set up a line of immensely secure fortifications between this bastion and the one now known as **Fort Napoléon**, 1km or so to the west at Chemin Marc Sangnier, which now houses a cultural centre and contemporary art gallery (open during exhibitions Tues–Sat 2–6pm; free; ☎ 04 94 30 42 80). Despite its ability to rain down artillery on any attacker, Balaguier was taken by Napoleon with a bunch of volunteers, who sent the enemies of revolutionary France packing, though not before they burnt the arsenal, the remaining French ships and part of the town.

Tamaris

Between Fort Balaguier and the sand spit of Les Sablettes is the peaceful former resort of **TAMARIS**, with its lovely shoreline of rickety wooden jetties and fishing huts on stilts overlooking the mussel beds of the Baie du Lazaret. The beautiful oriental building on the front, formerly the University of Lyon's Michel Pacha Marine Physiology Institute, was built in the nineteenth century by a local man who made his fortune in Turkey.

Les Sablettes and the Cap Sicié beaches

At **Les Sablettes** you can lounge on an impressive, south-facing sandy beach with a view towards **Cap Sicié**. It's very much bucket-and-spade, family territory, with no St-Tropez-style airs and graces, and there's a smattering of bar-*glaciers* and restaurants catering to day-trippers. To the southwest is a series of charming and progressively more low-key bays, from the perfect sandy cove of **Anse de Fabrégas** to a trio of idyllic naturist beaches on the eastern side of Cap Sicié, reached by a steep footpath from the Jonquet car park on the D2816. Access to these was restricted at the time of writing due to recent landslides.

St-Mandrier-sur-Mer

Beyond Les Sablette's neck of sand is the pretty little port of **ST-MANDRIER-SUR-MER**, with the security gates of a *terrain militaire* beyond it. The juxtaposition of portside cafés and hulking frigates anchored offshore is delightfully odd; that aside, there are beaches, including the rocky **plage de la Coudoulière** and sandy, pine-fringed **plage de Ste-Asile**.

Mont Faron

Cable car Bd Amiral Vence • Daily: Feb & Nov 10am–5.30pm; March 10am–6pm; April & Oct 10am–6.30pm; May, June & Sept 10am–7pm; July & Aug 10am–7.45pm; closed in high winds • €7.80 • ☎ teleferique-faron.com • Bus #40, direction "Super Toulon"

The best way to appreciate the magnificence of Toulon's harbour is to ascend the 542m **Mont Faron**. By road, avenue Emile-Fabre becomes route du Faron, snaking up to the top and descending again from the northeast, a journey of 18km in all. The **road** is a one-way slip of tarmac with few barriers on the hairpin bends, looping up and down through a pristine landscape of pine and rock – and with a wonderful if somewhat vertigo-inducing belvedere just before the summit. For speed of access, the **cable car** is the way to go.

The summit

Mont Faron's **summit** is threaded with paths and dotted with picnic spots, and the views over Toulon are quite breathtaking. The peak area also holds a **memorial museum** (Nov–March Mon & Wed–Sun 10am–12.30pm & 1.15–5.15pm; April–June & Sept–Oct Mon & Wed–Sun 10am–12.30pm & 1.15–7.15pm; July–Aug daily 10.15am–7.15pm; €5), dedicated to the Allied landings in Provence that took place in August 1944, with gripping screenings of original newsreel footage. There's a **restaurant**, *Le Drap d'Or*, close to the museum and another by the cable-car station.

6

Le Mourillon

Bus #3 (direction "Mourillon") or #23 (direction "Quatre Saisons") from the centre

Neat artificial beaches stretch along the shoreline of Toulon's smart eastern suburb of **Le Mourillon**, east of the city centre. In the mid-nineteenth century it became the favoured residence of naval officers, before developing as a bathing resort around the turn of the twentieth century. The artificial beaches were constructed in the 1960s; nowadays Le Mourillon's pleasant coastal strip is also home to many of the city's most fashionable bars and restaurants.

ARRIVAL AND INFORMATION
TOULON

By train The *gare SNCF* is on place de l'Europe on the northern side of the city centre, next to the *gare routière*. Destinations Hyères (every 30min–1hr 30min; 20min); Les Arcs-Draguignan (roughly half hourly; 32–59min); La Seyne-Six-Fours (every 30min–1hr 30min; 5min); Marseille (every 10–12min at peak times; 43min–1hr 6min); Ollioules–Sanary (up to every 12min at peak times; 9min).

By bus The *gare routière* is on Bd Tessé on the northern side of the city centre, next to the *gare SNCF*. Destinations Aix (up to 13 daily; 1hr 15min); Bandol (10 daily; 20–50min); Brignoles (up to 4 daily Mon–Fri, 2 on Sat; 1hr 35min); Collobrières (2 daily; 1hr 50min); Draguignan (2 daily; 1hr 50min); Hyères (every 20–30min;

1hr 9min); Le Lavandou (8 daily; 1hr 15min); St-Tropez (14 daily; 1hr 40min–2hr 10min); Sanary (approx. hourly; 40min); Six-Fours (every 30min; 40–45min); Toulon-Hyères airport (6 daily; 45min).

By ferry Corsica Ferries (ⓦcorsicaferries.com) operates ferry services between Toulon and Corsica; frequency depends on the season, but even in winter there's a daily sailing to Bastia (10hr) and Ajaccio (10hr).

Tourist office 12 place Louis Blanc (Sept–June Mon & Wed–Sat 9am–6pm, Tues 10am–6pm, Sun 9am–1pm; July–Aug Mon & Wed–Sun 9am–6pm, Tues 10am–6pm; ☎04 94 18 53 00, ⓦtoulontourisme.com).

GETTING AROUND

By bus and ferry Buses and the ferries across the Rade are run by Réseau Mistral (☎04 94 03 87 03, ⓦreseaumistral.com). The tourist office can supply you with a city bus map. **Tickets** Single fares on buses cost €1.40 and on the ferries €2; these are sold only on the bus or ferry. Abonnement 1

Jour tickets (€3.90) allow unrestricted travel for one day on buses and ferries. One-day tickets are sold in *bar-tabacs* and newsagents, Réseau Mistral offices and at the ferry terminal.

ACCOMMODATION
SEE MAP PAGE 258

Best Western Plus La Corniche 17 littoral Frédéric Mistral ☎04 94 41 35 12, ⓦhotel-corniche.com. Very pleasant hotel overlooking a small fishing port in the seaside suburb of Le Mourillon, with a/c, soundproofed rooms, modern decor and parking. Some rooms have sea views. **€152**

Grand Hôtel Dauphiné 10 rue Berthelot ☎04 94 92 20 28, ⓦgrandhoteldauphine.com. Impressively stylish three-star *Logis de France* in the pedestrian zone close to the Opéra, with 55 soundproofed, a/c rooms and a rooftop pool and sun terrace. There's no parking, but guests get concessionary rates at a nearby car park. **€77**

6

Jaurès 50 rue Jean-Jaurès ☎ 04 94 92 83 04, ⓦ hotel jaures.fr. One of the cheapest in town, close to the Base Navale, with soundproofed, a/c rooms with flat screen TV. There are also inexpensive singles (from €45) at its nearby sister, the *Hôtel des Allées*. **€55**

Little Palace 6 rue Berthelot ☎ 04 94 92 26 62, ⓦ hotel-littlepalace.com. Smart and comfortable two-star hotel in the *vieille ville* close to the Opéra, with 23 rooms decorated in attractive, Provençal style. There's also secure parking nearby sand a cheaper sister hotel, the *3 Dauphins*, opposite. **€65**

EATING

SEE MAP PAGE 258

There's a strip of **brasseries**, **cafés** and **restaurants** facing Toulon's port, though greater culinary ambition is to be found in the cluster of streets around the Opéra; there's plenty of choice, too, along the littoral Frédéric-Mistral in Le Mourillon.

Au Sourd 10 rue Molière ☎ 04 94 92 28 52, ⓦ ausourd. com. Toulon's oldest restaurant serves wonderful fish dishes like marinated oysters and squid in parsley sauce. *Menus* €28 and €37. Tues–Sat noon–2pm & 7.15–10pm.

Bistrot du Boucan 223 rue Jean-Jaurès ☎ 04 94 92 64 35, ⓦ lebistrotduboucan.com. Charming bistro serving seasonally changing *cuisine du marché*: slow roasted lamb with artichokes and polenta for €19. Lunch *formule* €21. Mon–Wed noon–2.30pm, Thurs–Sat noon–2.30pm & 7.30–10pm.

Carré 2 Vigne 14 rue de Pomet ☎ 04 94 92 98 21, ⓦ carre2vigne.com. Provençal and Italian influences blend on the menu of this chic small restaurant close to the Opéra, with dishes like roast monkfish with cuttlefish and chorizo fricassée, tentacle jus and seasonal veg. *Menus* €29–49. Tues–Sat noon–1.30pm & 7–9.30pm.

Grand Café de la Rade 224 av République ☎ 04 94 62 76 69, ⓦ restaurant-la-rade.com. Bustling brasserie with a terrace facing the port and a versatile menu with everything from main course salads to fish and pasta: spiced octopus salad €14.90, mussels from €7.90, meat mains from around €15.90. Mon–Thurs noon–2.30pm & 7–10.30pm, Fri–Sun 7–11pm.

La Reine des Tartes 3 place Louis Blanc ☎ 06 45 68 84 87. Homely and completely gluten free *tarterie* serving up home-made goodies such as quiches and meringue pies. *Menus* from €9.95. Mon 10am–2.30pm, Tues–Sat 8.30am–8pm.

Les Tables de la Fontaine Place Lambert ☎ 06 59 25 37 28. Appealingly positioned beside Place Lambert's old stone fountain one block from the harbour, and priding itself on quality ingredients and creative, modern French cooking and presentation. The good value *menu* at €16.50 can include braised lamb, homemade burger or vegetable and walnut tart. Wed, Thurs & Sun 11.45am–2pm, Fri & Sat 11.45am–2pm & 7.30–9pm.

DRINKING AND NIGHTLIFE

SEE MAP PAGE 258

Bar à Thym 32 bd Dr Cuneo ☎ 04 94 41 90 10, ⓦ barathym.net. Big, Irish-pub-style bar and live venue midway between the city centre and Le Mourillon's beaches, with regular live rock bands and DJ sets. Daily 6pm–3am.

Côté Jardin 437 littoral Frédéric Mistral, Le Mourillon ☎ 04 94 41 38 33. Big, slick Le Mourillon bar-brasserie with a bougainvillea-shaded terrace facing the sea, pool table and sport on TV. A perfect spot after a day at the beach, with a happy "hour" from 6 to 8pm including cheap cocktails and wheat beers, followed by live music into the evening. Excellent light meals from €6. Daily 7am–2am.

Havana 35 rue Muiron ☎ 04 94 31 25 55, ⓦ havanacafe. eu. Cuban-themed café/bar with a sprawling terrace on the square outside, rum-based cocktail and regular DJ sets. Daily 7am–2am; until 3am in summer.

Le Satyn's Promenade Henri Fabre, Le Mourillon ☎ 04 94 75 94 23, ⓦ lesatyns-toulon.com. Lively bar/lounge/restaurant and "before" club right on the beach, with a different theme every night, from salsa to reggae and students' nights, and occasional free entry. Hours vary, but generally 9pm–3am, closed Mon & Tues.

SHOPPING

SEE MAP PAGE 258

La Cigale 21 quai Cronstadt ☎ 04 94 93 58 56. An Aladdin's cave of gifts and nautical ephemera, from beautiful handmade wooden ship models to the likes of plan chests, steamer trunks and binnacles. Daily 9am–7pm.

Cap Garonne

Beyond Le Mourillon, Toulon merges with **Le Pradet**, from where the D86 winds south along the eastern side of Cap Garonne to the little resort of **La Garonne**, which has a pleasant west-facing shingle-and-sand beach and a scattering of restaurants. Further on, at **Les Oursinières**, there's a small curve of shingly beach, clear water and a diving school.

Musée de la Mine de Cap Garonne

Chemin du Baou Rouge, Le Pradet • Wed, Sat & Sun 2.30–4pm; guided tours only • €7 • ⓦ mine-capgaronne.fr

Between La Garonne and Les Oursinières a side road leads to the protected, pine-clad 300-hectare headland of Cap Garonne and the **Musée de la Mine de Cap Garonne**, a chilly treasure-trove of semiprecious minerals, including malachite, azurite and cyanotrichite. There's also some information on the history of the miners themselves. Napoléon III granted the licence for mining of copper and lead on this site in the mid-nineteenth century; the first miners were Italians and the raw copper was exported to Swansea in the UK for processing. The history of mineral extraction here was of frequent changes of ownership interspersed with lengthy periods of idleness; the mine closed for good in 1917. From the mine's entrance a circular path, the **Sentier de découverte Jean-François Juby**, winds 1.5km around the headland giving lovely views of Toulon, the Rade and the mountains beyond.

6

ARRIVAL AND DEPARTURE   CAP GARONNE

By bus #23 from Toulon Gare (direction "4 Saisons", stop "Flamencq"; every 30–40min; 30min), then bus #91 (direction "Oursinières") from Le Pradet to La Garonne and Les Oursinières (approx hourly; 12min).

ACCOMMODATION AND EATING

L'Escapade 1 rue de la Tartane, Port des Oursinières ☎ 04 94 08 39 39, ⓦ hotel-escapade.com. Delightful, small, family-run hotel just back from the port at Oursinières, tucked into a quiet lane, with plenty of exposed wood and stone, beautiful lush gardens and a pool. The hotel also has an excellent restaurant, *La Chanterelle*, with two-course *formules* from €24. **€189**

Hyères

HYÈRES is the oldest resort of the Côte d'Azur, listing among its pre-twentieth-century admirers Empress Joséphine, Queen Victoria, Tolstoy and Robert Louis Stevenson. It was particularly popular with the British, being closer, and more southerly, than its rival Nice. To winter at Hyères in style one needed one's own villa, hence the expansive gardened residences that spread seawards from the **vieille ville**, giving the town something of the atmosphere of a spa. By the early twentieth century, however, Nice and Cannes began to upstage Hyères, and when the foreign rich switched from winter convalescents to summer sunbathers, Hyères, with no central seafront, lost out.

Today it has the rare distinction on the Côte of not being totally dependent on the summer influx, with the export of flowers, exotic plants and trees important to the local economy. It's also a garrison town, home to the French army's 54th artillery regiment and to a naval air station. Hyères is consequently rather appealing: the *vieille ville* is neither a sanitized tourist trap nor a slum, and the locals aren't out to squeeze maximum profit from the minimum number of months.

Vieille ville

Hyères' **vieille ville** lies on the slopes of Casteou hill, 5km from the sea, with avenue des Îles d'Or and its continuation, avenue Général-de-Gaulle, marking its border with the modern town to the south. The best approach to the *vieille ville* is through the **Porte Massillon**, a medieval gatehouse that opens onto rue Massillon, a street lined with tempting shops selling fruit and vegetables, chocolate, soaps, olive oil and wine.

Tour des Templiers

Place Massillon • Open during exhibitions: Sept–June Tues–Sat 10am–5pm; July–Aug Tues–Sat 10am–1pm & 4–7pm • Free

The twelfth-century **Tour des Templiers**, the remnant of a Knights Templar lodge, overshadows place Massillon, a perfect Provençal square filled with café terraces. The tower now hosts art exhibitions, though these are sometimes less impressive than their dramatic setting: don't miss the narrow staircase that leads to the roof for a bird's-eye view of the medieval centre.

Place St-Paul

The **place St-Paul** gives panoramic views over a section of medieval town wall to the Golfe de Giens. It's around here, where the crumbly lanes are festooned with bougainvillea, wisteria and yuccas, that the real charm of the *vieille ville* becomes apparent.

Collégiale St-Paul

Place St-Paul • Sept–June Tues–Sat 10am–5pm; July–Aug Tues–Sat 10am–1pm & 4–7pm • Free

Dominating place St-Paul is the former collegiate church of **St-Paul**, whose wide steps fan out from a Renaissance door. Its distinctive belfry is pure Romanesque, as is the choir, though the simplicity of the design is masked by the collection of votive offerings hung inside. The decoration also includes some splendid wrought-iron candelabras and a Christmas crib with larger-than-life-sized *santons*.

Parc Ste-Claire

Entrance on rue Ste-Claire • Daily: Jan–March & Nov–Dec 8am–5.30pm; April–May & Sept–Oct 8am–6pm; June–Aug 8am–7pm • Free

The exotic gardens of **parc Ste-Claire** surround **Castel Ste-Claire**, which now houses the offices of the Parc National de Port Cros; the castle was originally owned by the French archeologist Olivier Voutier (who discovered the Vénus de Milo), before becoming home to the American writer Edith Wharton.

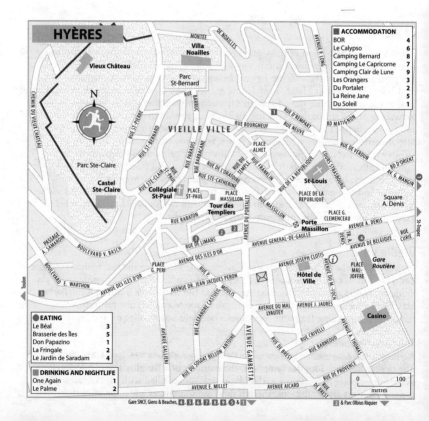

INTERNATIONAL SAILING IN HYÈRES

Thanks to its idyllic waters and consistently strong winds, the Hyères bay is one of the world's best-known **sailing** centres, bustling year-round with windsurfers, kite surfers and sailors alike. For forty-odd years the town was the venue each April for the **Semaine Olympique de Voiles**, a major six-day regatta when some fifty national teams and more than a thousand boats descended on the bay in what amounted to a rehearsal for the Olympic Games. Since 2014, however, the Semaine Olympique has been supplanted in the town's sailing calendar by the ISAF Sailing World Cup (W swc.ffvoile.com), one of several regattas organized by the International Sailing Federation. Like its predecessor it takes place in April.

6

Parc St-Bernard and around
Montée de Noailles • Daily: Jan–March & Oct–Dec 8am–5pm; April until 6.30pm; May & Sept until 7pm; June–Aug until 7.30pm • Free

Parc St-Bernard is an enjoyable warren full of almost every Mediterranean flower known. To the west of the park and further up the hill you come to the remains of Hyères' **Vieux Château** (free access), whose keep and restored outer walls outreach the oak and lotus trees with stunning views out to the Îles d'Hyères and east to the Massif des Maures. The site is a bit of a scramble.

Villa Noailles
Montée de Noailles • July–Sept Mon, Wed, Thurs, Sat & Sun 2–7pm, Fri 4–10pm; Oct–June Wed, Thurs, Sat & Sun 1–6pm, Fri 3–8pm • Free • ☎ 04 98 08 01 98, W villanoailles-hyeres.com

Sitting at the top of the parc St-Bernard, the **Villa Noailles**, an angular Cubist mansion, was designed by Mallet-Stevens in the 1920s, with gardens enclosed by part of the old citadel walls. All the luminaries of Dada and Surrealism stayed here and left their mark, including Man Ray who used it as the setting for one of his most inarticulate films, *Le Mystère du Château de Dé*. It now hosts contemporary art and design exhibitions.

The modern town
The switch from medieval to eighteenth- and nineteenth-century Hyères is particularly abrupt, with wide boulevards and open spaces, opulent villas, waving palm fronds and fanciful Moorish architectural details marking the modern town. Most of the former aristocratic residences and grand hotels now have more prosaic functions, though the **casino** is still in use (see page 267). Unfortunately its elegant Beaux Arts exterior and interior have lost much of their original character due to modernization, and the interior will disappoint if you're expecting *fin-de-siècle* opulence.

Parc Olbius Riquier
Av Ambroise Thomas • Daily: April–Sept 7.30am–8pm; closing times vary in winter • Free

South of the casino, at the bottom of avenue Ambroise Thomas, is Hyères' botanic garden, the **Parc Olbius Riquier**, which opened in 1868. Pride of place is given to the palms, of which there are 28 varieties, plus yuccas, agaves and bamboos. There's a hothouse full of exotics including banana, strelitzia, hibiscus and orchids, and a small zoo and miniature train for the kids.

The coast
Buses from Hyères' *gare routière* to Tour Fondue (#67; up to 4/hr; 36min), L'Almanarre (#39; every 20min–1hr; 14min), Hyères-Plage (#63; 6 daily; 15min; or #67; up to 4/hr; 14min) and Le Ceinturon (#102; 6 daily; 7min)

Hyères' coastal suburbs offer plenty of opportunities for bathing, though mosquitoes can be a problem, so bring insect repellent. Hyères' main port is at **Hyères-Plage**, with the village-resorts of **Le Ceinturon**, **Ayguade** and **Les Salins d'Hyères** strung out along the coast to the northeast. Traffic fumes and proximity to the airport detract from the charms of the seaside between Hyères-Plage and Le Ceinturon, despite the pines and ubiquitous palms, but it's more pleasant further up by the little fishing port of Les Salins. East of here, where the coastal road finally turns inland, you can follow a path between abandoned salt flats and the sea to a secluded beach, part of which is naturist.

Presqu'île de Giens

The peculiar **Presqu'île de Giens** is leashed to the mainland by an isthmus, known as **La Capte**, and a parallel sandbar enclosing the salt marshes. The eastern side of the isthmus is a series of narrow sand-and-pebble beaches, with warm, shallow water, packed out in summer; **plage de la Bergerie** in the south is about the nicest. The **route du Sel** (closed 9pm–5am & Oct–April) leads down the sandbar on the western side of the Presqu'île, giving you glimpses of the salt pans and flamingos that lie between the sandbar and the beach resorts on the eastern side; the windy **L'Almanarre** beach parallel to the route du Sel is a popular kitesurfers' hangout. At the south end of the sandbar sits the placid seaside community of **Giens**, with its **Tour Fondue**, built by Richelieu, on the eastern side overlooking the port that serves Porquerolles on the Îles d'Hyères (see page 267).

Site Archéologique d'Olbia

April, May, Sept & Oct Mon & Wed–Fri 9.30am–noon & 2–5.30pm, Sat & Sun 2–5.30pm; June– Aug Mon–Fri 9.30am–noon & 2.30pm–6pm, Sat & Sun 2.30–6pm; Nov–March groups only, by appointment • €3 • ☎ 04 94 65 51 49

L'Almanarre is the site of the ancient town of **Olbia**, a maritime trading post founded by Greeks from Marseille in the fourth century BC on a small knoll by the sea. Excavations here have revealed Greek and Roman remains, including a baths complex strikingly over-lavish for such a workaday, austere settlement, plus parts of the medieval abbey of St-Pierre de L'Almanarre. Note too the remains of the brick-built Roman jetty, clearly visible in the surf across the road from the site.

ARRIVAL AND DEPARTURE **HYÈRES**

By plane Toulon-Hyères airport (☎ 08 25 01 83 87, ⓦ toulon-hyeres.aeroport.fr) lies between Hyères and Hyères-Plage, 3km from the centre, to which it's connected by two bus services (#63 & 102; 10–20min). Destinations Southampton (1 weekly; 2hr 25min); Paris Orly (up to 8 daily; 1hr 25min).

By train The *gare SNCF* is on place de l'Europe, with frequent buses (#29, #39 or #67) to the town centre, 1.5km north, and eight daily runs to Toulon (21min).

By bus Buses arrive and depart from place Mal-Joffre, two blocks south of the entrance to the old town (☎ 04 94 03 82 03, ⓦ reseaumistral.com). Destinations Collobrières (2–4 daily Mon–Fri; 50min–1hr 10min); La Croix-Valmer (8 daily; 1hr 20min); Le Lavandou (8 daily; 35min); St-Tropez (8 daily; 1hr 35min); Toulon (frequent; 1hr); Tour Fondue (for Porquerolles): every 15– 30min; 35min).

INFORMATION AND ACTIVITIES

Tourist office Near the *gare routière* at *Rotonde du Park Hôtel*, 16 Av de Belgique (April–June & Sept Mon–Fri 9am– 6pm, Sat 9am–4pm; July & Aug Mon–Sat 9am–6pm, Sun 9am–1pm; Oct–March Mon–Fri 9am–5pm, Sat 9am–4pm; ☎ 04 94 01 84 50, ⓦ hyeres-tourisme.com).

Bike rental À Motos, 10 rue Jean d'Agrève, near port St-Pierre (☎ 04 94 38 79 45, ⓦ amotos.fr).

Kitesurfing Le Spot Kiteschool at La Bergerie (☎ 06 16 18 49 91, ⓦ kitesurf-var.com) has courses at all levels from €110; Robinson (☎ 06 30 08 79 84, ⓦ kite-hyeres.fr) offers introductory sessions from €90 and courses from €130.

Sailing The International Yacht Club de Hyères (IYCH), 61 av du Docteur-Robin (☎ 04 94 57 00 07, ⓦ iych.fr), has a sailing school.

ACCOMMODATION **SEE MAP PAGE 264**

BOR 3 allée Emile-Gérard, Les Pesquiers ☎ 04 94 58 02 73, ⓦ hotel-bor.com. Smart, timber-clad designer hotel right on the beach, with an elegant but rather pricey restaurant (lunch *formule* €25). Rooms have TV and a/c. Closed Nov to mid-March. **€180**

Le Calypso 36 av de la Méditerranée ☎ 04 94 58 02 09, ⓦ hotelcalypso.fr. Basic and friendly hotel close to Port St-Pierre, handy for the beach and for trips to the islands. The eleven rooms have double glazing and en-suite facilities; some also have a terrace or small garden. Closed Dec to mid-Feb. **€58**

Les Orangers 64 av des Îles d'Or ☎ 04 94 00 55 11,

ⓦ orangers-hotel.com. This pleasant small hotel is situated in a historic villa district, west of the modern centre, and has an attractive garden and terrace. Closed mid-Nov to mid-Feb. **€72**

Du Portalet 4 rue de Limans ⓣ 04 94 65 39 40, ⓦ hotel-portalet-hyeres.fr. In the lower and busier part of the old town, with tastefully designed rooms – including triples and a junior suite with terrace – with en-suite bath or shower, double glazing and satellite TV. Pets are accepted for a small fee. **€62**

La Reine Jane le port de l'Ayguade ⓣ 04 94 66 32 64, ⓦ reinejane.com. Small a/c hotel overlooking the port at Ayguade and just 30m from the beach, with a restaurant, bar and terrace to make up for its out-of-town location. Closed two weeks in Nov and from Jan to early Feb. **€108**

Du Soleil Rue du Rempart ⓣ 04 94 65 16 26, ⓦ hotel-du-soleil.fr. Twenty assorted en-suite rooms in a renovated house at the top of the *vieille ville*, close to parc St-Bernard and the Villa Noailles. Decor is simple, and the location peaceful. **€110**

CAMPSITES

Camping Bernard Rue des Saraniers 5 ⓣ 04 94 66 30 54. Two-star campsite just 50m from the sea in Le Ceinturon, with one hundred pitches and plenty of shade; facilities include a free wi-fi point and children's games. Closed Oct–Easter. **€21.90**

Camping Le Capricorne 1545 rte des Vieux Salins ⓣ 04 94 66 40 94, ⓦ campingcapricorne.com. Three-star site 1.5km from the beach at Les Salins, with a pool, volleyball and basketball courts and *boules* pitch and a snack bar. Closed Oct–March. **€36**

Camping Clair de Lune 27 av du Clair de Lune ⓣ 04 94 58 20 19, ⓦ campingclairdelune.com. Four-star campsite and caravan park on the Presqu'île de Giens, with free wi-fi. They also have bungalows and mobile homes. Closed mid-Nov to early Feb. Camping **€34**; mini-bungalow per week **€498**; mobile homes per week **€554**

EATING

SEE MAP PAGE 264

The most atmospheric places to eat and drink in Hyères are the **restaurant** terraces on place Massillon. There's a farmer's **market** on place Clemenceau on Tuesday mornings and a larger market in place Clemenceau and the pedestrian zone on Saturday morning.

Le Béal 24 rue de Limans ⓣ 04 94 20 84 98, ⓦ lebeal. com. Unpretentious *restaurant gastronomique* with a menu bursting with comfort food like the beef and dauphinoise potatoes or salmon parcel in dill cream. Lunch *plat du jour* €15.50. *Menus* €30 and €45. Mon & Fri–Sun noon–1.30pm & 7–9.30pm, Thurs 7–9.30pm.

Brasserie des Îles Port St-Pierre ⓣ 04 94 57 49 75, ⓦ brasserie-des-iles.com. A swish brasserie at the port serving a luxurious choice of *plateaux de fruits de mer* from €40. Wed–Sun 9am–10.30pm.

Don Papazino 14 av Mangin ⓣ 04 94 21 00 00. Standout pizzeria a short walk east of the centre that also offers a speedy delivery service. The pizzas are visually appealing and creatively conceived and consequently cost a little more than usual, starting at €13.50. Daily 6–10pm.

La Fringale 12 rue de Limans ⓣ 04 94 35 42 52. Bustling little restaurant with tables spilling out onto the quiet pedestrianized street. Interesting comfort food on offer here like rabbit cannelloni, as well as daily vegetarian options, like wild mushroom risotto. *Menus* €30. Mon–Wed & Fri noon–1.30pm & 7–10pm, Sat–Sun 7–10pm.

★ **Le Jardin de Saradam** 35 av de Belgique ⓣ 04 94 65 97 53. Reliable North African restaurant close to the *gare routière*, with a pretty garden and filling couscous and tagines on offer from around €17. Book ahead. July & Aug daily 7–9.30pm; Sept–June Tues–Sat noon–2pm & 7–9.30pm, Sun noon–2pm.

DRINKING AND NIGHTLIFE

SEE MAP PAGE 264

Hyères' **nightlife** is a rather scattered affair, with the portside café terraces having the edge over the more sedate old town. The **casino** (1 av Ambroise Thomas; daily 9am–4am; ⓦ casinohyeres.com) is south of the tourist office.

One Again 494 rue Nicéphore Niepce ⓣ 04 94 21 36 06. Right on the fringe of the airport, this club has a variety of themed nights ranging from house to salsa, hip-hop, soul and r'n'b – though the strip nights (Wed) won't be to everyone's taste. Entry €15. Wed–Sun 11.45pm–5.30am.

Le Palme 15 Av du Docteur Robin, Port St-Pierre ⓣ 06 19 21 10 05. A popular bar and disco down on the port with a huge, lively terrace. Regular live music performances from around 8.30pm and DJ sets from 11pm onwards. Tues 6pm–3am, Wed–Sun 9am–3am.

Îles d'Hyères

The wild, scented greenery and fine sand beaches of the **Îles d'Hyères** are a reminder of what much of the mainland was like half a century ago. You can stay on all three main islands – **Porquerolles**, **Port-Cros** and **Levant** – though accommodation is scarce, coveted and expensive. Today the Parc National de Port-Cros and the Conservatoire

Botanique de Porquerolles protect and document the islands' rare species of wild flowers. Port-Cros and its small neighbour Bagaud are just about uninhabited, so the main problem there is controlling the flower-picking and litter-dropping habits of visitors. On Levant, the military controls all but a tiny morsel of the island.

Make sure to observe signs forbidding smoking (away from the ports). The **fire risk** in summer is extreme: at times large sections of the islands are closed off and visitors must stick to marked paths.

Some history

A haven from tempests in ancient times, then the peaceful habitat of monks and farmers, in the Middle Ages the Îles d'Hyères (also known as the Îles d'Or) became a base for **piracy** and coastal attacks by a relentless succession of aggressors, against whom the few islanders were powerless. In 1550, Henri II tried to solve the problem by turning the islands into penal colonies, but the convicts themselves turned to piracy, even attempting to capture a ship of the royal fleet from Toulon. **Forts** were built all over the islands from the sixteenth century onwards, when François I started a trend of fort building that lasted into the twentieth century, when the German gun positions on Port-Cros and Levant were knocked out by the Americans. The military presence endures, and has at least spared the islands from the otherwise inevitable pressure for development.

ARRIVAL AND DEPARTURE   ÎLES D'HYÈRES

There are **ferries** to the Îles d'Hyères from numerous ports along the Côte d'Azur, though some services only operate in summer. Compagnies Maritimes TLV-TVM – which operates the ferry services from La Tour Fondue (the closest port to Porquerolles) and Port d'Hyères – also runs **glass-bottomed boat trips** from Tour Fondue to see the national park's marine treasures (June–Sept daily except Sat 9am–noon & 2–4pm; hourly; 35min; €19.50; ⊕tlv-tvm.com).

From Bandol Atlantide, Quai d'Honneur (☎04 94 32 51 41, ⊕atlantide1.com). Three weekly excursions to Porquerolles in spring, six in summer and one in Autumn; the trip includes 8–9hrs on the island.

From Cavalaire Vedettes Îles d'Or (☎04 94 00 45 77, ⊕vedettesilesdor.fr). To Porquerolles (April–June & Sept Tues & Fri; July & Aug daily) and Port-Cros (April–June & Sept Tues & Fri; July & Aug Tues–Fri).

From La Croix-Valmer Vedettes Îles d'Or (⊕vedettes ilesdor.fr). To Porquerolles (July & Aug daily) and Port-Cros (July & Aug Tues–Fri).

From La Tour Fondue, Presqu'île de Giens Compagnies Maritimes TLV-TVM (☎04 94 58 21 81, ⊕tlv-tvm.com). Year-round services to Porquerolles (daily).

From Le Lavandou Vedettes Îles d'Or, gare maritime (☎04 94 71 01 02, ⊕vedettesilesdor.fr). The closest port

to Port-Cros and Levant, with services to both destinations (April–June & Sept Tues, Wed, Fri & Sat; July & Aug daily; Oct Wed & Sat); plus services to Porquerolles (April to June Wed, Fri & Sat; July & Aug daily; Sept Tues, Wed & Fri–Sun; Oct Wed & Sat).

From La Londe Bateliers de la Côte d'Azur, Port Miramar (☎04 94 05 21 14, ⊕bateliersdelacotedazur.com). To Porquerolles (April–Aug daily; Sept daily [except Sat]; Oct Tues, Wed & Sun) and Port-Cros (April–June & Sept Tues, Wed, Fri & Sun; July & Aug daily [except Sat]; Oct Tues, Wed & Sun).

From Port d'Hyères Compagnies Maritimes TLV-TVM, Hyères-Plage (☎04 94 57 44 07, ⊕tlv-tvm.com). Year-round services to Port-Cros and Levant (April–Sept daily; Oct Mon, Wed & Fri–Sun; Nov–March Mon, Wed, Fri & Sat).

From Sanary Croix du Sud V, Port de Sanary (☎06 75 71 81 76, ⊕croixdusud5.com). To Porquerolles (mid-April–June & Sept–Nov Wed; July & Aug Mon, Wed & Sat).

From St-Raphaël Les Bateaux de Saint-Raphaël, Quai Nomy, Vieux Port (☎04 94 95 17 46, ⊕bateauxsaintraphael. com). Excursions to Porquerolles (July & Aug Mon).

From Toulon Bateliers de la Côte d'Azur, Quai Cronstadt (☎04 94 93 07 56, ⊕bateliersdelacotedazur.com). Excursions to Porquerolles (mid-May–June & Sept Tues, Wed, Fri & Sun; July & Aug daily).

Porquerolles

Porquerolles is by far the most easily accessible of the Îles d'Hyères, with a permanent village around the port, a few hotels and plenty of places to eat. In summer, the island's population expands dramatically, but there is some activity year-round. The only cultivated island, it has its own **wine**, with three Côte de Provence *domaines* that can be visited. Traffic-free and not too hilly, Porquerolles is a pleasure to explore on foot or by bike – and the further you get from the village the more beautiful it gets. The north coast is characterized by sandy bays, while the south coast is largely rugged and rocky, with just a handful of modest *calanques* where you can get to the water's edge.

The village
The **village** began life as a nineteenth-century military settlement, with its central square, the place d'Armes, being the old parade ground. It achieved notoriety of the non-military kind in the 1960s, when Jean-Luc Godard filmed the bewildering finale of his film *Pierrot le Fou* here, as well as at the Calanque de la Treille, at the far end of the plage de Notre-Dame.

Maison du Parc and around
Daily: March–Oct 9.30am–12.30pm & 2–6pm • Free • ⓦ porcros-parcnational.fr

Five minutes south of the village is the **Maison du Parc**, which organizes themed guided walks and has a garden full of stately palms. Immediately south, you're free to wander around the plantations of the otherwise private **Conservatoire Botanique**; there are more than two hundred varieties of olive and 230 of fig. The plantations stretch south towards the lighthouse at the island's southern tip.

Beaches
The most fabled (and distant) of the beaches is the **plage de Notre-Dame**, 3km northeast of the village just before the *terrain militaire* on the northeastern tip. The nearest to the village is the sandy **plage de la Courtade,** which you pass on the way to Notre-Dame. Facilities are minimal – there are earth toilets and places to park bikes at Courtade. The smaller **plage d'Argent** west of the village has a good **restaurant**, while at the island's Mistral-blasted western tip idyllic beaches bracket an isthmus that leads to the pink-painted, seventeenth-century **Fort du Grand Langoustier**. You can rent **kayaks** from Aventures Porquerolles (ⓦ aventuresporquerolles.com) on the plage d'Argent and **boats** and **kayaks** at the port from Locamarine 75 (ⓦ locamarine75.com).

INFORMATION AND GETTING AROUND   **PORQUEROLLES**

Tourist office There's a booth by the harbour (April–June & Sept Mon–Fri 9am–6pm, Sat 9am–1pm; July & Aug Mon–Sat 9am–6pm, Sun 9am–1pm; Oct–March Mon–Fri 9am–5pm, Sat 9am–4pm; ☎ 04 94 58 33 76, ⓦ porquerolles.com).

Bike rental Gravel tracks crisscross the island, so it's worthwhile renting bikes. Among several outlets in the village are Le Cycle Porquerollais, rue de la Ferme (☎ 04 94 58 30 32) and L'Indien, place d'Armes (☎ 04 94 58 30 39, ⓦ lindien.fr).

ACCOMMODATION AND EATING

In the village, **place d'Armes** is ringed by restaurant terraces, though they tend to be pricey for what they are. There are places selling ice creams and sandwiches to take away, plus a small supermarket and a fruit stall.

L'Arche de Porquerolles Place d'Armes ☎ 04 94 58 33 71, ⓦ larchedeporquerolles.fr. Eleven modernized, a/c rooms above a restaurant in the village, with modern decor, en-suite showers, wooden floors and TVs. The best rooms have terraces and sea views while the cheaper ones face the inner courtyard and suffer a little from restaurant noise. Closed mid-Nov to March. **€170**

Les Mas du Langoustier Western tip of the island, near the beach ☎ 04 94 58 30 09, ⓦ langoustier.com. The most luxurious hotel on Porquerolles, with a gourmet restaurant, pool, spa treatments and a minibus link to the port. It insists on *demi-pension*. Closed Oct–April. *Demi-pension* for two from **€500**

Les Mèdes 2 rue de la Douane ☎ 04 94 12 41 24, ⓦ hotel-les-medes.fr. Quite smart, modern three-star aparthotel close to place d'Armes, with a/c and a garden with an artificial waterfall. Closed early Nov to late Dec. **€195**

L'Olivier Le Mas du Langoustier ☎ 04 94 58 30 09, ⓦ langoustier.com. If you want gourmet cuisine you'll need to make the trek to the idyllic and Michelin-starred restaurant of the *Mas du Langoustier* hotel in the west of the island, with *menus* starting at €70 and dishes such as lobster tail with pomelo butter on the *carte*. May–Sept daily 12.30–2pm & 7–9.30pm.

Le Pélagros Place d'Armes ☎04 94 58 38 63. One of the more affordable options in the village, with grilled meats and fish for around €13–18, including sea bream in mango sauce with basil. April–Dec daily noon–2.30pm & 7.30–10pm.

La Plage d'Argent Plage d'Argent ☎04 94 58 32 48, ⓦplage-dargent.com. Gault Millau-listed place right on the beach, serving salads from around €20 and seafood from around €24, plus snacks. Mid-April to June & Sept daily 9am–6pm; July & Aug Mon, Wed, Fri & Sun 9am–6pm Tues, Thurs & Sat 9am–10/11pm.

6 Port-Cros

With around thirty permanent residents, the island of **Port-Cros** is France's smallest national park and a protected zone – dogs, smoking and fires are forbidden outside the port area, as is recreational fishing and picking flowers. It's the only one of the islands with natural springs, and boasts the richest **fauna and flora**. Kestrels, eagles and sparrowhawks nest here, and, along with common species such as broom, lavender, rosemary and heather in abundance, there are shrubs that flower and bear fruit at the same time.

The dense vegetation and hills make **exploring** considerably slower and harder going than on Porquerolles, even though it is less than half the size. Pick up the map from the **Maison du Parc** (hours vary according to boat arrivals; ☎04 94 01 40 70, ⓦportcrosparcnational.fr) at the port. Aside from forts and a handful of buildings around the port, the only significant interventions on the island's wildlife are the paths: the **Circuit des Crêtes** that circles the west, taking in the easily accessible beaches of **Anse de la Fausse Monnaie** and **plage du Sud**; the **route des Forts** that slashes northwest to southeast across the island from the port; the ambitious **circuit de Port-Man** towards the distant **plage de Port-Man** – a four-hour circular hike; and the beautiful but overgrown **Sentier des Plantes**, which zigzags across the clifftops to the **plage de la Palud**. If this beach is your goal there is, however, a more direct route (see opposite). You are not supposed to stray from these paths, though given the thickness of the undergrowth, doing so would be difficult. Divers will want to head for the island's southern shore to explore the waters round the **îlot de la Gabinière**.

Plage de la Palud and the Fort de l'Estissac

One kilometre northeast of the port is the nearest beach, **plage de la Palud**, backed by dense vegetation and with an underwater trail for snorkellers – the **Sentier Sous-Martin** (mid-June to mid-Sept; free); Sun Port Cros, which operates out of the *Sun Bistro* at the port (ⓦsun-portcros.com), rents equipment and organizes dives. On the way to the beach, you'll find the **Fort de L'Estissac** (July & Aug daily 10.30am–1pm; free), which houses an exhibition on the national park and the island's protected marine life – most easily seen by taking a glass-bottomed boat trip (see page 268) from La Tour Fondue.

ACCOMMODATION AND EATING   PORT-CROS

Le Manoir ☎04 94 05 90 52, ⓦhotel-lemanoirportcros. com. The island's principal hotel, in a leafy garden beneath tall eucalyptus and with a pool. Doubles with bath or shower; *demi-pension* only. *Prix-fixe menu* in its *restaurant gastronomique* €75. Closed Oct–April. **€230**

Provençale ☎04 94 05 90 43, ⓦhostellerie-provencale. com. En-suite, a/c rooms above a restaurant, with terrace or balcony. More luxurious rooms have sea views and access to a swimming pool. Closed Nov to mid-April. **€200**

Île du Levant

Ninety percent military missile testing range, **Île du Levant** is almost always humid and sunny. Cultivated plant life grows wild, with the result that giant geraniums and nasturtiums climb 3m hedges, overhung by immense eucalyptus trees and yucca plants. The tiny bit of the island spared by the military is dominated by the nudist colony of **Héliopolis**, founded in the early 1930s; nudity is compulsory on the beach of Les Grottes and is only forbidden in public buildings, at the port and in the village square, where residents wear sarongs or a tiny costume known as a *minimum*. About sixty people live at Héliopolis year-round, joined by thousands of summer visitors and many more day-trippers. Visitors who come just for a few hours tend to be treated as voyeurs. If you stay, even for one night, you'll generally receive a much friendlier reception, but in summer without advance booking you'd be lucky to find a room.

La Brise Marine ⊕ 06 14 68 71 10, ⊛ labrisemarine. net. One of the better-value options, this small hotel has fourteen simple en-suite rooms with sea views. There's a pool and a restaurant, too. €115

Héliotel ⊕ 04 94 00 44 88, ⊛ heliotel.net. Larger and a bit more fancy than the *Brise Marine*, this three-star hotel has a pool, a terrace with sea views and a vegetarian friendly restaurant (two-course *formule* €25, three courses €30). Rooms have a/c. €135

La Pinède ⊕ 04 94 05 92 81, ⊛ lapinede-iledulevant. com. A naturist accommodation comprising two furnished apartments with a terrace or balcony, plus two categories of bungalows, all with a kitchenette. There's a pool, jacuzzi and sauna. Closed mid-Oct to late April. Bungalows from €90; apartments €125

Corniche des Maures

The Côte d'Azur really gets going to the east of Hyères in the resorts of the **Corniche des Maures**, a 20km stretch of coast from Le Lavandou to the Baie de Cavalaire. Multimillion-dollar residences lurk in the hills, pricey yachts are moored in the bays, and seafront prices start edging up, yet the attractions are primarily natural: beaches that shine silver from the mica crystals in the sand, shaded by tall dark pines, oaks and eucalyptus; glittering rocks of purple, green and reddish hue; and chestnut-forested hills keeping the winds away. There are even unspoiled stretches where it's possible to imagine what all this coast looked like in bygone years, notably around **Cap de Brégançon**, at the **Domaine de Rayol gardens**, and between **Le Rayol** and the resort of **Cavalaire-sur-Mer**.

By car The coast road is narrow and littered with hairpin bends, so progress is slow, particularly in high season. **By bus** Regular buses on the Toulon–St-Tropez route #7801

link the settlements along this stretch of coast. **By bike** A cycle track runs parallel to the coast.

Bormes-les-Mimosas

You can almost smell the money as you spiral uphill from the D559 into immaculate **BORMES-LES-MIMOSAS**, 20km east of Hyères. It's indisputably medieval, with a restored castle at the top, protected by spiralling lines of pantiled houses backing onto short-cut flights of steps. The castle is private, but there is a public terrace alongside it with attractive views. The winding alleys of the village, with odd names such as "alleyway of lovers", "street of brigands", "gossipers' way" and "arse-breaker street", are stuffed full of arts and crafts ateliers.

Bormes-les-Mimosas' name is apt, particularly in February when you'll see a spectacular display of the tiny yellow pompoms. Incidentally, despite its popularity along the whole of the Côte d'Azur, **mimosa** is no more indigenous to the region than Porsches, having been introduced from Mexico in the 1860s.

Musée d'Art et d'Histoire

103 rue Carnot • June–Sept Tues & Thurs–Sat 10am–noon & 3–6.30pm, Wed 3–6.30pm, Sun 10am–noon; Oct–April Tues–Fri 10am–noon & 2–5.30pm; May, June & Sept Tues–Sun 10am–12.30pm & 2–6pm; July & Aug Tues–Sun 10am–12.30pm,& 2–7pm • Free • ☏ 04 94 71 56 60

Bormes' small **Musée d'Art et d'Histoire** occupies a renovated seventeenth-century house and displays nineteenth- and early twentieth-century painting by artists associated with the region. It also stages temporary exhibitions.

The coast

Bormes' bland pleasure port at **La Favière** is flanked by spot-the-spare-metre-of-sand beaches. A coastal footpath winds south from it around **Cap Bénat** passing numerous smaller (and harder to reach) coves along the way. West of Cap Bénat the **Fort de Brégançon** dominates the shore. A fortress of Merovingian origin, since 1968 it has been the holiday home of the president of the Republic. It can be visited in summer on a pre-booked guided tour (July & Sept Mon–Fri 9am–2.15pm; access by shuttle bus from Fort gates only; book through Bormes tourist office, visits last 3hr; €10; ☏ bregancon.monuments-nationaux.fr).

West of the fort is the long, sandy **Plage de Cabasson**, backed by pines and with views of the fort and towards Porquerolles; continuing west towards La Londe there are similar pine-backed sandy beaches including the gorgeous **Plage de l'Estagnol** and **Plage du Pellegrin**. In summer you will have to pay for parking if you want to drive down to the shore from the La Londe–Cabasson road, but on foot you can wander freely from beach to beach along the *sentier littoral*.

ARRIVAL AND INFORMATION · BORMES-LES-MIMOSAS

By bus Hyères–St-Tropez buses stop at Pin, some distance below the medieval village, from where there's a free shuttle bus daily outside high season; in July and Aug it may be easier to continue the short distance to Le Lavandou (up to 7 daily; 25min) and change there.

Tourist office Place Gambetta (April, May & June Mon–Sat 9.30am–12.30pm & 2–6pm, Sun 9am–1pm; July & Aug 9.30am–12.30pm & 2.30–6.30pm; Sept Mon–Sat 9am–12.30pm & 2–6pm; Oct–March Mon–Sat 9am–12.30pm & 2–5.30pm ☏ 04 94 01 38 38, ☏ bormeslesmimosas.com).

ACCOMMODATION AND EATING

Bellevue Place Gambetta ☏ 04 94 71 15 15, ☏ bellevue bormes.com. Simple but attractive hotel/restaurant at the entrance to the medieval village with a/c, en-suite rooms with TV and safe. Full or half board available. Closed mid-Nov to late Jan. **€71**

Camp du Domaine Rte de Bénat, La Favière ☏ 04 94 71 03 12, ☏ campdudomaine.com. Five-star site right by the sea, with plenty of sports facilities including tennis courts and *pétanque*, plus karaoke and cabaret nights. Closed Nov–March. Camping **€46**; mobile homes per week **€840**

Clau Mar Jo 895 chemin de Bénat ☏ 04 94 71 53 39, ☏ camping-clau-mar-jo.fr. Four-star mobile-home park just below the main road between the village and Le Lavandou, with good facilities including a swimming pool, children's play area and a gym. Closed mid-Nov to mid-March. Four people/week, high season **€1013**

Hostellerie du Cigalou Place Gambetta ☏ 04 94 41 51 27, ☏ hostellerieducigalou.com. Classy three-star hotel opposite the *Bellevue*, and a member of Châteaux & Relais de France. It has a mimosa-shaded swimming pool and twenty tastefully decorated a/c rooms with bath, safe and TV. **€175**

Le Jardin 1 ruelle du Moulin ☏ 04 94 71 14 86, ☏ lejardinrestaurant-bormes.com. Provençal specialities in unpretentious surroundings on a pretty terrace in the medieval village. Three-course *menu* €37, otherwise €14 and up for the likes of slow cooked lamb with stew. Wed–Sun noon–1.30pm & 7–10pm.

Les Palmiers 240 chemin du Petit Fort, Cabasson ☏ 04 94 64 81 94, ☏ hotellespalmiers.com. Very attractive and peaceful three-star hotel by the coast, with pool, private parking and its own path to the beach. Closed Nov–Jan. **€144**

Pâtes…et Pâtes Place du Bazar ☏ 04 94 64 85 75. At the foot of the medieval village, this restaurant serves good home-made pasta from around €9.90; there's also charcuterie boards and generous salads for around

€15. Mon–Wed noon–2pm & 7–10.30pm, Fri–Sun 7–10.30pm.

La Tonnelle de Gil Renard Place Gambetta ☎04 94 71 34 84, ⓦrestaurant-la-tonnelle.com. Rather chic, *Gault Millau*-listed restaurant at the entrance to the old village, with dishes such as foie gras with chestnuts and morels. *Menus* from €33, *plats* around €24. Wed–Sun noon–1.30pm & 7–9pm.

Le Lavandou

LE LAVANDOU, 5km from Bormes, is an out-and-out seaside resort, with sandy beaches, a scattering of pastel-painted high-rise hotels and an unpretentious atmosphere. Its origins as a Mediterranean fishing village are betrayed by the handful of remaining fishing vessels in the port, kept in business by the region's upmarket seafood restaurants. Merging with Bormes to the west and St-Clair to the east, Le Lavandou concentrates its charm in the tiny area between avenue du Général-de-Gaulle and Quai Gabriel-Péri, where café tables overlook the *boules* pitch and the traffic of the seafront road. Three narrow stairways lead back from here to rue Patron-Ravello, place Argaud and rue Abbé Helin, each lined with specialist shops and cafés.

However, it's the coast that is the real attraction, and there's no shortage of watersports and boat trips on offer: the CIP Lavandou diving school offers initiation **dives** (☎04 94 71 54 57, ⓦcip-lavandou.fr; from €70) while the École de Voile Municipale (☎06 26 58 39 55, ⓦle-lavandou.fr/ecole-de-voile) offers **sailing lessons** to groups and individuals from March to November. For **bathing**, the sands of St-Clair and the very pleasant cove of Aiguebelle mark the start of a string of excellent beaches, with crescents of silver sand interspersed with rocky headlands between here and Cavalaire-sur-Mer.

ARRIVAL AND INFORMATION
LE LAVANDOU

By bus Hyères–St-Tropez buses stop at the *gare routière* on Av de Provence, a short walk from the waterfront and tourist office.

Destinations Hyères (8 daily; 35min); Toulon (8 daily; 1hr 25min); St-Tropez (8 daily; 55min).

By ferry Ferries from the Îles d'Hyères arrive and depart from the *gare maritime* in Le Lavandou's port.

Destinations Porquerolles (April–June Wed, Fri & Sat; July & Aug daily; Sept Tues, Wed & Fri–Sun; Oct Wed & Sat); Port-Cros and Levant (April–June & Sept crossings on Tues, Wed, Fri & Sat; July & Aug daily; Oct Wed & Sat).

Tourist office Opposite the port at Quai Gabriel-Péri (mid-June to mid-Sept Mon–Sat 9am–12.30pm & 2–7pm, Sun 9.30am–12.30pm & 3.30–6.30pm; mid-season Mon–Sat 9am–12.30pm & 2.30–6pm; low season Mon–Fri 9am–noon & 2.30–5.30pm, Sat 9am–noon; ☎04 94 00 40 50, ⓦot-lelavandou.fr).

ACCOMMODATION AND EATING

Auberge de la Calanque 62 av du Général-de-Gaulle ☎04 94 71 05 96, ⓦaubergelacalanque.fr. Upmarket and spacious hotel close to the centre of town, with a shady garden, pool and a/c rooms including some with balconies and sea views. Room styles vary quite widely. Closed Nov–March. **€160**

Bistr'eau Ryon Bd des Dryades, plage St-Clair ☎04 94 15 26 97. A cut above the average tourist fare, right on the beach at St-Clair, with a short, weekly-changing market-based regional *carte* and a €34 three-course *menu*. April–Oct daily noon–1.30pm & 7–10pm; Nov–March Thurs–Sat noon–1.30pm & 7–9pm, Sun noon–1.30pm.

Brasserie du Centre 5 place Ernest Reyer ☎04 94 71 10 50, ⓦlabrasserieducentre.fr. Much the most animated of Le Lavandou's bar/brasseries, with a big shady terrace and a woody, yacht-like interior. Cocktails from €8; tapas from €8, breakfast €5.90. Daily: 7am–3am in high season; otherwise 7.30am–midnight.

L'Oustaou 20 av Général-de-Gaulle ☎04 94 71 12 18, ⓦlavandou-hotel-oustaou.com. Le Lavandou's best budget option – a clean, family-run two-star in the town centre, just minutes from the beach and port. It's well known and gets busy, so it's worth booking ahead. **€56**

Pazzi Plage Av des Trois Dauphins, Aiguebelle ☎04 94 05 81 20, ⓦpazziplage.fr. Fish and meat grilled over charcoal at this deceptively simple bar/restaurant right on the beach at Aiguebelle; grilled sardines €16; catch of the day €8 per 100g. Mon–Sat 9am–11pm, Sun 9am–5pm.

La Plage 14 rue des Trois-Dauphins ☎04 94 05 80 74, ⓦlhoteldelaplage.com. Classy, modernized three-star hotel right on the pretty sandy cove of Aiguebelle, with uncluttered modern decor, a restaurant (three-course *menu* €25) and a broad terrace with bar. Rooms have en-suite bath and a/c. **€104**

The silver beaches

The D559 east from Le Lavandou curves its way through steep wooded hills that reach down to the sea. This, along with the St-Tropez peninsula it leads to, is the most beautiful part of the Côte d'Azur, boasting silvery beaches and sections of unspoiled tree-backed coastline.

Each of Aiguebelle, there's silver sand at the **Plage de Jean Blanc** in Rossignol before you come to the tiny, secluded *calanques* either side of **Pointe du Layet**, at Plage de l'Éléphant, Plage du Rossignol and the naturist Plage du Layet. The village of **CAVALIÈRE** has a particularly fine beach: long, wide and pale, with undeveloped hilltops that at last outreach the houses. A couple of kilometres further on at **PRAMOUSQUIER**, you can look up from the turquoise water to woods undisturbed by roads and buildings.

Le Rayol and around

Some 4km east of Pramousquier, the villages of **LE CANADEL** and **LE RAYOL** have gradually merged and colonized the hills behind them. At Le Canadel, the sinuous D27 to **La Môle** leaves the coast road and spirals up past cork-oak woodland to the **Col du Canadel**, giving unbeatable views en route.

Domaine du Rayol gardens

Av des Belges, Le Rayol-Canadel-sur-Mer • Daily: April–June, Sept & Oct 9.30am–6.30pm; July & Aug 9.30am–7.30pm; Nov–March 9.30am–5.30pm; snorkelling tours of the "Jardin Marin" bookable in advance mid-June to mid-Sept • €12; English audioguide €2.50; snorkelling tours €30 • ☎ 04 98 04 44 00, ⓦ domaineredurayol.org

Le Rayol is best known for the beautiful **Domaine du Rayol gardens**, which extend down to the Figuier bay and headland. The land originally belonged to a banker who, before going bust at Monte Carlo in the 1930s, built the Art Nouveau mansion through which you enter the gardens; it's nowadays rather dilapidated, whereas the beautifully situated Art Deco villa at the far side of the *domaine* is undergoing restoration. Areas of the garden are dedicated to plants from different parts of the world that share the climate of the Mediterranean: Chile, South Africa, China, California, Central America, Australia and New Zealand. Apart from the extraordinary diversity of the vegetation, the garden is memorable for the loveliness of its setting, with cooling breezes and views of its small sandy beach (off-limits to visitors) and crystal-clear turquoise waters, which you can explore on **snorkelling tours**. There are also various engaging themed tours of the garden given by professional gardeners.

Cavalaire-sur-Mer

East from Le Rayol, the corniche climbs away from the coast through 3km of open countryside, sadly scarred most years by fire, before ending with the sprawl of **CAVALAIRE-SUR-MER**. Here the tiny *calanques* give way to a long stretch of sand and flat land that has been exploited for the maximum rentable space. In its favour, Cavalaire is very much a family resort and not too stuck on glamour.

INFORMATION	THE SILVER BEACHES

LE RAYOL
Tourist office Place Michel-Goy (July–Aug Mon–Sat 9.30am–1pm & 2.30–6.30pm, Sun 9.30am–12.30pm; April–June & Sept Mon–Fri 9.30am–1pm & 2–5.30pm, Sat 9.30am–noon; Oct–March 9.30am–1pm & 2–5pm; ☎ 04 94 05 65 69, ⓦ lerayolcanadel.fr).

CAVALAIRE-SUR-MER
Tourist office In the Maison de la Mer on the seafront (mid-June to mid-Sept daily 9am–7pm; mid-Sept to mid-June Mon–Fri 9am–12.30pm & 2–6pm, Sat 9am–12.30pm; ☎ 04 94 01 92 10, ⓦ cavalairesurmer.fr).

6

ACCOMMODATION AND EATING

Le Bailli de Suffren Av des Américains, Le Rayol-Canadel-sur-Mer ☎04 98 04 47 00, ⓦlebaillidesuffren.com. Four-star luxury in an idyllic beachside setting, with a/c suites, a heated pool and a *restaurant gastronomique*. Closed mid-Nov to mid-April. **€475**

La Calanque Rue de la Calanque, Cavalaire-sur-Mer ☎04 94 01 95 00, ⓦhoteldelacalanque.com. Small, upmarket hotel beautifully perched on a low cliff overlooking the sea a little way out of town. Closed mid-Oct to late March. **€398**

Le Maurin des Maures Av du Touring Club, Le Rayol ☎04 94 05 60 11, ⓦmaurin-des-maures.com. Lively place with sea views on the main road through Le Rayol,

serving fresh grilled fish, bouillabaisse and *daube de boeuf*. Menus €31.50 and €36.50. Daily noon–2pm & 7–9.30pm.

L'Émeraude Nouveau Port, Cavalaire-sur-Mer ☎04 94 64 06 88, ⓦrestaurant.emeraude.free.fr. Popular seafood place on the port with a €24 *menu* that starts with oysters, moves on to *moules-frites* and finishes with *l'île flottante*. Daily noon–2.30pm & 7–10.30pm.

Camping de Pramousquier Chemin de la Faverolle, Pramousquier ☎04 94 05 83 95, ⓦcamping pramousquier.com. Two-star site 400m from Pramousquier's fine sandy beach, with a bar, restaurant and food store on site. Closed early Oct to mid-April. Camping **€31.50**; bungalows per week **€888**

La Croix-Valmer and Cap Lardier

At the eastern end of Cavalaire-sur-Mer's bay lies another exceptional stretch of wooded coastline, the **Domaine de Cap Lardier**. This pristine coastal conservation area snakes around the southern tip of the St-Tropez peninsula, and is best accessed from **LA CROIX-VALMER**, even though the somewhat bland village centre is around 2.5km from the sea; some of the land between is taken up by vineyards that produce a decent wine.

To reach the best beach in the vicinity, **plage de Gigaro**, catch the *navette* or **shuttle bus** (see below).

ARRIVAL AND INFORMATION   LA CROIX-VALMER AND CAP LARDIER

By bus Buses stop at plage du Débarquement and at the Croix de Constantin in La Croix-Valmer. From mid-June to mid-Sept free shuttle buses connect the village centre with plage de Gigaro (every 45 min) and plage du Débarquement (every 30min).
Destinations Hyères (8 daily; 1hr 15min); Le Lavandou (8 daily; 35min); St-Tropez (up to 8 daily; 20min).

Tourist office 287 rue Louis Martin, La Croix-Valmer, just up from the junction of the D559 and D93 (April–June & Sept Mon–Sat 9.15am–noon & 2–6pm, Sun 9.15am–noon; July & Aug daily 9.30am–12.30pm & 3.30–7pm; Oct–March Mon–Fri 9.15am–noon & 2–6pm, Sat 9.15am–noon; ☎04 94 55 12 12, ⓦlacroixvalmertourisme.com).

ACCOMMODATION AND EATING

La Bienvenue Rue Louis Martin, La Croix-Valmer ☎04 94 17 08 08, ⓦhotel-la-bienvenue.com. Family-run, *two-star hotel* close to the tourist office, with light, neutral decor; cheaper rooms lack a/c and share facilities. Breakfast is served in the garden, and there's private parking. Closed Dec–Feb. **€115**

Brigantine Plage de Gigaro ☎04 94 79 71 11, ⓦlesmoulinsdepaillas.com. Near the conservation area, this beach-front Italian restaurant has menus ranging from pasta (from €12) and pizza (from €12) to more elaborate meat and fish *plats* chalked up on the blackboard (€28–36). Mid-May to Sept daily 12.30–2pm & 7.30–9.30pm.

Le Château de Valmer Bd de Gigaro, Plage de Gigaro ☎04 94 55 15 15, ⓦchateauvalmer.com. Luxurious old mansion in an idyllic setting between pines, palms and vines just back from the beach, with double and three- and four-bed family rooms, cottages and a few treehouses. Spa and leisure facilities include two pools, sauna, hamam and gym. Closed Oct–April. **€475**

Sélection 310 bd de la Mer, La Croix-Valmer ☎04 94 55 10 30, ⓦselectioncamping.com. Four-star campsite, 400m from the sea and with excellent facilities including a heated pool, bar, restaurant, takeaway, shop and plenty of activities. Closed mid-Oct to mid-March. **€50**

St-Tropez and around

As the summer playground of Europe's youthful rich, the one-time fishing village turned VIP hangout of **ST-TROPEZ** remains undeniably glamorous, its oversized yachts and infamous champagne "spray" parties creating an air of hedonistic excess; on warm nights there's a delicious buzz of excitement around the **port**. Be warned, however, that its **beaches** aren't the cleanest, and that if you don't have the holiday budget of a supermodel or Formula One racing driver, St-Tropez's sheer expense and occasional haughtiness towards visitors, particularly in high season, can make it feel like a party you're not invited to. Time your visit for a fine late spring or early autumn day, though, and the crowds will be more manageable – and you may just discern some of the old St-Tropez magic.

Vieux Port

6

The **Vieux Port**, rebuilt after its destruction in World War II, is where you get the classic St-Tropez experience: the quayside café clientele eyeing the Martini-sippers on their gin-palace motor yachts, with the latest fashions parading in between. It's the very definition of the French word *frimer* (derived from "sham") which means exactly this – to stroll ostentatiously in places like St-Tropez. You may be surprised at how entertaining the spectacle can be, though it's undeniably a little vulgar – a sort of human zoo in which the conspicuously rich are willing exhibits. The portside is at its most magical in late September and early October during **Les Voiles**, the regatta that sees the harbour swap ugly motor yachts for beautiful sailing vessels, and cruise liners dot the Golfe de St-Tropez beyond.

Musée de l'Annonciade

Place Grammont • Dec–Feb Tues–Sun 10am–5pm; March–June & Oct–Nov Tues–Sun 10am–6pm; July & Aug daily 10am–7pm • €6 • ☏ 04 94 17 84 10, ⓦ sainttropeztourisme.com

---

ST-TROPEZ AND THE ARTS: INSPIRATION AND INDULGENCE

The origins of St-Tropez are not unusual for this stretch of coast: a fishing village that grew up around a port founded by the Greeks of Marseille. It was destroyed by the Saracens in 739 and finally fortified in the late Middle Ages. Its sole distinction was its inaccessibility, stuck out on a peninsula that never warranted real roads. St-Tropez could be reached easily only by boat as late as the 1880s, when the novelist **Guy de Maupassant** sailed his yacht into the port during his final high-living binge before the onset of syphilitic insanity. Soon after Maupassant's visit, the Neo-Impressionist painter **Paul Signac** sailed down the coast in his boat, named after Manet's notorious painting *L'Olympia*. Bad weather forced him to moor in St-Tropez and – being rich and impulsive – he decided to have a house built there: *La Hune*, on what is now rue Paul-Signac, was designed by fellow painter Henri van de Velde. Signac opened his doors to impoverished friends who could benefit from the light, the beauty and the distance from the respectable convalescent world of Cannes and Nice. **Matisse** was one of the first to take up his offer; the locals were shocked again, this time by Madame Matisse modelling in a kimono. **Bonnard**, **Marquet**, **Dufy**, **Derain**, **Vlaminck**, **Seurat**, **Van Dongen** and others followed, and by the end of World War I St-Tropez was fairly well established as a hangout for bohemians.

The 1930s saw a further artistic influx, this time of writers as much as painters: **Jean Cocteau** came here, **Colette** lived for fourteen years in a villa outside the village, describing her main concerns as "whether to go walking or swimming, whether to have rosé or white, whether to have a long day or a long night", while **Anaïs Nin**'s journal records "girls riding bare-breasted on the back of open cars; an intensity of pleasure" and undressing between bamboo bushes that rustled with concealed lovers.

But it wasn't until after World War II that St-Tropez achieved international celebrity. In 1955 movie director Roger Vadim arrived to film **Brigitte Bardot** in *Et Dieu Créa La Femme*, and the cult of Tropezian sun, sex and celebrities took off, creating a tourist boom. The village has been groaning under the sheer weight of visitor numbers ever since.

6

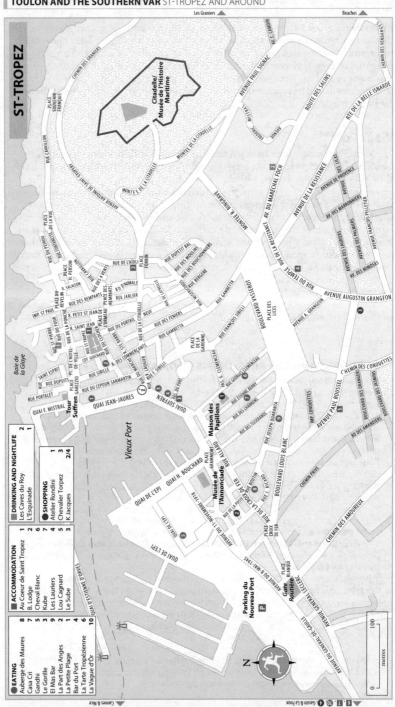

ST-TROPEZ

Les Graniers ▲

Beaches ▲

Citadelle/
Musée de l'Histoire
Maritime

Baie de
la Glaye

Tour
Suffren

Vieux Port

Maison des
Papillons

Musée de
l'Annonciade

Parking du
Nouveau Port
P

Gare
Routière

N

0	100
metres	

Cannes & Nice ◀

Gassin & La Foux ◀

Plage du Pampelonne ▶

Plage de Pampelonne ▶

● EATING	
Auberge des Maures	8
Casa Cri	7
Gandhi	5
Le Gorille	3
El Mas Bar	9
La Part des Anges	2
La Petite Plage	1
Bar du Port	4
La Tarte Tropézienne	6
La Vague d'Or	10

■ ACCOMMODATION	
Au Coeur de Saint Tropez	8
B. Lodge	7
Cheval Blanc	5
Kube	3
Les Lauriers	9
Lou Cagnard	2
Le Sube	4

■ DRINKING AND NIGHTLIFE	
Les Caves du Roy	2
L'Esquinade	1

● SHOPPING	
Atelier Rondini	1
Chevalier Torpez	3
K.Jacques	2/4

The marvellous **Musée de l'Annonciade**, occupying a deconsecrated sixteenth-century chapel right on the Vieux Port, is reason in itself for a visit to St-Tropez. It was Paul Signac who originally suggested setting up a permanent exhibition space for the Neo-Impressionists and Fauves who painted here, but it was not until 1955 that collections owned by various individuals were put together in this building. The museum features representative works by Signac, Matisse and most of the other artists who congregated in St-Tropez: grey, grim, northern scenes of Paris, Boulogne and Westminster, and then local, brilliantly sunlit landscapes by the same brush. Two winter scenes of the village by Dufy contrast with Camille Camoin's springtime *Place des Lices* and Bonnard's boilingly hot summer view. The museum is a real delight, both for its contents – unrivalled outside Paris for the 1890 to 1940 period – and for the fact that it is often the least crowded place on the port.

Place des Lices and around

Southeast of the Vieux Port is the other pole of St-Trop life, **place des Lices**, with its battered old plane trees, *pétanque* players and benches on which to sit and watch – a rather nicer option than the café-brasseries fringing the *place*, which are a bit too smugly Champs-Élysées in style. In the streets between here and the port – rue François Sibilli and rue Georges Clemenceau – and the smaller lanes in the heart of the old village you can window-shop or buy haute couture, antiques, *objets d'art* and classy trinkets.

Maison des Papillons

17 rue Etienne Berny • April–early Nov Mon–Sat 10am–12.30pm & 2–6pm, Sun 10am–12.30pm & 2–5pm • €2 • ☎ 04 94 97 63 45

One of the narrowest lanes in St-Tropez is rue Etienne Berny, where you'll find the **Maison des Papillons**, a butterfly museum housing more than twenty thousand pinned specimens, including many rare and endangered species.

Quartier de la Ponche

Heading east from the port, from the top end of Quai Jean-Jaurès, you pass the **Tour Suffren**, originally built in 980 by Count Guillaume I of Provence, and enter the **quartier de la Ponche,** the oldest and most atmospheric part of the village. Here, place de l'Hôtel-de-Ville is dominated by the *mairie*, which, with its attractive earthy pink facade and dark green shutters is one of the few reminders that this is a real town. A street to the left takes you down to the tiny, rocky **Baie de la Glaye**; straight ahead, rue de la Ponche passes through an ancient gateway to place du Revelin, which overlooks the lovely **fishing port** and its tiny beach.

Citadelle

1 Montée de la Citadelle • Daily: April–Sept 10am–6.30pm; Oct–March 10am–5.30pm• €3 • ☎ 04 94 97 59 43, ⓦ sainttropeztourisme.com

If you turn inland from the sea and walk upwards, you finally reach the open space around the sixteenth-century **citadelle**, which offers glorious views of the gulf and town that haven't changed much since they were painted by St-Tropez's bohemian newcomers a century ago. It houses the well-presented **Musée de l'Histoire Maritime**, which charts St-Tropez's long and often surprising association with the sea – from its historic role as a centre for coastal trade and participation in the "maritime caravan" between ports of the Ottoman Empire to the torpedo factory built here by the British on the eve of World War I.

6

ARRIVAL AND DEPARTURE   ST-TROPEZ

By bus Buses drop you at the *gare routière*, southwest of the Vieux Port on Av du Général-de-Gaulle.

Destinations La Garde-Freinet (1–2 daily; 45min); Grimaud (2 daily; 30min); Hyères (up to 12 daily; 50min–1hr 40min; Le Lavandou (up to 8 daily; 55min); Ste-Maxime (10–12 daily; 35–40min); St-Raphaël (10–12 daily; 1hr 25min); Toulon (10–12 daily; 1hr 45min–2hr 10min).

By car Beware of driving to St-Tropez in summer – traffic jams start in earnest at Ste-Maxime, where the D25 from the autoroute joins the coast road; it can take 2hr to crawl the remaining 16km into St-Tropez. There is (paid) parking in the vast Parking du Nouveau Port at the entrance to the village.

By ferry The quickest way to reach St-Tropez in summer – other than by helicopter – is the ferry from Ste-Maxime (see page 287) on the opposite side of the gulf. In summer there are also ferries from Port Grimaud and Les Issambres with Les Bateaux Verts (☎ 04 94 49 29 39, ⊚ bateauxverts. com), and from Port Grimaud with Les Navettes Bateaux (⊚ navette-bateau.com).

Destinations Les Issambres (June–Sept; hourly, 25min); Port Grimaud (Les Bateaux Verts: mid-April–early Oct, every 30min to 1hr; 20–30min; Les Navettes Bateaux: May to early Oct; hourly); Ste-Maxime (mid-Feb to Dec; every 15min in high season; 15min).

INFORMATION AND GETTING AROUND

Tourist office Quai Jean-Jaurès (April–June, Sept & Oct daily 9.30am–12.30pm & 2–7pm; July & Aug daily 9.30am–12.30pm & 2.30–7pm; Oct [after Les Voiles] to March Mon–Sat 9.30am–12.30pm & 2–6pm; ☎ 04 94 97 45 21, ⊚ sainttropeztourisme.com). In July and Aug there's

also an office at the Parking du Nouveau Port (Tues–Sat 9.30am–12.30pm & 2.30–7pm).

Bike rental Bikes and motorbikes can be rented at Rolling Bikes, 50 av G.-Leclerc (☎ 04 94 97 09 39, ⊚ rolling-bikes. com).

ACCOMMODATION   SEE MAP PAGE 278

You'll be lucky to find a room in **high season**. The tourist office can help (for a fee), but – transport permitting – you might be better off staying elsewhere. A lot of the classiest accommodation is out of town on the peninsula. There's no price advantage but you may gain in tranquillity what you lose in convenience; some outlying hotels run shuttles into town. Campsites are out on the peninsula (see page 283) and are geared more towards **glamping** than pitches for tents. In summer it's worth checking out the signs for **camping à la ferme** that you'll see along the D93, but make sure you know the charges first.

Au Coeur de Saint Tropez 15 rue Saint-Jean ☎ 06 16 05 21 76. Stylish *chambres d'hôtes* with two individually decorated rooms in the oldest part of the village. The larger of the two is a duplex with views of the citadelle and sea; it sleeps up to three. **€145**

B. Lodge 12 rue de l'Aïoli ☎ 04 94 97 06 57, ⊚ hotel-b-lodge.com. Overlooking the citadelle, this attractive boutique-style hotel is in a quieter setting than places in the centre and has stylish decor and its own bar. There is a/c and pets are welcome, but parking is a headache. **€220**

Cheval Blanc Plage de la Bouillabaisse ☎ 04 94 55 91 00, ⊚ chevalblanc.com. With a wonderful location on its own private beach, this luxurious hotel has just 36 spacious

rooms and suites tastefully decorated in pale colours. Past guests include Audrey Hepburn and Brigitte Bardot. Prices are eye-watering, though. Closed mid-Oct to mid-April. **€990**

★ **Kube** Rte de St-Tropez ☎ 04 94 97 20 00, ⊚ kube hotel-saint-tropez.com. Gorgeous boutique hotel on the road from La Foux, with an infinity pool facing the sea and designer decor. Rooms have coffee makers and a TV with video on demand. **€586**

Les Lauriers 5 Rue du Temple ☎ 04 94 97 04 88, ⊖ hotel leslauriers@wanadoo.fr. Just behind place des Lices, this friendly, relaxed three-star has eighteen a/c rooms and a garden. **€197**

Lou Cagnard 18 av Paul-Roussel ☎ 04 94 97 04 24, ⊚ hotel-lou-cagnard.com. Pretty, affordable option with Provençal-style rooms – fifteen of them with a/c – in a relatively tranquil location with a garden and secure private parking. Seven-night minimum stay June–Sept and during Les Voiles (see page 277). **€185**

Le Sube 23 quai Suffren ☎ 04 94 97 30 04, ⊚ hotel subesainttropez.com. One of St-Tropez's oldest hotels, in the thick of the action, with 22 rooms, two suites, a/c and a classy bar. Some rooms offer fantastic views over the port. Closed Nov–March. **€180**

EATING   SEE MAP PAGE 278

The **eating** scene in St-Tropez is notoriously expensive. The correlation between price and quality is weaker here than anywhere else on the Côte d'Azur, even at the top end of the market. As a rule of thumb, avoid the obvious

hot spots of the Vieux Port or place des Lices, and instead browse the menus in the lanes that climb towards the church and citadelle to find the best value. Place aux Herbes has a daily fish **market**; the main food market is on place des Lices on Tuesday and Saturday mornings from 7am to 1pm.

RESTAURANTS

Auberge des Maures 4 rue du Dr-Boutin ☎ 04 94 97 01 50, ⊛ aubergedesmaures.fr. Twee, pretty Michelin- and *Gault Millau*-rated place specializing in classic Provençal cooking, chargrilled fish and meat, with a *menu* at €59. Mid-April–Nov daily 7pm–midnight.

Casa Cri 20 rue Berny ☎ 04 94 97 42 52. Classy Italian, set in a lovely courtyard garden down a quiet side street just back from the Vieux Port. *Menus* €20–42; there are also chalked-up specials on the blackboard. May, June, Sept & Oct Tues–Sat noon–3pm & 7.30pm–11pm, Sun 7.30pm–11pm; July & Aug daily 7.30pm–late.

Gandhi 3 quai de l'Épi ☎ 04 94 97 71 71. Near the Parking du Nouveau Port, this small, busy Indian restaurant has earned a good reputation for its familiar line-up of tandooris, vindaloos and biryanis. Lunch *formule* €18.50, main dishes from around €13.50. Feb–Nov Mon & Wed 7–10.30pm, Tues & Thurs–Sun noon–1.30pm & 7–10.30pm.

El Mas Bar 5 rue Quaranta ☎ 04 94 97 00 60. A veritable world away from the swanky quayside hangouts, this place is popular with locals for its exciting and relatively cheap French-Spanish tapas and *raciones*. Expect to fill up for around €16 to €20. Daily noon–1am.

La Part des Anges 7 rue de l'Église ☎ 04 94 96 19 50. Very pleasant little restaurant serving decent food at modest prices in a pretty, atmospheric lane just down from St-Tropez's church, with two course menus of grilled meat, fish or a veggie option for €18. April–Oct Mon–Sat noon–3pm & 7–11pm.

La Petite Plage 9 quai Jean-Jaurès ☎ 04 94 17 01 23. Upmarket restaurant and lounge on the Vieux Port with a stylish beach shack inspired interior with sand scattered on the floor. Lots of fish on the menu with some interesting ideas like spice prawn carpaccio with olive oil from around €24 upwards. Daily 9am–3am.

La Vague d'Or Résidence La Pinède, Plage de la Bouillabaisse ☎ 04 94 55 91 00, ⊛ vaguedor.com. Michelin three-star chef Arnaud Donckele presides over the kitchens at St-Tropez's most renowned restaurant, where you might feast on loin and cheek of sea bass poached in seawater with lime cress and seaweed; *menus* €300–375; main courses à la carte from €98 upwards. Daily 7.30–10pm.

CAFÉS AND SNACKS

Le Gorille 1 quai Suffren ☎ 04 94 97 03 93. Straightforward quayside café, where you can get a *croque-madame* for €8.50, omelettes for €12 and salads from €15.50. Daily 6.30am–7pm.

Bar du Port 7 quai Suffren ☎ 04 94 97 00 54, ⊛ barduport.com. With its stylish, modern but vaguely retro-1960s decor, this café-bar is the epitome of St-Tropez idling – and not as expensive as some. Cocktails from €16, or try the refreshing peach-flavoured fizz, *Ice Tropez* (€8.50). Daily 7.30am–3am.

★ **La Tarte Tropézienne** 36 rue G.-Clemenceau ☎ 04 94 97 71 42, ⊛ latartetropezienne.fr. Patisserie claiming to have invented the moreish eponymous sponge and custard cake (€4), though you no longer have to come to St-Tropez to sample it – the company is now a chain. Daily 7am–8pm.

DRINKING AND NIGHTLIFE
SEE MAP PAGE 278

In season, St-Tropez stays up late, as you'd expect. The **pétanque games** on place des Lices continue till well after dusk, the portside spectacle doesn't falter till the early hours, and even the shops stay open late into the evening. Prime **drinking** spots are along the port and on place des Lices. **Clubs** open every night in summer, and usually weekends only in winter; your chances of getting in will depend on who's on the door, and whether they think you look the part.

Les Caves du Roy Byblos, Av du Maréchal Foch ☎ 04 94 56 68 00, ⊛ lescavesduroy.com. Still the place to see and

be seen, where you'll mix with rap stars and supermodels – if your face and clothes pass muster on the door. Check with your bank manager first: cheapest drink €26, bottle of champagne €290, bottle of nebuchadnezzer €75,000. Late April to June & Sept to early Oct Fri & Sat midnight–6am; July & Aug nightly midnight–6am.

L'Esquinade 2 rue du Four ☎ 04 94 56 26 31. Gay-friendly club spinning house, disco and electro music. Unlike most of St-Tropez's clubs it's open year-round. Daily midnight–7am; in winter Thurs–Sat only.

SHOPPING
SEE MAP PAGE 278

As you'd expect, St-Tropez attracts a plethora of designer names, though the local brands that stay true to the village's **hippy chic** ethos make for more interesting – if scarcely less expensive – shopping. In addition, the peninsula's **wines** are well worth seeking out.

Atelier Rondini 18–18bis rue Georges Clemenceau

☎ 04 94 97 19 55, ⊛ rondini.fr. Old-established manufacturer of "*tropéziennes*" – the distinctive flat "slave" sandals that epitomize St-Tropez's casual chic. Mon–Sat 9.30am–12.30pm & 2–7pm, Sun 10am–1pm & 3–7pm.

Chevalier Torpez Av Paul Roussel ☎ 04 94 97 01 60,

ⓦvignobles-saint-tropez.com. Wine cooperative a short walk from the Place des Lices. A good place to taste and buy the wines produced on the peninsula. Mon–Sat 9.30am–12.30pm & 3.30–7pm.
K Jacques 39 bis rue Allard & 28 rue Seillon ☎04 94 56 26 31, ⓦkjacques.fr. K Jacques' elegant, strappy flat sandals are available worldwide, but their easy yet dressy style makes particular sense here – at a couple of hundred euros a pair. Mon–Sat 10am–1pm & 3–8pm, Sun 10.30am–1pm & 3–7.30pm; closes later in high season, earlier in the off-season.

6 St-Tropez peninsula

St-Tropez's fabled **beaches** stretch along the eastern flank of the **St-Tropez peninsula**. They may lack the Blue Flags of their neighbours but more than make up for it in glamour; it was here back in the 1960s that topless bathing and G-string bikinis were seen for the first time. The nearest beach to St-Tropez, within easy walking distance, is **Les Graniers**, below the citadelle beyond the Port des Pêcheurs along rue Cavaillon. From here a path follows the coast around the **Baie des Canebiers**, which has a small beach, to Cap St-Pierre, Cap St-Tropez, the crowded **Salins** beach and round to **Plage Tahiti** at the top end of the famous **plage de Pampelonne**, 12.5km from St-Tropez.

In contrast to its crowded coastline, the **interior** of the St-Tropez peninsula is almost uninhabited, thanks to government intervention, complex ownerships and the value of some local wines. The best view of this richly green, wooded and flowering countryside is from the hilltop village of **Gassin**, its lower neighbour **Ramatuelle**, or the tiny road between them, the beautiful route des Moulins de Paillas where the ruined windmills once caught every wind.

Plage de Pampelonne and beyond

The almost straight 5km north–south **plage de Pampelonne** is the famous bronzing belt of St-Tropez and initiator of the topless bathing cult. The water is shallow for 50m or so and exposed to the wind, and it's sometimes scourged by dried sea vegetation, not to mention slicks of pollutants from the offshore traffic. But spotless glitter comes from the rash of **beach bars and restaurants** built out over the coarse sand, all with patios and sofas, all serving cocktails and ice creams (as well as full-blown meals) and all renting out beach mattresses and matching parasols. Nevertheless you're free to stroll along the shore – it's actually a public beach – and there are a few patches of sand that don't have restaurants and celebrities on them.

The beach ends with the headland of **Cap Camarat**, beyond which the private residential settlement of Villa Bergès grudgingly allows public access to the Plage de l'Escalet. Another coastal path leads to the next bay, the **Baie de la Briande**, where you'll find the least populated beach of the whole peninsula. You can continue on the *sentier littoral* to **Cap Lardier** and beyond it all the way round to Gigaro (see page 276).

Gassin

The highly chic village of **GASSIN** gives the impression of a small ship perched on a summit. Once a Moorish stronghold, it's a perfect place to have a dinner (see below), as you sit outside by the village wall enjoying a spectacular panorama east over the peninsula.

Ramatuelle

RAMATUELLE is bigger than its neighbour Gassin, though just as old, and is surrounded by some of the best Côtes de Provence **vineyards** – the top selection of wines can be tasted at Les Maîtres Vignerons de la Presqu'île de St-Tropez by the La Foux junction on the N98. The twisting and arcaded streets of Ramatuelle itself are inevitably full of arts and crafts shops selling works by artists of dubious talent, but the village is very pleasant nonetheless. The central Romanesque **Église Notre Dame**

that formed part of the old defences has heavy gilded furnishings from the Chartreuse de la Verne (see page 285) and an impressive early seventeenth-century door carved out of serpentine.

ARRIVAL AND DEPARTURE   ST-TROPEZ PENINSULA

By bus From St-Tropez a summer minibus runs from place des Lices to Salins (4–6 daily; 15min), and bus #7705 runs to Ramatuelle (6 daily in summer; 9min).

By car If you come by car, you'll have to pay for parking at all the beaches – the approach roads are designed to make it impossible to park for free on the verge.

ACCOMMODATION

La Croix du Sud Rte des Plages, 3km from Ramatuelle ☎ 04 94 55 51 23, ⓦ campingramatuelle.com. A three-star campsite 3km from Ramatuelle towards the plage de Pampelonne, with plenty of shade and a pool. Closed Oct–March. **€50**

L'Ecurie du Castellas Rte des Moulins de Peillas, Ramatuelle ☎ 04 94 79 20 67, ⓦ lecurieducastellas. com. Just outside Ramatuelle village on the road to Gassin,

with panoramic views over the village to the sea, and eleven stylish en-suite rooms; some have terraces. **€90**

Yelloh! Village Les Tournels Rte des Tournels, 3km from Ramatuelle ☎ 04 94 55 90 90, ⓦ tournels.com. Five-star campsite with a big heated outdoor pool with slides, plus an indoor pool and spa. It's more geared to chalet lets than tents, but they do welcome campers too. Closed Nov–March. **€70**

EATING

Au Fil à la Pâte 7 rue Victor Léon, Ramatuelle ☎ 04 94 79 16 40. Diminutive, rustic place on the main street in the old village, serving fresh pasta (think ravioli stuffed with ceps and truffles for €21), salads from around €18 and meat or fish mains from €19. Mid-March to early Nov daily noon–2pm & 6–10pm; until midnight in high season.

★ **Bello Visto** 9 place des Barrys ☎ 04 94 56 17 30, ⓦ bellovisto.eu. Good Provençal specialities on a €33 *menu*, with dishes like rosemary roasted rabbit thigh and pear clafoutis. They have rooms, also. Tues–Sun noon–2.30pm & 7–9.30pm; closed Nov–Dec 20 & Jan 5 to Easter.

Club 55 43 bd Patch, plage de Pampelonne ☎ 04 94 55 55 55, ⓦ leclub55.fr. The classic among Pampelonne's chic

beach concessions, named after the year when Vadim's film crew scrounged food from what was then a family beach hut. Expect to pay around €27 for an omelette. April–Oct & Christmas daily 9am–5pm.

L'Ecurie du Castellas Rte des Moulins de Peillas, Ramatuelle ☎ 04 94 79 11 59, ⓦ lecurieducastellas.com. Michelin-listed restaurant with a pretty outdoor terrace and dishes such as asparagus salad on summer truffle scrambled eggs for €19. Daily noon–2pm & 7–10pm.

Nikki Beach Rte de l'Epi ☎ 04 94 79 82 04, ⓦ nikkibeach. com. The hot celebrity haunt on the plage de Pampelonne, with simple fare at VIP prices: crudités with *bagna cauda* €38, breaded langoustines €30, gazpacho with blue lobster €35. Mid-April to end Sept daily 11.30am–8pm.

Massif des Maures

The secret of the Côte d'Azur is that despite the crowds and traffic of the coast, Provence is still just behind – old, sparsely populated, village-oriented and dependent on the land for its produce, not its real-estate value. Between Marseille and Menton, the most bewitching hinterland is the sombre, darkly forested **Massif des Maures** that stretches from Hyères to Fréjus.

The highest point of these darkly forested hills – the name derives from the Provençal and Latin words for dark, *mauram* and *mauro* – stops short of 800m, but the quick succession of ridges, the sudden drops and views, and the curling, looping roads are pervasively mountainous. Where the lie of the land gives a wide bowl of sunlit slopes, vines are grown. Elsewhere the hills are thickly forested, with Aleppo pines, holly, sweet chestnuts and gnarled cork oaks, their trunks scarred in great bands where their bark has been stripped.

Exploring the massif

Much of the massif is inaccessible even to **walkers**. However, the GR9 follows the most northern and highest ridge from Pignans on the N97 past Notre-Dame-des-Anges, La Sauvette, La Garde-Freinet and down to the head of the Golfe de St-Tropez. There are other paths and tracks, such as the one following the Vallon de Tamary from north of La Londe-des-Maures to join one of the roads snaking down from the Col de Babaou to Collobrières. Some of the smaller back roads don't go very far and many are closed to the public in summer for fear of forest fires, but when they are open, this makes exceptional countryside for exploring by mountain bike or on foot. Bear in mind, however, that at certain times of the year the entire massif is thick with rifle-toting hunters. Local tourist offices have information on routes.

For **cyclists**, the stunning D14 that runs through the middle of the massif, parallel to the coast, from Pierrefeu-du-Var north of Hyères to Cogolin near St-Tropez, is manageable.

Collobrières

At the heart of the massif is the ancient village of **COLLOBRIÈRES**, reputed to have been the first place in France to adopt **cork-growing** from the Spanish. From the Middle Ages until recent times, cork production has been the major business of the village; however, the main industry now is *marrons glacés* and every other confection derived from sweet chestnuts. The annual *Fête de la Châtaigne*, the **chestnut fair**, takes place at the height of the harvest on the last three Sundays of October, when special dishes are served in restaurants and roast chestnuts sold in the streets.

Confiserie Azurienne

Bd Koenig • Daily: summer 9.30am–12.30pm & 1.30–7.30pm; winter 9.30am–12.30pm & 2–6pm • T 04 94 48 07 20, W confiserieazureenne.con

The **Confiserie Azurienne** factory has a small exhibition of old machinery used for processing chestnuts, and a shop that sells the signature *marrons glacés* plus ice cream, jam, nougat and bonbons, all made with chestnuts, as well as a sunny terrace on which to enjoy the delicious chestnut-flavoured ice cream.

ARRIVAL AND INFORMATION — COLLOBRIÈRES

By bus Collobrières is served by infrequent buses from Hyères (2 daily; 50min) and Toulon (2 daily; 1hr 50min).

By car Parking can be a headache, with the main tourist car park a 5min walk from the village centre.

Tourist office Bd Charles-Caminat (Mon 3–6.30pm, Tues–Sat 10am–12.30pm & 3–6.30pm, Sun 10am–12.30pm; closed Mon, Sun & Thurs morning in low season; T 04 94 48 08 00, W collobrieres-tourisme.com). They can supply details of walks in the surrounding hills.

ACCOMMODATION AND EATING

Camping Just outside the eastern side of the village on the D14 T 04 94 48 08 00, W collobrieres-tourisme.com. A small signposted field by the side of the road is set aside for camper vans. Facilities are limited to a bin but there is a septic tank disposal facility 1km further along the road. Always open. Free

La Ferme du Peïgros South of the village, signed off the D41 to Bormes at the Col de Babaou T 04 94 48 03 83. An isolated farmhouse in wonderful surroundings serving its own produce, including goat's cheese and – in season – ceps. Dishes from around €18. Lunch all year round, plus dinner in July & Aug.

Des Maures 19 bd Lazare Carnot T 04 94 48 07 10, W hoteldesmaures.fr. Simple but spacious and very good-value rooms above a restaurant and bar in the centre of the village, facing the river at the back. Half-board available. €60

★ **Notre Dame** 15 av de la Libération T 04 94 48 07 13, W hotel-notre-dame.eu. Surprisingly chic for the deeply rural location, this boutique-style hotel has ten individually decorated rooms with huge bathrooms, a lovely patio restaurant by the river and a pool. There's limited parking – reserve in advance. €102

★ **La Petite Fontaine** 6 place de la République T 04 94 48 00 12. Congenial, affordable *Gault Millau*-listed restaurant, serving hearty, rustic food – *daube de boeuf*, home-made *terrines*, *tarte aux poires* with chestnut purée – with *menus* from €26 and €33. Tues–Sat noon–1.30pm & 7–9pm, Sun noon–1.30pm.

SHOPPING

Les Vignerons de Collobrières Near Notre Dame hotel at the western entrance to the village ☎ 04 94 48 07 26. A good place to buy the local Côtes de Provence wines. Summer Mon 2–6pm, Tues–Sat 8.30am–noon & 2–6pm; winter Tues–Fri 2–5.30pm, Sat 8.30am–noon & 2–5.30pm.

La Chartreuse de la Verne

Off the D14 • Feb–May & Sept–Dec daily except Tues 11am–5pm; June–Aug daily except Tues & during high fire risk 11am–6pm • €6 • ☎ 04 94 43 48 28 or ☎ 04 94 48 08 00 for fire-risk information, ⓦ diocese-frejus-toulon.com/Monastere-Notre-Dame-de-Clemence • Drivers have to park at the visitor car park, several hundred metres from the monastery

Writing at the end of the nineteenth century, Maupassant declared that there was nowhere else in the world where his heart had felt such a pressing weight of melancholy as at the ruins of **La Chartreuse de la Verne**. Since then a great deal of restoration work has been carried out on this Carthusian monastery, abandoned during the Revolution and hidden away in total isolation, 12km east of Collobrières on a winding but largely paved track off the D14 towards Grimaud. It remains a desolate spot, though; the buildings of this once vast twelfth-century complex, in the dark reddish-brown schist of the Maures, combined for decorative effect with local greenish serpentine, appear gaunt and inhospitable, but the atmosphere is indisputable.

Le Village des Tortues

5 miles west of Gonfaron on D97 • Daily 9am–7pm; winter 9.30am–5pm • €12 • ☎ 04 89 29 14 10, ⓦ www.villagetortues.com

About 20km north west of Collobrières, **Le Village des Tortues** is not simply a tourist attraction but also a serious conservation project to repopulate the native Hermann tortoise. A million years ago the tortoises populated a third of France, but now, due to the ever-increasing threat of urbanization, forest fires, theft of eggs and sale as pets, this rare creature only just survives in the Massif des Maures. The tortoises are cared for and protected here, and you can look round their large enclosures where you'll see the tiny babies, "juveniles" and those soon to be released back into the wild.

Grimaud and around

GRIMAUD looks like a film set of a *village perché*, where the cone of houses enclosing the twelfth-century church, culminating in the spectacular ruins of a medieval castle, appears as a single, perfectly unified entity, decorated by its trees and flowers. The most vaunted street in this ensemble is the narrow **rue des Templiers**, which leads up past the arcaded Gothic house of the Knights Templar to the pure Romanesque **Église St-Michel**. The views from the **château ruins** (free access) are superb, and the monumental, sharply cut serpentine window frames of the shattered edifice stand in mute testimony to its former glory.

Port Grimaud

The main visitor entrance is well signed 800m off the D559, surrounded by parking areas • Boat rental €25 for 30min, €50 for a day; boat tours €6.50 • Buses from St-Tropez (7 daily; 5min)

Avoiding the St-Tropez traffic chaos is tricky if you're visiting **PORT GRIMAUD**, the ultimate Côte d'Azur property development, half standing, half floating at the head of the Golfe de St-Tropez just north of La Foux and quite separate from Grimaud village itself, though it's part of the same *commune*. It was created in the 1960s by developer François Spoerry – whose tomb is in the village church – as a private pleasure lagoon with waterways for roads and yachts parked at every door. The houses are in exquisitely tasteful old Provençal style, and their owners, among them Joan Collins, are extremely well heeled. Anyone can wander in for a gawp: you don't pay to get in, but you can't

6

explore all the islands without renting a **boat** or taking a crowded boat tour. There are plenty of places to eat and drink, though they are clearly aimed at visitors rather than the residents.

ARRIVAL AND INFORMATION   GRIMAUD

By bus Buses link St-Tropez to Grimaud (2 daily; 30min). There are also connections from Grimaud to La Garde-Freinet (4–5 daily; 15min) and Ste-Maxime (6–8 daily; 20min).

Tourist office On the RD558 next to the lift up to the old village (April–June & Sept Mon–Sat 9am–12.30pm & 2–6pm; July & Aug daily 9am–1pm & 2.30–7pm; Oct– March 9am–12.30pm & 2–5.30pm; ☎04 94 55 43 83, ⓦgrimaud-provence.com).

ACCOMMODATION AND EATING

Apopino Place des Pénitents ☎04 94 43 25 26, ⓦapopinorestaurant.com. Stylish place at the western end of the village, with an imaginative *carte*: rock fish soup with cod and garlic, for example, asparagus, asparagus pesto and parmesan crumble. *Menus* €20/€33. June–Aug Mon–Sat 7–9pm; Sept–May Tues–Sat noon–1.45pm & 7–9pm.

Le Café de France 5 place Neuve ☎04 94 43 20 05. Pleasant place in the old village, with a shady terrace, a two-course lunchtime *formule* for €18 and interesting à la carte options like tuna tataki for €18. Noon–2pm & 7.15– 10pm, closed all day Tues & Mon & Sun eve.

Camping Charlemagne Le Pont de Bois, rte de Collobrières ☎04 94 43 22 90, ⓦcamping-charlemagne.

com. Four-star campsite on the road to Collobrières. Facilities include a restaurant, pizzeria, barbecue, bakery and games room, and there's wi-fi, too. €33

Le Pâtissier du Château Bd des Aliziers ☎04 94 43 21 16, ⓦpatisserieduchateau.com. Bakery and tearoom selling wonderful cakes and fresh, nutty breads, plus breakfasts (€5.50 for coffee & €2.50 for a croissant). Daily (except Wed): July & Aug 7am–8pm; Sept, Oct & April– June 7am–7pm.

Le Verger Maelvi Rte de Collobrières ☎04 94 55 57 80, ⓦhotel-grimaud.com. Lovely country hotel in a peaceful riverside setting 1km west of the village, with a pool and individually decorated, spacious a/c double rooms with terraces. €210

La Garde-Freinet

The attractive village of **LA GARDE-FREINET**, 10km north of Grimaud, was founded in the late twelfth century by people from the nearby villages of St-Clément and Miremer. The original fortified settlement sat further up the hillside, and the foundations of its **fort** are visible above the present-day village. To explore it, you'll have to make the steep 1km clamber along a path from the car park at place de la Planète; the tourist office can supply a simple map, and it's also signposted from place de l'Hubac above the tourist office.

Although attempts have been made to give La Garde-Freinet the chic airs of the nearby coast, it still retains an authentic, rural feel for now, with tempting food shops selling organic produce and good local wines. The **Conservatoire du Patrimoine** (Mon– Sat: April–Oct 9am–1pm & 2–5pm; Nov–March Mon–Fri 9am–1pm & 2–5pm; free), next to the tourist office, has displays on local natural and cultural interest. For hikers, the spectacular 21km GR9 **route des Crêtes** to the west of the village passes along a tremendously scenic forested ridge, though if the fire risk is high the paths are likely to be closed; the tourist office has information (in English) on the route.

ARRIVAL AND INFORMATION   LA GARDE-FREINET

By bus Buses from Grimaud (4–5 daily; 15min) and St-Tropez (1–2 daily; 45min) arrive at Parking du Stade on the main road at the entrance to the village.

Tourist office Chapelle St-Jean (April–June & Sept Mon–Fri 9am–12.30pm & 2–5.30pm, Sat 9am–12.30pm; July & Aug Mon–Sat 9.30am–1pm & 2.30–6.30pm, Sun 9.30am–12.30pm; Oct–March Mon–Fri 9.30am–12.30pm & 2–5pm; ☎04 94 56 04 93, ⓦla-garde-freinet-tourisme. fr). They can provide details for the Maures region, with suggested walks and hikes (in English) including the GR9 rte des Crêtes.

ACCOMMODATION AND EATING

Camping de Bérard 5km along the RD558 to Grimaud ☎ 04 94 43 21 23, ⑩ campingberard.com. Three-star campsite with a swimming pool, free wi-fi, a shop, restaurant and bar, plus musical evenings and plenty of games facilities. Closed Nov–Feb. **€18**

Le Carnotzet 7 place du Marché ☎ 04 94 43 62 73. Lively bar, art gallery and restaurant with a terrace on the village's most exquisite square. *Plats du jour* from €12, *menu* €25; live jazz Thurs evenings in July & Aug. Daily noon–2.30/3pm & 7–10/10.30pm; Sept–June closed Tues & Wed.

La Faucado Bd de l'Esplanade ☎ 04 94 79 67 37, ⑩ lafaucado.fr. *Restaurant gastronomique* with mains around €35; it's overpriced, but serves beautiful dishes such as razor clam with pickled veg or artichoke ravioli with basil from local produce in a pretty garden setting. Noon–2pm & 7.30–9.30pm, closed Mon & Tues lunch.

Le Mouron Rouge Quartier Le Défend Nord, 1km north of La Garde-Freinet ☎ 04 94 43 66 33, ⑩ lemouronrouge. com. Lovely *chambres d'hôtes* in a rustic setting, with well-equipped apartments and studios (all for two to four people) and a double room with private terrace. In high season rooms are rented by the week only. There's a *boules* pitch and a large pool. Per week: doubles **€875**; studios **€1450**; apartments **€1650**

Ste-Maxime and around

STE-MAXIME, which faces St-Tropez across the gulf, is an archetypal Côte resort: palmed corniche and enormous pleasure-boat harbour, beaches crowded with confident, bronzed windsurfers and waterskiers, a local history museum in a defensive tower that no one goes to, and a proliferation of estate agents. It sprawls a little too far – most of the coast road to Fréjus is built up – but the magnetic appeal of the water's edge is hard to deny. Compared to its more famous neighbour, though, it's all rather lacking in atmosphere.

Its sandy **beaches**, however, have the Blue Flags for cleanliness that St-Tropez's lack, and there's a string of fancy concessions along the east-facing **Plage de la Nartelle**, 2km from the centre round the Pointe des Sardinaux towards Les Issambres. The Plage de la Nartelle merges seamlessly into the **Plage des Eléphants**, named after the cartoons of Jean de Brunhoff, creator of Babar the elephant, who had a holiday home in Ste-Maxime. There are more opportunities to cool off inland at the **Aqualand** water park, just off the D25 (late June to end Aug daily 10am–6/7pm; €28; ⑩ aqualand.fr).

Beyond Ste-Maxime, its suburb **Val d'Esquières** merges with **Les Issambres**, the seaside extension of Roquebrune, and **St-Aygulf**, belonging to the *commune* of Fréjus, along the fast and rather dangerous coast road. For all its relentless suburban sprawl, this stretch has its attractions, notably a shoreline of rocky coves and *calanques*, shaded by shapely pines and alternating with golden crescents of sand.

Musée du Phonographe et de la Musique Mécanique

Parc St-Donat, rte de Muy • May–June & Sept Wed–Sun 10am–noon & 3–6pm; July & Aug 10am–noon • €4 • ☎ 04 94 96 50 52

Some 10km north of town on the road to Le Muy, the marvellous **Musée du Phonographe et de la Musique Mécanique** is the result of one woman's forty-year obsession with collecting audio equipment. The facade may resemble Hansel and Gretel's fantastical biscuit house, but it is actually modelled on an eighteenth-century Limonaire mechanical music machine. Inside, displays include one of Thomas Edison's "talking machines" of 1878, the first recording machines of the 1890s and an amplified

---

THE MARKETS OF STE-MAXIME

Ste-Maxime's rather pretty *vieille ville* has several good **markets**: a covered flower and food market on rue Fernand-Bessy (July & Aug Mon–Sat 8am–1pm & 4.30–8pm, Sun 8am–1pm; Sept–June Tues–Sun 8am–1pm); a daily fish market on the port (8am–noon); a Thursday morning food market on place du Marché; a weekly flea and antiques market on promenade Simon-Lorière (Wed 8am–6pm) and arts and crafts in the pedestrian streets (April to mid-Sept daily 4–11pm).

lyre (1903). Almost half the exhibits still work, and you may find yourself listening to the magical, crackling sounds of an original wax cylinder recording from the 1880s played on the equipment it was made for.

ARRIVAL AND INFORMATION

STE-MAXIME

By bus Buses from St-Tropez (up to 12 daily; 35min) and St-Raphaël (up to 15 daily; 50min) stop outside the tourist office.

By ferry Ferries to and from St-Tropez run all year except in Jan and early Feb (every 20min in high season; 15min; ☎ 04 94 94 49 29 39, ⊛ bateauxverts.com).

Tourist office 1 promenade Simon-Lorière (April–June & Sept Mon–Sat 9am–12.30pm & 2–6.30pm; July & Aug daily 9am–7pm; Oct–March daily 9am–noon & 2–6pm; ☎ 0826 20 83 83, ⊛ sainte-maxime.com).

Bike rental Rent Bike Location, 15 rue Magali (☎ 04 94 43 98 07, ⊛ rentbike-location.com).

ACCOMMODATION AND EATING

La Beaumette 142 rte du Plan de la Tour ☎ 04 94 96 10 92, ⊛ www.labeaumette.com. Three-star campsite some 2km inland from the port, up in the hills off the D25, with a pool, ping-pong and *pétanque*. Closed Oct–March. **€35**

La Belle Aurore 5 bd Jean-Moulin ☎ 04 94 96 02 45, ⊛ belleaurore.com. Elegant *restaurant gastronomique* with a stunning setting on the water's edge with views across to St-Tropez. There's a €49 six-course *menu*; otherwise it's around €31 for a main course. Tues & Thurs–Sun 12.15–2pm & 7.30–9pm.

Castellamar 8 av G.-Pompidou ☎ 04 94 96 19 97. The best of the cheaper hotels, on the west side of the river, but still close to the town centre and the sea, with a bar, lounge and tree-shaded terrace. Closed mid-Oct to mid-March. **€86**

Les Cigalons 34 av du Croiseur Léger le Malin ☎ 04 94 96 05 51, ⊛ campingcigalon.com. Two-star seaside campsite east of town, just 50m from the beach, with wi-fi, children's games and *boules*. It also rents out holiday bungalows. Closed mid-Oct to late March. Camping **€35**; bungalows per week **€650**

La Dérive 14 rue Courbet ☎ 06 12 43 30 75, ⊛ laderive. fr. Lively brasserie with a small terrace in an atmospheric part of the old town. Good value lunch menu of mussels or pasta, dessert and coffee for €15.50. Daily noon–2.30pm & 7–9.30/10.30pm.

Matisse 11 bd Frédéric-Mistral ☎ 04 94 96 18 33, ⊛ hotel-matisse.com. Stylish and central three-star hotel with Matisse-themed decor and a pool. There are various categories and styles of room but all have a/c and either bath or shower. **€150**

Inland: the Argens Valley

The **River Argens** meets the Mediterranean in unspectacular style between St-Aygulf and St-Raphaël. It's an important source of irrigation for orchards and vines, but as a waterway it has little appeal, being sluggish, full of breeding mosquitoes and on the whole inaccessible. The geographical feature that dominates the lower Argens Valley, and acts as an almost mystical pole of attraction, is the **Rocher de Roquebrune** between the village of **Roquebrune-sur-Argens** and the town of Le Muy.

Roquebrune-sur-Argens and around

The village of **ROQUEBRUNE-SUR-ARGENS** lies on the edge of the Massif des Maures, 12km from the sea, facing the flat valley of the Argens that opens to the northeast. Some of its sixteenth-century defensive towers and ramparts remain, and almost every house within them is four hundred years old or more, joined together by vaulted passageways and tiny cobbled streets. Two fountains face each other across picturesque rue des Portiques, where the houses are arcaded over the pavement; beyond it, ancient houses huddle around the imposing village church. Close by there's a **Maison du Patrimoine** (Tues–Sat 10am–12.30pm & 2.30–5.30/6.30pm; daily in high season) where you can buy local produce.

Maison du Chocolat

Chapelle Saint-Jacques, rue de l'Hospice • Wed–Sat 9am–12.30pm & 1.30–5pm; also open Tues during high season and school holidays • Free • ☎ 09 67 08 42 65

A seventeenth-century chapel in Roquebrune village is the setting for the **Maison du Chocolat**, a delightful collection of chocolate-related ephemera from antique packaging and advertising to toys and even a chocolate sculpture. It's the private collection of *maître chocolatier* Gérard Courreau, whose boutique is nearby at 2 montée St-Michel.

Rocher de Roquebrune

Three kilometres west of Roquebrune, the rust-red mass of the **Rocher de Roquebrune** erupts unexpectedly out of nothing, as if to some purpose. Even the A8 autoroute thundering past its foot fails to bring it into line with the rest of the coastal scenery glimpsed from the fast lane. To reach it, coming from Roquebrune, take the left fork just after the village, signed to La Roquette; at the next fork you can go left or right depending on which side of the mountain you want to skirt. The right-hand route runs alongside the highway towards **Notre Dame de la Roquette**, an erstwhile place of pilgrimage (now closed to the public), while the left-hand fork takes you round the quieter, steeper southern side.

Four **hiking routes** ascend the rock from the north, east and west. All but one are challenging in their latter stages, so wear appropriate walking boots. The tourist office has information, with route descriptions and downloadable GPX tracks for smartphone or GPS on their website (see below).

Chapelle de Ste-Roseline

Near Les-Arcs-sur Argens, on the D91 • **Chapelle de Ste-Roseline** April & May Tues–Sun 2.30–5.30pm; June–Sept Tues & Wed 2.30–6.30pm, Thurs–Sun 2.30–6pm; Oct–March Tues & Wed 2–5pm, Thurs–Sun 2.30–5pm • Free • **Château de Ste-Roseline** Wine-tasting & buying Mon–Fri 9am–12.30pm & 2–6.30pm, Sat & Sun 10am–12.30pm & 2–6pm; cellar tours Mon–Fri 2.30pm • Cellar tours free • ☎ 04 94 99 50 30, ⊕ sainte-roseline.com

Beneath a crudely buttressed ceiling, the crumbly interior of the **Chapelle de Ste-Roseline** is really rather ghoulish. St Roseline was born in 1263 and spent her adolescence disobeying her father by giving food to the poor. On one occasion he caught her and demanded to see the contents of her basket; the food miraculously turned into rose petals. She became the prioress of the abbey and when she died her body refused to decay and now, supposedly, lies in a glass case in the chapel, shrivelled and brown but not quite a skeleton. What's worse are her eyes – one lifeless, the other staring at you – displayed in a gaudy frame on a wall. Horror objects apart, the chapel has a fabulous mosaic by **Chagall** showing angels laying a table for the saint; some beautifully carved seventeenth-century choir stalls; and an impressive Renaissance rood-loft in which peculiar things happen to the legs of the decorative figures.

The old abbey buildings of which the chapel is part are a private residence belonging to a **wine** grower, and you can also taste and buy the *cru classé* named after the chapel and visit the château's cellars. The château is also a venue for classical music concerts in summer.

Les Arcs-sur-Argens

Eighteen kilometres west of Roquebrune, the picturesque medieval village of **LES ARCS-SUR-ARGENS** has been immaculately restored, with its skyline dominated by a Saracen lookout tower, the sole remnant of a thirteenth-century castle. Les Arcs is one of the centres for the Var wine industry, and at the **Maison des Vins** (daily: Mon–Sat 10am–6pm, Sun 10am– 5pm; ⊕ maison-des-vins.fr) you can taste and buy wine and regional products and pick up details of local *routes du vin* and *vignerons*: it's on the DN7 just west of the village towards Vidauban.

6

ARRIVAL AND INFORMATION

THE ARGENS VALLEY

ROQUEBRUNE-SUR-ARGENS

Tourist office La Gallery, ZA des Garillans on the DN7 (July & Aug Mon–Sat 9am–7pm, Sun 9am–1pm & 3–7pm; Sept Mon–Sat 9am–12.30pm & 2.30–7pm, Sun 9am–1pm; Oct–June Mon–Sat 9am–12.30pm & 2.30–6pm, Thurs opens 10.30am except in June & Sept; ☎ 04 94 19 89 89, ⓦ roquebrunesurargens.fr).

LES ARCS-SUR-ARGENS

By train Les Arcs' *gare SCNF* is on the south side of the village; turn left out of the station and then right into Av Jean-Jaurès to reach the centre.

Destinations Fréjus (14 daily; 13min); St-Raphaël (roughly every 30min; 14–17min); Toulon (roughly every 30min to 1hr; 36min–1hr).

ACCOMMODATION AND EATING

ROQUEBRUNE-SUR-ARGENS

Le Jardin de l'Orangeraie 401 bd Jean-Jaurès ☎ 04 94 81 22 16. Creative cooking in an inconspicuous setting on the edge of the old village, close to the Maison du Terroir, with a garden terrace, open kitchen and dishes like corn fed chicken with roasted polenta. Lunchtime *plat* €14.50, two courses €17 and €19 for three. Tues–Fri noon–1.30pm & 7–9pm, Sat 7–9pm, Sun noon–2pm.

LES ARCS-SUR-ARGENS

Le Logis du Guetteur Place du Château ☎ 04 94 99 51 10, ⓦ logisduguetteur.com. Charming three-star hotel in a lovely setting at the top of Les Arcs' beautiful *vieux village*, clustering at the base of the Saracen tower and with just fifteen rooms and suites. The good restaurant has *menus* from €29 to €79. Daily noon–2pm & 7.15–9.30pm. **€170**

Fréjus and around

FRÉJUS – along with its neighbour St-Raphaël (see page 295) 3km east – dates back to Roman times. It was established as a naval base under Julius Caesar and Augustus, and its ancient port, known as Forum Julii, consisted of 2km of quays connected by a walled canal to the sea (which was considerably closer then). After the battle of Actium in 31 BC, the ships of Antony and Cleopatra's defeated fleet were brought here. Little exists of the Roman walls that circled the city, and the

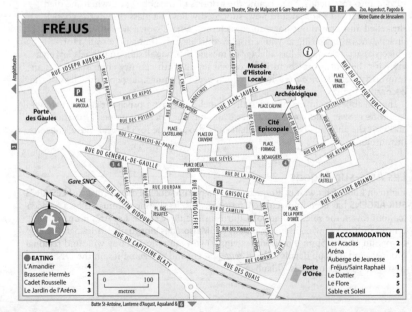

FRÉJUS PASSES

If you're planning to visit most of Fréjus' sights, it may be worth getting the seven-day **Fréjus Pass** (€6), which gives access to the amphitheatre, Musée Archéologie and Notre Dame de Jerusalem, or the **Pass Intégral** (€9), which adds to these access to the cathedral cloisters.

once-important port silted up and was filled in after the Revolution. Today you can see a scattering of **Roman remains**, along with the medieval **Cité Episcopale**, or cathedral complex, which takes up two sides of **place Formigé**, the marketplace and heart of both contemporary and medieval Fréjus. The area between Fréjus and the sea is now the suburb of **Fréjus-Plage**, with its vast 1980s marina, **Port-Fréjus**, a little over 2km from the centre of the old city. Both Fréjus and Fréjus-Plage merge seamlessly with St-Raphaël, which in turn merges with **Boulouris** to the east.

The environs of Fréjus hold a couple of reminders of France's **colonial past**, a beautiful chapel decorated by **Jean Cocteau** and the **Site de Malpasset**, evidence of a terrible disaster that befell Fréjus half a century ago (see page 292). More light-hearted diversions are to be found in the town's **zoo** and **water park**.

Roman remains

A tour of the **Roman remains** gives you a good idea of the extent of Forum Julii, but they are scattered throughout and beyond the town centre and take a full day to get around. As you turn right out of the *gare SNCF* it's a 400m walk down boulevard Séverin-Decuers to the **Butte St-Antoine**, against whose east wall the waters of the port would have lapped, and which once was capped by a fort. It was one of the port's defences, and one of the ruined **towers** may have been a lighthouse. A lane around the southern wall follows the quayside (some stretches are visible) the short distance from boulevard Séverin-Decuers to the medieval **Lanterne d'Auguste**, which was built on the Roman foundations of a structure marking the entrance of the canal into the ancient harbour. Retracing your steps to the centre, on rue des Moulins, you will come to the arcades of the **Porte d'Orée**, positioned on the former harbour's edge alongside what was probably a **bath complex**.

Amphitheatre

Rue Henri Vadon • April–Sept Tues–Sun 9.30am–12.30pm & 2–6pm; Oct–March Tues–Sat 9.30am–noon & 2–4.30pm • €3, or included in Fréjus Pass and Pass Intégral • ☎ 04 94 51 34 31, 🌐 frejus.fr

On the southwestern fringe of the old town, the Roman **Porte des Gaules** marks the approach on rue Henri Vadon to the **amphitheatre**, which had a capacity of around ten thousand. Fit to host concerts again after a refurbishment in 2012, its upper tiers have been reconstructed, but the vaulted galleries on the ground floor are largely original.

Roman theatre and around

Av du Théâtre Romain • April–Sept Tues–Sun 9.30am–12.30pm & 2–6pm; Oct–March Tues–Sat 9.30am–noon & 2–4.30pm • Free • ☎ 04 94 53 58 75, 🌐 frejus.fr

The **Roman theatre** is immediately north of the old town, around 300m from the tourist information office. Its original seats have long gone, though it's still used for shows in summer. To the northeast, in the parc Aurélien at the far end of avenue du XVème-Corps-d'Armée, six arches are visible of the 40km **aqueduct**, which was once as high as the ramparts.

6

THE MALPASSET DAM DISASTER

The bleakest day in Fréjus's recent history is recalled by the **Site de Malpasset**, deep in the Forêt Communale de Fréjus and signposted off the Rond-point du Gargalon on the D37. At 9.13pm on the rainy night of December 2, 1959, the new **Malpasset Dam** across the Reyran Valley collapsed, releasing 50 million cubic metres of water to create a 40m wave that swept along the narrow valley, obliterating everything – including the construction workers' camp on the site of the A8 autoroute, just below the dam. As the wave neared the coast it fanned out, widening the trail of destruction; it was still 3m high when it raced through Fréjus twenty minutes later. **Fifty farms** were swamped and some 423 people killed; the death toll was never accurately established as many victims were swept out to sea.

Afterwards, it was found that the **geological survey** had failed to **pinpoint a fault line** at the site, which allowed pressure to build up under the dam. Far from failing structurally, the entire left side of the dam was simply pivoted off its foundations by the water. The access road fords the insignificant looking stream in the valley bottom before passing beneath the autoroute to a car park, from which a path leads to the broken dam. Long before you reach it, house-sized chunks of steel-reinforced concrete litter the riverbed like outsized boulders. The dam is left more or less as it was, its graceful arc poignantly terminated a few metres from the valley side. Forest has **recolonized** the valley floor behind it.

Cité Episcopale and around

The **Cité Episcopale**, or cathedral close, takes up two sides of **place Formigé**, the marketplace and heart of both contemporary and medieval Fréjus. It comprises the cathedral, flanked by the fourteenth-century bishop's palace, now the Hôtel de Ville, the baptistry, cloisters and archeological museum. You can wander through the modern courtyard of the Hôtel de Ville, but you get a better view of the orange Esterel stone walls of the Episcopal Palace from rue de Beausset.

Cloisters, baptistry and cathedral

Cloisters 48 rue de Fleury • Daily: May–Aug 10am–6pm; Sept–April 10am–1pm & 2–5pm • €6, or included in Pass Intégral; info sheets in English available • ☎ 04 94 52 14 01, ⓦ monuments-nationaux.fr

By far the most beautiful and engaging component of the Cité Episcopale ensemble is the **cloisters**. Slender marble columns, carved in the twelfth century, support a fourteenth-century ceiling of wooden panels painted with apocalyptic creatures. Out of the original 1200 pictures, four hundred remain; subjects include multiheaded monsters, mermaids, satyrs and scenes of bacchanalian debauchery.

The oldest part of the complex is the **baptistry**, one of France's most ancient buildings, built in the fourth or fifth century and, as such, contemporary with the decline and fall of the city's Roman founders. Its two doorways are of different heights, signifying the enlarged spiritual stature of the baptized; it was used in the days of early Christianity when adult baptism was still the norm.

Parts of the early Gothic **cathedral** may belong to a tenth-century church, but its best features, apart from the coloured diamond-shaped tiles on the spire, are Renaissance: the choir stalls, a wooden crucifix on the left of the entrance, and the intricately carved doors with scenes of a Saracen massacre.

Musée Archéologique

Place Calvini • April–Sept Tues–Sun 9.30am–12.30pm & 2–6pm; Oct–March Tues–Sat 9.30am–noon & 2–4.30pm • €3, or included in Fréjus Pass and Pass Intégral • ☎ 04 94 52 15 78, ⓦ frejus.fr

The **Musée Archéologique**, on the upper storey of the cloisters, has as its star pieces a complete Roman mosaic of a leopard and a copy of a renowned double-headed bust of Hermes, alongside various archeological finds from the Roman town, from workaday ceramics to domestic artefacts and tombs.

Musée d'Histoire Locale

153 rue Jean-Jaurès • April–Sept Tues–Sun 9.30am–12.30pm & 2–6pm; Oct–March Tues–Sat 9.30am–noon & 2–4.30pm • €3 • ☎ 04 94 51 64 01

Close to the Cité Episcopale in an old bourgeois townhouse, the small **Musée d'Histoire Locale** has reconstructions of days gone by, including an old school classroom, plus displays on traditional local trades and a film about the Malpasset Dam tragedy of 1959 (see box above).

Pagode Hong Hien and around

13 rue Henri-Giraud • Daily: summer 9am–9pm; winter 9am–6pm • €2

About 2km north of Fréjus centre at the junction of rue Henri-Giraud and the DN7 to Cannes, the Vietnamese **Pagode Hong Hien**, built by colonial troops, is still maintained as a Buddhist temple and open to visitors. Alongside stands a massive **memorial** to the dead of the Indo-Chinese wars of the 1940s and 1950s. It is inscribed with the name of every fallen Frenchman; it's clear to see that the years 1950–54 were the most bloody. A small but evocative photo **exhibition** inside the memorial adds human interest (Mon & Wed–Sun 10am–5.30pm; free; ☎ 04 94 44 42 90).

Mosquée Missiri de Djenné

Rte des Combattants d'Afrique du Nord • Closed but viewable from the road

An unlikely remnant of France's imperial past comes in the shape of an abandoned mosque, built by French colonial troops. The **Mosquée Missiri de Djenné** is on the left off the D4 to Bagnols, in the middle of an army camp 2km from the RN7 junction. A strange, guava-coloured, fort-like building, it's a replica of a Sudanese mosque in Mali, sadly fenced off most of the time, though much of the interior is visible from outside.

Notre Dame de Jérusalem

Rte de Cannes • April–Sept Tues–Sun 9.30am–12.30pm & 2–6pm; Oct–March Tues–Sat 9.30am–noon & 2–4.30pm • €3, or included in Fréjus Pass and Pass Intégral (see page 291) • ☎ 04 94 53 27 06

Just off the DN7 at La Tour de Mare, 5.6km from the centre of Fréjus, is the last of **Jean Cocteau**'s artistic landmarks, the chapel of **Notre Dame de Jérusalem**. Conceived as the church for a failed artistic community, the octagonal building was not completed until after Cocteau's death in 1963, and the interior was completed to Cocteau's plans by Edouard Dermit. *The Last Supper* scene inside includes a self-portrait of Cocteau; the building's exterior is covered in elegantly simple mosaics and its floors with vibrant blue tiles.

KIDS' ACTIVITIES AROUND FRÉJUS

Opposite the Base Nature (see page 294), west of Port-Fréjus, Fréjus's water park, **Aqualand**, has all manner of water slides and pools (mid-June to mid-July & first week Sept Wed 10am–9pm, Thurs–Tues 10am–6pm; mid-July to end Aug daily 10am–7pm; second week Sept Wed, Sat & Sun 10am–6pm; €28; ☎ 04 94 51 82 51, ⓦ aqualand.fr). Equally appealing to children is the **zoo** in Le Capitou, close to exit 38 from the autoroute on the D4 heading north, which has everything from big cats, marsupials and apes to small reptiles and exotic birds (daily: March–May, Sept & Oct 10am–5pm; June–Aug 10am–6pm; Nov–Feb 10.30am–4.30pm; €17; ☎ 04 98 11 37 37, ⓦ zoo-frejus.com; bus #1 or #2).

6

OUTDOOR ACTIVITIES AROUND FRÉJUS

Around Fréjus, rugged terrain for **cyclists** is found in the forested hills of the **Massif de l'Esterel** to the northeast of town; there are more than 100km of signposted trails in and around Fréjus. Tourist offices in Fréjus and St-Raphaël sell maps and **guides** to the Esterel. There are also cycle trails at the **Base Nature François Léotard** (daily: July & Aug 7.30am–midnight; Sept–June 7.30am–11pm; free; ✆04 94 51 91 10), a large public park just west of Port-Fréjus on the coast, as well as a beach, a public swimming pool and sports pitches.

ARRIVAL AND INFORMATION
FRÉJUS

By train Trains to St-Raphaël are much more frequent than those to Fréjus, so it's often easiest to alight there and take the #1, #2, #3, #4, #A or #B Agglobus, which run between the two towns (12–30min). There are also trains between St-Raphaël and Fréjus *gare SNCF*, which is on the south side of the *vieille ville* (7 daily; 3min).

By bus The *gare routière* is on the north side of the town centre at rue Gustave Bret close to the tourist office (✆04 94 53 78 46). Note that the inter-town coastal bus route #7601 doesn't serve Fréjus town centre but continues to St-Raphaël's *gare routière*.

Destinations St-Raphaël (frequent; 15–35min).

Tourist office Le Florus II, 249 rue Jean-Jaurès (June & Sept Mon–Sat 9.30am–12.30pm & 2–6.30pm; July & Aug daily 9.30am–7pm; Oct–May Mon–Sat 9.30am–noon & 2–6pm; ✆04 94 51 83 83, 🔁frejus.fr).

Market days Wed and Sat morning.

ACCOMMODATION
SEE MAP PAGE 290

Aréna 145 rue du Général-de-Gaulle ✆04 94 17 09 40, 🔁hotel-frejus-arena.com. Comfortable four-star hotel in three buildings grouped around a pool and luxuriant garden, close to the *gare SNCF*. Rooms have TV and a/c. There's also a good restaurant. Closed late Oct to late Nov. **€133**

Auberge de Jeunesse Fréjus/Saint Raphaël 627 chemin Counillier ✆04 94 53 18 75, 🔁fuaj.org. Fréjus' hostel is set amid ten hectares of umbrella pines 2km northeast of the centre. It's close to the pagoda Hong Hien and served by the infrequent bus #10 from Fréjus or St-Raphaël *gare routière*. Reception 8.30am–noon & 5.30–10pm. **€19.80**

Le Flore 35 rue Grisolle ✆04 94 51 38 35, 🔁hotels-frejus.fr. The nicest budget option in the old town is this pretty, wisteria-clad two-star. It won't win any awards for decor but rooms have a/c and TV, and there are two triples and one four-bed room. **€69**

Sable et Soleil 158 rue Paul-Arène, Fréjus-Plage ✆06 73 09 84 44, 🔁hotel-sableetsoleil.com. A pleasant, small, modern hotel, 300m from the sea near the port. Most rooms have a private terrace; there's also secure parking. **€90**

CAMPSITES

Les Acacias 370 rue Henri-Giraud, 2.5km from the old town, close to the pagoda Hong Hien ✆04 94 53 21 22, 🔁campingacacias.fr. Leafy, moderate-sized three-star campsite with 81 pitches, play facilities, a swimming pool, spa and gym. Closed Nov–March. **€34**

Le Dattier 1156 rue des Combattants d'Afrique du Nord ✆04 94 40 88 93, 🔁camping-le-dattier.com. A four-star site 3.5km north of Fréjus, with a restaurant and bar, pool and sports faciltiies. They also rent mobile homes. Closed Oct–March. Camping **€35.50**; mobile homes per week **€760**

EATING
SEE MAP PAGE 290

Fréjus is not a bad place for menu-browsing and café-lounging, with a scattering of reasonably priced places to **eat** in the *vieille ville*. There's a string of options to choose from at Fréjus-Plage, and more upmarket seafood outlets at Port-Fréjus. For **bars and nightlife**, head for the port and beach.

L'Amandier 19 rue Desaugiers ✆04 94 53 48 77, 🔁restaurant-lamandier-frejus.com. Critically lauded restaurant in the *vieille ville*, serving dishes such as squid cooked in fish soup with rice and aioli; *menus* €31 and €43. Mon & Wed 7.30–9.30pm, Tues & Thurs–Sat noon–1.30pm & 7.30–9.30pm.

Brasserie Hermès 15 place Formigé ✆04 94 17 26 02. Unpretentious and affordable brasserie with a terrace facing the cathedral. There's a €15.50 two-course lunchtime *formule* and a big choice of salads and pizza from around €11, plus sandwiches and snacks from around €6.50. Mon–Sat 7am–11pm; July & Aug also open Sun eve.

Cadet Rousselle 25 place Agricola ✆04 94 53 36 92. Perennially popular crêperie with a wide choice of sweet crêpes and savoury *galettes* and a three-course weekday *menu* for €14.50. They also serve main-course-sized salads from €9. Daily 11am–2pm & 6.30–10.30pm.

Le Jardin de l'Aréna 145 rue du Général-de-Gaulle ✆04 94 17 09 40, 🔁lejardin-frejus.com. You can dine on the leafy terrace at the *Aréna* hotel's *restaurant gastronomique*, and enjoy dishes like lobster *parmentier* or veal with thyme *jus*. Lunchtime *formule* €20; *menus* €46–99. Mon 7–9.30pm, Tues–Sat noon–2.30pm & 7–9.30pm, Sun noon–2.30pm.

St-Raphaël

A large resort and now one of the wealthiest towns on the Côte, **ST-RAPHAËL** became fashionable at the turn of the twentieth century. It lost many of its *belle époque* mansions and hotels in the bombardments of World War II; some, like the *Continental*, have been rebuilt from scratch in a modern style, others have undergone more subtle restoration. The sea is the main draw, with family-friendly sandy beaches and plenty of watersports options.

Vieille ville

The **vieille ville**, beyond place Carnot on the inland side of the railway line, is no longer the town's commercial focus but a good place to stroll and browse. On rue des Templiers the fortified Romanesque church of **San Raféu** has fragments of the Roman

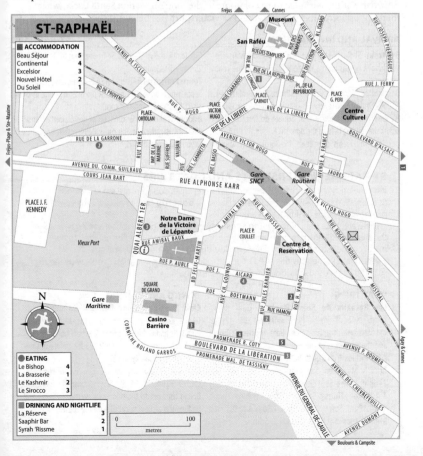

aqueduct that brought water from Fréjus in its courtyard, along with a local **history and underwater archeology museum** (March–June & Oct Tues 2–5pm, Wed–Sat 9am–12.30pm & 2–5pm; July–Sept Tues–Sat 10am–6pm; Nov–Feb Tues 2–5pm, Wed–Fri 10am–12.30pm & 2–5pm, Sat 10am–12.30pm; free; ⓦmusee-saintraphael.com). You can climb to the top of the fortified tower for views over the town and sea.

The modern town

Dominating the **modern town** is St-Raphaël's principal landmark, the towering, florid late nineteenth-century church of **Notre Dame de la Victoire de Lépante**, on boulevard Félix-Martin. Its interior houses a representation of St-Raphaël, the symbol of the city. From here, it's a brief stroll to the broad promenade René Coty, which is lined with grand hotels – look out for the opulent stucco flowers adorning La Rocquerousse apartment buildings, next to the *Hôtel Beau Séjour*. The promenade culminates with the grandiose Résidence La Méditerranée, built in 1914, at 1 avenue Paul Doumer: continue along here, and you'll find a fine *fin-de-siècle* villa, Les Palmiers.

The beaches and coast

St-Raphaël's **beaches** stretch west of the port into Fréjus-Plage and east of the Jardin Bonaparte at the entrance to the old port to the modern **Marina Santa Lucia**, where there are opportunities for every kind of **watersport** (see below).

ARRIVAL AND INFORMATION   ST-RAPHAËL

By train St-Raphaël's *gare SNCF*, on the Marseille–Ventimiglia line, is on rue Waldeck-Rousseau in the centre of town.

Destinations Cannes (every 10–30min; 21–38min); Fréjus (7 daily; 3min); Nice (every 10–30min; 50min–1hr 15min).

By bus The *gare routière* is at Square du Docteur Régis, across the rail line behind the *gare SNCF*.

Destinations Fréjus (frequent; 15–35min); Ste-Maxime (up to 15 daily; 50min); St-Tropez (up to 11 daily; 1hr 25min–1hr 45min).

Tourist office Quai Albert 1er (July & Aug daily 9am–7pm; Sept–June Mon–Sat 9am–12.30pm & 2–6.30pm; ☎04 94 19 52 52, ⓦsaint-raphael.com).

Bike rental Riviera Evasion, 60 av des Clairettes (☎06 22 48 21 73, ⓦrivieraevasion.com); delivers to tourist office or to your accommodation.

ST-RAPHAËL WATERSPORTS AND BOAT TRIPS

With the pristine coast of the Corniche de l'Esterel on its doorstep, the sea is a strong draw at St-Raphaël. You can explore the Esterel coast on a **boat trip**, dive to discover the coast's rich marine archeology or simply rent a boat.

There are more than thirty **diving sites** between the bay of St-Raphaël and Agay, and the area is well known for its numerous wrecks, ranging from Gallo-Roman ships to the minesweepers, barges and landing ships lost during the 1944 Allied landings.

In addition to the activities listed here, the tourist office has information on a wide range of sea- and land-based activities in and around St-Raphaël.

BOAT TRIPS

Les Bateaux de Saint Raphaël Quai Nomy, south side of Vieux Port ☎04 94 95 17 46, ⓦbateauxsaintraphael.com. Boat trips to St-Tropez and the *calanques* of the Esterel coast. Also trips from Agay, including on a glass-bottomed boat. Ticket office April & May Mon–Sat 9am–noon & 2–6pm, Sun 2–6pm; June & Sept daily 9am–noon & 2–6pm; July & Aug Mon–Thurs & Sat 9am–7pm, Fri 9am–7pm & 9–10.30pm, Sun 9–11.45am & 1.30–7pm; Oct Mon 2–5pm, Tues–Sat 9am–noon & 2–5pm.

DIVING AND SAILING

Club Nautique Saint Raphaël Bd Général de Gaulle ☎04 94 95 11 66, ⓦcnsr.fr. Sailing courses for adults and children during the school holidays: one-week catamaran course €165 (€125 for children). One-hour windsurfing tuition €57.

Club Sous l'Eau Port Santa Lucia, east of the town centre ☎04 94 95 90 33, ⓦclubsousleau.com. Diving trips out to the numerous wartime wrecks and underwater archeological sites off the coast.

ACCOMMODATION SEE MAP PAGE 295

Beau Séjour Promenade René-Coty ☎ 04 94 95 03 75, ⓦ beausejour-hotel.com. Seafront hotel, with a pleasant bar and terrace and 41 soundproofed rooms – some of them a/c and some very spacious, with balconies and sea views, and all with TV. **€109**

Continental Promenade René-Coty ☎ 04 94 83 87 87, ⓦ hotels-continental.com. A modern seafront hotel built on the site of its illustrious predecessor, with a/c, parking and light, spacious, soundproofed non-smoking rooms, each with minibar, satellite TV and safe. **€133**

Excelsior 192 bd Félix Martin ☎ 04 94 95 02 42, ⓦ excelsior-hotel.com. The handsome old *Excelsior* is one of the rare seafront survivors from St-Raphaël's prewar heyday, with forty tastefully decorated a/c rooms plus a restaurant and English-style pub. More expensive rooms have sea views. **€184**

Nouvel Hôtel 66 av Henri Vadon ☎ 04 94 95 23 30, ⓦ nouvelotel.net. Pleasant two-star hotel between the *gare SNCF* and the beach; all the rooms are different, and they have singles and triples as well as doubles. There's also a restaurant, so *demi-pension* is possible for €25pp extra. **€110**

Du Soleil 47 bd du Domaine du Soleil ☎ 04 94 83 10 00, ⓦ hotel-dusoleil.com. Charming hotel in a very pretty old villa east of the town centre. All twelve rooms have TV, bath or shower and most have a balcony or terrace. Bus #8 to Les Plaines. **€120**

EATING SEE MAP PAGE 295

Pizzerias, crêperies and restaurants fill the Vieux Port, Port Santa Lucia and the promenades; inland options are more interesting. There are **food markets** on place Victor Hugo (daily) and place de la République (every morning except Monday).

Le Bishop 84 rue Jean Aicard ☎ 04 94 95 04 63. Popular restaurant dishing up Provençal staples at reasonable prices, a couple of blocks back from the beach. Beef with morels €26, *aïoli* €22; *menus* from €24. July & Aug Mon–Sat noon–2pm & 7–10pm; Sept–June Tues–Sat noon–2pm & 7–10pm, Sun noon–2pm.

La Brasserie 6 av de Valescure ☎ 04 94 95 25 00. Traditional Provençal dishes are cooked to a high standard at this smart modern restaurant on the edge of the *vieille ville*. You can get a lunchtime *plat du jour* for €14.60, and there's a *formule* at €18.20, with an evening *menu* at €30. Tues–Sat noon–2.30pm & 7–10.30pm.

Le Kashmir 159 rue de la Garonne ☎ 04 94 19 42 77, ⓦ kashmir83700.fr. Highly regarded Pakistani restaurant with a couple of Kashmiri specialities such as kofta Kashmiri, as well as plenty options for vegetarians. *Menus* range from €14.50 lunch to €21.90 dinner. Daily noon–2pm & 7–11pm.

Le Sirocco 35 quai Albert 1er ☎ 04 94 95 39 99, ⓦ lesirocco.fr. This chic portside restaurant specializes in fish, offering extravagant *plateaux de fruits de mer* (€42) along with optional lobster mayonnaise (€26 extra). *Menus* at €17.90 (week-day lunch) & €19.90 to €49.90. Daily noon–2pm & 7–10pm; closed Mon outside of high season.

NIGHTLIFE SEE MAP PAGE 295

If you're in St-Raphaël in early July, try to catch some of the bands playing in the international **Festival des Jazz**: ask at the tourist office for details of venues. St-Raphaël's **casino** is on Square de Gand overlooking the Vieux Port (daily 9am–3/4am; ☎ 04 98 11 17 77, ⓦ casinosbarriere.com).

La Réserve Promenade René-Coty ☎ 06 27 13 88 99, ⓦ la-reserve.fr. Swish seafront disco, improbably situated beneath a road junction, that attracts some big-name international DJs. Entry with *conso* (free drink) €20. Summer nightly 11.30pm–7am; winter Fri & Sat only.

Saaphir Bar 133 rue Jules Barbier ☎ 06 62 67 83 83. Seafront nightclub with regular guest DJs and the occasional gay night. Can be a bit of a slow burner out of high season. Entry €15. Thurs–Sat midnight–6am.

Syrah 'Rissime 12 rue de la République ☎ 06 37 09 77 25, ⓦ syrahrissime.fr. A couple of blocks in from the *quai*, this convivial wine bar offers a range of cheeses and sushi to pair with their extensive wine collection. They also offer light lunches like salads or fish for around €12. Mon–Fri 10am–3pm & 6pm–midnight.

The Esterel

The 32km **Corniche de l'Esterel**, the sole stretch of wild coast between St-Raphaël and the Italian border, remains untouched by property development – at least between **Anthéor** and **Le Trayas** – its backdrop a 250-million-year-old arc of brilliant red volcanic rock tumbling down to the sea from the harsh crags of the **Massif de l'Esterel**. Because of the fire risk the entire massif is subject to

6

closure during the summer months and when the Mistral blows: call the **fire information line** on ☎04 98 10 55 41 or check ⊕var.gouv.fr to check the current situation. Fires and smoking are banned, and vehicle access is limited – from the D100 heading out of Agay a forestry road penetrates deep into the interior of the massif, but otherwise you'll get no further than the car parks on its fringes, beyond which you'll have to continue on foot or by bike. This makes **walking** all the more enjoyable: the tourist office in St-Raphaël (see page 290) can provide details of paths and of the peaks that make the most obvious destinations. The **shoreline**, meanwhile, is a mass of little beaches – some sand, some shingle – cut by rocky promontories.

The inland route

The high, hairpin **inland route** along the old DN7 route de Cannes is a dramatic drive, and once you pass Notre Dame de Jérusalem on the northernmost tip of the Fréjus-St-Raphaël agglomeration it's largely free of development. It's an ancient route, in parts following the Roman Via Aurelia. The highest point is **Mont Vinaigre**, which you can almost reach by road on the DN7; from the car park at the **Maison Forestière du Malpey** a broad, signposted footpath leads up to the summit. At 618m it's hardly a mountain, but the view from the top is spectacular. From Malpey an authorized mountain bike route crosses the massif.

The corniche

The long, winding D559 coastal route east of St-Raphaël is one of the most exhilarating drives on the Côte d'Azur, its rugged scenery and deep-blue waters made more memorable still by the extraordinary, rust-red colour of the rock. Along the twisting coast road between Anthéor and Le Trayas, each easily reached **beach** has its summer snack-van, and by clambering over rocks you can usually find a near-deserted cove.

Prior to the twentieth-century creation of the corniche, the coastal communities here were linked only by sea; these days, the coast is altogether more accessible even for nondrivers. **Hikers** can follow the *sentier littoral* as far as Agay, though the route is occasionally blocked by the campsites along the shoreline.

Le Dramont

The merest snatch of clear hillside separates Boulouris from the hamlet of **LE DRAMONT**, 7km east of St-Raphaël, where the landing of the 36th American Division in August 1944 is commemorated by a memorial and by the name of the largest beach – plage du Débarquement. The path around the wooded, lighthouse-capped **Cap du Dramont** gives fine views out to sea, with the Île d'Or – a rocky islet, 200m offshore, capped by a mock-medieval tower – providing a popular target for camera-snapping. East of the Cap du Dramont there's another modest crescent of beach at Camp Long.

Agay and Anthéor

Le Dramont's close neighbour **AGAY** is one of the least pretentious resorts of the Côte d'Azur, beautifully situated around a deep horseshoe bay edged by sand beaches, red porphyry cliffs and pines. Both Agay and its eastern neighbour **ANTHÉOR** suffer a little from the housing estates clinging to their hillsides, but once you get above the concrete line, at the **Sommet du Rastel** (a forest track ascends from the far end of boulevard du Rastel and avenue du Bourg in Agay), you can begin to appreciate this wonderful terrain. The residential roads leading off the corniche are private, so you'll have to make the ascent on foot.

Le Trayas

LE TRAYAS is on the highest point of the corniche and its shoreline is the most rugged, with wonderful inlets to explore. You can also trek to the Pic de l'Ours from here (7.9km; the route starts from the *gare SNCF*).

ARRIVAL AND DEPARTURE   THE ESTEREL

By train The Esterel boasts half a dozen train stations, including Agay, Anthéor-Cap Roux and Le Trayas.

By bus There are bus services between St-Raphaël and Le Trayas (Mon–Fri, 3 daily; 50–55min).

By boat Boat trips ply the coast from Agay and St-Raphaël's *gare maritime*.

ACCOMMODATION AND EATING

Agay Soleil 1152 bd de la Plage, Agay ☎ 04 94 82 00 79, ⓦ agay-soleil.com. Three-star campsite on the horseshoe-shaped bay of Agay, with mobile homes and chalets to rent as well as pitches. Closed Nov to late March. **€34**

Les Flots Bleus 83 rte Saint-Barthélemy, Anthéor ☎ 04 94 44 80 21, ⓦ hotel-cote-azur.com. Good-value two-star *Logis de France* hotel, with sea views, individually decorated rooms, parking and a restaurant. Closed Nov–March. **€94**

Les Rives de l'Agay Av du Gratadis, Agay ☎ 04 94 82 02 74, ⓦ camping-lesrivesdelagay.com. Well-equipped campsite 400m inland on the D100 road to Valescure, with a diving club, grocery store and pizzeria and just 133 pitches. Closed mid-Nov to March. **€45**

Why Not 643 bd de la Plage, Agay ☎ 04 94 82 70 49. Amiable place on the seafront, with a relaxed holiday vibe and eclectic comfort food such as Iberian burger (beef with chorizo, manchego and grilled peppers) for €18 and prawn, garlic and girolle linguine for €20. Tues–Sun noon–2pm & 7pm–9pm.

Cannes and the western Riviera

304 Cannes

312 Îles de Lérins

313 Around Cannes

316 West of Cannes

318 Juan-les-Pins

320 Antibes

325 Biot

326 Villeneuve-Loubet

327 Cagnes

329 Grasse

333 Around Grasse

335 Vence

339 St-Paul-de-Vence

BOULEVARD DE LA CROISETTE, CANNES

Cannes and the western Riviera

The stretch of coast between the Massif de l'Esterel and the River Var makes up the western French Riviera. As much legend as reality, the region has been a playground for the rich and famous for the better part of two centuries. Such names as Cannes, Juan-les-Pins and Antibes conjure up powerful images, of a fantasy land where the sparkling blue sea is speckled with boards, bikes and skis, and where extravagant yachts moor tantalizingly out of reach, disgorging their privileged cargo to fill the glamorous bars and restaurants or populate the latest event in the celebrity-studded calendar. To some extent, that's still true, even though the region has long since lost any sense of exclusivity: this now ranks among the most developed and densely populated coastal strips in Europe. Summer crowds and traffic can make travelling slow and unpleasant – speedy train connections offer a convenient alternative to driving – but once you're here, each individual resort has its own appeal. It's also possible simply to visit the coast on day-trips, and stay inland in historic towns like Vence and Grasse, or lovely villages such as St-Paul-de-Vence and Tourrettes-sur-Loup.

Though it shares much in common with the coast east of the Var, the western Riviera has a rather different **history**. Unlike the formerly Savoyard (and strongly Italianate) Nice and Menton, Cannes and Antibes were always Provençal, the latter almost a border town, just west of the frontier on the Var. The fishing village of **Cannes** itself was "discovered" in the 1830s by a retired British chancellor, Lord Brougham, who couldn't get to Nice because of a cholera epidemic. From the start, tourism here was more exclusive than in bustling, raffish Nice (see page 344), with aristocrats and royals from across Europe and North America building opulent mansions in the years before World War I. During the 1920s, as Coco Chanel popularized the suntan and the glamorous *Eden Roc* on **Cap d'Antibes** stayed open year-round for the first time, the season switched from winter to summer. A new kind of elite took centre stage, notably film stars including Charlie Chaplin and Maurice Chevalier; the era was immortalized in F. Scott Fitzgerald's *Tender is the Night*. Then, in 1936, the socialist government of Léon Blum granted French workers their first paid holidays, and the **democratization** of the Riviera began.

War in 1939 interrupted everything – including Cannes' first film festival – but by the 1950s **mass tourism** took off in earnest and the real transformation began. Locals quickly realized that catering to visitors was far more profitable than working on the land or at sea, and over-zealous property development and sheer pressure of numbers have been problems ever since. The coast is now built-up for its entire length, while inland the hills between the villages are carpeted with disorientating, featureless suburbia. The appeal of the coast, however, remains clear enough, most notably in the legacies of the **artists** who stayed here: from the castles turned **Picasso** museums in Antibes and Vallauris to the stunning museum devoted to **Léger** in Biot; and from **Matisse's** unique chapel in Vence to **Renoir's** studio in Cagnes-sur-Mer – not to mention the unmatched fusion of modern art and architecture at the **Fondation Maeght** in St-Paul-de-Vence.

Highlights

❶ Boulevard de la Croisette, Cannes Pop on your shades, tune in to the *Rough Guide to Everywhere* podcast and rollerblade along the Riviera's most glamorous seafront. See page 305

❷ Îles de Lérins Clean, pine-scented air, peaceful walks and shimmering rocks andwater, just minutes from the centre of Cannes. See page 312

❸ Musée d'Art Classique, Mougins As well as Classical and contemporary art, this museum owns a staggering array of beautiful ancient arms and armour. See page 314

❹ Jazz à Juan The Riviera's most renowned jazz festival brings big names to Juan-les-Pins every summer. See page 320

❺ Plage de la Salis, Cap d'Antibes This beautiful, sandy public beach is the laziest way to enjoy the millionaires' cape. See page 323

❻ Chapelle du Rosaire Matisse's final masterpiece – the modern master oversaw every stunning detail of this profoundly moving convent chapel in Vence. See page 338

❼ St-Paul-de-Vence A favourite haunt of Riviera artists, this quintessential Provençal hill village makes an exhilarating escape from the coast. See page 339

❽ Fondation Maeght Art and architecture fuse with landscape and the dazzling Provençal light to create this astonishing museum of contemporary art and sculpture. See page 340

HIGHLIGHTS ARE MARKED ON THE MAP ON PAGE 304

Cannes

With its immaculate seafront hotels and exclusive beaches, glamorous yachts and glitzy designer boutiques, **CANNES** is in many ways the definitive Riviera resort. It's a place where appearances truly count, especially during the **film festival** in May, when the orgy of self-promotion reaches its annual peak.

Although its urban sprawl stretches several kilometres east, west and inland, Cannes lacks the must-see sights and general dynamism of a genuine city. At heart, it's just a beach resort, and while the central **Plage de la Croisette** remains the preserve of an opulent elite, it's actually possible to come here for a straightforward, unpretentious seaside holiday, as there are plenty of free sandy **beaches** west of the port, and hotels and restaurants to suit all pockets. In terms of sightseeing, the two most enjoyable

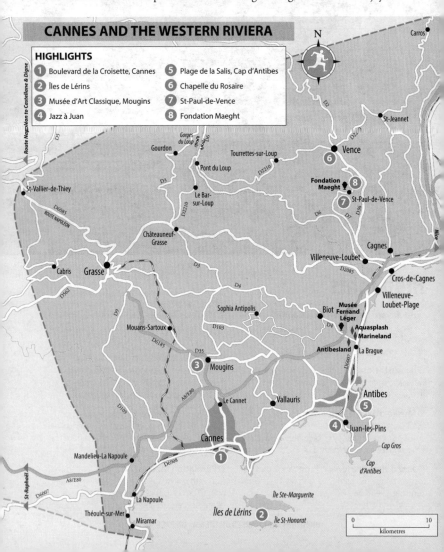

CANNES AND THE WESTERN RIVIERA

N

HIGHLIGHTS

1 Boulevard de la Croisette, Cannes
2 Îles de Lérins
3 Musée d'Art Classique, Mougins
4 Jazz à Juan
5 Plage de la Salis, Cap d'Antibes
6 Chapelle du Rosaire
7 St-Paul-de-Vence
8 Fondation Maeght

THE FLOODS OF 2015

The valleys and coastal towns of the western Riviera were particularly badly hit by the devastating **floods** that coursed through the Alpes-Maritimes on the evening of October 3, 2015, when the region received two months' worth of rain in just two hours. There were nineteen deaths, in some cases caused by local residents trying to retrieve their cars from underground car parks ahead of the deluge; in Biot, three residents of a retirement home were trapped on the ground floor and drowned. Many local businesses in **Biot**, **Mougins** and **Mandelieu-La Napoule** – including some mentioned in this guide – were badly affected and have taken some time to get back on their feet.

attractions are the self-contained old-town quarter of **Le Suquet**, and the sublimely peaceful **Îles de Lérins**, just a short boat-ride out to sea.

Modern Cannes is not as large as you might expect, consisting basically of the five or so blocks between the seafront boulevard of **La Croisette** and the parallel rue d'Antibes. Old Cannes, or Le Suquet, is even smaller, just a few tight streets spiralling up the hill immediately west. If you're just popping into Cannes for a quick look, take a stroll beside the main beach then climb up to the fortifications atop Le Suquet, and you'll have seen the best of both.

La Croisette

Although Cannes' *raison d'être*, the celebrated, swanky **Plage de la Croisette**, stretches for well over 1km, only a few meagre scraps of sand are freely accessible to the public. The rest is swallowed up by chic private beach concessions, many belonging to specific hotels and clubs. During the film festival especially, you can spot the most exclusive and expensive by the paparazzi who buzz around them. Those that allow mere mortals entry tend to cost upwards of €20 per day, with supplementary charges for parasols or prime locations on their jetties (*pontoons*), as well, of course, for food and drink.

If you can't get onto the beach, you can at least take advantage of the little blue chairs provided free along the elegant **boulevard de la Croisette**, the broad promenade which curves all the way from the Pointe de la Croisette to the Vieux Port. Here you can watch the endless display of rollerbladers, rubbernecking visitors and genteel retired folk with tiny dogs.

The buildings of La Croisette

Much of central Cannes has fallen victim to redevelopment, but a few palatial hotels from the town's nineteenth-century golden age remain on La Croisette, notably the Art Deco **Martinez** and the **Carlton InterContinental**, whose cupolas were inspired by the breasts of a famous courtesan. Rather overshadowed by the seafront glitz, the beautiful **La Malmaison**, at no. 47, started life as the tearoom of the now-vanished *Grand Hotel*, which was built in 1863 and demolished a century later. It now stages temporary **exhibitions** of modern and contemporary art (July–Sept daily 10am–7pm; late Nov to late Feb Tues–Sun 10am–1pm & 2–6pm; admission varies; ☎04 97 06 45 21). Further east is the **Espace Miramar**, which also hosts short-term exhibitions of art and photography (hours vary; usually free; ☎04 93 43 86 26).

Palais des Festivals

Dominating the western end of La Croisette, the vast, ugly **Palais des Festivals** resembles a misplaced concrete missile silo. The main focus of the film festival, it also hosts a steady stream of conferences, tournaments and trade shows throughout the year.

Outside, you can compare hand sizes with film icons from Catherine Deneuve to Quentin Tarantino, whose **imprints** were traditionally set, Hollywood-style, in tiles on the pavement. In recent years the original ceramic plaques have been gradually replaced with stainless steel facsimiles.

Vieux Port

Cannes' **Vieux Port**, west of the Palais des Festivals, fills up with extraordinarily sumptuous yachts in summer; tourists gather to watch white-frocked crews serve dinner to millionaires on their decks. Immediately to the east, the western end of La Croisette, the rue d'Antibes and the streets between form the South of France's most extensive luxury **shopping** district, stuffed with designer names such as Bulgari, Cartier, Chanel, Lacroix and Vuitton, and also hold the city's most stylish **nightclubs**. This part of town looks its best in the weeks leading up to Christmas,

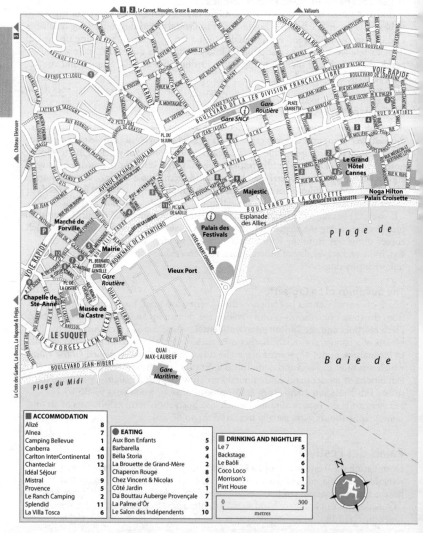

■ ACCOMMODATION	
Alizé	8
Alnea	7
Camping Bellevue	1
Canberra	4
Carlton InterContinental	10
Chanteclair	12
Idéal Séjour	3
Mistral	9
Provence	5
Le Ranch Camping	2
Splendid	11
La Villa Tosca	6

● EATING	
Aux Bon Enfants	5
Barbarella	9
Bella Storia	4
La Brouette de Grand-Mère	2
Chaperon Rouge	8
Chez Vincent & Nicolas	6
Côté Jardin	1
Da Bouttau Auberge Provençale	7
La Palme d'Or	3
Le Salon des Indépendants	10

■ DRINKING AND NIGHTLIFE	
Le 7	5
Backstage	4
Le Baôli	6
Coco Loco	3
Morrison's	1
Pint House	2

when the streets glitter with tasteful white lights and the crowds of summer are long forgotten.

Le Suquet

Back in the eleventh century, the hill known as **Le Suquet** became the property of the Îles de Lérins monks. It still holds a castle built by the *abbé* in 1088, with the white stone twelfth-century Romanesque **Chapelle de Ste-Anne** alongside. After several centuries in which a small town took root around the religious settlement, a dispute arose between the monks and the townsfolk who wanted their own parish and priest. Two hundred years after their initial demand in 1648, **Notre Dame de l'Espérance** was finally built beside the Chapelle de Ste-Anne.

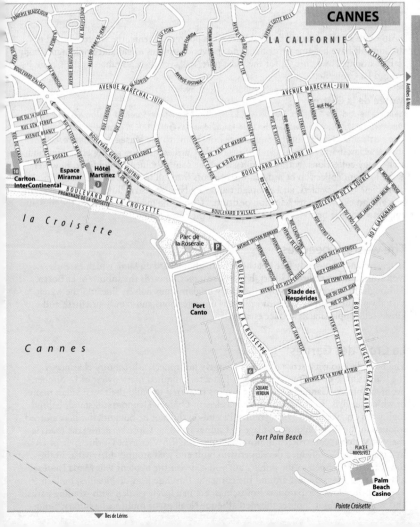

THE CANNES FILM FESTIVAL

In mid- to late May each year, Cannes hosts the world's most famous movie festival, the **Festival International du Film** (⟨w⟩festival-cannes.com). It was first conceived in 1939, as an alternative to the Venice film festival, which had fallen under the influence of Mussolini – only pro-Fascist films had any chance of winning prizes there. However, World War II intervened, and the first Cannes festival eventually took place in 1946.

Winning Cannes' top prize, the **Palme d'Or**, may not compete with Oscars for box-office impact, but for prestige within the movie world it remains unrivalled, and alongside all the attendant glitz and froth, the festival has become renowned for rewarding politically committed (and/or controversial) film-makers.

The event is strictly for film professionals and the associated media, and without proper accreditation you won't get to any of the screenings or sessions at the Palais des Festivals. However, the open-air **Cinéma de la Plage** – a series of free screenings of current and classic selections – is open to all.

7

Although Le Suquet used to house the city's poorer residents, the streets leading to the summit have become gentrified, and the various places to **eat** and **drink** increasingly tourist-oriented and chic, if, for the most part, less overtly trendy than in the streets behind La Croisette.

Musée de la Castre

Rue de la Castre • April–June & Sept Tues–Sun 10am–1pm & 2–6pm, June & Sept Wed until 9pm; July & Aug Mon, Tues & Thurs–Sun 10am–7pm, Wed 10am–9pm; Oct–March Tues–Sun 10am–1pm & 2–5pm • €6 • ☎ 04 89 82 26 26, ⟨w⟩ cannes-destination.com

The castle and chapel atop Le Suquet are now home to the **Musée de la Castre**, which, as well as fascinating pictures and prints of old Cannes, displays strong ethnology and archeology collections, with an emphasis on the south Pacific. Its highlight, however, is the brilliant collection of musical instruments from all over the world, including Congolese bell bracelets, an Ethiopian ten-string lyre, an Asian "lute" with a snakeskin box and an extraordinary selection of drums. Climb the medieval tower in the museum courtyard for the best view of Le Suquet and the town below.

The western beaches

Extensive and very sandy **free beaches** line the **boulevard du Midi**, which extends west from boulevard Jean-Hibert, below Le Suquet, towards the suburb of **La Bocca**. Although the road is backed by a distinctly unglamorous railway line and the water isn't always the cleanest, the atmosphere is unpretentious and family-oriented, and kiosks sell simple snacks and ice creams.

La Croix des Gardes

The best place to get a sense of Cannes' largely lost nineteenth-century elegance is the leafy suburb of **La Croix des Gardes**, just a few hundred metres west of Le Suquet. From the outset, Cannes' aristocratic visitors preferred to build their own villas, many of which survive. Thus Lord Brougham's elegant **Château Eléonore** still stands behind high walls on avenue du Dr Raymond-Picaud on the plot he bought after his enforced sojourn in the then-unknown village of Cannes in 1834. Close by, across the road, is the **Villa Victoria**, constructed in unmistakeably English Victorian Gothic style in 1852 by Sir Thomas Woolfield, a developer who built and sold around thirty villas in the town. Neither is open to the public, but you can visit the opulent **Villa Maria Thérèse**, a Beaux-Arts mansion just around the corner at 1 avenue Jean-de-Noailles, built in 1881 for the Dowager Baroness Rothschild. Set in a lovely garden with winding paths and waterfalls, it now houses the **Mediathèque Noailles**, or multimedia library, along with the city archive (July & Aug Tues–Sat 8am–3pm; Sept–June Tues–Thurs & Sat 9.30am–6pm, Fri 9.30am–7pm; ☎04 97 06 44 83).

Le Cannet

Although nominally a town in its own right, **Le Cannet**, 4km northeast of the city centre along the busy boulevard Carnot, forms an indistinguishable part of Cannes' urban sprawl. It was originally built on land belonging to the Îles de Lérins monks to house 140 Ligurian families brought here to tend the orange trees, and its old quarter, along rue St-Sauveur, still preserves a certain villagey charm.

Musée Bonnard

16 bd Sadi-Carnot • July & Aug Tues, Wed & Fri–Sun 10am–8pm, Thurs 10am–9pm; Sept–June Tues–Sun 10am–6pm; occasional closures between temporary exhibitions • €5, or €7 during exhibitions • ☎04 93 94 06 06, ⓦmuseebonnard.fr • Bus #1A or #4 from the Hôtel de Ville to Le Cannet

Perhaps the most private of the Riviera's great artists, **Pierre Bonnard** bought the Villa le Bosquet in Le Cannet in 1926. He lived here from 1939 until his death in 1947, and is buried in the town's Notre Dame des Anges cemetery. Born in the suburbs of Paris in 1867, Bonnard found fame early as a member of "Les Nabis", followers of Gauguin, and subsequently created his own style, distinguished by intense colour and a highly domestic choice of subject matter.

Opened in 2011, the **Musée Bonnard** is housed not in Bonnard's former home but in a *belle époque* villa transformed by recent concrete-and-glass extensions. As well as displaying an extensive collection of Bonnard's own work, it hosts temporary exhibitions focusing on the artist and his contemporaries – during these, some or all of the permanent collection may not be on view.

ARRIVAL AND INFORMATION   CANNES

By bus There are two *gares routières*: one on place B.-Cornut-Gentille between the *mairie* and Le Suquet, serving coastal destinations; and the other, next to the *gare SNCF*, for local buses. In addition some services for destinations inland, including Grasse, depart from Bd d'Alsace on the north side of the Voie Rapide.

Destinations Aéroport Nice-Côte-d'Azur (every 30min; 50min); Antibes (every 15min; 30min); Grasse (every 15–30min; 50–55min); Juan-les-Pins (every 15min; 25min); Mougins (every 1hr 30min–2hr 15min; 20min); Nice (every 15min; 1hr 20min–1hr 40min); Vallauris (every 15min; 25min).

By train The *gare SNCF* is on rue Jean-Jaurès, five blocks north of the Palais des Festivals.

Destinations Antibes (up to 5 hourly; 8–13min); Biot (roughly every 30min; 17min); Cagnes-sur-Mer (every 18–25min; 22min); Cros-de-Cagnes (roughly every 30min; 28min); Grasse (roughly hourly; 30min); Juan-les-Pins (every 10–25min; 10min); Marseille (roughly every

30min at peak times; 2hr 6min–2hr 21min); Nice (up to 4 hourly; 27–44min); St-Raphaël (every 5min–1hr 29min; 22–39min).

By car Cannes' narrow, traffic-clogged streets are cramped and unpleasant for drivers. Multistorey car parks in the centre charge around €3.60/hr, or €22 overnight; outside high season certain car parks including the Parking Suquet-Forville on rue Louis Pasteur and the Parking parc Croisette at Port Canto offer the first hour free. There are free car parks in La Bocca.

Tourist offices There are two tourist offices in Cannes (both ☎04 92 99 84 22, ⓦcannes-destination.com): Palais des Festivals, 1 bd de la Croisette (daily: March–June, Sept & Oct 9am–7pm; July & Aug 9am–8pm; Nov–Feb 10am–7pm); 1 rue Pierre-Sémard in La Bocca (Tues–Sat: April–Oct 9am–12.30pm & 2.30–6pm; Nov–March 9am–12.30pm & 1.30–5pm); 8 bis, Place de la Gare (daily 9am–1pm & 2–6pm).

GETTING AROUND

By bus Palm Bus (☎08 25 82 55 99, ⓦpalmbus.fr) runs more than thirty lines and five night buses, serving all of Cannes and the surrounding area from the *gare routière* outside the Hôtel de Ville, facing the Vieux Port, and from the *gare SNCF*. A single ticket costs €1.50, a carnet of ten €12.50, a 1/3 day pass €4/8 and a weekly pass, the

Carte Palm'Hebdo, €15. You can also pay via their new smartphone app (see the website for details). The enjoyable Palm Imperial bus #8 (€3) runs along the seafront from the Quai Max-Laubeuf to Palm Beach Casino on Pointe Croisette, at the other end of the bay.

By taxi Taxi Cannes (☎04 93 99 27 27, ⓦtaxis-cannes.net).

Bike rental Bikes can be rented from Elite Rent a Bike, 19 av Maréchal Juin (☎ 04 93 94 30 34, ⓦ elite-rentabike. com), or Holiday Bikes, 44 bd Lorraine (☎ 04 97 06 30 63, ⓦ motorbike-rentals.com).

ACCOMMODATION
SEE MAP PAGE 306

Cannes has **hotels** to suit all budgets, though it has to be said that €80 or €90 here doesn't get you nearly as nice a room as it might inland. Book well in advance for the cheaper options. Room rates in winter (Nov–March) can be little more than half what's indicated below. The tourist office runs a **reservation website**, on ⓦ cannes-hotel-reservation.fr.

Alizé 29 rue Bivouac Napoleon ☎ 04 97 06 64 64, ⓦ hotel-alize-cannes.fr. A central hotel with large, renovated and soundproofed rooms with a/c and cable TV – great value in this price range. **€94**

Alnea 20 rue Jean de Riouffe ☎ 04 93 68 77 77, ⓦ hotel-alnea.com. Centrally located two-star with pleasant service and simple but colourful and well-equipped rooms with individual a/c, flatscreen TV and double glazing. **€71**

★ **Canberra** 120 rue d'Antibes ☎ 04 97 06 95 00, ⓦ hotel-cannes-canberra.com. Classy, understated and intimate four-star hotel with elegant, 1950s-inspired decor and large rooms with a/c and flatscreen TV. There's a heated pool in the garden plus a sauna, gym, restaurant and cocktail bar. **€274**

Carlton InterContinental 58 bd de la Croisette ☎ 04 93 06 40 06, ⓦ carlton-cannes.com. Legendary landmark *belle époque* seafront palace hotel that featured in Hitchcock's *To Catch a Thief*. Rooms are a/c and decorated in a tasteful but conservative style, with pay-per-view movies and marble bathrooms. **€857**

Chanteclair 12 rue Forville ☎ 04 93 39 68 88, ⓦ hotel chanteclair.com. Almost as cheap as you'll get in the centre of Cannes, right next to the old town, and with a private courtyard where you can eat breakfast. Rooms are small but all have shower; most also have WC. **€80**

Idéal Séjour 6 allée du Parc-des-Vallergues ☎ 04 93 39 16 66, ⓦ ideal-sejour.com. Nicely restored, gay-friendly villa hotel, set in spacious hillside gardens a 15min walk up from the centre. Small but very tasteful rooms, with attractive common areas that include an extensive library. Free parking; cheaper single rooms available. **€120**

Mistral 13 rue des Belges ☎ 04 93 39 91 46, ⓦ mistral-hotel.com. Smart little modernized hotel, in a great position just back from the Croisette, with ten funky rooms, all crisp, clean and en suite, with a/c. **€141**

Provence 9 rue Molière ☎ 04 93 38 44 35, ⓦ hotel-de-provence.com. Charmingly decorated and well-appointed three-star hotel just off rue d'Antibes, with pale colours, a/c, a bar and a luxuriant garden. Some rooms have balconies; the deluxe suite has a large terrace. **€169**

Splendid 4 rue Félix-Faure ☎ 07 63 77 22 23, ⓦ splendid-hotel-cannes.fr. Charmingly old-fashioned *belle époque* hotel. Many of the tasteful rooms have wrought-iron balconies; expect to pay extra for those that overlook the yachts of the old port. **€170**

La Villa Tosca 11 rue Hoche ☎ 04 93 38 34 40, ⓦ villa-tosca.com. Smartly renovated three-star hotel a few blocks from the sea, with well-equipped, a/c rooms with flatscreen TV; some also have balconies. There is a cheaper two-star sister hotel – the *PLM* – a few doors down. **€122**

CAMPSITES

Camping Bellevue 67 av Maurice-Chevalier ☎ 04 93 47 28 97, ⓦ parcbellevue.com. Three-star campsite, complete with pool, bar, shop and restaurant, 3km northwest of the centre in the suburb of Ranguin; bus #2 from Hôtel de Ville (stop "Ste-Jeanne"). Closed Oct–March. **€33**

Le Ranch Camping Chemin St-Joseph, l'Aubarède ☎ 04 93 46 00 11, ⓦ leranchcamping.com. Three-star site, with pool, set on a wooded hillside 4km northwest of the centre in Le Cannet, very close to the A8 autoroute; bus #10 from the Hôtel de Ville (direction "Les Pins Parasols", stop "Le Ranch"). Closed mid-Oct to mid-April. **€37**

EATING
SEE MAP PAGE 306

Cannes has hundreds of **restaurants**, though quality across the board can be patchy. Many stay open very late, so getting a meal after midnight is no great problem. The best areas for **inexpensive dining** are rue Meynadier, Le Suquet and Quai St-Pierre on the Vieux Port, which is lined with brasseries and cafés. Reserving a table is advisable at almost all the places listed here. Thanks to the **Forville market**, two blocks north of the Vieux Port (Tues–Sun 7am–1pm, ⓦ marcheforville.com), local chefs have access to the finest and freshest ingredients. Note that many Cannes visitors also eat in nearby **Mougins** (see page 314), renowned for its gourmet restaurants.

Aux Bons Enfants 80 rue Meynadier ⓦ aux-bons-enfants-cannes.com. Small, friendly and rustic, this family-run stalwart – established in 1920 – serves very reliable Provençal cuisine with *plats du jour* at €18 and dishes such as stuffed lamb with figs or grilled *andouillette*. Cash only. Jan–Nov Tues–Sat noon–2pm & 7–10pm; open Mon during school holidays and conferences.

Barbarella 16 rue St-Dizier, Le Suquet ☎ 04 92 99 17 33. Stylish, fun and LGBTQ-friendly restaurant and cabaret, with themed evenings and quality cosmopolitan bar food such as avocado toast, salads for around €15 and pizza and pasta for around €20. Mon–Thurs & Sun 8.30am–9pm, Fri & Sat 8.30am–10pm.

Bella Storia 51 rue Félix Faure ☎ 04 93 39 03 95. Contemporary, unpretentious and locally popular Italian restaurant serving pizza from €12 and clam linguine or truffle fettucine for €22, as well as a trio of similarly priced standard fish and meat dishes. Lunch *formule* €14. Daily noon–2.30pm & 7–10.30pm.

La Brouette de Grand-Mère 9 bis rue d'Oran ☎ 04 93 39 12 10, ⊛labrouettedegrandmere.fr. Something of a Cannes institution, with a resolutely traditional €46 *menu* featuring the likes of home-made *terrine*, Ardeche sausage or pork fillet with camembert cream. The price includes half a bottle of wine. Daily 7pm–late.

Chaperon Rouge 17 rue St-Antoine ☎ 04 93 99 06 22. Friendly dinner-only restaurant, with tables squeezed onto a terrace beside a steep alley leading up to Le Suquet; this is a very touristy district, but the evening hurly-burly is fun and the food is actually pretty good, with a daily vegetarian *plat* (€26) and a €28 *menu* that features such dishes as veal with truffle risotto or rack of lamb Provençal style. Tues–Sun 6.30–11.30pm.

Chez Vincent & Nicolas 90 rue Meynadier ☎ 04 93 68 35 39, ⊛chezvincentetnicolas.fr. Slightly quirky and original choice, with a lovely setting in a small square, serving such time honoured French delicacies as sautéed frogs legs and Bourgogne *escargots*. Meat or fish mains start at around €20. Tues–Sun 7–11.30pm.

Côté Jardin 12 av St-Louis ☎ 04 93 38 60 28, ⊛restaurant-cotejardin.com. Intimate family-run restaurant with a small garden and terrace. Classic Provençal cuisine with *plats du jour* at €12 and steaks and whole roasted fish at €22, as well as the occasional tapas-style *formule* at €21. Tues–Fri noon–2pm & 7.30–9.30pm, Sat noon–2pm & 7.30–10pm.

Da Bouttau Auberge Provencale 10 rue St-Antoine, Le Suquet ☎ 04 92 99 27 17, ⊛dabouttau.com. Established in 1860, this stylish restaurant is the oldest in Cannes. It serves Niçois specialities and creative dishes such as chicken tagine with green olives, apricots, lemon, quinoa and dried fruit. *Menu gourmand* €35; two-course lunch *formule* €26. Daily noon–2.30pm & 7–10.30pm.

La Palme d'Or Hôtel Martinez, 73 bd de la Croisette ☎ 04 92 98 74 14. The place to go and celebrate if you've just won a film festival prize; it has held two Michelin stars for a quarter of a century. *Menus* (including a vegetarian option, alongside those dedicated to lobster and pigeon) from €136. Tues–Fri 7.30–10pm, Sat noon–2pm & 7.30–10pm.

Le Salon des Indépendants 11 rue Louis Perrissol ☎ 04 93 39 97 06. Inventive and very popular dinner-only restaurant on one of Le Suquet's quieter alleys, featuring dishes – and live music – from around the Mediterranean. The one *menu* is priced at €49 including wine, €35 without. No credit cards. Tues–Sat 7–9pm.

DRINKING AND NIGHTLIFE
SEE MAP PAGE 306

Cannes abounds with exclusive **bars** and **clubs**, nowhere more so than in the tight little grid of streets bounded by rue Macé, rue V. Cousin, rue Dr G Monod and rue des Frères Pradignac. As is so often the case in the South of France, the boundaries between restaurant, bar and club are somewhat blurred, so that you can frequently dine, drink and dance – at a price – in the same venue. Cannes' **LGBTQ** bar scene is smaller than that in Nice, but smart and a good deal more relaxed, and some venues attract hetero as well as LGBTQ visitors. If you are determined to lose money, choose from three **casinos**: at the Palais des Festivals; at 50 bd de la Croisette; and at the *Palm Beach* at the eastern end of La Croisette.

Le 7 7 rue Rouguière ☎ 06 09 55 22 79. Gay disco and cabaret club just off rue Félix-Faure, with regular events year round, including drag shows and live music. Daily midnight–dawn.

Backstage 17 rue Gérard Monod ☎ 09 81 48 07 03, ⊛facebook.com/BackstageClubCannes. The biggest and flashiest of the trendy lounge/bar/clubs in the tight little knot of streets between rue d'Antibes and la Croisette, with hyper-bling decor, various free themed nights and a terrace at the front. Daily 6pm–2.30am.

Le Baôli Port Pierre Canto ☎ 04 93 43 03 43, ⊛baoli-group.com. If you want to rub shoulders with celebrities and big-name international DJs, head to this exclusive exotic (and expensive; reckon on spending at least €70) outdoor disco-restaurant with palms lit up at night. Dress the part. Fri & Sat 8pm–5am.

Coco Loco 4 rue des Frères Pradignac ☎ 04 97 06 31 90. Cocktails and a Creole vibe, with a drinks buffet and litre sharing bottles of punch, sex on the beach et al in the €25–40 bracket; rum's the speciality. Everything really kicks off here during the film festival. Mon–Sat 6.30pm–2.30am.

Morrison's 10 rue Teisseire ☎ 04 92 98 16 17, ⊛cannes-nightlife.com.morrisons. The inevitable Irish pub, a few blocks back from the seafront, with British and Irish sport on TV and an upscale lounge. Daily happy hour 5–8pm. Mon–Fri 5pm–2.30am, Sat & Sun noon–2.30am.

Pint House 19 rue des Frères Pradignac ☎ 04 93 38 90 10, ⊛pinthouse.fr. Pub with live rugby on TV; the beers are mostly French or Belgian (*pression* from €3.80, bottles from €5). A bit of a relief after the trying-too-hard excess of much Cannes bar life. Daily 6pm–5am.

DIRECTORY

Bookshop Cannes English Bookshop, 11 rue Bivouac Napoleon (Mon–Sat 10.30am–6.30pm; ☎ 04 93 99 40 08).
Emergencies SOS médecins (☎ 08 25 00 50 04); Hôpital de Cannes, Av des Broussailles (☎ 04 93 69 70 00, ⊛www.ch-cannes.fr).

Pharmacy After 7.30pm call ☎ 3237 (⊛www.3237.fr) for the address of the nearest emergency pharmacy.
Police Commissariat Central de Police, 1 av de Grasse (☎ 04 93 06 22 22).
Post office 22 rue Bivouac Napoleon.

Îles de Lérins

The **Îles de Lérins** would be lovely anywhere, but at just a fifteen-minute ferry ride from Cannes, they make an idyllic escape from the modern city. Known as Lerina, or Lero, in ancient times, the two tiny islands, **Ste-Marguerite** and **St-Honorat**, have a long historical pedigree and today offer the gentle pace and tranquillity the Riviera so often lacks.

Ste-Marguerite

The more animated of the Îles de Lérins, **Ste-Marguerite**, has plenty of day-trippers and a working boatyard, but also offers clear water and beautiful scenery. It's large enough to find seclusion if you're prepared to leave the crowded port and follow paths through the thick woods of Aleppo pines and evergreen oaks.

Fort Ste-Marguerite

April & May daily 10.30am–1.15pm & 2.15–5.45pm; June–Sept daily 10am–5.45pm; Oct–March Tues–Sun 10.30am–1.15pm & 2.15–4.45pm • €6, includes museum • ☎ 04 93 38 55 26

The imposing **Fort Ste-Marguerite**, reached by a very obvious path that leads up from the ferry dock, past the boatyard, was a Richelieu commission that failed to prevent the Spanish occupying both Lérins islands between 1635 and 1637; the fortifications were later completed by Vauban.

A cell within is renowned for having held the **Man in the Iron Mask** for eleven years of his long captivity, between 1687 and 1698; a quasi-mythical character who died in the Bastille in 1703, and whose true identity has never been proved, his legend was popularized by novelist Alexandre Dumas. Other prisoners here included Huguenots imprisoned for refusing to submit to Louis XIV's vicious suppression of Protestantism. A series of murals created in the 1990s covers the cell walls, and depicts painter Jean le Gac as a prisoner.

As well as three Roman **cisterns** – Ste-Marguerite has no natural springs, so water supply has always been a problem – the fort also holds a barracks-style hostel used by school and youth groups, and the **Musée de la Mer**, which displays artefacts discovered by underwater archeologists, such as amphorae from a Roman shipwreck and ceramics from a tenth-century Arab vessel.

Exploring the island

The quickest route to Ste-Marguerite's peaceful southern shore, the **allée des Eucalyptus**, heads south from roughly halfway around the fort. Follow the outer perimeter of the walls, and keep going straight on when you come to a sign pointing left towards *La Guérite* (see page 313). A pleasant fifteen-minute stroll from here ends abruptly at the seashore, where you can look across the lovely turquoise channel that separates Ste-Marguerite from St-Honorat. Picnic tables are scattered at the water's edge, and many visitors swim here, though the shore is lined by compacted masses of dried vegetation.

The most enjoyable way to get back to the ferry is to follow the coastal **Chemin de la Ceinture**, which offers great views back to Cannes once you round the headland at either end.

St-Honorat

St-Honorat, the smaller and southernmost of the Îles de Lérins, is an idyllic spot, devoid of cars and hotels, though with enough summer visitors that you're unlikely to mistake it for a desert island. It has belonged to monks almost continuously since Honoratus, a former Roman noble seeking peace and isolation, founded a monastery here in 410 AD. Visitors soon began to arrive, and a monastic order was established. By the end of Honoratus' life, the Lérins monks had monasteries all over France, held bishoprics in Arles and Lyon, and were renowned throughout the Catholic world for their contributions to theology. **St Patrick** trained here for seven years before setting out for Ireland.

Most of the present **abbey** buildings date from the nineteenth century, though vestiges of medieval and earlier construction survive in the church and cloisters. You can visit the austere church, but not the residential areas, where 25 Cistercian monks live and work, tending an apiary and a vineyard that produces a sought-after white wine, sold in the abbey's two shops. Behind this complex, on the sea's edge, stands an eleventh-century **fortress**, a monastic bolthole connected to the original abbey by a tunnel, and used to guard against invaders, especially the Saracens. Of all the protective forts along this coast, only this one looks as if it could still serve its original function.

The other buildings on St-Honorat are the churches and chapels that served as retreats. **St-Pierre**, beside the modern monastery, **La Trinité**, to the east, and **St-Sauveur**, west of the harbour, remain more or less unchanged. By **St-Cabrais**, on the eastern shore, a furnace with a chute for making cannonballs shows that the monks did not lack worldly defensive skills.

The rest of the island is given over to cultivated vines, lavender, herbs and olive trees, mingled with wild poppies and daisies. Pine and eucalyptus trees shade the paths beside the white rock shore, mixing their scent with rosemary, thyme and wild honeysuckle.

ARRIVAL AND DEPARTURE   **ÎLES DE LÉRINS**

STE-MARGUERITE

From Cannes Three companies – Horizon (☎ 04 92 98 71 36, �🌐 horizon-lerins.com), Riviera Lines (☎ 04 92 98 71 31, �🌐 riviera-lines.com) and Trans Côte d'Azur (☎ 04 92 98 71 30, �🌐 trans-cote-azur.com) – run to Ste-Marguerite (up to 17 daily 7.30am–4.30pm; last boat back to Cannes 5pm; €15).

From Juan-les-Pins Riviera Lines offers day-trips to Ste-Marguerite (early April to mid-June & Sept 5–6 daily except Mon; mid-June to end Aug 56 daily; €19; ☎ 04 92 98 71 31, �🌐 riviera-lines.com).

From Nice Trans Côte d'Azur offers day-trips to Ste-Marguerite in summer (late May to June & Sept Tues, Thurs, Sat & Sun 9am; July & Aug Tues–Sun 9am; €41; ☎ 04 92 00 42 30, �🌐 trans-cote-azur.com).

ST-HONORAT

From Cannes Compagnie Planaria (Jan & Feb 4 daily; March & mid- to late-Oct 7 daily; May–Sept & early to mid-Oct 9–10 daily. The last boat back to Cannes leaves 4.30pm in winter, 5.30pm in spring and autumn & 6.30pm in high summer; €16.50; ☎ 04 92 98 71 38, �🌐 cannes-ilesdelerins.com).

EATING

Ste-Marguerite is an expensive place to eat and drink, and options are limited, so at the very least it's worth bringing plenty of **water**. A couple of summer-only snack stalls sell *pan bagnats* close to the ferry dock.

La Guérite Ste-Marguerite ☎ 04 93 43 49 30, �🌐 laguerite.fr. Walk all the way around the inland side of the fort, drop back down to sea level via the steep stairway on the far side, and you'll come to this absurd but very welcome beachfront *Club-Med*-style place, divided between a very expensive à la carte restaurant with mains

in the €40–50 bracket, and a shaded terrace snack bar serving sandwiches for €10–15. Late April to June, Sept & Oct lunch only; July & Aug lunch & dinner.

La Tonelle St-Honorat ☎ 04 92 99 54 08, ⌂ tonnelle-abbayedelerins.fr. St-Honorat's one restaurant, a short walk from the landing stage, is open for lunch only, with a tree-shaded terrace, salads from €14 and fish and meat mains for around €35. On weekdays, a two/three-course set *menu* costs €29/34. Daily noon–2.30pm; closed mid-Nov to mid-Dec.

Around Cannes

A couple of small towns in the hills immediately inland from Cannes are worth visiting before you head further afield. The hilltop village of **Mougins** is renowned as being home to some of the finest restaurants in Provence, while the pottery town of **Vallauris**, a short way west, was where Pablo Picasso made his fascinating postwar experiments with ceramics.

Mougins

If **MOUGINS**, 8km north of Cannes, is the first Provençal village you visit, you may well be charmed by its hilltop site, exquisitely preserved lanes and associations with Man Ray and with Picasso, who had his last studio here and died here in 1973. If, however, you arrive with villages such as Cotignac, Simiane la Rotonde or even St-Paul-de-Vence fresh in mind, Mougins itself may strike you as rather over-praised, a pretty bauble adrift amid bland suburbs and lacking character of its own. Its winding streets are, however, thick with ateliers and small galleries, including the superb **Musée d'Art Classique**.

More than anything else, modern Mougins is effectively a **culinary** theme park. It was at the **Moulin de Mougins** restaurant, across the Cannes–Grasse highway from the old village on avenue Notre Dame de Vie, that legendary, now-retired chef Roger Vergé perfected his *Cuisine of the Sun*, a modern reworking of Provençal cooking that won him (and Mougins) international acclaim in the 1970s. The *village* remains a pilgrimage destination for fans of contemporary Provençal cuisine – especially the moguls and megastars who attend the Cannes Film Festival – and an astonishing number of high-class restaurants is crammed into the gorgeous medieval centre. In September each year, the community hosts the **Festival International de Gastronomie Mougins** (ⓦlesetoilesdemougins.com).

Musée d'Art Classique

32 rue du Commandeur • Daily: late June to end Sept 10am–8pm; Oct to late June 10am–6pm • €14 • ☎04 93 75 18 65, ⓦ mouginsmusee.com

Opened in 2011, Mougins' small but exquisite **Musée d'Art Classique** displays a remarkable collection of art, artefacts and sculpture acquired by British hedge-fund manager Christian Levett. Placing its emphasis on the continuing exploration by contemporary artists of themes from Egyptian, Greek and Roman art, it repeatedly juxtaposes original Classical works – for example some stunning Roman bronzes – with pieces by the likes of Keith Haring, Yves Klein and Andy Warhol. Picasso is especially well represented.

The most extraordinary section of the museum is the **armoury** on its topmost floor, which holds an array of superbly preserved ancient arms and armour. Highlights include bronze Urartian helmets from Mesopotamia, dating from the eighth century BC; Thracian helmets, as worn by the troops of Alexander the Great; and Roman cavalry helmets, adorned with eagles.

Musée de la Photographie

Porte Sarrazin • Daily: July & Aug 10am–1pm & 2–7pm; Sept–June 10am–12.30pm & 2–6pm • Free • ☎04 93 75 85 67, ⓦ mougins.fr

Mougins' excellent **Musée de la Photographie**, just beyond the Porte Sarrazine, hosts changing exhibitions by contemporary photographers. Its own small permanent collection includes some stunning portraits of Pablo Picasso, taken by Jacques Lartigue (1894–1986) during the 1950s. Lartigue, who was also a painter himself, had first met Picasso in Paris in 1915.

Le Lavoir de Mougins

Av J.C.-Mallet • Hours vary according to exhibition • Free • ☎04 92 92 50 08, ⓦ mougins-tourisme.fr

At the top end of the village, the old wash house, **Le Lavoir de Mougins**, serves as an exhibition space for the visual arts. Its wide basin of water plays reflecting games with the images and the light, making it well worth checking out each year's changing temporary exhibitions.

ARRIVAL AND INFORMATION
MOUGINS

By bus Mougins is served by frequent #600 buses between Cannes and Grasse, but they don't go up to the *vieux village*; alight at Val de Mougins then catch Palmbus #27 to reach the village. Alternatively, walk up – it's a little under 1km from Val de Mougins.

Destinations Cannes (every 20–30min; 25min); Grasse (every 20–30min; 35min).

By car Driving up to Mougins involves negotiating a fiendishly complicated road network; just trust the signs,

even when they seem to make no sense. Parking once you're there is straightforward, though; the village itself is pedestrianized, so you'll be directed to one of the peripheral car parks just below the hilltop.

Tourist office 39 place des Patriotes, just below the village centre (April & May Mon–Sat 10am–6pm; June & Sept daily 10am–6pm July & Aug daily 10am–7pm; Oct–March Mon–Sat 10am–5pm; ☎ 04 92 92 14 00, ⓦ mougins-tourisme.fr).

ACCOMMODATION AND EATING

L'Amandier 48 av J.C.-Mallet ☎ 04 93 90 00 91, ⓦ amandier.fr. The attractive Michelin-listed former cooking school of the *Moulin de Mougins*, close to the main car park, has a lunch *formule* at €22, and evening *menus* from €33 up to a €55 tasting *menu* featuring the likes of red quinoa soup and cauliflower with sour cream. Daily noon–2pm & 7–10pm.

Les Liserons de Mougins 608 av St-Martin ☎ 04 93 75 50 31, ⓦ hotel-liserons-mougins.com. A good-value alternative to staying in Mougins itself, well beyond walking distance 2km north towards Mouans-Sartoux. It's a pretty old country house, with sun-splashed rooms of varying sizes, climbing flowers, a pleasant breakfast terrace and a pool. **€70**

Le Mas Candille Bd Clément-Rebuffel ☎ 04 92 28 43 43, ⓦ lemascandille.com. Forty-five romantic, tastefully decorated rooms in a gorgeous traditional farmhouse, complete with deluxe Shiseido spa and three swimming pools amid the olive groves and cypresses, 1km southwest of the village centre. Its renowned restaurant, under chef Xavier Burelle, serves exquisite lunches and dinners daily

year-round, on the €98 Discovery *menu* and the €135, eight-course *Signature*. **€373**

La Méditerranée 32 place du Commandant Lamy ☎ 04 93 90 03 47, ⓦ brasseriemediterranee.fr. Bright, cheerful brasserie on the main square, with a three-course *menu tradition* for €27 and a €49 *menu gourmande*, which includes lobster ravioli in a saffron emulsion. Daily noon–3pm & 7–11pm.

Paloma 47 av du Moulin de la Croix ☎ 04 92 28 10 73, ⓦ restaurant-paloma-mougins.com. Wielding two Michelin stars and flaunting baroque-bling in black with gold accents, *Paloma* is the seductive domain of noted chef Nicolas Decherchi, whose lunch and dinner *menus* range from €59 to €195 and might feature the likes of foie gras with raspberries and sweet almond milk or lobster roasted in red curry butter. Mon–Sat noon–2pm & 7.30–9.30pm.

Rendez-Vous de Mougins 84 place du Commandant Lamy ☎ 04 93 75 87 47, ⓦ rendezvousdemougins.com. Excellent Provençal food, with indoor and outdoor seating on the village's central square. Dinner *menus* €28 and €37. Daily 11.45am–2.45pm & 6.45–10.45pm.

Vallauris

The small town of **VALLAURIS**, 6km east of Cannes above Golfe-Juan, is remarkable only for its long-standing tradition of making **pottery**, and its more recent association with **Picasso**. Despite being set on sloping hills, it's not a hill village in the usual sense; it's just an ordinary little town. That said, the very fact that it feels genuinely lived-in, with back streets close to the centre bustling with day-to-day activity, makes it a refreshing change from so many prettified Riviera communities.

Ceramics became established here in the sixteenth century, when the bishop of Grasse rebuilt Vallauris following a plague, and settled Genoese potters in the town to exploit the clay soil and abundant timber. By the end of World War II, however, aluminium had become a much more popular material for pots and plates. It took the intervention of Picasso to reverse Vallauris' decline. In 1946, while installed in the castle at Antibes, the artist met some of the town's few remaining potters, and was invited to Vallauris by the owner of a ceramics studio, Georges Ramié. Hooked on clay, Picasso spent the next two years working at Ramié's Madoura workshop.

A gift from Picasso to the town, the bronze **Man with a Sheep**, stands in the main square, beside the church and neat little castle. The municipality had some misgivings as to whether the sculpture might prove to be too "modern", but decided that the possible affront to their conservative tastes was outweighed by the benefits to tourism of Picasso's international reputation. They needn't have worried; the statue looks quite simply like a shepherd boy and sheep.

Today the main street, avenue Georges-Clemenceau, is almost entirely given over to **pottery shops**, while **L'Atelier Madoura** (corner rue Suzanne et Georges Ramié and Av Gerbino; Mon–Fri 10am–1pm & 2–5pm; free), off to the left halfway up, is now a beautiful exhibition space. Classy commercial galleries include **Galerie Agnès Sandahl**, 65 av Georges-Clemenceau (Mon–Sat 10am–1pm & 3–6pm; ☎04 93 64 65 71, ⓦgalerie-agnes-sandahl.com).

Musée National Picasso

Place de la Libération du 24 Août 1944 • July & Aug daily 10am–12.45pm & 2.15–6.15pm; Sept–June Mon & Wed–Sun 10am–12.15pm & 2–5pm • €6, includes Musée de la Céramique/Musée Magnelli • ☎ 04 93 64 71 83, ⓦmusee-picasso-vallauris.fr

In 1952, Pablo Picasso took up the offer from local authorities and redecorated the early medieval deconsecrated **chapel** in the courtyard of Vallauris' castle. The tiny vault – now the **Musée National Picasso** – is covered with painted panels and has the architectural simplicity of an air-raid shelter, which indeed it was during the war. Picasso's subject is *War and Peace*. At first glance it's easy to be unimpressed (as many critics still are) – it looks mucky and slapdash, with paint runs on the unyielding plywood surfaces. Stay a while, however, and the passion of this violently drawn pacifism slowly emerges. On the *War* panel a music score is trampled by hooves and about to be engulfed in flames; the figure of "valiant resistance" tenuously holds the scales of justice; a shield bears the outline of a dove; and skeletons unleash creepy-crawlies and pestilence from a deathly chariot. *Peace* is represented by symbols of creativity and fecundity, including Pegasus; people dancing and suckling babies; trees bearing fruit; owls; books; and general innocent mischief.

The ticket for the chapel also gives admission to the castle's **Musée de la Céramique/Musée Magnelli**, which exhibits many of the ceramics Picasso made at the Madoura, ranging from plates and more complicated vessels to carved woodblocks, as well as works by the Florentine painter Alberto Magnelli.

ARRIVAL AND INFORMATION   VALLAURIS

By bus Regular buses from Cannes (#9 from Bd Alsace north of the *gare SNCF*) arrive at the rear of the castle. **Destinations** Antibes (every 15–20min; 30–35min); Cannes (hourly; 21min).
By car The main tourist car park is near the tourist office on

square du 8-Mai-1945.
Tourist office 4 av Georges-Clemenceau in the heart of the old town (Mon–Sat 9am–noon & 1–5pm; ☎04 93 63 38, ⓦvallauris-golfe-juan.fr).

EATING AND DRINKING

l'Escalier Gourmand 47 av Georges-Clemenceau ☎04 93 00 08 74. The pick of the restaurants, cafés and bars along the main tourist drag; lunch specials served on the airy upstairs terrace cost around €12/13. Mon–Sat noon–3pm & 6.30–11pm, Sun noon–3pm.

Café Llorca Place Paul Isnard ☎04 93 33 11 33, ⓦalainllorca.net/cafe-llorca. Classy bistro and patisserie run by renowned chef/restaurateur Alain Lorca, close to the Picasso museum and with a two/three-course *menu du jour* for €19/25 and *menu gourmand* at €33. Tues–Sun noon–2pm & 7.30–10pm.

West of Cannes

Immediately **west of Cannes**, the western end of the Riviera holds a handful of little resorts, such as **La Napoule** and **Théoule-sur-Mer**. While they're not worth going out of your way to see, the coastal D6908 makes an enjoyable route west towards St-Raphaël (see page 295), running beyond Théoule-sur-Mer along the dramatic **Corniche de l'Esterel**.

La Napoule

The small former fishing port of **LA NAPOULE** stands 8km west of Cannes, beyond the city's small airport. Technically, it's just the seaside portion of the larger community of **Mandelieu-La Napoule**. Mandelieu, up the hill away from the sea, is a characterless golfing resort with minimal appeal for casual visitors.

Château de la Napoule

Gardens Early Feb to early Nov daily 10am–6pm; early Nov to early Feb Mon–Fri 2–5pm, Sat & Sun 10am–5pm • €3.50 • **Castle tours** Early Feb to early Nov daily 11.30am, 2.30pm, 3.30pm & 4.30pm; early Nov to early Feb Mon–Fri 2.30pm & 3.30pm, Sat & Sun 11.30am, 2.30pm & 3.30pm • €6 • ☎ 04 93 49 95 05, ⓦ www.chateau-lanapoule.com

The fantasy castle that dominates the waterfront of La Napoule, the **Château de la Napoule**, was erected atop the three towers and gateway of a fourteenth-century fort by American sculptor Henry Clews and his wife, Marie. A classic pre-World War I folly, it features beautiful gardens, which host a quirky and hugely enjoyable treasure hunt for children, and also holds a collection of Clews' odd and gloomy works, represented on the exterior by the grotesques on the gateway.

Théoule-sur-Mer and around

The ruggedly picturesque **Corniche de l'Esterel** extends for 20km westwards from **THÉOULE-SUR-MER**, 2.5km down the coast from La Napoule, all the way to St-Raphaël. Théoule itself is a quiet, rather low-key place with a sandy beach, large marina, and a small castle that can't be visited. Beyond it the coast runs south, becoming wilder and more dramatic around the Pointe de l'Esquillon as it approaches the little village of **Miramar**.

INFORMATION   **WEST OF CANNES**

LA NAPOULE

Tourist office 806 av de Cannes, Mandelieu-La Napoule (April–June, Sept & Oct Mon–Sat 9.30am–12.30pm & 2–5.30pm, Sun during school holidays 9.30am–1.30pm; July & Aug Mon–Sat 9.30am–1pm & 3–6pm, Sun 9.30am–1pm & 3–5pm; Nov–March Tues–Sat 9.30am–12.30pm & 2–5pm; ☎ 04 93 93 64 64, ⓦ ot-mandelieu.fr).

THÉOULE-SUR-MER

Tourist office 2 corniche d'Or (May to mid-June & last two weeks in Sept Mon–Sat 9am–7pm; mid-June to Aug and first two weeks in Sept Mon–Sat 9am–7pm, Sun 10am–1pm & 3–7pm; Oct–April Mon–Sat 10am–5.30pm; ☎ 04 93 49 28 28, ⓦ theoule-sur-mer.org).

THE ROUTE NAPOLÉON

The pines and silver sand between Juan-les-Pins and Cannes, now **Golfe-Juan**, witnessed Napoleon's return from exile in 1815. Having been in command of the Mediterranean defences as a general in 1794, with Antibes' Fort Carré as his base, the emperor knew the bay well. This time, however, his emissaries to Cannes and Antibes were taken prisoner upon landing, though the local men in charge decided not to capture him. The lack of enthusiasm for his return was enough to persuade the ever-brilliant tactician to head north, bypassing Grasse, and take the most isolated snowbound mule paths up to Sisteron and onwards – the path commemorated by the modern **Route Napoléon**. By March 6 he was in Dauphiné; on March 19 he was back in Paris's Tuileries Palace. One hundred days later he lost the battle of Waterloo and was finally and absolutely exiled on St Helena.

It's said that on the day he landed at Golfe-Juan, Napoleon's men accidentally held up the prince of Monaco's coach travelling east along the coast. The Revolution incorporated Monaco into France but the restored Louis XVIII had just granted back the principality. When the prince told the former emperor that he was off to reclaim his throne, Napoleon replied that they were in the same business and waved him on his way.

Other sections of the Route Napoléon are covered in our accounts of Grasse (see page 330) and Sisteron (see page 176).

ACCOMMODATION AND EATING

LA NAPOULE

La Corniche d'Or place de la Fontaine ☏ 04 93 49 92 51, ⊚ cornichedor.com. Modern, functional rooms with balconies in this basic hotel overlooking a square a few blocks back from the beach. Buffet breakfast €10. **€60**

MIRAMAR

Tour de l'Esquillon Place Vert Bisson ☏ 04 93 75 41 51, ⊚ esquillon.com. This splendidly located three-star hotel, high up on the corniche in Miramar, is the most memorable place to stay on this stretch of coast. Pretty, authetically retro a/c rooms enjoy breathtaking views, and it has its own beach and restaurant. Closed Nov–March. **€160**

Juan-les-Pins

Though perhaps not as glamorous as it once was, **JUAN-LES-PINS**, just 9km east of Cannes, is still an appealing resort, with sandy beaches, haunting reminders of its former Art Deco glory, plenty of nightlife and a renowned **jazz festival**, **Jazz à Juan**. The one real drawback is that so much of its 2km stretch of fine sheltered sand is obscured by private beach and restaurant concessions.

Unlike St-Tropez, Juan-les-Pins was never a fishing village, just a pine grove by the sea. Its casino was built in 1908, but only in the late 1920s did it take off as the original summer resort of the Côte d'Azur. It was here, in the 1930s – when Charlie Chaplin and Maurice Chevalier were regular visitors – that revealing swimsuits were reputedly first worn, and waterskiing was invented. Juan-les-Pins' trail-blazing style continued to attract aristocrats, royals, writers, dancers and screen stars throughout the 1950s and 1960s.

For more than thirty years after it closed in 1976, the town's central landmark, the eerily beautiful Art Deco **Hotel Provençal** – built by the American railroad magnate Frank Jay Gould, who was also responsible for the Palais de la Méditerranée in Nice – slipped gradually into utter dereliction, and seemed to symbolize the decline in local fortunes. Plans to restore it and convert it into high-end apartments were stalled by the 2008 property market crash. At the time of writing, work is ongoing, with a proposed completion date of 2022/2023. Gould's own home, the 1912 **Villa Vigie**, stands behind high walls across the road.

Another wonderfully eccentric remnant from Juan's heyday stands at the western end of the seafront; complete with minaret, cupolas and domes, the **Villa El Djezair**, at 1 bd Charles-Guillaumont, was built in exuberant neo-Moorish style by Antibes architect Ernest Truch in 1922.

An ancient, beautiful pine grove near the eastern end of the promenade, **Jardin de la Pinède** (known simply as La Pinède), plays host to the jazz festival, and boasts a Hollywood-style **celebrity walk** with the handprints of Sydney Bechet, B.B. King, Stéphane Grappelli, Dave Sanborn and others.

ARRIVAL AND INFORMATION

By train The *gare SNCF* is 200m from the sea, on Av de l'Esterel.
Destinations Cannes (every 10–25min; 10min).
By bus The most central bus stops are "Pin Doré" and "Rond-point Joffre".
Destinations Antibes (#1; every 15min; 6min); Cannes (every 15; 25min).

Tourist office 60 chemin des Sables in the Palais des Congrès, facing La Pinède (Jan & Nov Mon–Sat 9am–12.30pm & 1.30–5pm; Feb, March, Oct & Dec Mon–Sat 9am–12.30pm & 1.30–5pm, Sun 9am–1pm; April–June & Sept Mon–Sat 9.30am–12.30pm & 2–6pm, Sun 9am–1pm; July & Aug daily 9am–7pm; ☏ 04 22 10 60 01, ⊚ antibesjuanlespins.com).

GETTING AROUND AND TOURS

Bike rental Holiday Bikes, 93 bd Wilson (☏ 04 93 61 51 51).

Boat trips Boats from Ponton Courbet run regular cruises around Antibes' fabled "bay of millionaires", east of Pointe

7

JAZZ À JUAN

Juan's international jazz festival – known simply as **Jazz à Juan** and by far the best in the region (ⓦjazzajuan.com) – is held in the middle two weeks of July in the Jardin de la Pinède and on square Gould above the beach by the casino. The music is always chosen with serious concern for every kind of jazz, both contemporary and traditional, rather than commercial popularity, and Juan-les-Pins is twinned with New Orleans, so there's always a strong contingent of performers from the Crescent City.

---

de l'Îlette (April–June & Sept 4 departures daily, 11am–4.30pm; July & Aug 7 departures daily, 9.25am–6pm; ☎06 36 65 50 08, ⓦvisiobulle.com; €15). It is also possible to make day-trips to the Îles de Lérins (see page 312).

ACCOMMODATION

Belles Rives 33 bd Edouard-Baudoin ☎04 93 61 02 79, ⓦbellesrives.com. This gorgeous Art Deco hotel preserves Juan-les-Pins' most authentic aura of jazz age glamour – F. Scott Fitzgerald and wife Zelda stayed here in 1925–6 – but luxury comes at a price, and it's not the most tranquil spot in summer. **€600**

La Marjolaine 15 av du Dr Fabre ☎04 93 61 06 60; ⓦlamarjolainefrance.com. Sixteen traditionally styled rooms in a beautiful a/c villa with a leafy terrace and a handy location between the train station and the beach. Two night minimum stay last two weeks in May, June & Sept; three night minimum stay July & Aug. Closed Oct–March. Three nights **€338.40**

Mimosas Rue Pauline ☎04 93 61 04 16, ⓦhotel mimosas.com. Grand but very welcoming white villa, in lush gardens a 10min walk up from the sea, with rooms of varying sizes – the cheapest are rather small – and a lovely pool, but no restaurant. Free parking. Closed Oct–April. **€100**

Pré Catelan 27 av des Palmiers ☎04 93 61 05 11, ⓦprecatelan.fr. Peaceful and very comfortable hotel, in attractive gardens on the corner of Av des Lauriers, near the sea and the station, with large spacious rooms, some sleeping four, and a heated swimming pool. **€169**

EATING AND DRINKING

Le Pam–Pam 137 bd Wilson ☎04 93 61 11 05, ⓦpampam.fr. Popular cocktail bar with a Polynesian-meets-Brazilian ambience and frequent live music and dance spectacles. Fruit and gewgaw-bedecked cocktails from €12. Daily 3pm–4.30am.

★ **La Passagère** Hotel Belles Rives, 33 bd Edouard-Baudoin ☎04 93 61 02 79, ⓦbellesrives.com. Modern Mediterranean delights using regional produce served in lovely, restored Art Deco surroundings with wonderful views over the bay; *menus* range from the "culinary adventure" of

the mystery *Invitation au Voyage* to the gourmet vegetarian feast of *Menu de la Fourche à la Fourchette* (both €105) *menus*. March–May & Oct–Dec Wed–Sun 7.30–9.30pm; June–Sept daily 7.30–10pm.

Café de la Plage 1 bd Edouard-Baudouin ☎04 93 61 37 61. This pleasant seafront spot offers everything from seafood to cocktails and ice cream, with pizzas from €10.90, salads from around €13 and meat and fish mains around €16 up. Daily: June–Sept 8am–midnight; Oct–May 8am–7pm.

Antibes

Centring on its walled old town, abutting against the waves 1.5km east of Juan-les-Pins and a total of 11km east of Cannes, the delightful resort of **ANTIBES** has largely escaped the overdevelopment that blights so many of its neighbours. Graham Greene lived here for more than twenty years and described it as the only place on the Riviera to have preserved its soul. It remains a bustling little town, its animated streets full of bars and restaurants swarming with Anglophones and yachting types, and hosting one of the finest **markets** along the coast. In addition to its stupendous seafront setting, its castle holds an extensive **Picasso collection**, and the views up from the ramparts towards the Alps are wonderful.

Very little remains of the medieval centre of Antibes, owing to border squabbles from the fifteenth century until the Revolution, when Antibes belonged to France and Nice to Savoy. The finest surviving stretch of **walls** lines the seafront near the little crescent of the old port, with a tiny beach in front. Immediately north, luxury yachts and humble fishing boats jostle amicably for space in the harbour. The headland at its northern end is topped by the splendidly situated **Fort Carré** (Feb–May Tues–Sun 10am–12.30pm & 1.30–5pm; June–Oct Tues–Sun 10am–1pm & 2–6pm; Nov–Jan Tues–Sat 10am–12.30pm & 1.30–4.30pm; €3 including 30min guided tour or €10 pass with other Antibes museums; ⓦ antibes-juanlespins.com/culture/fort-carre), which was transformed by Vauban in the seventeenth century into an impregnable fortress.

Musée Picasso

Place Mariejol • Mid-June to mid-Sept Tues–Sun 10am–6pm; mid-Sept to mid-June Tues–Sun 10am–1pm & 2–6pm • €8, or €10 pass with other Antibes museums • ⓣ 04 92 90 54 20, ⓦ antibes-juanlespins.com/culture/musee-picasso

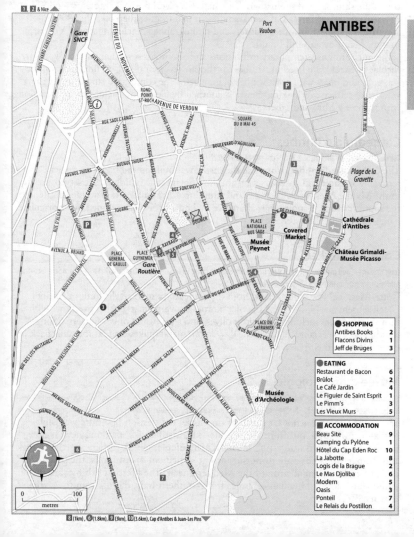

Lording it over the ramparts, Antibes' **Château Grimaldi**, rebuilt in the sixteenth century but still with its twelfth-century Romanesque tower, is a beautifully cool, light space. In 1946, Picasso was offered this dusty old building – by then already a museum – as a studio. Several prolific months followed before he moved to Vallauris (see page 315), leaving all his Antibes output to what is now the **Musée Picasso**. Although he donated other works later on, the bulk of the collection belongs to this one period, when he was involved in one of his better relationships, with Françoise Gilot; Matisse was just up the road in Vence; the war was over; and the 1950s had not yet changed the Côte d'Azur forever.

For all but devotees, the Picassos on display will not be familiar; instead, the museum offers a chance to see lesser-known works in beautiful surroundings. There's an uncomplicated exuberance in the numerous still lifes of sea urchins, the goats and fauns and the wonderful *Ulysses and the Sirens*, a great round head against a mast, around which the ship, sea and sirens swirl. The materials reveal postwar shortages – odd bits of wood and board instead of canvas, and boat paint rather than oils. Picasso himself also makes a subject for other painters and photographers, including André Villers, Brassai, Man Ray and Bill Brandt.

The museum hosts temporary exhibitions and also holds several anguished works by **Nicolas de Staël**, who lived in Antibes for the last few months of his life, painting the sea, gulls and boats with great washes of grey before he committed suicide in 1955. A wonderful terrace overlooking the sea is adorned by Germaine Richier sculptures, along with works by Miró and others.

Cathédrale d'Antibes

Rue du St-Esprit • Daily 8am–noon & 3–6.30pm • ☎ 04 93 34 06 29

The **Cathédrale d'Antibes**, alongside the castle, was built on the site of an ancient temple. The choir and apse survive from the Romanesque building that served the city in the Middle Ages, while the nave and stunning ochre facade are Baroque. Inside, in the south transept, a sumptuous altarpiece by Louis Bréa is surrounded by immaculate panels of tiny detailed scenes.

Covered market

Cours Masséna • **Food market** June–Aug daily 6am–1pm; Sept–May Tues–Sun 6am–1pm • **Craft market** Mid-June to Sept Tues–Sun 3pm–midnight; Oct to mid-June Fri–Sun 3pm–midnight

Cours Masséna, one block inland from the castle, once marked the limit of Antibes' Greek settlement. Now it's the site of a morning **covered market** that overflows with Provençal goodies including delicious olives, and a profusion of cut **flowers**, a long-standing local speciality. Later in the day, a **craft market** takes over; as the stalls pack up, café tables take their place.

Musée d'Archéologie

Bastion St-André • Feb–Oct Tues–Sun 10am–12.30pm & 2–6pm; Nov–Jan Tues–Sat 10am–1pm & 2–5pm • €3, or €10 pass with other Antibes museums • ☎ 04 93 95 85 98, ⓦ antibes-juanlespins.com/culture/musee-d-archeologie

Set into the ramparts not far south of the castle, the Bastion St-André was built by Vauban in 1698, but from the outside at least still looks spanking new. It now houses the small but interesting **Musée d'Archéologie**, which gathers together Greek and Roman finds not only from the ancient settlement of Antipolis, the precursor of Antibes, but from all around the Mediterranean. The prettiest exhibits are the oldest: some lovely Duanian ceramics from southern Italy, dating from the sixth century BC.

ANTIBES THEME PARKS

Several large-scale attractions for **children** line up along the main coast road between Antibes and Biot – everything from performing dolphins at Marineland to water slides at Aquasplash.

Marineland On the N7 ⓦmarineland.fr. Dolphin, killer whale and sea lion shows, aquariums, a shark tunnel and plenty of other marine animals, from penguins to polar bears, spread over an expansive site. Adults €39, children €32. Daily: early April to mid-July 10am–7pm; last two weeks in July & Aug 10am–10pm; Sept 10am–6pm; Oct to early Jan and first week in April 10am–5pm.

Aquasplash Next to Marineland, on the D4 ⓦmarineland.fr. Water toboggans, chutes and slides. Adults €29, children €20.90. Daily: mid-June to early July 10am–6pm; last three weeks in July & Aug 10am–7pm.

Antibesland Almost opposite Aquasplash ⓦazurpark.com. Large funfair with plenty of rollercoasters and rides. Passes €17–29. April daily 4–11pm; May Tues–Sun 6pm–midnight; June daily 7pm–midnight; July–Sept daily 8pm–1am.

Cap d'Antibes

7

South of the walled town, the peninsula known as the **Cap d'Antibes** is dominated by the world's super-rich, many of whom live – or at least maintain homes – here, though the southern Cap still retains pinewoods that hide the exclusive mansions. As well as offering intermittent access to the wonderful rocky shore and a couple of sandy beaches, the Cap holds a couple of beautiful gardens, the **Jardin Thuret** and the **Villa Eilenroc**. Walking or cycling up the western side of the Cap is a joy; you pass the tiny **Port de l'Olivette**, full of small, unflashy boats, as well as rocks, jetties, tiny sandy beaches and grand villas hiding behind high walls.

The beaches

Antibes' longest beach, the sandy and utterly irresistible **Plage de la Salis**, runs along the eastern neck of the **Cap d'Antibes**. It's a rarity along the Riviera: access to it is free, with no big hotels blocking the way – the success of Juan-les-Pins spared this side of the Cap from unchecked development in the days before planning laws were tightened.

Above the southern end of the beach, at the top of chemin du Calvaire, stands the **Chapelle de la Garoupe** (daily 10am–6pm; ⓦantibes-juanlespins.com/culture/chapelle-de-la-garoupe), full of ex votos for deliverances from accidents ranging from battles with the Saracens to collisions with speeding Citroëns. Much the best reason to make the trail up here, however, is for the stunning panoramic **views** across Cap d'Antibes towards both Juan-les-Pins and Antibes; you can see as far as the Esterel and to Nice and beyond. Next to the church is a powerful lighthouse whose beam is visible 70km out to sea.

A second public beach, **Plage de la Garoupe**, smaller than de la Salis but similarly sandy, stretches along boulevard de la Garoupe before the promontory of Cap Gros.

Villa Eilenroc

Av L.D. Beaumont • Wed 2–5pm, every first & third Sat of the month 2–5pm • €2 • ☎04 93 67 74 33, ⓦantibes-juanlespins.com/culture/villa-eilenroc

At the southern end of the Cap d'Antibes stands the grandiose **Villa Eilenroc**, completed in 1867 and designed by Charles Garnier, architect of the casino at Monte Carlo. Its unusual name is (almost) the Christian name of the wife of its original owner, spelled backwards – Cornelia. Both the house and its 27 acres of lush gardens are now owned by the municipality, and open to visitors; the real highlight is the superb **rose garden**.

From the gardens you may catch a glimpse of the villa's equally magnificent neighbour, the **Château de la Croë**. Home, after the 1936 abdication, to the Duke and Duchess of Windsor, it now belongs to Russian billionaire Roman Abramovich.

Espace Mer et Littoral

Bd J.-F.-Kennedy • Mid-June to mid-Sept Tues–Sat 10am–6.30pm • Free • ☎ 04 93 61 45 32, ⊛ antibes-juanlespins.com/culture/espace-mer-et-littoral

The **Espace Mer et Littoral**, at the Napoleonic coastal battery of Graillon, close to the southwestern extremity of the Cap d'Antibes, presents changing exhibitions on the marine and coastal environments. Both the fort itself, and the slightly grubby public beach alongside, enjoy lovely views.

Jardin Thuret

90 chemin Raymond • Mon–Fri: summer 8am–6pm; winter 8.30am–5.30pm • Free • ☎ 04 97 21 25 00

Dominating the middle of the Cap, the **Jardin Thuret** was established in the nineteenth century by botanist Gustav Thuret. It now tests and acclimatizes subtropical trees and shrubs in order to diversify the Mediterranean plants of France.

ARRIVAL AND INFORMATION   ANTIBES

By train The *gare SNCF* is a 3min walk north of the old town along Av Robert Soleau.

Destinations Cannes (up to 5 hourly; 7–12min); Nice (up to 5 hourly; 18–30 min).

By bus The *gare routière* is on place Guynemer (☎ 04 89 87 72 00, ⊛ envibus.fr).

Destinations Aéroport Nice-Côte-d'Azur (every 35–45min; 38min); Biot (#10; every 30–40min; 27–30min); Cannes (every 15min; 30min); Cap d'Antibes (#2; every 30min–1hr; 14min); Juan-les-Pins (#1; every 15min; 6min); Nice (every 15min;1hr–1hr 5min); Vallauris (#8; every 15–20min; 30–35min).

By car Driving in and around Antibes can be a nightmare; best to follow signs to one of the city's multistorey car parks as soon as you arrive. The most convenient for the walled town is Parking J-M Poirier, accessed on Av Tourre.

Tourist office 42 av Robert Soleau (July & Aug daily 9am–7pm; Sept–June Mon–Fri 9am–12.30pm & 1.30–6pm, Sat 9am–noon & 2–6pm, Sun 9am–1pm; ☎ 04 22 10 60 10, ⊛ antibesjuanlespins.com).

ACCOMMODATION   SEE MAP PAGE 321

Beau Site 141 bd Kennedy, Cap d'Antibes ☎ 04 93 61 53 43, ⊛ hotelbeausite.net. This white-painted inn, set in a lovely garden amid some of the most exclusive villas on the Cap d'Antibes, offers spacious, plain, airy rooms that represent great value, plus a very welcome pool. Closed Nov–Feb. **€110**

Hôtel du Cap Eden Roc Bd Kennedy, Cap d'Antibes ☎ 04 93 61 39 01, ⊛ hotel-du-cap-eden-roc.com. A celebrity haunt since F. Scott Fitzgerald used it as the setting for *Tender is the Night*, this luxury hotel has a prime seafront position in 25 acres on Cap d'Antibes. Along with all the comforts you'd expect at this price, it even has its own landing stage. Closed mid-Oct to mid-April. **€1900**

La Jabotte 13 av Max Maurey ☎ 04 93 61 45 89, ⊛ jabotte.com. Just a short walk from the plage de la Salis, this friendly place is big on statement wallpaper and original design touches – book in advance. Three night minimum stay June–Sept. **€144**

Le Mas Djoliba 29 av de Provence ☎ 04 93 34 02 48, ⊛ hotel-djoliba.com. Three-star *Logis de France* with a pool, *boules* and a fabulous garden; it's a great hideaway from the bustle of town and not too far from the beach. Closed mid-Nov to Feb. **€260**

Modern 1 rue Formilière ☎ 04 92 90 59 05, ⊛ modernhotel06.com. Welcoming and inexpensive little hotel, tucked away in a pedestrian lane in the heart of the old town, though the very plain modern rooms are duller than the cute exterior might suggest. **€62**

Oasis 20 Rue des Casemates ☎ 06 16 66 28 43. The best budget option in town, stylishly incorporating the stone and wooden beams of a period building into its design-hostel chic, with a central location, huge kitchen and three-bed en-suite dorms. Great value. **€38**

Ponteil 11 impasse Jean-Mensier ☎ 04 93 34 67 92, ⊛ leponteil.com. Friendly, pretty hotel with the feel of a B&B, in a quiet location at the end of a cul-de-sac near the sea, and surrounded by luxuriant vegetation. Small plain rooms, and free parking. Closed mid-Nov to mid-Feb. **€150**

Le Relais du Postillon 8 rue Championnet ☎ 04 93 34 20 77, ⊛ relaisdupostillon.com. In Antibes old town, this charming two-star above a low-key bar feels like an old inn, with its individually styled a/c rooms and lots of exposed stonework. **€85**

CAMPSITES

Camping du Pylône v du Pylône, La Brague ☎ 04 93 33 52 86, ⊛ campingdupylone.com. Two-star campsite near Biot train station and 200m from the sea, with twenty camping spaces plus a pool and restaurant. Closed Oct–March. **€31.90**

Logis de la Brague 1221 rte de Nice ☎ 04 93 33 54 72, ⊛ camping-logisbrague.com. As with all campsites near Antibes, this three-star site is north of the city in the *quartier* of La Brague (one train stop to "Gare de Biot"); this one is closest to the station. Closed Oct–April. **€29**

EATING

SEE MAP PAGE 321

Old Antibes has places to eat at every turn: place Nationale and cours Masséna are lined with **cafés** and rue Thuret and its side streets also offer numerous menus to browse through. Places to **drink** are especially thick on the ground by the port.

Restaurant de Bacon 664 bd de Bacon, Cap d'Antibes ☎ 04 93 61 50 02, ⓦ restaurantdebacon.com. With excellent fish and a sea view, this locally renowned restaurant offers a €55 set lunch; otherwise, *menus* from €85 except during high season. Tues 7.30–10pm, Wed–Sun noon–2pm & 7.30–10pm.

Brûlot 3 rue Frédéric Isnard ☎ 04 93 34 17 76, ⓦ brulot. fr. A stalwart of the restaurant scene in Antibes' old town, dishing up classic regional dishes like *socca, salade niçoise* and tripe. Lunch *formule* €14.90, *menus* €23.90–44.90. Mon–Wed 4pm noon–11pm, Thurs–Sat noon–1.30pm & 4–11pm.

Le Café Jardin 23 rue des Bains ☎ 04 93 34 42 66, ⓦ lecafejardin.fr. Friendly, cluttered, slightly twee little brasserie/café in a very peaceful spot in the back lanes of the old town, with a nice bar, and a courtyard filled with ceramic frogs. A fair sized array of tapas (€6) includes guacamole, chorizo and the likes, while lunch *menus* start at €15.50. Mon–Sat 8am–7pm.

Le Figuier de Saint Esprit 14 rue ste Esprit ☎ 04 93 34 50 12, ⓦ restaurant-figuier-saint-esprit.fr. Tucked down a cobbled street with terrace tables spreading beneath a trellis of vines, *Le Figuier* is the creation of Michelin-starred chef Christian Morriset. Served in a rustic yet elegant interior, his lunch *menu* comes in at €42–55 and there's even a drinks *formule* at €12. Tasting *menu* €142. May–Oct Mon 7.15–9.30pm, Wed–Sun 12.15pm–1.30pm & 7.15–9.30pm; late Nov to April Mon & Thurs–Sun 12.15pm–1.30pm & 7.15–9.30pm.

Le Pimm's 3 rue de la République ☎ 04 93 34 04 88, ⓦ pimms.cabanova.com. Daytime brasserie, with carousel decor and a friendly atmosphere, where the pavement tables on the corner of place Guynemer guard the approach to the old town. Whether you order salad, pasta, or a daily *plat*, it will cost around €13; more substantial dishes from around €14–19. Regular live music. Daily 7am–8.30pm.

Les Vieux Murs 25 promenade Amiral-de-Grasse ☎ 04 93 34 06 73, ⓦ lesvieuxmurs.com. *Restaurant gastronomique* serving classy food such as green asparagus tart with diced *confit* veal or swordfish with lobster broth, in a perfect setting on the castle ramparts. *Menus* from €36 for both lunch and dinner, main courses from €25. Daily 12.30–2pm & 7–10pm.

SHOPPING

SEE MAP PAGE 321

Antibes Books 13 rue Georges Clemenceau ☎ 04 93 61 96 47, ⓦ antibesbooks.com. A well-stocked and very friendly English-language bookshop in Antibes' old town. Summer daily 10am–7pm; winter Mon & Sun 10am–6pm, Tues–Sat 10am–7pm.

Flacons Divins 6 rue du Docteur Rostan ☎ 04 97 04 70 40, ⓦ flaconsdivins.fr. A very professional, knowledgeable and accommodating *cave à vin* with expert sommeliers on

hand so you can try before you buy. A large selection of artisan and organic wines; tasting classes also available. Tues–Sat 9.30am–7pm.

Jeff de Bruges 5 bd Wilson ☎ 04 93 34 12 40, ⓦ magasins.jeff-de-bruges.com. Swanky *chocolatier* which also sells artisan ice cream as well regional delicacies such as *calissons*. Chocolate bars (€3.75) come in a numbered series. Mon–Sat 9am–12.15pm & 2.30–7.15pm.

Biot

The pretty *village perché* of **BIOT**, 4km from the coast and 5km northwest of Antibes, is famous for its rich arts and crafts tradition. Long a centre of **pottery** production and now home to several glassworks, Biot is usually packed out in high season, as visitors drawn by the excellent **Fernand Léger museum** nearby stay on to browse around the village itself.

Most of Biot's wide array of shops, studios and galleries line up along the long, straight **rue St-Sébastien**, which runs along the crest of the hill to reach the old **walled village**, a much less developed labyrinth of narrow lanes and tiny squares.

Musée d'Histoire et de Céramique Biotoises

8 rue St-Sébastien • Mid-June to mid-Sept Tues–Sun 10am–6pm; mid-Sept to mid-June Wed–Sun 2–6pm • €4 • ☎ 04 93 65 54 54, ⓦ musee-de-biot.fr

The artist **Fernand Léger**, who lived in Biot for a few years at the end of his life, was first attracted to the village by its potteries; one of his old pupils had set up shop here to produce ceramics of his master's designs. Today, the former Chapelle des Pénitents Blancs houses a small **Musée d'Histoire et de Céramique Biotoises**, which underlines the importance of the potteries to the historical development of the village.

Verrerie de Biot

Chemin des Combes • **Verrerie de Biot** Mid-June to mid-Sept Mon–Sat 9.30am–8pm, Sun 10.30am–1.30pm & 2.30–7.30pm; mid-Sept to mid-June Mon–Sat 9.30am–6pm, Sun 10.30am–1.30pm & 2.30–6; closed last 2 weeks in Jan • Free • **Eco-musée du Verre** Mid-June to mid-Sept Mon–Sat 9.30am–7.30pm, Sun 10.30am–1.30pm & 2.30–7.30pm; mid-Sept to mid-June Mon–Sat 9.30am–6pm, Sun 10.30am–1.30pm & 2.30–6pm; closed last 2 weeks in Jan • €3 ; guided tour €6 • ☎ 04 93 65 03 00, ⓦ verreriebiot.com

Biot's **glass-makers** do all they can to encourage visitors to admire, and ideally buy, the famous and beautiful hand-blown bubble glass (*verre bullé*). You can watch glass-blowers at work at the **Verrerie de Biot** – established in 1956, a year after Léger's death – just north of the centre, and learn more by taking a tour of the on-site **Eco-musée du Verre**.

Musée Fernand Léger

316 chemin du Val de Pôme • Mon & Wed–Sun: May–Oct 10am–6pm; Nov–April 10am–5pm • €5.50 (€7.50 during temporary exhibitions) • ☎ 04 92 91 50 20, ⓦ musee-fernandleger.fr • Bus #10 (every 30–40min: from Antibes 25min, from Biot *gare SNCF* 5min) to "F. Leger" stop

A stunning, life-affirming collection of paintings by Fernand Léger is displayed at the **Musée Fernand Léger**, 1km southeast of Biot. Even the museum building is a pleasure: with its giant mosaic murals, it transcends its suburban setting.

Léger was turned off from the abstraction of Parisian painters by his experiences of fighting alongside ordinary working people in World War I. Not that he favoured realism, but he wanted his paintings to have popular appeal. Understanding that in the modern world, art competes with images generated by advertising, cinema and public spectacle, he set about producing work with a similar visual power. Without any realism in the form or facial expressions, the people in such paintings as *Four Bicycle Riders* or the various *Construction Workers* are forcefully present as they engage in their work or leisure, and are visually on an equal footing with the objects. Almost all the collection is displayed in two spacious white galleries upstairs; while it's not scrupulously chronological, Léger's earlier, Cubist works come first.

ARRIVAL AND INFORMATION   BIOT

By train Although Biot does officially have a *gare SNCF*, it's not near the village itself, but down by the sea at La Brague, 4km south, along a road that's much too dangerous and unpleasant to walk.

By bus Regular buses between Biot and Antibes (#10; every 30–40min; 27–30min) call at the *gare SNCF*.

Tourist office 4 Chemin Neuf (April–June & Sept Mon–Fri 9.30am–12.30pm & 1.30pm–6pm, Sat & Sun 11am–5pm; July & Aug Mon–Fri 9.30am–6pm, Sat & Sun 11am–5pm; Oct–March Mon-Fri 9.30am–12.30pm & 1.30–5pm, Sat 11am–5pm; ☎ 04 93 65 78 00, ⓦ biot-tourisme.com).

ACCOMMODATION AND EATING

La Bastide de Biot 625 rte de la Mer ☎ 04 93 65 50 50, ⓦ labastidedebiot.fr. Plush, if slightly plain, modern rooms in a newly renovated complex with centrepiece swimming pool on the road south. €240

Des Arcades 16 place des Arcades ☎ 04 93 65 01 04, ⓦ hotel-restaurant-les-arcades.com. Book well in advance to stay in this appealing old hotel/restaurant in the medieval centre of the village, full of old-fashioned charm and with huge rooms and an excellent restaurant that doubles as an art gallery (*menu* €35). Very good value for this neck of the woods. €60

L'Eden 243 chemin du Val-de-Pôme ☎ 04 93 65 63 70, ⓦ camping-eden.fr. Three-star campsite, a couple of hundred metres from the Léger museum, with a pool, bar and restaurant. Closed Nov–March. €28

Café de la Poste 24 rue St-Sébastien ☎ 04 93 65 19 32. The best of several restaurants that have outdoor tables in the main village square, as well as indoor dining rooms just off it. Either way, you can choose between *salade niçoise*, ravioli with goat's cheese or *moules* for around €16, or try the €13.50 *plat du jour*. Tues–Thurs & Sun 8.30am–7.30pm, Fri & Sat 8.30am–11.45pm.

Villeneuve-Loubet

The Riviera shore reaches its trashy nadir at **Villeneuve-Loubet-Plage**, 6km straight up the coast from Antibes, where the giant **Baie des Anges** marina dominates the waterfront. The marina was built in the 1970s, and the petrified sails of its colossal residential blocks – a clever, well-maintained but hugely intrusive slice of modernism – are visible all the way from Cap d'Antibes to Cap Ferrat. The commercial squalor that surrounds it is rather harder to stomach – an unsightly mess of drive-in restaurants, petrol stations and out-of-town retail sheds wedged between the autoroute and the sea.

Across the autoroute, the quieter, more attractive village of **VILLENEUVE-LOUBET**, on the River Loup, clusters around an undamaged twelfth-century castle, once home to François I.

Musée de l'Art Culinaire

3 rue Escoffier • Daily: July & Aug 10am–1pm & 2–7pm; Sept, Oct & late Dec to June 10am–1pm & 2–6pm • €6 • ☎ 04 93 20 80 51, ⓦ fondation-escoffier.org

7

The small village house in Villeneuve-Loubet where legendary chef **Auguste Escoffier** (1846–1935) was born is now the **Musée de l'Art Culinaire**, The son of a blacksmith, Escoffier began his restaurant career at 13, skivvying for his uncle in Nice, and was by the end of the century known as "the king of chefs and the chef of kings". In London he was the *Savoy*'s first head chef, then the *Carlton*'s; he fed almost every European head of state, and personally trained almost two thousand chefs. *Pêche melba* was his most famous creation, but his significance for the history of haute cuisine was in breaking the tradition of health-hazard richness and quantity. He was also a technical innovator, who invented dried potato and a breadcrumb maker.

As well as items related to Escoffier's own life, the museum tells the history of French cuisine, and includes a re-creation of an eighteenth-century Provençal kitchen. The invention of the stove or *potager* during that century revolutionized French cooking: by making it possible to cook dishes simultaneously at a wide range of temperatures, it paved the way for the development of elaborate menus. The top floor displays a collection of historic menus, while another entire floor, reeking of chocolate and sugar, is devoted to the art of the pastry chef.

ARRIVAL AND DEPARTURE
VILLENEUVE-LOUBET

By train Villeneuve-Loubet's *gare SNCF* is on the coast some distance from the village, a long and potentially dangerous walk along busy roads.

By bus The #200 Nice–Cannes bus comes no closer than the Mairie annexe next to the autoroute; the #500 Nice–Grasse bus serves the village itself.

Destinations Cagnes-sur-Mer (every 20–45min; 6min); Grasse (every 20–45min; 35–40min); Nice (every 20–45min; 50–55min).

ACCOMMODATION AND EATING

L'Auberge Fleurie 11 rue des Mesures ☎ 04 93 73 90 92, ⓦ laubergefleurievilleneuveloubetvillage.com. It's not just the web address that's flowery at this pretty, bloom-bedecked village restaurant, which serves the likes of kidneys in *cassoulet* and ravioli with ceps in a formal setting. *Menus* from €16.90 at lunch & €30 at dinner. Tues–Thurs & Sun noon–3pm, Fri & Sat noon–3pm & 7–10pm.

Au Garçon Boucher 4 place de Verdun ☎ 04 93 08 86 80, ⓦ augarconboucher.fr. Good local restaurant in the pedestrianized centre serving unpretentious brasserie standards. Steak, hamburgers and brochettes go for around €15–20. Summer Mon–Thurs & Sun 7am–3pm, Fri & Sat 7am–3pm & 7–10pm; winter daily 7am–3pm.

Ô Villagio 1 av de la Libération ☎ 04 93 20 88 13, ⓦ hotel-ovillagio.com. Two-star hotel, beside the bridge at the busy road junction at the entrance to the old town, with fifteen simple, a/c rooms, a restaurant serving Niçoise cuisine and a rather smart terrace overlooking the river. **€70**

Cagnes

Slashed through by three major roads and with an awe-inspiring traffic problem, **CAGNES** is a confusing agglomeration. The narrow coastal strip, known as **Cros-de-Cagnes**, consists of a small, pleasant old quarter, with fishing boats pulled up on its broad, pebbly beach. Scruffy, modern **Cagnes-sur-Mer**, which constitutes the town centre, is inland above the autoroute, a bustling but rather characterless place notable only for **Renoir's house**. The original medieval village, **HAUT-DE-CAGNES**, overlooks both town and coast from the northwest heights, and has a stunning **castle** that contains the fabulous **Donation Solidor**.

In early July Cagnes celebrates all manner of sea-related activities as part of the **Fête de la Saint-Pierre et de la Mer**; in early August there's free **street theatre** on place du Château and on the seafront; and late August sees a bizarre **square boules** competition down montée de la Bourgade.

Les Collettes – Musée Renoir

Chemain des Colettes • Mon & Wed–Sun: April & May 10am–noon & 2–6pm; June–Sept 10am–1pm & 2–6pm; Oct–March 10am–noon & 2–5pm • €6, or €8 with Château Grimaldi (see page 328) • ☎ 04 93 20 61 07, ⓦ cagnes-tourisme.com • Free shuttle bus #45 from Cagnes-sur-Mer bus station; it's about 10min on foot

Surrounded by olive and rare orange groves, **Les Collettes**, the house that **Renoir** had built in 1907 and where he spent the last twelve years of his life, is now the **Musée Renoir**. Renoir was captivated by the olive trees and by the difficulties of rendering "a tree full of colours". One of the two studios in the house, north-facing to catch the late afternoon light, is arranged as though Renoir had just popped out. Despite the rheumatoid arthritis that had forced him to seek a warmer climate than Paris, he painted every day at Les Collettes, strapping the brush to his hand when moving his fingers became too painful.

Portraits of Renoir here by his closest friends, displayed in the house, include Albert André's *À Renoir Peignant*, showing the ageing artist hunching over his canvas; a bust by Aristide Maillol; a crayon sketch by Richard Guido; and Dufy's *Homage to Renoir*. Renoir's work is represented by several sculptures including two bronzes – *La Maternité* and a medallion of his son Coco – some beautiful, tiny watercolours in the studio, and ten paintings from his Cagnes period (the greatest, the final version of *Les Grandes Baigneuses*, hangs in the Louvre).

Haut-de-Cagnes

As perfect a hilltop village as you'll find on the Riviera, **HAUT-DE-CAGNES**, a short but steep walk up from Cagnes-sur-Mer and also accessible on the free bus #44, was for many years the haunt of successful artists. No architectural excrescences spoil its tiers of tiny streets, and even the flowers spilling over terracotta pots or climbing soft stone walls appear perfect.

Château Grimaldi

Place du Château • Mon & Wed–Sun: April–June & Sept 10am–noon & 2–6pm; July & Aug 10am–1pm & 2–6pm; Oct–March 10am–noon & 2–5pm • €4, or €8 with Musée Renoir • ☎ 04 92 02 47 35, ⓦ cagnes-tourisme.com • Free shuttle bus #44 from bus station; on foot, it's a steep ascent from Av Renoir along rue Général-Bérenger and montée de la Bourgade

Ancient Haut-de-Cagnes backs up to the crenellated **château**, which once belonged to the Grimaldis of Monaco and now houses the **Château Grimaldi**. Here you will find a number of museums, including the **Musée de l'Olivier** – which explains the history and practice of olive cultivation and oil production, with sundry old wooden presses and other artefacts – along with the **Donation Solidor** and exhibition space for **contemporary art**.

The castle's Renaissance interior is itself a masterpiece, with tiers of arcaded galleries, vast frescoed ceilings, stuccoed historical reliefs and gorgeously ornamented chambers and chapels.

Donation Solidor

The **Donation Solidor** consists of wonderfully diverse portraits of cabaret star **Suzy Solidor**, by the likes of Dufy, Cocteau, Laurençin, Lempicka, Van Dongen and Kisling. Solidor's career spanned the 1920s to the 1970s, and she spent her last 25 years in Cagnes. She was quite a character: extremely talented and independent, she declared herself a lesbian years before the word, let alone the preference, was remotely acceptable, and was the inspiration for the British music-hall song "If you knew Suzy, like I know Suzy". Each canvas clearly reveals the qualities that most endeared her to each artist, or the fantasies she provoked, giving a fascinating insight into the art of portraiture as well as a multifaceted image of the woman.

ARRIVAL AND INFORMATION   CAGNES

By train The Cagnes-sur-Mer *gare SNCF* (as opposed to Cros-de-Cagnes, one stop along) is southwest of the centre alongside the autoroute. If you're walking from the station, turn right on the northern side of the autoroute along Av de la Gare to head into town; the sixth turning on your right, rue des Palmiers, leads to the Cagnes-sur-Mer tourist office. Buses #42, #49 and #200 make the short run from the *gare SNCF* to the *gare routière* on place M. Bourdet in Cagnes-sur-Mer.

Destinations Antibes (roughly every 30min; 10min); Cannes (every 18–25min; 22min); Nice (roughly every 25–35min; 15min).

By bus The *gare routière* is on place M. Bourdet in Cagnes-sur-Mer. Bus #41 runs to Cros-de-Cagnes and the seafront; bus #45 to the Renoir museum; and #44 up to Haut-de-Cagnes.

Destinations Cannes (roughly every 15min; 57min); Grasse (every 20–45min; 45min); Nice (roughly every 15; 40min); Villeneuve-Loubet (every 20–45min; 6min).

By car The narrow lanes of Haut-de-Cagnes present a phenomenal challenge to drivers. The extraordinary hilltop car park is well worth experiencing, however; you leave your vehicle in what looks like a car wash, from which it's whisked away and filed in some subterranean cavern until you return.

Tourist office Each component of Cagnes has its own office. In Cagnes-sur-Mer, it's at 6 bd Maréchal-Juin (July & Aug Mon–Sat 9am–1pm & 2–6pm; Sept–June Mon–Fri 9am–noon & 2–6pm, Sat 9am–noon; ☎ 04 93 20 61 64, ✆ cagnes-tourisme.com); up in Haut-de-Cagnes, it's on place du Dr-Maurel (July & Aug daily 10am–1pm & 2–6pm; Sept–June Mon–Sat 2–6pm; ☎ 04 92 02 85 05).

ACCOMMODATION AND EATING

Although the largest choice of **hotels** is down in Cros-de-Cagnes, assuming you don't mind not being by the sea it's much nicer to stay up in the peace of Haut-de-Cagnes. There are also plenty of **campsites**, most of them located in wooded areas inland.

Aéva 22–23 promenade de la Plage, Cros-de-Cagnes ☎ 04 93 73 39 52, ✆ hotel-aeva.fr. Stylishly revamped seafront hotel. Elegant, modern, a/c en suites have soundproofing, satellite TV and safes. There's a classy restaurant facing the sea, and a separate *aparthotel*, too. **€135**

Fleur de Sel 85 montée de la Bourgade ☎ 04 92 20 33 33, ✆ www.restaurant-fleurdesel.com. This lovely old hilltop house serves dishes such as Scottish lobster with black truffle oil or scallops with carrot tagliatelle, lemon juice, caviar and yuzu; *menus* from €36. April–Sept Mon, Tues & Thurs–Sun from 7pm; Oct–March also closed Thurs.

Le Grimaldi 6 place du Château, Haut-de-Cagnes ☎ 04 93 08 67 12, ✆ hotelgrimaldi.com. Charming old village house, with four atmospheric rooms plus a top floor suite

with rooftop terrace, set behind a large terrace restaurant on the square. It's really hard to get a car anywhere near here, but once you find it, it's a delightful place to spend a few days, absorbing the life of the village. **€119**

Josy-Jo 2 rue du Planastel ☎ 04 93 20 68 76, ✆ restaurant-josyjo.com. Charming restaurant in the space that served as Soutine's workshop in the interwar years, with an oleander-shaded terrace and refined Provençal dishes. *Formule* €25, otherwise around €25–40 for main courses. Tues–Sat noon–2pm & 7.30–10pm.

Les Terrasses du Soleil Place Notre Dame de la Protection, Haut-de-Cagnes ☎ 04 93 73 26 56, ✆ terrassesdusoleil.com. Attractive *chambres d'hôtes* in the former village home of songwriter Georges Ulmer, with one B&B room and two suites. **€125**

Le Val Fleuri 139 chemin Vallon des Vaux ☎ 04 93 31 21 74, ✆ campingvalfleuri.fr. Three-star campsite approximately 4km from the sea (bus #41) with a heated pool, snack bar and children's play area. They also rent out studio flats and mobile homes. Closed Oct to early April. **€30**

Grasse

Enjoying stunning uninterrupted views over the Côte d'Azur from its hillside location 16km inland from Cannes, **GRASSE** has been capital of the **perfume industry** for almost three hundred years. It's a far cry now, though, from the medieval town depicted in Patrick Süskind's novel *Perfume*. If you're at all interested in the scent business, various perfume museums and factories make Grasse worthy of a day-trip, and it also has a gritty sense of being a genuine lived-in community that many of its neighbours lack, but it's not really a place to plan a long stay, especially as it's very short of decent hotels.

By the time Grasse experienced the aristocratic tourist boom of the late nineteenth century, its most desirable addresses – including one where Queen Victoria stayed for a month in 1891 – lay outside the old town, to the east. These days, however, the residential suburbs hold minimal appeal for the visitors who flock to the restored **vieille ville**, a hubbub of life and noise where the former homes of sixteenth-century tanning merchants, seventeenth-century perfumed-glove manufacturers and eighteenth-century *parfumiers* have become museums, boutiques and municipal offices. Walking the narrow lanes of the old town is a pleasure in itself, as is emerging into the public gardens at the southern end, where the terrace above Boulevard Fragonard commands fabulous views down to the distant Mediterranean.

At the north end of town, **Place aux Aires** hosts a daily **flower and vegetable market** (mornings only). Ringed by arcades of different heights, it was at one time the exclusive preserve of the tanning industry.

Musée International de la Parfumerie

2 bd du Jeu-de-Ballon • **Museum** daily: May–Sept 10am–7pm; Oct–March 10am–5.30pm; **gardens** April & Sept–Nov 10am–5.30pm; May–Aug 10am–7pm; also full programme of guided tours (see website) • **Museum** €4 (includes Musée d'Art et d'Histoire de Provence and Villa-Musée Fragonard) or €2 upon presentation of a gardens ticket; **gardens** €4 or €2 upon presentation of a museum ticket • Ⓦ museesdegrasse.com

Housed in a much-altered eighteenth-century mansion alongside two hectares of gardens filled with aromatic plants, the **Musée International de la Parfumerie** tells the story of the creation and uses of scent ever since ancient Egyptian priests became the first *parfumiers*. A fascinating parallel account describes how perfumes have been marketed and sold – often using Egyptian or other "exotic" iconography – and there's also a general history of the beauty and make-up industries. Prize exhibits include a travelling case that belonged to Marie Antoinette, and there's a greenhouse filled with gently scented herbs and flowers. Visits culminate in an exploration of Grasse's role in industrializing the whole process.

Musée Provençal du Costume et du Bijou

2 rue Jean-Ossola • Daily 10am–1pm & 2–6pm • Free • ☎ 04 93 36 44 65, Ⓦ fragonard.com

The small **Musée Provençal du Costume et du Bijou**, owned by the Parfumerie Fragonard, does exactly what it claims. Besides a room filled with jewels, several more hold mannequins dressed in various traditional regional costumes, and are dimly lit to preserve their vivid colours.

Musée d'Art et d'Histoire de Provence

2 rue Mirabeau • Daily: May–Sept 10am–7pm; Oct–April 10–5.30pm • €2 including Villa-Musée Fragonard • Ⓦ museesdegrasse.com

A luxurious townhouse commissioned by the sister of the Comte de Mirabeau, a leading figure in the French Revolution, now serves as the **Musée d'Art et d'Histoire de Provence**. As well as retaining many of its gorgeous fittings and original eighteenth-century kitchen, it displays a historical collection that includes wonderful eighteenth- to nineteenth-century faïence from Apt and Le Castellet; Mirabeau's death mask; a tin bidet; six prehistoric bronze leg bracelets; *santons*; and oil presses.

Villa-Musée Fragonard

23 bd Fragonard • Daily: late April to early May 1–5.30pm; July–Sept 1–6.30pm • €2 including Musée d'Art et d'Histoire de Provence • Ⓦ museesdegrasse.com

The delightful **Villa-Musée Fragonard** celebrates Rococo painter Jean-Honoré Fragonard. The son of an early and not very successful Grassois perfumed-glove maker, he returned to live in this villa when his work fell out of favour after the Revolution. The staircase features impressive wall paintings by his son Alexandre-Evariste, while the salon is graced by copies of the panels depicting *Love's Progress in the Heart of a Young Girl*, which Jean-Honoré painted for Louis XV's mistress, Madame du Barry.

Cathédrale Notre Dame du Puy

Place du Petit Puy • Mid-April to early Nov Mon 9am–noon & 2–6pm, Tues–Sat 10am–noon & 1–6pm; early Nov to mid-April Tues–Sat 9am–noon & 1–5pm • Free

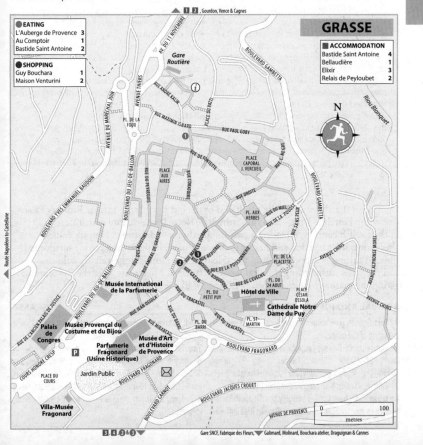

SCENTS AND SENSIBILITY: THE PARFUMERIES OF GRASSE

Making **perfume** is usually presented as a mysterious process, an alchemy, turning the soul of the flower into a liquid of luxury and desire. The reality – including traditional methods of *macération* (mixing the blossoms with heated animal fat) and *enfleuration* (placing the flowers on cold fat, then washing the result with alcohol and finally distilling it into the ultimately refined essence) – is distinctly less romantic, but every bit as intriguing.

There are thirty or so **parfumeries** in and around Grasse, most of them making not perfume but essences-plus-formulas, that are then sold to Dior, Lancôme, Estée Lauder and the like, who make up their own brand-name perfumes. Although synthetic ingredients have long formed an essential part of their repertoire, they still use copious amounts of locally grown lavender, jasmine and roses. To extract 1kg of essence of lavender takes 200kg of lavender; 1kg of cabbage rose essence needs more than 3000kg of roses. Perfume contains twenty percent essence (eau de toilette contains ten percent; eau de Cologne five or six percent), and the bottles are extremely small. The major cost to this multibillion-euro business is marketing. On strictly cost-accounting grounds, the clothes created by the grand Parisian couturiers serve simply to promote their latest fragrances.

7

For a fairly close-up look at production, visit the **Parfumerie Fragonard**, which is spread over two venues. The first, the **Usine Historique** at 20 bd Fragonard (daily 9am–6.30pm; free guided tour in French and English; ⓣ 04 93 36 44 65, ⓦ fragonard.com), shows traditional methods of extracting essence and has a collection of antique cosmetics bottles and bejewelled flagons. The second, the **Fabrique des Fleurs** – 3km southeast towards Cannes, at Les Quatre Chemins (daily: March–Oct 9am–6pm; Nov–Feb 9am–1pm & 2–6pm; free guided tour in French and English; ⓣ 04 93 77 94 30, ⓦ fragonard.com), is more informative, and at least admits to modernization of the processes. A world map shows the origins of various strange ingredients: resins, roots, moss, beans, civet (extract of a wild cat's genitals), ambergris (whale intestines), bits of beaver and musk from Tibetan goats all help to produce the array of scents that the "nose" – as the creator of the perfume's formula is known – has to play with. A professional "nose" (of whom there are fewer than fifty) can recognize five or six thousand different scents.

Two other *parfumeries* offer tours in French and English: **Galimard**, 4km southeast of the centre at 73 rte de Cannes (daily: April–June & Sept 9am–noon & 2–6pm; July & Aug 9am–6.30pm; Oct–March 9am–noon & 2–6pm; free; ⓣ 04 93 09 20 00, ⓦ galimard.com), and **Molinard**, 1.5km southwest of the centre at 60 bd Victor-Hugo (July & Aug daily 9.30am–7pm; Sept–June Mon–Sat 9.30am–6.30pm, Sun 10am–6pm; free; ⓣ 04 93 36 01 62, ⓦ molinard.com).

Cradled in the alleyways at the south end of the old town is the former Bishop's Palace – now the Hôtel de Ville – and the **Cathédrale Notre Dame du Puy** which were built in the twelfth century, replacing a two-hundred-year-old fortress. Despite endless alterations, the cathedral still has its high gaunt nave, in which the starkly unadorned ribbed vaulting is supported from the side walls. Its astonishing, weighty columns and the walls surrounding the altar were fractured in a fierce fire after the Revolution, giving the masonry an incredible, organic cave-like feel.

ARRIVAL AND INFORMATION — GRASSE

By bus Grasse's *gare routière* is on place de la Buanderie, just north of the old town.

Destinations Le-Bar-sur-Loup (9 daily; 17min); Cagnes (every 20–45min; 45min); Cannes (every 15–30min; 40min–1hr); Digne (1–2 daily; 2hr 25min); Mougins (every 20–30min; 35min); Nice (every 20–45min; 1hr 30min).

By train Trains from Cannes (roughly hourly; 30min) arrive at Grasse's *gare SNCF*, south of the *vieille ville*; it's a stiff walk uphill, so take the Funix shuttle bus (Mon–Sat every 15min; €1.50) to reach the centre of town.

Tourist office At the *gare routière*, place de la Buanderie (May, June & Sept Mon–Fri 9am–6pm, Sat & Sun 10am–1pm & 2–5pm; July & Aug Mon–Sat 9am–7pm, Sun 10am–7; Oct–April Mon–Fri 9am–1pm & 2–5pm, Sat 10am–1pm & 2–5pm; ⓣ 04 93 36 66 66, ⓦ grasse.fr).

ACCOMMODATION
SEE MAP PAGE 331

The fact that Grasse sprawls over an extended and very hilly urban area means that it would be preferable to stay right in the heart of town. However, not only does the centre have surprisingly few **hotels**, but some of the few there are best avoided. Many visitors choose to stay instead in more rural locations nearby.

Bastide Saint Antoine 48 av Henri-Dunant ✆04 93 70 94 94, ⓦjacques-chibois.com. Gorgeous and extremely luxurious country-house hotel, 1km south of the centre, that's best known for its restaurant (see below). Its nine rooms and seven even fancier suites cost up to €1000; even breakfast will cost you the price of a midday meal. €340

Bellaudière 78 av Pierre Ziller ✆04 93 36 02 57, ⓦlabellaudiere.com. Two-star *Logis de France* hotel enjoying long-distance sea views from the slopes 3km east of town. Set in an eighteenth-century farmhouse, it has seventeen simple, good-value rooms and a nice terrace restaurant. €89

Elixir rue Martine Carol ✆04 93 70 70 70, ⓦbestwestern-elixir-grasse.com. Best western hotel in Les Quatre Chemins near the Fabrique des Fleurs (see page 332), with standard issue modern rooms, a restaurant and a large swimming pool. €135

Relais de Peyloubet 65 chemin de la Plâtrière ✆06 16 90 67 39, ⓦrelais-peyloubet.com.fr. Five very comfortable B&B rooms and suites, in an eighteenth-century *bastide* perched on a hillside 2km east of town, with magnificent views, a large pool, and barbecue facilities in summer. €120

EATING
SEE MAP PAGE 331

Old Grasse is disappointingly short of good **restaurants**, though one or two hidden gems are tucked away in the lanes. As for **bars**, there a couple of lively spots on the place aux Aires; sitting outside here makes a very pleasant way to spend a summer evening, and offers the best chance to meet the locals.

L'Auberge de Provence 2 place St Donat, Plascassier ✆04 93 42 40 83. Located in the village of Plascassier just to the southeast of Grasse on the D4, this bright airy restaurant serves up traditional Provençal cooking with a lunch *menu* at €15 and dinner *menu* at €27. Mon, Tues, Thurs & Sun noon–2pm, Fri & Sat noon–2pm & 7–9.30pm.

Au Comptoir 9 rue Dominique Conte ✆04 93 36 90 25. Lively little *bar à vins* on the fringe of the *vieille ville*, with a chalked-up selection of tapas and sharing platters (around €12) to soak up the wines. Tues–Sat 11am–11pm.

Bastide Saint Antoine 48 av Henri-Dunant ✆04 93 70 94 94, ⓦjacques-chibois.com. The best place to eat in Grasse is the Michelin-starred restaurant at this elegant small hotel, which serves *cuisine gourmande* with a Provençal twist in dishes such as spelt risotto with prawns and squid, shellfish foam and saffron. *Menus* €66 (at lunch) or from €105. Daily noon–2.30pm & 8–10pm; closed early Nov to early Dec.

SHOPPING
SEE MAP PAGE 331

Guy Bouchara 14 rue Marcel-Journet ✆04 93 40 07 29, ⓦguybouchara.com. Artisan *parfumier* in the old town, with two signature fragrances – Théosiris and l'Eau de Grasse. You can also visit their museum and atelier on rte de Cannes a little way out of town. Boutique March–Oct daily 9.30am–7pm; atelier daily 10am–7pm.

Maison Venturini 1 rue Marcel-Journet ✆04 93 36 20 47. *Confiserie* where you can buy *fougassettes* – a sweet flatbread flavoured with orange blossom (€1.80). It also sells candied fruits, candied rose petals and Marseille-style *navettes* (€3 for 100g). Tues–Sat 9am–12.30pm & 3–6.30pm.

Around Grasse

The main highlight of the countryside surrounding Grasse is the attractive village of **Cabris**, but two routes out of the area offer wonderful scenic views. The **Route Napoléon** heads northwest through the mountains towards Castellane, while to the northeast the gorges of the **Loup river** pass the cliff-hanging stronghold of **Gourdon**, and **Le-Bar-sur-Loup**, home to an intriguing medieval chapel. East of the river, the hillside road towards Vence holds one final treat, the delightful village of **Tourrettes-sur-Loup**.

7

OUTDOOR ACTIVITIES IN THE GORGES DU LOUP

Several outfits organize day and half-day **canyoning** expeditions in the spectacular setting of the **Gorges du Loup**, catering for a broad range of abilities and experience. Expect to pay around €50 for a half day's canyoning. Some also offer **via ferrata** and **rock-climbing**. For information (in French) and maps of hiking trails in and around the Gorges du Loup – several of which start from Gourdon – consult the website ⓦ randoxygene.org.

ACTIVITY TOUR OPERATORS
Altitude 06 Mougins ☎ 06 09 55 80 67, ⓦ altitude06.com.

Funtrip Tourrettes-sur-Loup ☎ 06 19 66 03 65, ⓦ funtrip.fr.
Les Geckos Vence ☎ 06 75 24 93 40, ⓦ lesgeckos.fr.

Cabris

CABRIS, 6km southwest of Grasse, has all the trappings of a picture-postcard village: a ruined château providing panoramas from the Lac de St-Cassien to the Îles de Lérins, sometimes as far as Corsica; arty residents who decamped here from Grasse; and no shortage of *immobiliers* trading on fat local property prices. It's a lovely place to stroll around for an hour or two, but most visitors press on to the region's larger towns.

Route Napoléon

Built in the 1930s to commemorate the path taken by the emperor in March 1815 after his escape from Elba, the D6085 north from Grasse is known as the **Route Napoléon**. The road doesn't follow the imperial boot-tracks precisely, going far off course in places, but it serves a useful purpose. After several kilometres of zigzagging bends you get fantastic views back to Grasse, its basin and the coast.

The first village you come to – **ST-VALLIER-DE-THIEY**, 12km from Grasse – holds some prehistoric dolmens and tumuli. From here, the Route Napoléon heads, almost uninterrupted by settlements, towards Castellane (see page 223). Wayside stalls sell honey and perfume; each little hamlet has a hotel-restaurant; and every so often you see a commemorative plaque carved with Napoleon's winged eagle.

Gorges du Loup

Of the two alternative routes that follow the stunning **Gorges du Loup**, the lower, along the east bank of the Loup, is the more compelling. Both leave the main D2085 at **Châteauneuf-Grasse**, 6km east from Grasse.

Le Bar-sur-Loup

The lower Gorges du Loup road, the D2210, passes through the pretty hillside village of **LE BAR-SUR-LOUP** after just 3.5km. The little **Église de St-Jacques** here contains an altarpiece attributed to the Niçois painter Louis Bréa, while a tiny but detailed fifteenth-century *Danse Macabre*, painted on a wooden panel, shows courtly dancers being picked off by Death's arrows, and their souls being thrown by devils into the toothed and tongued mouth of hell.

From **Pont du Loup** immediately to the north, you can follow the **gorge road** itself, the D6, through dark, narrow twists of rock beneath cliffs that look as if they might tumble at any minute, through the sounds of furiously churning water, to corners that appear to have no way out.

Gourdon

The higher of the two roads from Châteauneuf-Grasse, the D3, climbs 8km along the northern balcony of the gorges to tiny **GOURDON**, a *village perché* teetering on the very brink of the abyss. The village itself is swamped in souvenir shops, but the view from place Victoria at the top is extraordinary.

Tourrettes-sur-Loup

TOURRETTES-SUR-LOUP is an artisans' paradise, preserving just the right balance between crumbly attractiveness and modern comforts. The three towers from which the village derives its name – and the rose-stone houses that cling to the high escarpment – almost all date from the fifteenth century; the best views can be had from the curious rock shelf known as Les Loves, just above the town.

The oldest and most charming part of the village is accessed via two gateways that lead south from the main place de la Libération, which adjoins the D2210. Beyond the fine portals, the Grande Rue loops between the two, lined with expensive ateliers selling clothes, sculpture, jewellery, leather, fine art and the like. A viewing platform at the southern end commands a majestic prospect all the way to the Mediterranean.

During Tourrettes' famous **violet festival**, on the last two days of February, floats are decorated with thousands of blooms. Violets, which thrive in the mild microclimate, are grown here in vast quantities for the perfume trade as well as for subsidiary cottage industries such as old-fashioned candied violets; be sure to try the local violet-flavoured ice cream while you're here.

INFORMATION

AROUND GRASSE

ST-VALLIER-DE-THIEY
Tourist office 101 Allée Charles Bonome (Mon–Fri 9am––6pm , Sat 9am–noon & 3–6pm; also Sun 10am–noon in July & Aug; ☎ 04 89 04 52 60, ⓦ saintvallierdethiey.com).

TOURRETTES-SUR-LOUP
Tourist office 2 place de la Libération (April, May, June & Sept Mon–Sat 9am–1pm & 2–5.30pm; July & Aug daily 9am–1pm & 2–6.30pm; Oct–March Mon–Sat 9am–1pm & 2–5pm; ☎ 04 93 24 18 93, ⓦ tourrettessurloup.com).

ACCOMMODATION AND EATING

CABRIS
★ **Auberge du Vieux Château** Place du Panorama ☎ 04 93 60 50 12, ⓦ aubergeduvieuxchateau.com. With just four tasteful rooms, this lovely hotel is a great place to stay, with wonderful views, though dinner *menus* in its high-class dining room (closed Mon & Tues; July & Aug open Tues eve) start at €49. **€89**
Petit Prince 15 rue Frédéric-Mistral ☎ 04 93 60 63 14. Traditional delicacies at this warm and welcoming restaurant, overlooking a park lined with chestnut trees, include tripe *à la provençale* with steamed potatoes (€17). *Menu* €28. Mon, Tues & Fri–Sun noon–2pm & 7–9.30pm, Wed noon–2pm.

ST-VALLIER-DE-THIEY
Le Préjoly Place Rougière ☎ 04 93 60 03 20, ⓦ leprejoly. com. Presentable, reasonably priced two star hotel at the entrance to the village. Some of the en-suite rooms have large mountain-view terraces. **€86**

TOURRETTES-SUR-LOUP
Bistro Gourmand Clovis 21 Grand Rue ☎ 04 93 58 87 04, ⓦ clovisgourmand.fr. Largely organic Michelin-starred restaurant in the historic core, using such choice ingredients as Perigord truffles and Andalucian figs. *Formules* from €40, tasting *menu* €75. Mon 12.30–2pm & 7.30–9pm, Thurs, Fri & Sun 12.30–2pm & 7.30–9.30pm, Sat 7.30–9.30pm.
★ **Histoires de Bastide** 26 rue de la Bourgade ☎ 06 67 79 08 73, ⓦ histoiresdebastide.com. Classy *chambres d'hôtes* on the fringe of the old village with stunning views, a pool, and just four simple but stylish rooms, two of which have private jacuzzi. **€170**
Médiéval 6 Grand' Rue ☎ 04 93 59 31 63. Good restaurant in the historic core, serving the likes of lamb *noisette* with basil and garlic and rabbit *terrine* with baby vegetables on traditional Provençal *menus* at €20, €25 and €35. Mon, Tues & Fri–Sun noon–2pm & 7–9pm.
Rives du Loup 2666b rte de la Colle ☎ 04 93 24 15 65, ⓦ rivesduloup.com. Fancy three-star campsite – just a

couple of kilometres south of the village on the other side of the gorges but 9km by road – with a restaurant, snack bar and pool, and offering hotel-style rooms as well as tent pitches and mobile homes. Closed Oct–March. Camping **€28**; doubles **€90**

Vence

Sheltered by the Pre-Alpes that rise to its rear, the delightful hill town of **VENCE**, 10km up from the sea, is unusual in having an appealing modern quarter that for once complements rather than simply engulfs its ravishing historic core, **Vieux Vence**. It helps, of course, that **Henri Matisse** chose the new town as the site of his magnificent **Chapelle du Rosaire**, but more generally the bustle of the boulevards outside the walls, and particularly the lively main place du Grand-Jardin, with its cafés, carousel and summer concerts, make a pleasing contrast to the tranquil ancient lanes of the old town. In July, during **Les Nuits du Sud** (ⓦnuitsdusud.com), big-name Latin, Brazilian and World musicians perform open-air concerts on the *place*, mostly on Thursday, Friday and Saturday evenings.

Brief history

Vence was founded by a Ligurian tribe, the Nerusii. They put up stiff opposition to Augustus Caesar, but to no avail; Roman funeral inscriptions and votive offerings remain embedded in the fabric of its cathedral. During the Dark Ages, the local bishop, **St Véran**, organized the city's defence. The Saracens, however, subsequently razed both the town and St Véran's cathedral to the ground. Thereafter, Vence was plagued until the Revolution by rivalry between its barons and its bishops.

In the 1920s the town became a haven for **painters and writers**: André Gide, Raoul Dufy, D.H. Lawrence (who died here in 1930 while being treated for tuberculosis

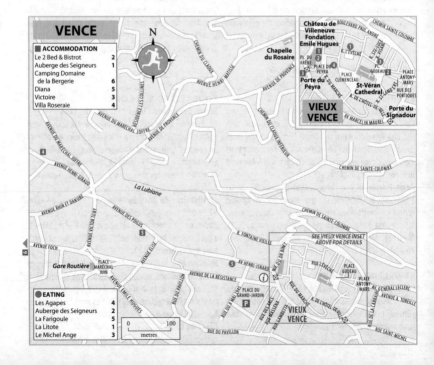

contracted in England) and Marc Chagall were all long-term visitors. Matisse moved here towards the end of World War II, to escape the Allied bombing of the coast.

Vieux Vence

With its ancient houses, gateways, fountains and chapels, the diminutive old town of **Vieux Vence** is absolutely exquisite. It remains encircled by medieval ramparts, though they're not so much walls as the backs of people's homes. While holding its fair share of chic boutiques and arty restaurants, it also has an everyday feel, with ordinary townsfolk going about their business, seeking out the best market deals, and stopping for a chat and a *petit verre* at little cafés.

More or less untouched since the twelfth century, the **Porte du Peyra**, and the tower that surmounts it, provide the best entry into Vieux Vence. **Place du Peyra**, within the walls, focuses on the town's oldest fountain. The narrow, cobbled **rue du Marché** off to the right is a busy street of tiny and delectable food shops, all with stalls (and all closed Mon). Behind it, **place Clemenceau**, centring on the cathedral, hosts a Tuesday and Friday clothes **market**.

East of the cathedral is **place Godeau** which is almost totally medieval save for the column in the fountain, presented to the city, along with its twin on place du Grand-Jardin, by the Republic of Marseille during the third century. Follow rue St-Lambert and rue de l'Hôtel-de-Ville down from here to reach the original eastern gate, the **Porte du Signadour**, outside which another fifteenth-century fountain on place Antony-Mars celebrates the town's expansion.

St-Véran Cathedral

Place Godeau • Free

St-Véran Cathedral is a tenth- and eleventh-century replacement for the church over which St Véran presided in the fifth century, which had in turn been built on the ruins of a Roman temple to Mars and Cybele. Like so many of the oldest Provençal churches, it's basically square in shape, with an austere exterior. Although centuries of subsequent alterations have left none of the clear lines of Romanesque architecture, fragments of its Merovingian and Carolingian predecessors, and of Roman Vence, still remain.

In the chapel beneath the belfry, two reliefs from the old church show birds, grapes and an eagle, while more stone birds, flowers, swirls of leaves and interlocking lines are embedded in the walls and pillars throughout the church. The purported **tomb of St Véran**, in the southern chapel nearest the altar, is a pre-Christian sarcophagus. Later adornments include some superb, irreverent Gothic carved **choir stalls**, housed alongside powerfully human, if crude, polychrome wooden statues of the Calvary, up above the western end of the nave. In the baptistry, a Chagall **mosaic** depicts the infant Moses being saved from the Nile by the Pharaoh's daughter.

Château de Villeneuve Fondation Emile Hugues

2 place du Frêne • Tues–Sun 11am–6pm • €6 • ☎ 04 93 58 15 78, ⓦ vence.fr/musee-de-vence-fondation-emile-hugues

Vence's castle, the **Château de Villeneuve Fondation Emile Hugues,** was built just outside the city walls during a calm period of fifteenth-century expansion. Rebuilt in the seventeenth century, it was renovated in 1992 to become a beautiful space for displaying modern and contemporary art. Each year sees a different themed exhibition. Out in front, **place du Frêne** is named for its 450-year-old ash tree.

7

MATISSE AND THE CHAPELLE DU ROSAIRE

In 1941, while convalescing from an operation for cancer, Matisse advertised for a "young and pretty nurse". Having developed a strong rapport with successful applicant Monique Bourgeois, who also posed for him, he bought a home in Vence after she joined the Dominican convent here, in 1943, as Sister Jacques-Marie. Although he did not consider himself a Christian, Matisse agreed to help the young nun with the new convent chapel, the **Chapelle du Rosaire**. As he later put it "my only religion is the love of the work to be created, the love of creation, and great sincerity".

The artist moved back to his huge rooms in Nice in 1949, to work on the designs using the same scale as the chapel. A photograph shows him in bed, drawing studies for the figure of St-Dominic on the wall with a paintbrush tied to a long bamboo stick. It's not clear how much this bamboo technique was a practical solution to his frailty, and how much a solution to an artistic problem. Some critics suggest Matisse wanted to pare down his art to the basic essentials of human communication, and thus needed to remove his own stylistic signature from the lines.

Matisse's Chapelle du Rosaire

466 av Henri-Matisse • March–Oct Tues, Thurs & Fri 10am–noon & 2–6pm, Wed & Sat 2–6pm; Nov–Feb Tues, Thurs & Fri 10am–noon & 2–5pm, Wed & Sat 2–5pm • €7 • ☎ 04 93 58 03 26, ⓦ chapellematisse.com

It's worth travelling a very long way indeed to see the beautiful and profoundly moving **Chapelle du Rosaire**, which **Henri Matisse** spent four of the final years of his life designing in every meticulous detail; be sure to time your visit to Vence to coincide with its limited opening hours. A simple modern structure, the chapel is inconspicuous but for its blue-and-white tiled roof, topped by a wrought-iron cross. Matisse was too ill to attend its dedication in 1951, but in a statement read out at the ceremony he said "in spite of all its imperfections, I consider it as my masterpiece".

The **murals** on the chapel walls – faceless black outlines on white tiles – leave some visitors disappointed, not finding the "Matisse" they expect. The east wall is the most shocking; it shows the *Stations of the Cross*, each one numbered and scrawled as if it were an angry doodle on a pad. The full-length windows in the west and south walls are the aspect of the chapel most likely to live up to expectations. They provide the only source of colour, which changes with the day's light through opaque yellow, transparent green and watery blue, playing across the black-and-white murals, floor and ceiling.

Despite the prominent signs requesting silence, the chapel repeatedly fills with excited, chattering tour groups. A nun is usually on hand to calm things down, and point out the symbolism of every aspect of Matisse's vision: the overall configuration of the chapel; the stone of the east-facing altar, chosen for its resemblance to bread; the raw anguish of the figures; the door of the confessional, alluding to the artist's trips to Morocco; and the chasubles, crucifix and candelabra.

Matisse was even responsible for the various resplendently colourful silk **vestments**, which match different moments in the liturgical calendar; ideally you'd see them worn by the priest at Sunday Mass, but during the week they're displayed in the gallery beyond, which also holds a gift shop.

ARRIVAL AND INFORMATION
VENCE

By bus Vence's *gare routière* is at place Maréchal Juin, a short walk from the tourist office.
Destinations Nice (every 20–50min; 55min–1hr 15min) via St-Paul-de-Vence (5min) and Cagnes (26min).
By car The best place to park is the large underground car park beneath place du Grand-Jardin.

Tourist office Place du Grand-Jardin (April–June, Sept & Oct Mon–Sat 9am–6pm; July & Aug Mon–Sat 9am–7pm, Sun 10am–6pm; Nov–March Mon 1–5pm, Tues–Sat 9am–5pm; ☎ 04 93 58 06 38, ⓦ vence-tourisme.fr).
Bike rental Tendances Cycles, Av Henri-Giraud (☎ 04 93 32 59 92).

ACCOMMODATION   SEE MAP PAGE 336

Home to an excellent range of well-priced **hotels**, Vence makes a popular and peaceful base for visitors who plan to explore not just the town itself, and the surrounding hills, but all the way down to the coast as well.

Le 2 Bed & Bistrot 2 rue des Portiques ☎04 93 24 42 58, ⓦle2avence.fr. Four stylish a/c rooms – including a junior suite and a loft with private roof terrace that gives stunning views over the surrounding hills – in a *chambres d'hotes* in the heart of Vieux Vence, above a bistro. **€108**

Auberge des Seigneurs 1 rue du Dr Binet ☎04 93 58 04 24, ⓦauberge-seigneurs.fr. Lovely, very friendly seventeenth-century inn, set into the walls of Vieux Vence, with six rooms named after artists associated with the town. The restaurant is superb, too (see p.339). Closed mid-Dec to mid-Jan. **€90**

Camping Domaine de la Bergerie 1330 chemin de la Sine ☎04 93 58 09 36, ⓦcamping-domaine delabergerie.com. Three-star campsite 3km west of town off the road to Tourrettes-sur-Loup, with a pool and a

pétanque pitch. They also rent small chalet-like pods (€42). Closed mid-Oct to late March. **€28**

Diana 79 av des Poilus ☎04 93 58 28 56, ⓦhotel-diana.fr. Smart, family-run three-star hotel in a quiet and convenient location just 200m west of the centre, and enjoying lovely views. Comfortable rooms, some with balconies and half with kitchenettes, and an open-air jacuzzi. **€135**

Victoire 4 place du Grand-Jardin ☎04 93 24 15 54, ⓦhotel-victoire.com. Soundproofed, very central three-star hotel beside the tourist office on the main square in the modern town, and offering spruced-up rooms at reasonable prices. **€90**

Villa Roseraie Av Henri-Giraud ☎04 93 58 02 20, ⓦvillaroseraie.com. Three-star comforts in a villa that dates from 1929, with a palm-fringed pool, a garden, private parking and a bar. The rooms are decorated in Provençal style and some have private patio or terrace. **€104**

EATING   SEE MAP PAGE 336

The squares and lanes of **Vieux Vence** abound in restaurants, bars and cafés in all price ranges, and there are also several appealing alternatives in the newer streets beyond.

Les Agapes 4 place Clemenceau ☎04 93 58 50 64, ⓦles-agapes.net. Lively, sophisticated old-town restaurant, in a quiet spot close to the cathedral, serving dishes like green asparagus panna cotta with parmesan emulsion; lunch *formule* €15–24, *menu gourmand* €35. June–Sept Tues–Sat noon–2pm & 7–10pm; Oct–May Tues–Sat noon–2pm & 7–9.30pm.

★ **Auberge des Seigneurs** 1 rue du Dr Binet ☎04 93 58 04 24, ⓦauberge-seigneurs.fr. The restaurant of this lovely hotel (see above), which spreads onto a panoramic terrace just outside the walls, serves a fine array of Provençal specialities (*menus* from €25 at lunch, gourmet *menu* €36). Mid-Jan to mid-Dec Tues–Sat noon–1.30pm & 7–9pm.

La Farigoule 15 av Henri-Isnard ☎04 93 58 01 27, ⓦlafarigoule-vence.fr. This very pretty restaurant just outside the old town – with white limed beams inside and a courtyard garden – is a good bet for a special meal, with

mains in the €30 bracket and serving Côtes de Provence wines. Wed–Sun noon–1pm & 7.30–9pm; closed late Nov to Christmas.

★ **La Litote** 5 rue l'Évêché ☎04 93 24 27 82, ⓦlalitote-vence.com. The outdoor tables of this lovely, secluded old-town restaurant fill the delightful little place de l'Évêché, beneath its single spreading tree. Changing daily chalked-up selections here might include sea bream with apple, celery and a cider *jus*; prices start at €18 for two courses at lunch, €22 for three. Unusually, they also have a specific vegan *menu* priced from €29, featuring the likes of coconut curry and dark chocolate with blood orange and pecan nuts. Tues–Sun noon–2pm & 7–9.30pm; closed early Nov to early Dec.

Le Michel Ange 1 place Godeau ☎04 93 58 32 56. Tiny place in Vieux Vence, in a pretty location close to the cathedral with seats out on the square, serving resolutely straightforward Niçois dishes at fair prices, with *menus* from €17 and a *plat du jour* at €14. Tues–Thurs & Sun noon–2pm, Fri & Sat noon–2pm & 7–9.30pm.

St-Paul-de-Vence

The beautiful fortified village of **ST-PAUL-DE-VENCE** squeezes onto a hilltop just 3km south of Vence towards Cagnes, although the combination of twisting roads and undulating hills can make it unexpectedly hard to find. While the village itself is a delight, and is usually crammed with visitors throughout the summer, its popularity owes as much to the **Fondation Maeght**, a wonderful museum of modern art and sculpture tucked into the woods nearby, as it does to its medieval core. As most visitors just come for the day, St-Paul is a very quiet place to spend a night.

7

St-Paul stands on its own separate eminence alongside the D7. You can't miss its most famous landmark, right outside the walls on the only approach road – the **Colombe d'Or**, a hotel-restaurant (see page 341) that's celebrated not so much for its food as for the art on its walls, donated in lieu of payment for meals by the then-impoverished Braque, Picasso, Matisse and Bonnard in the lean years following World War I.

The walled village

Beyond the *Colombe d'Or* hotel, you pass through the ramparts to find a miniature jewel of a village, where the old stone cottages that line the winding lanes hold around seventy contemporary **art galleries and ateliers**. Most of those are concentrated along the central rue Grande, so it's normally possible to escape the crowds simply by exploring any alleyway that catches your eye, or heading for the walls.

Up on the top of the hill, facing the stark whitewashed belfry of the Église Collégiale across place de l'Église, a peculiar little **museum** holds dioramas of local history (daily: May–Sept 10am–12.30pm & 2–6pm; Oct–April 10.30am–12.30pm & 2–4pm; €4). At the far end of the village, a small **cemetery** (daily: summer 7.30am–8pm; winter 8am–5pm) outside the ramparts, perched above the fields, holds the simple grave of **Marc Chagall**.

Fondation Maeght

623 chemin des Gardettes • Daily: July & Aug 10am–7pm; Sept–June 10am–6pm • €16 • ☎ 04 93 32 81 63, Ⓦ fondation-maeght.com

The remarkable **Fondation Maeght**, ten minutes' walk west of the village, encapsulates the link between the Côte d'Azur and modern European art. It was established in 1964 by art collectors Aimé and Marguerite Maeght, who knew all the great artists who worked in Provence. Spanish architect José Luis Sert designed the building, and it was decorated by assorted painters, sculptors, potters and designers. Both structure and ornamentation were conceived as a single project, to create a museum in which the concepts of entrance, exit and *sens de la visite* would not apply.

Once through the gates, any idea of dutifully checking off a catalogue of priceless museum pieces crumbles. Giacometti's *Cat* is sometimes stalking along the edge of the grass, Miró's *Egg* smiles above a pond, and his totemed *Fork* is outlined against the sky. It's hard not to be bewitched by the Calder mobile swinging over watery tiles, by Léger's flowers, birds and a bench on a sunlit rough stone wall, by Zadkine's and Arp's metallic forms hovering between the pine trunks, or by the clanking tubular fountain by Pol Bury. And all this is just a portion of the garden.

The **building** itself is superb: multilevelled and flooded with daylight, with galleries opening on to terraces and courtyards, blurring the boundaries between inside and outside. It houses an impressive collection, including sculpture, ceramics, paintings and graphic art by Braque, Miró, Chagall, Léger, Kandinsky, Dubuffet, Bonnard, Derain and Matisse, along with work by more recent artists. Not all the works are exhibited at any one time, however, and in summer, when the main annual exhibition is mounted, only those that make up the decoration of the building are on show.

ARRIVAL AND INFORMATION	**ST-PAUL-DE-VENCE**

By bus St-Paul is on bus route #400 between Nice and Vence, via Cagnes. There are two stops: to reach the Fondation from the first, beside the roundabout on the way up from Nice, head left up the hill; from the village centre, head uphill along the steep street opposite the village entrance.

Destinations Nice (every 20–50min; 1hr 3min); Vence (every 20–50min; 10min).

By car or bike Parking is limited and expensive; if you're visiting both the Fondation and the village for the day, you could park at the Fondation, which is clearly signposted off both the D7 and the D2 – though be aware that the car park there closes not long after the Fondation itself.

Tourist office 2 rue Grande, just inside the walled village (June–Sept Mon–Fri 10am–7pm, Sat & Sun 10am–1pm & 2–7pm; Oct–May Mon–Fri 10am–6pm, Sat & Sun 10am–1pm & 2–6pm; ☎04 93 32 86 95, ⊛saint-pauldevence. com).

ACCOMMODATION AND EATING

As St-Paul-de-Vence is primarily a day-trip destination, it has many more places to eat than to sleep. You'll need to book well in advance if you want to stay overnight in summer; if you manage to find a **room**, though, you'll find it delightfully tranquil once the crowds have gone. As for **restaurants**, most are firmly poised at the more expensive end of the spectrum, but a few reasonably priced options are scattered through the village.

La Colombe d'Or Place du Général-de-Gaulle ☎04 93 32 80 02, ⊛www.la-colombe-dor.com. Famous for its stellar collection of modern art, the *Colombe d'Or* also has a *restaurant gastronomique*, valet parking, a heated outdoor pool, sauna and gardens, plus thirteen rooms and twelve apartments. Closed Nov–Christmas. **€330**

Hostellerie Les Remparts de St-Paul 72 rue Grande ☎04 93 24 10 47, ⊛hostellerielesremparts.com. The least expensive central option, in the heart of the village, occupies a nicely shaded terrace with huge views out over the hills. There are eight pretty but far from luxurious rooms, and a good-value restaurant (closed Mon outside high season). Closed Nov to late Dec. **€60**

La Sierra Rempart Ouest, just below rue Grande ☎04 93 32 82 89. Anything from salads (from €16) to pizzas (around €12) and chalked-up Niçois specials served on a lovely garden terrace beside the western ramparts. Daily: June–Sept noon–2.30pm & 7–10.30pm; Oct–May Mon–Wed & Fri–Sun noon–6pm.

7

Nice and the eastern Riviera

344 Nice

361 The Arrière-Pays Niçois

366 The Corniche Inférieure

371 The Moyenne Corniche

372 The Grande Corniche

375 Monaco

382 Menton

388 Around Menton

COURS SALEYA MAIN MARKET

Nice and the eastern Riviera

East of the River Var, the Riviera is subtly different. For much of its history the coastline between Nice and the Italian border was part of the Kingdom of Savoy, only becoming securely French in 1860. Even today a certain Italian influence lingers, not least in the cooking of Nice and in the architecture of Vieux Nice, Villefranche and Menton. The landscape changes, too: east of Nice the Alpes-Maritimes come crashing down to the sea and the coastline is often thrillingly scenic. The contrast between the littoral and the interior is stark: opulent villas dot the coast's green hillsides and jostle for the best position on its headlands, while behind the coast the landscape is rugged and unspoiled and the villages timeless in their appeal.

The Riviera's largest city, **Nice** became fashionable as a winter resort in the eighteenth century, as aristocratic visitors – many of them invalids – made the journey south to escape the brutal northern winters. Right up to World War I they built their villas here or sojourned in the opulent palace hotels, most of which have long since been converted to apartments, though their architecture remains and often lends the city an appealing, eccentric face. Gradually, other resorts grew to rival Nice, each with its own speciality: **Menton** was the destination for tuberculosis sufferers; **Monte Carlo** in the comic-opera principality of Monaco boasted its smart casino.

After World War I many of the old aristocratic visitors never returned: many had died, others were now impoverished or scattered by revolution and war. In their place came artists and intellectuals: **Matisse** and **Dufy** made Nice their home, where **Isadora Duncan** met her end; **Cocteau**, meanwhile, favoured Villefranche, and **Somerset Maugham** Cap Ferrat. The introduction of *congés payés* (paid holiday) in 1936 brought thousands of ordinary French people to a coast that had hitherto been an elite retreat. The democratization continued after the war, and though the marriage in 1956 of film star Grace Kelly to Prince Rainier of Monaco set the seal on the Riviera's glamour image, the reality was increasingly different. It's impossible to picture today the bucolic coast as described by the author Tobias Smollett in the eighteenth century.

Nevertheless, there's much to enjoy: the food, vivacious street life and superb culture of **Nice**, and the unspoiled **villages** in the city's hinterland; the thrills of the **corniches** along the mountainous coast between Nice and Menton; and – last but not least – the vicarious pleasures of the independent principality of **Monaco**.

Nice

The capital of the Riviera and fifth-largest town in France, **NICE** lives off a glittering reputation, its former glamour now gently faded. First popularized by English aristocrats in the eighteenth century, Nice reached its zenith in the *belle époque* of the late nineteenth century.

Today, the city has retained its historical styles almost intact: the medieval labyrinth of **Vieux Nice**, the Italianate facades of **modern Nice** and the rich exuberance of *fin-de-siècle* residences dating from when the city was Europe's most fashionable winter retreat. It also preserves mementoes from the **Roman** period, when the region was ruled from here, and from the era of its Greek founders. Nice may be a politically conservative – at times even reactionary – city, but it does not rest on its laurels, as a recent extensive **refurbishment** of its public spaces and the construction of a **tramway**

VILLA EPHRUSSI

Highlights

❶ Vieux Nice From the flower market at dawn to bar-hopping in the early hours, Nice's mellow, Mediterranean heart buzzes with street life night and day. See page 347

❷ Musée Chagall, Nice Custom-built to house Marc Chagall's Biblical Message paintings, the Musée Chagall is unmissable for fans of the artist's work. See page 355

❸ Niçois villages Explore craggy Peillon and unspoiled Lucéram, the *villages perchés* of Nice's wild and underpopulated hinterland, where locals still live off the land, producing olives, goat's cheese, herbs and vegetables. See pages 362 and 364

❹ Villa Ephrussi Visit this handsome mansion and its exquisite gardens to find out how the Riviera's aristocratic other half used to live. See page 369

❺ Plage Mala Relax on this secluded, idyllic Riviera beach in classy Cap d'Ail, just a leisurely stroll along the coast from the hustle and bustle of Monaco. See page 371

❻ The Casino at Monte Carlo Break the bank – or merely admire the *belle époque* architectural and decorative opulence – at the world's most famous casino. See page 375

HIGHLIGHTS ARE MARKED ON THE MAP ON PAGE 346

shows. The many **museums**, meanwhile, are a treat for art lovers: within France, Nice is second only to Paris for the sheer range.

Far too large to be considered simply a resort, Nice has all the advantages and disadvantages of a major Mediterranean city: superb cultural facilities, wonderful street life and excellent shopping, eating and drinking, but also a high crime rate, graffiti blight and horrendous traffic. Yet for all that, the sun shines, the sea sparkles and a thousand sprinklers keep the lawns and flowerbeds lush. On summer nights, when the old town buzzes with contented crowds, it's hard not to be utterly seduced by the place.

Parc de la Colline du Château

Daily: April–Sept 8.30am–8pm; Oct–March 8.30am–6pm • Free • Take the lift by the Tour Bellanda at the eastern end of Quai des États-Unis (April, May & Sept 8am–7pm; June–Aug 8am–8pm; Oct–March 8am–6pm; free), climb montée du Château from the old town or take the tourist train from place Masséna (10am–5/6/7pm; €10)

For initial orientation, with brilliant sea and city views, fresh air and a cooling waterfall, head for the **Parc de la Colline du Château**. There's no fortress here today; it was destroyed by the French in the early eighteenth century when Nice belonged to Savoy. This is, however, where Nice began as the ancient Greek city of Nikea – hence the mosaics and stone vases in mock Grecian style. Excavations have revealed Greek

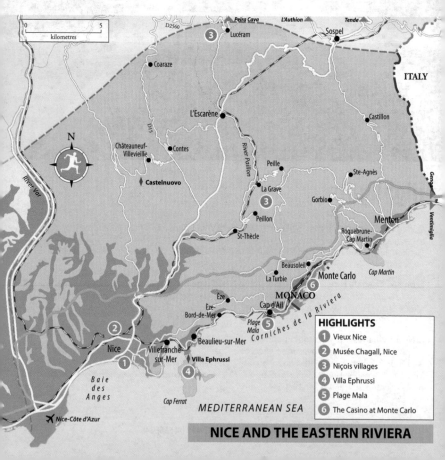

NICE AND THE EASTERN RIVIERA

HIGHLIGHTS

1. Vieux Nice
2. Musée Chagall, Nice
3. Niçois villages
4. Villa Ephrussi
5. Plage Mala
6. The Casino at Monte Carlo

NICE ORIENTATION

Shadowed by mountains that curve down to the Mediterranean east of its port, Nice divides fairly clearly between old and new. **Vieux Nice**, the old town, groups about the hill of **Le Château**, its limits signalled by **boulevard Jean-Jaurès**, which was built along the course of the River Paillon.

Along the seafront, the celebrated **promenade des Anglais** runs a cool 5km until forced to curve inland by the sea-projecting runways of the airport. The central square, **place Masséna**, is at the bottom of the modern city's main street, **avenue Jean-Médecin**; to the north is the exclusive hillside suburb of **Cimiez**, while the port lies on the eastern side of **Le Château**.

and Roman levels beneath the foundations of the city's first, eleventh-century cathedral on the eastern side of the summit.

Rather than ruin-spotting, however, the real pleasure here lies in looking down on the scrambled rooftops and gleaming mosaic tiles of Vieux Nice, the yachts and fishing boats in the port on the eastern side, and along the sweep of the promenade des Anglais. In the **cemetery** to the north of the park are buried the two great Niçois revolutionaries, Giuseppe Garibaldi and Léon Gambetta, though casual visitors aren't particularly welcome. A moving Jewish war memorial includes an urn of ashes from the crematoria of Auschwitz.

Vieux Nice

Most of Nice's wonderful street life – and a fair amount of its street crime – is concentrated in the dense warren of medieval streets that make up **Vieux Nice**. Once considered little more than a slum, it has changed markedly over the years, yet despite decades of gradual gentrification, the teeming *quartier* is still very far from sanitized. It's an intriguing and often charming place, full of contradictions: churches of the most opulent Italianate Baroque rub shoulders with mean, scruffy alleyways where washing hangs high overhead, while the flipside of the elegant restaurant terraces and colourful markets is a dodgy undercurrent, particularly at night. Vieux Nice is, without doubt, the repository of Nice's Mediterranean soul, but though it has an almost Neapolitan vibrancy and chaos in high summer, it can seem eerie and deserted in winter once the tourists have departed.

The streets are too narrow for buses and much of it is effectively car- (though not necessarily scooter-) free. It's an area made for **walking**.

Place Rossetti

The central square of Vieux Nice is **place Rossetti**, where the soft-coloured Baroque **Cathédrale de Ste-Réparate** (Mon–Fri 9am–noon & 2–6pm, Sat 9am–noon & 2–7.30pm, Sun 9am–1pm & 3–6pm; free; ⓦ cathedrale-nice.fr) just manages to be visible from the eight narrow streets that meet here. There are cafés to relax in, with the choice of sun or shade, and a magical ice-cream parlour, *Fenocchio* (see page 359).

Cours Saleya

The real magnet of Vieux Nice is the **cours Saleya**, with its splendidly Baroque **Chapelle de la Miséricorde** (currently closed for renovation), and its adjacent places Pierre Gautier and Charles-Félix. These wide-open, sunlit spaces, lined with grandiloquent municipal buildings and Italianate chapels, are the site of the city's main **market** (see page 361), where there are gorgeous displays of fruit, vegetables, cheeses and sausages – along with cut and potted flowers and scented plants. Summer nights see café and restaurant tables filling the *cours* to create the Riviera's most animated free show.

Leading west off the *cours* is rue St-François-de-Paule, home to the suitably grand *belle époque* **Opéra**, which opened in 1885.

8

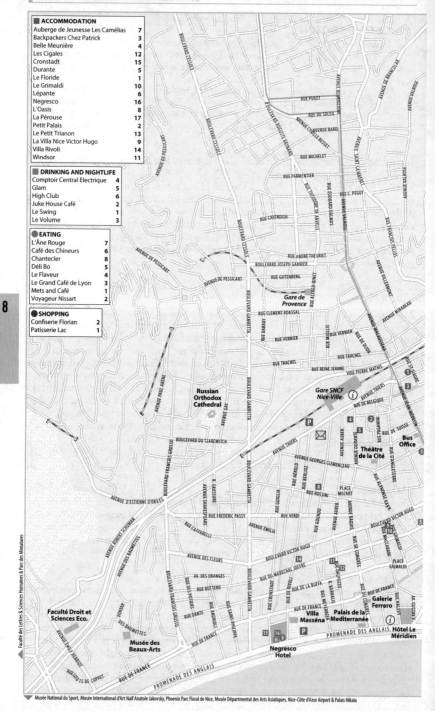

ACCOMMODATION

Auberge de Jeunesse Les Camélias	7
Backpackers Chez Patrick	3
Belle Meunière	4
Les Cigales	12
Cronstadt	15
Durante	5
Le Floride	1
Le Grimaldi	10
Lépante	6
Negresco	16
L'Oasis	8
La Pérouse	17
Petit Palais	2
Le Petit Trianon	13
La Villa Nice Victor Hugo	9
Villa Rivoli	14
Windsor	11

DRINKING AND NIGHTLIFE

Comptoir Central Electrique	4
Glam	5
High Club	6
Juke House Café	2
Le Swing	1
Le Volume	3

EATING

L'Âne Rouge	7
Café des Chineurs	6
Chantecler	8
Déli Bo	5
Le Flaveur	4
Le Grand Café de Lyon	3
Mets and Café	1
Voyageur Nissart	2

SHOPPING

Confiserie Florian	2
Patisserie Lac	1

8

Faculté des Lettres & Sciences Humaines & Parc des Miniatures

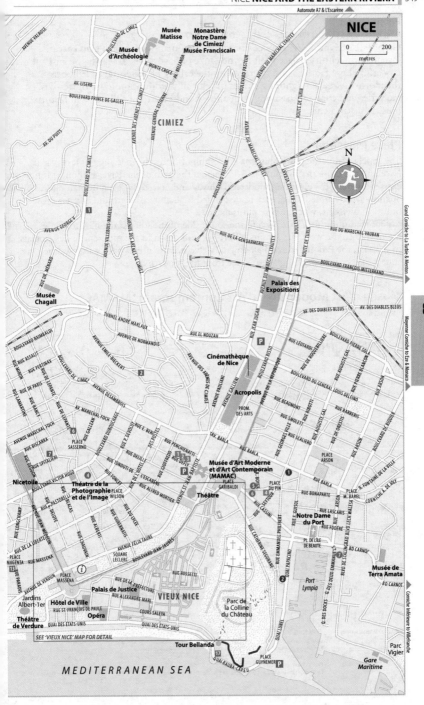

NICE

0   200
metres

Autoroute A7 & L'Escarène

AVENUE VALROSE

Musée Matisse

Monastère Notre Dame de Cimiez/ Musée Franciscain

Musée d'Archéologie

AVENUE DU MARÉCHAL LYAUTEY

BOULEVARD DE CIMIEZ

R. MONTE-CROCE

AV. BELLANDA

BOULEVARD PASTEUR

AV. LISERB

BOULEVARD PRINCE DE GALLES

AVENUE DES ARÈNES DE CIMIEZ

AVENUE ÉDOUARD ESTIENNE

AVENUE DU MARÉCHAL LYAUTEY

ROUTE DE TURIN

AV. DU PUITS

CIMIEZ

BOULEVARD DE CIMIEZ

AVENUE VILLEBOIS-MAREUIL

AVENUE DES ARÈNES DE CIMIEZ

AVENUE DU MARÉCHAL LYAUTEY

BOULEVARD JEAN-BAPTISTE VÉRANY

RUE DU MARÉCHAL VAUBAN

AVENUE GEORGE V

BOULEVARD PASTEUR

RUE DE LA GENDARMERIE

ROUTE DE TURIN

N

Grand Corniche to La Turbie & Menton

BOULEVARD FRANÇOIS MITTERRAND

RUE DE MIRABEL

Musée Chagall

TUNNEL ANDRÉ MALRAUX

Palais des Expositions

AV. DES DIABLES BLEUS   AV. DES DIABLES BLEUS

Moyenne Corniche to Èze & Monaco

8

BOULEVARD RAIMBALDI

RUE ASSAUT

RUE PERTINAX

BOULEVARD DE CIMIEZ

AVENUE ÉMILE-BIECKERT

AVENUE DE NORMANDIE

RUE EL NOUZAH

AVENUE DES ARÈNES DE CIMIEZ

RUE JEAN JIGAN

BOULEVARD RISSO

RUE LÉOTARDI

BOULEVARD PIERRE SOLA

Cinémathèque de Nice

BOULEVARD DU GÉNÉRAL LOUIS DELFINO

RUE DE BONNEFILLIÈRE

RUE AUGUSTE GAL

RUE PIERRE BLANQUIN

BOULEVARD DE RIQUIER

RUE AMIRAUX

RUE DE PARIS

RUE BEAUMONT

RUE RIQUETTI

RUE 24 ORESTIS

RUE ARSON

RUE LAMARTINE

RUE DE LA BUFFA

AVENUE DESAMBROIS

AVENUE GALLIENI

AVENUE PAULIANI

Acropolis

RUE SMOLETT

AVENUE DE LA RÉPUBLIQUE

RUE GEORGES VILLE

RUE AUGUSTE GAL

PLACE ARSON

RUE NANCY

AV. MARÉCHAL FOCH

AV. BARLA

PROM. DES ARTS

RUE BEAUMONT

RUE GEORGES VILLE

RUE SCALIERO

BOULEVARD DE RIQUIER

AVENUE MARÉCHAL FOCH

RUE BISCARRA

PLACE SASSERNO

BOULEVARD DUBOUCHAGE

RUE E. BERLIER

RUE DES POTIERS

RUE PENCHIENATTI

RUE BARLA

RUE BARLA

PLACE FONTAINE DE LA VILLE

RUE SPITALIÉRI

RUE GALLEAN

RUE DEFLY

RUE GODFROY

RUE SCALIERO

CORNICHE A. DE L'ISLY

Nicetoile

BOULEVARD VICTOR HUGO

RUE TUNDUTT DE L'ESCARÈNE

RUE DEUILLE

Musée d'Art Moderne et d'Art Contemporain (MAMAC)

PLACE DU PIN

RUE BONAPARTE

PLACE M. BAREL

RUE PASTORELLI

RUE GUBERNATIS

RUE DE FRANCE

RUE FONCET

RUE DE L'HÔTEL

AVENUE ST-JEAN BAPTISTE

PLACE GARIBALDI

Théâtre de la Photographie et de l'Image

PLACE WILSON

RUE ALFRED MORTIER

Théâtre

RUE CASSINI

RUE SEGURANE

RUE LASCARIS

RUE PASTORELLI

RUE ALBERTI

RUE GIOFFREDO

AVENUE FÉLIX FAURE

RUE CHAUVAIN

Notre Dame du Port

RUE EMMANUEL PHILIBERT

RUE FODÉRÉ

BD STALINGRAD

RUE CATHERINE SEGURANE

RUE DE LA LIBERTÉ

SQUARE LECLERC

PLACE MAGENTA

RUE PARADIS

RUE MASSÉNA

PLACE MASSÉNA

BOULEVARD JEAN-JAURÈS

RUE ROSSETTI

RUE DE LA PRÉFECTURE

PL. DE L'ÎLE-DE-BEAUTÉ

BLVD CARNOT

BLVD DEUX EMMANUEL

Musée de Terra Amata

Jardins Albert-1er

AVENUE DE VERDUN

Palais de Justice

RUE ALEXANDRE MARI

VIEUX NICE

RUE PAPACINO

Port Lympia

BD CARNOT

Théâtre de Verdure

Hôtel de Ville

RUE ST-FRANÇOIS DE PAULE

Opéra

COURS SALEYA

QUAI DES ÉTATS-UNIS

Parc de la Colline du Château

QUAI LUNEL

QUAI DES DOCKS

Corniche Inférieure to Villefranche

QUAI DES ÉTATS-UNIS

SEE 'VIEUX NICE' MAP FOR DETAIL

Tour Bellanda

QUAI RAUBA-CAPEU

PLACE GUYNEMER

Parc Vigier

Gare Maritime

MEDITERRANEAN SEA

Palais Lascaris

15 rue Droite • Mon & Wed–Sun 10am/11am–6pm • €10 • ☏ 04 93 62 72 40

Grandest survivor of Vieux Nice's Baroque town mansions is the **Palais Lascaris**, a seventeenth-century palace built by the Duke of Savoy's Field-Marshal, Jean-Paul Lascaris, whose family arms, engraved on the ceiling of the entrance hall, bear the motto "Not even lightning strikes us". It's all very sumptuous, with frescoes, tapestries and chandeliers, along with a five-hundred-strong collection of historic musical instruments.

Place Masséna

The stately, red-ochre **place Masséna** is the hub of Nice, the meeting point of Vieux Nice and the modern city. Built in 1835 across the path of the River Paillon, it is now crossed by the city's gleaming modern tramway and graced by seven human figures by Spanish artist Jaume Plensa; they're suspended high above the ground and are most beautiful by night, when they're illuminated.

Steps lead up from Vieux Nice to the south side of the square; the new town lies to the north. To the west, the **Jardins Albert-1er** lead down to the promenade des Anglais; to the east, the **Promenade du Paillon** – a twelve-hectare urban park – follows the course of the river, dividing Vieux Nice from the modern city.

Musée d'Art Moderne et d'Art Contemporain (MAMAC)

Place Yves Klein • Tues–Sun: May–Oct 10am–6pm; Nov–April 11am–6pm • €10 • ☏ 04 97 13 42 01, ⊛ mamac-nice.org

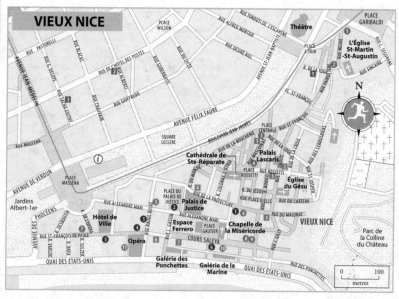

■ ACCOMMODATION		● EATING		■ DRINKING & NIGHTLIFE		● SHOPPING	
Villa La Tour	1	Café de Turin	1	Akathor	7	Alziari	5
Villa Saint-		La Civette du Cours	9	Blue Whales	1	Cave Bianchi	3
Exupery Beach	3	L'Escalinada	2	Les Distilleries Idéales	5	Cours Saleya markets	6
Wilson	2	Fenocchio	4	Ma Nolan's	6	Maison Auer	4
		Le Festival de la Moule	10	Shapko	3	Marché aux Peintures	2
		Le Frog	11	The Snug and Cellar	2	Patisserie Lac	1
		Lou Pilha Leva	3	Wayne's	4		
		La Merenda	5				
		Pasta Basta	6				
		Le Safari	8				
		Terres de Truffes	7				

THE GALLERIES OF VIEUX NICE

Vieux Nice has some small art galleries worth seeking out. The municipal **Galerie des Ponchettes**, 77 quai des États-Unis (Tues–Sun: late June to mid-Oct 10am–6pm; mid-Oct to late June 11am–6pm; €10), and the neighbouring **Galerie de la Marine**, 59 quai des États-Unis (same hours and ticket), host temporary exhibitions of contemporary artists; the Galerie de la Marine focuses in particular on the work of young artists. Also worth tracking down is the **Espace Ferrero**, place Pierre Gautier (same hours and ticket) which displays works by contemporary artists of the Nice school; the collection was donated to the city of Nice in 2013 by photographer and collector Jean Ferrero, a key figure on the Côte d'Azur's art scene.

One of the cultural highlights of Nice, and not to be missed, the futuristic **Musée d'Art Moderne et d'Art Contemporain (MAMAC)** is composed of four marble-clad towers linked by steel and glass bridges, with the giant **Tête Carrée** sculpture terminating the view to the northeast. It's a bold and confident work of architecture – though at night it is a favourite gathering place for the city's drunks. Rotating shows draw on the museum's collection of avant-garde French and American movements of the 1960s to the present. **Pop Art** highlights include Lichtenstein cartoons and Warhol's Campbell's soup tins, while more contemporary artists include Ai Weiwei. An entire room is devoted to Nice's own **Yves Klein**, his celebrated 1960s happenings and his uniquely vibrant shade of blue, and there's also a room given over to the colourful work of the Franco-American sculptor, painter and Vogue fashion model Niki de Saint Phalle, who died in 2002 having donated 170 works to the museum. Don't miss the roof terrace, which offers wonderful views over Vieux Nice.

The modern city

Running north from place Masséna, **avenue Jean-Médecin** is the city's rather dull main **shopping** street. The late nineteenth-century architecture and trees make it indistinguishable from any other big French city, as do the usual chain stores – including FNAC and Galeries Lafayette – though the extensive refurbishment work on the Nicetoile mall and the opening of the tramway have cheered things up a little. More inviting shopping, including Nice's densest knot of **designer boutiques**, is concentrated west of place Masséna on rue du Paradis and rue Alphonse Karr. Both intersect with the pedestrianized **rue Masséna**, an out-and-out tourist haunt full of bars, *glaciers* and fast-food outlets.

Théatre de la Photographie et de l'Image

27 bd Dubouchage • Tues–Sun: late June to mid-Oct 10am–6pm; mid-Oct to late June 11am–6pm • €10 • ☎ 04 97 13 42 20, Ⓦ museephotographie.nice.fr

A side turning off avenue Jean-Médecin brings you to the **Théatre de la Photographie et de l'Image**: a photographic museum which displays the fascinating works of Charles Nègre, who shot local views of Nice between 1863 and 1866, just after the city and surrounding area had been ceded to France. There are also regular temporary exhibitions on photographic themes.

Russian Orthodox Cathedral

Av Nicolas II • Daily 9am–6pm • Bus #17, #71, stop "Tzaréwitch" • Ⓦ sobor.fr

The chief interest of the modern town is its architecture: eighteenth- and nineteenth-century Italian Baroque and Neoclassical, florid *belle époque*, the occasional slice of Art Deco, and unclassifiable exotic aristo-fantasy. The most gilded, elaborate edifice is the early twentieth-century **Russian Orthodox Cathedral**, beyond the train station, at the end of avenue Nicholas II, off boulevard du Tsaréwitch. The subject of a bitter battle over its ownership in recent years, it is now under the aegis of the Moscow patriarchate.

8

NICE MUSEUM PASSES

Entry to municipal museums in Nice is via one of two passes: the **Ticket Individuel 24hr** (€10) and the €20 **Ticket 7 Jours**, both of which offer unlimited access (ⓦbilletterie-museesnice.tickeasy.com). Note, however, that the Musée Chagall and Musée Départemental des Arts Asiatiques are not municipal museums, and are thus not part of the deal. The **French Riviera Pass** (€26/24hr, €38/48hr, €56/72hr; ⓦfrenchrivierapass.com) gives access to all the city's museums, and to numerous other museums and attractions along the Riviera.

Promenade des Anglais

The point where the Paillon flows into the sea marks the start of the famous palm-fringed **promenade des Anglais**, which began as a coastal path created by nineteenth-century English residents for their afternoon stroll. It was here that the dancer **Isadora Duncan** met a dramatic death one September evening in 1927, throttled by her own scarf as it caught in the wheel of the open car in which she was travelling. Today, the broad beachfront promenade itself is separated from the town by multiple lanes of traffic, which crawl past some of the most fanciful architecture on the Côte d'Azur.

Beyond the first building, the glittery Casino Ruhl, is the 1930s Art Deco facade of the **Palais de la Méditerranée**, all that remains of the original municipal casino, closed due to intrigue and corruption, and finally demolished; a new casino and hotel have subsequently been inserted behind the original facade.

Galerie Ferrero

2 rue du Congrès • Mon–Sat 2–6.30pm • Free • ☎ 04 93 88 34 44, ⓦgalerieferrero.com

Something of an institution in the art world, the commercial **Galerie Ferrero** is associated strongly with the artists of the Nice School and with Nouveau-Réalisme, and nowadays also sells works by a new generation of artists from the Côte d'Azur.

Villa Masséna

65 rue de France/35 promenade des Anglais • Mon & Wed–Sun: late June to mid-Oct 10am–6pm; mid-Oct to late June 11am–6pm • €10 • ☎ 04 93 91 19 10

The **Villa Masséna**, the city's local history museum, charts Nice's development from Napoleonic times up to the 1930s. It was built at the turn of the twentieth century as a private residence for Prince Victor d'Essling, Duc de Rivoli, and it's worth a look to see the sumptuous interior of an aristocratic villa from Nice's heyday.

Negresco Hotel

37 promenade des Anglais • ☎ 04 93 16 64 00, ⓦhotel-negresco-nice.com

Most celebrated of all the Riviera's hotels is the **Negresco**, built in 1906 and occupying the block between rues de Rivoli and Cronstadt. It's one of the great surviving European palace hotels, still independently run and with an interior that is both opulent and occasionally downright odd. You'll have to be staying there or dining at one of the restaurants if you want to see it though, as they don't encourage casual visitors.

Musée des Beaux-Arts

33 av des Baumettes • Tues–Sun: late June to mid-Oct 10am–6pm; mid-Oct to late June 11am–6pm; guided tours in French Wed 3pm • €10, tours €6 • ☎ 04 92 15 28 28, ⓦmusee-beaux-arts-nice.org • Bus #3, #9 #10, #22, stop "Rosa Bonheur"

A kilometre or so west of the *Negresco Hotel* and a couple of blocks inland is the **Musée des Beaux-Arts**, housed in a mansion built by a Ukrainian princess in 1878. Highlights include 28 works by Raoul Dufy, a bequest to the city from his wife. There are also works by Monet, Sisley, Degas and Ziem, as well as whimsical canvases by Jules Chéret, who died in Nice in 1932, a room dedicated to Vanloo, and some amusing Van Dongens.

Musée International d'Art Naïf Anatole Jakovsky

Château Sainte-Hélène, Av de Fabron • Mon & Wed–Sun late June to mid-Oct 10am–6pm; mid-Oct to late June 11am–6pm • €10 • ☎ 04
93 71 78 33 • Bus #9, #10, #23, #34, stop "Fabron/Art Naïf"

A kilometre or so west of the Musée des Beaux-Arts and on the inland side of the
Voie Rapide expressway is the **Musée International d'Art Naïf Anatole Jakovsky**, home
to a surprisingly good collection of amateur art from around the world. Housed in
the former home of the *parfumier* Coty, the museum displays six hundred examples
of art naïf from the eighteenth century to the present day, including works by Vivin,
Rimbert, Bauchant and the Croatian masters Ivan and Josep Generalić.

Phoenix Parc Floral de Nice

405 promenade des Anglais • Daily: April–Sept 9.30am–7.30pm; Oct–March 9.30am–6pm • €3 • ☎ 04 92 29 77 01, ⊚ parc-phoenix.org •
Exit St-Augustin from the highway from Nice or Promenade des Anglais from Cannes; bus #9, #10 or #23 from Nice

The **Phoenix Parc Floral de Nice**, right out by the airport, is a cross between a botanical
garden, bird-and-insect zoo and theme park, with everything from Mediterranean
and acid-tolerant plants to caimans, wallabies and free-flying exotic birds, all grouped
around a lake with fountains. The centrepiece is one of the largest greenhouses in
Europe, with six different tropical zones.

Musée Départemental des Arts Asiatiques

Phoenix Parc Floral • **Museum** Mon & Wed–Sun: July & Aug 10am–6pm; Sept–June 10am–5pm; guided tour third Sat of month 3pm •
Free; tour €4 • **Tea ceremony** Sun 3pm • €10 • ☎ 04 92 29 37 00, ⊚ arts-asiatiques.com

The Phoenix Parc Floral is home to the **Musée Départemental des Arts Asiatiques**, beside
the lake. Housed in a beautiful building designed by Japanese architect Kenzo Tange,
the museum displays artworks from India, China, Japan and Cambodia, as well as
hosting touring exhibitions; there is also a weekly tea ceremony.

Musée National du Sport

Bd des Jardiniers, Stade Allianz Riviera • Tues–Sun: May–Sept 10am–6pm, Thurs until 9pm; Oct–April 11am–5pm • €5, €7 including
temporary exhibitions • ⊚ museedusport.fr • Bus #11 or #59, stop "St-Isidore"

The Allianz Riviera stadium, hard by the River Var on Nice's northwestern outskirts, is
the setting for the **Musée National du Sport**, which spans the sixteenth century to the
present. The focus is on French sport, but many of the artefacts – from Marcel Cerdan's
boxing gloves and Yannick Noah's tennis racquet to the football used in the 1998
World Cup – have international resonance.

The beaches

Nice's main **beach** stretches west of Le Château along the shores of the Baie des Anges and
is backed by the promenade des Anglais. Although the water is reasonably clean, the beach
itself is painfully pebbly, and though much of it is public it's broken up by fifteen private
concessions that, from April to October, charge fees for loungers, parasols, mattresses and
towels, and are more interested in serving you a meal or cocktail than in the state of your
tan. East of the port a string of rocky coves includes the **Plage de la Réserve** opposite Parc
Vigier (bus #30 or #T32), and **Coco Beach**, popular with the local LGBTQ community.

The port and around

The **port**, flanked by gorgeous red-ochre eighteenth-century buildings and headed by
the Neoclassical **Notre Dame du Port**, is full of bulbous yachts but has little quayside life
despite the restaurants along Quai Lunel, though a new programme of improvement
has somewhat tamed the ferocious traffic. There is a **flea market** at place Robilante
(Tues–Sat: June–Sept 10am–7pm; Oct–May 10am–6pm).

Musée de Terra Amata

25 bd Carnot • Mon & Wed–Sun: May–Oct 10am–6pm; Nov–April 10am–5pm • €10 • ☎ 04 93 55 59 93, Ⓦ musee-terra-amata.org • Bus #81 or #100, stop "Gustavin"

Just east of the port is the **Musée de Terra Amata**, a museum of human paleontology on the site of an early human settlement dating back 400,000 years – a time when the sea level was much higher than it is today and much of what is now present-day Nice was submerged. The settlement was the camp of a tribe of hunters, located on a pebbly beach.

Cimiez

Nice's northern suburb, **Cimiez**, has always been posh. The approach up boulevard de Cimiez is punctuated by vast *belle époque* piles, many of them former hotels; at the foot of the hill stands the gargantuan *Majestic*, while the summit is dominated by the equally vast *Hôtel Régina*, built for a visit by Queen Victoria.

Musée d'Archéologie

160 av des Arènes de Cimiez • Mon & Wed–Sun: May–Oct 10am–6pm; Nov–April 10am–5pm • €10 • ☎ 04 93 81 59 57 • Take bus #15, #17 or #20, stop "Arènes-Musée Matisse"

The heights of Cimiez were the social centre of the town's elite some 1700 years ago, when the city was Cemenelum, capital of the Roman province of Alpes-Maritimes. Part of a small amphitheatre still stands, and excavations of the Roman baths have revealed enough detail to distinguish the sumptuous facilities for the top tax official and his cronies from the plainer public and women's baths. The **archeological site** is overlooked by the impressive, modern **Musée d'Archéologie**, which displays all the finds and illustrates the city's history up to the Middle Ages.

Musée Matisse

164 av des Arènes de Cimiez • Mon & Wed–Sun: May–Oct 10am–6pm; Nov–April 10am–5pm • €10 • ☎ 04 93 81 08 08, Ⓦ musee-matisse-nice.org • Take bus #15, #17 or #20, stop "Arènes-Musée Matisse"

Adjacent to the Musée d'Archéologie is the **Musée Matisse**, housed in a seventeenth-century villa painted with trompe l'oeil. The collection has work from every period of Matisse's long career, including an almost complete set of his bronze sculptures; sketches for one of the *Dance* murals; models for the Vence chapel (see page 338) and priests' robes; book illustrations, including for a 1935 edition of Joyce's *Ulysses*; and excellent examples of his cut-out technique, of which the most delightful are *The Bees* and *The Creole Dancer*. Not everything is necessarily on view at any one time, and temporary exhibitions highlight particular aspects of Matisse's life and work.

MATISSE IN NICE

Matisse wintered in Nice from 1916 onwards, staying in hotels on the promenade – from where he painted *Storm over Nice* – and then, from 1921 to 1938, renting an apartment overlooking place Charles-Félix. It was in Nice that he painted his most sensual, colour-flooded canvases, featuring models as oriental odalisques posted against exotic draperies. In 1942, when he was installed in the *Régina* hotel, he said that if he had gone on painting in the north "there would have been cloudiness, greys, colours shading off into the distance". As well as the Mediterranean light, Matisse loved the cosmopolitan life of Nice and the presence of fellow artists Renoir, Bonnard and Picasso in neighbouring towns. He returned to the *Régina* from Vence in 1949, having developed his solution to the problem of "drawing in colour" by cutting out shapes and putting them together as collages or stencils. He died in Cimiez in November 1954, aged 85, and is buried in the local cemetery (see below).

Monastère Notre Dame de Cimiez

Place Jean Paul II • **Monastery** Mon–Sat 7.30am–6.30pm • Free • **Gardens** Daily: April, May & Sept 8am–7pm; June–Aug 8am–8pm;
Oct–March 8am–6pm • Free • **Musée Franciscain** Mon–Fri 10am–noon & 3–5.30pm, Sat 10am–noon • Free • ◍ stemariedesanges.
free.fr • Bus #17 to "Monastère Cimiez" stop

The Musée Matisse and the Roman remains back onto an old olive grove, the **Parc
des Arènes de Cimiez**, one of the best open spaces in Nice. At its eastern end is the
Monastère Notre Dame de Cimiez, which has a flamboyant pink Gothic facade of
nineteenth-century origin topping a much older and plainer porch. Inside there's
more gaudiness, reflecting the rich benefactors the Franciscan order had access to, but
also three masterpieces of medieval art: a *Pietà* and *Crucifixion* by Louis Bréa and a
Deposition by Antoine Bréa.

Adjoining the monastery is the **Musée Franciscain**, which paints a picture of the
mendicant friars and relates the gruesome fate that befell some early martyrs. You can
also look into the first cloister of the sixteenth-century **monastic buildings**, and visit the
peaceful **gardens**.

Matisse is buried in the Cimiez **cemetery** (daily: March, April, Sept & Oct 8am–
5.45pm; May–Aug 8am–6.45pm; Nov–Feb 8am–4.45pm), on the north side of the
monastery; his simple tomb is signposted on the left-hand side.

Musée Chagall

Av Docteur Ménard • Mon & Wed–Sun: May–Oct 10am–6pm; Nov–April 10am–5pm • €8; €10 during temporary exhibitions; free first Sun
of month • ☎ 04 93 53 87 20, ◍ en.musees-nationaux-alpesmaritimes.fr/chagall • Bus #15, stop "Marc Chagall"

At the foot of Cimiez hill, just off boulevard de Cimiez, the **Musée Chagall** was
custom-built to house the artist's Biblical Message paintings, and opened by Chagall
himself in 1972. The rooms are light, white and cool, with windows allowing us to
see the greenery of the garden beyond the pinky red shades of the five *Song of Songs*
canvases. The seventeen paintings of the Biblical Message are all based on the Old
Testament and are complemented by etchings and engravings. To the building itself,
Chagall contributed a mosaic, the painted harpsichord and the *Creation of the World*
stained-glass windows in the auditorium.

8

ARRIVAL AND DEPARTURE   NICE

BY PLANE
Airport Aeroport Nice Côte d'Azur (☎ 0820 42 33 33,
◍ nice.aeroport.fr) is at the western end of the Promenade
des Anglais.

Getting into town Two fast buses (both €6) connect
with the city: #99 goes to the *gare SNCF* on Av Thiers (every
30min, 7.53am–8.53pm); #98 goes to the Promenade
des Arts (up to every 16min, 5.40am–11.45pm). A new
tram line (#2) also serves the airport (€1.50; up to every
12min, 7.07am–8.15pm), terminating at the port. Taxis are
plentiful and cost about €25–32 into the centre.

Airlines Aer Lingus (☎ 0821 23 02 67); Air France (☎ 36
54); Air Transat (☎ 0176 54 28 96); British Airways (☎ 0825
82 54 00); Delta (☎ 04 93 21 34 86); EasyJet (☎ 0820 42 03
15); Ryanair (☎ 0892 56 21 50).

Destinations Belfast (mid-May to early Oct 2–3 weekly; 2hr
35min–2hr 40min); Bristol (April–Oct 1 daily; Nov–March 2
weekly; 2hr 10min); Cork (April–Oct 2 weekly; 2hr 50min);
Dublin (daily (3–7 weekly Ryanair; 1–2 daily Aer Lingus; 2hr
30min–2hr 40min); Edinburgh (up to 5 weekly; 2hr 35min);
Liverpool (April–Oct 1 daily; Nov–March up to 5 weekly;

2hr 20min); London City (up to 2 daily; 1hr 55min); London
Gatwick (up to 8 daily; 2hr 5min); London Heathrow (up to
8 daily; 2hr–2hr 20min); London Luton (2 daily; 2hr 5min);
London Stansted (1–2 daily; 2hr 5min); Lyon (up to 3 daily;
55min–1hr); Manchester (April–Oct 3 weekly; Nov–March
2 weekly; 2hr 20min); Montreal (May–Oct 2–3 weekly;
8hr 35min); Newcastle (May–Sept 3 weekly; Nov–March 2
weekly; 2hr 25min); New York JFK (1 daily; 8hr 50min–9hr);
Paris CDG (7 daily; 1hr 35min); Paris Orly (19 daily; 1hr
25min–1hr 30min).

BY TRAIN
Nice's *gare SNCF* (☎ 04 92 14 85 62) is on Av Thiers on the
northern edge of the city centre next to the voie Pierre
Mathis trunk road.

Destinations Antibes (up to 5 hourly; 18–30min);
Beaulieu-sur-Mer (every 15–30min 11–13min); Breil-
sur-Roya (11 daily; 1hr 7min–1hr 22min); Cannes (up
to 4 hourly; 27–44min); Cap d'Ail (every 15min–1hr;
20–21min); Digne (daily; 3hr 25min); Entrevaux (5 daily;
1hr 21min–1hr 30min); L'Escarène (11 daily; 38–46min);

CHEMINS DE FER DE PROVENCE

The **Chemins de Fer de Provence** (⊛ trainprovence.com) runs one of France's most scenic and fun railway routes, from the Gare de Provence on rue Alfred-Binet (4 daily; 3hr 25min; €24 one-way). The line runs up the Var Valley into the hinterland of Nice to Digne-les-Bains (see page 211), and climbs through some spectacular scenery as it goes. There are also special steam train excursions on Sundays from May to October.

Èze-sur-Mer (every 30min–1hr; 16min); Marseille (every 30min–3hr; 2hr 36min–2hr 42min); Menton (every 15min; 34–49mins); Monaco (every 15min; 21–26mins); Peille (11 daily; 28–35mins); Peillon (11 daily; 22–28min); Roquebrune-Cap Martin (every 30min–1hr; 31–41mins); St Raphaël (16 daily; 50min–1hr 4min); Sospel (11 daily; 54min–1hr 9min); Tende (4 daily; 1hr 55min–2hr 9min); Villefranche (every 15min; 8min).

BY BUS

Buses generally pull in along Av de Verdun near place Masséna; Menton and Monaco buses arrive at the port. Buses from the Arriére-Pays Niçois and Èze village arrive at Av des Diables Bleus, 1km north of the old town.

Destinations Antibes (every 15min; 1hr–1hr 5min); Cannes (every 15min; 1hr 20min–1hr 40min); Coaraze (1 daily; 1hr); Contes (every 30min–1hr 15min; 30min); Èze-sur-Mer (every 10–35min; 25min); Èze village (15 daily; 38min); Grasse (every 20–45min; 1hr 30min); La Turbie (5 daily; 45min); L'Escarène (8 daily; 50min); Lucéram (9 daily; 50min–1hr); Menton (every 10–35min; 1hr –1hr 40min); Monaco (every 10–35min; 40min); Peille (3 daily; 55min); Peillon (2 daily; 45min); St-Paul-de-Vence (every 20–50min; 1hr 3min); Vence (every 20–50min; 55min–1hr 15min); Villefranche-sur-Mer (every 10–35min; 15min).

BY FERRY

Corsica Ferries Services from the port to Ajaccio, Bastia, Vecchio and Île Rousse in Corsica (frequencies vary according to season; ☎ 04 95 32 95 95, ⊛ corsica-ferries.fr).

INFORMATION AND TOURS

Tourist office In front of the *gare SNCF* on Av Thiers (June–Sept daily 9am–7pm; Oct–May Mon–Sat 9am–6pm, Sun 10am–5pm; ☎ 04 92 14 46 14, ⊛ en.nicetourisme.com). There's an additional office at 5 promenade des Anglais (Carnival & May Mon–Sat 9am–6pm, Sun 10am–5pm, June–Sept daily 9am–7pm; Oct–April Mon–Sat 9am–6pm).

Boat trips Trans Côte d'Azur, Quai Lunel (☎ 04 92 00 42 30, ⊛ trans-cote-azur.com), runs summer trips to Cannes or the Îles de Lérins (late May to June and Sept Tues, Thurs, Sat & Sun; July & Aug daily except Mon), Monaco (mid-May to Sept Tues, Thurs & Sat) and St-Tropez (late May to June & Sept Tues, Thurs, Sat & Sun; July & Aug daily except Mon).

GETTING AROUND

BY BUS AND TRAM

Lignes d'Azur, 1 rue d'Italie (Mon–Sat 7am–8pm, Sun 8am–6pm; ☎ 08 1006 1006, ⊛ www.lignesdazur.com), provides bus and tram service in Nice and surrounding towns.

Trams A single tram line loops in a "V" shape from the northern suburbs through the city centre to the northeastern suburbs. Services continue until 1.35am to Henri Sappia and until 12.50am to Hôpital Pasteur. A second line links the port to the airport (see page 355).

Buses Buses run a frequent service until early evening (roughly 8.30–9.40pm), after which five Noctambus night buses serve most areas from the promenade des Arts next to MAMAC (until 1.10am).

Tickets and passes You can buy a single ticket (€1.50), day pass (€5), ten-journey multipasses (€10) and seven-day passes (€15) from machines at tram stops (using coins or credit cards); passes are also available from *tabacs*, kiosks, newsagents and from the Lignes d'Azur office, where you can also pick up a free route map. A mobile app, the NFC Nice Ticket, is available on the website (see above), facilitating both ticket purchase and validation.

BY TAXI

Taxis cost €2.12/km by day and €2.90/km by night (7pm–7am) and on Sun and public holidays. Note that there are supplementary charges for the airport run, for each item of baggage and for being stuck in traffic; the minimum fare is €7.10. Firms include Central Taxi Riviera (☎ 04 93 13 78 78, ⊛ taxis-nice.fr) and Taxis Niçois Indépendents (☎ 04 93 88 25 82).

BY BIKE

Vélo Bleu Nice's on-street bicycle rental scheme, Vélo Bleu (☎ 04 93 72 06 06, ⊛ www.velobleu.org), has 175 rental stations scattered throughout the city, extending into Cagnes-sur-Mer and St-Laurent-du-Var. You have to sign up online or call toll-free from the bike station (€1.50/day, €5/

week), after which the first 30min is free; it costs €1 for the next 30min and €2/hr thereafter. Payment is by credit card.

Bike, scooter and motorbike hire If you want to rent a mountain bike, electric bike, scooter or motorbike, try Holiday Bikes, 9 rue Massenet (☎ 04 93 04 15 36, ⊚ loca-bike.fr).

BY CAR

Car rental You can rent an electric car using the Renault Mobility mobile app (⊚ renault-mobility.com), with over three hundred charging points due to be rolled out across the Nice area. For a Twingo, different hourly rates are charged by day and night, as well as for an entire day, night or weekend, varying by model and starting at €4/5 hour by day/night. Otherwise, conventional commercial agencies are based at the airport and *gare SNCF*.

Car parks There are pay car parks at Acropolis conference centre; promenade des Arts; Av Thiers (*gare SNCF*); palais Masséna, and cours Saleya.

ACCOMMODATION

SEE MAPS PAGES 348 AND 350

Before hunting for **accommodation**, it's worth taking advantage of the **online reservation service** on the tourist office website (see page 356). The area around the station teems with cheap hotels, some of them seedy, though there are a few gems. Sleeping on the beach is illegal and for campsites you'll need to head west to Cagnes-sur-Mer (see page 329).

Les Cigales 16 rue Dalpozzo ☎ 04 97 03 10 70, ⊚ hotel-les-cigales.fr. Clean, a/c and smart three-star hotel 150m from the promenade des Anglais, with soundproofed, recently redesigned en-suite rooms with satellite TV and safe, plus a sun terrace for guests. Good value for the price and location. €134

Cronstadt 3 rue Cronstadt ☎ 04 93 82 00 30, ⊚ hotel cronstadt.com. Hidden inside the garden courtyard of a large residential block, slightly gloomy but extremely tranquil for its location, close to the *Negresco* and the sea, with old-fashioned, clean and comfortable rooms including some triples. €120

Durante 16 av Durante ☎ 04 93 88 84 40, ⊚ hotel-durante.com. Great-value mid-range hotel in a quiet suite turning near the *gare SNCF*, with smart, pretty a/c rooms with flatscreen TV, limited free parking and an attractive garden. €119

★ **Le Floride** 52 bd de Cimiez ☎ 04 93 53 11 02, ⊚ www.hotel-floride.fr. Clean, friendly, good-value two-star hotel in Cimiez, with some spacious en-suite doubles and a few cheap singles with WC and shower. Rooms at the front have a/c – those at the shadier back make do with fans. There's also private parking. €81

Le Grimaldi 15 rue Grimaldi ☎ 04 93 16 00 24, ⊚ le-grimaldi.com. Highly successful boutique-style reworking of a *belle époque* hotel on the fringe of Nice's prime designer shopping district: smart, central, and with attractive, individually designed rooms. €184

Lépante 6 rue de Lépante ☎ 04 93 62 20 55, ⊚ hotel lepante.com. LGBTQ-friendly two-star hotel in a central *belle époque* building, with a/c and a first-floor sunny terrace where breakfast is served in fine weather. Rooms have soundproofing and private bath. €86

Negresco 37 promenade des Anglais ☎ 04 93 16 64 00, ⊚ hotel-negresco-nice.com. This legendary, free-spirited seafront palace hotel is a genuine one-off, with its own private beach, masses of art and a few wacky touches, including some occasionally garish colour schemes. €470

★ **L'Oasis** 23 rue Gounod ☎ 04 93 88 12 29, ⊚ hotel niceoasis.com. Tucked off the street in a palm-shaded garden setting, this three-star former Russian guesthouse – Lenin and Chekhov are former guests – has nice, upgraded a/c rooms, secure private parking and a terrace where you can take breakfast in fine weather. €134

La Pérouse 11 quai Rauba-Capeu ☎ 04 93 62 34 63, ⊚ hotel-la-perouse.com. The best-situated hotel in central Nice, at the foot of Le Château, and with a rooftop pool and fabulous views over the promenade des Anglais and Baie des Anges. Rooms have marble bathrooms and individually controlled a/c. €428

Petit Palais 17 av Émile-Bieckert ☎ 04 93 62 19 11, ⊚ petitpalaisnice.com. Set in hilly Cimiez, this attractive, quiet and comfortable *belle époque* mansion was the former home of writer and actor Sacha Guitry. There are 25 rooms, some with views over the Baie des Anges. €165

Le Petit Trianon 11 rue du Paradis ☎ 04 93 87 50 46, ⊚ lepetittrianon.fr. Prettily renovated, in a modern yet slightly frou-frou style, these a/c and soundproofed rooms have a great location in an old apartment block in the pedestrian zone close to the beach. €104

La Villa Nice Victor Hugo 19 bd Victor Hugo ☎ 04 93 87 15 00, ⊚ hotel-villa-nice-centre.com. Another magnificent *belle époque* pile occupying a central spot just outside the old town, with contemporary, low key-verging-on-monochrome decor and a tranquil ambience despite the busy road below. All rooms are a/c and en suite, and some are fronted with Juliet balconies. €149

Villa Rivoli 10 rue de Rivoli ☎ 04 93 88 80 25, ⊚ villa-rivoli.com. Sweet hotel in a *belle époque* building a short walk from the promenade des Anglais and beach, with refurbished, a/c en-suite rooms with pretty, traditional decor. Some rooms have small balconies. €143

Villa la Tour 4 rue de la Tour ☎ 04 93 80 08 15, ⊚ villa-la-tour.com. Located in the heart of Vieux Nice, with seventeen a/c en-suite rooms with satellite TV and safe, including a few with balconies or views over the city. Room

8

styles (and rates) vary quite widely. There's also a bar-restaurant. **€154**

Wilson 39 rue de l'Hotel des Postes ☎ 04 93 85 47 79, ⊕ hotel-wilson-nice.com. A stylish and gay-friendly budget guesthouse on the third floor in a great location, with individually themed rooms, the cheapest of which have washbasin only. No lift. **€62**

★ **Windsor** 11 rue Dalpozzo ☎ 04 93 88 59 35, ⊕ hotel windsornice.com. Smart boutique-style and LGBTQ-friendly "art hotel" with individually styled rooms, some with frescoes, and many of them quite striking. There's also a spa with sauna and steam bath, and small pool in a partially shaded garden, overgrown with bamboo. **€160**

HOSTELS

Auberge de Jeunesse Les Camélias 3 rue Spitalieri ☎ 04 93 62 15 54, ⊕ hifrance.org. Very central HI hostel in a fine old villa with a pretty garden tucked behind the Nicetoile shopping centre, with accommodation in three-to seven-bed dorms, plus wi-fi, bar, laundry and kitchen facilities. Closed Christmas week. **€29.90**

Backpackers Chez Patrick First floor (the hostel downstairs is nothing to do with them), 32 rue Pertinax ☎ 04 93 80 30 72, ⊕ backpackerschezpatrick.com. Clean, a/c hostel close to the station. There are no breakfast facilities but there's a fridge, microwave, washing machine, safe, and no curfew. Accommodation is in four- to six-bed dorms or doubles. Dorms **€30**; doubles **€76**

Belle Meunière 21 av Durante ☎ 04 93 88 66 15, ⊕ bellemeuniere.com. Efficient, clean and friendly hostel in a lovely old bourgeois house, with double, twin, triple and four-bed rooms, and dorms that sleep up to five. There's a laundry service, parking and a terrace. They can also advise on renting apartments for longer stays. Very keen on guests booking direct. Dorms **€32**; doubles **€77**

★ **Villa Saint-Exupery Beach** 6 rue Sacha Guitry ☎ 04 93 16 13 45, ⊕ villahostels.com. Well-equipped, a/c hostel near Place Masséna and Vieux Nice with bar, 24hr gym, movie lounge, secure lockers and free wi-fi. There are doubles, twins and private three- or four-bed rooms, plus dorms sleeping three to fourteen, some of which are women-only. Dorms **€39.95**; doubles **€130**

EATING

SEE MAPS PAGES 348 AND 350

Nice is a great place for **food**, whether you're picnicking on market fare, snacking on **Niçois specialities** like *pan bagnat* (a bun stuffed with tuna, salad and olive oil), *salade niçoise*, *pissaladière* (onion tart with anchovies) or *socca* (a chickpea flour pancake), or dining in the palace hotels. The **Italian** influence is strong, with pasta on every menu; **seafood** and **fish** are also staples, with good *bourride* (fish soup), *estocaficada* (stockfish and tomato stew), and all manner of sea fish grilled with fennel or Provençal herbs. The local Bellet **wines** from the hills behind the city provide the perfect light accompaniment. For **snacks**, many of the cafés sell sandwiches with typically Provençal fillings such as fresh basil, olive oil, goat's cheese and mesclun, the green-salad mix of the region. Despite the usual fast-food chains and tourist traps dotted around, there are plenty of reasonable **restaurants**. Vieux Nice has a dozen on every street catering for a wide variety of budgets, while the port quaysides have excellent, if pricey, places to eat fish and seafood. From June till September it's wise to **reserve** tables, or turn up before 8pm, especially in Vieux Nice – and though browsing menus is half the fun it's best not to leave it too long, as not all Niçois kitchens stay open late.

VIEUX NICE

RESTAURANTS

Café de Turin 5 place Garibaldi ☎ 04 93 62 29 52, ⊕ cafedeturin.fr. A local institution, the *Café de Turin* dominates one corner of place Garibaldi. The emphasis is on raw seafood, with *panachés* of *fruits de mer* from €37, plus

cooked options such as octopus linguine in a tomato and aniseed sauce (€20). No reservations; be prepared to queue. Daily 8am–10pm.

L'Escalinada 22 rue Pairolière ☎ 04 93 62 11 71. Good Niçois specialities at this old restaurant, at the foot of a stepped side street, include stockfish (€26), ravioli with *daube* sauce (€21) and courgette fritters with mesclun (€12.50);. Service is efficient, but occasionally a bit gruff. Daily 11.30am–3.30pm & 6.30–11.30pm.

Le Festival de la Moule 20 cours Saleya ☎ 04 26 85 36 38, ⊕ lefestivaldelamoule.com. This unpretentious all-you-can-eat *moules-frites* place offers various sauces; a pot is €15.90 with free refills. They also serve omelettes, salads, pizza, paella and fish; *menus* at €19 and €29. Daily 11.45am–2.30pm & 6.30–10.30pm.

★ **Le Frog** 3 rue Milton Robbins ☎ 04 93 85 85 65, ⊕ restaurantgroupesnice.fr. Quirky, trendy little restaurant serving up cheeky variations on classic French cooking, with a €31 *menu* featuring frogs' legs and snails. The *tourte de blette* – sweet Swiss chard tart – is seriously good. Daily noon–2.30pm & 7–11pm.

Lou Pilha Leva 10 rue Collet ☎ 04 93 13 99 08. Piping-hot *socca* (€2.80) fresh from the pan is much the best thing to eat at this rock-bottom street food place – much of the rest is microwaved. *Pissaladière* €3.20, *pan bagnat* €4.30. Take away, or eat at the benches outside. Daily 10am–10pm.

★ **La Merenda** 4 rue Raoul Bosio ⊕ lamerenda. net. Chef Dominique le Stanc quit the Michelin-starred *Chantecler* to cook classic Niçois dishes at this tiny, legendary place in Vieux Nice. *Plats du jour* include *tripes à la niçoise* at

€15; stockfish €22. Booking in person only. No cards. Mon–Fri noon–2pm & 7–11pm.

Pasta Basta 18 rue de la Préfecture ☎ 04 93 80 03 57, ⊛ pastabasta.fr. No-frills pasta place with six types of fresh and two dried pasta varieties and a choice of eighteen sauces. Pasta from €5.50, sauces from €4, and rough wine by the *pichet* from €4. Try the *merda de can* (buckwheat gnocchi). Mon–Wed & Fri–Sun 10am–2pm & 7–10pm.

Le Safari 1 cours Saleya ☎ 04 93 80 18 44, ⊛ restaurant safari.fr. Hearty portions of authentic Niçois cuisine – from cod *beignets* to wood-roast rabbit or *daube* with ravioli – make this one of the cours Saleya's better culinary bets. *Menu* €29; chalked-up specials from around €14. Daily noon–11pm.

Terres de Truffes 11 rue St-François-de-Paule ☎ 04 93 62 07 68, ⊛ terresdetruffes.com. Intimate, upmarket and tasteful restaurant with a wide variety of dishes – from pasta to meat and fish – all cooked or served with truffles. *Menus* €39–89. Tues–Sat noon–2pm & 7–10pm.

CAFÉS AND BARS

La Civette du Cours 1 cours Saleya ☎ 04 93 80 80 59, ⊛ civette-cours-nice.fr. Classier and more intimate than its neighbours, this is the best-loved of the *cours*' café terraces, with a mixed LGBTQ/straight crowd, a vaguely Art Deco look and a wide terrace for people-watching. Sandwiches around €10, pasta and salads around €13/14; expect to pay around €14–20 for *plats du jour*. Daily 7.30am–11.30pm.

★ **Fenocchio** 2 place Rossetti ☎ 04 93 80 72 52, ⊛ fenocchio.fr. A firm Vieux Nice favourite, this excellent *glacier* serves 59 varieties of ice creams and 35 sorbets, with flavours like salty caramel and violet alongside more familiar offerings. On warm nights, skip the restaurant desserts and head here instead. One scoop €2.50, two €4. March–Nov daily 9am–midnight.

GREATER NICE

RESTAURANTS

L'Âne Rouge 7 quai des Deux-Emmanuel ☎ 04 93 89 49 63, ⊛ anerougenice.com. Lobster is the speciality of this portside gastronomic haunt, which has a bias towards fish and seafood but also features the likes of stuffed shoulder of *confit* lamb with *tian* of courgettes. Lunch *menu* €27, dinner *menus* from €39. Mon, Tues & Fri–Sun noon–2pm & 7.30–10pm, Thurs 7.30–10pm.

Chantecler 37 promenade des Anglais ☎ 04 93 16 64 00, ⊛ hotel-negresco-nice.com. The *Negresco's restaurant gastronomique* is the grandest in Nice, with two Michelin stars. Chef Virginie Basselot's sublime creations included mullet and squid with stuffed peppers, petit pois and a Sobressada jus, and there's even a seven-course vegetarian *menu*. *Menus* €150–230. Tues–Sat 7–10pm.

Le Flaveur 25 rue Gubernatis ☎ 04 93 62 53 95, ⊛ restaurant-flaveur.com. Stylish gastro restaurant with striking abstract interior design and creative dishes such as smoked swordfish with salted citron confit and fresh herbs, making it a firm local favourite. *Menus* €110–175. Tues–Fri noon–1.30pm & 7.15–10pm, Sat 7.15–10pm.

Mets and Café 28 rue Assalit ☎ 04 93 80 30 85. Busy budget brasserie close to many of the backpacker hostels, serving up traditional French food and with a €13 lunchtime *formule* (till 3pm). Mon–Sat 7.30am–9.30pm.

★ **Voyageur Nissart** 19 rue Alsace Lorraine ☎ 04 93 82 19 60, ⊛ voyageurnissart.com. Excellent food like *maman* used to make, in a setting that couldn't be more typically French – chequered tablecloths and all. *Menus* start at €15.90; one focuses on Niçois specialities such as *tripes* and *petits farcis*. Tues–Fri & Sun noon–2.30pm & 7–10.30pm, Sat 7–10.30pm.

CAFÉS AND BARS

Café des Chineurs 1 rue Cassini ☎ 04 93 89 09 62. Hipster bar-bistro in the "Petit Marais" (see below), with a prettily shabby interior, lively, see-and-be-seen terrace and a versatile menu, from tapas (around €6) and sharing platters (around €15–20) to full meals. Regular live music. Mon–Sat 11am–midnight.

Déli Bo 5 rue Bonaparte ☎ 04 93 56 33 04, ⊛ delibo.fr. Seasonal and organic nibbles are the order of the day at this charming little café-deli, with breakfast served until 11am (everything from a pastry at €0.70 to scrambled eggs and truffles at €16), followed by afternoon tea (organic tea blends €3.50), and brunch on Sunday. Mon–Sat 7am–7pm, Sun 10am–5pm.

Le Grand Café de Lyon 33 av Jean-Médecin ☎ 04 93 88 13 17, ⊛ cafedelyon.fr. Large bar/brasserie/café on Nice's main shopping street, with Art Deco touches and a big terrace for people-watching. *Plats du jour* are €12.70, and there's a decent selection of beer and wine (draught beer from €3.80, *pichets* of Côtes de Provence €7.50). Daily 7am–11pm.

8

DRINKING AND NIGHTLIFE   **SEE MAPS PAGES 348 AND 350**

Vieux Nice's British- and Irish-style **pubs** have long been very popular with young expat travellers – in fact, you're more likely to hear English than French spoken in some of them. Along with their encyclopaedic range of beers or whiskies they often feature live **bands**, though the

music tends to be not very original. For the older, more affluent generation, the luxury **hotel bars** with their jazzy singers and piano accompaniment have held sway for decades. There are two big casinos – the Casino Ruhl (1 promenade des Anglais; ☎ 04 97 03 12 22) and the Palais de la Méditerranée (15 promenade des Anglais; ☎ 04 92 14 68 00). As for the **clubs**, bouncers judging your wallet or exclusive membership lists are the rule. Nice's **LGBTQ scene** is quite sizeable; rue Bonaparte is the focus of a LGBTQ district between place Garibaldi and the port – the so-called "Petit Marais". The annual Pink Parade takes place in early summer.

VIEUX NICE

Akathor 32 cours Saleya ☎ 04 93 62 49 90, ⓦ pub-akathor.com. Much the busiest of cours Saleya's rock and sports bars, with live bands and DJs from 9pm (no cover), salsa nights, happy hour 5–9pm and a good choice of draught beers from €5.50/pint. English-language stand-up comedy, too. Mon & Fri–Sun 10am–2am, Tues–Thurs 5pm–2am.

Blue Whales 1 rue Mascoïnat ☎ 04 93 62 90 94. Intimate late-night bar and diner with a friendly, boozy atmosphere and live music; doesn't get busy till well after midnight, once other places begin to close. Daily 4pm–4.30am.

★ **Les Distilleries Idéales** 24 rue de la Préfecture ☎ 04 93 62 10 66. Probably the prettiest bar in Vieux Nice, with high vaulted ceilings and a florid, *fin de siècle* steampunk look including murals by a local artist. No less than twenty draught beers, including Grimbergen and Afflighem (both €7.50); cocktails are €9. Charcuterie and cheese platters (around €10–15), too. Daily 9am–12.30am.

Ma Nolan's 2 rue St-François-de-Paule ☎ 04 93 85 42 67, ⓦ ma-nolans.com. Vast, slick Irish pub with live bands most nights at 10pm, televised Irish and British sport, and a good range of draught and bottled beer from €3.50, with burgers (from €11.90) and even bangers and mash (€14.90) to eat. You might as well not be in France, but it's popular with a younger crowd. There's a second branch on the port. Daily 11am–2am.

★ **Shapko** 5 rue Rossetti ☎ 07 55 67 89 89, ⓦ shapko bar.fr. Intimate and friendly two-storey music bar, with a relaxed crowd and eclectic live music from slap bass jazz to funk, soul, hip hop, samba and bossa nova. Mon night is an open jam session; all musicians welcome. Daily 6pm–2.30am.

The Snug and Cellar 22 rue Droite ☎ 09 63 08 02 12. Smaller and lower-key than most of Nice's Irish bars, with a friendly, pub-like atmosphere, live music, open mic night (Mon) and Guinness for €5 during happy hour (6–8pm).

Mon–Thurs 4pm–12.30am, Fri 4pm–2am, Sat noon–2am, Sun noon–12.30am.

Wayne's 15 rue de la Préfecture, ☎ 04 93 13 46 99, ⓦ waynes.fr. This big, boisterous bar is one of the linchpins of the Vieux Nice nightlife scene, very popular with Anglophone expats. There's sport on big-screen TVs and nightly live rock music. Daily 10am–2am.

GREATER NICE

★ **Comptoir Central Electrique** 10 rue Bonaparte ☎ 09 60 46 30 72. Stylishly distressed café-bar in the hip "Petit Marais", converted from an electrical lighting store, with 1950s furniture, obligatory Edison lights, a few tables facing the street, a long list of wines by the glass (€5.50), and cocktails from €8. There's food, too. Mon–Sat 8.30am–12.30pm, Sun noon–12.30pm.

Glam 6 rue Eugène Emanuel ☎ 04 93 87 29 67. Nice's liveliest lesbian and gay club, with guest DJs, a dance and pop-oriented music policy and theme nights ranging from bears to pop. Entry with free drink (*conso*) €10 Fri and Sun, €15 Sat. Fri–Sun 11.45pm–5am.

High Club 45 promenade des Anglais ☎ 06 16 95 75 87, ⓦ highclub.fr. Large seafront disco that attracts big-name international DJs and live PAs. There's also an Eighties-themed club, *Studio 47*, aimed at the over-25s, plus a LGBTQ-friendly club, *Sk'high*. Expect to pay €10, except for the occasional free nights. Fri–Sun 11.45pm–6am.

Juke House Café 8 rue Defly ☎ 04 93 80 02 22. Tiny American-style cocktail and tapas bar that draws a young crowd. Happy hour (6–8pm) sees cocktails at €5.50–7 and draught beers from €2.30. Tapas, burgers and salads are on offer, and as the name suggests, there's a jukebox. Tues–Thurs 11.30am–2pm & 5pm–midnight, Fri & Sat 11.30am–2pm & 5pm–2.30am.

Le Swing 10 rue Defly, ☎ 06 86 31 40 45, ⓦ facebook. com/LESWING06. One of the more recent additions to Nice's LGBTQ scene, and located amid the nightlife hub that is rue Defly, this bar specialises in karaoke, cabaret, drag shows and the like; always busy. Tues–Sun 6pm–2.30am.

Le Volume 6 rue Defly ☎ 04 93 26 75 20. Underground music venue with an emphasis on local bands, from indie and rock to dubstep and drum'n'bass. Monthly open jam sessions .Hours vary.

ENTERTAINMENT

The best place for up-to-date **listings** for concerts, plays, films and sporting events is FNAC at 44–46 av Jean-Médecin (Mon–Sat 10am–7.30pm), where you can also buy **tickets** for most events.

Cinémathèque de Nice 3 esplanade Kennedy ☎ 04 92 04 06 66, ⓦ cinematheque-nice.com. Arthouse cinema which shows subtitled films in the original

language (*v.o*), including black-and-white classics and documentaries.

Opéra de Nice 4 & 6 rue St-François-de-Paule ☎ 04 92 17 40 00, ⓦ opera-nice.org. Nice's opulent late nineteenth-century opera house provides a magnificent venue for classical opera, ballet and concerts. Opera tickets range €10–100. Performances generally start at 8pm.

NICE FESTIVALS AND SPORTING EVENTS

Of Nice's many **festivals** – which begin with the celebrated Mardi Gras **Carnival** and associated flower processions in February – probably the most interesting is the **Nice Jazz Festival**, staged in July (ⓦnicejazzfestival.fr). The city's biggest sporting event is the **Ironman France Nice** in June, when competitors from all round the world swim 3.8km in the Baie des Anges, cycle 180km in the hills behind the city and run 42km, ending up along the promenade des Anglais.

Palais Nikaïa 163 bd du Mercantour ❶04 92 29 31 29, ⓦnikaia.fr. This indoor auditorium in the west of the city is Nice's major venue for big-name touring rock concerts, major musicals and ice spectaculars.

Théâtre de la Cité 3 rue Paganini ❶04 93 16 82 69, ⓦtheatredelacite.fr. Small, independent theatre with an eclectic programme for adults and children that embraces

everything from live chanson and flamenco to cabaret, drama and dance.

Théâtre National de Nice Promenade des Arts ❶04 93 13 19 90, ⓦtnn.fr. Nice's most prestigious stage for serious drama is part of the same iconic arts complex as MAMAC, staging everything from Molière to new works by up-and-coming dramatists.

SHOPPING

SEE MAPS PAGES 348 AND 350

Alziari 14 rue St-François-de-Paule ❶04 93 62 94 03, ⓦalziari.com.fr. Legendary (and very pretty) olive oil emporium established in 1868. You can taste and buy the oils, and they sell beautifully wrapped packs of oil, tapenade, olives, honey and other luxury nibbles to take home. Mon–Sat 9am–7pm, Sun 10am–7pm.

Cave Bianchi 7 rue Raoul Bosio ❶04 93 85 65 79, ⓦcave-bianchi.fr. This old-established wine merchant is a good place to sample wines from Nice's own *appellation contrôlée*, Bellet; it has a lovely vaulted stone wine cellar. Mon–Thurs & Sun 9.30am–7.30pm, Fri & Sat 9.30am–10.30pm.

Confiserie Florian 14 quai Papacino ❶04 93 55 43 50, ⓦconfiserieflorian.com. Venerable artisan confectioner on the port, with wonderful displays of sweets and candied fruits, jams and chocolates; you can take a free guided tour and watch sweets and jams being made, too. Mon–Sat 9am–7pm, Sun 9am–1pm & 2–7pm.

Cours Saleya markets Cours Saleya, place Pierre Gautier and Charles Félix. The city's famous market sells much more than just flowers, with fresh fruit, veg, cheeses and sausages all fresh from local farms; on Mon it's given

over to bric-a-brac and secondhand clothes, and on summer evenings a makers' market burns the midnight oil. Mon 7.30am–6pm, Tues–Sun 6am–1.30pm.

Maison Auer 7 rue St-François-de-Paule ❶04 93 85 77 98, ⓦmaison-auer.com. Lovely old *confiserie* and *chocolatier* that has been selling its famous candied fruits, chocolates and *marrons glacés* from beautiful premises close to the Opera since the nineteenth century. Tues–Sat 9am–6pm.

Marché aux Peintures Place du Palais. Monthly art market, with the opportunity to see artists at work. Second Sat of month: summer 7am–7pm; winter 7am–5pm.

Patisserie Lac 18 rue Barla ❶04 93 55 37 74; 12 rue de la Préfecture ❶04 93 55 37 74, ⓦpatisseries-lac.com. Classy *chocolatier* selling beautifully presented chocolate, *macarons*, nougat, *marrons glacés* and chocolate-coated ginger. Rue Barla Mon– Fri 9am–12.30pm & 3–7.30pm, Sat 9am–1pm & 3–7.30pm, Sun 9am–1pm & 4–7pm; rue de la Préfecture Mon–Sat 9.30am–7.30pm, Sun 9.30am–1.30pm & 3–7pm.

DIRECTORY

Consulate Canada, 10 rue Lamartine (❶04 93 92 93 22).
Health SAMU ❶15; Riviera Emergency Medical Services (English-speaking doctors; ❶04 93 26 12 70); Hôpital Pasteur, 30 voie Romaine (❶04 92 03 77 77); Centre de Santé Dentaire de Nice (❶04 22 13 06 26).
Laundry Laverie Asselit, 25 rue Assalit.

Lost property 42 rue Dabray (❶04 97 13 44 10).
Pharmacy 66 av Jean-Médecin (Mon–Sat 24hr, Sun 7pm–midnight; ❶04 93 62 54 44).
Police 1 av Maréchal Foch (❶04 92 17 22 22).
Post office 21 av Thiers (Mon–Wed & Fri 8am–6.30pm, Thurs 8am–noon & 2–6.30pm, Sat 8.30am–12.30pm).

The Arrière-Pays Niçois

The **foothills of the Alps** come down to the northern outskirts of Nice, and right down to the sea on the eastern side of the city: a majestic barrier, with the highest peaks snowcapped for much of the year. From the sea, the wide course of the Var to the west appears to be the only passage northwards. But the hidden river of Nice, the **Paillon**, also cuts its way to the sea through the mountains past small, fortified medieval settlements. The **Nice–Turin railway line** follows the Paillon for part of its way – one of the many spectacular train journeys of this region. If you have your own transport you'll find this is serious, hairpin-bend country where the views are a major distraction. **Buses** from Nice to its villages are infrequent.

With their proximity to the metropolis, the *villages perchés* of **Peillon**, **Peille**, **Lucéram**, **L'Escarène**, **Coaraze** and **Contes** are no longer entirely peasant communities, though the social make-up remains a mix. You may well hear Provençal spoken and the **traditional festivals** are still communal affairs, even when the participants include well-off Niçois escaping the coastal heat. The links between the city and its hinterland are strong: the villagers still live off the land and sell their olives and olive oil, goat's cheese or vegetables and herbs in the city's markets; many city dwellers' parents or grandparents still have homes within the mountains, and for every Niçois this wild and underpopulated countryside is the natural remedy for city stress.

Peillon

For the first 10km or so along the River Paillon, after you leave the last of Nice, the valley is marred by quarries that supply the city's constant demand for building materials. However, shortly after Ste-Thècle – site of Peillon's nearest *gare SNCF* – a side road begins to climb, looping through olive groves, pine forest and brilliant pink and yellow broom to reach the gates of **PEILLON**'s medieval enclave. The ascent is little more than 1km from the valley floor as the crow flies, but in reality the journey is considerably further because of the twisting, circuitous road.

Peillon is beautifully maintained, right up to the lovely place de l'Église at the top. There is very little commerce and very little life during the week – most of the residents commute to their jobs in Nice. Just outside the village stands the **Chapelle des Pénitents Blancs**, which is decorated with violent fifteenth-century frescoes similar to those by Jean Canavesio at La Brigue (see page 244). You can peer through the grille across the chapel door; depositing a fifty-cent coin illuminates the interior. From the chapel a path heads off across the hills northwards to Peille. It's a two-hour walk along what was once a Roman road, and a more direct route than going via the valley.

Peille

PEILLE lies at the end of a 6km climb from the valley below, the journey up from the *gare SNCF* replete with hairpin bends. The atmosphere here is very different to that in Peillon. The village was excommunicated several times for refusing to pay its bishop's tithes, and its republicanism was later manifested by the domed thirteenth-century Chapelle de St-Sébastien being turned into the **Hôtel de Ville**, and the Chapelle des Pénitents Noirs into a communal **oil press**. Peille claims to be the birthplace of the Roman emperor Pertinax, who was assassinated within thirteen weeks of his election on account of his egalitarian and democratic tendencies.

The village

The main square, **place de la Colle**, is graced with a Gothic fountain and two half-arches supporting a Romanesque pillar. It's also home to the medieval **courthouse**,

which bears a plaque recalling Peille's transfer of its rights over Monaco to Genoa. On nearby rue St-Sébastien the former salt tax office, the **Hôtel de la Gabelle**, still stands. The only thing detracting from the beauty of the village is the view to the southwest, which is marred by the cement-quarrying around La Grave, its suburb down in the valley by the rail line. You can, however, take labyrinthine winding routes to La Turbie, Ste-Agnes or L'Escarène from the village, on which precipitous panoramas – and slow progress – are assured. More adventurous visitors make the circuit of Peille's **Via Ferrata**, which includes a rope bridge and rock face, though it's now closed until further notice; check with the tourist office for updates.

L'Escarène

At **L'ESCARÈNE** the rail line leaves the Paillon and heads northeast to Sospel (see page 243). In the days before train travel, this was an important staging post on the road from Nice to Turin, when drivers would harness up new horses to take on the 100m Braus pass, which the rail line now tunnels under. There's not a great deal to see, other than the great Baroque church of **St-Pierre-ès-Liens**, with its wonderful eighteenth-century church organ.

Lucéram

Following the Paillon upstream for 6km from L'Escarène, you reach unpretentious but beautiful **LUCÉRAM**, with its outwardly unobtrusive fifteenth-century **Chapelle de St-Grat**, with gorgeous frescoes by Jean Beleison, a colleague of Louis Bréa, at the entrance to the village. You'll need to visit the tourist office (see page 365) to gain entry to the village's museums or church, which are otherwise locked; it's a good idea to phone in advance.

Circuit des Crèches and Musée de la Crèche

Lucéram is well known locally for its annual **Circuit des Crèches**, which brings thousands of visitors to the village in the weeks before Christmas. During this period more than four hundred nativity scenes are displayed in the streets of Lucéram and the neighbouring community of Peïra-Cava; there's a smaller selection at the **Musée de la Crèche** (daily during the Circuit des Crèches; free; for admission at other times enquire at tourist office; €2), which is midway between the tourist office (see page 365) and the church of Ste-Marguerite.

Ste-Marguerite

The belfry of the church of **Ste-Marguerite** rises proudly above the village houses, its Baroque cupola glittering with polychrome Niçois tiles. Inside are some of the best late medieval artworks in the Comté de Nice, though several have been removed and taken to Nice's Musée des Beaux-Arts (see page 352). All these works belong to the School of Nice, and both the Retable de Ste-Marguerite, framed by a tasteless Baroque baldaquin, and the painting of Sts Peter and Paul, with its cliff-hanging castle in the distance, are attributed to Louis Bréa.

Chapelle de Notre Dame de Bon Coeur

There are examples of work by Jean Beleison on the walls and ceilings of the **Chapelle de Notre Dame de Bon Coeur**, 2km northwest of the village off the road to the St-Roch pass and Coaraze. Although you can't go in to the chapel, you can view the paintings from outside.

Coaraze

COARAZE overlooks the valley of the Paillon de Contes, a tributary running west of the main Paillon. From Lucéram the D2566 ascends to the pass of St-Roch, from which the D15 hangs over near-vertical descents, turning corners onto thrilling vistas of these beautiful but inhospitable mountains.

Coaraze is one of the more chic Niçois villages, with many an artist and designer in residence, and it doesn't pander to the tourist trade in the slightest. The facades of the post office and *mairie*, and place Félix-Giordan near the top of the village, are decorated with **sundials** signed by various artists including Jean Cocteau and Ponce de Léon. The latter decorated the **Chapelle Notre Dame du Gressier**, northwest of the village, in 1962, known now as the Chapelle Bleue for the single colour he used in the frescoes. Place Félix-Giordan also has a **lizard mosaic** and a Provençal poem engraved in stone. The **church**, destroyed and rebuilt three times, is famous for the number of angels in its interior decoration, 118 in all. The tourist office (see page 365) holds the key to the church and chapel.

Châteauneuf-Villevieille and around

Across the river from Contes, 9km downstream from Coaraze, the D815 road winds up the mountainside to **CHÂTEAUNEUF-VILLEVIEILLE**, a hilltop gathering of houses around an eleventh-century Romanesque church.

Castelnuovo

About 2km beyond Châteauneuf-Villevieille, a rutted track to the left leads to a more recent **ruined village**, the Bourg Mediéval (also called **Castelnuovo**) which was established by Châteauneuf-Villevieille's inhabitants in the sixth century for reasons of defence, but gradually abandoned from the first half of the eighteenth century as the political situation stabilized and defence was no longer the highest priority, at which point the community "deperched" itself to return to the village's original site. Ivy-clad towers and crumbling walls rise up among once-cultivated fig trees and rose bushes, while insects buzz in the silence and butterflies flit about the wild flowers that have replaced the gardens. The views over Contes, Coaraze and the surrounding rugged landscape are superb. A boom across the track leading to the site supposedly closes at night, but there's otherwise nothing to stop you wandering around at will.

Sentier de découverte Mont Macaron

From Castelnuovo a well-marked 4.8km footpath, the **Sentier de découverte Mont Macaron**, loops around the summit of the mountain, offering breathtaking views in every direction; at one point Nice and the entire sweep of the Baie des Anges are laid out beneath you as if on a map. The walk is particularly lovely in the spring, when the hillsides are a mass of wild flowers.

ARRIVAL AND INFORMATION   THE ARRIÈRE-PAYS NIÇOIS

PEILLON

By bus Bus #360 from Nice (2 daily; 45min) will get you as far as the "Le Moulin" stop after Ste-Thècle, from where it is a stiff walk uphill.

Tourist office 4 Carriera Centrale (Tues–Sat 1–5pm; ☎06 24 97 42 25).

PEILLE

By bus Bus #116 makes the connection between Nice and Peille via La Turbie (3 daily; 55min).

By train The *gare SNCF* is at La Grave, 7km from the village via a twisting road.

Tourist office Pointe Info, 15 rue Centrale (Wed–Sun 10am–noon & 1–6pm; ☎04 93 82 14 40, ⓦ peille.fr).

LUCÉRAM

By bus Buses #340 and #360 run from Nice (9 daily; 50min–1hr).

Tourist office Place Adrien-Barralis (Mon, Tues & Thurs–Sat 9am–noon & 2–6pm; ☎04 93 79 46 50, ⓦ luceram.com).

COARAZE

By bus Bus #300 serves Contes from Nice, with the daily

4pm service continuing on to Coaraze (1hr 20min).
Tourist office 7 Montée du Portal (Tues & Thurs–Sat 9.30am–12.30pm & 2.30–5pm, Wed 9.30am–12.30pm;

☎ 04 93 79 37 47). As it's volunteer-run and not always staffed, it's best to phone ahead.

ACCOMMODATION AND EATING

PEILLON

Auberge de la Madone 3 place August Arnulf ☎ 04 93 79 91 17, ⊕ auberge-madone-peillon.com. Lovely, rambling hotel/restaurant at the entrance to the *vieux village*, with plenty of old-fashioned charm, a good restaurant gastronomique, *L'Authentique*, serving *menus* at €40, €55 and €65 and a bistro, *La Table d'Augustine*, serving two-course lunch *formules* for €19 and three-course for €25. Closed mid-Nov to Christmas and second half of Jan; reception closed Wed. Restaurants daily 12.30–2.30pm & 7–10pm. **€110**

PEILLE

Chez Mimi 1 place de la Republique ☎ 07 70 26 83 72. Friendly restaurant in the *vieux village*, where highly regarded wood-fired pizza goes for around €12. In summer, the expansive terrace occasionally plays host to live music and Valencian-style uber-paella. May–Oct Wed, Thurs &

Sun noon–2pm & 6.30–9.30pm, Fri & Sat noon–2pm & 6.30–10pm; Nov–April Thurs & Sun 6.30–9pm, Fri & Sat 6.30–10pm.

★ **Restaurant Cauvin/Chez Nana** Place Carnot ☎ 04 93 79 90 41. For a real slap-up feed like your (Provençal) mother would make, it's worth making the pilgrimage to this wonderful restaurant for the €28 lunch buffet, complete with a generous selection of hors d'oeuvres. Thurs–Sun noon–1.15pm.

LUCÉRAM

Bocca Fina Place Adrien Barralis ☎ 04 93 79 51 54. Unpretentious restaurant with a striking cave-like interior on the main road through the village, close to the tourist office, serving Niçois favourites like *socca* for around €5 and main courses for around €15. Tues–Sun noon–2.30pm & 7–10pm.

The Corniche Inférieure

The characteristic **Côte d'Azur mansions** that represent the unrestrained fantasies of the original owners parade along the **Corniche Inférieure**, creating a series of pale dots among the lush pines. Others pepper the promontory of **Cap Ferrat**, where some of the planet's priciest real estate hides behind high walls and equally high security.

Villefranche-sur-Mer

VILLEFRANCHE-SUR-MER, the resort closest to Nice, marks the beginning of one of the most picturesque and unspoiled sections of the Riviera, though the cruise liners attracted by the deep anchorage in Villefranche's beautiful bay ensure a steady stream of tour buses climbing the hill from the port. However, as long as your visit doesn't coincide with the shore excursions, the old town on the waterfront, with its active fishing fleet and its covered, medieval **rue Obscure** running beneath the houses, is a charming place to while away an afternoon.

Chapelle de St-Pierre

Mon & Wed–Sun: mid-March to mid-Sept 10am–noon & 3–7pm; mid-Sept to mid-March 10am–noon & 2–6pm • €3

The fishing harbour is overlooked by the tiny medieval **Chapelle de St-Pierre**, decorated by **Jean Cocteau** in 1957 in shades he described as "ghosts of colours". In the guide to the chapel written by Cocteau, the artist invites travellers to enter without any aesthetic preconceptions. Those ghostly colours fill drawings in strong and simple lines, portraying scenes from the life of St Peter and homages to the women of Villefranche and to the gypsies. Above the altar Peter walks on water supported by an angel, to the amusement of Christ. The fishermen's eyes are drawn as fishes; the ceramic eyes on either side of the door are the flames of the Apocalypse.

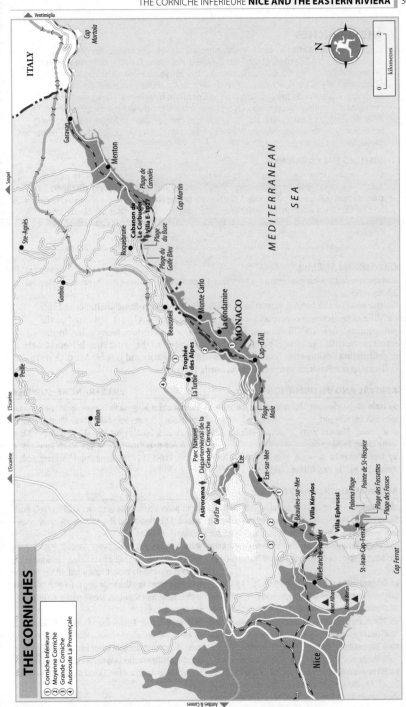

THE CORNICHES

1. Corniche Inférieure
2. Moyenne Corniche
3. Grande Corniche
4. Autoroute La Provençale

N

0 — 2 kilometres

ITALY

Ventimiglia
Cap Mortola
Garavan
Menton
Plage de Camolés
Cap Martin
Ste-Agnès
Roquebrune
Cabanon de Le Corbusier
Villa E-1027
Plage du Buse
Gorbio
Plage du Golfe Bleu
Monte Carlo
Beausoleil
MONACO
La Condamine
Trophée des Alpes
La Turbie
Cap-d'Ail
Peille
Plage Mala
Peillon
Parc Naturel Départemental de la Grande Corniche
Astrorama
Col d'Èze
Èze
Èze-sur-Mer
Beaulieu-sur-Mer
Villa Kérylos
Villa Ephrussi
Pointe de St-Hospice
Paloma Plage
Plage des Fossettes
Villefranche-sur-Mer
St-Jean-Cap-Ferrat
Plage des Fosses
Cap Ferrat
Nice
Mont Alban
Mont Boron

MEDITERRANEAN SEA

Sospel
L'Escarène
L'Escarène

Antibes & Cannes

8

THE CORNICHES

Three **corniche roads** run east from Nice to the independent principality of Monaco and on to Menton, the last town of the French Riviera. Napoleon built the **Grande Corniche** on the route of the Romans' Via Julia Augusta. The **Moyenne Corniche** dates from the first quarter of the twentieth century, when aristocratic tourism on the Riviera was already causing congestion on the coastal road, the **Corniche Inférieure**. The upper two are popular for shooting car commercials and action films, but they're dangerous roads: Grace Kelly, princess of Monaco, who was filmed driving the corniches in *To Catch a Thief*, died more than 25 years later when she took a bend too fast as she descended from La Turbie to the Moyenne Corniche.

VISITING THE CORNICHES

Buses serve all three routes; the train follows the lower corniche; and all three are superb means of seeing the most mountainous stretch of the Côte d'Azur. For **long-distance panoramas** you follow the Grande Corniche; for **precipitous views** the Moyenne Corniche; and for **close-up encounters** with the architectural riot of the continuous coastal resort, take the Corniche Inférieure. If you want to **stay**, you'll find that the biggest choice is along the Corniche Inférieure, or in the chic (and expensive) *village perché* of Èze.

Citadelle de St-Elme

Museums June–Sept Mon–Sat 10am–noon & 3–6.30pm, Sun 3–6.30pm; Oct & Dec–May Mon–Sat 10am–noon & 2–5.30pm, Sun 2–5.30pm • Free

To the west of the fishing port, the massive **Citadelle de St-Elme** shelters the Hôtel de Ville, a conference centre and a series of **art museums**. One is dedicated to the voluptuous works of Villefranche sculptor **Volti**, whose bronze woman lies in the fountain outside the citadel gates; another, dedicated to the artist couple **Henri Goetz** and **Christine Boumeester**, contains two works by Picasso and one by Miró. A third collection, the **Roux**, is given over to ceramic figurines.

ARRIVAL AND INFORMATION   VILLEFRANCHE-SUR-MER

By train Villefranche's *gare SNCF* is just above the beach, a short walk from the port.
Destinations Monaco (every 15min; 12–17min); Nice (every 15min; 8min).
By bus Villefranche is served by the #100/101 Nice–Menton bus and the local #81 bus from Nice.

Tourist office In the Jardin François-Binon just below the corniche as it changes from Av Foch to Av Albert-1er (April–June, Sept & Oct Mon–Sat 9am–12.30pm & 2–5.30pm; July & Aug daily 9am–6.30pm; Nov–March 9am–noon & 1–5pm; ☎ 04 93 01 73 68, ⌨ villefranche-sur-mer.com).

ACCOMMODATION AND EATING

★ **La Darse** 32 av du Général de Gaulle ☎ 04 93 01 72 54, ⌨ hoteldeladarse.com. Two-star hotel in a charming spot overlooking the nineteenth-century naval harbour, with renovated a/c rooms, some with sea-facing balconies and some sleeping up to three. Closed mid-Nov to mid-Feb. **€90**

La Grignotière 3 rue du Poilu ☎ 04 93 76 79 83, ⌨ la-grignotiere-restaurant-villefranche-sur-mer.com. An affordable option in Villefranche's old town, with fillet of sea bream Provençal-style or spaghetti with mussels and basil cream on a three-course lunch *menu* (€19.50 and main courses from around €14. Daily noon–2.30pm & 6.30–9.30pm.

La Mère Germaine 7–9 quai Amiral-Courbet ☎ 04 93 01 71 39, ⌨ meregermaine.com. The most famous of the quayside fish restaurants, founded in 1938 and known

for its pricey bouillabaisse (well over €100 for two); mains around €40. Closed mid-Nov to mid-Feb. Daily noon–2.30pm & 7–10pm.

Villa Patricia 310 av de l'Ange Gardien, Pont St-Jean ☎ 04 93 01 06 70, ⌨ hotel-patricia.riviera.fr. Good-value, gay and eco-friendly budget option just off the Corniche Inférieure between Villefranche and Cap Ferrat, with nine rooms, some with sea views. There's private parking and a shady garden.. **€95**

Welcome 3 quai Amiral-Courbet ☎ 04 93 76 27 62, ⌨ welcomehotel.com. Highly recommended four-star hotel in the former convent where Cocteau used to stay, in a prime position overlooking the port. The 35 rooms have a/c, balconies and sea views. Closed mid-Nov to early Jan. **€235**

Cap Ferrat

Closing off Villefranche's bay to the east is **Cap Ferrat**, justifiably among the Côte d'Azur's most desirable addresses due to the lack of through traffic and its pretty, indented coast; past residents include assorted Rothschilds, the King of Belgium and writer Somerset Maugham. The one town, **ST-JEAN-CAP-FERRAT**, is a typical Riviera hideout for the wealthy: old houses overlooking modern yachts in a fishing port turned millionaires' resort.

East of St-Jean's pleasure port you can follow avenue Jean-Mermoz and then a **coastal path** out along the little peninsula, past the Plage Paloma to **Pointe de St-Hospice**, where a nineteenth-century chapel cowers behind a 12m-high turn-of-the-twentieth-century metal *Virgin and Child*. Back in St-Jean, another coastal path runs from avenue Claude-Vignon right round to chemin du Roy on the opposite side of the peninsula. The Cap's coastal walks are delightfully traffic-free – if you don't count the endless yachts and motorboats offshore – and there are beaches to discover: **Paloma Plage** on the north side of Pointe de St-Hospice, dominated by its restaurant, and the rather more appealing, south-facing **Plage des Fosses** and **Plage des Fossettes**.

Villa Ephrussi

St-Jean-Cap-Ferrat • Feb–June, Sept & Oct daily 10am–6pm; July & Aug daily 10am–7pm; Nov–Jan Mon–Fri 2–6pm, Sat & Sun 10am–6pm • €15 • ☎ 04 93 01 33 09, ⊕ villa-ephrussi.com

The one exception to the Cap's formidable privacy is the **Villa Ephrussi**, which was built in 1912 for Baroness Ephrussi, née Rothschild, a woman of unlimited wealth and eclectic tastes. The result is a wonderful profusion of decorative art, paintings and sculpture of European to Far Eastern origin from the fourteenth to the nineteenth century. Highlights include a fifteenth-century d'Enghien tapestry of hunting scenes; paintings by Carpaccio and other works of the Venetian Renaissance; Sèvres and Vincennes porcelain; Ming vases; and Mandarin robes. The baroness had a particular love of the eighteenth century, and would receive guests dressed as Marie Antoinette; in order to make the beautiful **gardens**, she had a hill removed to level out the space for her formal French design, but funds eventually ran out so one part of the park – the eastern slope – remained wild. Today, highlights include the **musical fountains**, which gush into life every twenty minutes, and – when in bloom – the stunning **rose garden**, which offers wonderful views over the bay of Villefranche.

8

ARRIVAL AND INFORMATION   CAP FERRAT

By bus The #81 bus from Nice and Villefranche (every 25–35min) serves St-Jean's port.
Tourist office 5 av Denis-Séméria, on St-Jean's port

(May–Sept Mon–Sat 9–6.30pm, Sun 9am–1pm & 2–5pm; Oct–April Mon–Sat 9am–1pm & 2–5pm; ☎ 04 93 76 08 90, ⊕ saintjeancapferrat-tourisme.fr).

ACCOMMODATION AND EATING

Brise Marine 58 av J-Mermoz, St-Jean ☎ 04 93 76 04 36, ⊕ hotel-brisemarine.com. Attractive old Italianate villa in an idyllic garden setting close to the sea. Rooms are a/c and en suite; the more expensive options have a balcony or terrace. Closed Nov–Feb. **€206**

Capitaine Cook 11 av Port, St-Jean ☎ 04 93 76 02 66. Not quite fronting St-Jean's port but near enough, this local institution specialises in their own take on the Provençal seafood soup, bisquebouille. Be sure to finish up with their trademark strawberry and ice cream soup. *Menu* €34. Summer Mon & Thurs–Sun noon–2/3pm & 7–10pm, Tues & Wed 7–10pm; rest of year Mon & Thurs–Sun same hours, Tues & Wed noon–2/3pm.

La Frégate 11 av Denis-Séméria, St-Jean ☎ 04 93 76 04 51, ⊕ hotellafregate.jimdo.com. The best budget option, in a central location by the port, characterful and even slightly eccentric with ten rooms, some with a/c and sea views, and a pleasant, art-filled garden where you can take breakfast in fine weather. **€60**

Grand-Hôtel du Cap Ferrat 71 bd du Général-de-Gaulle ☎ 04 93 76 50 50, ⊕ fourseasons.com/capferrat. Classic Riviera palace hotel in a stunning site near the southern tip of the Cap, with elegant, all-white rooms and suites – the very fanciest have their own swimming pools – and an excellent restaurant. **€1360**

Le Pacha du Sloop Quai du Nouveau Port, St-Jean ☏04 93 01 48 63, ⓦle-pacha-du-sloop-restaurant-st-jean-cap-ferrat.com. The pick of the restaurants fronting St-Jean's port, serving fresh fish cooked in delicate and original ways. Lunch *formule* €18; mains around €20. Mon & Thurs–Sat noon–3pm & 7.30–9pm, Sun 12.30–3pm.

Beaulieu-sur-Mer

To the eastern side of the Cap Ferrat peninsula, overlooking the pretty Baie des Fourmis and accessible by foot from St-Jean along the promenade Maurice-Rouvier, is **BEAULIEU-SUR-MER**, sheltered by a ring of craggy hills that ensures its temperatures are among the highest on the Côte, and that the town itself is one of its less developed spots. It's an appealing place, more tranquil than the bigger resorts and with a working harbour where you can buy freshly caught fish from the quayside, and it retains a couple of fine examples of *belle époque* architecture – most notably La Rotonde on avenue Fernand-Dunan, an opulent former hotel.

Villa Kérylos

Impasse Gustave Eiffel • Daily: May–Aug 10am–7pm; Sept–April 10am–5pm • €11.50 • ☏04 93 01 01 44, ⓦvillakerylos.fr • 5min walk from Beaulieu train station

Beaulieu's star attraction is the **Villa Kérylos**, a near-perfect reproduction of an ancient Greek villa, just east of the casino. The only concessions made by Théodore Reinach, the archeologist who had it built, were glass in the windows, a concealed piano, and a minimum of early twentieth-century conveniences. He lived here for twenty years, eating, dressing and behaving as an Athenian citizen, taking baths with his male friends and assigning separate suites to women. However bizarre the concept, it's visually stunning, with faithfully reproduced frescoes, ivory and bronze copies of mosaics and vases, authentic antiquities and lavish use of marble and alabaster; the more intimate upstairs rooms are particularly appealing. The waterside setting is fabulous, with views across to St Jean-Cap-Ferrat.

ARRIVAL AND INFORMATION
BEAULIEU-SUR-MER

By train The *gare SNCF* is on place Georges-Clemenceau. **Destinations** Monaco (every 11min–1hr; 8–13min); Nice (every 15–30min; 11–13min).

By bus Beaulieu is served by the Nice–Menton bus #100/101 and local bus #81 from Nice and Villefranche. **Destinations** Nice (every 10–35min; 25min); St-Jean-Cap-Ferrat (every 20–35min; 6min); Villefranche (every 10–35min; 6min).

Tourist office Next to the *gare SNCF* (mid-April to June & Sept to mid-Oct Mon–Fri 9am–12.15pm & 2–6pm, Sat 9am–12.15pm & 2–5pm; July & Aug daily 9am–1pm & 2–6.30pm; mid-Oct to mid-April Mon–Fri 9am–12.15pm & 2–5pm, Sat 9am–1pm; ☏04 93 01 02 21, ⓦotbeaulieusurmer.com).

ACCOMMODATION AND EATING

Le Beaulieu 45 bd Marinoni ☏04 93 01 03 36. Smart and central café/bar that's a good bet for drinks and coffee, with a chalked-up menu of salads, platters and simple main courses – including some low-calorie choices – from around €12.50. Live music on Fri from 6pm. Mon–Thurs & Sat 7am–10.30pm, Fri 7am–midnight, Sun 7am–2pm.

Le Petit Darkoum 18 bd du Maréchal Leclerc ☏04 93 01 48 59, ⓦlepetitdarkoum-beaulieusurmer.fr. Atmospheric Moroccan restaurant serving up tagines and couscous with a lunch *formule* at €13.50 and *menu* at €27. It doesn't look much from the outside but has a beautiful tiled interior and a good reputation locally. Wed–Sun noon–1.30pm & 7–9.30pm.

La Restaurant des Rois La Réserve, 5 bd du Maréchal Leclerc ☏04 93 01 00 01, ⓦreservebeaulieu.com. Beaulieu's best restaurant is in its best hotel, with a Michelin star and a suitably palatial setting for dishes such as oven-baked sea bass with *pastis* and pan-seared fennel bulb broth or lobster in a yuzu emulsion. Main courses cost €68–92; *menus* €70–165; there's a more informal regional restaurant, *La Table de la Réserve*, and in summer a poolside restaurant, *Vent Debout*, at lunchtime. Daily 7.30–9.30pm.

Riviera 6 rue Paul Doumer ☎ 04 93 01 04 92, ⓦ hotel-riviera.fr. A tempting, economical option, this family-run three-star hotel is on a quiet side street close to the Villa Kérylos and the sea. Tastefully decorated rooms have a/c and double glazing. **€79**

Select 1 rue André Cane ☎ 04 93 01 05 42, ⓦ hotelselect-beaulieu.com. Good-value two-star hotel in the centre of Beaulieu, facing the market and close to the *gare SNCF* and restaurants, with nineteen simple but modern rooms, a/c and soundproofing. **€96**

Èze-sur-Mer

The little seaside extension of **Èze** village (see page 372) on the Moyenne Corniche, **ÈZE-SUR-MER** has a long but narrow shingle beach and fewer pretensions than its western neighbours. When you tire of the beach, you can struggle up the steep Sentier Nietzsche (see page 372) to reach Èze's *vieux village* – the uphill hike takes an hour and a half, or take the easy way with the #83 bus from the *gare SNCF* (roughly hourly 10am–6.20pm; 15min; €2).

Cap d'Ail

CAP D'AIL has an informal (but extremely affluent) feel, though it suffers from the noise and congestion of the lower and middle corniches running closely parallel. As you descend to the sea from the main road, however, the noise is quickly left behind, for Cap d'Ail's delightful secret is that its coast is fringed not by some multi-laned boulevard but by a peaceful and beautiful coastal path.

From the tiny promontory of **Pointe des Douaniers**, the **sentier du Littoral** leads east into **Monaco** and also – rather more temptingly – winds west around the headland to the pretty little **Plage Mala**, one of the most secluded and attractive beaches on the eastern Riviera. The way there is dotted with imposing old villas; in places the path is a bit of a scramble, and it can get slippery if the sea is rough.

8

ACCOMMODATION AND EATING   CAP D'AIL

Hôtel de Monaco 1 av Pierre-Weck ☎ 04 92 41 31 00, ⓦ hoteldemonaco.com. Chic boutique-style hotel in a quiet and classy residential area close to Plage Mala, with tasteful contemporary decor and a private bar/terrace. **€179**

La Pinède 10 av R. Gramaglia ☎ 04 93 78 37 10, ⓦ restaurantlapinede.com. In a pine grove right on the water's edge on the sentier du Littoral, with a *carte* ranging from steak tartare to *moules marinières*, and *menus* from €37. March–Oct Mon, Tues & Thurs–Sun noon–2.30pm & 7–10.30pm.

Thalassa Relais International de la Jeunesse 2 av R. Gramaglia ☎ 04 93 81 27 63, ⓦ clajsud.fr. Youth hostel right on the sentier du Littoral close to the *gare SNCF*, with accommodation in four- to ten-bed dorms overlooking the sea. Closed Nov–March. **€20**

The Moyenne Corniche

The first views from the **Moyenne Corniche** are back over Nice as you grind up Mont Alban, which, with its seaward extension, Mont Boron, separates Nice from Villefranche. The wooded summit is crowned by a perfect little sixteenth-century fortress, the **Fort du Mont Alban,** a surprisingly endearing structure with its four tiny turrets glimmering in glazed Niçois tiles. You can wander freely around the fort and see why Villefranche's citadel, so unassailable from the sea, was so vulnerable from above. To reach it you turn sharp right off the corniche along route Forestière before you reach the Villefranche pass. The #14 bus from Nice stops at Chemin du Fort, from where the fort is signed. At the opposite (southern) end of the summit, an old military battery has been laid out as a **belvedere** and public park, with views over the coast and a nature trail through lush woodland. Once through the pass, the cliff-hanging car-chase stretch of the Moyenne Corniche begins, with great views, sudden tunnels and barely any habitation.

Èze

ÈZE is unmistakeable long before you arrive, its streets wound around a cone of rock below the corniche, whose summit is 470m above the sea. From a distance the village has the monumental medieval unity of Normandy's Mont St-Michel and is a dramatic sight to behold, but seen up close, its secular nature exerts itself. Of the *villages perchés* in Provence, only St-Paul-de-Vence can compete with Èze for catering so single-mindedly to tourists, and it takes a mental feat to recall that the labyrinth of tiny vaulted passages and stairways was designed not for charm but from fear of attack.

Jardin Exotique

Daily: April–June & Oct 9am–6.30pm; July–Sept 9am–7.30pm; Nov–Feb 9am–4.30pm • €6 • ⓦ jardinexotique-eze.fr

Èze's ultimate defence, the castle, no longer exists, but the **Jardin Exotique** which replaces it is worth a visit for the fantastic views it offers from the ruins – and for a respite from the commerce below. Cacti, agave and aloe thrive on the dry, stony site.

Sentier Frédéric-Nietzsche

From place du Centenaire, just outside the old village, you can descend to the shore on foot in around 45 minutes via the signposted, scenic and blissfully car-free **sentier Frédéric-Nietzsche**. The philosopher Nietzsche is said to have conceived part of *Thus Spoke Zarathustra* on this path. You arrive at the Corniche Inférieure at the eastern limit of Èze-sur-Mer (see page 371).

8

ARRIVAL AND INFORMATION ÈZE

By train Èze's *gare SNCF* is on the coast in Èze-sur-Mer, from where bus #83 ascends to the village (8 daily; 15). Destinations Monaco (every 30min–1hr; 8min); Nice (every 30min–1hr; 16min).

By bus Bus #83 from Èze's *gare SNCF* and buses from Nice arrive at the entrance to the village. Destinations Nice (15 daily; 38min).

Tourist office On place du Général-de-Gaulle just above the main car park (Jan, March, Nov & Dec Mon–Sat 9am–4pm; Feb, April, May & Oct daily 9am–6pm; June–Sept daily 9am–7pm; ☏ 04 93 41 26 00, ⓦ eze-tourisme.com). Pick up a free map here of the footpaths through the hills linking the three corniches.

ACCOMMODATION AND EATING

Château de la Chèvre d'Or Rue de Barri ☏ 04 92 10 66 66 (hotel), ☏ 04 92 10 66 61(restaurant); ⓦ chevredor. com. Luxury hotel (closed early Nov to early March) in the *vieux village* with a variety of rooms and suites, some very spacious with terraces and sea views; the panoramic suite has its own infinity pool. Nose-bleedingly high prices match the dizzying location at the two-Michelin-starred *restaurant gastronomique*. You'll pay from €85 for main courses à la carte; *menus* are €90 (lunch) and from €160 (dinner). March Tues–Sun 12.30–3pm & 7.30–10pm; April–June & Sept to early Nov daily 12.30–3pm & 7.30–10pm; July & Aug Mon–Wed 7.30–10pm, Thurs–Sun 12.30–3pm & 7.30–10pm. **€408.50**

Château Eza Rue de la Pise ☏ 04 93 41 12 24, ⓦ chateau eza.com. Award-winning luxury boutique hotel (closed Nov and first three weeks Dec) in the *vieux village*, with twelve a/c rooms and suites that range from prettily Provençal to grandly spacious, plus a Michelin-starred restaurant (*menus* €55–125) and fabulous views. Jan–March Wed–Sun 12.30–2.30pm & 7.30–10pm; April–Oct & last week in Dec daily 12.30–2.30pm & 7.30–10pm. **€380**

Le Golf Hôtel Place de la Colette ☏ 04 93 41 18 50, ⓦ hotel-du-golf.cotedazurhotel.net/en. A reasonably priced option on the main road at the entrance to the *vieux village*, with eight a/c rooms, a restaurant and parking nearby. Closed Jan. **€80**

The Grande Corniche

At every other turn on the **Grande Corniche** you're tempted to park your car and enjoy the distant views, which uniquely extend both seaward and inland – but there are frustratingly few truly safe places to do so. At certain points, such as **Col d'Èze**, you can turn off upwards for even higher views.

Col d'Èze

The upper part of Èze is backed by the **Parc Naturel Départemental de la Grande Corniche**, a wonderful oak forest covering the high slopes and plateaux of this coastal range. Paths are well signed, and there are picnic and games areas and orientation tables – in fact it's rather over-managed, but at least it isn't built on. If you take a left (coming from Nice) to cross the col and keep following route de la Revère, you come, after 1.5km or so, to an observatory, **Astrorama** (Jan, Feb, Nov & Dec Fri & Sat during school holidays 6–10pm; March–June, Sept & Oct Fri & Sat 6–10pm; July & Aug Tues–Sat 7–11pm; €10; ⓦastrorama.net), where you can admire the evening and night sky through telescopes.

ACCOMMODATION AND EATING   COL D'ÈZE

Èze Hermitage 1951 av des Diables Bleus ☎ 04 93 41 00 68, ⓦezehermitage.com. Three-star *Logis de France* hotel/restaurant on the Grande Corniche, with magnificent views of sea and forested hills, and a restaurant serving reasonable meals. April–Oct daily 12–1.30pm & 7–9.30pm. **€125**

La Turbie

Eighteen stunning kilometres from Nice, **LA TURBIE** boasts an eighteenth-century church, the **Église de St-Michel-Archange,** that is a Baroque concoction of marble, onyx, agate and oil paint, with pink the overriding colour, and, among the paintings, a superb *St Mark writing the Gospel* attributed to Veronese. In the old part of the village rough-hewn stone houses line rue Comte-de-Cessole, once part of the Roman Via Julia, leading to the **Trophée des Alpes**.

Trophée des Alpes

Av Albert 1er • Tues–Sun: mid-May to mid-Sept 9.30am–1pm & 2.30–6.30pm; mid-Sept to mid-May 10am–1.30pm & 2.30–5pm • €6 • ☎ 04 93 41 20 84, ⓦtrophee-auguste.fr • Infrequent buses (#116; 35min) from Nice

La Turbie's chief glory is the **Trophée des Alpes**, a sixth-century monument to the power of Rome and the total subjugation of the local peoples. Originally, a statue of Augustus Caesar stood on a 45m plinth, which was inscribed with the names of 45 vanquished tribes and an equally long list of the emperor's virtues. In the fifth century the descendants of the suppressed were worshipping the monument – to the horror of St Honorat, who did his best to have the graven image destroyed. However, it took several centuries of barbarian invasions, quarrying and incorporation into military structures before the trophy was finally reduced to rubble in the early eighteenth century by Louis XIV's engineers, who blew the fortress up to prevent it being used by the king's enemies. Its painstaking reconstruction was undertaken in the 1930s, and it now stands, statueless, at 35m.

Viewed from a distance along the Grande Corniche, however, the Trophée can still hold its own as an imperial monument. If you want to take a closer look and see a 3D virtual reconstruction of the original, you'll have to buy a ticket for the fenced-off plinth and its little **museum**. You can climb up to the viewing platform and enjoy the spectacular view, extending to the Esterel in the west and Italy in the east.

ACCOMMODATION AND EATING   LA TURBIE

Café de la Fontaine 4 av Général de Gaulle ☎ 04 93 28 52 79. Excellent bistro on the main road through La Turbie with a chalked-up selection of classic dishes like saddle of rabbit *à la niçoise* or lamb with shallots; main courses from €15. Daily noon–3pm & 7–11pm.

Hostellerie Jérôme 20 Comte-de-Cessole ☎ 04 92 41 51 51. There's plenty of style and atmosphere at this thirteenth-century hostelry on the Via Julia in the heart of the old village; its beautiful *restaurant gastronomique* has a Michelin star (*menus* €98 and €159). July & Aug and early Sept daily 7–11pm; mid-Sept to mid-Nov & mid-Feb to June Tues–Sat 7–11pm. **€180**

8

Roquebrune-Cap Martin

As the Grande Corniche descends towards Cap Martin, it passes the eleventh-century castle of **ROQUEBRUNE** and its fifteenth-century village nestling round the base of the rock. The village is a real maze of passages and stairways that eventually lead either to one of the six castle gates or to dead ends. If you find yourself on rue de la Fontaine you can leave the village by the Porte de Menton and see, on the hillside about 200m beyond the gate, an incredible spreading **olive tree** that was perhaps one hundred years old when the count of Ventimiglia first built a fortress on Roquebrune's spur in 870 AD.

Roquebrune castle

Daily: Feb–May daily 10am–12.30pm & 2–6pm; June–Sept daily 10am–1pm & 2.30–7pm; Oct daily 10am–12.30pm & 2–5pm; Nov–Jan Mon–Thurs, Sat & Sun 10am–12.30pm & 2–5pm • €5 including English audioguide • ☎ 04 93 35 07 22

Roquebrune castle might well have become yet another Côte-side architectural aberration, thanks to its English owner in the 1920s. He was prevented from continuing his "restorations" after a press campaign brought public attention to the mock-medieval tower by the gateway, now known as the *tour anglaise*. The local authority has since made great efforts to kit the castle out in medieval fashion, and one of the best, if perhaps not most authentic, ideas has been to create an **open-air theatre** for the concerts and dance performances held here in July and August, with a spectacular natural backdrop down the precipitous slopes to Monaco and the coast.

Cap Martin

Southeast of the old village, just below the joined middle and lower corniches and the station, is the peninsula of **Cap Martin**, where a **coastal path** gives access to a wonderful shoreline of white rocks and wind-bent pines. The path is named after **Le Corbusier**, who spent several summers in Roquebrune and drowned off Cap Martin in 1965. His grave – a work of art that he designed himself – is in the **cemetery** (square J, near the flagpole), high above the old village on promenade 1ère DFL. You can also visit his **cabanon** (beach house) and the architect Eileen Gray's stunning 1920s modernist **Villa E-1027** on a two-hour guided tour (early May to Oct daily 10am & 2pm; €18; book in advance on the website, ⓦcapmoderne.monuments-nationaux.fr). Both buildings are just above the shore east of the pretty **Plage du Buse**, the beach below the station. It's a restful, low-key spot, with a simple café, *Le Cabanon* (April–Oct daily roughly 10am–10pm; hours vary according to weather) right on the shingle. Further west, the **Plage du Golfe Bleu** is similar. East of Plage du Buse, the coastal path threads its way right round the tip of Cap Martin, linking up with avenue Winston Churchill on the eastern side to bring you to Roquebrune-Cap Martin's main beach, the **Plage de Carnolès**. It's a spacious enough stretch of shingle, though much less restful than the beaches west of the Cap.

At the junction of the Via Aurelian and Via Julia on avenue Paul Doumer is a remnant from the Roman station. Known as the **Tombeau de Lumone**, it comprises three arches of a first-century BC mausoleum, with traces of frescoes visible under the vaulting.

ARRIVAL AND INFORMATION   ROQUEBRUNE-CAP MARTIN

By train It's a steep walk uphill from the Roquebrune *gare SNCF*: turn right out of the station, ascending to Av de la Côte d'Azur from where a stepped route climbs to the Grande Corniche, crossing it to join the final stretch – the escalier Chanoine Grana – to reach the village. Alternatively, alight at Carnolès *gare SNCF* and get the #21

bus up to the village.

Destinations Èze-sur-Mer (roughly every 25min; 15min); Monaco (roughly every 25min; 4min).

By car There's limited parking at the entrance to Roquebrune's *vieux village*.

Tourist office In the modern town centre just up from

the beach, at 218 av Aristide-Briand (July& Aug Mon–Sat 9.30am–1pm & 2–6.30pm, Sun 9.30am–1.30pm; Sept–

June Mon–Sat 9am–12.30pm & 2–5.30pm; ☎ 04 93 35 62 87, ⚲ roquebrune-cap-martin.com).

ACCOMMODATION AND EATING

Au Grand Inquisiteur 18 rue du Château ☎ 04 93 35 05 37, ⚲ augrandinquisiteur.com. Atmospheric, almost cave-like restaurant in one of the darker crannies of Roquebrune's *vieux village*, with dishes like rabbit, and artichoke ravioli on €27 and €35 *menus*. Mon, Tues & Thurs–Sun 7–9.30pm.

Le Cabanon Plage du Buse ☎ 04 93 83 33 93. Simple café and restaurant in an idyllic setting on the beach below Roquebrune's *gare SCNF*, serving *plats du jour* from around €16, main course salads from €14, takeaway flan and pizza slices from as little as €5 and sandwiches from €6/7. April–Oct daily 10am–roughly 10pm; hours are weather dependent.

Les Deux Frères Place des Deux Frères ☎ 04 93 28 99 00, ⚲ lesdeuxfreres.com. The best-located hotel in Roquebrune village, worth booking in advance to try to get a sea-view room; there are just eight a/c rooms, varying widely in style and price. The hotel also has a good restaurant with €32 and €53 *menus*. Wed–Sun noon–1.30pm & 7.30–9.30pm. €120

Hôtel Victoria 7 promenade du Cap ☎ 04 93 35 65 90, ⚲ hotel-victoria.fr. Stylish, upmarket seafront hotel overlooking the Plage de Carnolès on the coast, with crisp, contemporary blue-and-white decor, a bar/terrace and a/c. Around half the rooms have balcony and sea view. €195

Monaco

Viewed from a distance, there's no mistaking the dense cluster of towers that is **MONACO** – a principality that is no bigger than London's Hyde Park. Though rampant property development rescued the principality from postwar decline, much of its former Italianate prettiness was elbowed aside in the process, leaving it looking like nowhere else on the Riviera. Not for nothing was **Prince Rainier**, who died in 2005, known as the Prince Bâtisseur ("Prince Builder"). For all its wealth it's nowadays a city-state of apartment dwellers, built up from end to end and almost entirely lacking the leisured elegance of the Riviera's other plutocrat hangouts. Despite this, Monaco actually has quite a lot to offer the visitor, from the famous **casino** to the Grimaldis' **Palais Princier** and a string of **museums**.

One time to avoid Monaco – unless you're a motor-racing fan – is the end of May, when racing cars burn around the port and casino for the **Formula 1 Monaco Grand Prix**. Every space in sight of the circuit is inaccessible without a ticket, making casual sightseeing – or sneaky free views of the race – out of the question.

8

Monte Carlo

The heart of **MONTE CARLO** is its **casino**, the one place not to be missed on a trip to Monaco. It forms the focus of place du Casino, which with its lush gardens, palace hotels and multi-million euro facelift is in turn the focus of Monte Carlo itself – the one part of the principality which, more than any other, usually lives up to the jet-set image. The *American Bar* of the newly renovated **Hôtel de Paris** is *the* place for the elite to meet, while the turn-of-the-twentieth-century **Hermitage** has a beautiful Gustave Eiffel iron-and-glass dome. While the highly controversial demolition of the 1932-built Art Deco Sporting d'Hiver may have encapsulated the principality's ongoing love affair with the hard hat and the wrecker's ball, its designer shops have now vacated their temporary cabins for permanent homes on a new pedestrianized street. It's at the heart of the swanky One Monte Carlo redevelopment, along with elegant glass fronted pavilions and a subterranean reincarnation of the old Salle des Arts gallery (yet to open at the time of writing).

Casino de Monte-Carlo and the Opera House

Place du Casino • Daily: tours 10am–1pm (last entrance 12.15pm); gaming from 2pm • **Tours** €17 including audioguide; **gaming** Atrium and Salle Renaissance free; **Salle Europe** €17 including restaurant/gaming voucher • Entrance restricted to over-18s and ID required;

dress code rigid, with shorts and T-shirts allowed until 7pm only, and, for men, jackets mandatory after 8pm; photography prohibited and bags and large coats checked at the door • ☎ +377 98 06 41 51, ⓦ montecarlocasinos.com • Bus #1, #5 or #6

The first halls within the **Casino de Monte-Carlo** are the **Salle Renaissance** – an anteroom – and the **Salle Europe**, where serried ranks of slot machines stand below ceilings of *fin-de-siècle* extravagance. The more subdued **Salle des Amériques** is devoted to table games – roulette, blackjack and craps. Of the **Salons Privés**, the giddily opulent **Salle Médecin** and the **Salles Touzet** are also devoted to table games; as their name suggests, the **Salons Super Privés** are more intimate, and you won't see them on tours.

Charles Garnier, the nineteenth-century architect of the Paris Opera, designed both the casino and the attached **Opera House**, though you'll need to take in a performance (see page 381) to see the auditorium, which is an excess of gold and marble with statues of pretty Grecian boys, frescoed classical scenes and figures waving palm leaves.

Nouveau Musée National de Monaco

NMNM Villa Sauber 17 av Princesse Grace • **NMNM Villa Paloma** 56 bd du Jardin-Exotique • Daily 10am–6pm • €6 for both • ☎ +377 98 98 91 26, ⓦ nmnm.mc

The **Nouveau Musée National de Monaco** presents interesting temporary art exhibitions, often on Monaco-related themes, and is divided between two buildings: the **NMNM Villa Sauber**, one of the few surviving *belle époque* villas in the principality, set incongruously amid towering concrete apartment blocks east of the casino towards Larvotto beach; and the **NMNM Villa Paloma**, a dazzling white villa set in an Italian garden in Fontvieille.

Monaco-Ville

Bus #1 or #2 from place d'Armes by the *gare SNCF*; vehicle access to Monaco-Ville is restricted – head for the Parking des Pêcheurs, from where there's a lift up to Av St-Martin by the Musée Océanographique

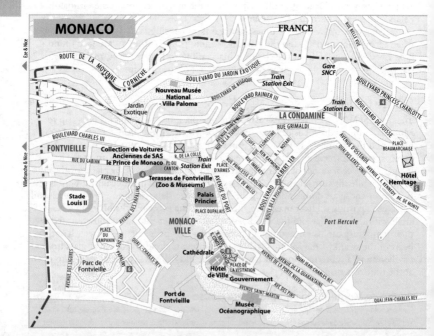

MONACO PRACTICALITIES

There are no **border** formalities for visitors arriving in Monaco from France, and the currency used is the euro. Note, however, that wearing just bathing costumes, or displaying bare feet or chests, is **illegal** once you step off the beach.

Monaco's international code is 00377 and **telephone numbers** have eight digits (omit 0 when dialing from outside the principality).

ORIENTATION

The 3km-long state consists of several distinct quarters. The pretty old town of **Monaco-Ville** around the palace stands on the high promontory, with the densely built suburb and marina of **Fontvieille** in its western shadow. **La Condamine** is the old port quarter on the other side of the rock; **Larvotto**, the rather ugly bathing resort with artificial beaches of imported sand, reaches to the eastern border; and **Monte Carlo** sits in the middle. French **Beausoleil**, uphill to the north, is merely an extension of the conurbation – the border is often unmarked and always easily crossed on foot.

Though rather over-restored and lifeless, **MONACO-VILLE** is the one part of the principality where the developers have been reined in, and it retains a certain toy-town charm despite the surfeit of shops selling Grimaldi mugs and assorted junk. This is the principality's royal, official and religious focus: you can tour the **Palais Princier** and afterwards see the tombs of Prince Rainier and Princess Grace in the slightly dull nineteenth-century **Cathédrale** (daily 8.30am–6/7pm; free).

Palais Princier

Daily: April–June & Sept to mid-Oct 10am–5.30pm; July & Aug 10am–6.30pm • €8; €14 with Collection de Voitures Anciennes • ☎ +377 93 25 18 31, ⓦ palais.mc

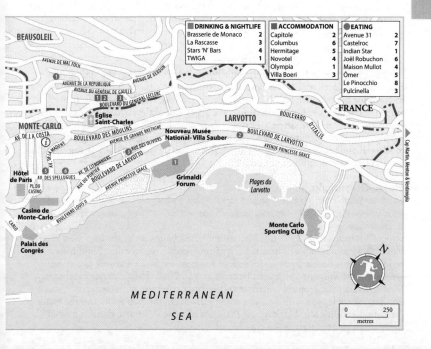

MONACO: A HISTORY OF INDEPENDENCE

It may have lost its looks, but the tiny state of **Monaco** retains its comic-opera independence. It has been in the hands of the **Grimaldi family** since the fourteenth century (save for the two decades following the French Revolution) and, in theory, Monaco would again become part of France were the royal line to die out. For the last hundred years the principality has lived off gambling, tourism and its status as a tax haven – among its inhabitants, French citizens outnumber native-born Monegasques.

Along with the pope and the house of Liechtenstein, **Prince Albert II** is one of Europe's few remaining constitutionally autocratic rulers, with right of refusal over any changes to the constitution – though since the late Prince Rainier's constitutional 1962 reforms, the monarch's power is no longer absolute. Monaco has a 24-member **parliament** of limited power, elected by universal suffrage and (since 2003) with competing parties, but the prince has the power to dissolve it. The only other authority is the **Société des Bains de Mer (SBM)**, which owns the casino, the opera house and some of the grandest hotels.

Along with its reputation for great wealth, Monaco more recently acquired an unwelcome reputation for wheeler-dealer **sleaze**. On his accession in July 2005, the US-educated Albert declared that he no longer wished the principality to be known – in the words of Somerset Maugham – as "a sunny place for shady people". He signalled that Monaco would be more discriminating in granting residence, and in 2005 Sir Mark Thatcher, the son of former British Prime Minister Margaret Thatcher, was declared persona non grata. Albert then set about complying with EU banking regulations and trying to get Monaco off an OECD list of uncooperative tax havens – a policy that finally came to fruition in 2009. The principality now levies a withholding tax on the interest income of EU citizens resident here, which it rebates to the resident's country of origin.

Even so, Monaco remains home to large numbers of non-French **expats**, many of them British – including Ringo Starr and Shirley Bassey. Hopes that Monaco under Albert might take a more sensitive line on **development** were dashed in 2009, when plans for the 49-storey Tour Odéon skyscraper hard against the French border were approved despite protests from residents in Beausoleil, who feared the tower – now complete – would blot out their views and cast them into perpetual shade. Further controversy followed with the 2015 demolition of the Art Deco Sporting d'Hiver building to make way for a state-of-the-art redevelopment.

Monaco-Ville is home to the **Palais Princier**, whose state apartments and throne room can be visited on a self-guided tour, with Prince Albert's voice on the audioguide. Despite the palace's modest size and military origins as a thirteenth-century Genoese fortress, the part you see certainly feels suitably palatial, thanks in part to major embellishment by the Grimaldis during the latter half of the sixteenth century. The courtyard conceals a massive sixteenth-century cistern designed to ensure a water supply in time of siege; these days, the main group besieging it is camera-clicking tourists. If you're outside the palace at 11.55am, you'll catch the daily changing of the immaculate, white-uniformed guard.

Musée Océanographique

Av St-Martin • Daily: April–June & Sept 10am–7pm; July & Aug 9.30am–8pm; Oct–March 10am–6pm • €11/14/16 in low/median/high season; with Palais Princier €19/20.50 in median/high season; with Jardin Exotique €15/17/18 in low/median/high season • ☎ +377 93 15 36 00, ⓦ oceano.org

One of Monaco's best sights is the aquarium in the basement of the imposing **Musée Océanographique**, where the fishy beings outdo the weirdest Kandinsky or Hieronymus Bosch creations. A serious scientific institution as well as a visitor attraction, the museum celebrated its centenary in 2010. The attractions include Mediterranean and tropical aquariums – the latter complete with coral reef – and a 6m-deep shark lagoon with non-distorting glass 30cm thick to withstand the water pressure. In addition to blacktip reef sharks, it is home to a nurse shark, a hawksbill turtle and a giant guitarfish – a type of ray.

Fontvieille

Tucked behind Monaco-Ville at Monaco's southwestern extremity, **Fontvieille** is the newest of the principality's main districts, built on land reclaimed from the sea. For the most part it's a standard-issue development of apartments and yacht moorings, but it's worth a visit for the museums in the **Terrasses de Fontvieille**.

Terrasses de Fontvieille

Collection de Voitures Anciennes Daily 10am–5.30pm • €8, €14 with Palais Princier • ☎+377 92 05 28 56, ⓦ mtcc.mc • **Musée Naval** Daily 10am–6pm • €4 • ☎+377 92 05 28 48 • **Musée des Timbres et des Monnaies** Daily: July–Sept 9.30am–6pm; Oct–June 9.30am–5pm • €3 • ☎+377 98 98 41 50, ⓦ oetp-monaco.com,

Overlooking Fontvieille's harbour and the Palais Princier, and with a public garden on its roof, the **Terrasses de Fontvieille** complex houses a number of interesting museums: the **Collection de Voitures Anciennes**, an enjoyable miscellany of old and not-so-old cars, with everything from a 1928 Hispano-Suiza worthy of Cruella de Vil to the beautiful blue Sunbeam convertible driven by the future Princess Grace in *To Catch a Thief*; the **Musée Naval**, crammed with 250 model ships; and a museum of stamps and coins, the **Musée des Timbres et des Monnaies**, which has rare stamps, money and commemorative medals dating back to 1640.

Jardin Exotique

62 bd du Jardin-Exotique • Daily: Feb–April & Oct 9am–6pm; May–Sept 9am–7pm; Nov–Jan 9am–5pm • €7.20 • ☎+377 93 15 29 80, ⓦ jardin-exotique.mc • Bus #2

High above Fontvieille there are breathtaking panoramas of the coast as far as Italy from the **Jardin Exotique**, where cacti and succulents native to South Africa, the Southwestern USA, Mexico and the Arabian peninsula, alternate with mineral-rich caverns.

La Condamine

Swimming pool Daily: late April to mid-June & first week in Sept to mid-Oct 9am–6pm; mid-June to first week in Sept 9am–8pm • Morning €3.30, afternoon €4.30, full day €6

The yachts in the **Port Hercule** in **LA CONDAMINE** are, as you might expect, gigantic. Also on the port at Quai Albert-1er is a fabulous public Olympic-sized, saltwater **swimming pool** with high-dive boards. From December to early February it's transformed into an **ice rink**.

ARRIVAL AND INFORMATION

MONACO

By train The *gare SNCF* is wedged between Bd Rainier III and Bd Princess Charlotte and has several exits, signposted clearly.

Destinations Menton (roughly every 30min; 12min); Nice (up to every 15min; 21–26min).

By bus Buses following the lower corniche or autoroute stop at place d'Armes by the *gare SNCF* and in Monte Carlo; there's also a service from Nice via Èze.

Destinations Èze (7 daily; 15min); Menton roughly hourly; 30min); Nice (every 10–35min; 40min); Nice airport (every 30min; 40–45min).

Tourist office Monaco's main tourist office, 2a bd des Moulins (mid-June to Sept Mon–Fri 9am–6.30pm, Sat 9am–7pm, Sun 10am–6pm; Oct to mid-June Mon–Fri 9am–6.30pm, Sat 9.45am–5.30pm; ☎+377 92 16 61 66, ⓦ visitmonaco.com) is helpful and friendly, with English-speaking staff and plenty of information in English; you can also pick up a free map here.

GETTING AROUND

By bus Municipal buses ply the length of the principality from around 7am to 9pm (€2 one-way, one-day pass €5.50; ⓦ cam.mc); from 9.20pm there is a single night bus route (Mon–Fri until 12.20am, Sat & Sun until 4am).

By ferry An ecofriendly ferry (8am–8pm; €2) shuttles across the harbour every 20min.

Lifts Clean and convenient lifts – marked on the tourist office's map – link the lower and higher streets and can save you a lot of breathless hill climbing.

8

ACCOMMODATION
SEE MAP PAGE 376

Monaco has relatively few **hotels**, and most are pitched firmly at the top end of the market. If you're on a tight budget, it's not really worth trying to stay in Monaco itself: you'll get more for your money by staying just across the invisible border in **Beausoleil**. The most prestigious hotels cluster around the casino in **Monte Carlo**. Monaco has no **campsite**, and **caravans** are illegal; camping vehicles must be parked at the Parking des Écoles in Fontvieille, but can't stay overnight.

Capitole 19 bd du Général-Leclerc, Beausoleil ☎ 04 93 28 65 65, ⌨ hotel-capitole.fr. This three-star is one of Beausoleil's nicest, just 300m from the Casino, with tastefully decorated renovated rooms with a/c, soundproofing, safe and flatscreen TV. There's a pleasant breakfast room. **€152**

Columbus 23 av des Papalins, Fontvieille ☎ 92 05 90 00, ⌨ columbushotels.com. Overlooking the sea in Fontvieille, offering boutique hotel comforts in cool shades and natural materials for a fraction of the price of the palace hotels. Rooms are soundproofed, with a/c, and there's a pool and a bar. **€237**

Hermitage Square Beaumarchais ☎ +377 98 06 41 51, ⌨ hotelhermitagemontecarlo.com. One of two opulent *belle époque* palace hotels owned by the Societé des Bains de Mer, the *Hermitage* boasts a glass dome by Gustav Eiffel, a Michelin-starred restaurant and fabulous views over the harbour. **€690**

Novotel 16 bd Princesse Charlotte ☎ +377 99 99 83 00, ⌨ novotel.com. One of the best mid-priced options, with 218 modern, comfortable rooms and suites – some with views over the principality – plus a pool, gym and sauna. **€226**

Olympia 17bis bd du Général-Leclerc, Beausoleil ☎ 04 93 78 12 70, ⌨ olympiahotel.fr. More traditional than its near neighbour *Capitole*, this comfortable three-star hotel is a good mid-range option. **€135**

Villa Boeri 29 bd du Général-Leclerc, Beausoleil ☎ 04 93 78 38 10, ⌨ hotelboeri.com. Cheerful and welcoming two-star with a nice terrace at the front. The a/c rooms are soundproofed, with satellite TV and bath or shower and WC. **€120**

EATING
SEE MAP PAGE 376

La Condamine and Monaco-Ville are replete with **restaurants**, **brasseries** and **cafés**, and there's a scattering of mid-priced options along Larvotto beach and the port, but good food and reasonable prices don't always coincide in Monaco: the best-value cuisine is usually Italian. The best daily food **market** is on rue du Marché in Beausoleil.

Avenue 31 31 av Princesse Grace ☎ +377 97 70 31 31, ⌨ avenue31.mc. Stylish, modern brasserie just across from the beach in Larvotto, with an eclectic *carte* that ranges from stir fries and fish to steaks and Italian dishes. Lunchtime *formules* from €18. Mon–Thurs noon–2.15pm & 7.30–10.45pm, Fri & Sat noon–2.15pm & 7.30–11.45pm, Sun noon–2.45pm & 7.30–10.15pm.

Castelroc Place du Palais ☎ +377 93 30 36 68, ⌨ castelrocmonaco.com. Opposite the Palais Princier, with a terrace overlooking Fontvieille, this smart restaurant isn't cheap, but it's a good place to sample traditional Monégasque dishes like *barbajuans* – samosa-like triangles stuffed with Swiss chard and cheese. Lunch *menus* from €24. Tues–Sat 9am–10pm, 9am–6pm.

Indian Star 23 bd de la République ☎ +04 93 41 94 34, ⌨ indianstar.fr. One of the best value meals you'll find in touching distance of Monaco and a cut above the average Indian restaurant in France, with *menus de midi* from €8 and plenty of vegetarian options. They also do takeaway – order on the website. Daily noon–2.30pm & 7–11.30pm.

Joël Robuchon Hôtel Metropole, 4 av de la Madone ☎ +377 93 15 15 10, ⌨ metropole.com. The inventive,

elegant, Mediterranean-accented cooking of this two-Michelin-starred restaurant was, until his death in summer 2018, under the aegis of one of the world's most respected chefs, Joël Robuchon. Still going strong under executive chef Christophe Cussac, it may not be the grandest dining room in the principality, but it's pretty close. À la carte mains such as roasted turbot with pistachio oil will set you back a budget-busting €170. Mon, Tues & Thurs–Sun 12.15–2pm & 7.30–10.30pm.

Maison Mullot 22 av de la Costa ☎ +377 93 50 17 59, ⌨ maisonmullot.mc. Clean, bright patisserie and *chocolatier* near Monte Carlo's main strip, with a wide selection of organic and artisan breads and pastries including fougasse Monegasques made to an old family recipe for €5. Mon–Sat 7.30am–3pm.

Ômer Hôtel de Paris, place du Casino ☎ +377 98 06 39 39, ⌨ hoteldeparismontecarlo.com. Alain Ducasse's Monaco flagship hotel, in the newly renovated *belle époque* splendour of one of the grandest palace hotels, has three Michelin stars and makes plentiful use of excellent local produce, with a defined Mediterranean/Middle Eastern focus. Lunch *menus* €42/55 for two/three courses; à la carte mains around €40–50. Mon–Fri noon–2.30pm & 7.30–10pm, Sat & Sun 12.30–2.30pm & 7.30–10pm.

Le Pinocchio 30 rue Comte-Félix-Gastaldi ☎ +377 93 30 96 20, ⌨ lepinocchiomonaco.com. A reliable, good-value Italian in a narrow street in Monaco-Ville dishing up hearty portions from a long menu of *antipasti* and pasta, including the likes of burrata with pine nuts, basil and

MONACO FESTIVALS AND SPORTING EVENTS

Monaco's **festivals** are spectacular, particularly the **International Fireworks** in July and August, which can be seen from as far away as Cap d'Ail or Cap Martin. Mid- to late January sees vast trailers entering Monaco for the **International Circus Festival** at the Espace Fontvieille, a rare chance to witness the world's best in this underrated performance art (ⓦmontecarlofestival.mc).

As for sporting spectaculars, the principality's name is synonymous with motorsport: the **Monte-Carlo Automobile Rally** takes place in mid-January and the **Formula 1 Grand Prix** at the end of May. Every space in sight of the circuit, which runs around the port and the casino, is inaccessible without a ticket (☏+377 93 15 26 00). Monaco also has a first-division **football team**, AS Monaco, whose home ground is the enormous Stade Louis II in Fontvieille, 7 av des Castelans (☏+377 92 05 37 54, ⓦasmonaco.com).

cuttlefish bread crumble or marinated pork with red fruits vinaigrette from €18. Daily noon–3pm & 7–10.30pm.
Pulcinella 17 rue du Portier ☏+377 93 30 73 61, ⓦpulcinella.mc. Traditional Italian restaurant between the Casino and Larvotto beach. The view – of a motorway flyover – isn't the best, but the food is relatively good value

for the location. *Malanzane alla parmigiana* €16, salmon tartare with asparagus tagliatelle and grapefruit sauce €19; more elaborate dishes include beef carpaccio with courgette salad, courgette flowers and black truffle (€22). Lunch *formule* €19. Daily noon–2pm & 7.30–11pm.

DRINKING AND NIGHTLIFE SEE MAP PAGE 376

There are better places for **nightlife** than Monaco. Prices can be astronomical, service haughty and the top nightclubs like *Jimmy'z* (in the Sporting Monte-Carlo in Larvotto) are not going to let you in unless you're decked out in designer finery.
Brasserie de Monaco 36 rte de la Piscine ☏+377 97 98 51 20, ⓦbrasseriedemonaco.com. Situated on the port and with Monaco's only organic craft beer brewed on the premises – including wheat beers and amber ale – this smart place has DJs nightly from 6pm and a burgers-to-salads food menu. Pints €7. Daily noon–2am.
La Rascasse 1 quai Antoine 1er ☏+377 98 06 16 16. Squeezed into – and named after – an iconic bend in the Grand Prix circuit, with an unusually varied programme featuring everything from salsa nights and live acoustic music to DJ battles. Daily 4pm–4.45am.

Stars 'N' Bars 6 quai Antoine 1er ☏+377 97 97 95 95, ⓦstarsnbars.com. Big, American-themed bar-diner on the port, with crash helmet and pit-stop motifs, games machines and sport on TV. Draught beers from €5, mojitos from €14, plus a huge food menu with everything from tapas to salad, burgers and Tex-Mex food, with dedicated vegetarian and vegan options. Daily 11am–midnight.
TWIGA 10 av Princesse Grace, 2er Grimaldi Forum ☏+377 99 99 25 50, ⓦtwigasumosan.com. In the space formerly occupied by *Zelo's* and still bringing le bling, this stylish combination of Italian/Japanese restaurant, cocktail lounge, DJ bar and dancefloor isn't shy about advertising its jet-set credentials, with a sea-facing terrace and plush interior. The place morphs from dinner-with-live-music into full-on club mode nightly at 1am. Tues–Sat 7pm–3am.

ENTERTAINMENT

The programme of **theatre**, **ballet** and **concerts** throughout the year is impressive, with the **Printemps des Arts** festival (March and April) seeing performances by famous classical and contemporary dance troupes from all over the world. The main **booking office** for ballet, opera and concerts is the casino foyer, place du Casino, Monte Carlo (Tues–Sat 10am–5.30pm; ☏+377 98 06 28 28).
Opera House Place du Casino, Monte Carlo ☏+377 98 06 28 00, ⓦopera.mc. Monaco's opera house is in

the Monte Carlo Casino. The season (Nov–April) is pretty exceptional, the SBM (see page 378) being able to book up star companies and performers before Milan, Paris or New York get hold of them.
Théâtre Princesse Grace 12 av d'Ostende, Monte Carlo ☏+377 93 25 32 27, ⓦwww.tpgmonaco.mc. The principality's main drama venue, housed in a building that dates from 1932, and with a repertoire that ranges from Pagnol to Shakespeare.

DIRECTORY

Banks Most banks (Mon–Fri 9am–noon & 2–4pm) have a branch in Monaco around Bd des Moulins, Av de Monte-Carlo and Av de la Costa.

Emergencies ☏18 or ☏+377 93 30 19 45; Centre Hospitalier Princesse Grace, Av Pasteur (☏+377 97 98 99 00); police ☏17.

Lost property 4 rue Louis-Notari (☎ +377 93 15 30 18).

Money exchange Cie Monégasque de Change, parking du Chemin des Pêcheurs; Monafinances, 17 av des Spélugues.

Pharmacy Call ☎ 141.

Post office PTT Palais de la Scala, Av Henri Dunant (Mon–Fri 8am–7pm & Sat 8am–1pm).

Public holidays Similar to those in France, with the addition of January 27 (Fête de Ste-Dévote) and November 19 (Fête Nationale Monégasque), and without Bastille (July 14), VE (May 8) or Armistice (Nov 11) days.

Radio Riviera Radio (106.5 FM; ⊕ rivieraradio.mc) is an English-language radio station.

Menton

Of all the big Riviera resorts, **MENTON**, the warmest and the most Italianate, is the one that most retains an atmosphere of genteel, aristocratic tourism. It's also a classic border town, and in summer the streets and beaches are thronged with relaxed Italian day-trippers enjoying ice cream. Menton does not go in for the ostentatious wealth of Monaco and it has little of Nice's big-city buzz: its lush gardens and associations with Cocteau aside, what it chiefly glories in is its **climate** and its famous lemon crop. Ringed by protective mountains, hardly a whisper of wind disturbs the suntrap of the city. Winter, when Menton is several vital degrees warmer than St-Tropez or St-Raphaël, is when you notice the difference most. The **beaches**, though stony, are popular, and in summer the gritty **plage des Sablettes** on the harbour has a fashionable edge.

Brief history

Menton's history almost took an independent path like that of Monaco. In the revolutionary days of 1848, Menton and Roquebrune, both at the time under Monaco's jurisdiction, declared themselves an **independent republic** under the protection of Sardinia. When the Prince of Monaco came to Menton in the hope that his regal figure would sway the people, he had to be rescued by the police from a furious crowd and locked up overnight for his own protection. Eventually, following an 1860 vote by Roquebrune and Menton to remain in France, Grimaldi agreed to the sale of the towns to the French state for four million francs.

Menton got its first boost as a resort the following year when a British doctor, James Henry Bennet, published a treatise on the benefits of Menton's mild winter climate to tuberculosis sufferers, and soon thousands of well-heeled invalids were flocking to the town in the vain hope of a cure. Menton's sedate feel and well-preserved historic architecture makes it easy to imagine the presence of archduchesses, grand dukes, tsars and other autocrats, as well as convalescing artists such as Guy de Maupassant and Katherine Mansfield.

The modern town

Roquebrune and Cap Martin merge into Menton along the 3km shore of the **Baie du Soleil**. The **modern town** is arranged around three main streets parallel to the promenade du Soleil, with an impressive boulevard – **avenue Boyer/de Verdun** – running inland from the sea.

Menton's old palace hotels, now almost all converted into apartments, add touches of architectural grandeur, whimsy and exotica to the townscape, but the main cultural draw is the town's association with Cocteau. The pedestrianized **rue St-Michel**, lined with cafés and restaurants, links the old and modern towns.

Salle des Mariages

Place Ardoïno • Mon–Fri 8.30am–noon & 2–4.30pm • €2 • ☎ 04 92 10 50 00

The **Salle des Mariages**, or register office, in the Hôtel de Ville, was decorated in inimitable style by **Jean Cocteau** (1889–1963) and can be visited by asking the receptionist by the main door.

On the wall above the official's desk a couple face each other, with strange topological connections between the sun, her headdress and his fisherman's cap. The *Saracen Wedding Party* on the right-hand wall reveals a disapproving mother of the bride, spurned girlfriend of the groom and her armed vengeful brother among the cheerful guests. On the left wall is the story of *Orpheus and Eurydice* at the doomed moment when Orpheus has just looked back. Meanwhile, on the ceiling are *Poetry Rides Pegasus*, tattered *Science Juggles with the Planets*, and *Love*, open-eyed, waiting with bow and arrow at the ready.

Musée de Préhistoire Régionale

Rue Lorédan-Larchey • Mon & Wed–Sun 10am–noon & 2–6pm • Free • ☎ 04 93 35 84 64

The **Musée de Préhistoire Régionale**, at the top of rue Lorédan-Larchey near the Hôtel de Ville, is one of the best on the subject. There are good films to watch, interactive displays on the origins of human life and a section on life in the Menton region between the Iron Age and late antiquity.

Musée Jean Cocteau Collection Séverin Wunderman

2 quai de Monléon • Musée Jean Cocteau closed for renovations at time of writing; bastion Mon & Wed–Sun 10am–noon & 2–6pm • Bastion €3 • ☎ 04 89 81 52 50, ⓦ museecocteaumenton.fr

The seafront's most diverting building is the striking structure opened in 2011 to house the **Musée Jean Cocteau Collection Séverin Wunderman**. Designed by North African-born Provençal architect Rudy Ricciotti, the museum exhibits all facets of

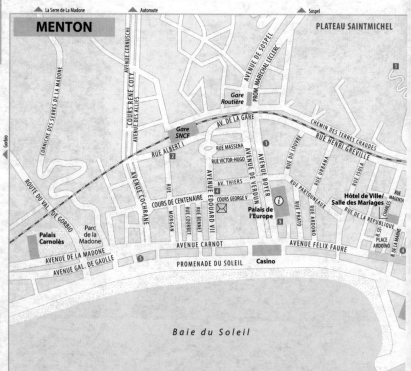

the polymath artist's work from before World War I to the 1950s; it also mounts temporary exhibitions. On the same ticket you can visit the seventeenth-century **bastion**, by the Quai Napoléon-III nearby, which was restored according to Cocteau's plans between 1958 and 1963. It contains ceramics and pictures of his Mentonaise lovers in the *Inamorati* series.

Palais de Carnolès

3 av de la Madone • Closed for renovation at time of writing • Free • ⓦ menton.fr/Musee-des-Beaux-Arts-Palais-de-Carnoles • Bus #7

At the far western end of the modern town, an impressive collection of paintings from the Middle Ages to the twentieth century can be seen in the sumptuous but rather crumbly **Palais de Carnolès**, the old summer residence of the princes of Monaco. Of the early works, the *Madonna and Child with St Francis* by Louis Bréa is exceptional, and there are excellent Dutch and Venetian portraits and an anonymous sixteenth-century École Française canvas of a woman holding a scale. The small modern and contemporary collection includes a wonderful Suzanne Valadon and works by Graham Sutherland, who spent some of his last years in Menton. The downstairs of the building is given over to temporary exhibitions, and there's a **sculpture garden** in the adjoining lime, lemon and orange grove.

La Serre de la Madone

74 rte du Val de Gorbio • Guided tours Tues–Sun 3pm • €8

Some 3km north of the Palais Carnolès is **La Serre de la Madone**, a botanical garden of great tranquillity created in the interwar years by an American, Lawrence Johnston, who had already created a celebrated garden at Hidcote Manor in England.

8

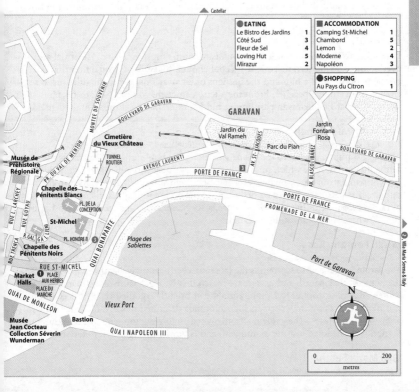

Vieille ville

Menton's fabulous **vieille ville** is the most Italianate and beautiful on the Riviera – a wonderful huddle of pastel campaniles and disappearing stairways east of the modern town, towering above the old port and the Baie de Garavan from its hillside site.

St-Michel

Parvis de la Basilique St-Michel • Aug Mon–Fri 10am–noon & 4–6pm; Sept–July Mon–Fri 10am–noon & 3–5pm

Where the *quai* bends round the western end of the Baie de Garavan a long flight of black-and-white pebbled steps leads to the **parvis St-Michel** and the perfect pink and yellow proportions of the **St-Michel** church. The interior is a stupendous Italian Baroque riot of decoration, with an impressive, vast organ casing, a sixteenth-century altarpiece in the choir by Antonio Manchello, and a host of paintings, sculptures, gilded columns, stucco and frescoes. Note that ongoing renovations mean parts of the building are currently obscured.

Cimetière du Vieux Château

Daily: April–Oct 8am–8pm; Nov–March 8am–5pm • Free

At the summit of the *vieille ville* you'll reach the bewitchingly beautiful and hauntingly sad **Cimetière du Vieux Château**. Its cream-coloured mid-nineteenth-century sculpted gravestones bear diverse foreign names from Russian princes to William Webb-Ellis, credited, in public schools throughout England, with the invention of rugby. Many of Menton's young, consumptive visitors were buried here, and the grief etched in the gravestones is palpable. If all this untimely death is a tad gloomy, there can at least be few lovelier final resting places, with sweeping views along the coast into Italy. The cemetery is gradually being restored, but some of it is still in rather crumbly condition.

Garavan

Extending to the Italian border, **Garavan** is Menton's most exclusive residential area, overlooking the modern marina. If it's cool enough for walking, you'll find that the public **parks** up in the hills and the **gardens** of Garavan's once-elegant villas make a change from shingle beaches. From the Vieux Cimetière you can walk or take bus #8 along boulevard de Garavan past houses hidden in their large, exuberant gardens.

Jardin du Val Rahmeh

Av St-Jacques • Mon & Wed–Sun: April–Sept 9.30am–12.30pm & 2–6pm; Oct–March 9.30am–12.30pm & 2–5pm • €7

The closest public garden to the *vieille ville* along the boulevard de Garavan is the **Jardin du Val Rahmeh**, which surrounds a nineteenth-century villa that acquired its current name from a past owner, a former British governor of Malta. Open to the public since 1967, it's nowadays dedicated to the acclimatization and conservation of rare species, including *sophora toromiro*, a species of flowering tree native to Easter Island, where it has almost disappeared.

Jardin Fontana Rosa

Av Blasco Ibáñez • Guided tours Mon & Fri 10am • €6

The **Jardin Fontana Rosa** surrounds the late nineteenth-century villa that was, from 1921, the home of the Spanish author Vicente Blasco Ibáñez. Figs, palms and bananas give the garden an almost tropical feel, emphasized by its brightly coloured ceramic decoration, and monuments to great writers include a rotunda dedicated to Cervantes, the "father of Spanish literature". The garden, recently voted among the top ten most beautiful in France, is a scheduled historic monument, and is slowly undergoing restoration.

Villa Maria Serena

21 promenade Reine Astrid • Guided garden tours Tues 10am, Fri 2.30pm • €6

MENTON FESTIVALS

In August the pebbled mosaic of the Grimaldi arms on the parvis St-Michel is covered by chairs, music stands, pianos and harps for the **Festival de Musique de Menton** (ⓦ festival-musique-menton.fr). The nightly concerts are superb and can be listened to from the quaysides without buying a ticket. If you want a proper seat, make a reservation at the tourist office. More bizarrely, Menton's biggest event of the year is the **Fête du Citron** in February, when the lemon-flavoured baccanalia includes processions of floats decorated entirely with the fruit.

The very last house on the seafront before the Italian border is the **Maria Serena Villa**, designed by Charles Garnier – architect of the Paris Opéra and the casino in Monte Carlo – for the family of Ferdinand de Lesseps. Its **garden**, reputed to be the most temperate in France, has an important collection of palms and tropical plants.

ARRIVAL AND INFORMATION   MENTON

By train Menton's *gare SNCF* is at the end of Av de la Gare, off Av de Verdun/Boyer.
Destinations Monaco (roughly every 30min; 12min); Nice (every 15min; 34–49min).
By bus The *gare routière* is north of the *gare SNCF* on Av de Sospel, which is the northern continuation of Av de Verdun. All local buses (€1.50; ⓦ zestbus.fr) pass through the *gare routière*.
Destinations Monaco (every 15–30min; 30–46min); Nice (roughly hourly; 30min); Nice airport (every 30min; 50min).
Tourist office 8 av Boyer (July & Aug daily 9am–7pm; Sept–June Mon–Sat 9am–12.30pm & 2–6pm; ☎ 04 92 41 76 76, ⓦ tourisme-menton.fr).

ACCOMMODATION   SEE MAP PAGE 384

Camping St-Michel 1 rte des Ciappes de Castellar ☎ 09 82 21 27 95, ⓦ campingscotedazur.com/menton. Menton's municipal campsite sits in an olive grove overlooking the town. It's a gruelling walk uphill, so take the bus (#6, via les Ciappes). Closed mid-Oct to March, except for the Fête du Citron. **€28.40**

Chambord 6 av Boyer ☎ 04 93 35 94 19, ⓦ hotel-chambord.com. Sister hotel to the *Moderne* (see below), and slightly swisher, with large, modern en-suite rooms, many with balconies. Near the tourist office, the sea and the town centre. **€110**

★ **Lemon** 10 rue Albert-1er ☎ 04 93 28 63 63, ⓦ hotel-lemon.com. Appealing, renovated budget hotel a couple of minutes' walk from the train station, run by a friendly young couple. Simple but modern en-suite rooms, and a pretty garden. A good choice for the price. **€70.80**

Moderne 1 cours George V ☎ 04 93 57 20 02, ⓦ hotel-moderne-menton.com. Good-value two-star between the *gare SNCF* and the tourist office. The a/c and soundproofed rooms have cable TV; some have balconies. The decor isn't as up-to-the-minute as the name might suggest, but it's comfortable enough. **€100**

Napoléon 29 porte de France, Baie de Garavan ☎ 04 93 35 89 50, ⓦ napoleon-menton.com. Menton's smartest hotel is modern, friendly and right on the seafront between the old town and Italian border, with understated contemporary decor, a pool, gym and stylish, jungly garden on site. **€166**

EATING   SEE MAP PAGE 384

The pedestrianized **rue St-Michel** is promising ground for cheap eats, with plenty of snack stops and an excellent Italian *gelato* stand, while the pretty **covered market** off Quai Monléon is a good place to assemble a picnic. In summer, the **Plage des Sablettes** between the Vieux Port and the Port de Garavan is lined with beach bars, some of them quite stylish.

Le Bistrot des Jardins 14 av Boyer ☎ 04 93 28 28 09, ⓦ le-bistrot-des-jardins.fr. Provençal cooking in a pretty garden setting close to the *gare routière* and tourist office, with the likes of prawn risotto with artichokes or scallop carpaccio. Two-course lunch *formule* or dinner *menu* both €33. Tues–Sat noon–2pm & 7.30–9.30pm, Sun noon–2pm.

Côté Sud 15–17 quai Bonaparte ☎ 06 31 11 48 70, ⓦ cotesudmenton.com. One of the more promising mid-range options facing the port, with stylish modern decor, homemade pasta, a vast selection of pizzas from around €12, and meat or fish mains around €25/30. Mon–Sat 7pm–midnight, Sun noon–3pm & 7pm–midnight.

Fleur de Sel 2 rue du Vieux Collège ☎ 04 93 44 87 34. Crêpes and galettes of distinction in a side street near the Salle des Mariages. Various combinations of cheese, nuts, seafood, sausage and salad, as well as lemon, sugar, caramel and chocolate, with prices starting at €3.50 for the most basic crêpe, rising to around €15 for something more substantial. Tues–Sun noon–2.30pm & 7–10.30pm.

8

Loving Hut 649 promenade du Soleil ☎04 92 07 32 57, ⓦmenton.lovinghut.fr. The Côte d'Azur outpost of this worldwide franchise, serving up the kind of creative and delicious vegan food – much of it organic – that has seen it win multiple awards. Salads around €10, mains around €15. Tues & Wed noon–2.30pm, Thurs–Sun 7–9pm.

Mirazur 30 av Aristide Briand ☎04 92 41 86 86, ⓦmirazur.fr. Rising Italo-Argentinian culinary star Mauro Colagreco has bagged a very impressive three Michelin stars for this swish 1930s-style dining room by the Italian border, famously using vegetables from their own farm; it's one of the Riviera's hottest culinary tickets. Menus €80–260. Wed–Sun 12.15–2pm & 7.15–10pm.

SHOPPING   **SEE MAP PAGE 384**

Au Pays du Citron 24 rue St Michel ☎04 92 09 22 85, ⓦaupaysducitron.fr. Slick boutique selling just about anything you can think of that could be flavoured or scented with lemon, from olive oil to limoncello, syrups and biscuits, plus delicious lemon marmalade (€3.50). Daily 10am–7pm.

Around Menton

Perched in the hills around Menton, the stunning little unspoiled village of **Ste-Agnès** is known for its arts and crafts studios and stunning views, while its near neighbour **Gorbio** is just as scenic, but more sleepy and traditional.

Ste-Agnès

Ten kilometres northwest of Menton and 800m above sea level, **STE-AGNÈS** claims to be the highest coastal village in Europe – something you'll readily believe after completing the tortuous journey up and getting a glimpse of the breathtaking views over Menton. Though packed with crystal engravers, painters, herbalists, jewellers and leather workers, it's still a peaceful spot. When it's not swathed in clouds Ste-Agnès commands breathtaking views, especially from the fascinating twentieth-century **fort** at the seaward end of the village (July–Sept Tues–Sat 3–6pm; Oct–June Sat & Sun 2–5.30pm; €5), tunnelled into the mountaintop as part of the Maginot Line defences of the 1930s. Clamber higher still and you'll reach the ancient Saracen fortress at the top of **Ste-Agnès crag**, from which you'll get proper 360-degree panoramas of sea and mountain – though if the views over Menton and the coast are all you're after save your breath, as the seaward view is no better than from the Maginot fort below.

Ste-Agnès is also an excellent starting point for **walks**; download route descriptions and maps from the Pays Côtier section of the Randoxygène website (ⓦrandoxygene. org), or pick up a copy from one of the local tourist offices. One popular route is the four-hour ascent and circuit of **Pointe Siricocca** (1051m).

ARRIVAL AND DEPARTURE   **STE-AGNÈS**

From the *gare routière* in Menton, **bus** #10 (6 daily; 18min) makes the trek up to the village.

EATING AND DRINKING

Le Righi 1 place du Fort ☎04 92 10 90 88, ⓦrestaurant-lerighi.fr. The views from this restaurant bar/*glacier* and *salon de thé* just beyond the fort are breathtaking; they serve home-made pasta or gnocchi with *daube* or *blettes* sauces, plus meat-based main courses. Menus €22 and €27. Mon, Tues & Thurs–Sun: July & Aug 9am–10pm; Sept to mid-Dec & mid-Feb to June 9am–6pm.

Gorbio

GORBIO, to the southwest of Ste-Agnès, is an exquisite hilltop village with very few arts and crafts boutiques or other tourist fodder, lending it a tranquil atmosphere that's rare for so scenic a place. Though the two villages are only 2km apart as the crow flies, by road it's a tortuous journey of around 8km.

On the Thursday after Corpus Christi in June, the annual rite of the **Procession des Limaces** takes place, when the streets are illuminated by tiny lamps of snail shells filled with olive oil – a custom dating back to medieval times and occurring in villages throughout this area (check with the tourist office in Menton for exact dates).

ARRIVAL AND DEPARTURE   GORBIO

From Menton's *gare routière*, bus #7 (Mon–Sat 6 daily, Sun 4; 30min) heads up to Gorbio.

EATING AND DRINKING

Beau Séjour Place de la République ☎ 04 93 41 46 15. Very pretty restaurant on Gorbio's main square, with a pergola-shaded terrace and *daube de boeuf* and *soupe de* *poisson* on its €29 *menu*. No cards. Daily (except Wed): April–June & Sept–Nov noon–2.30pm; July & Aug noon–2.30pm & 7–9.30pm.

8

MOSAIC IN MUSÉE ARCHÉOLOGIQUE, FRÉJUS

Contexts

391 History

407 Books

410 French

420 Glossary of French terms

421 Glossary of architectural terms

History

While it's hard today to think of Provence and the Côte d'Azur as anything other than definitively French, the region has a long and varied history. Colonized by the Greeks, occupied by the Romans, fought over by Normans and Saracens, and prized as the personal fiefdom of medieval counts and popes, it has only belonged to France for little more than five centuries.

From the Stone Age to the Celto-Ligurians

Although it can safely be assumed that Provence and southeastern France held substantial populations during the Stone Age – including in large areas that now lie beneath the sea – all the great French discoveries from that era are in the southwest of the country. A few Paleolithic traces have been found at Nice and in Menton, but there's nothing to compare with the cave drawings of Lascaux.

The development of farming, which characterizes the **Neolithic Era**, began in Provence around 6500 BC, with the domestication of wild sheep. Around 3000 BC, **Ligurian** settlers reached southern France from the east, and cultivated the land for the first time. These were the people responsible for the carvings in the Vallée des Merveilles, the region's few megalithic standing stones, and the earliest *bories*. Certain Provençal word endings, such as *-osc*, *-asc*, *-auni* and *-inc*, which endure in place names, derive from Ligurian dialects passed down through Greek and Latin.

At some later point **Celts** from the north moved into western Provence, bringing bronze technology with them. A new ethnic mix emerged, the **Celto-Ligurians**; they built the earliest fortified hilltop retreats, the *oppida*, of which traces remain in the Maures, the Luberon, the upper Durance and the hills in the Rhône Valley.

The Greeks discover Provence

As the Celto-Ligurian civilization developed, so did its trading links with other Mediterranean peoples. The River Rhône may have been named by traders from the Greek island of Rhodes (in French the name can be made into an adjective, *Rhodien*). Etruscans, Phoenicians, Corinthians and Ionians all had connections with Provence. Starting with **Massalia** (Marseille) around 600 BC, the **Greek colonies** that appeared along the coast were the result not of military conquest but of gradual economic integration. While Massalia was a republic with great influence over its hinterland, it was not a base for wiping out the indigenous peoples. Deriving prestige and wealth from its port, the city prided itself on its independence, which was to last well into the Middle Ages.

The Greeks introduced olives, figs, cherries, walnuts, cultivated vines and money. In the succeeding two centuries, further colonies were set up in La Ciotat, Almanarre (near Hyères), Bréganson, Cavalaire, St-Tropez (known as Athenopolis), Antibes, Nice and Monaco, while Mastrabala at St-Blaize and Glanum by St-Rémy-de-Provence developed within Massalia's sphere of influence. The **Rhône** was the

400,000 BC	6500 BC	3200 BC
Human beings inhabit the cave of Baume Bonne, near Quinson, and use fire at Terra Mata, Nice.	Neolithic shepherds introduce farming to the lower Alpine slopes.	Ligurian settlers create enigmatic rock carvings in the Vallée des Merveilles.

corridor for commercial expeditions, including journeys as far north as Cornwall to acquire tin. Away from the coast and the river, however, the Celto-Ligurian lifestyle was barely affected.

Roman conquest

Unlike the Greeks, the **Romans** were true imperialists, imposing their organization, language and laws by military subjugation on every corner of their empire. During the third century BC, Roman expansion focused on Spain, from where the Carthaginian general Hannibal set off with his elephants to cross first southern Gaul and then the Alps, before attacking the Romans in upper Italy. Massalia's good diplomatic relations with Rome served the city well when Spain was conquered, and the Romans set about securing the land routes to Iberia.

This they achieved remarkably quickly. Between 125 and 118 BC, **Provincia** (the origin of "Provence") became part of the Roman Empire. Encompassing all southern France from the Alps to the Pyrenees, it stretched as far north as Vienne and Geneva.

While Massalia and other areas remained neutral or collaborated with the invaders, many Ligurian tribes fought to the death. Thus the Oppidum d'Entremont of the Salyens was demolished, and a victorious new city, Aquae Sextiae (Aix), built at its foot in 122 BC. Pax Romana was still a long way off, however. **Germanic Celts** moving south from the Baltic managed to decimate several Roman legions at Orange in 105 BC, only to be defeated by a major campaign designed to keep the barbarians out of Italy. Massalia exploited every situation to gain more territories and privileges, while the rest of Provence grudgingly submitted. Finally, from 58 to 51 BC all of Gaul was conquered by **Julius Caesar**.

At that crucial moment, Massalia blew its hitherto successful diplomatic strategy by supporting Pompey in the Civil War. Caesar laid siege, defeated the city and confiscated all its territories, from the Rhône to Monaco. Unlike earlier emperors, Julius Caesar implanted his own people in Provence – St-Raphaël was founded for his veterans – and so too did his successor Octavian (later Augustus).

While the coastal areas duly Latinized themselves, the **Ligurians** in the mountains, from Sisteron to the Roya Valley, refused to give up their identity. They kept Roman troops busy until their eventual defeat in 14 BC, over which the Trophie des Alpes at La Turbie gloats to this day.

This monument to Augustus Caesar was erected on the newly built **Via Aurelia**, which linked Rome with Arles, by way of Cimiez, Antibes, Fréjus and Aix (pretty much the route of today's N7). The **Via Agrippa** continued north from Arles, through Avignon and Orange. Only the rebellious mountainous area was heavily garrisoned. Western Provence, with Arles as its main town, dutifully served the imperial interests, providing oil, grain and, most importantly, ships for the superpower that ruled western Europe and the Mediterranean for five centuries.

Christianity appeared in Provence during the third century and spread rapidly, becoming the official religion of the Roman Empire in the fourth. The **Lérins Monastery** was founded around 410 AD and the **Abbey of St-Victor** in Marseille six years later.

600 BC	450 BC	218 BC
Greek colonists establish a coastal settlement at Massalia (Marseille).	Arrival of the Gauls.	Hannibal, plus army and elephants, crosses the Rhône above Orange, en route for Italy.

Rome falls: more invasions

During the early fifth century, as the Roman Empire began to split apart, Germanic invaders initially bypassed Provence. By the time the Western Roman Empire finally collapsed in 476 AD, Provence was dominated by both the **Visigoths**, who had captured Arles and were terrorizing the lower Rhône valley, and the **Burgundians**, who had moved in from the east. The new rulers confiscated land, took slaves and generally made life miserable.

Over the next two centuries, **Goths** and **Franks** fought over Provence. Famine, disease and bloodshed diminished the population, lands that had been drained returned to swamp, and intellectual life declined. Under the eighth-century **Merovingian dynasty**, Provence, in theory, formed part of the **Frankish empire**. But a newly emergent world power – **Islam** – had spread from the Middle East into North Africa and most of Spain. In 732 a Muslim army reached as far as Tours before being defeated by the Franks at Poitiers. At this point the local ruler of Provence rebelled against the central authority, and called on the **Saracens** (Muslims) to assist. Armies of Franks, Saracens, Lombards and locals rampaged through Provence, putting the Franks back in control.

Though the ports had trouble continuing their lucrative trade while the Mediterranean was controlled by Saracens, agriculture developed under the Frankish **Carolingian dynasty**, particularly during the relatively peaceful reign of **Charlemagne**. When Charlemagne's sons and then grandsons squabbled over the inheritance, during the ninth century, Provence once again became easy prey.

Normans took over the lower Rhône, and the **Saracens** returned, pillaging Marseille and destroying its abbey in 838, sacking Arles in 842, and attacking Marseille again in 848. From a base at Fraxinetum (La Garde-Freinet), they controlled the whole Massif des Maures for a century.

In response to the Saracen threat, the people of Provence constructed the **hilltop villages** that still, albeit in much altered form, characterize the Provençal coast. Far inland, they similarly retreated to whatever defensive positions were available, which in cities would be the strongest building, for example the Roman theatre at Orange. Rhône Valley villagers took refuge in the Luberon and the Massif de la Ste-Baume.

Despite the terrors and bloodshed, the period also saw progress. The Saracens introduced basic medicine, the use of cork bark, resin extraction from pines, flat roof-tiles, and the most traditional Provençal musical instrument, the tambourine.

The counts of Provence

Towards the end of the tenth century, **Guillaume Le Libérateur**, count of Arles, expelled the Saracens and claimed Provence as his own feudal estate. A period of relative stability ensued. Forestry, fishing, irrigation, land reclamation, vine cultivation, beekeeping, salt-panning, river transport and renewed learning began to pull Provence out of the Dark Ages.

While Guillaume and his successors retained considerable independence from their overlords – first the kingdom of Burgundy, then the Holy Roman Empire – their influence was largely confined to the region around Arles and Avignon. Local lords held sway in rural areas, and the cities developed their own autonomy. Although the Rhône officially formed the border between France and the Holy Roman Empire, the old economic, cultural and linguistic links between its two sides endured.

175 BC	Second century BC	49 BC
Celto-Ligurian peoples establish the oppidum of Entremont, outside Aix-en-Provence.	Gallo-Greeks found Glanum, just outside modern St-Rémy; Provincia joins the Roman Empire, with Narbonne as its capital.	Having constructed a fleet in Arles and defeated Pompey's forces off Les Lecques, Julius Caesar successfully besieges Massalia.

During the **twelfth century**, Provence passed to the counts of Toulouse. It was then divided with the counts of Barcelona, although various fiefdoms – including Forcalquier, Les Baux and Beuil – refused integration. Power shifted repeatedly but, sporadic armed conflicts apart, who held title to Provence hardly affected ordinary people, bound in serfdom to their immediate *seigneurs*.

Thanks to the Crusades, **maritime commerce** flourished once again, as did trade along the Rhône, giving prominence to Avignon, Orange, Arles and, most of all, Marseille. In Nice, then under the control of the Genoese Republic, a new commercial town developed below the castle rock. The cities took on the organizational form of the Italian consulates, increasingly separating themselves from feudal power.

Troubadour poetry made its appearance in the *langue d'oc* language that was spoken from the Alps to the Pyrenees (and from which the **Provençal dialect** developed). Church construction looked back to the Romans for inspiration, producing the great Romanesque edifices of Montmajour, Sénanque, Silvacane, Thoronet and St-Trophime in Arles.

Raymond Béranger V, Catalan count of Provence in the early thirteenth century, took the unprecedented step of spending time in his domains. While fighting off the count of Toulouse and the Holy Roman Emperor, he made Aix his capital, founded Barcelonnette and travelled throughout the Alps and the coastal regions. For the first time since the Romans, Provence became an organized mini-state with a more or less **unified feudal system** of law and administration.

The Angevins

After Béranger's death, Provence turned towards France. It fell under the control of the **house of Anjou** until the end of the fifteenth century. The borders changed: Nice, Barcelonnette and Puget-Théniers passed to Savoy in 1388 and remained separate from Provence until 1860. Extraneous powers claimed or bought territories: the **popes at Avignon** (see page 117) and in the **Comtat Venaissin**; the Prince of Nassau in Orange. Though armed conflicts, revolts and even civil war chequered its medieval history, Provence was at least spared the Hundred Years War, which never touched the region.

By the end of this period the trading routes from the Orient to Genoa and Marseille, and from Marseille to Flanders and London, were forming the basis of **early capitalism**, and spreading new techniques and learning. Marseille was not a great financial centre, but its population became ever more cosmopolitan. For a shepherd or forester in the mountains, meanwhile, life in Marseille or in the extravagant papal city of Avignon would have appeared to belong to another planet.

Provençal Jews exercised equal rights with Christians, owning land and practising assorted professions in addition to finance and commerce. Though concentrated in the western towns, they were not always ghettoized. But the moment disaster struck, such as the **Black Death** in the mid-fourteenth century, latent hostility became violently manifest. The Plague itself made no distinctions: half the population died in the recurring epidemics.

In **cultural and intellectual life** the dominant centres were the **papal court at Avignon**, and later the court of **King René of Anjou** at **Aix**. However, Angevin rulers and foreign trade, art and architecture remained surprisingly unmarked by the major contemporary

First century AD	c.100 AD	410
According to legend, Mary Jacobé, Mary Salomé and their Egyptian servant Sarah, later the Gypsies' patron saint, land at Les-Saintes-Maries-de-la-Mer.	Completion of amphitheatre in Arles, the largest Roman building in Gaul.	Honoratus founds a monastery on the Île St-Honorat.

movements. Only in the mid-fifteenth century did native art develop around the **Avignon School**, while the **School of Nice**, more directly under Italian influence, also emerged. Avignon acquired great **Gothic architecture** – the Palais des Papes and many of the churches – but elsewhere the only major examples of the new style were Tarascon's castle and the basilica of St-Maximin-de-la-Ste-Baume.

Founded in 1303, the **university in Avignon** became famous for jurisprudence. Aix university was established a century later and in the mid-fourteenth century the first paper mills were in use. By King René's time, French was the official language of the court.

Union with France

After the short-lived Charles III of Provence, René's heir, bequeathed all his lands to **Louis XI of France**, the *parlement* of Aix glossed over, and approved, the transfer of power in 1482. Within twelve months every top Provençal official had been replaced by a Frenchman; the castles at Toulon and Les Baux were razed to the ground; and garrisons were placed in five major towns.

Louis XI's successors took a more careful approach to this crucial border province. The **Act of Union**, ratified by *parlement* in 1486, declared Provence to be a separate entity within France, enshrining the rights to its own law courts, customs and privileges. In reality, the ever-centralizing power of the French state systematically eroded these rights.

The **Jewish population** provided a convenient diversion for Provençal frustrations. Encouraged, if not instigated, by the Crown, there were massacres, expulsions and assaults in Marseille, Arles and Manosque at the end of the fifteenth century. The royal directive was convert or leave – some, like the parents of **Nostradamus**, converted, while others fled to the Comtat, where Jews lost their papal protection in turn in 1570.

Meanwhile Charles VIII, Louis XII and François I involved Provence in their **Italian Wars. Marseille** became a **military port** in 1488, and in 1496 **Toulon** was fortified and its first **shipyards** opened. While the rest of the province suffered troop movements and requisitions, Marseille and Toulon benefited from extra funds and unchecked piracy against the enemies of France. Genoese, Venetian and Spanish vessels were regularly towed into Marseille.

The war took a more serious turn in the 1520s. After the French conquered Milan, **Charles V**, the new Holy Roman Emperor, sent a large army across the Var and into Aix. The French sought to protect Marseille at all costs. When the imperial forces failed to take Marseille, the city was rewarded with a royal wedding between François' second son, the future Henri II, and **Catherine de Médicis**. The Château d'If was built to protect the roadstead.

Charles V then retook Milan, so the French invaded Savoy and occupied Nice. In 1536 an even bigger **imperial army invaded**, and again the French abandoned inland Provence to protect Marseille and the Rhône Valley. At **Le Muy**, fifty local heroes, subsequently hanged for their pains, stopped the emperor for one day. **Marseille** and **Arles** held out; French troops moved south down the Durance; and the weakened Savoyards returned whence they came.

As a result of the Italian Wars, Provence finally identified itself with France. That made it easier for the Crown to diminish the power of the *États*, impose greater

Fifth century	Ninth century	973
With the Roman Empire collapsing, Visigoths and Burgundians contend for control.	Saracen armies sack Arles in 842 and Marseille in 848.	Count Guillaume of Arles expels the Saracens from Provence, following the battle of Tourtour.

numbers of French administrators, and, in 1539, decree that all administrative laws were to be translated from Latin into French, not Provençal.

Life in the early sixteenth century

Sixteenth-century Provence was ruled by two royal appointees – a governor and grand *sénéchal* (the chief administrator) – but the **feudal hierarchy** had little control over the structure of society. Those few nobles who lived on their estates were often poorer than the merchants and financiers of the major cities. In remoter areas people cultivated their absent *seigneur's* land as if it were their own; elsewhere towns bought land off the feudal owners, and nearly half the population owned land. Advances in irrigation, such as **Craponne's canal through the Crau**, were carried out independently from the aristocracy.

While not self-sufficient in grain, Provence exported wine, fish and vermilion from the Camargue; textiles, tanneries, soap and paper thrived; and new foods, such as oranges, pepper, palm dates and sugar cane, were imported. Olives provided the basic oil for food, commercial orchards appeared, and most families kept pigs and sheep: only vegetables were rare luxuries. People lived on their land, with the **old fortified villages** populated only in times of insecurity. Epidemics continued, however, and sanitation left much to be desired.

Certain larger towns set up **free schools**, while Aix, Marseille, Arles and Avignon established secondary colleges. **Nostradamus** (1503–66) achieved renown throughout France, although his books had to be printed in Lyon – there was as yet no market for printers in Provence.

The Wars of Religion

While the Italian Wars disrupted social and productive advances, they were nothing compared with the **Wars of Religion** that threw all France into **civil war** later in the sixteenth century. The clash between the reforming ideas of Luther and Calvin and the old Roman Catholic order was particularly violent in Provence. Avignon was a rigid centre of Catholicism, whereas Orange allowed Huguenots to practise freely. Haute Provence and the Luberon became centres for the new religion due to the influx of Dauphinois and Piedmontais settlers.

Incidents built up in the 1540s, culminating in the massacre of Luberon Protestants and the destruction of Mérindol (see page 169). In Avignon heretics were displayed in iron cages; in Haute Provence churches were smashed by the reformers; and in Orange Protestants pillaged the cathedral and seized control of the city. The regent Catherine de Medici's **Edict of Tolerance** in 1562 only made matters worse. *Parlement* chose to resign rather than ratify a new Edict of Tolerance in 1563, even though by now Orange had been won back to the established Church, the garrison of Sisteron had been massacred for protecting the Protestants, and the last armed group of reformers had fled north.

When Catherine de Médicis and her son Charles XIV toured Provence in 1564, all seemed well. But within a few years fighting again broke out, with Sisteron once more under siege. This state of civil war was only terminated by another major outbreak of **plague** in 1580.

Twelfth century	1309	1334	1388
The Cistercian order establishes the Abbaye de Sénanque.	Clement V becomes the first pope to move to Avignon.	Benedict XII builds the Vieux Palais.	Civil war in Provence; Nice and Barcelonnette pass to Savoy.

The *Guerres de Religion* hotted up after the Protestant **Henri de Navarre** (the future Henri IV) became heir to the throne in 1584. The pope excommunicated Henri, and the leaders of the French Catholics (the de Guises) formed the **European Catholic League**, seized Paris and drove out the king, Henri III. Provence found itself with two governors – the king's and the League's appointees; two capitals – Aix and Pertuis; and a split *parlement*. After Henri III's assassination, Catholic Aix called in the duke of Savoy, whose troops trounced Henri de Navarre's supporters at Riez. By now the main issue for the Provençaux was loyalty to the French Crown against invaders, rather than religion. Even the Aix *parlement* stopped short of giving Savoy the title to Provence, and after Marseille again withstood a siege, the duke gave up and went back home to Nice in 1592. For another year battles continued between the Leaguers and the Royalists. Finally Henri IV said his Mass; troops entered Marseille; and Provence reverted, war-damaged and impoverished, to **royal control**.

Louis XIII and Louis XIV

The **consolidation of the French state** initiated by Louis XIII's minister, **Richelieu**, saw Provençal institutions and ideas of independence whittled away, along with ever-increasing tax demands and enforced "free gifts" to the king.

As the power and prestige of the *États* and *parlement* dwindled, political power switched to *intendants*, servants of the state with powers over every aspect of provincial life, including the military. Having refused to provide the royal purse with funds in 1629, the *États* were not convoked again. The *noblesse d'épée* (the real aristos) were left disgruntled but impotent, while the clergy (the First Estate) also lost a measure of power.

It was a time of **plague**, **famine**, and yet more **religious strife and conflict. War with Spain** increased taxation, decimated trade and cost lives. When Marseille attempted to preserve its ancient independence by setting up a rebel council in 1658, the royal response was swift. Troops were sent in, rebels condemned to the rack or the galleys, and a permanent garrison established.

Despite taxes and upheavals, progress in manufacture (including the faïence industry), education and social provision carried on apace. The townhouses of Aix, Marseille and Avignon, the Hospice de la Charité in Marseille, the Baroque additions to churches and chapels, all show wealth accumulating – gained, as ever, by maritime commerce.

As the reign of **Louis XIV**, the **Sun King**, became more grandiose and more aggressive, Provence, like all France beyond Versailles and Paris, was eclipsed. The **war with Holland** saw Orange and the valley of Barcelonnette annexed; Avignon and the papal Comtat swung steadily into the French orbit; attempts to capture Nice were renewed. As the *ancien régime* slowly dug its own grave, the rest of France stagnated. The pattern for Provence of wars, invasions and trade blockades became entrenched. Aix had its grandiose town planning, Avignon its mansions, and Grasse its perfume industry, but elsewhere there was complete stagnation.

The Revolution

Conditions in Provence were ripe for **revolution**. The region had suffered a disastrous silk harvest and a sharp fall in the price of wine in 1787, and the severe winter of

1409	1434–80	1482	1503
The antipope Benedict XIII, following a siege that prompts him to build Avignon's still-extant walls, flees the city.	Under King René of Anjou, Aix-en-Provence reaches its apogee as capital of Provence.	Provence passes into French control, following the death of Charles III of Provence.	Nostradamus is born in St-Rémy.

1788–89 killed off olive trees. Unemployment and starvation were rife and the soaring cost of bread provoked riots in the spring of 1789.

In **July 1789**, while the Bastille was stormed in Paris, Provençal peasants pillaged local châteaux and urban workers rioted against the mayors, egged on by the middle classes. There was only one casualty, at Aups. The following year **Marseillaise revolutionaries** seized the forts of St-Jean and St-Nicolas, with again just one dose of violence when the crowd lynched St-Jean's commander. **Toulon** was equally fervent in its support for the new order, and at **Aix** a counter-revolutionary lawyer and two aristocrats were strung up on lampposts.

Counter-revolutionaries regrouped in Carpentras, but 1792 saw Marseille's staunchly Jacobin National Guard, the **Féderés**, demolish counter-revolutionary forces in the Comtat and aristocratic Arles. Marseille's authorities declared kingship to be contrary to the principles of equality and national sovereignty. When the Legislative Assembly summoned the Féderés to Paris, five hundred Marseillais marched north singing Rouget de Lisle's **Hymn to the Army of the Rhine**. Written for troops in that April's war with Germany and Austria, it was a major hit with the Parisian *sans-culottes*, and as the **Marseillaise** it became France's national anthem – especially after the attack on the Tuileries Palace was swiftly followed by the dethronement of the king.

Provence had by now incorporated the papal states and was divided into **four départements**. Peasants were once again on the pillage, and still starving, while royalists and republicans fought it out in the towns. In 1793 the Var military commander was ordered to take Nice, a hotbed of émigré intrigue. Twenty thousand people fled the city but no resistance was encountered. The Alpes-Maritimes *département* came into existence.

That summer, political divisions between the factions of the Convention and the growing fear of a dictatorship by the Parisian *sans-culottes* provoked the **provincial Federalist revolt**. Fed up with conscription to wars on every frontier, the populace hankered after their former Provençal autonomy. Revolutionary cities found themselves fighting against government forces – a situation exploited by the real **counter-revolutionaries**. In Toulon the entire fleet and the city's fortifications were handed over to the English. Besides the almost daily executions of the Terror, reprisals cost thousands of lives.

Much of Provence, however, had remained Jacobin, and fell victim to the **White Terror of 1795** that followed the execution of Robespierre. The prisons of Marseille, Aix, Arles and Tarascon overflowed with people picked up on the street with no charge. Cannons were fired into the cells at point-blank range and sulphur or lighted rags thrown through the bars. The Revolution abandoned all hope of being revolutionary, and **anarchy reigned**. Provence was crawling with returned émigrés who readily attracted violent followers motivated by frustration, exhaustion and famine.

Napoleon and restoration

Provence's experience of **Napoleon** was much like that of the rest of France, despite the emperor's close connection with the region (childhood at Nice; military career at Antibes and Toulon; then the escape from Elba). Order was restored and power became even more centralized, with *préfets* enlarging on the role of Louis XIV's *intendants*. Although the **concordat with the pope** re-establishing Catholicism as the state religion

1584	1632	1661	1720
With the Wars of Religion at their peak, Provence finds itself with two governors, and two capitals – Aix and Pertuis.	Louis XIII of France destroys the feudal citadel at Les Baux.	Louis XIV, the "Sun King", introduces absolute monarchy to France.	Plague kills half the population of Marseille.

was widely welcomed, secular power often reverted to the old *seigneurs* – the new mayor of Marseille, for example, was a marquise.

It was the **Napoleonic wars** that cost the emperor his Provençal support. Marseille's port was again blockaded; conscription and taxes for military campaigns were as detested as ever; the Alpes-Maritimes *département* became a theatre of war and in 1814 was handed over (with Savoy) to Sardinia. Monaco followed suit the following year, though with the Grimaldi dynasty reinstalled in their palace.

The **restoration of the Bourbons** after Waterloo unleashed another White Terror. Provence was again bitterly divided between royalists and republicans, but there was no major resistance to the **1830 revolution** that put Louis-Philippe, the "Citizen King", on the throne. The new regime represented liberalism – tinged with anti-clericalism and a dislike of democracy – and was welcomed by the Provençal bourgeoisie.

1848 and 1851

The first half of the nineteenth century saw the first major **industrialization** of France, and, overseas, the conquest of Algeria. Marseille was linked by rail with Paris and expanded its port to take steamships; iron bridges over the Rhône and new roads were built; many towns demolished their ramparts to extend their main streets into the suburbs. By the 1840s the arsenal at Toulon employed over three thousand workers.

This emerging proletariat was highly receptive when socialist and feminist **Flora Tristan** toured France in 1844. A year later all the arsenal's different trades went on strike. Throughout industrialized Provence workers overturned their traditional *compagnons* (guilds) to form radical trade unions. Things hardly changed inland, however, as protectionist policies hampered the exchange of foodstuffs, and the new industries' demand for fuel eroded forestry rights. By 1847 the country (and most of Europe) was in severe economic crisis.

When news of the **1848 revolution** arrived from Paris, town halls, common lands and forests were instantly and peacefully reclaimed by the populace. The ensuing elections returned very moderate republicans, albeit including three manual workers in Marseille, Toulon and Avignon. Two months later, however, the economic situation was deteriorating again, and employers were clawing back newly won improvements in working hours and wages. A demonstration in Marseille turned nasty and the **barricades** went up.

Elsewhere, the most militant action was in Menton and Roquebrune, both under the rule of **Monaco**, where locals refused to pay the prince's high taxes on oil and fruit. Sardinian military assistance failed to quell the revolt and the two towns declared themselves independent. His main source of income gone, the Grimaldi prince turned his focus shrewdly towards **tourism** – already well-established in Nice and Hyères – and opened the casino at Monte Carlo.

The 1848 revolution turned sour with the election of **Louis-Napoleon** as president in 1850. Universal male suffrage was effectively annulled by a new residency requirement. Laws against "secret societies" and "conspiracies" followed. Ordinary *paysans* discussing prices over a bottle of wine could be arrested; militants from Digne and Avignon were deported to Polynesia for belonging to a democratic party; and cooperatives were seen as hotbeds of sedition.

1789	1792	1793
French Revolution ends the monarchy.	Written for troops in the war with Germany and Austria, the Hymn to the Army of the Rhine becomes, as the *Marseillaise*, the French national anthem.	Revolutionary forces recapture Toulon, in an engagement that brings the young Napoleon to public attention.

When Louis-Napoleon made himself emperor in the **coup d'état of 1851**, Provence, like many other regions, turned again to revolt. Initially there were insufficient forces in the small towns and villages to prevent the rebels taking control. In order to take the *préfectures*, villagers and townspeople, both male and female, organized themselves into "*colonnes*" that marched beneath the red flag. Digne was the only *préfecture* they held, though, and then for only two days. Reprisals were bloody, with thousands of rebels caught as they tried to flee. Of all the insurgents shot, imprisoned or deported in France, one in five was from Provence.

The Second Empire

The **Second Empire** saw huge changes in everyday life. **Marseille** became France's premier port, its trade enormously expanded by the colonization of North and West Africa, Vietnam and parts of China. The depopulation of inland Provence suddenly became a deluge of migration to the coast and Rhône Valley. While the railway was extended along the coast, communications inland were ignored.

At the end of the **war for Italian unification** in 1860, **Napoléon III** regained the Alpes-Maritimes as reward for supporting Italy against Austria. A plebiscite in Nice gave majority support for **reunion with France**. To the north, Tende and La Brigue voted almost unanimously for France but the result was ignored: Italy's new king wished to keep his favourite hunting grounds. Menton and Roquebrune also voted for France. While making noises about rigged elections, Charles of Monaco agreed to sell the two towns – despite their independence – to France. The sum was considerably greater than the proceeds from the fledgling gambling and tourism industry, and saved the principality from bankruptcy. **Monaco's independence**, free from any foreign protector, was finally established.

One casualty of this dispersal of traditional Provence was the Provençal language. This prompted the formation of the **Félibrige** in 1854, by a group of poets including **Frédéric Mistral** – a nostalgic, backward-looking and intellectual movement in defence of literary Provençal. Other, more populist, Provençal writers of the time were similarly conservative, railing against gas lighting and any other innovation. The attempt to associate the language with some past golden age of ultra-Catholic primitivism only encouraged the association of progress with the French tongue – particularly for the Left.

By the end of the 1860s the **socialism** of the First International was gaining ground in the industrial cities, and in Marseille most of all. In the plebiscite of 1870, in which the country as a whole gave Napoleon III their support, the Bouches-du-Rhône *département* was second only to Paris in the number of "nons". It was not surprising therefore that Marseille had its own commune (see page 55) when the Parisians took up arms.

Honoré Daumier, the Marseillais caricaturist and fervent republican, was the great illustrator of both the 1851 and the 1871 events. In the middle of the century the **Marseille school of painting** developed under the influence of foreign travel and Orientalism, attracting such artists as Puvis de Chavannes and Félix Ziem. Provence's greatest native artist, **Cézanne**, though living in Paris from the 1860s to the 1880s, spent a few months of every year in his home town of Aix, or in Marseille and

1815	1830	1834
Napoleon defeated at Waterloo; monarchy re-established.	Frédéric Mistral, the writer largely responsible for re-establishing a Provençal identity, is born near St-Rémy.	Cholera sweeps Provence; Jean Giono later records its impact on his native Manosque in *A Horseman On The Roof*.

L'Estaque. He was sometimes accompanied by his childhood friend **Zola**, and by **Renoir**, whom he introduced to this coast. Meanwhile **Van Gogh** travelled south to Arles, and briefly persuaded **Gauguin** to join him.

Third Republic: 1890–1914

Under the **Third Republic**, the division between inland Provence and the coast and Rhône Valley accentuated. Port activity at Marseille quadrupled with the opening of new trade routes along the Suez Canal and further colonial acquisitions in the Far East. Manufacturing began to play an equal role with commerce. The Rhône Valley orchards were planted on a massive scale, and light industries developed in Aix and elsewhere to export clothes, foodstuffs and paper to the North African colonies. Chemical works in Avignon produced the synthetics that ensured the decline of the traditional industries of the interior – tanning, dyeing, silk and glass. Wine production, meanwhile, was devastated by phylloxera.

An especial area of brilliance was **art**, and painting in particular. A younger generation of artists discovered the Côte d'Azur, while the **Post-Impressionists** and Fauves flocked to St-Tropez in the wake of the ever-hospitable Paul Signac. Matisse, Dufy, Seurat, Dérain, Van Dongen, Bonnard, Braque, Friesz, Marquet, Manguin, Camion, Vlaminck and Vuillard were all intoxicated by the Mediterranean light, the climate and the ease of living. The escape from the rigours of Paris released a massive creative energy and resulted in works that, in addition to their radical innovations, have more *joie de vivre* than those of any other period in French art. Renoir retired to Cagnes for health reasons in 1907; for Matisse, Dufy and Bonnard the Côte d'Azur became their permanent home.

Meanwhile, the **winter tourist season** on the coast was taking off. **Hyères** and **Cannes** had been "discovered" in the first half of the nineteenth century (and Nice even earlier). But increased ease of travel and the temporary restraint of simmering international tensions encouraged aristocratic mobility. The population of **Nice** trebled between 1861 and 1911; luxury trains ran from St Petersburg, Vienna and London; *belle époque* mansions and grand hotels rose along the Riviera seafronts; and gambling, particularly at Monte Carlo, won the patronage of the Prince of Wales, the Emperor Franz Josef and scores of Russian grand-dukes.

The native working class, meanwhile, were forming the first **French Socialist Party**, which held its opening congress in Marseille in 1879. In 1881 Marseille elected the first socialist *député*. By 1892 the municipal councils of Marseille, Toulon, La Ciotat and other industrial towns were in socialist hands. In Aix, however, the old legitimist royalists (those favouring the return of the Bourbons) still held sway.

World War I and the interwar years

The battlefields of **World War I** may have seemed far away in northern France and Belgium, but conscription brought the people of Provence into the war. The socialists divided between pacifists and patriots, but when, in 1919, France took part in the attack on the Soviet Union, soldiers, sailors and workers joined forces in Toulon and Marseille to support mutinies on French warships in the Black Sea. The struggle to

1856	1871	1888	1907
Monte Carlo opens its first casino.	Marseille establishes its own commune, in response to events in Paris.	Following a confrontation with Paul Gauguin in Arles, Vincent van Gogh cuts off his ear.	The game of *pétanque* is invented in La Ciotat on the Côte d'Azur.

have the mutineers freed continued well into 1920, the year in which the **French Communist Party** (PCF) was born.

War casualties led to severe depopulation in the already dwindling villages of inland Provence. **Land use** also changed dramatically, from mixed agriculture to a monocrop of vines, to provide the army ration of one litre of wine per soldier per day. Quantity rather than quality was the aim, leaving acre upon acre of unviable vineyards after demobilization. With the growth in tourism, it was easiest to sell the land for construction.

The **tourist industry** recovered fairly quickly from the war. The *Front Populaire* of 1936 introduced paid holidays, encouraging native visitors to the still unspoiled coast. International literati – Somerset Maugham, Katherine Mansfield, Scott and Zelda Fitzgerald, Colette, Anaïs Nin, Gertrude Stein – and a new wave of artists, including Picasso and Cocteau, replaced the defunct grand-dukes.

Marseille during the interwar years saw the emergence of characteristics that have yet to be obliterated. The activities of the fascist *Action Française* led to deaths during a left-wing counter-demonstration in 1925. Modern-style **corruption** snaked its way through the town hall and gangsters on the Chicago model moved in on the vice industries. Elections were rigged; revolvers were used at the ballot box. The increasing popularity of the Communist Party in the city was due to its anti-corruption platform. After the failure of the *Front Populaire* (for which the great majority of Provençaux had voted, electing several Communist *députés*), Marseille saw constant pitched battles between Left and Right.

World War II

France and Britain declared **war on Germany** together on September 3, 1939. The French Maginot line, however, swiftly collapsed, and by June 1940 the Germans controlled Paris and all of northern France. On June 22, Marshal Pétain signed the **armistice with Hitler**, which divided France between the Occupied Zone – the Atlantic coast and north of the Loire – and "unoccupied" Vichy France in the south. Menton and Sospel were occupied by the Italians, to whom the adjoining Roya Valley still belonged.

With the start of the British counteroffensive in 1942, **Vichy France** joined itself with the Allies and was immediately occupied by the Germans. When the port of Toulon was overrun in November, the French navy scuppered its fleet rather than letting it fall into German hands.

Resistance fighters and passive citizens suffered executions, deportations and the wholesale destruction of Le Panier quarter in Marseille (see page 49). The **Allied bombings** of 1944 caused high civilian casualties and considerable material damage, particularly to Avignon, Marseille and Toulon. The **liberation** of the two great port cities was aided by armed popular revolt, but the fighting by the local populace was at its most heroic in the Italian sector, in Sospel and its neighbouring villages.

Modern Provence

Before surrendering **Marseille**, the Germans made sure its harbours were blown to bits. In the immediate **postwar years** the task of repairing the damage was compounded by a

1920s	1936	1939–45
Celebrities including Charlie Chaplin, Maurice Chevalier, F. Scott Fitzgerald and the Prince of Wales flock to the Côte d'Azur.	The *Front Populaire* introduces paid holidays, encouraging French visitors to the coast.	World War II; Paris and northern France occupied by Nazis; the south, ruled at first by the puppet Vichy regime, falls under German occupation in 1942.

slump in international trade and passenger traffic. The nationalization of the Suez Canal also hit the city, ending its prime position on world trading routes.

Marseille's solution was to orient its **port** and industry towards the Atlantic and the inland route of the Rhône. The **oil industries** that had developed in the 1920s around the Étang de Berre and Fos were extended. The mouth of the Rhône and the Golfe de Fos became a massive tanker terminal. **Iron and steel works** filled the spaces behind the new Port de Marseille that stretched for 50km beyond the Vieux Port. In the process, the city's population boomed. To meet the urgent demand for housing, badly designed, low-cost, high-rise estates proliferated out from the congested city centre.

While never halted, the depopulation of **inland Provence** was slowed by massive **irrigation and hydroelectric schemes**. The isolated *mas* or farmhouses, positioned wherever there happened to be a spring, were left to ruin or linked to the mains. Orchards, lavender fields and olive groves became larger, competition for early fruit and vegetables fiercer, and the market for luxury foods greater. The rich **Rhône Valley** continued to export fruit, wine and vegetables, while the river was exploited for irrigation and power, both nuclear and hydroelectric, and made navigable for sizeable ships.

After Algeria won back its independence in 1962, hundreds of thousands of French settlers, the **pieds noirs**, returned, bringing a virulent hatred of Arabic-speaking people. At the same time, the government encouraged immigration from its former colonies, North Africa in particular, with the (unkept) promise of well-paid jobs, civil rights and social security. The resulting tensions, not just in Marseille but all along the coast, made perfect fodder for the **parties of the Right**. From being a bastion of socialism at the end of World War II, Provence turned towards intolerance and reaction.

Ethnic tensions and the rise of the Front National

Corruption, waste and incompetence in the region's town halls was a significant element in the 1995 electoral breakthrough of **Jean-Marie Le Pen's neo-fascist Front National** (FN) party. Under the slogan "Priority for the French", by which it meant the "ethnically pure" French, it took control in Orange, Marignane and Toulon. The most important factor was fear, born of a toxic brew of racism, unemployment and high crime rates.

Le Pen returned in full force for the 2002 **presidential elections**, with first-round victories in five out of six *départements* in the PACA (Provence, Alpes, Côte d'Azur) region (changed to *Région Sud* in 2017), soundly defeating both Chirac and Jospin. At about the same time, **ethnic tensions** of other kinds began to manifest themselves, notably among France's Arab and Jewish communities – both the largest of their kind in Europe.

After the region's most prominent FN mayor, Jacques Bompard of Orange, defected to the rival *Mouvement pour la France* (MPF) in 2005, the FN tide seemed to be ebbing. Elections in 2012, however, showed that the far right remained a force to be reckoned with in Provence. Neighbouring districts in the Vaucluse elected both Le Pen's 22-year-old granddaughter Marion Maréchal-Le Pen, and Jacques Bompard, nominally independent but with FN support, to the National Assembly. Bompard was re-elected as mayor of Orange in 2014, while in the regional **elections of 2015**, held in the immediate aftermath of terrorist attacks in Paris, Marion Maréchal-Le Pen

1946	1947	1951
Cannes stages its first Festival International du Film; Pablo Picasso at work in Antibes' Château Grimaldi.	Tende and the upper Roya Valley revert from Italy to France.	Matisse's final masterpiece, the Chapelle du Rosaire, is dedicated in Vence.

CRIME, CORRUPTION AND POLITICS

The hidden ties between the Provençal mafia – known as the **milieu** – and the region's town halls date back to the 1920s, but only after the shocking assassination of Hyères' *député*, **Yann Piat**, in 1994 did the demand for a "clean hands" campaign begin in earnest.

Drug trafficking became a major problem in Marseille in the early 1970s as the notorious **French Connection** routed heroin from Turkey to the United States through the port, then controlled by Corsican mobsters. At the same time, regional politics were ripe for exploitation. **Municipal fiefdoms** evolved, offering opportunities for patronage, nepotism and corruption, along with the financial muscle that, until all too recently, ensured incumbents a more-or-less permanent position.

In 1982, Graham Greene accused Nice's police and judiciary of protecting organized crime; he claimed he slept with a gun under his pillow after he detailed the corruption in *J'Accuse* (which was banned in France). The late **Jacques Médecin**, who succeeded his father as mayor of Nice in 1966, controlled public life in the city until his downfall in 1990 for political fraud and tax evasion; only when he fled to Uruguay were his mafioso connections finally discussed. Despite this, most Niçois gladly supported his sister Geneviève Assémat-Médecin as his successor; and those who didn't backed his daughter, Martine Catinchi-Médecin, a Le Pen supporter. Finally extradited in 1994, Médecin served a short prison term and used his popularity to back **Jacques Peyrat**, a former member of the *Front National*, who was mayor of Nice from 1995 until 2008, since when the mayor has been **Christian Estrosi** of the centre-right UMP party.

Toulon was another classic fiefdom, run for four decades by **Maurice Arreckx** and his clique of friends with their underworld connections, until he was put away when financial scandals finally came to light. His successor, and former director of finances, tried in vain to win back the voters but merely ran up more debts and lost to the *Front National* in 1995.

François Léotard, the right-wing mayor of Fréjus, who held cabinet office (under Chirac in the late 1980s) and a seat in the *Assemblée Nationale*, was investigated for financial irregularities, but the case eventually ran out of time and the charges were dropped. Cannes' mayor, **Michel Mouillot**, was debarred from public office for five years and given a fifteen-month suspended sentence in 1989, then won his appeal and returned to the town hall only to be given an eighteen-month suspended sentence in 1996. **Pierre Rinaldi**, mayor of **Digne**, was investigated for fraud; **Jean-Pierre Lafond**, mayor of **La Ciotat**, for unwarranted interference; two successive mayors of **La Seyne** for corruption and abuse of patronage … and so the list goes on.

Meanwhile, though the French Connection was ultimately smashed, **organized crime** continued to flourish, controlled both by the Italian mafia and – increasingly – by eastern European gangs. The faces and nationalities may change, but the criminals of the Côte d'Azur preserve their reputation for resourcefulness. The activities of the newer arrivals have included boat-jacking: yachts stolen to order, and often used for drug trafficking and smuggling illegal immigrants before being resold in the ports of the Black Sea.

narrowly failed to seize control of the Provence-Alpes-Côte d'Azur region, which was won instead by the Republicans, under Nice's conservative mayor **Christian Estrosi**.

Mass tourism and the environment

A crucial factor in the postwar history of Provence has been the rise of **mass tourism**. From the 1960s onwards the number of visitors to the Côte d'Azur soared beyond

1953	1962	1967
Roger Vadim films *Et Dieu Créa La Femme*, introducing St-Tropez, and Brigitte Bardot, to the world.	Following Algerian independence, former French settlers and North Africans add to the mix of Marseille and other cities.	British cyclist Tom Simpson dies on Mont Ventoux during the Tour de France.

what – in any sane sense – could be considered manageable proportions. By the mid-1970s the coast had become a nearly uninterrupted wall of concrete; agricultural land, save for a few profitable vineyards, was transformed into campsites, hotels and holiday housing. **Property speculation** and construction became the dominant economic activities, while the flaunting of planning laws and the ever-increasing threat to the **environment** were ignored.

When **Brigitte Bardot** complained in the 1980s that her beloved **St-Tropez** was becoming a mire of human detritus, the media saw it as a sexy summer story. Then **ecologists** began to warn that the Mediterranean's principal oxygenating sea grasses were disappearing. A non-native toxic algae, *Caulerpa taxifolia*, has spread from the Côte d'Azur around the Mediterranean, obliterating sea grasses and replacing them with largely sterile algal beds.

More environmental controversy followed in 2016 when people took to the streets of Marseille in their thousands to protest the official sanctioning of continued dumping of toxic red mud (bauxite residues) from aluminium production into the coastal waters of the Parc National des Calanques.

Urban expansion on the coast

Since the first three postwar decades, when sun-worshipping set the region's tone, different forces have been at work. While summer tourism exacted a heavy toll, a new type of visitor and resident has also become prevalent: the expense-account delegate to **business conferences** and the well-paid employee of **multinational firms**. Towns like Nice and Cannes led the way in attracting the former, while the business park of **Sophia-Antipolis** north of Antibes showed how easily information-technology firms could be persuaded to relocate to the beautiful Côte d'Azur hinterland. The result is a further erosion of Provençal identity and greater pressure on the environment. Rather than countering the seasonal imbalance of tourism, business visitors have made consumption and congestion a year-round factor.

The money from business services and industry on the Riviera now outstrips income from tourism. In the big cities, the distinctive Marseillais and Niçois identities have endured, but elsewhere along the coast, continuities with the past have become ever harder to detect.

Inland Provence

Inland Provence has undergone a parallel transformation – more social than physical, with less property development but a great deal of property price inflation, as high-salaried professionals from all over northern Europe buy their place in the sun. The Luberon in particular is especially prized as **second-home territory**.

While the influx rescued some villages from extinction, many are now lifeless out of season. In the Alpine valleys, the growth of ski resorts reversed centuries-old population decline, and the resultant damage to trees, soil and habitats was in part offset by the creation of the **Parc National du Mercantour**, which saved several Alpine animal and plant species.

Meanwhile, ever fewer *paysans* can support themselves by keeping goats and bees, a few vines and a vegetable plot. The cheeses and honey, the vegetables, olive oil and wine (unless it's AOP) must compete with Spanish, Italian and Greek produce, from

1986	1989	1994
Film director Claude Berri releases *Jean de Florette* and *Manon des Sources*, based on the books by Marcel Pagnol, themselves novelizations of his own 1952 movie, *Manon des Sources*.	Peter Mayle publishes *A Year in Provence*, inspiring a new wave of British visitors to explore the region.	Following extradition from Uruguay, former Nice mayor Jacques Médecin is convicted of corruption.

land that doesn't have the ludicrously high values of Provence. The emergence of successful international companies such as l'Occitane en Provence and Oliviers & Co, however, offers one pointer to a viable economic future, trading on the magic of a Provençal image to target upmarket consumers, with prices to match.

Transport mania

Fast access to the Côte d'Azur has long obsessed planners in Paris. The **TGV** was extended to Marseille in 2001, and has since been extended to Nice, while there are now direct trains from London to Marseille year-round. Increasing accessibility, however, serves to exacerbate existing transport problems within Provence. An attenuated but densely populated linear conurbation without a proper regional mass transportation system, the Riviera is particularly badly affected. Heavy traffic and gridlocks are the norm on the roads, with the temptation to drive everywhere promoted by the suburban and commercial sprawl that has long since eliminated any clear distinction between individual coastal towns. At least things have somewhat improved in Marseille and Nice, with the opening of new **tramways** and **public bike rental** schemes.

Terror and political turmoil

On 14th July 2016, the large-scale **terror** caused by so-called **Islamic State** which had thus far mainly confined itself to Paris was visited upon Nice as a nineteen tonne truck was deliberately driven into Bastille Day crowds on the Promenade des Anglais, killing 86 people and injuring hundreds more. In response the authorities constructed an extensive, multi-million euro defence of steel cables and concrete bollards, permanently altering the face of one of the most iconic seafronts in France. The long term socio-political, economic and cultural consequences on both the city and the region remain to be seen but with the country still on high alert and right-wing populism mushrooming across both France and Europe amid the continuing fallout of the EU-wide migrant crisis, harmony is in short supply.

Nor has Provence been immune to the civil unrest of the **gilet jaunes** (yellow vest) movement, sparked in October 2018 by opposition to President Emmanuel Macron's economic reforms, and specifically by a proposed fuel tax. Nice, Marseille, Avignon and Arles have all seen disruption, while images of an elderly female activist in Nice knocked unconscious after police charged protesters defying a ban, hasn't done the city any favours.

2005	2011	2015	2016
Prince Albert II succeeds his father Prince Rainier in Monaco.	Parc National des Calanques created near Marseille.	Eurostar inaugurates year-round direct train service between London and Marseille.	Terrorist attack in Nice results in 86 people dead and 458 injured.

Books

In addition to their seminal role in French history and the cultural and artistic life of Europe, Provence and the Côte d'Azur have inspired many modern English, American and French writers, whether indulging in the high life like F. Scott Fitzgerald, slumming it with the bohemians like Anaïs Nin, or trying to regain their health like Katherine Mansfield. The two best-known Provençal writers of the twentieth century, Jean Giono and Marcel Pagnol, chronicled peasant life in inland Provence. Titles marked with the ★ symbol are particularly recommended.

FICTION

★ **Sybille Bedford** *Jigsaw: an Unsentimental Education.* Bedford's own precarious childhood on the Côte d'Azur provides rich source material for her evocative novel, which roams between Germany, France and London and depicts the bohemian life of 1930s Sanary-sur-Mer in delicious detail. Sanary also features in Bedford's autobiographical memoir *Quicksands.*

Alexandre Dumas *The Count of Monte Cristo.* A runaway success when initially serialized during the 1840s, Dumas' long, engrossing tale of the prisoner of the Île d'If, who plots escape and revenge on those who wronged him, has never lost its grip on the public imagination.

Lawrence Durrell *The Avignon Quintet.* Five interlinked novels that offer a creative and romantic vision of a fast-disappearing way of life, both rural and urban, in Provence.

★ **F. Scott Fitzgerald** *Tender is the Night.* Glitter is interwoven with darkness in this dense but beautifully written tale of mental illness among the millionaire smart set, played out against the glamorous backdrop of the Riviera in the interwar years.

★ **Jean Giono** *The Horseman on the Roof.* This gripping and extraordinary novel of one man's odyssey through a Provence ravaged by a nineteenth-century cholera epidemic has a very contemporary, postapocalyptic feel. Giono's other works, such as *To the Slaughterhouse, Two*

Riders of the Storm, Blue Boy and *The Man Who Planted Trees* are also recommended.

Sébastien Japrisot *One Deadly Summer.* Suspenseful modern novel of a girl's revenge; noir to the nth degree.

★ **Marcel Pagnol** *The Water of the Hills: Jean de Florette* and *Manon of the Springs.* These rich evocations of hardship, intrigue and family vengeance in rural Provence in the early twentieth century have a humour, warmth and depth that's lacking in Claude Berri's admittedly ravishing 1986 films.

Patrick Süskind *Perfume.* Hugely successful story of an orphan born with no smell, who gravitates to Grasse and becomes both a master *parfumier* and a mass murderer.

James Thomas (ed) *Grains of Gold: An Anthology of Occitan Literature.* Award winning collection of Occitan writing from the Middle Ages to the present day with English translations.

Bert Wagendorp *Ventoux.* The intriguing and often entertaining tale of an ill-fated cycling trip to Mont Ventoux by a group of young Dutch cyclists.

Émile Zola *The Masterpiece.* Born in Aix-en-Provence, Zola draws on his own life and that of his boyhood friend Paul Cézanne to tell the contrasting stories of a successful novelist and an artist obsessed with the creation of one great canvas. The novel offended Cézanne and ended their friendship.

HISTORY, SOCIETY AND POLITICS

Mary Blume *Côte d'Azur: Inventing the French Riviera.* This 1990s attempt to analyse the myth only reconfirmed it, mainly because all the people interviewed had a stake in maintaining the image of the Côte as a cultured millionaires' dreamland. Great black-and-white photos, though.

Robin Briggs *Early Modern France, 1560–1715.* Readable account of the period when the French state started to assert control over the whole country. Strong perspectives on the provinces, including coverage of the Marseille rebellion of 1658.

James Bromwich *The Roman Remains of Southern France.* A comprehensive guide: detailed, well-illustrated and

approachable. In addition to accounts of well-known sites, it will lead you off the map to all sorts of discoveries.

Alfred Cobban *A History of Modern France.* Very complete, three-volume political, social and economic history, from Louis XIV to de Gaulle.

Margaret Crosland *Sade's Wife.* An expert on Provence's most notorious resident examines how Renée-Pélagie de Montreuil coped with being married to the Marquis de Sade.

Lawrence Durrell *Caesar's Vast Ghost.* Durrell long promised to write a huge and all-encompassing book about Provence; this much slimmer volume, published just before his death, is probably an easier read, with entertaining essays on, for example, bulls and Arles.

★ **John Noone** *The Man Behind the Iron Mask*. Fascinating enquiry into the mythical or otherwise prisoner of Ste-Marguerite Fort on the Îles de Lérins, immortalized by Alexander Dumas.

Jim Ring *Riviera: The Rise and Fall of the Côte d'Azur*. Highly readable social history of the French Riviera and of the many nationalities that have shaped the region's history, culture and architecture.

Graham Robb *The Discovery of France*. Captivating study of the evolution and "civilization" of France since the Revolution, which makes a superb antidote to conventional narratives of kings and state affairs.

Simon Schama *Citizens*. A fascinating, accessible treatment of the history of the Revolution, with a fast-moving narrative and a reappraisal of the customary view of a stagnant, unchanging nobility in the years preceding the uprising.

Richard Vinen *The Unfree French*. The best account of the French experience under Nazi occupation, from politicians and collaborators to heroes of the Resistance.

Laurence Wylie *Village in the Vaucluse*. Sociological study of Roussillon, full of interesting insights into Provençal village life in the postwar years.

★ **Theodore Zeldin** *France 1845–1945*. Five thematic volumes on French history.

TRAVEL

Carol Drinkwater *The Olive Farm*. Soft-focus memoir of the joys of expatriate life in rural Provence, written by a well-known British actress.

★ **M.F.K. Fisher** *Two Towns in Provence*. Evocative memoirs of life in Aix-en-Provence and Marseille during the 1950s and 1960s.

William Fotheringham *Put Me Back on My Bike: In Search of Tom Simpson*. An in-depth study of Simpson's life as a cyclist, leading up to his tragic death on Mont Ventoux.

Peter Mayle *A Year in Provence*. Though it's often blamed for contributing to the anglicization of rural Provence, there's really nothing to dislike about this bestselling memoir. A month-by-month account of the charms and frustrations of moving into an old Provençal farmhouse, it entertainingly covers everything from tips for wooing fickle French contractors to handicapping goat races. The posthumous *My 25 Years in Provence* followed Mayle's death in early 2018, a collection of anecdotes and musings on his quarter century as an expat.

ART AND ARTISTS

★ **Martin Bailey (ed)** *Van Gogh: Letters from Provence*. Attractively produced in full colour – very dippable, and very good value.

Martin Gayford *The Yellow House*. A tense and absorbing account of the nine extraordinary weeks in 1888 when Vincent van Gogh and Paul Gauguin shared a tiny house in Arles.

Françoise Gilot *Matisse & Picasso: A Friendship in Art*. A fascinating subject – two more different men in life and art would be hard to find.

D. and M. Johnson *The Age of Illusion*. Links French art and politics in the interwar years, featuring Provençal works by Le Corbusier, Chagall and Picasso.

Jacques Henri Lartigue *Diary of a Century*. Book of pictures by a great photographer from the day he was given a camera in 1901 through to the 1970s. Contains wonderful scenes of aristocratic leisure and Côte d'Azur beaches.

Sarah Whitfield *Fauvism*. Good introduction to a movement that encompassed Côte d'Azur and Riviera artists Matisse, Dufy and Van Dongen.

FOOD AND DRINK

Luke Barr *Provence, 1970*. Fascinating oddity of a book recounting a rendezvous of America's culinary great and good in deepest Provence in 1970 to chew over the future of Stateside fine dining; among them was *Two Towns in Provence* author M.F.K. Fisher.

Alain Ducasse *Flavours of France*. Celebrity cookbook that follows Ducasse from the kitchens of the *Louis XV* restaurant (latterly re-christened *Ômer*) in Monte Carlo to *La Bastide de Moustiers*.

Hubrecht Duijker *Touring in Wine Country: Provence*. Still the best guide to the top vineyards and wine cellars of Provence.

Kenneth James *Escoffier: the King of Chefs*. Biography of the famous chef who started his career on the Côte d'Azur.

Richard Olney *Lulu's Provençal Table*. Classic Provençal recipes and interesting commentary from Lulu Peyraud, long the proprietor of the Domaine Tempier vineyard in Bandol. Great black-and-white photos.

Roger Vergé *Cuisine of the Sun*. The classic cookbook of modern Provençal cuisine, from the legendary chef of the *Moulin de Mougins*, who sadly passed away in 2015.

Patricia Wells *The Provence Cookbook*. More than two hundred recipes rooted in the *terroir*, plus vignettes on suppliers and markets, and wine-pairing suggestions.

BOTANY

W. Lippert *Fleurs de Haute Montagne*. Palm-sized guide to flowers of the Haute Montagne, with colour photos and botanical names; available from French bookshops in the trekking areas.

CYCLING

Jeremy Whittle *Ventoux: Sacrifice and Suffering on the Giant of Provence*. An in-depth deconstruction of the iconic mountain and its place in competitive cycling from *The Times* correspondent Jeremy Whittle.

French

French can be a deceptively familiar language because of the number of words and structures it shares with English. Despite this, it's far from easy, though the bare essentials are not difficult to master and can make all the difference. Even just saying "Bonjour, Madame/Monsieur" and then gesticulating will usually get you a smile and helpful service. People working in tourist offices, campsites, hotels and so on almost always speak English and tend to use it if you're struggling to speak French – for which be grateful, not insulted.

On the Côte d'Azur you can get by without knowing a word of French, with menus printed in at least four languages, and half the people you meet fellow foreigners. In Nice, Sisteron and the Roya Valley a knowledge of Italian would provide a common language with many of the natives. But if you can hold your own in **French** – however imperfectly – speak away and your audience will warm to you.

We've covered a lot of ground in this section, but for more detail, the *Rough Guide French Phrasebook* is a useful mini dictionary-style **phrasebook** with both English–French and French–English sections, along with a menu reader and cultural tips. Meanwhile ⌯www.bbc.co.uk/languages/french features assorted **online audio courses** tailored to suit all levels.

Provençal and accents

The one language you don't have to learn – unless you want to understand the meaning of the names of streets, restaurants or cafés – is **Provençal**. Itself a dialect of the *langue d'oc* (Occitan), it evolved into different dialects in Provence, so that the languages spoken in Nice, in the Alps, on the coast and in the Rhône Valley, though mutually comprehensible, were not precisely the same. In the mid-nineteenth century the *Félibrige* movement established a standard literary form in an attempt to revive the language. But by the time Frédéric Mistral won the Nobel Prize in 1904 for his poem *Mirèio*, Provençal had already been superseded by French in ordinary life.

Two hundred years ago everybody – counts, shipyard workers, peasants – spoke Provençal. Today you might (if you're lucky) hear it spoken by the older generation in some of the remoter villages. It just survives as a literary language: it can be studied at school and university and some newspapers publish columns in Provençal. But unlike Breton or Occitan proper, it has never been the fuel of a separatist movement.

The French that people speak in Provence has, however, a very marked **accent**. It's much less nasal than northern French, words are not run together to quite the same extent, and there's a distinctive sound for the endings *in* and *-en*, and for *vin*, and so on, that is more like *ung*.

Pronunciation

Consonants are much as in English, except that: "*ch*" is always sh, "*c*" is s, "*h*" is silent, "*th*" is the same as t, "*ll*" is like the y in "yes", "*w*" is v, and "*r*" is growled (or rolled). One easy rule to remember is that consonants at the ends of words are usually silent. *Pas plus tard* (not later) is thus pronounced "pa-plu-tarr". But when the following word begins with a vowel, you run the two together: *pas après* (not after) becomes "pazaprey". **Vowels** are the hardest sounds to get right.

a as in hat	**i** as in machine
e as in get	**o** as in hot
é between get and gate	**o, au** as in over
è between get and gut	**ou** as in food
eu like the u in hurt	**u** as in a pursed-lip version of use

More awkward are the **combinations** *in/im, en/em, an/am, on/om, un/um* at the ends of words, or followed by consonants other than norm.

in/im like the an in anxious	**on/om** like the don in Doncaster said by someone with
an/am, en/em like the don in Doncaster when said	a heavy cold
with a nasal accent	**un/um** like the u in understand

Basic words and phrases

French nouns are divided into **masculine** and **feminine**. This causes difficulties with adjectives, whose endings have to change to suit the gender of the nouns they qualify. If you know some grammar, you will know what to do. If not, stick to the masculine form, which is the simplest – that's what's done in this glossary.

ESSENTIALS

today aujourd'hui	**that one** cela
yesterday hier	**open** ouvert
tomorrow demain	**closed** fermé
in the morning le matin	**big** grand
in the afternoon l'après-midi	**small** petit
in the evening le soir	**more** plus
now maintenant	**less** moins
later plus tard	**a little** un peu
at one o'clock à une heure	**a lot** beaucoup
at three o'clock à trois heures	**cheap** bon marché
at ten-thirty à dix heures et demie	**expensive** cher
at midday à midi	**good** bon
man un homme	**bad** mauvais
woman une femme	**hot** chaud
here ici	**cold** froid
there là	**with** avec
this one ceci	**without** sans

TALKING TO PEOPLE

When addressing people you should always use *Monsieur* for a man, *Madame* for a woman, or *Mademoiselle* for a young woman; plain *bonjour* by itself is not enough. This isn't as formal as it seems, and it has its uses when you've forgotten someone's name or want to attract someone's attention.

Excuse me Pardon	**…Scottish** écossais[e]
Do you speak English? Vous parlez anglais?	**…Welsh** gallois[e]
How do you say it in French? Comment ça se dit en	**…American** américain[e]
français?	**…Australian** australien[ne]
What's your name? Comment vous appelez-vous?	**…Canadian** canadien[ne]
My name is… Je m'appelle…	**…a New Zealander** néo-zélandais[e]
I'm … Je suis …	**yes** oui
…English anglais[e]	**no** non
…Irish irlandais[e]	**I understand** Je comprends

I don't understand Je ne comprends pas
Can you speak slower? S'il vous plaît, parlez moins vite
OK/agreed d'accord
please s'il vous plaît
thank you merci
hello bonjour
goodbye au revoir
good morning/afternoon bonjour
good evening bonsoir
good night bonne nuit

How are you? Comment allez-vous?/Ça va?
Fine, thanks Très bien, merci
I don't know Je ne sais pas
Let's go Allons-y
See you tomorrow À demain
See you soon À bientôt
Sorry Pardon, Madame/Excusez-moi
Leave me alone! Fichez-moi la paix! **(aggressive)**
Please help me Aidez-moi, s'il vous plaît

FINDING THE WAY

bus autobus/bus/car
bus station gare routière
bus stop arrêt
car voiture
train/taxi/ferry train/taxi/ferry
boat bateau
plane avion
train station gare (SNCF)
platform quai
What time does it leave? Il part à quelle heure?
What time does it arrive? Il arrive à quelle heure?
a ticket to... un billet pour...
single ticket aller simple
return ticket aller retour
validate your ticket compostez votre billet
valid for valable pour
ticket office vente de billets
how many kilometres? combien de kilomètres?
how many hours? combien d'heures?
hitchhiking autostop

on foot à pied
Where are you going? Vous allez où?
I'm going to... Je vais à...
I want to get off at... Je voudrais descendre à...
the road to... la route pour...
near près/pas loin
far loin
left à gauche
right à droite
straight on tout droit
on the other side of à l'autre côté de
on the corner of à l'angle de
next to à côté de
behind derrière
in front of devant
before avant
after après
under sous
to cross traverser
bridge pont

QUESTIONS AND REQUESTS

The simplest way of asking a question is to start with *s'il vous plaît* (please), then name the thing you want in an interrogative tone of voice. For example:

Where is there a bakery? S'il vous plaît, la boulangerie?
Which way is it to the Pont du Gard? S'il vous plaît, la route pour le Pont du Gard?
We'd like a room for two S'il vous plaît, une chambre pour deux
Can I have a kilo of oranges? S'il vous plaît, un kilo d'oranges?

QUESTION WORDS
where? où?
how? comment?
how many/how much? combien?
when? quand?
why? pourquoi?
at what time? à quelle heure?
what is/which is? quel est?

ACCOMMODATION

a room for one/two people une chambre pour une personne/deux personnes
a double bed un grand lit
a room with a shower une chambre avec douche
a room with a bath une chambre avec salle de bain
for one/two/three nights pour une nuit/deux/trois nuits

Can I see it? Je peux la voir?
a room on the courtyard une chambre sur la cour
a room over the street une chambre sur la rue
first floor premier étage
second floor deuxième étage
with a view avec vue
key clef

to iron repasser
do laundry faire la lessive
sheets draps
blankets couvertures
quiet calme
noisy bruyant
hot water eau chaude
cold water eau froide
Is breakfast included? Est-ce que le petit déjeuner est compris?

I would like breakfast Je voudrais prendre le petit déjeuner
I don't want breakfast Je ne veux pas de petit déjeuner
Can we camp here? On peut camper ici?
campsite un camping/terrain de camping
tent une tente
tent space un emplacement
youth hostel auberge de jeunesse

DRIVING

service station garage
service service
to park the car garer la voiture
car park un parking
no parking défense de stationner/stationnement interdit
petrol station station essence/station service
fuel essence
(to) fill it up faire le plein
oil huile
air line ligne à air

put air in the tyres gonfler les pneus
battery batterie
the battery is dead la batterie est morte
spark plugs bougies
to break down tomber en panne
petrol can bidon
insurance assurance
green card carte verte
traffic lights feux
red light feu rouge
green light feu vert

HEALTH MATTERS

doctor médecin
I don't feel well Je ne me sens pas bien
medicines médicaments
prescription ordonnance
I feel sick Je suis malade
I have a headache J'ai mal à la tête

stomach ache mal à l'estomac
period règles
pain douleur
it hurts ça fait mal
chemist pharmacie
hospital hôpital

OTHER NEEDS

bakery boulangerie
food shop alimentation
supermarket supermarché
to eat manger
to drink boire
camping gas camping gaz
tobacconist tabac
stamps timbres

bank banque
money argent
toilets toilettes
police police
telephone téléphone
cinema cinéma
theatre théâtre
to reserve/book réserver

NUMBERS

1 un
2 deux
3 trois
4 quatre
5 cinq
6 six
7 sept
8 huit
9 neuf
10 dix
11 onze

12 douze
13 treize
14 quatorze
15 quinze
16 seize
17 dix-sept
18 dix-huit
19 dix-neuf
20 vingt
21 vingt-et-un
22 vingt-deux

30 trente	**100** cent
40 quarante	**101** cent-et-un
50 cinquante	**200** deux cents
60 soixante	**300** trois cents
70 soixante-dix	**500** cinq cents
75 soixante-quinze	**1000** mille
80 quatre-vingts	**2000** deux mille
90 quatre-vingt-dix	**5000** cinq mille
95 quatre-vingt-quinze	**1,000,000** un million

DAYS AND DATES

January janvier	**Monday** lundi
February février	**Tuesday** mardi
March mars	**Wednesday** mercredi
April avril	**Thursday** jeudi
May mai	**Friday** vendredi
June juin	**Saturday** samedi
July juillet	**August 1** le premier août
August août	**March 2** le deux mars
September septembre	**July 14** le quatorze juillet
October octobre	**November 23** le vingt-trois novembre
November novembre	**1999** dix-neuf-cent-quatre-vingt-dix-neuf
December décembre	**2019** deux-mille-dix-neuf
Sunday dimanche	

Food and drink terms

When in a restaurant or café always call the waiter or waitress *Monsieur* or *Madame* (*Mademoiselle* if a young woman). Never use *garçon*.

BASIC TERMS

pain bread	**cuillère** spoon
beurre butter	**cure-dent** toothpick
céréales cereal	**table** table
lait milk	**l'addition** bill
huile oil	**offert/gratuit** free
confiture jam	**(re)chauffé** (re)heated
poivre pepper	**cuit** cooked
sel salt	**cru** raw
sucre sugar	**emballé** wrapped
vinaigre vinegar	**Sur place ou à emporter?** Eat in or take away?
moutarde mustard	**à emporter** takeaway
bouteille bottle	**fumé** smoked
verre glass	**salé** salted/spicy
fourchette fork	**sucré** sweet
couteau knife	

SNACKS (CASSE-CROÛTE)

un sandwich/une baguette a sandwich	**au plat(s)** fried eggs
...**au jambon/fromage** ...with ham/cheese	**à la coque** boiled eggs
...**au jambon beurre** ...with ham and butter	**durs** hard-boiled eggs
...**fromage beurre** ...with cheese and butter	**brouillés** scrambled eggs
...**au pâté (de campagne)** ...with pâté (country-style)	**pochés** poached eggs
oeufs... eggs...	**omelette...** omelette

...**nature/aux fines herbes** plain/with herbs
...**au fromage** with cheese
croque-monsieur grilled cheese and ham sandwich
croque-madame grilled cheese, ham or bacon and
  fried egg sandwich

pan bagnat bread roll with egg, olives, salad, tuna,
  anchovies and olive oil
tartine buttered bread or open sandwich

SOUPS (SOUPES) & STARTERS (HORS D'ŒUVRES)

bisque shellfish soup
baudroie fish soup with vegetables, garlic and herbs
bouillabaisse soup with five fish other tasty seafood
  morsels
bouillon broth or stock
bourride thick fish soup with garlic, onions and
  tomatoes
consommé clear soup
pistou parmesan, basil and garlic paste or cream added
  to soup

potage thick vegetable soup
rouille red pepper, garlic and saffron mayonnaise
  served with fish soup
velouté thick soup, usually fish or poultry
assiette anglaise plate of cold meats
crudités raw vegetables with dressings
hors d'œuvres variés combination of *crudités* plus
  smoked or marinated fish

PASTA (PÂTES), PANCAKES (CRÊPES) & SAVOURY FLANS (TARTES)

crêpe au sucre/aux œufs pancake with sugar/eggs
nouilles noodles
panisse thick chickpea flour pancake
pissaladière tart of fried onions with anchovies and
  black olives

pâtes fraîches fresh pasta
raviolis pasta parcels of meat or chard, a Provençal, not
  Italian, invention
socca thin chickpea flour pancake

FISH (POISSON), SEAFOOD (FRUITS DE MER) & SHELLFISH (CRUSTACES/COQUILLAGES)

aiglefin small haddock or fresh cod
anchois anchovies
amande de mer small sweet-tasting shellfish
anguilles eels
araignée de mer spider fish
baudroie monkfish or anglerfish
barbue brill
bigourneau periwinkle
brème bream
bulot whelk
cabillaud cod
calmar squid
carrelet plaice
chapon de mer Mediterranean fish (related to scorpion
  fish)
claire type of oyster
colin hake
congre conger eel
coques cockles
coquilles St-Jacques scallops
crabe crab
crevettes grises shrimp
crevettes roses prawns
daurade sea bream
écrevisse freshwater crayfish
éperlan smelt or whitebait
escargots snails
favou(ille) tiny crab

flétan halibut
friture assorted fried fish
gambas king prawns
girelle type of crab
grenouilles (cuisses de) frogs' (legs)
grondin red gurnard
hareng herring
homard lobster
huîtres oysters
langouste spiny lobster
langoustines saltwater crayfish (scampi)
limande lemon sole
lotte de mer monkfish
loup de mer sea bass
maquereau mackerel
merlan whiting
morue salt cod
moules (marinière) mussels (with shallots in white
  wine sauce)
oursin sea urchin
pageot sea bream
palourdes clams
poissons de roche fish from shoreline rocks
poulpe octopus
poutine small river fish
praires small clams
paie skate
rascasse scorpion fish

rouget red mullet
rouquier Mediterranean eel
St-Pierre John Dory
saumon salmon
sole sole
telline tiny clam
thon tuna
truite trout
turbot turbot
violet sea squirt

FISH TERMS

aïoli garlic mayonnaise – also applies to the name of the dish itself when served with salt cod and vegetables
anchoïade anchovy paste or sauce
arête fish bone
assiette de pêcheur assorted fish
Béarnaise sauce of egg yolks, white wine, shallots and vinegar

beignets fritters
bonne femme with mushroom, parsley, potato and shallots
brandade crushed cod with olive oil
colbert fried in egg with breadcrumbs
croûtons toasted bread, often rubbed with garlic, to dip or drop in fish soups
darne fillet or steak
la douzaine a dozen
en papillote cooked in foil
estocaficada stockfish stew with tomatoes, olives, peppers, garlic and onions
frit fried
friture deep-fried small fish
fumé smoked
fumet fish stock
gelée aspic
gigot de mer baked fish pieces, usually monkfish
goujon several types of small fish, also deep-fried pieces of larger fish coated in breadcrumbs

MEAT (VIANDE) & POULTRY (VOLAILLE)

agneau (de pré-salé) lamb (grazed on salt marshes)
andouille, andouillette tripe sausage
bœuf beef
bifteck steak
boudin blanc sausage of white meats
boudin noir black pudding
caille quail
canard duck
caneton duckling
cervelle brains
châteaubriand porterhouse steak
cheval horse meat
contrefilet sirloin roast
coquelet cockerel
dinde, dindon, dindonneau turkey of different ages and genders
entrecôte ribsteak
faux filet sirloin steak
fricadelles meatballs
foie liver
foie gras fattened (duck/goose) liver
gésier gizzard
gibier game
graisse fat
jambon ham
langue tongue
lapin, lapereau rabbit, young rabbit
lard, lardons bacon, diced bacon
lièvre hare
magret de canard duck breast
merguez spicy, red sausage
mouton mutton

museau de veau calf's muzzle
oie goose
os bone
pintade guinea fowl
porc, pieds de porc pork, pig's trotters
poulet chicken
poussin baby chicken
ris sweetbreads
rognons kidneys
rognons blancs testicles
sanglier wild boar
saucisson dried sausage
steack steak
taureau/toro bull meat
tête de veau calf's head (in jelly)
tournedos thick slices of fillet
travers de porc spare ribs
tripes tripe
veau veal
venaison venison

MEAT & POULTRY DISHES

aïado roast shoulder of lamb, stuffed with garlic and other ingredients
bœuf à la gardane beef or bull meat stew with carrots, celery, onions, garlic and black olives, served with rice
canard à l'orange roast duck with an orange-and-wine sauce
canard périgourdin roast duck with prunes, pâté de foie gras and truffles
cassoulet a casserole of beans and meat

choucroute pickled cabbage with peppercorns, sausages, bacon and salami

coq au vin chicken cooked until it falls off the bone with wine, onions and mushrooms

gigot (d'agneau) leg (of lamb)

grillade grilled meat

hâchis chopped meat or mince hamburger

pieds et paquets mutton or pork tripe and trotters

steak au poivre steak in a black (green/(**vert/rouge**) red) peppercorn sauce

steak tartare raw chopped beef, topped with a raw egg yolk

MEAT & POULTRY TERMS

aile wing

blanc breast or white meat

blanquette, civet, daube, types of stew estouffade, hochepôt, navarin, ragoût

brochette kebab

carré best end of neck, chop or cutlet

confit meat preserve/slow-cooked

côte chop, cutlet or rib

cou neck

cuisse thigh or leg

èpaule shoulder

médaillon round piece

pavé thick slice

en croûte in pastry

farci stuffed

au feu de bois cooked over wood fire

au four baked

broche spit-roasted

garni with vegetables

grillé grilled

mariné marinated

marmite casserole

mijoté stewed

rôti roast

sauté lightly cooked in butter

FOR STEAKS

bleu almost raw

saignant rare

à point medium

bien cuit well done

très bien cuit very well cooked

GARNISHES & SAUCES

américaine white wine, Cognac and tomato

arlésienne with tomatoes, onions, aubergines, potatoes and rice

au porto in port

auvergnat with cabbage, sausage and bacon

beurre blanc sauce of white wine and shallots, with butter

bonne femme with mushroom, bacon, potato and onions

bordelaise in a red wine, shallots and bone-marrow sauce

boulangère baked with potatoes and onions

bourgeoise with carrots, onions, bacon, celery and braised lettuce

chasseur white wine, mushrooms and shallots

chatêlaine with artichoke hearts and chestnut purée

diable strong mustard seasoning

forestière with bacon and mushroom

fricassée rich, creamy sauce

galantine cold dish of meat in aspic

mornay cheese sauce

pays d'Auge cream and cider

piquante gherkins or capers, vinegar and shallots

provençale tomatoes, garlic, olive oil and herbs

véronique grapes, wine and cream

VEGETABLES (LÉGUMES), HERBS (HERBES) & SPICES (ÉPICES)

ail garlic

anis aniseed

artichaut artichoke

asperges asparagus

avocat avocado

basilic basil

betterave beetroot

blette/bette swiss chard

cannelle cinnamon

câpre caper

cardon cardoon, a beet related to artichoke

carotte carrot

céleri celery

champignons: cèpes, chanterelles, girolles, morilles mushrooms of various kinds

chou (rouge) (red) cabbage

chou-fleur cauliflower

ciboulettes chives

concombre cucumber

cornichon gherkin

échalotes shallots

endive chicory

épinards spinach

épis de maïs corn on the cob

estragon tarragon

fenouil fennel

férigoule thyme (in Provençal)

fèves broad beans

flageolets white beans

fleur de courgette courgette flower

frisé(e) curly lettuce
genièvre juniper
gingembre ginger
haricots verts string (French) beans
...**rouges** ...kidney beans
...**beurres** ...butter beans
...**blancs** ...white beans
laitue lettuce
laurier bay leaf
lentilles lentils
maïs corn
marjoline marjoram
menthe mint
navet turnip
oignon onion
panais parsnip
pélandron type of string bean
persil parsley
petits pois peas
pignons pine nuts
piment pimento
poireau leek
pois chiches chickpeas
pois mange-tout snow peas
poivron (vert, rouge) sweet pepper (green, red)
pommes de terre potatoes
radis radishes
raifort horseradish
riz rice
romarin rosemary
safran saffron
sarrasin buckwheat
sauge sage
serpolet wild thyme
thym thyme
tomate tomato
truffes truffles

DISHES & TERMS

Il y a des plats sans viande? Are there any non-meat dishes?
Je suis végétarien(ne) I'm a vegetarian

à l'anglaise boiled
à la grecque cooked in oil and lemon
à la parisienne sautéed in butter (potatoes); with white wine sauce and shallots
à la vapeur steamed
biologique organic
farci stuffed
gratiné browned with cheese or butter
râpé(e)s grated or shredded
sauté lightly fried in butter
beignet fritter
duxelles fried mushrooms and shallots with cream
fines herbes mixture of tarragon, parsley and chives
gousse d'ail clove of garlic
gratin dauphinois potatoes baked in cream and garlic
herbes de Provence mixture of bay leaf, thyme, rosemary and savory
jardinière with mixed diced vegetables
mesclun salad combining several different leaves
parmentier with potatoes
petits farcis stuffed tomatoes, aubergines, courgettes, peppers
pistou ground basil, olive oil, garlic and parmesan
pommes château, fondantes quartered potatoes sautéed in butter
pommes lyonnaise fried onions and potatoes
primeurs spring vegetables
raclette melted cheese served with potatoes, gherkins and onions
ratatouille mixture of aubergine, courgette, tomatoes and garlic
rémoulade mustard mayonnaise, sometimes with anchovies and gherkins, also salad of grated celeriac with mayonnaise
salade niçoise salad of tomatoes, radishes, cucumber, hard-boiled eggs, anchovies, onion, artichokes, green peppers, beans, basil and garlic (though rarely includes all those ingredients, even in Nice)
salade verte lettuce with vinaigrette
tapenade olive and caper paste
tomates à la provençale tomatoes baked with breadcrumbs, garlic and parsley

FRUITS (FRUITS), NUTS (NOIX) & HONEY (MIEL)

abricot apricot
amandes almonds
ananas pineapple
banane banana
brugnon, nectarine nectarine
cacahouète peanut
cassis blackcurrants
cerises cherries
châtaignes chestnuts
citron lemon

citron vert lime
dattes dates
figues figs
fraises (de bois) strawberries (wild)
framboises raspberries
fruit de la passion passion fruit
grenade pomegranate
groseilles redcurrants
mangue mango
marrons chestnuts

melon melon
miel de lavande lavender honey
mirabelles small yellow plums
myrtilles blueberries
noisette hazelnut
noix nuts/walnut
noix de cajou cashew nut
orange orange
pamplemousse grapefruit
pastèque watermelon
pêche (blanche) (white) peach
pistache pistachio
poire pear
pomme apple
prune plum

pruneau prune
raisins grapes
reine-Claude greengage

TERMS

agrumes citrus fruits
beignet fritter
compôte stewed fruit
coulis sauce of puréed fruit
crème de marrons chestnut purée
flambé set aflame in alcohol
fougasse bread flavoured with orange flower water or
almonds; can also be savoury
frappé iced

DESSERTS (DESSERTS OR ENTREMETS), PASTRIES (PATISSERIES) & CONFECTIONERY (CONFISERIE)

bombe a moulded ice-cream dessert
brioche sweet, high-yeast breakfast roll
calissons almond sweets
charlotte custard and fruit in lining of almond fingers
chichis doughnuts shaped in sticks
clafoutis heavy custard and fruit tart
crème Chantilly vanilla-flavoured and sweetened
whipped cream
crème fraîche sour cream
crème pâtissière thick eggy pastry-filling
crêpes suzettes thin pancakes with orange juice and
liqueur
fromage blanc cream cheese
gaufre waffle
glace ice cream
île flottante/œufs à la neige soft meringues floating
on custard
macarons macaroons
madeleine small sponge cake
marrons chestnut purée and cream on a Mont Blanc
rum-soaked sponge cake
mousse au chocolat chocolate mousse
nougat nougat
palmiers caramelized puff pastries
parfait frozen mousse, sometimes ice cream
petit Suisse a smooth mixture of cream and curds
petits fours bite-sized cakes/pastries

poires Belle Hélène pears and ice cream in chocolate
sauce
tarte Tropézienne sponge cake filled with custard
cream topped with nuts
tiramisu layered pudding of mascarpone cheese,
alcohol and coffee
truffes truffles
yaourt, yogourt yoghurt

DISHES & TERMS

barquette small, boat-shaped flan
bavarois refers to the mould, could be a mousse or
custard
biscuit a kind of cake
chausson pastry turnover
chocolat amer unsweetened chocolate
coupe a serving of ice cream
crêpes pancakes
en feuilletage in puff pastry
fondant melting
galettes buckwheat pancakes
gênoise rich sponge cake
pâte pastry or dough
sablé shortbread biscuit
savarin a filled, ring-shaped cake
tarte tart
tartelette small tart

CHEESE (FROMAGE)

The cheeses produced in Provence are all either *chèvre* (made from goat's milk) or *brebis* (made from sheep's milk). The most renowned are the *chèvres*, which include Banon, Picodon, Lou Pevre, Pelardon and Poivre d'Ain.

Le plateau de fromages is the cheeseboard, and bread (but not butter) is served with it. Some useful phrases: *une petite tranche de celui-ci* (a small piece of this one); *je peux le goûter?* (may I taste it?).

Glossary of French terms

abbaye abbey

arrondissement district of a city

assemblée nationale the French parliament

AJ (Auberge de Jeunesse) youth hostel

bastide medieval military settlement, constructed on a grid plan

Beaux-Arts fine arts museum (and school)

borie dry-stone wall, or building made with same

calanque steep-sided inlet on coast, similar to Norwegian fjord, but not glacially formed

car/autocar bus

chambres d'hôtes Guestrooms in a private house – roughly equivalent to a B&B

chasse, chasse gardée hunting grounds

château mansion, country house or castle

château fort castle

chemin path

col mountain pass

consigne luggage store

côte coast

cours combination of main square and main street

couvent convent, monastery

défense de… It is forbidden to…

dégustation tasting (wine or food)

département county – more or less

donjon castle keep

église church

en panne out of order

entrée entrance

faubourg suburb, often abbreviated to *fbg* in street names

ferme farm

fermeture closing period

fouilles archeological excavations

gare station; **routière** – bus station; **SNCF** – train station

gîte d'étape basic hostel accommodation, primarily for walkers

GR (grande randonnée) long-distance footpath

halles covered market

hôtel a hotel, but also an aristocratic townhouse or mansion

hôtel de ville town hall

jours fériés public holidays

mairie town hall

marché market

mas Provençal farmhouse

place square

porte gateway

presqu'île peninsula

puy peak or summit

quartier district of a town

relais routiers truckstop café-restaurant

RC (Rez-de-chaussée) ground floor

RN (Route Nationale) main road

santon ornamental figure, used especially in Christmas cribs

SI (Syndicat d'Initiative) tourist information office; also known as OT, OTSI and *maison du tourisme*

SNCF French railways

sortie exit

tabac bar or shop selling stamps, cigarettes, etc

table d'hôte meal served in lodging at the family table

tour tower

transhumance routes followed by shepherds for taking livestock to and from suitable grazing grounds

Vauban seventeenth-century military architect – his fortresses still stand all over France

vieille ville old quarter of town

vieux port old port

village perché hilltop village

zone bleue restricted parking zone

zone piétonnée pedestrian precinct

Glossary of architectural terms

ambulatory covered passage around the outer edge of a choir of a church

apse semicircular termination at the east end of a church

Baroque High Renaissance period of art and architecture, distinguished by extreme ornateness

Carolingian dynasty (and art, sculpture, etc) founded by Charlemagne, late eighth to early tenth century

chevet east end of church, consisting of apse and ambulatory, with or without radiating chapels

Classical architectural style incorporating Greek and Roman elements – pillars, domes, colonnades, etc – at its height in France in the seventeenth century and revived in the nineteenth century as Neoclassical

clerestory upper storey of a church, incorporating the windows

Flamboyant florid form of Gothic

fresco wall painting – durable through application to wet plaster

Gallo-Roman period of Roman occupation of Gaul (first to fourth century AD)

Gothic architectural style prevalent from the twelfth century to the sixteenth century, characterized by pointed arches and ribbed vaulting

Merovingian dynasty (and art, etc) ruling France and parts of Germany from the sixth to mid-eighth century

narthex entrance hall of church

nave main body of a church

Renaissance art-architectural style developed in fifteenth-century Italy and imported to France in the early sixteenth century by François I

retable altarpiece

Romanesque early medieval architecture distinguished by squat, rounded forms and naive sculpture

stucco plaster used to embellish ceilings, etc

transept cross arms of a church

tympanum sculpted panel above a church door

voussoir sculpted rings in arch over church door

Small print and index

423 Small print

425 Index

432 Map symbols

A ROUGH GUIDE TO ROUGH GUIDES

Published in 1982, the first Rough Guide – to Greece – was a student scheme that became a publishing phenomenon. Mark Ellingham, a recent graduate in English from Bristol University, had been travelling in Greece the previous summer and couldn't find the right guidebook. With a small group of friends he wrote his own guide, combining a contemporary, journalistic style with a thoroughly practical approach to travellers' needs.

The immediate success of the book spawned a series that rapidly covered dozens of destinations. And, in addition to impecunious backpackers, Rough Guides soon acquired a much broader readership that relished the guides' wit and inquisitiveness as much as their enthusiastic, critical approach and value-for-money ethos. These days, Rough Guides include recommendations from budget to luxury and cover more than 120 destinations around the globe, from Amsterdam to Zanzibar, all regularly updated by our team of roaming writers.

Browse all our latest guides, read inspirational features and book your trip at **roughguides.com**.

Rough Guide credits

Authors: Neville Walker, Greg Ward
Updater: Brendon Griffin
Editor: Aimee White
Cartography: Katie Bennett
Managing editor: Rachel Lawrence

Picture editor: Aude Vauconsant
Cover photo research: Aude Vauconsant
Senior DTP coordinator: Dan May
Head of DTP and Pre-Press: Rebeka Davies

Publishing information

Tenth edition 2020

Distribution

UK, Ireland and Europe
Apa Publications (UK) Ltd; sales@roughguides.com
United States and Canada
Ingram Publisher Services; ips@ingramcontent.com
Australia and New Zealand
Woodslane; info@woodslane.com.au
Southeast Asia
Apa Publications (SN) Pte; sales@roughguides.com
Worldwide
Apa Publications (UK) Ltd; sales@roughguides.com
Special Sales, Content Licensing and CoPublishing
Rough Guides can be purchased in bulk quantities
at discounted prices. We can create special editions,
personalised jackets and corporate imprints tailored to
your needs. sales@roughguides.com.

roughguides.com
Printed in China by CTPS
All rights reserved
© 2020 Apa Digital (CH) AG
License edition © Apa Publications Ltd UK
All rights reserved. No part of this publication may be
reproduced, stored in or introduced into a retrieval system,
or transmitted in any form, or by any means (electronic,
mechanical, photocopying, recording or otherwise) without
the prior written permission of the copyright owner.
A catalogue record for this book is available from the
British Library
The publishers and authors have done their best to ensure
the accuracy and currency of all the information in **The
Rough Guide to Provence and Cote d'Azur**, however,
they can accept no responsibility for any loss, injury, or
inconvenience sustained by any traveller as a result of
information or advice contained in the guide.

Help us update

We've gone to a lot of effort to ensure that this edition
of **The Rough Guide to Provence and Cote d'Azur** is
accurate and up-to-date. However, things change – places
get "discovered", opening hours are notoriously fickle,
restaurants and rooms raise prices or lower standards. If
you feel we've got it wrong or left something out, we'd like
to know, and if you can remember the address, the price,
the hours, the phone number, so much the better.

Please send your comments with the subject line
"Rough Guide Provence and Cote d'Azur Update" to
mail@uk.roughguides.com. We'll credit all contributions
and send a copy of the next edition (or any other Rough
Guide if you prefer) for the very best emails.

Acknowledgements

Sylvie Anquetil, Marie-Pierre Arnaud, Estelle Barlet, Olivia Brindle, Christian Brizion, Marion Cirino,
Philippe and Jean Pierre Estevenin, Julia Gensbeitel-Ortiz, Angélique Giraud, Nadine Lopez, Fabrice
Meynadier, Manuel Pennequin, Mickaël Piccardi, Adrien Ricard, Edith Ricotta, Manon Tourtoulon.

ABOUT THE AUTHOR

Brendon Griffin has co-authored and edited numerous Rough Guides covering Europe, Africa
and Latin America. His initiation into French culture came as a – not altogether successful -
ad-hoc interpreter for a love-struck classmate on a mid-80s exchange trip. Language skills long
since honed, he's been back more times than he cares to remember.

Photo credits

(Key: T-top; C-centre; B-bottom; L-left; R-right)

Index

A

Abbaye de Montmajour 93
Abbaye de Sénanque 193
Abbaye de Silvacane 167
Abbaye du Thoronet 206
accommodation 29
activities 222
adventure activities 35
Aéroport Marseille-Provence 58
Aeroport Nice Côte d'Azur 355
Agay 298
Aiguines 223
Ail, Cap d' 371
Aix-en-Provence 154
    accommodation 162
    arrival and information 162
    Arts, the 164
    Atelier Cézanne 161
    bars 163
    bike rental 162
    buses 162
    bus station 162
    cafés 163
    Camp des Milles 161
    campsites 163
    car rental 162
    Cathédrale St-Sauveur 159
    Caumont Centre d'Art 160
    cinemas 164
    Citypass 159
    Cours Mirabeau 157
    directory 165
    drinking 164
    eating 163
    entertainment 164
    festivals 165
    Fondation Vasarely 160
    Granet XXe – Collection Planque
        160
    health 165
    history 157
    hotels 162
    Jas de Bouffan 160
    laundry 165
    Les Deux Garçons 157
    markets 164
    Musée des Tapisseries 159
    Musée du Vieil Aix 159
    Musée Granet 159
    nightlife 164
    Oppidum d'Entremont 161
    police 165
    post office 165
    Quartier Mazarin 159
    restaurants 163
    shopping 165
    taxis 162
    Terrain des Peintres 161
    theatres 164
    tourist office 162
    train station 162
    transport 162
    Vieil Aix 157
Aix-en-Provence, the Durance
    and the Luberon 154
Allos 233
Alpha wolf reserve 241
Alps 361
Annot 235
Anse de Figuerolles 72
Ansouis 170
Anthéor 298
Antibes 320
Antiques, Les 97
Apt 188
Aqualand 293
Aquasplash 323
Arcs-sur-Argens, Les 289
Argens Valley 288
Arles 84
    accommodation 91
    Alyscamps, Les 89
    Arènes, Les 86
    arrival and information 91
    bars 93
    bike rental 91
    buses 91
    cafés and ice cream 93
    campsites 92
    car parks 91
    Cirque Romaine 89
    Cryptoportiques 87
    drinking 93
    eating 92
    Église St-Trophime 89
    Fondation Vincent van Gogh 90
    hotels 91
    Luma Arles 91
    Musée Départemental Arles
        Antique 88
    Musée Réattu 91
    nightlife 93
    Place de la République 89
    restaurants 92
    Théâtre Antique 87
    Thermes de Constantin 87
    tourist office 91
    train station 91
Arles and the Camargue 84
Arrière-Pays Niçois 361
art 8, 277, 400, 401. See
    also artists by name
ATMs 39
Aubagne 73
Aups 209
Auron 238
Avignon 114
    accommodation 124
    airport 124
    arrival and departure 123
    bars 126
    bike, scooter and motorbike rental
        124
    boats 124
    boat trips 124
    buses 124
    bus station 124
    cafés 126
    campsites 125
    car parks 123
    Cathédrale Notre Dame des Doms
        121
    Chapelle Ste-Claire 122
    cinemas 126
    clubs 126
    Collection Lambert 123
    directory 128
    drinking 126
    driving 123
    eating 125
    Festival d'Avignon 120
    history 117
    hotels 124
    information 124
    laundry 128
    Maison Jean Vilar 121
    markets 128
    medical emergencies 128
    Musée Angladon 122
    Musée Calvet 123
    Musée du Petit Palais 120
    Musée Lapidaire 122
    Musée Requien 122
    Musée Vouland 123
    nightlife 126
    Palais des Papes 117
    Palais du Roure 121
    Place de l'Horloge 121
    Place Pie 122
    police 128
    Pont d'Avignon 120

Pont St-Bénézet 120
popes 117
post office 128
Quartier de la Banasterie 122
restaurants 125
Rocher des Doms 121
salons de thé 126
shopping 126
swimming pool 128
taxis 124
theatre 126
tourist office 124
train stations 123
transport 124
wine bars 126
Avignon and the Vaucluse 114
Avignon-Caumont Airport 124

B

Bandol 254
Banon 184
Barbegal aqueduct 94
Barbegal watermill 94
Barbentane 101
Barben Zoo 80
Barcelonnette 229
Bardot, Brigitte 277, 405
Bargemon 217
Barjols 206
Barroux, Le 139
Bar-sur-Loup, Le 334
Basses Gorges du Verdon 210
Baux-de-Provence, Les 94
beaches 35, 180, 323
Beaucaire 104
Beaulieu-sur-Mer 370
Beaumes-de-Venise 139
bed and breakfast 29
Bedford, Sybille 256
Bédoin 141
Beuil 240
bike rental 91, 162
bikes 28
Biot 325
birdwatching 108, 110, 232
boat trips 73, 107, 124, 296, 356
Bonette, La 237
Bonnard, Pierre 277, 401
Bonnieux 196
books 407
Bormes-les-Mimosas 271
Bouilladoires, Les 193
Brecht 256
Breil-sur-Roya 244
Brexit 37
Briançonnet 227
Brignoles 205
Brigue, La 244

Brusc, Le 257
bungee jumping 222, 235
buses 26

C

Cabris 333
Cadenet 168
Cagnes 328
Calanque de Sugiton 68
Calanques, Massif des 67
Calanques, Parc National des 68
calanques, safety in 67
Callas 217
Camargue, Arles and the 84
Camargue, The 105
camping 30
Cannes 304
    accommodation 310
    arrival and information 309
    beaches 305, 308
    bike rentals 310
    bookshop 311
    buses 309
    bus stations 309
    campsites 310
    Cannes Film Festival 308
    Cannet, Le 309
    car parks 309
    casinos 311
    Croisette, La 305
    Croix des Gardes, La 308
    directory 311
    drinking 311
    eating 310
    emergencies 311
    hotels 310
    Mediathèque Noailles 308
    Musée Bonnard 309
    Musée de la Castre 308
    nightlife 311
    Palais des Festivals 305
    pharmacy 311
    police 311
    post office 311
    restaurants 310
    Suquet, Le 307
    taxis 309
    tourist offices 309
    train station 309
    transport 309
    Vieux Port 306
Cannes and the western Riviera 302
canoeing 107
canyoning 334
Cap d'Ail 371
Cap d'Antibes 323

Capelière, La 110
Cap Ferrat 369
Cap Garonne 262
Cap Lardier 276
Cap Martin 374
Cap Sicié 257, 260
Cap Sicié peninsula 255
Carpentras 144
car rental 28
Carrières de Lumières 95
Carry-le-Rouet 75
Carzou, Jean 172
Cassis 69
Castellane 223
Castelnuovo 365
Cavaillon 150
Cavalaire-sur-Mer 275
Cézanne, Paul 160, 400
Chagall, Marc 340, 355
Chaîne de la Ste-Baume 202
chambres d'hôtes 29
Chapelle des Pénitents Blancs 362
Chapelle du Rosaire 337, 338
Chartreuse de la Verne, La 284
Chartreuse du Val de Bénédiction, La 129
Château-Arnoux 176
Château de la Barben 80
Château de la Tour d'Aigues 172
Château de Sauvan 183
Château d'If 66
Châteaudouble 216
Châteauneuf-du-Pape 131
Châteauneuf-Villevieille 365
Châteaurenard 100
cheese 184, 419
Chemins de Fer de Provence 213, 356
Chèvre de Banon 184
children, travelling with 41
Chorégies 134
Cians Valley 240
Ciotat, La 71, 72
climate 10
Clues de Haute Provence 226
Coaraze 364
Cocteau, Jean 277
Col de Turini 242
Col d'Èze 373
Colette 277
Collobrières 284
Colmars-les-Alpes 234
Colorado Provençal 186
Commune de Valdeblore 241
Comps-sur-Artuby 223
consulates 37, 66
Corniche des Crêtes 70
Corniche des Maures 271
Corniche, Grande 368

Corniche Inférieure 366, 368
Corniche, Moyenne 368
corniches 368
Corniche Sublime 223
corruption 404
Cosquer Cave 69
costs 36
Côte Bleue 75
Cotignac 206
Coursegoules 227
Crêtes, Corniche des 70
Crillon-le-Brave 141
crime 36, 404
Croix-Valmer, La 276
Cucuron 170
cycling 28

D

Daumier, Honoré 400
Dentelles, The 138
Digne-les-Bains 211
Digue à la Mer 109
disabilities, travellers with 40
Domaine de la Palissade 111
Draguignan 214
Draille de Cacharel 107
Dramont, Le 298
drinking 32
driving
    from the UK 24
    within Provence and Côte d'Azur 27
Drummond, Sir Jack 176
Duncan, Isadora 352
Durance River 167

E

electricity 36
embassies 37
emergency numbers 36
Entrecasteaux 206
Entrevaux 236
entry requirements 36
environmental issues 404
Ernst, Max 217
Escoffier, Auguste 327
Espace 324
Esterel, Corniche de l' 297
Èze 372
Èze-sur-Mer 371

F

Fabre, Jean Henri 136
Fayence 218
Ferrat, Cap 369

ferries 26, 111
festivals 33
    Aix-en-Provence, The Durance and
        The Luberon 165, 188
    Arles and The Camargue 89, 98,
        103, 111
    Avignon and The Vaucluse 114, 120,
        132, 134, 139, 145
    Cannes and the Western Riviera
        308, 314, 318, 320, 335, 336
    Marseille and around 72
    Marseille and Around 78
    Monaco 381
    Nice and the Eastern Riviera 361, 387
film 72
flamingos 108
flights
    from Australia, New Zealand and
        South Africa 24
    from the UK and Ireland 23
    from the US and Canada 23
flora 108
Fondation Maeght 340
Fontaine-de-Vaucluse 148, 245
Fontvieille 94
food and drink 30
Forcalquier 181
Fort de Buoux 187
Fort St-André 128
Foux d'Allos, La 233
Fréjus 290
French Foreign Legion 75

G

Gaméou 72
Garde-Freinet, La 286
gardians 108
Garonne, Cap 262
Gassin 282
Gauguin, Paul 90, 401
Gémenos 202
Gigondas 139
Giono, Jean 172, 173
gîtes 29
Glanum 97
Gorbio 388
Gordes 192
Gordolasque Valley 242
Gorges de Châteaudouble 217
Gorges de Daluis 235
Gorges du Cians 240
Gorges du Loup 334
Gorges du Verdon 219
Gourdon 334
Grand Canyon du Verdon 219, 222
Grande Corniche 372
Grande Crau, La 93
Grasse 330

Greene, Graham 320
Gréolières 227
Gréolières-les-Neiges 227
Grimaud 285
Grottes de Calès 79
Guillaumes 235

H

Haut-de-Cagnes 328
Haute Provence seasons 203
Haut Var 205
Haute Provence 200
Haut-Var Valley 235
Haut-Verdon Valley 233
health 37
Héliopolis 270
hiking 166, 184
history 391
horseriding 107, 111, 187
hostels 29
hot-air ballooning 187
hotels 29
hot springs 157
Huxley, Aldous 256
Hyères 263
Hyères, Îles d' 267

I

Île de Bendor 254
Île des Embiez 257
Île du Levant 270
Îles de Frioul 66
Îles de Lérins 312
Îles d'Hyères 267
insurance 37
internet 37
Isola 2000 238
itineraries 20

J

Jazz à Juan 320
Jean de Florette 74
jeep safaris 107
Juan-les-Pins 318

K

kayaking 107
Klein, Yves 351

L

Lac d'Allos 233
Lac de Castillon 225
Lac de Ste-Croix 221
Lacoste 195
Lamanon 78
language 410
laundry 37
Lavandou, Le 274
Lecques, Les 250
Léger, Fernand 326
L'Escarène 364
L'Estaque 75
Levant, Île du 270
LGBTQ travellers 38
L'Isle-sur-la-Sorgue 147
literature 400, 407
Long, Lac 245
Lourmarin 169
Lower Var Valley 235
Luberon, The 186
Lucéram 364
Lumière brothers 72
Lurs 174

M

magazines 33
mail 38
Maillane 101
Malaucène 141
Malpasset Dam disaster 292
Mane 183
Mann, Thomas 256
Manon des Sources 74
Manosque 172
Man Ray 314
maps 39
    Aix-en-Provence 158
    Aix-en-Provence, the Durance and
        the Luberon 156
    Antibes 321
    Apt 188
    Arles 88
    Arles and the Camargue 86
    Avignon 118
    Avignon and the Vaucluse 116
    Cannes 306
    Cannes and the western Riviera 304
    Carpentras 144
    Digne-les-Bains 212
    Fréjus 290
    Grand Canyon du Verdon 220
    Grasse 331
    Hyères 264
    Itineraries 21
    Marseille 48
    Marseille and around 46
    Marseille: around the Vieux Port 50
    Menton 384
    Monaco 376
    Nice 348
    Nice and the eastern Riviera 346
    Orange 133
    Parc National du Mercantour 230
    Provence and the Côte d'Azur 6
    Salon-de-Provence 78
    Sisteron 177
    St-Raphaël 295
    St-Tropez 278
    Tarascon 102
    The Camargue 106
    The Corniches 367
    The Haut Var and Haute Provence
        202
    Toulon 258
    Toulon and the southern Var 252
    Vence 336
    Vieux Nice 350
    Villeneuve-lès-Avignon 129
Marineland 323
Marseille 44, 402
    Abbaye St-Victor 49
    accommodation 60
    Aéroport Marseille-Provence 58
    arrival and departure 58
    bars 62
    Belsunce, quartier 55
    Bibliothèque Alcazar 55
    bike rental 59
    boat trips 68
    buses 59
    bus station 59
    cafés 61
    Canebière, La 54
    car parks 59
    car rental 59
    Cathédrale de la Major 54
    cinemas 64
    Cité Radieuse 57
    City Pass 47
    clubs 64
    Commune 55
    concert halls 64
    consulates 66
    corniche Président J.F. Kennedy 58
    Cours Julien 56
    directory 66
    drinking 62
    eating 61
    entertainment 64
    Euroméditerranée project 52
    ferries 59
    Fort St-Jean 53
    FRAC 54
    Friche la Belle de Mai, La 54
    Goudes, Les 58
    health 66
    history 44
    Hospice de la Vieille Charité 52
    hostels 60
    hotels 60
    information 59
    J4 52
    laundry 66
    MAC 57
    Maison de l'Artisanat et des Métiers
        d'Art 49
    Malmousque 58
    markets 57, 65
    Mémorial de la Marseillaise 55
    metro 59
    Montredon 58
    Musée Cantini 56
    Musée d'Archéologie
        Méditerranéenne 52
    Musée de la Marine et de
        l'Économie 54
    Musée des Arts Africains, Océaniens
        et Amérindiens 52
    Musée des Beaux-Arts 56
    Musée des Civilisations d'Europe et
        de la Méditerranée (MuCEM) 52
    Musée des Docks Romains 50
    Musée d'Histoire de Marseille 55
    Musée d'Histoire Naturelle 56
    Musée du Santon 49
    Musée Grobet-Labadié 56
    Musée Regards de Provence 53
    nightlife 64
    Notre Dame de la Garde 47
    Olympique de Marseille 57
    opera 64
    orientation 47
    Palais de Longchamp 56
    Palais des Sports 57
    Panier, Le 49
    Parc Borély 57
    Parc Chanot 57
    Parc Valmer 58
    Pass Musées 47
    Plage du Prado 58
    Pointe Rouge 58
    police 66
    Porte d'Aix 55
    post office 66
    Préfecture 55
    restaurants 61
    shopping 65
    Stade Vélodrome 57
    taxis 59
    theatres 64
    tourist office 59
    tours 59
    train station 59
    trams 59
    transport 59
    Unité d'Habitation 57

Vallon des Auffes 58
Vieux Port 46
Villa Méditerranée 53
Martigues 76
Martin, Cap 374
Massif des Maures 283
Massif les Monges 228
Matisse, Henri 277, 335, 337, 338, 354, 355, 401
Maupassant, Guy de 277
media 33
Ménerbes 194
Menton 382
Mercantour, Parc National du 229
Merveilles, Lac des 245
Merveilles, Vallée de 245
Mines de Bruoux 190
Mistral, Frédéric 101, 400
Monaco 375
  accommodation 380
  arrival and information 379
  banks 381
  bars 381
  buses 379
  bus station 379
  Casino de Monte-Carlo 375
  Collection de Voitures Anciennes 379
  Condamine, La 379
  directory 381
  drinking 381
  eating 380
  emergencies 381
  entertainment 381
  ferry 379
  festivals 381
  Fontvieille 379
  history 378
  hotels 380
  Jardin Exotique 379
  lifts 379
  lost property 382
  Monaco-Ville 376
  money exchange 382
  Monte Carlo 375
  Musée des Timbres et des Monnaies 379
  Musée Naval 379
  Musée Océanographique 378
  nightlife 381
  Nouveau Musée National de Monaco 376
  Opera House 375, 381
  orientation 377
  Palais Princier 377
  pharmacy 382
  post office 382
  practicalities 377
  public holidays 382

  radio 382
  restaurants 380
  sporting events 381
  Terrasses de Fontvieille 379
  theatre 381
  tourist office 379
  train station 379
  transport 379
money 39
Mons 218
Montagne de Lure 184
Montagne Ste-Victoire 165, 166
Monte Carlo 375
Mont Faron 260
Mont Ventoux 140
Mont Vinaigre 298
Mosquée Missiri de Djenné 293
motels 29
motorbikes 28
Mougins 314
Moulin, Jean 79
Mourillon, Le 261
Moustiers-Ste-Marie 219
Moyenne Corniche 371
Musée de la Camargue 107
Musée de Préhistoire des Gorges du Verdon 210
Musée du Vigneron 138
Musée Fernand Léger 326
Musée National Picasso 316
Musée Picasso 321
Musée Renoir 328

N

Napoleon 178, 317, 398
Napoleon III 209
Napoule, La 316
national holidays 39
national parks 66, 68, 229, 270, 405
Naturoptère 136
newspapers 33
Nice 344
  accommodation 357
  airport 355
  arrival and departure 355
  bars 359
  beaches 353
  bike rental 356
  boat trips 356
  buses 356
  bus station 356
  cafés 359
  Canadian Consulate 361
  car parks 357
  car rental 357
  Cathédrale de Ste-Réparate 347
  Chapelle de la Miséricorde 347

  Cimiez 354
  cinema 360
  Cours Saleya 347
  directory 361
  drinking 359
  eating 358
  entertainment 360
  ferries to Corsica 356
  festivals 361
  flea market 353
  Galerie Ferrero 352
  galleries 351
  health 361
  hostels 358
  hotels 357
  information 356
  laundry 361
  lost property 361
  Monastère Notre Dame de Cimiez 355
  Musée Chagall 355
  Musée d'Archéologie 354
  Musée d'Art Moderne et d'Art Contemporain (MAMAC) 350
  Musée Départemental des Arts Asiatiques 353
  Musée des Beaux-Arts 352
  Musée de Terra Amata 354
  Musée Franciscain 355
  Musée International d'Art Naïf Anatole Jakovsky 353
  Musée Matisse 354
  Musée National du Sport 353
  museum passes 352
  Negresco Hotel 352
  nightlife 359
  Notre Dame du Port 353
  Opéra 347, 360
  orientation 347
  Palais de la Méditerranée 352
  Palais Lascaris 350
  Palais Nikaïa 361
  Parc de la Colline du Château 346
  Parc des Arènes de Cimiez 355
  pharmacy 361
  Phoenix Parc Floral de Nice 353
  Place Masséna 350
  Place Rossetti 347
  police 361
  port 353
  post office 361
  Promenade des Anglais 352
  restaurants 358, 359
  Russian Orthodox Cathedral 351
  shopping 361
  sport 361
  taxis 356
  Théatre de la Photographie et de l'Image 351
  theatres 361

tourist office 356
tours 356
train station 355
trams 356
transport 356
Vieux Nice 347
Villa Masséna 352
Nice and the eastern Riviera 344
Nice–Turin railway line 362
Nin, Anaïs 277
Nostradamus 78, 97, 217, 396
Notre Dame de Jérusalem 293
Notre Dame des Fontaines 245

O

Observatoire de Haute Provence 183
ochre quarrying 186, 190, 191
Olbia 266
olives 77
opening hours 39
Oppède-le-Vieux 194
Orange 133
outdoor activities 34, 187, 334

P

Pagnol, Marcel 73, 74
Pagode Hong Hien 292
Paillon River 362
Palud-sur-Verdon, La 221
Pampelonne, Plage de 282
paragliding 187
Parc National des Calanques 66
Parc National du Mercantour 229, 405
Parc Naturel Régional du Luberon 186, 189
Parc Ornithologique de Pont de Gau 107
parfumeries of Grasse 332
Pays de Forcalquier 180
Peille 362
Peillon 362
Pénitents des Mées 176
perfume industry 329
Pernes-les-Fontaines 146
Pertuis 171
Petite Crau, La 100
Petit Luberon, The 194
pets, travelling with 41
phones 39
Picasso 314, 315, 316
Plage de Pampelonne 282
plantlife 108, 232
politics 403, 404
Pont de Gau 107, 131

Porquerolles 268
Port-Cros 270
Port Grimaud 285
post offices 38
pottery 315
Presqu'île de Giens 266
public holidays 39
Puget-Théniers 236
Puyloubier 166

Q

Quinson 210

R

radio 33
Ramatuelle 282
Rayol, Le 275
regional delicacies 31
Rencontres d'Arles 89
Renoir 401
Renoir, Pierre-Auguste 328, 401
restaurants 31
Rhône Valley 403
Riez 211
Rocher de Roquebrune 288
rock climbing 138, 187, 222, 334
Roquebillière 242
Roquebrune 374
Roquebrune, Rocher de 288
Roquebrune-sur-Argens 288
Roquebrussanne, La 203
Roubion 238
Rougon 222
Roussillon 191
Route des Crêtes 221, 228
Route des Vins 166
Route Napoléon 317, 334
Roya Valley 243

S

Sablettes, Les 260
safety 36
Saignon 186
sailing 35, 265, 296
Saintes-Maries-de-la-Mer, Les 108
Salernes 207
Salin-de-Giraud 110
Salon 77
Salon-de-Provence 77
Sanary-sur-Mer 256
Saorge 244
Sault 142
scuba-diving 296
Séguret 139

Seillans 217
self-catering 29
Sentier de découverte Mont Macaron 365
Sérignan-du-Comtat 135
Seyne-les-Alpes 229
Seyne-sur-Mer, La 260
shopping 40
Signac, Paul 277, 401
Signes 203
Sillans-la-Cascade 207
Simiane-la-Rotonde 185
Sisteron 176
Six-Fours-les-Plages 257
skiing 35, 184, 227, 231, 238, 240
smoking 40
snowboarding 35
Sorgue River, source of 148
Sospel 243
southern Var, Toulon and the 250
sports 34
St-André-les-Alpes 226
St-Auban 227
St-Cyr-sur-Mer 250
Ste-Agnès 388
Ste-Marguerite 312
Ste-Maxime 287
St-Étienne-de-Tinée 238
St-Honorat 312
St-Julien-du-Verdon 226
St-Mandrier-sur-Mer 260
St-Martin-Vésubie 241
St-Maximin-de-la-Ste-Baume 204
St-Paul-de-Vence 339
St-Raphaël 294
St-Rémy-de-Provence 96
St-Sauveur-sur-Tinée 238
St-Tropez 276
St-Tropez peninsula 282
studying in Provence 38

T

Tamaris 260
Tanning, Dorothea 217
Tarascon 101
Tarasque, the 103
Tartarin 103
television 33
temperature 10
Tende 245
theme parks 323
Théoule-sur-Mer 317
Tholonet, Le 166
time zone 40
Tinée Valley 237
Tortues, Le Village des 285
Touët-sur-Var 236

Toulon 257
tourism 401, 404
tourist information 40
Tourrettes-sur-Loup 334
tours 107
Tourtour 207
Train des Pignes 213
trains 24, 26, 356, 362, 406
transport 23, 406
Trayas, Le 298
Turbie, La 373
Turini, Col de 242

U

Utelle 242

V

Vacqueyras 139
Vaison-la-Romaine 136
Valdeblore, Commune de 241
Val d'Enfer 94
Val Joanis 171
Vallauris 315

Vallée de Fontanable 245
Vallée des Merveilles 245
Van Gogh, Vincent 90, 401
Var, southern 250
Vauvenargues 165
Venasque 147
Vence 335
Vésubie Valley 241
via ferrata 334, 364
Villa Ephrussi 369
Village des Bories 193
Village des Tortues, Le 285
Villa Kérylos 370
Villecroze 207
Villefranche-sur-Mer 366
Villeneuve-lès-Avignon 128
Villeneuve-Loubet 327

W

walking
Aix-en-Provence, The Durance and
The Luberon 166
Arles and The Camargue 107,
109, 111

Haut Var and Haute Provence
203, 219, 222, 226, 228, 231,
244, 245
Marseille and Around 67, 68
Toulon and the Southern Var 283,
289, 297
Wars of Religion 169
water parks 35, 287, 293, 323
watersports 35, 222, 226, 296
weather 10
websites 40
wildlife 108, 232
wine 4, 32, 131, 132, 139, 166,
196, 254
World War I 401
World War II 49, 402

Y

youth hostels 30

Z

Zola, Émile 401
zoo 293

Map symbols

The symbols below are used on maps throughout the book

——	International boundary	——	Ferry route	⊠	Gate	⌂	Abbey
——	Regional boundary	——	Wall	∴	Ruins/archeological site	⸸	Chapel
– – –	Chapter boundary	✈	Airport	⌂	Refuge	⌂	Monastery
	Motorway	★	Transport stop	⬛	Chateau	↔	Church
	Main road	Ⓜ	Metro station	♟	Fort		Building
⊓⊓⊓⊓	Steps	ⓘ	Tourist office	⌒	Cave	⬭	Stadium
	Pedestrianized street	✉	Post office	⛩	Lighthouse	⬚	Park
– – – –	Footpath	♟	Museum	🦤	Bird/nature sanctuary	⬚	Beach
═══	Railway	♦	Place of interest	⑊	Viewpoint	⊞	Christian cemetery
═══	TGV	Ⓟ	Parking	⸗	Cliffs	⬚	Jewish cemetery
——	Tramway	⊙	Statue	▲	Mountain peak		

Listings key

 Accommodation

 Eating

■ Drinking/Nightlife

● Shopping